GERMAN CAPITAL SHIPS *of the* SECOND WORLD WAR

GERMAN CAPITAL SHIPS *of the* SECOND WORLD WAR

**SIEGFRIED BREYER,
MIROSŁAW SKWIOT**

FRONTISPIECE:
Gneisenau at the A10 mooring buoy in the Heikendorf roadstead off Kiel. This picture was probably taken in September 1938 and shows the detail of the bow before modification.
ADM

© Seaforth Publishing 2012

Text translated from Polish by Jarosław Głodek © Seaforth Publishing 2012

This edition first published in Great Britain in 2012 by
Seaforth Publishing
An imprint of Pen & Sword Books Ltd
47 Church Street, Barnsley
S Yorkshire S70 2AS

www.seaforthpublishing.com
Email info@seaforthpublishing.com

British Library Cataloguing in Publication Data
A CIP data record for this book is available from the British Library

ISBN 978 1 84832 143 4

All rights reserved. No part of this publication may be reproduced or transmitted in any form or by any means, electronic or mechanical, including photocopying, recording, or any information storage and retrieval system, without prior permission in writing of both the copyright owner and the above publisher.

The right of Siegfried Breyer and Mirosław Skwiot to be identified as the authors of this work has been asserted in accordance with the Copyright, Designs and Patents Act 1988

Typeset and designed by Roger Daniels
Printed and bound in China by 1010 Printing International Limited

Contents

The Authors	6
Siegfried Breyer	
Mirosław Skwiot	
Preface	9
1. Battleships of the Reichsmarine and the Kriegsmarine	10
2. Reconstruction of the Reichsmarine: The First Battleship Concepts	42
Deutschland/Lützow	60
ADOLF VON LÜTZOW	
Admiral Scheer	104
REINHARD SCHEER	
Admiral Graf Spee	152
MAXIMILIAN JOHANNES GRAF VON SPEE	
3. The Evolution of Battleships D and E	190
Scharnhorst	202
GERHARD JOHANN DAVID VON SCHARNHORST	
Gneisenau	248
AUGUST WILHELM ANTON NEIDHARDT VON GNEISENAU	
4. The Evolution of Battleships F and G	302
Bismarck	316
OTTO VON BISMARCK	
Tirpitz	366
ALFRED VON TIRPITZ	
Appendix: The Aircraft Carrier *Graf Zeppelin*	422

The Authors

SIEGFRIED BREYER

Siegfried Breyer was born in 1926 and was associated with the Kriegsmarine from the age of 12. In 1941, while still of school age, he had a chance to enter the naval NCO school, as the Kriegsmarine followed the Wehrmacht and opened their own NCO schools for juniors. He left school and enlisted. After two years of education his first active posting was to a destroyer, and then on other small warships.

During his school years Germany was at war with the Allies both in the West and in the East. After the Kriegsmarine was destroyed, in the last months of the war Breyer found his way to the marine infantry fighting the British in the West. He was captured a few days before the war ended but managed to escape from the POW camp in France in autumn 1945. Hidden under the load on a coal train, he returned to his devastated homeland. In 1947 he joined the civil service where he worked until his retirement in 1980.

From early postwar days he contributed to naval publications where he was able to use his drawing skills. He drew several hundred silhouette drawings for the annual *Weyers Flottentaschenbuch*, and from 1958 he wrote for *Soldat und Technik*, the armed forces journal, and published several hundred articles on naval subjects. He specialised in the Soviet Navy and over the years he became one of the most renowned experts on Russian naval forces. His articles appeared in both the German and foreign press: in *Marinerundschau*, *Die Seekiste*, *Wehr und Wissenschaft*, *Atlantische Welt*, the French *Revue Maritime*, *Internationale Wehrrevue*, and *Leinen Los*.

He also published many books, and became one of the best-selling naval and maritime authors. In 1963 J F Lehmanns Verlag in Munich published his first book, *Die Seerüstung der Sowjetunion* (Naval Armament of the Soviet Union). In 1969 he wrote the classic *Schlachtschiffe und Schlachtkreuzer 1905-1970*, which was reprinted four times, and also published in English in 1973 by MacDonald & Janes as *Battleships and Battlecruisers 1905-1970*. Then Bernard & Graefe published his three-volume illustrated *Großkampfschiffe 1905-1970*, which was also soon published in Britain as *Battleships of the World 1905-1970*. In 1978 another of Breyer's book was co-written with his wartime friend Gerhard Koop: it was a two-volume history of German major warships called *Von der Emden zur Tirpitz* (From Emden to Tirpitz). In 1981 he collaborated with Koop on another book, *Die Schiffe und Fahrzeuge der deutschen Bundesmarine* (Ships and Vessels of the German Federal Navy), reprinted in 2000. His next books were co-written with a Swiss historian, Jürg Meister (*Die Marine der Volksrepublik China* – The Navy of the People's Republic of China), and with Dr Peter Lapp, (*Die Volksmarine der DDR* – People's Navy of the GDR). In the years 1987-1993 Koehlers Verlag of Herford published the three-volume *Enzyklopädie des sowjetischen Kriegsschiffbaus* (Encyclopedia of Soviet Warships); the first two volumes were published in English by Conway Maritime Press. In the years 1986-1991 Podzun-Pallas Verlag published his seven-volume series on *Die deutsche Kriegsmarine 1935-1945* (The German Navy 1935-1945), in 1997 *Stapelläufe auf deutschen Schiffswerften* (Ships Launched in German Yards), in 1998 *Flottenparaden und Präsentationen der Marine 1925-1940* (Fleet Parades and Reviews 1925-1940), in 1995 a collaboration with several other authors produced the *Handbuch für Ubootkommandanten* (U-Boat Commanders' Manual), and in 1992 and 1993 a two-volume illustrated book *Schlachtschiffe 1905-1992* (Battleships 1905-1992). Some of the most popular of Breyer's works were the 'Marine-Arsenal' series published by Podzun-Pallas (more than 70 booklets since 1986). Also the *Handbuch der Warschauer Paktflotten* (Manual of Warsaw Pact Fleets) series, published by Bernard & Graefe Verlag of Bonn in the years 1982-1996, proved very successful (with 29 updates released).

Breyer has also co-written several serious scientific works. In 1970 J F Lehmanns published Prof Friedrich Forstmeier's *Deutsche Großkampfschiffe 1915-18* (German Capital Ships 1915-18), now available in a new edition; Breyer wrote the second part of the book. In early 2002 Breyer planned to retire from writing with his final *magnum opus*, entitled *Schlachtschiffe und Schlachtkreuzer 1921-1997* (Battleships and Battlecruisers 1921-1997). However, bowing to pressure from Mirosław Skwiot, he decided to prepare one last work – a photo album on German capital ships in the Second World War, co-written with his younger Polish friend.

Unfortunately Siegfried Breyer did not live to see this work published. He died after a prolonged illness on 22 March 2010.

MIROSŁAW SKWIOT

Mirosław Skwiot was born in 1964, in Gdynia, Poland. German warships first came to his notice at the age of 6 or 7, when he heard a mysterious conversation between his father and his brothers in which the name of a Kriegsmarine battleship was mentioned, a ship which had docked in Gdynia (then called the Gotenhafen) more than once during the war. Young Mirek was hooked, and the mighty battleship became his obsession. In the following years his knowledge of history broadened and facts replaced many myths. His second contact with the Kriegsmarine did not come until 1979, when he travelled outside the Eastern bloc for the first time, to Austria. It was a great adventure for Mirek, who witnessed the culture-clash between East and West. But he was more interested in maritime books and magazines and these he saw in almost all of the larger bookstores, even though Austria has no access to the sea. He spent all of his pocket money on a copy of the Marine-Arsenal volume on *Tirpitz* and the then current issue of *Marine Rundschau*. That was all he could afford. But buying these publications was the easy part – now he had to smuggle his 'contraband' across the Czechoslovak and Polish borders. Dreading the loss of such valuable treasures, he somehow managed to pass the border controls for both intervening countries. Now he could rejoice over his discoveries at home in Gdańsk.

Since then his interest in warships has focused on several thematic groups. His greatest passion are still the Third Rate sailing warships of the 1740-1815 era. Second place is occupied by the Imperial Japanese Navy, and the third – his childhood hobby – Axis battleships of the Second World War.

Since 1979 Skwiot has been expanding his knowledge of historic sailing ships as an assistant to Lech Nowicz, chief of the Underwater Exploration Team at the Central Maritime Museum in Gdańsk. In 1980 he completed a scuba diving course and since then he has been a regular member of the underwater exploration team working in the Bay of Gdańsk and the Baltic Sea aboard the MS *Wodnik*, the museum's own ship. His tasks include exploring the wrecks, but he is also responsible for drawing the visual documentation of each of the sites. As he says, 'Drawing in 27 metres of water, and to scale at that, is not an easy task.' The expeditions allowed him test many of the common assumptions about the construction of wooden sailing ships. The current CMM Director, Jerzy Litwin, had a strong influence on what Skwiot is doing now: it was he who put him in touch with the *Modelarz* (Modeller) magazine that drew him into the world of modelmaking. Skwiot's first work in that field was a reconstruction of the British 74-gun ship HMS *Hero*.

In 1986-87 he served his compulsory military service in the Polish Navy, and then returned to the Museum, to their new ship, the MS *Kaszubski Brzeg*.

In 1990 Adam Jarski set up a publishing business to fulfil his ambition of producing an aviation magazine. During one of numerous meetings with interested parties, it was decided to widen the scope of AJ-Press and include a series on warships. Thus the Monografie Morskie series was launched.

'Neither of us had any doubts,' Skwiot recollects, 'the first issue just had to be devoted to *Bismarck*.' Then came a volume on the Japanese aircraft carrier *Akagi*. Another change in his life came with Elżbieta T Prusinowska, with whom he wrote several other monographs. Their first joint work was the monograph on the battleship *Nagato*, for which they translated the Japanese texts needed to prepare this book together. Later they wrote books on Pearl Harbor, on Operation Rheinübung, a *Tirpitz* monograph and a book devoted to the Battle of the Coral Sea, after which their paths separated.

During the following years Skwiot published new editions of the monographs on *Bismarck and Tirpitz*, *Nagato* and *Akagi*, but his next work was devoted to German naval artillery, which was also published in English. In the last twenty years the contacts he maintains with other naval historians from various countries has allowed him to build up a collection of unpublished documents, photographs and other visual material devoted to the warships of the Kriegsmarine and the Imperial Japanese Navy.

During his work on the *Tirpitz* monograph, Skwiot began corresponding with Siegfried Breyer. As a result of this co-operation, he received a lot of original material that fundamentally changed his position on the history and perfomance of the Kriegsmarine in the Second World War. In the course of this fascinating voyage of discovery, he put up the idea of collaborating on a jointly-written book on German battleships. After much discussion, and a digression into publishing a *Bismarck* monograph, both agreed that a photo album would be the ideal approach to the subject. And so, after many years spent on their shared hobby, they managed to assemble a unique collection of photographs depicting German capital ships of the Second World War.

This book is the final fruition of that project.

The newly completed *Bismarck* in the river Elbe on 15
September 1940, escorted by a tug belonging to Blohm & Voss.
Blohm & Voss, via Jörg Schmiedeskamp

ABBREVIATIONS USED IN THE CREDITS

ADM	Archiwum Dokumentacji Mechanicznej w Warszawie - Archive of Audiovisual Records, Warsaw
CAW	Centralne Archiwum Wojskowe w Warszawie - Central Military Archive, Warsaw
CMM	Centralne Muzeum Morskie w Gdańsku - Polish Maritime Museum, Gdańsk
IWM	Imperial War Museum, London
MMG	Muzeum Miasta Gdyni - Museum of the City of Gdynia
MMW	Muzeum Marynarki Wojennej - Polish Navy Museum, Gdynia
NHC	National Historical Center, Washington DC
NARA	National Archives and Records Administration, Washington DC

Preface

No warships of any era have been given as much press coverage as the German battleships of the Second World War era.

There were not many of these – only four ships worthy of the term were built between 1935 and 1941. The *Scharnhorst* and *Gneisenau* were ready before the war broke out, the *Bismarck* and *Tirpitz* shortly thereafter. These four ships were the greatest success of the German Navy rearmament program driven by Adolf Hitler.

Earlier there were three ships built to replace the elderly pre-dreadnought battleships that Germany was allowed to retain under terms of the Treaty of Versailles. These new ships were radically different from traditional categories and were simply called *panzerschiffe* (literally 'armoured ships') by the Germans, but they were soon dubbed 'pocket battleships' by the foreign press. As battleship replacements, *Deutschland*, *Admiral Scheer* and *Admiral Graf Spee* have a historical claim to be regarded as capital ships, but they were reclassed as heavy cruisers at the beginning of war, which was closer to their true role.

The four genuine battleships were in service together for only a quarter of a year or so – to be precise, from late February until late May 1941. During that time the *Scharnhorst* and *Gneisenau* were in the French port of Brest, the *Bismarck* was prepared for the Atlantic commerce-raiding mission, and *Tirpitz* was finishing her sea trials awaiting commissioning into active service. The *Scharnhorst* and *Gneisenau* had already successfully operated on British sea lanes, but by remaining in western France they were risking air attack. After the initial triumph of sinking the *Hood*, the *Bismarck* was herself sunk, before she had a chance to start the commerce-raiding mission against British convoys. The aftermath of this disaster was even worse, in that the British managed to destroy the entire German supply network in the Atlantic. Thereafter German heavy ships were unable to operate in distant waters due to lack of fuel and stores. The Allied grip on the Atlantic grew ever tighter, and because of this the *Scharnhorst* and the *Gneisenau* had to force their way back to Germany through the British-controlled English Channel. This daring plan succeeded, proving a great tactical success, but in the longer term it was a strategic defeat. Hitler, fearing an Allied invasion of Norway, then ordered all German capital ships redeployed to the north, to bolster Norwegian defences. Before this order could be executed, *Gneisenau* was bombed and so badly damaged that she was never able to return to action during the remainder of the war.

This left the *Scharnhorst* and *Tirpitz* as the only serviceable capital ships that could be transferred to Norway. There they hid in the fjords as a 'fleet in being', but were continually harassed by lack of fuel and petty air raids. After the disastrous Operation Regenbogen of July 1942, Hitler pronounced them unfit for operational service and even wanted them decommissioned. This debacle brought down Grand Admiral Raeder, the Kriegsmarine C-in-C, to be replaced by the commander of the U-boat arm, Admiral Dönitz. The latter resisted Hitler's orders and managed to retain the operational status of the battleships, but fortune had deserted the German capital ships for good.

Only twice were they able to leave their Norwegian hideouts to take part in any major naval actions. In September 1943 *Tirpitz* and *Scharnhorst* bombarded the Allied base on Spitsbergen, and then in December the *Scharnhorst* had to undertake her last mission alone, because *Tirpitz* had been damaged in a British midget submarine attack. The damage was not critical, nor were the injuries sustained in carrier-launched air attacks. However, the British were focused on destroying the only remaining German capital ship. Three times they tried with four-engined heavy bombers, twice failing to accomplish their goal. Then, on the fatal third time, on 12 November 1944, they dropped the 5-ton Tallboy bombs on her and finally sealed her fate. A direct hit with a Tallboy set off the ammunition magazines under C turret, and the *Tirpitz* capsized. The last of the Kriegsmarine battleships was gone. It was clear that the reign of the battleship was over, because they were unable to defend themselves against air attack. And thus the history of German battleships came to an end.

The Second World War at sea demonstrated that the battleship had been superseded by the aircraft carrier as the capital ship in the world's major navies. Germany made only one serious attempt to build a carrier – the uncompleted *Graf Zeppelin* – and this book concludes with pictorial coverage of the project.

Siegfried Breyer, Hanau, 2002

1 Battleships of the Reichsmarine and the Kriegsmarine

Battleship *Friedrich der Grosse*, flagship of Rear Admiral Reuter, commander of the German fleet interned in Scapa Flow.
Photograph by Drüppel, from the collection of A Jarski

THE KAISER'S NAVY, at the time the second largest battle fleet in the world, met its end on 21 June 1919 when Rear Admiral Ludwig von Reuter, commander of the interned remnant of the High Seas Fleet (Hochseeflotte) decided to scuttle all ships. On the following day, a fleet consisting of eleven battleships, five battlecruisers, eight light cruisers and fifty destroyers sank in the Scapa Flow anchorage. As the rear admiral made his decision to scuttle the fleet, the Reichstag decided to accept the terms of the Versailles Treaty, which brought the war to a definitive end. These provisions also formed the basis for the creation of the new German navy – the Reichsmarine. Its composition was to be very limited, so that it would no longer pose a threat to any European country. In practice its tasks were limited to patrolling borders, police operations to maintain peace at sea and the protection of fisheries. The largest ships the Germans were entitled to keep were six very old

Among the ships scuttled in the British naval base was the battleship *Kaiser*, seen here with the crew manning the side.
Photograph by Finke, from the collection of A Jarski

Battleship *Friedrich der Grosse*.
CAW

Battleship *Bayern* of the Third Squadron.
Photograph by Drüppel, from the collection of A Jarski

Battleship *Helgoland* of the *Nassau* class, an overhead view taken in the North See. Note the recognition markings in the form of white circles on the forward and aft turrets. They were intended to identify German ships to their own aircraft.
Photograph by Drüppel, from the collection of A Jarski

battleships built at the beginning of the century and two similar ships in reserve; six light cruisers, twelve destroyers and twelve torpedo boats completed the composition of the new small fleet. The Navy was not allowed to have any submarines, which did so much damage to the Allies during the war. The restrictions of the Versailles Treaty were also to dominate the development of the next generation of German battleships. The displacement of these ships was limited to 10,000 tons, which soon became the new international limit for cruisers under the 1922 Washington Treaty. With such strict limits imposed, it was obvious that no German capital ship could ever rival battleships built in other countries.

However, in the year 1919 no one in the German Navy thought about building new battleships, even though it was permitted to replace any old battleships which remained in service longer than twenty years. The eight remaining battleships belonged to the pre-dreadnought category: five of the *Braunschweig* class (*Braunschweig, Elsass, Hessen, Preussen* and *Lothringen*) and three of the slightly newer *Deutschland* class (*Hannover, Schlesien* and *Schleswig-Holstein*). All of them had been obsolete for a decade. Yet, in the new post-Versailles reality the Reichsmarine had no option but to modernise them and assign them to training duties. Even these modestly ambitious plans did not come to fruition because of the economic crisis which struck the country – there was simply no money for the

Two views of the battlecruiser *Seydlitz*, flagship of the First Scouting Group.
Photograph by Drüppel, from the collection of M Skwiot

The other ships of the First Scouting Group that were scuttled were the battlecruisers *Von der Tann* (above) and *Derfflinger*.
Photographs by Drüppel, from the collection of A Jarski

immediate modernisation of old battleships. The financial crisis also had an impact on the construction of new battleships. It is worth noting at this point that the situation was theoretically favourable for Germany, as they could have begun the construction of new ships on the day the Versailles Treaty was ratified. The battleships *Braunschweig* and *Elsass* had entered service in 1904 and so in 1924 they could have been replaced by new ships. Yet, in the defeated and crisis-struck Germany there was neither the money nor the appetite for the construction of new warships. The fleet command, however, was duty-bound to plan for the future reinforcement of the Navy.

Having only 10,000 tons of displacement at their disposal, the German designers had to accept massive compromises. Such a small hull could not possibly accommodate strong armament, heavy armour and powerful engines at the same time. Two schools of thought soon emerged, one opting for the construction of a small, well-armoured monitor – something like a coast defence battleship – while the other

At the end of the Great War the High Seas Fleet (Hochseeflotte) was eliminated as a fighting force; most of the ships were scuttled in Scapa Flow and the remainder were broken up.
ABOVE: The turrets of the scuttled battlecruiser *Hindenberg*.
TOP RIGHT: One of this ship's turrets with the guns removed.
Both photographs CAW

Salvage work on the wreck of the German capital ship *Hindenburg* after it was scuttled in Scapa Flow.
CAW

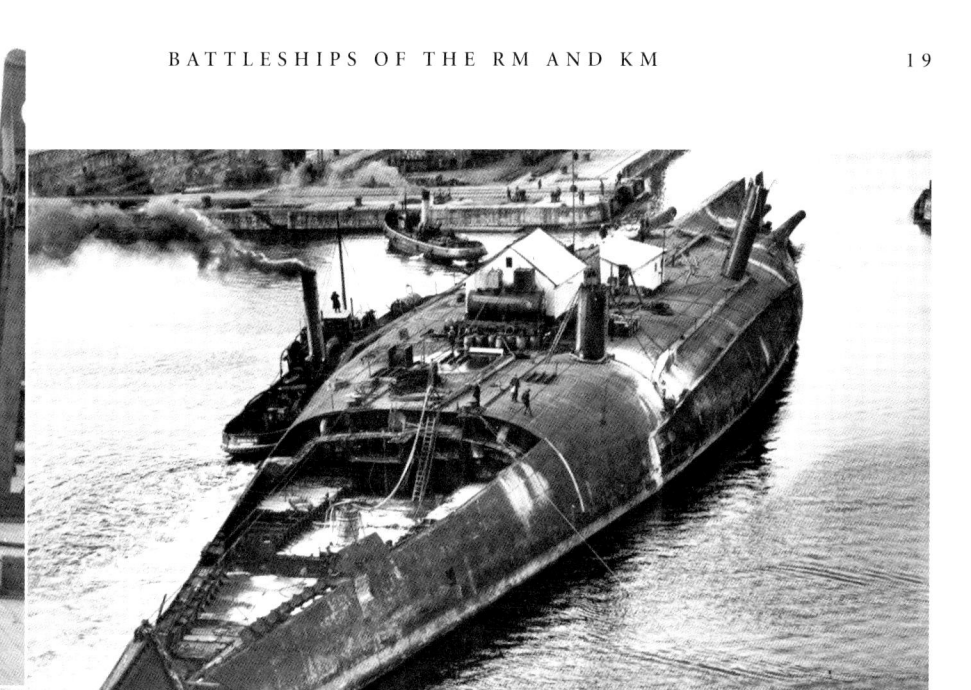

Wreck of the battlecruiser *Moltke* being broken up after being raised from the bottom of Scapa Flow.
CAW

LEFT: Wreck of the battlecruiser *Derfflinger* towed to the dockyard for breaking up.
ADM

The capsized hulk of the battleship *König Albert* after being raised from the bottom of Scapa Flow.
CAW

A squadron of German battleships photographed about 1930 from the *Schlesien* in the Marinearsenal (naval base) in Kiel. In the foreground is the old battleship *Hessen*, the *Hannover* (with three funnels) astern, and *Schleswig-Holstein* in the background.
CAW

Preparations for a German fleet review in the Swinemünde (present-day Świnoujście) naval base on 17 April 1932. Until the *Deutschland* type ships entered service the core of the fleet was comprised of these old pre-dreadnought battleships. Only after 1930 were they replaced with new ships.
CAW

preferred a heavily armed ship with very limited armour, but fast enough to be able to break contact with a more powerful opponent. This second concept had more support, as it implied active operations and was not limited to coastal defence in the vicinity of home ports. The first sketch designs were produced as early as 1923, but before final versions were accepted, a prolonged debate took place over every detail of the new ship: armour, armament, power plant and the financial resources required to complete the project. Even the idea of using 38cm (15in) guns was considered, as the Allies had not imposed any limitations on gun calibre. However the final decision to build the new 'battleship' was postponed for some time as a result of the economic crisis, hyperinflation and political instability. A breakthrough came in 1927 when a firm decision on main gun calibre and the number of barrels was finally made. Yet, only after the parliamentary elections in May 1928 and the advent of a new political cli-

Of the battleships that the Germans were allowed to retain after the war, five were of the *Braunschweig* class. This photograph shows one of them, the *Hessen*, photographed in 1929 during repainting of the underwater hull in dry dock in the Marinewerft (naval dockyard) in Wilhelmshaven.
A Jarski collection

mate was the Navy able to begin replacing its old pre-dreadnoughts with new ships. The new Reichstag included twelve NSDAP (Nazi Party) representatives, who strongly supported the fleet development plan. Very soon all obstacles to financing the expansion of any armed forces in the German Reich were removed. The first ship, the so-called 'Panzerschiff A', was ordered on 17 August 1928 from Deutsche Werke in Kiel and the keel was laid on 9 February in the following year. The launching ceremony took place on 19 May 1931 and after two years of fitting-out the ship was commissioned on the 1 April 1933 as the *Deutschland*.

The German panzerschiffe turned out to be extraordinary ships. Their armament comprised six 28cm (11in) guns, which made them superior to all Washington treaty cruisers armed with 8in (203mm) guns. With their maximum speed of 28 knots, only three British ships were both faster and more powerful; these were the battlecruisers *Hood*, *Renown* and *Repulse*. Ironically, the treaty limitations designed to neutralise any German naval threat

The old battleship *Hessen* moored at the A9 buoy in Schwentine. The ship survived the Second World War as a target ship and after the war was transferred to the Soviet Union where she remained in service until the early 1950s in the Tisiel naval base.
A Jarski collection

Battleships *Hessen* (in the foreground) and *Schleswig-Holstein* photographed in April 1929 at Kiel. The ships are entering the Holtenau lock at the beginning of a voyage to Spain.
ADM

Schleswig-Holstein photographed in April 1929 in the Holtenau lock in the Kiel Canal, the first stage of a cruise to Spain.
ADM

The situation of the German fleet began to change in 1936 when Adolf Hitler unilaterally renounced all disarmament treaties. The old pre-dreadnought battleships, here photographed during exercises in April 1932, were to be supplemented by two new ships referred to as D and E.
CAW

The second *Braunschweig* class battleship which was returned to service in accordance with the Versailles Treaty was *Elsass*, seen here from the Levensau bridge while steaming to Wilhelmshaven.
L Trawicki collection

The other battleships which returned to active duty belonged to the *Deutschland* class and among them was the *Hannover*. This ship was the first to be refitted and the first to re-enter service. During her career the ship made several representative international voyages. Here the battleship is seen in Wilhelmshaven in June 1930 after returning from the Mediterranean.
ADM

RIGHT: *Schleswig-Holstein* seen before refit. After Hitler renounced the disarmament treaties in 1936, it was planned to replace this old ship by Battleship G, but this was never completed.
ADM

MAIN PICTURE: *Schleswig-Holstein* after refitting, with two funnels. This was the ship which fired the first shots of the Second World War.
M Cieślak collection

Kiel, 19 May 1931: high ranking Reichsmarine officers are introduced to the president, Field Marshal von Hindenburg.
ADM

Battleship *Schleswig-Holstein* dressed overall in the Bay of Kiel, 31 May 1933 or 1934, celebrating the anniversary of the Battle of the Skagerrak (as the Germans referred to Jutland).
ADM

The crew of the *Schlesien* taking a line from the *Hessen* during a training cruise in the North Sea.
A Jarski collection

succeeded in creating heavily armed cruisers without an exact equivalent in other fleets. Designed primarily to destroy enemy merchant shipping, they had typical raider characteristics – by employing diesel main engines, the ships had an almost unbelievable range of 18,600 nautical miles at 15 knots. Foreign experts were left wondering how it was possible to design such a fast and powerful ship on a displacement of just 10,000 tons: no one even suggested that these values were understated. However, the Germans themselves muddied the waters by claiming unrealistic weight-savings achieved through the use of electric welding and lightweight diesel machinery. In reality the *Deutschland*'s hull was only partially welded and the true standard displacement was 11,700 tons, full load being as high as 15,200 tons.

Before the third ship, Panzerschiff C (*Admiral Graf Spee*), was laid down, the political situation in Germany had changed again. In January 1933 Adolf Hitler became the Chancellor of the Third Reich and introduced a policy of expanding the country's position in the world. It was widely expected that Germany would soon refuse to comply with the Versailles Treaty limitations. Since the Washington Treaty of 1922 the five major naval powers (which did not include Germany) had agreed limits on the size and numbers of new warships, most notably a ban on the construction of any new battleships. This agreement broke down during the naval conference in London in 1930, when the representatives of France and Italy refused to extend the Washington Treaty's 'battleship holiday', justifying their decision by the fact that the Germans had begun a program of replacing their old battleships with new units. Finally, the Versailles Treaty was unilaterally renounced

Battleship *Schleswig-Holstein* photographed in 1932 from the Levensau bridge in the suburbs of Kiel. The ship flies the flag of the C-in-C Battleships (BdL). **CAW**

The task of building the first post-war German capital ship, Panzerschiff A, was given to Deutche Werke in Kiel on 27 August 1928. However, the keel was not laid until 5 February 1929. The German term translated simply as 'armoured ship', but they were soon called 'pocket battleships' by the British. CAW

Deutschland, in light condition prior to commissioning, proceeding under the Levensau bridge in the Nord-Ostsee (or Kiel) Canal on 27 February 1933.
M Skwiot collection

Side view of the hull of Panzerschiff A, to be called the *Deutschland*, on the slipway of the Deutsche Werke in Kiel shortly before launching.
CAW

Admiral Scheer photographed in 1936 in Wilhelmshaven. In the background are the old battleships *Schleswig-Holstein* and *Schlesien*.
A Jarski collection

Panzerschiff *Admiral Scheer*.
Photograph by Urbahns, from the collection of A Jarski

Panzerschiff *Admiral Graf Spee*, mid-1936.
M Skwiot collection

by Hitler on 16 March 1935, which put an end to all illusions regarding the peaceful character of the Third Reich. In the naval sphere this was of more concern to Britain than any of the other powers and secret negotiations on arms limitations ended with the German Chancellor offering Britain a bilateral treaty. The British accepted the German proposal to voluntarily limit the size of their fleet to 35 per cent of the tonnage of the Royal Navy. Furthermore, the Germans also undertook to respect current and future treaties on tonnage and gun calibre limitations. It is worth remembering that in 1935 the provisions of the Washington Treaty, reaffirmed in 1930, were still in force, limiting the displacement of battleships to 35,000 tons and their gun calibre to 406mm (16in). Thus, the Germans were able to proceed towards the construction of real battleships with no more restrictions than any other power.

The battleships *Gneisenau* and *Scharnhorst*, which entered service in late 1938 and early 1939 respectively, had the weakest main armament of any battleships built after the First World War. The Germans published 26,000 tons as the official figure, but in fact each ship displaced 34,800 tons standard. A ship of such size could easily have carried 38cm (15in) guns, but the decision to choose the smaller calibre was made by Hitler, who did not want to antagonise other countries with the power of his new battleships. Another consideration was the instant availability of triple 28cm turrets, whereas at that time the Germans did not have a twin 38cm turret design finished. Hitler in fact wanted the new ships for political reasons and the calibre of their guns was of secondary importance. The new battleships adopted an armour protection system similar to that used in pre-First World War designs. The main armoured

The French battleship *Dunkerque*. This ship became an important reference point when establishing technical requirements for subsequent new capital ship designs. In Germany it affected the construction of the *Deutschland* class and led to a reformulation of the new D and E designs. **ADM**

deck was placed low in the hull and was inclined downwards to meet the bottom edge of the side armour. Other navies preferred an armoured deck higher in the hull and connected to the upper edge of the armour belt. The German designers assumed that their battleships would operate in the foggy North Sea, where the fighting distances would be shorter, so any shell hits would be on a flatter trajectory. The low-lying armoured deck would then back up the side armour by stopping any shells or fragments that penetrated the belt. Other navies assumed that improvements in fire control would mean engagements at longer ranges, when shells striking at steep angles would reach the inside of the hull from above the side armour. Placing the armoured deck as high as possible would explode the shell far from the vital parts of the ship. The Germans, however, stood firmly by their assumptions and repeated the layout in the battleships *Bismarck* and *Tirpitz*. The experience of the war, and particularly the unforeseen threat from aerial bombs, proved the German concept to be wrong.

For the battleships that became *Bismarck* and *Tirpitz*, the Kriegsmarine Construction Office started preliminary design on a ship of 35,000 tons with an armament of eight 33cm (13in) guns in the year 1934. This gun calibre, identical to that of the French battleship *Dunkerque*, was soon considered too light to meet the requirements of the new German battleships.

Scharnhorst in the Bay of Kiel, photographed in April 1939.
M Skwiot collection

Scharnhorst at Gotenhafen in May 1940, after the refit which extended the bow and relocated the mainmast to the after superstructure.
S Gonera collection

After the Washington Treaty was renounced the calibre was changed to 38cm (15in). Although the gun calibre might have been a matter for discussion, the ship's dimensions were fixed by the necessity to pass through the locks of the Kiel Canal and into the Wilhelmshaven Naval Base. The smallest lock in the Kiel Canal was 250m long and 38m wide so the future battleship could not exceed those dimensions, and the final displacement of both ships was planned to be 41,700 tons. *Bismarck* and *Tirpitz*, were the last ships of this kind to be built for the Kriegsmarine. During a meeting between the C-in-C of the German fleet Admiral Erich Raeder and Adolf Hitler in 1933, the future chancellor declared that he had no intention of building another great battle fleet to rival the Royal Navy. The five capital ships that entered service in the interwar period were required more for political reasons than to pursue a co-

Gneisenau during speed trials in the Bay of Kiel, photographed in May 1938.
Photograph by E Crull, from the collection of M Skwiot

herent naval policy. This was confirmed during the war by the way in which these ships were employed, and Hitler's low opinion of battleships was finally demonstrated by his order to remove them all from active duty after the lost battle of the Barents Sea (Operation Regenbogen).

The strategy of using large surface ships as commerce raiders did not work out well during the war, as it brought only limited success while putting very valuable ships at risk of loss. The sinking of the *Admiral Graf Spee* in December 1939 and the hunt for *Bismarck* in May 1941 were proof of British determination to prevent such operations. The advent of radar and long-range maritime reconnaissance gradually reduced the areas of ocean that remained unpatrolled, until only submarines could be considered relatively safe.

Gneisenau photographed with the new bow in the summer of 1939, a few days before the outbreak of war.
A Jarski collection

Bismarck (below) as first commissioned in August 1940 with much of the fire control equipment still missing, most noticeably in this view the main armament directors. To the right the ship is seen in Grimstadfjord on 21 May 1941, about to sail on her one and only operational sortie.
S Breyer collection

Three views of *Tirpitz* dating from her working-up period in the summer of 1941. As can be clearly seen in the quarter view, the ship does not yet have the after main armament director fitted.
S Breyer collection

2 Reconstruction of the Reichsmarine:
THE FIRST BATTLESHIP CONCEPTS

The first step in the reconstruction of the postwar German navy, the new panzerschiff *Deutschland* is seen on the day before her launch.
CAW

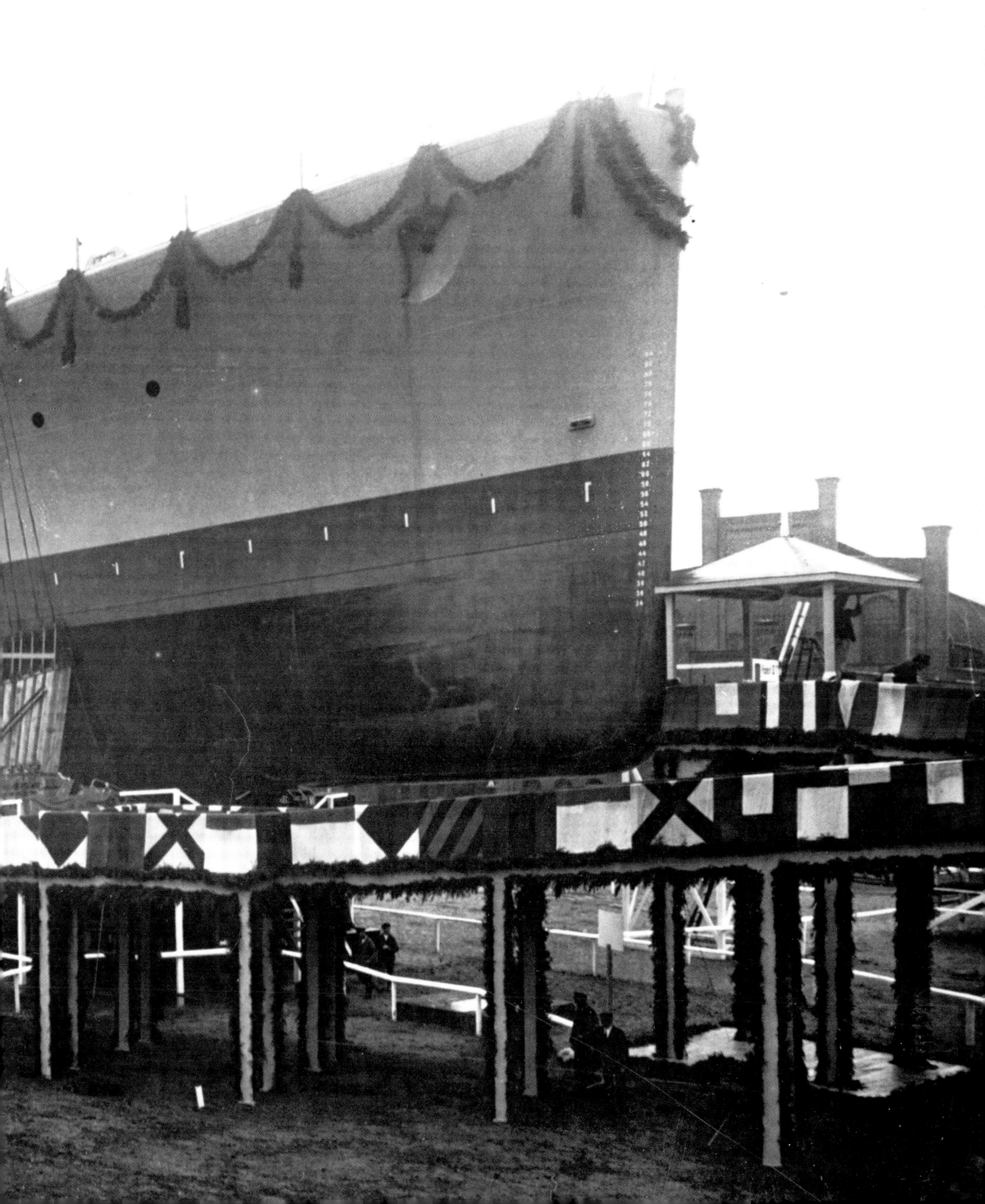

THE NEW GERMAN NAVY, the Reichsmarine, was created on 31 March 1921 and Admiral Paul Behncke became its first commander-in-chief. Immediately on taking post he initiated a discussion of concepts for the replacement of the obsolete battleships the Germans were entitled to keep under the Versailles Treaty. This was straightforward: Germany was forbidden to build battleships exceeding 10,000 tons displacement and the construction of a fast and powerful ship within this limit was a very difficult task – difficult, but not impossible. In 1923 initial concept work began on the future ship to replace the ageing pre-dreadnought *Preussen*. In the same year the Navy Construction Office prepared two preliminary designs. The first ship, designated Entwurf II/10, was armed with four 38cm (15in) guns. While not breaching the displacement limit of 10,000 tons, its maximum speed was only 22 knots; the protection consisted of 200mm side armour and a 30mm armoured deck. The other design, designated Entwurf I/10, was armed with eight 21cm (8.2in) guns in twin turrets and was able to reach 32 knots, but this required the protection to be much reduced; the main armour belt was only 80mm thick and the armoured deck 30mm.

The debate lasted well into the following year until Admiral Hans Zenker took over as head of the Reichsmarine on 18 October 1924. Initially the Navy's high command favoured the concept of a slow, heavily armed ship, similar to a monitor or a coast defence battleship, but after a more considered analysis this design was abandoned and the other concept, a battle-cruiser-type ship, was selected. From then on, all discussion about the future battleship concentrated on one crucial issue – the selection of the main armament calibre. Admiral Behncke had suggested 38cm guns, which he believed

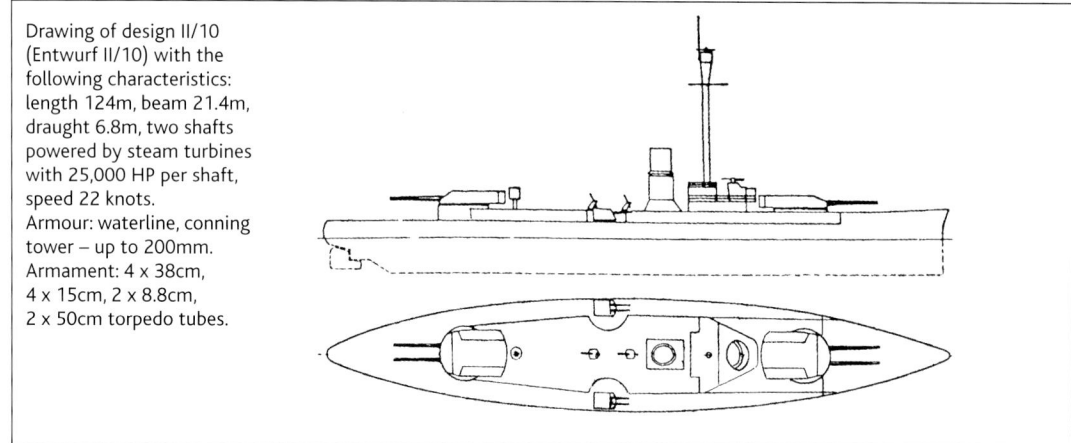

Drawing of design II/10 (Entwurf II/10) with the following characteristics: length 124m, beam 21.4m, draught 6.8m, two shafts powered by steam turbines with 25,000 HP per shaft, speed 22 knots.
Armour: waterline, conning tower – up to 200mm.
Armament: 4 x 38cm, 4 x 15cm, 2 x 8.8cm, 2 x 50cm torpedo tubes.

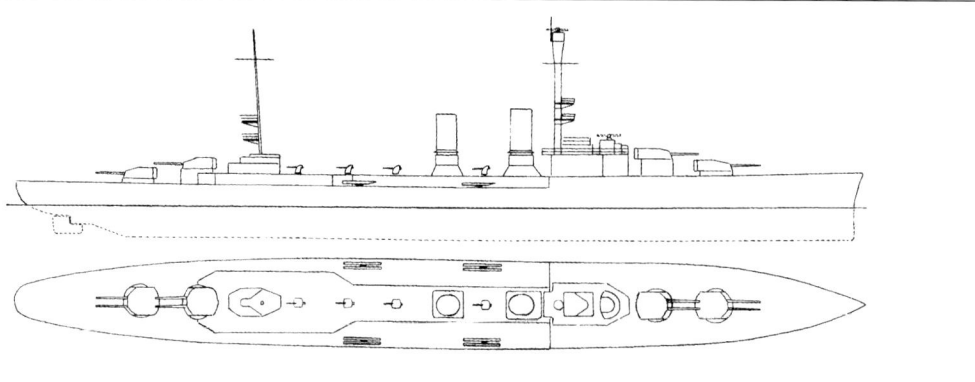

Drawing of design I/10 (Entwurf I/10) with the following characteristics: length 176m, beam 18.8m, draught 6.5m, two shafts powered by steam turbines with 80,000 HP per shaft (6 single and 4 double oil-fired boilers), speed 32 knots.
Armament: 8 x 21cm, 4 x 8.8cm, 8 x 50cm torpedo tubes.
Drawing by S Breyer

Drawing of design II/30 (Entwurf II/30) with the following characteristics: length 132m, beam 22m, draught 6.5m, three shafts powered by diesel engines with 24,000 HP per shaft, speed 21 knots. Armour: vertical – up to 200mm, deck 25mm. Armament: 6 x 30.5cm, 4 x 10.5cm, 2 x 53cm torpedo tubes.

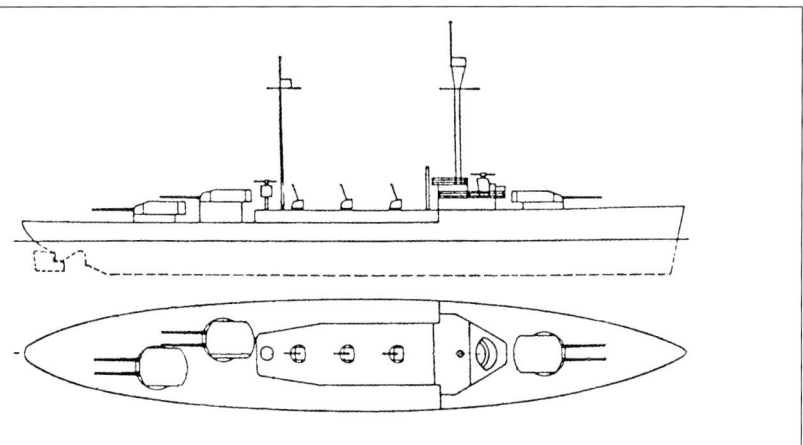

Drawing of design I/35 (Entwurf I/35) with the following characteristics: length 126m, beam 21m, draught 7.2m, two shafts powered by diesel engines with 16,000 HP per shaft, speed 19 knots. Armour: waterline 300mm, conning tower 300mm, turret 300mm, deck 30mm. Armament: 3 x 35cm, 4 x 15cm, 4 x 8.8cm, 4 x 53cm torpedo tubes.
Drawing by S Breyer

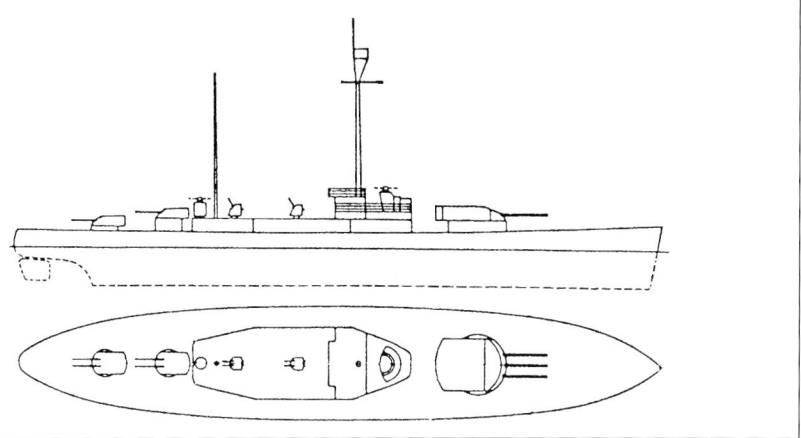

Drawing of design VII/30 (Entwurf VII/30) with the following characteristics: length 141m, beam 20.20m, draught 7m, three shafts powered by diesel engines with 36,000 HP per shaft, speed 24 knots. Armament: 4 x 30.5cm, 6 x 15cm, 6 x 8.8cm, 2 x 53cm torpedo tubes.
Drawing by S Breyer

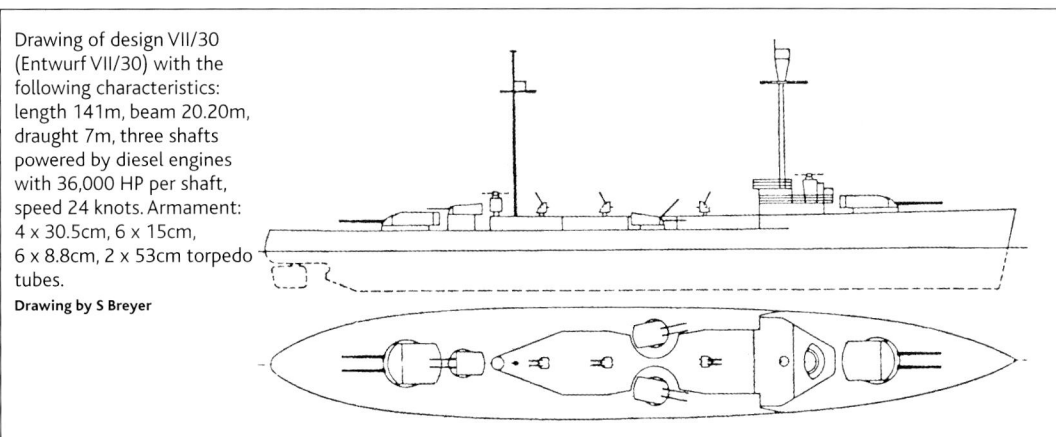

I/M26 (Entwurf I/M26) with the following characteristics: length 138m, beam 20.70m, draught 5.5m, three shafts powered by diesel engines with 54,000 HP per shaft, speed 28 knots. Armour: waterline, conning tower – up to 100mm. Armament: 6 x 28mm, 8 x 12mm.
Drawing by S Breyer

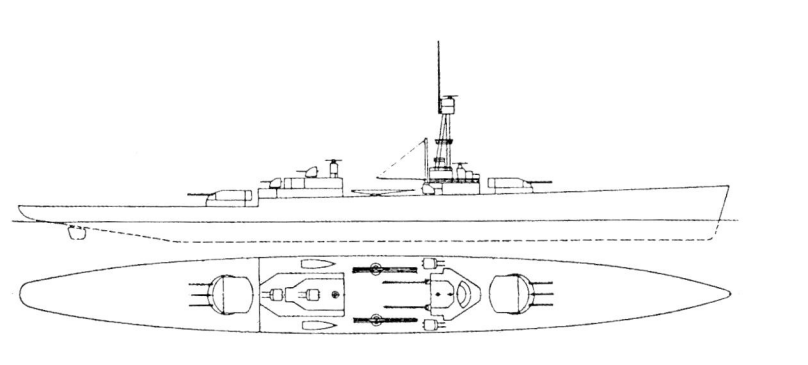

could have been used in this design. Officially the Allies did not impose any limitation on gun calibre, but they later decided that 30.5cm (12in) was to be the largest the Germans were allowed to manufacture; in the event, this was to apply only to coast defence weapons and did not affect the battleship designs. Nevertheless, at that time it appeared beneficial, for political reasons, to equip the new ship with 30.5cm guns. The second design, Entwurf II/30, adopted this calibre – six guns in three twin turrets. The maximum thickness of the main armour was to be 200mm, which at that time was more than enough to protect the ship. The novelty in this design was the use of diesel engines, which allowed the ship to reach 21 knots. However, this design was not approved by naval officers because of its weak secondary battery, but it became the starting point for new variants, which included different secondary guns and, what is more important, other armour protection schemes. Triple turrets were also suggested, as was the case with the Entwurf V/30 design. These lengthy discussions were to be finally closed at a conference planned for 15 May 1925.

During this debate all parties found some shortcomings in the designs presented which they argued should be immediately eliminated. For example, the Armament Office (Marinewaffenabteilung) was not satisfied with the proposed armament, and in particular with the secondary battery, which it wanted changed at any cost. Yet their biggest concern was the production of the new main guns. In post-war

After being decommissioned the battleship *Preussen* was replaced by Panzerschiff A – *Deutschland*. This is why in the early stages the designs were also referred to as 'Ersatz [literally 'replacement'] *Preussen*'.
A Jarski collection

An artist's impression of one of the *Deutschland* designs.
CAW

Another impression of the 'Ersatz *Preussen*' designs.
CAW

Germany there was only capacity to manufacture one 30.5cm gun per year; some land-service guns held in reserve could be quickly modified for marine use, but only three additional guns were available from this source, so the ship's main armament would have to be reduced to four guns. This was definitely not enough for the future ship. Therefore, it was decided to consider 28cm (11in) guns, and designs Entwurf I/28 and Entwurf II/28 showed various arrangements of armament, but they both included two additional 15cm (5.9in) guns. The differences between the designs applied to the number, calibre and positions of secondary artillery. In the end the conference did not solve the 30.5cm main armament problem and Admiral Zenker called another meeting for two weeks later, on 27 May 1925. This meeting did not come up with a solution either. The availability of 30.5cm guns was limited at that time because the French occupied the industrial Ruhr region and so the Krupp factory was only able to supply one gun per year. In this situation equipping a single ship with 30.5cm guns, provided nine were needed, would take almost a decade. This was out of the question, so it was

The Second Squadron of the High Seas Fleet in the Great War era grouped all pre-dreadnought battleships together when at sea. Leading the squadron is the battleship *Preussen*, which survived the war and served with the fleet of the Weimar Republic.
S Breyer collection

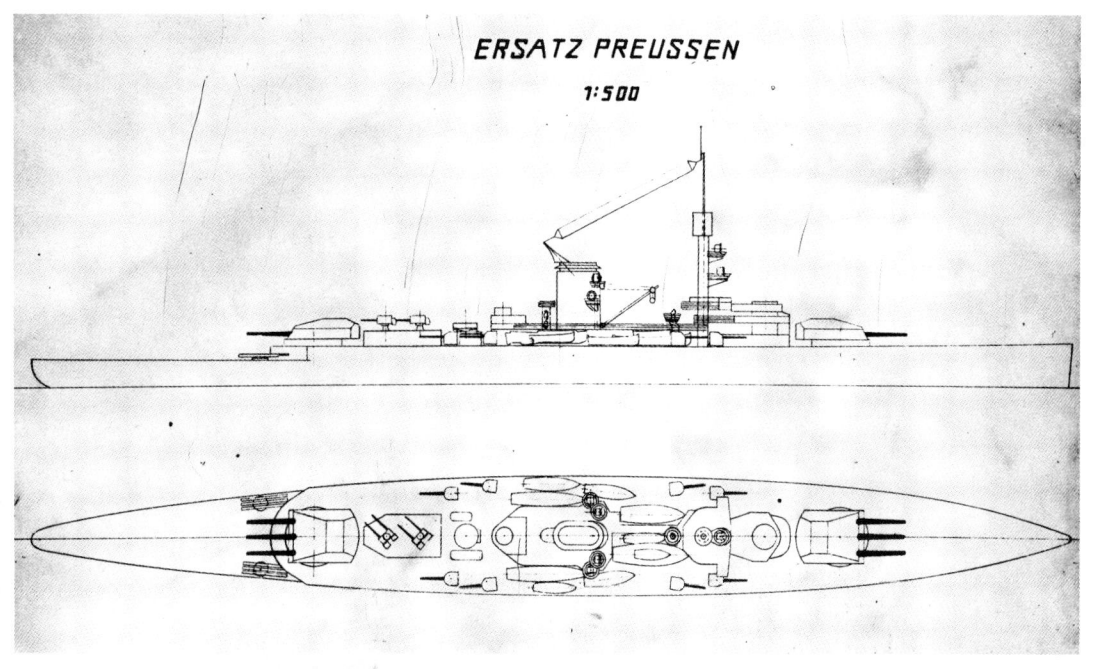

Drawings of the preliminary design for the *Deutschland* that was the basis for the final detailed design.
CAW

One 'Ersatz *Preussen*' design.
CAW

decided to leave the question of armament until autumn and focus on building smaller craft such as cruisers and torpedo boats.

In the absence of precise direction the Construction Office produced further concept designs: Entwurf I/35 and Entwurf VII/30. In comparison with earlier designs these ships were smaller and not as heavily armed, but had better armour protection, similar to a monitor or a coast defence battleship. The designs were presented to Admiral Zenker, who rejected them and sent them back, as he put it, 'for reconsideration'. In the year 1926 two further designs, Entwurf I/M26 and Entwurf II/M26, were prepared and officially presented. Both designs called for an armament of six 28cm guns and twelve anti-aircraft guns. The first design would reach a speed of 28 knots and would have 100mm belt armour. The second variant of the design carried additional 3.7cm anti-aircraft guns. The two conferences called in the first quarter of 1927 did not result in the selection of any of these designs; on the contrary, supplementary requirements for the new vessels were added. Finally, after long discussion and numerous changes to the design, a compromise was reached. The new battleship must have very good seakeeping qualities; at the same time it was required that the ship carry six 28cm guns and six to eight 12cm guns and be able to maintain a speed of 26-27 knots. This concept, if realised, would revolutionise shipbuilding as it combined the qualities of a cruiser and of a battleship in a single ship. While fighting cruisers, it would have the advantage of more powerful guns and better armour, while in confrontation with battleships it had superior speed. At that time the German designers preferred to use diesel engines over steam propulsion systems. Initially it was planned to use 54,000 HP diesel engines, which would increase the ship's range considerably. With the design of the *Deutschland*, therefore, the Fleet Command began to think of oceanic warfare, a scenario which the victorious Allied powers did not expect. While maintaining the 10,000-ton limit, the ship was to be more powerful than all faster ships and faster than all stronger ships. At that time only three British ships (*Hood*, *Renown* and *Repulse*) were both faster and more heavily armed – although even this was theoretical, as Germany did not then wish to provoke an armed conflict with Great Britain.

Several factors conspired to hold up further construction work on the new battleship. The situation inside the Navy became very difficult when the Lohmann affair threatened to expose the Weimar Republic's clandestine efforts to circumvent the military restrictions of the Versailles Treaty. In addition, the hyperinflation raging in the German Reich allowed very little money to be spent on the Reichsmarine and its new building program. The final roadblock was a dispute in parliament, where the upper chamber (Reichsrat) was against building a battleship; during a session on 17 December 1927 it refused to approve the decision to build the ship, citing the difficult financial situation of the Reich. When the question of building a battleship reached the lower house (Reichstag), it met opposition from the SDP and KPD (Socialist and Communist) parties. They argued that the German people at that time needed many things but a battleship was not one of them. The discussion about the real need for the battleship lasted until almost the end of 1927. Surprisingly, a breakthrough came on 27 March 1928 when the lower house approved the construction of the ship. However, fearing the upper house would reject the project once more, the voting was postponed until autumn. During that time the press began a campaign against the construction of the new battleship, using a very powerful slogan: 'Kinderspeisung statt Panzerkreuzer' (Food for children not armoured cruiser). In May 1928 new parliamentary elections were held and the result finally allowed the Navy to begin replacing the old pre-dreadnoughts with new battleships. The new Reichstag included among its members twelve NSDAP (Nazi Party) representatives, fully in support of the fleet development plan.

There were still problems with settling the

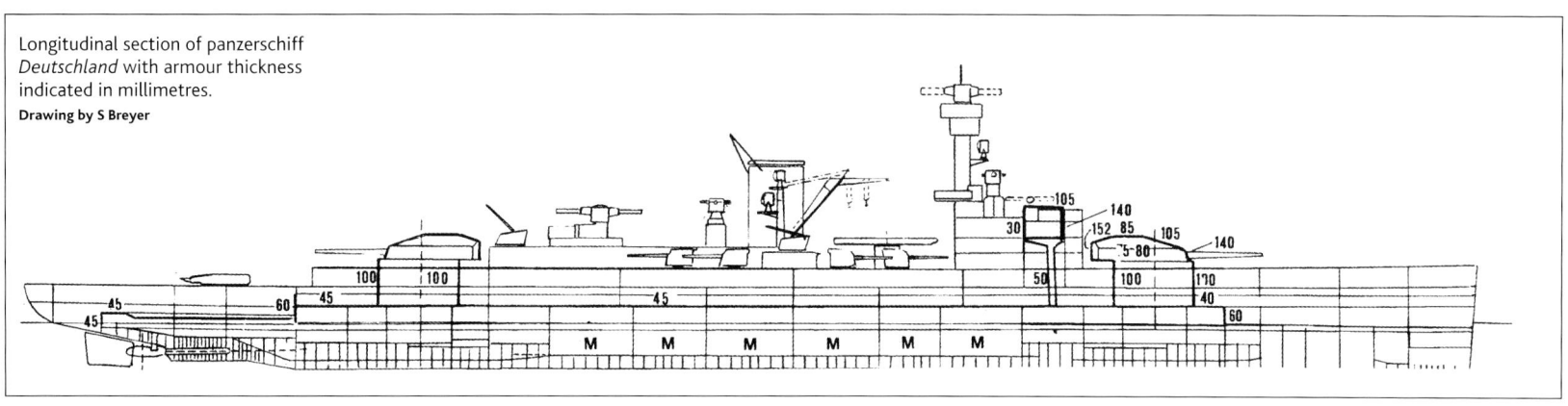

Longitudinal section of panzerschiff *Deutschland* with armour thickness indicated in millimetres.
Drawing by S Breyer

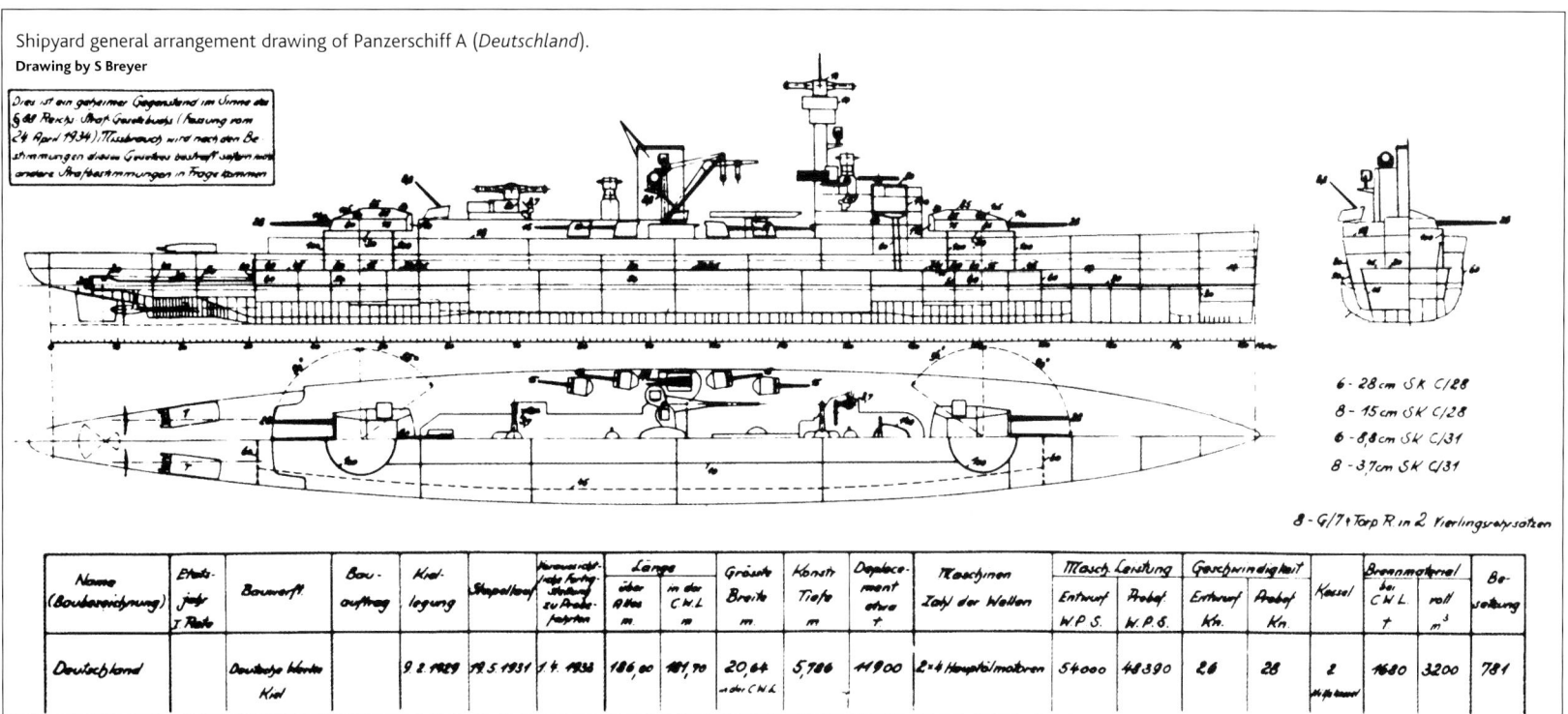

Shipyard general arrangement drawing of Panzerschiff A (*Deutschland*).
Drawing by S Breyer

technical details of the ship's equipment while keeping the design under the 10,000-ton limit, but another step forward was made on 11 April 1928, when Admiral Zenker formally accepted the preliminary design. This then required the Construction Office to prepare all the necessary drawings within the next quarter, so that a shipyard could be selected where the Navy would place an order for the new ship. The Construction Office did its job on time and the design work was completed on 28 December 1928. The final design characteristics of 'Panzerschiff A' were as follows: waterline length 181.7m, length overall 185.7m, total beam 20.5m, draught 5.77m, displacement 10,000 tons, propulsion by eight diesel engines with a total power of 54,000 HP, maximum speed 27 knots. Armament was: six 28cm guns, eight 15cm guns, five 8.8cm anti-aircraft guns, four 3.7cm anti-aircraft guns and six 53.3cm torpedo tubes. The design was produced under the supervision of senior constructor Blechschmidt.

This was not the end of the difficulties surrounding the first German panzerschiff. Before the drawings and calculations were complete, there were major upheavals in the German Navy and in the world of politics. First

The hull of Panzerschiff A ready for the christening and launching ceremony. In the front, the launching platform is already erected and decorated with flags. This picture was probably taken on the day before launch as the battleship's hull is decorated as well.
CAW

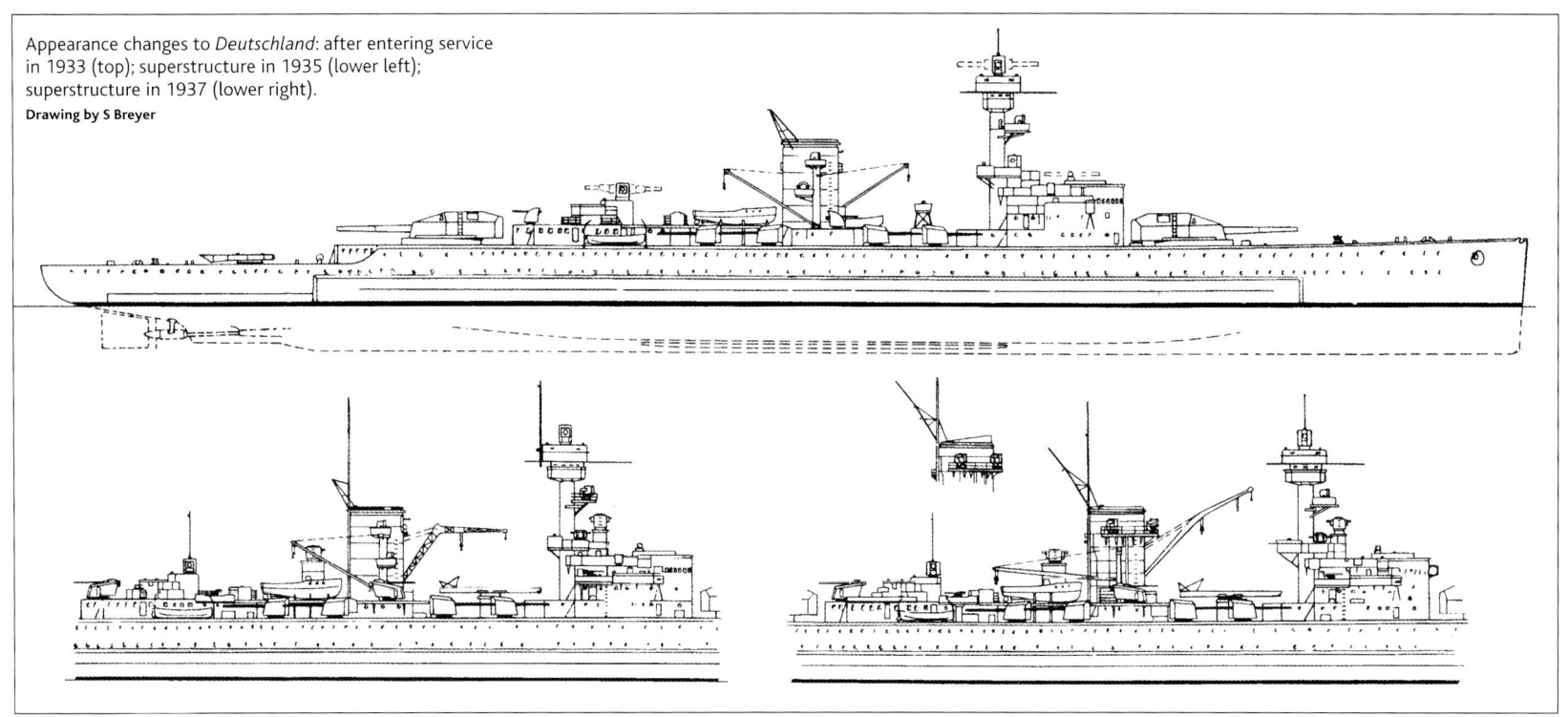

Appearance changes to *Deutschland*: after entering service in 1933 (top); superstructure in 1935 (lower left); superstructure in 1937 (lower right).
Drawing by S Breyer

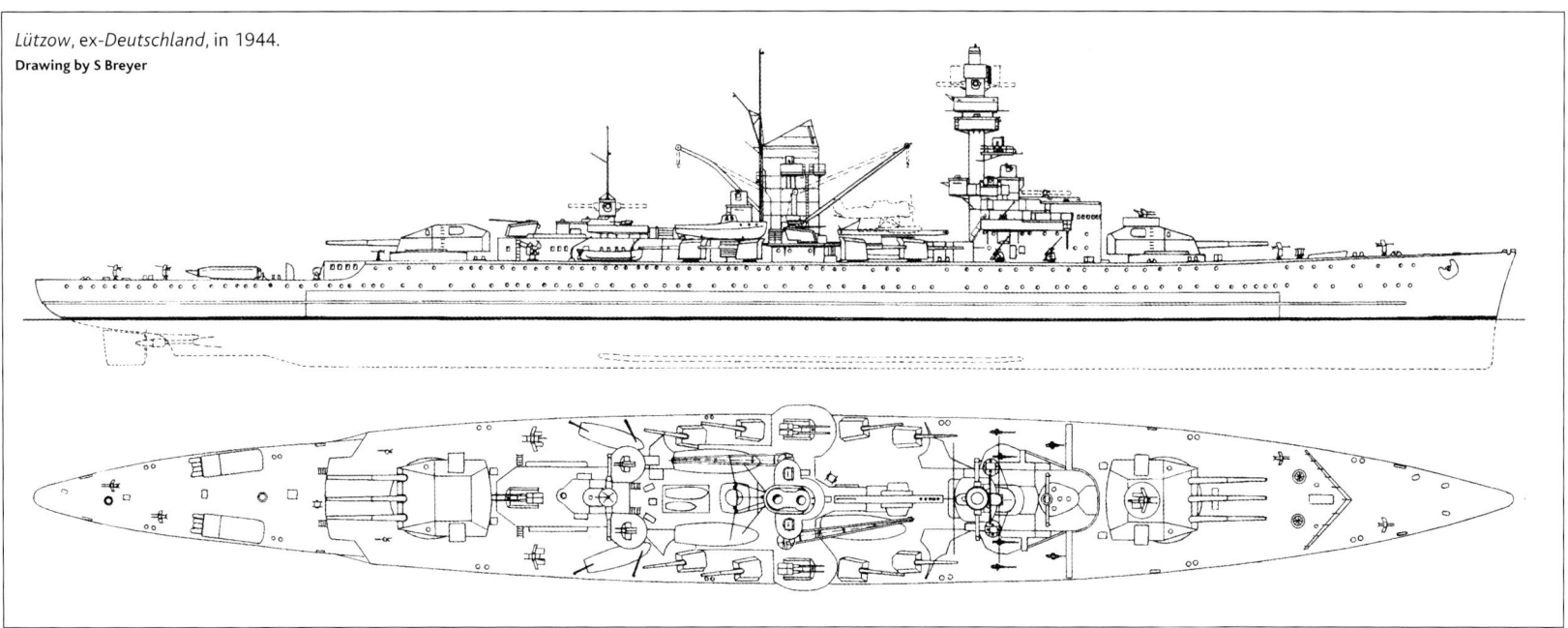

Lützow, ex-*Deutschland*, in 1944.
Drawing by S Breyer

of all, as a result of the Lohmann scandal, the C-in-C, Admiral Zenker, resigned from his post in August 1928, to be succeeded on 24 September by Admiral Erich Raeder, who systematically worked to introduce changes to the modest characteristics of Panzerschiff A. In 1929 it was planned to build two ships to the approved design known in the German Reich as Panzerschiffe A and B ('Ersatz *Preussen*', 'Ersatz *Lothringen*'), but there was a chance that the second ship would be built to slightly different specifications. The following sums (in Reichsmarks) were assigned for the project in the budget years: 1930 RM 11.75 million; 1931 RM 15.60 million; 1932 RM 21.55 million; and in 1933 RM 24.10 million. It was planned to start the construction of another ship, Panzerschiff C ('Ersatz *Braunschweig*') in the early 1930s.

In the meantime two disarmament conferences had been held, the first in 1927 in Geneva and the second in 1930 in London. During these conferences the governments of Britain and the United States sought to maintain the dominant position they had established under the Washington Treaty, preventing the construction of battleships of 'uncontrolled' displacement. Much to their surprise, other countries clearly believed that the limitations imposed by the earlier treaties would soon be lifted, which was confirmed by the fact that most of them unofficially prepared sketch designs for battleships exceeding those limits. Another surprise was that in 1930 Germany joined the new global arms race. This was indicated by the construction of the fourth battleship, Panzerschiff D, as part of the fleet development plan for the years 1931–1934. This program, known as the 'Reconstruction of the Reichsmarine', was prepared by the Weimar Republic a few weeks before Adolf Hitler came to power. It called for the construction of six ships of the panzerschiff type, which was in accordance with the provisions of the Versailles Treaty. However, the

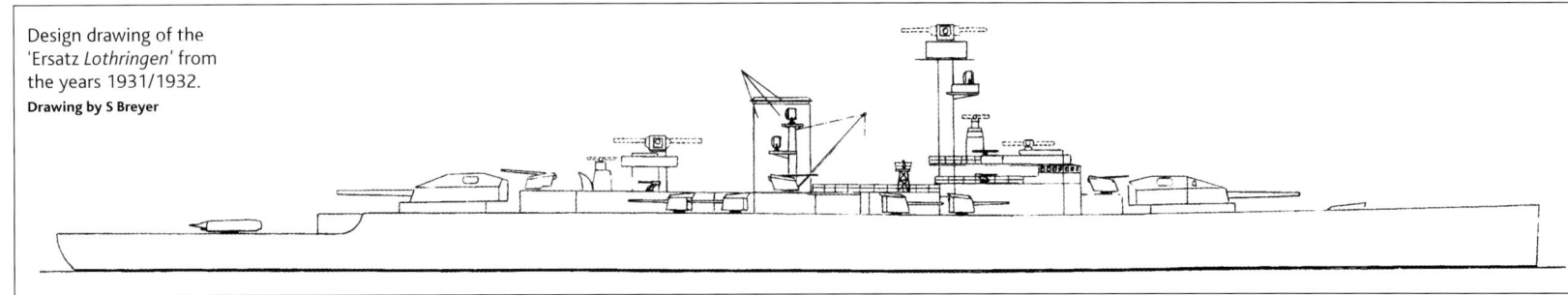

Design drawing of the 'Ersatz *Lothringen*' from the years 1931/1932.
Drawing by S Breyer

The old pre-dreadnought battleship *Lothringen*, for which the *Admiral Scheer* was the formal replacement.
A Jarski collection

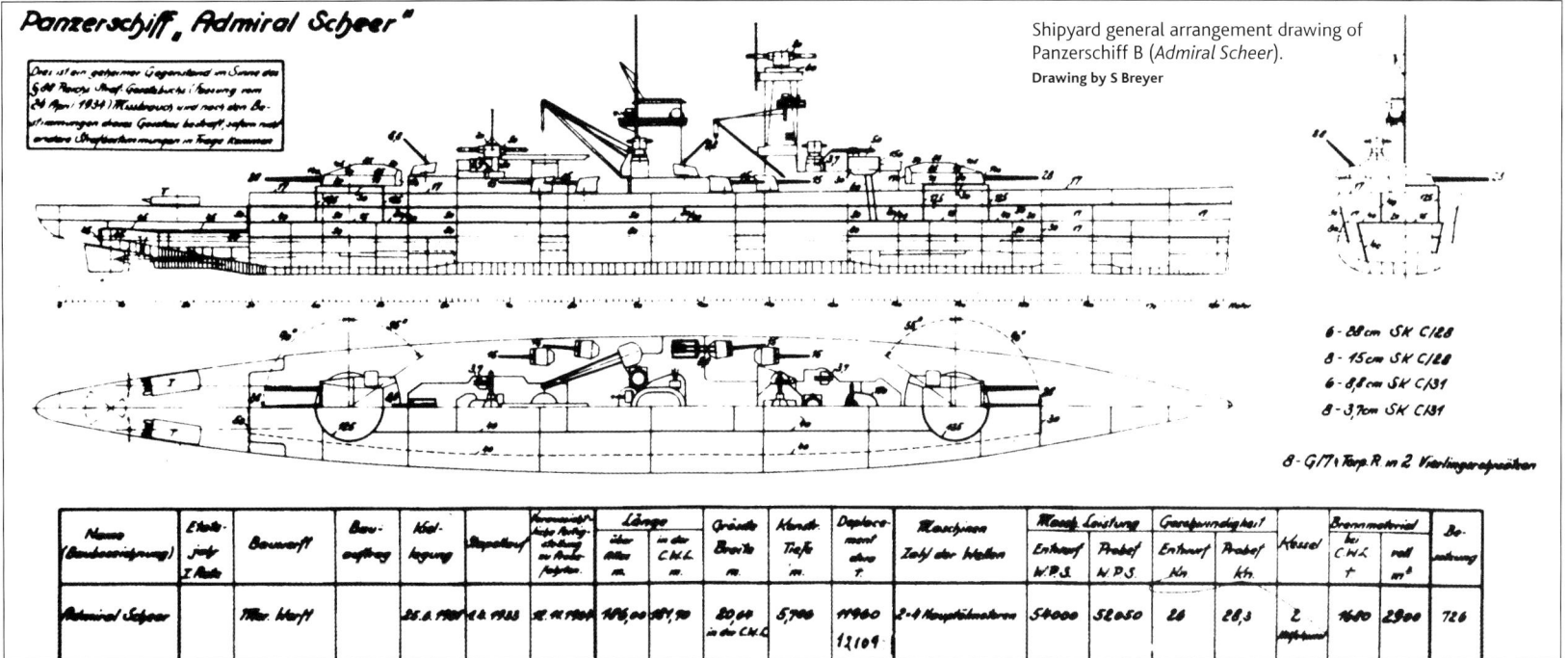

Shipyard general arrangement drawing of Panzerschiff B (*Admiral Scheer*).
Drawing by S Breyer

nationalists who came to power radically altered the political balance, which gave the Navy hope for a faster and more comprehensive expansion plan. At first the tenets of the Treaty of Versailles were not to be openly violated but it was planned to use diplomacy to circumvent the treaty restrictions at a later time.

Such an ambitious fleet expansion program could not pass unnoticed in Europe. France, which was afraid that it would no longer be able to protect the trade routes to its colonies spread around the world, was the first to react. Work commenced on building an opponent for the German *Deutschland*, the result of which was the *Dunkerque* class battleships, for which the first keel was laid in December 1932. Under the Washington Treaty of 1922, France could begin the construction in 1926 of two battleships with a displacement of 35,000 tons each. During the conference the French had forced this concession as compensation for having built so few battleships during the First World War. In 1926 the Staff of the French Navy (État-Major de la Marine) ordered the Naval Technical Service (Section Technique de Constructions Navales) to create a design for the new 'croiseur de combat' (literally, combat cruiser, or battlecruiser). The requirements for those ships were summarised under three main heads: first, they had to be able to destroy any existing treaty cruiser; second, to be capable of attacking convoys protected by battleships steaming at 20–25 knots; and third, to become part of a reconnaissance force, in the event of signing agreements with other naval powers under which the French fleet would become a partner. As can be appreciated, these requirements were not very onerous and were the result of the colonial character of France, which first and foremost needed to protect its trade routes. The initial 17,500-ton designs were created in 1926, but the situation changed in 1928 when the Germans made public their plan to build 10,000-ton *Deutschland* type battleships. As a result, new designs were drafted with better armour protection and more powerful armament. When intelligence provided some additional information on the *Deutschland*, new requirements for the 'combat cruisers' were drawn up. The new design studies displaced between 23,000 and 35,000 tons, with an armament consisting of 30.5cm or 33cm (12in or 13in) guns, although 38cm or 40.6cm (15in or 16in) guns would have been allowable by treaty. In addition, the French Navy increased the requirements for protection and in 1930 demanded that the armour be able to resist the 28cm shell planned for the *Deutschland*. The design prepared by the Naval Technical Service (STCN) was a 25,000-ton ship, armed with eight 30.5cm guns mounted in two quadruple turrets, and capable of 29–30 knots. The design for the battleship *Dunkerque* was completed in 1931, but the final version was only accepted on 27 April 1932, by which time the ship was to carry 33cm guns on a standard displacement of 26,500 tons. Although the requirements were not particularly demanding, the *Dunkerque* exceeded all initial expectations. The concept turned out to be such a success that it influenced to some degree the design of most subsequent battleships in other navies.

In the German Reich the construction of the third panzerschiff was planned for 1929, but the

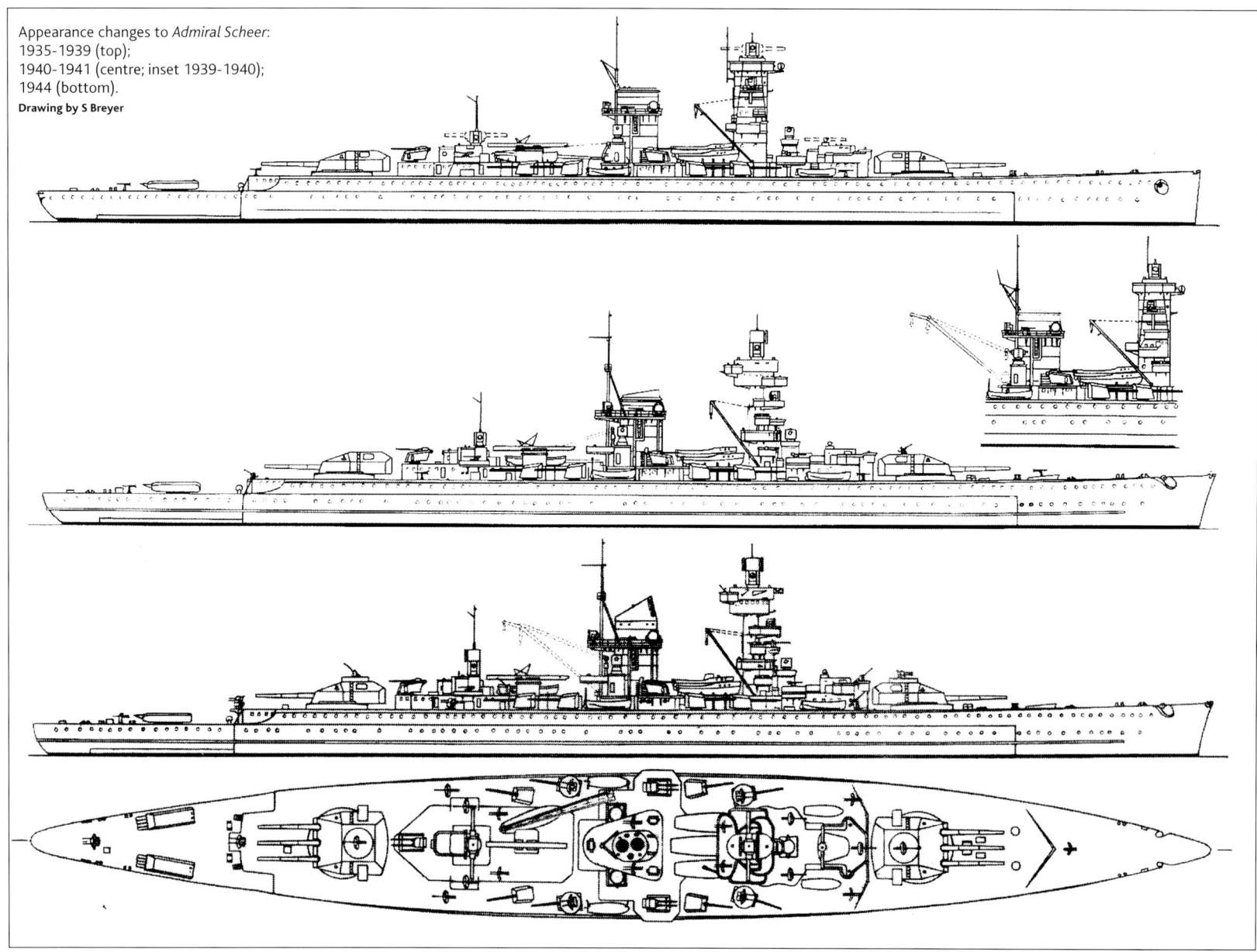

Appearance changes to *Admiral Scheer*:
1935-1939 (top);
1940-1941 (centre; inset 1939-1940);
1944 (bottom).
Drawing by S Breyer

The launching of Panzerschiff B ('Ersatz *Lothringen*') on 1 April 1933 marked the completion of the first stage of the new battleship construction. After releasing the chocks the hull slid safely into the water from the Number 2 slipway.
CAW

Germans feared a strong reaction by the western powers and in particular France. In addition, the construction of the new *Dunkerque* class with 33cm guns cast doubt on the wisdom of ordering further *Deutschland* type ships. The Germans quickly created new sketch designs for Battleship C, some of them even proposing a reduction in the calibre of the main guns to 21cm (8.2in), an inferiority to the new French ships that was impossible to accept. The follow-up concepts for Panzerschiff C were versions equipped with 24cm (9.4in) guns in three triple turrets. However, Germany's toughest opponent was time, which was running out. If the change of armament to 24cm guns was accepted while maintaining the 30-knot speed, it would take too long to design a ship with the same level of protection within the 10,000-ton displacement limit. By the time such a ship entered service it would already have been outdated.

Admiral Scheer was launched on 1 April 1933 at the Marinewerft in Wilhelmshaven. Shown here, the guard of honour is inspected by the Reich's defence minister Werner von Blomberg followed by the commander of the Reichsmarine Admiral Erich Raeder.
CAW

During the time the panzerschiffe were being built, significant political upheavals continually influenced their design and construction. After the second, Panzerschiff B, was laid down, the future of the German battleship construction program was not entirely clear. In 1932 Admiral Raeder suggested increasing the displacement of Battleship C to 15,000/18,000 tons and equipping it with three 28cm turrets; a second variant proposed by the admiral was a ship with twin 20.3cm turrets. However, at that time it was impossible to circumvent the Versailles Treaty openly, so in 1932 it was decided to order the third ship, Panzerschiff C, to the same specification as the previous two. The circumstances surrounding the construction of capital ships changed dramatically when Adolf Hitler came to power, but in the interim the *Deutschland* design was incrementally improved, which resulted in the creation of three individual ships. Officially, they shared the same characteristics but these figures, and especially the dis-

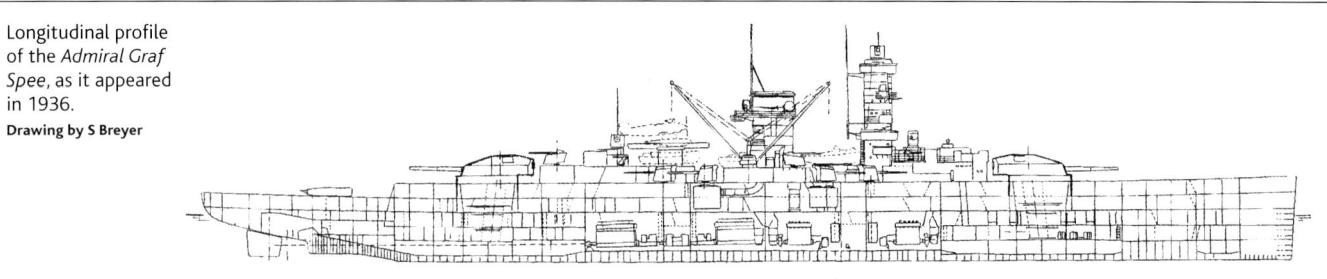

Longitudinal profile of the *Admiral Graf Spee*, as it appeared in 1936.
Drawing by S Breyer

Panzerschiff C ('Ersatz *Braunschweig*') was named *Admiral Graf Spee* on launching, a ceremony witnessed by numerous inhabitants of Wilhelmshaven as with previous warship launches. The ship was christened by Huberta von Spee, the daughter of the Rear Admiral after whom the ship was named, and surviving members of crews commanded by Admiral von Spee participated in the ceremony. After the christening ceremony the battleship's nameplate was uncovered.
CAW

The old battleship *Braunschweig* was replaced by *Admiral Graf Spee*.
A Jarski collection

placement, were identical only on paper. Even judging from their external appearance a careful observer could see that their characteristics did not match the official figures. However, a comparison was only really possible when all three ships were in commission in 1936, by which time Hitler was powerful enough to ignore earlier undertakings and treaties.

At that point it was possible to identify numerous major differences among the three ships. The most visible was the command tower structure (Kommandoturm), which was systematically improved. The cylindrical tower installed on the *Deutschland* proved too cramped, especially when the ship was acting as a flagship. The next ship, *Admiral Scheer*, had this tower greatly enlarged and more functional in layout, but at sea it was soon discovered that in strong headwinds it acted like a backed sail, reducing speed by 1–2 knots. Because of this shortcoming, combined with experience garnered on Spanish 'neutrality' patrols, it was quickly decided to rebuild the tower to a modified version of the cylindrical form on the *Deutschland*. *Admiral Graf Spee*, which entered service last, had the most numerous external changes, but even these modifications turned out to be insufficient. This ship was also supposed to have its command tower remodelled along similar lines to *Admiral Scheer* but the outbreak of war and the early scuttling of the ship made it impossible. This panzerschiff design, later reclassified as a heavy cruiser, formed the basis for all later German battleship concepts. Finally, it is worth noting that the total costs and building times of the ships were as follows:

Deutschland: 4 years, total cost RM 80 millions.

Admiral Scheer: 3 years and 4 months, total cost RM 90 millions.

Admiral Graf Spee: 3 years and 3 months, total cost RM 82 millions.

Deutschland/Lützow

Deutschland photographed with the crew manning the side. The He 60 floatplane on the ship's catapult carries the markings 60 + D 91.
S Breyer collection

Panzerschiff A ('Ersatz *Preussen*') was ordered on 17 August 1928 from the Deutsche Werke shipyard in Kiel, where the ship received hull number 219. According to the construction progress log, the keel was laid on 5 February 1929. Lofflund, the shipyard director, supervised all construction works on the ship with the assistance of principal engineers Malsius and Senst. The launching ceremony took place on 19 May 1931, performed by Feldmarshal Paul von Hindenburg (Paul Ludwig Hans Anton von Beneckendorff und von Hindenburg). The first in the series of panzerschiffe started her builder's sea trials on 19 January 1933. Apart from naval personnel, shipyard workers and employees from some of the sub-contracting companies were also involved in the trials, which lasted until the end of the month. In mid-February the *Deutschland* commenced her first gunnery and torpedo shoots. After the completion of trials on 28 February 1933 the ship was officially taken over from the shipyard and prepared for commissioning. This ceremony took place on 1 April 1933 in the Wilhelmshaven naval base. The first commander of the new ship was Captain (Kpt z S) Hermann von Fischel. In the shipyard on the same day, *Deutschland*'s sister ship was launched; Panzerschiff B was named *Admiral Scheer*.

The *Deutschland* spent the period immediately after commissioning on trials and working-up cruises. Until the second half of May the ship carried an extra hundred MAN factory personnel, tasked with sorting out the teething troubles of the main diesels. The manager of the Marinewerft shipyard in Wilhelmshaven, Rear Admiral Massman, remained with the ship until the trials were over. The ship next undertook a VIP cruise out into the Skagerrak, where the distinguished guests included Adolf Hitler, who came on board on 23 May for his first sea voyage. The ship sailed to Norway, the Faroe Islands and Iceland, but during the cruise numerous technical shortcomings became apparent. These were addressed by the Marinewerft shipyard in Wilhelmshaven in May and June and after the necessary repairs the ship left for main engine trials. Unfortunately, the results were again disappointing and the ship had to return to the yard once more. Solving all the problems took until the second half of August and only on the 23rd was the ship committed to the measured mile for main engine trials, where she reached a maximum speed of 28.03 knots at 48,390 HP. This was repeated near Bornholm on 31 August and 4 and 5 September 1933. During the trials the ship experienced some minor machinery vibration which affected the rangefinders located in B turret and higher on the ship. After that the ship conducted practice firings against the target ship *Baden*. The ship was exercised intensively around Eckernförde, Flensburg, Kiel and Wilhelmshaven until the end of the year. On 10 December 1933 the *Deutschland* was declared fully combat ready and was assigned to C-in-C Battleships (BdL, Befehlshaber der Linienschiffe), although trials and training exercises continued through the first quarter of 1934.

The ship sailed from Kiel on 10 April 1934 for a cruise off Norway, when the guest list included Hitler; the minister of the Reichswehr, Generalleutnant von Blomberg; the C-in-C of land forces von Fritsch; and the C-in-C of the Reichsmarine, Admiral Raeder. During the cruise both the army and the naval commanders assured Hitler of their personal support in his power struggle with the commander of the SA (Sturmabteilung), Ernst Röhm, which was to come to a bloody end on 30 June 1934 during the so-called Night of the Long Knives (Nacht der langen Messer). The ship returned to Kiel on 14 April, and in May took part in fleet manoeuvres in the Baltic. From 9 to 23 June 1934 *Deutschland* and the light cruiser *Köln* undertook a training cruise for gunnery practice in the central Atlantic. In August the panzerschiff paid an official visit to the Swedish port of Göteborg, followed in September by participating in the autumn fleet manoeuvres; on 1 October 1934 the C-in-C Battleships, Rear Admiral R Carls, hoisted his flag on the ship. Later that month the ship paid a visit to Scotland where from 16 to 20 October the ship was open to the public at Edinburgh.

On her return to Wilhelmshaven the ship began a refit in the Marinewerft that lasted until 21 February 1935 when the ship assumed the duties of fleet flagship. In the following years the ship conducted intensive exercises in the Atlantic and in the Mediterranean. In 1937, while carrying out patrols off

Spain during the civil war, the ship was bombed near Ibiza by republican aircraft; twenty-three men were killed in this attack. After bringing back the bodies of the dead to Germany, the ship was repaired and *Deutschland* returned to Spanish waters in 1938.

Before September 1939 the ship conducted intensive training cruises in the North Sea and in the Atlantic, but when hostilities seemed imminent, the panzerschiff was sent to the North Atlantic to await further orders for conducting raids against enemy shipping. On 25 January 1940 the ship was renamed *Lützow* and reclassified as a heavy cruiser. The decision to change the name was driven by a concern that if a ship bearing the name *Deutschland* (Germany) was to be sunk, it would hand the enemy a massive propaganda coup. Not long before, in December 1939 the Royal Navy had trapped the *Graf Spee*, which was then scuttled off Uruguay, so losing another ship was a real fear. This name-change was possible because the incomplete hull of the heavy cruiser *Lützow* had just been sold to the Russians. The first operation under the new name and designation was a redeployment to the Bay of Gdańsk for sea trials and gunnery practice. After returning to Gotenhafen (present-day Gdynia) the ship took part in Operation Weserübung – the invasion of Denmark and Norway – where she was damaged by Norwegian coastal artillery. The ship's bad luck continued as during the return to Kiel she was hit by torpedoes from the British submarine *Spearfish*. A two-day struggle to tow the cruiser back to Kiel eventually ended successfully and on 13 April 1940 the ship entered a dry dock. Repairs took until the end of the year and were closely monitored by British aerial reconnaissance. In March 1941 the *Lützow* returned to combat duties under the command of Captain (Kpt z S) Leo Kreisch. In June she took part in Operation Sommerreise, an attempted breakout into the Atlantic, but was once again hit by a torpedo, this time dropped from a British Beaufort bomber. The *Lützow* returned to the Deutsche Werke shipyard in Kiel, where she remained under repair for another six months. At the beginning of 1942, when all work was complete, it was decided to relocate the ship to the Gotenhafen naval base for sea trials and gunnery practice. In the middle of the year the ship sailed to Norway to reinforce the German forces in Bergen and Altafjord. During Operation Rösselsprung the heavy cruiser ran aground on underwater rocks near Tjeldsund and had to abort the operation and return to the fjord because of the damage sustained. The patched-up ship left Norway on 9 August 1942 for the Deutsche Werke shipyard in Kiel, where repairs lasted until the end of October. Following sea trials in the Baltic, *Lützow* returned to Norway, entering Bogen Bay near Narvik on 12 December. At the end of the year the ship was part of the German force that attacked convoy JW51B near Bear Island (Operation Regenbogen). Despite their overwhelming advantage in firepower the Germans were unable to sink any of the merchantmen and, what is more, lost one of their own destroyers in what the British call the Battle of the Barent Sea. In the early months of 1943 *Lützow* lay at anchor in Bogen Bay but in March was relocated further north to Kaafjord near Altafjord. Throughout this time the ship was suffering from engine trouble which kept her from any combat operations, but in September she was sent to Germany for repairs, and from there to Gotenhafen (Gdynia). Even this naval base was being systematically bombed by Allied air forces, so it was no longer considered safe and the repairs to the *Lützow* had to be performed in Libau (present-day Liepāja).

In March 1944, with the dockyard work complete, *Lützow* conducted sea trials in the roadstead and was assigned to training units based in Gotenhafen (Gdynia). The ship's status was changed once again at the end of July, when she was assigned to the 2nd Battle Group under the command of Rear Admiral Thiele. Around this time the *Lützow*'s anti-aircraft armament was improved by the installation of additional 20mm Flakvierling mounts. At the turn of the year *Lützow* was employed bombarding the positions of the advancing Russian and Polish troops until mid-March 1945 when the front moved closer to the Bay of Gdańsk and the Vistula Spit. At the end of March the *Lützow* was again in action against enemy troops advancing on Danzig and Gotenhafen (Gdańsk and Gdynia.). On the night of 4/5 April the ship took part in Operation Walpurgisnacht, during which German ships transported 35,000 refugees and soldiers from Oksywie Heights to the Hel Peninsula.

The final chapter began on 16 April 1945 during British air raids on Swinemünde (Świnoujście) when the ship was heavily damaged and ran aground. As Russian troops approached Stettin (Szczecin) on 4 May 1945, the ship was scuttled by the remaining crew. The hulk was taken over by the Russians and salvaged, but had to wait two years for a decision on its final fate. In the event, the ship was used for tests of aerial bombs. The tests began at 08.00 on 20 June 1947, when *Lützow* was towed by five tugs through the Piast Canal. Towing the ship to the Świnoujście roadstead took until 13.40. There, the icebreaker *Volynetsch* carrying the fleet command representatives joined the other ships. Two days later, on the 22nd, the *Lützow* reached the assigned test location near Kołobrzeg. During the initial tests, bombs from 100kg to 1000kg were placed on the ship and connected with wires to the detonators on the icebreaker. It was also planned to perform a torpedo attack using a squadron of Tu-2 aircraft. The experiment started at 10.25 by detonating almost 1.5 tons of explosives on board the *Lützow*. At 16.16 the ship began to sink on a an even keel; eight minutes later the bow was under water, the stern rising slowly as the ship sank.

Adolf von Lützow

Ludwig Adolf Wilhelm Freiherr von Lützow was born on 18 May 1783 in Berlin. He was a Prussian officer, who took part in the Battle of Auerstedt, and later commanded a volunteer corps during the Napoleonic Wars, rising to the rank of general. When Frederick Wilhelm III launched his appeal for men to join the Freikorps in February 1813, Lützow, then a major, formed a volunteer corps to fight Napoleon's army. Consisting mainly of university students, the corps of 3000 men under his command first went into battle with the French on 27 March 1813, fighting with valour against Napoleon's seasoned troops. Effective use of manoeuvre and hit-and-run tactics soon became the hallmark of the corps under von Lützow's command. However, in June 1813 his corps was decimated and the remaining men joined the regular army. In 1814 he fought in the Ardennes and during the 1815 campaign he commanded a cavalry brigade which fought at Ligny, where von Lützow was wounded and captured by the French. He was released after the Battle of Waterloo. Von Lützow died on 6 December 1834 in Berlin.

Last-minute checks by shipyard workers and other personnel responsible for the launching to see whether everything is ready for the ceremony.
CAW

One of the most important days in the history of Deutsche Werke in Kiel: 19 May 1931 saw the launch of the first post-war German capital ship. In the foreground the guard of honour salutes President Paul von Hindenburg and the Reich Chancellor Heinrich Brunning.
CAW

On the launching platform, President Hindenburg is about to give Panzerschiff A ('Ersatz *Preussen*') the name *Deutschland*.
CAW

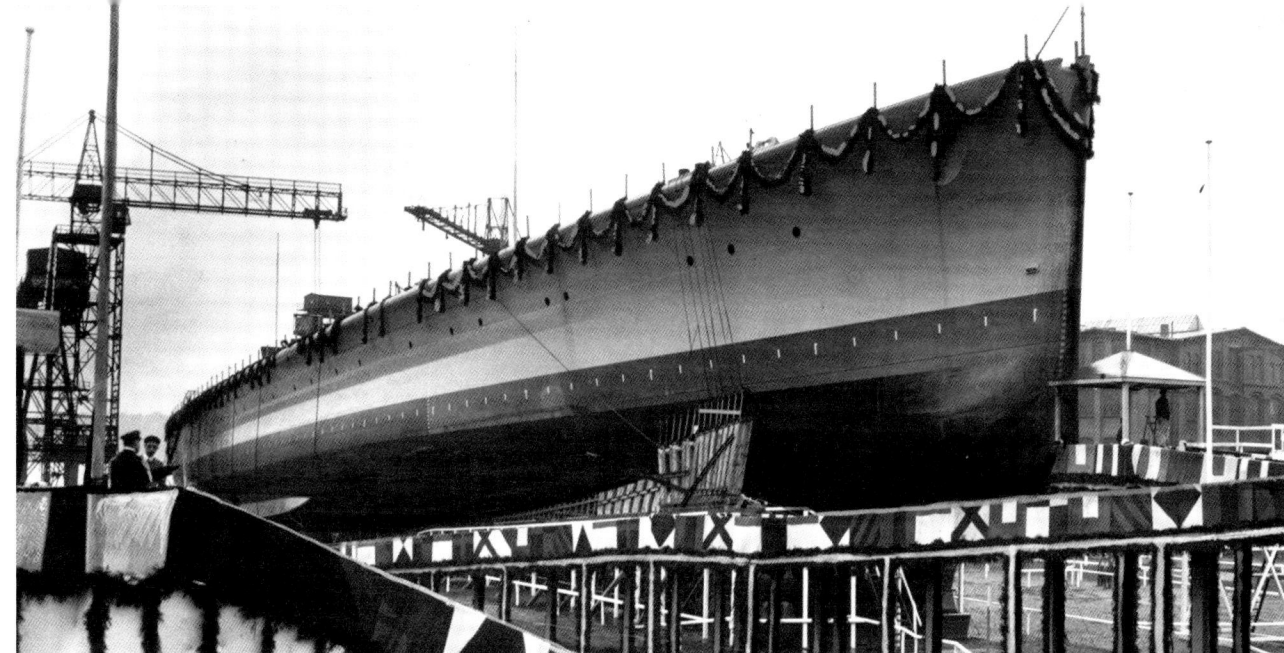

RIGHT: One last look from the launching platform at the slipway and the hull of 'Ersatz Preussen' which will soon slide down to the water.

BELOW: Almost 60,000 people gathered to witness the launching ceremony, most of whom were the local inhabitants of Kiel. A view over the grandstands on both sides of the slipway, this picture was taken moments before the ship was given its name and the nameplate was uncovered.

CAW

During the speech by Chancellor Brunning, the ship started to slide down the ways because the chocks supporting the hull were released too early. A considerable commotion arose on the launching platform, but President Hindenburg was quick to react: he was able to press the button releasing the bottle of champagne which just managed to hit the ship's bow.
CAW

No one has foreseen that the ceremony would go off half-cock, and some of the numerous reporters did not even manage to photograph the moment of christening. A shot of the *Deutschland* safely leaving the slipway.
ADM

The *Deutschland* being turned in the shipyard basin shortly after launch.
CAW

Scaffolding surrounds the director tower and funnel of *Deutschland* and stages are rigged over the hull sides as fitting out proceeds in the basin of Deutsche Werke.
CAW

Installing an armoured turret roof plate over the 28cm guns in the forward turret.
M Skwiot collection

A retouched view of the ship proceeding to the fitting-out berth, with the main gun turrets already in place.
CAW

Deutschland fitting out: a close-up of the forward superstructure and conning tower under construction.
S Breyer collection

The last of the starboard 15cm MPL C/28 single mountings being hoisted into place.
S Breyer collection

Deutschland moored at the fitting-out quay in the Deutche Werke shipyard in Kiel, 1932. The work is picking up pace and the main gun turrets look complete, as do many of the smaller deck fittings.
S Breyer collection

Deutschland fitting out: work continuing on the after superstructure and around the mast.
CAW

Deutschland's sea trials in open water on 18 and 19 January 1933. The battleship's main rangefinders and quarterdeck torpedo tubes have not been installed yet.
Photograph by Drüppel, from the collection of A Jarski

Another early view of *Deutschland*, but by this time the torpedo tubes have been fitted on the quarterdeck.
Photograph by Drüppel, from the collection of A Jarski

Deutschland sailing under a bridge on the Kaiser Wilhelm Canal after leaving the Holtenau locks at Kiel.
M Krzyżan collection

After the successful completion of sea trials the *Deutschland* sailed from Kiel to the Wilhelmshaven naval base to be officially commissioned. Note the ship's crest either side of the stemhead and a second anchor on the port side only.
CAW

Deutschland photographed on 27 February 1933 during her first transit voyage, seen under the Levensau bridge over the Nord-Ostsee (Kiel) Canal en route for Wilhelmshaven where the ship was to be commissioned on 1 April 1933.
A Jarski collection

Deutschland making her way to Wilhelmshaven. After the ship arrived, ammunition was embarked and the ship sailed to the Cuxhaven area for gunnery exercises.
A Jarski collection

At this period the crew's life was rather monotonous, with most of their time spent on drills and preparations for the commissioning ceremony. This picture shows the crew arriving on board the ship.
CAW

A speech by the first commanding office, Captain (Kpt z S) Hermann Fischel, given to the crew assembled on the quarterdeck was one element of the commissioning ceremony on 1 April 1933.
CAW

The Reichsmarine ensign is hoisted at the stern of the panzerschiff, 1 April 1933.
CAW

Deutschland berthed at Wilhelmshaven a few days before commissioning. To the right the old battleship *Hannover* can be seen.
A Jarski collection

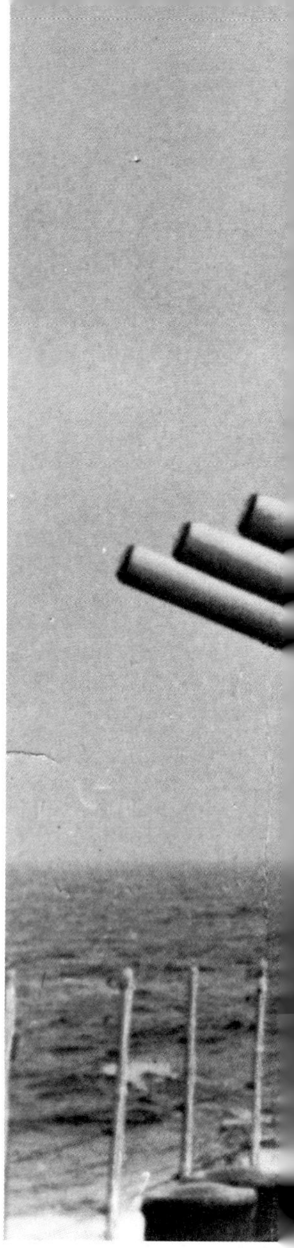

On 10 April 1934 the *Deutschland* left Kiel and sailed to Norway. On board the ship were the Reich's Chancellor Adolf Hitler, minister of the Reichswehr Generalleutnant Werner von Blomberg, commander of land forces Werner von Fritsch and the commander of the Reichsmarine Admiral Erich Raeder. The picture shows the *Deutschland* in Sognefjord.
CAW

Deutschland's main gun turrets received individual names and crests. A Turret was named *Hitler* and had the NSDAP emblem installed on its sides together with the nameplate. B Turret was named *Hindenburg* and had the Hindenburg family crest and the nameplate on its sides.
T Klimczyk collection

Deutschland in Hamburg during her visit of 28 May–1 June 1934. In the background the old battleship *Schleswig-Holstein* is visible.
S Breyer collection

The *Deutschland*'s crew manning the side as the ship enters Hamburg in May 1935. It is difficult to establish whether the censor removed the background or if it was the publisher attempting to improve the photo for a commemorative postcard.
Photograph by Urbahns, from the collection of T Klimczyk

LEFT: Panzerschiff *Deutschland* in Hamburg in May 1935.
CAW

OPPOSITE: *Deutschland*'s forward superstructure photographed during the ship's visit to Hamburg at the end of May 1935. The dark grey turret roofs are visible, a type of camouflage used on the ship since early 1934. Additionally, a white circle is painted on the roof of A turret which was an identification marking for friendly aircraft.
S Breyer collection

Details of the *Deutschland*'s stern as the ship sails into the Bay of Kiel. Note the stern anchor and the Nazi eagle emblem.
A Jarski collection

Deutschland at a mooring buoy in the Heikendorf Bay roadstead near Kiel. This picture was taken in 1936, probably in early May when the *Deutschland* participated in a fleet review. Interestingly, the ship's bow coat of arms was removed from the photograph.
W Danielewicz collection

Deutschland photographed near Wilhelmshaven in the first half of 1935.
W Danielewicz collection

The *Deutschland* shortly after a refit that included the installation of a seaplane catapult and other aviation equipment. This photograph was taken in the second half of 1935 during exercises with an embarked aircraft. The launching and landing trials were conducted with a Heinkel He 60 floatplane with the civilian registration D-IPEN.
T Klimczyk collection

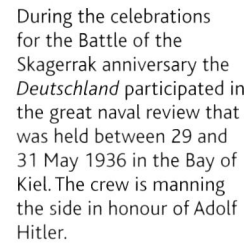

During the celebrations for the Battle of the Skagerrak anniversary the *Deutschland* participated in the great naval review that was held between 29 and 31 May 1936 in the Bay of Kiel. The crew is manning the side in honour of Adolf Hitler.
A Jarski collection

Deutschland leaving Wilhelmshaven in June 1936, flying the flag of Rear Admiral Carls. This picture was taken either shortly before or shortly after the battleship's visit to Copenhagen.
CAW

Another view of the ship from the same period shows the *Deutschland* alongside a pier.
CAW<None>

Deutschland photographed in the summer of 1936 before a deployment to Spain on 'neutrality' patrols during the Civil War. On the fore topmast the ship flies the flag of Commander of Battleships (BdL – Befehlshaber der Linienschiffe), Rear Admiral Carls. The seaplane catapult installed in 1935 is clearly visible. As with most battleship pictures of the time, this too was retouched by the censors.
Photograph by Klein, from the collection of A Jarski

The battleship's crew enjoying their free time on board the ship. This picture was taken during the *Deutschland*'s first tour of duty in Spanish waters (26 July–25 August 1936). On 31 July 1936 the crew was ordered to paint the German national colours on the main gun turrets for clearer identification.
M Krzy an collection

Battleship *Deutschland* (in the foreground) together with the battleship *Admiral Scheer* during their first deployment to Spain.
Photograph by Drüppel, from the collection of A Jarski

Two pictures of the *Deutschland* taken after returning from her first Spanish tour. They were probably taken in Kiel in autumn 1936. On both photographs the ship's crests were removed by the censor.
M Krzy an collection

The second shot taken a few seconds after the first one – note how quickly the men have changed position. Both pictures were retouched by the censor who in this case 'moved' the ship to the open sea by removing the background of the Kiel naval base.
W Danielewicz collection

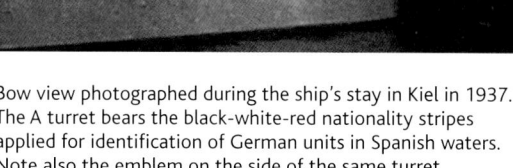

Bow view photographed during the ship's stay in Kiel in 1937. The A turret bears the black-white-red nationality stripes applied for identification of German units in Spanish waters. Note also the emblem on the side of the same turret.
M Skwiot collection

Superstructure of the *Deutschland* with the He 60 floatplane visible. The aircraft on the catapult bears the markings 60 + H 91. The panzerschiff was photographed in autumn 1936.
Photograph by Urbahns, from the collection of T Klimczyk

Deutschland leaving for another operation in Spanish waters, taken in 1937 prior to the ship's refit.
Photograph by Urbahns, from the collection of T Klimczyk

The crew is assembled for the daily hoisting of the ensign at the stern. This picture was also taken during the ship's stay in Kiel. Details of the torpedo tube mountings can be clearly seen.
M Skwiot collection

Deutschland near Gazelebrücke. Surrounding B turret are the coffins of the dead sailors which will soon be transferred to trucks waiting on the pier.
CAW

The evening of 16 June 1937: the coffins of the seamen killed in the air attack off Ibiza are ceremonially carried ashore.
CAW

During one Spanish deployment the *Deutschland* was bombed by Republican aircraft off the island of Ibiza on 29 May 1937. Two bomb hits killed 23 men and another 11 died of wounds. Initially the dead were buried in Gibraltar but on Hitler's orders they were disinterred and the bodies brought back to Germany on board the *Deutschland*. The coffins with the dead sailors were placed under B turret. In the evening of 16 June 1937 a funeral service was held on board the ship. After the speeches were made the coffins were brought ashore.
CAW

Deutschland took part in a total of five 'neutrality' patrols off Spain. Here, the ship was photographed in late 1937 or in early 1938 with the markings used during the Spanish deployments but following a refit that included the addition of a funnel cap (the inset photo shows the ship before the refit). She flies the flag of the new Commander of Naval Forces in Spain Rear Admiral Hermann von Fischel.
M Skwiot collection

TOP LEFT AND MAIN PICTURE: *Deutschland* photographed with the crew manning the side. The He 60 floatplane on the ship's catapult carries the markings 60 + D 91.
S Breyer collection

The launch of a new battleship, to be named *Tirpitz*, on 1 April 1939 was an occasion for a fleet review in the Wilhelmshaven roadstead. In this picture the *Deutschland*'s crew is preparing to man the side during the parade.
CAW

The panzerschiffe *Admiral Graf Spee* (in the foreground) and *Deutschland* photographed on 1 April 1939 during the fleet review in the Wilhelmshaven roadstead.
CAW4

On 15 February 1940 the panzerschiff *Deutschland* was reclassified as a heavy cruiser and renamed *Lützow*, seen here after the replacement of the main gun barrels, 24 May 1941 at Kiel.
S Breyer collection

Another shot taken during the fleet review in April 1939, this time from the rear of the line with the *Deutschland* in the foreground and *Admiral Graf Spee* ahead.
A Szewczyk collection

Operation Weserübung, the invasion of Norway, did not end well for the ship. While attacking Oslofjord the heavy cruiser was hit by coastal artillery several times. Once the area was secured, the ship retired but on 11 April 1940 at approximately 01.29 the *Lützow* was hit by torpedoes from the British submarine HMS/M *Spearfish*. There followed a two-day struggle to tow the crippled cruiser back to safety at Kiel. In the end the operation was successful and on 13 April the ship entered the dry dock in the Deutsche Werke shipyard. In the close-up photograph opposite the serious structural damage to the stern is clearly visible even before water is pumped out of the dock.
Photograph by Drüppel, from the collection of S Breyer

The *Lützow* returned to combat service on 31 March 1941, and in April carried out machinery trials and gunnery exercises. While stationed at Kiel the heavy cruiser received a striped camouflage pattern. The ship only used this scheme while in the Baltic sea.
S Breyer collection

The first attempt to deploy the cruiser to Norway in June 1941 was interrupted by Bristol Beaufort aircraft, which attacked the ship with torpedoes. The ship was damaged and had to be withdrawn from service until the end of the year. The second attempt, Operation Walzetraum, was made in May 1942 and this time it was successful. This photograph shows the *Lützow* surrounded by torpedo nets off Trondheim in May-June 1942.
Photograph by Klemm, from the collection of S Breyer

Bow of the *Lützow* photographed during the ship's stay in Swinemünde.
A Jarski collection

The heavy cruiser *Lützow* in Kaafjord in 1942, seen from on board a destroyer.
S Breyer collection

The heavy cruiser *Lützow* at Gotenhafen (Gdynia) in November 1942. During a refit in the Danziger Werft (from 2 April 1942) a new FuMB 4 radar with the Samos antenna and an additional FuMO 22 antenna were installed.
CAW

Lützow in the Baltic, October 1944. On 28 July 1942 the ship became part of Kampfgruppe 2, whose tasks included providing artillery support for the Wehrmacht troops fighting in Estonia and East Prussia, providing supplies and ammunition and covering the evacuation of soldiers and civilians.
CAW

After firing the last remaining shells on 3 May 1945, the crew prepared the ship for scuttling. On the next day the demolition charges were detonated and the ship sank in the Kaiserfahrt (the present Paistowski Kanał) near the estuary of Alte Swine (Stara Świna).
M Skwiot collection

Admiral Scheer

The second ship of the type, Panzerschiff B, was ordered from the Marinewerft shipyard in Wilhelmshaven. Officially the replacement for the old battleship *Lothringen*, the keel of the new ship was laid on 25 June 1931 and received the shipyard number 123. The construction was supervised by directors Schultz and Lottman with the assistance of engineer Wischer. On 1 April 1933 the first of the class, *Deutschland*, was formally commissioned, while the hull of the second panzerschiff was launched from Number 1 slipway. The sponsor was Marianne Besserer, daughter of Admiral Reinhard Scheer. Officers of the old Kaiserliche Marine and the current Reichsmarine, including Admiral Raeder, were present at this dual event.

The new ship's first machinery trials were conducted in March 1934 off the River Jade estuary. The trials revealed the usual technical problems, which were not entirely rectified until the end of the year, when the ship was prepared for commissioning. The ensign hoisting ceremony took place on 12 November 1934 and Captain (Kpt z S) Wilhelm Marschall became the *Admiral Scheer*'s first commander. The first crew consisted mostly of men from the recently decommissioned battleship *Hessen*. After taking on fuel and stores, *Admiral Scheer* left for another set of trials, this time of the combat systems. These were conducted between 3 and 6 December followed on the 12th by the first live-fire gunnery practice. On the 13th the ship was inspected by Rear Admiral R Carls before the planned visit the following day by Adolf Hitler, the Defence Minister, and the C-in-C of the Reichsmarine, Admiral Erich Raeder.

On 20 December 1934 *Admiral Scheer* began preparations for machinery trials in the Baltic, conducted on 22 and 23 January 1935 on the measured mile near Heisternest (Jastarnia) and in February and March on the Neukrug (Piaski) measured mile. During the test runs the ship reached a maximum speed of 29 knots, but compared to her sister ships the *Admiral Scheer* turned out to be a 'noisy' ship. In addition, at speeds between 21 and 23 knots the ship suffered from excessive vibration, which was especially felt amidships. The trials and training cruises continued through the first half of 1935. Only on 18 April 1935 was *Admiral Scheer* declared operational and assigned to the Commander of Battleships.

Throughout May *Admiral Scheer* was employed in training, engine trials and testing equipment. Between 30 May and 2 June the ship took part in the celebrations of the anniversary of the Battle of the Skagerrak, which were held in Stettin (Szczecin), when she was flagship of Admiral Richard Foerster, the fleet commander. During the celebrations almost 10,000 people visited the ship. Later, *Admiral Scheer* participated in Navy Week at Kiel. During the four days

Admiral Scheer at sea. The year is 1935 and the ship has the seaplane catapult and other aviation equipment already installed.
Photograph by Klein, from the collection of T Klimczyk

the ship was visited by 38,000 people, including the Chancellor of the Reich Adolf Hitler, Rudolf Hess and C-in-C of the Navy Admiral Raeder.

The ship's first combat operation was a naval patrol of Spanish waters in July 1936. There the ship was principally employed evacuating German civilians escaping the civil war, but the ship also fired on Republican positions in Almería on 31 May 1937; the bombardment was German retaliation for the bombing of the panzerschiff *Deutschland*. During the civil war, the ship conducted seven tours of duty in Spanish waters before the end of June 1938, the last being completed on the 29th. Before the outbreak of the Second World War the ship took part in numerous fleet manoeuvres, reviews and later in the annexation of Klaipėda and in a cruise to Portugal. Early in May 1939 the ship returned to Wilhelmshaven, for intensive training and sea trials in preparation for wartime operations. As soon as the war began the ship was attacked by RAF Blenheim bombers on 4 September 1939, during a raid on the Wilhelmshaven naval base and other German ships. *Admiral Scheer* was hit by three bombs, but no major

Reinhard Scheer

Reinhard Scheer was born on 30 September 1863 into a pastor's family in Obernkirchen. In April 1879 he began his naval career as a Cadet in the Imperial Navy, going to sea a year later in the sailing frigate *Niobe*. As a Cadet he served in the gunnery training ship *Renown*, armoured frigate *Friedrich Karl*, corvette *Hertha* and the training ship *Mars*.

He received his commission and the rank of Sub Lieutenant on 16 November 1882. While serving in German West Africa in 1884 he was decorated for conducting an attack on a fortified native village. As an officer he served on the battleship *Bayern*, corvettes *Bismarck* and *Sophie*, aviso *Grief* and the battleships *Sachsen* and *Kurfurst Friedrich Wilhelm*. In that period he specialised in torpedo warfare, seeing service in the torpedo training ship *Blücher*. At the end of 1900 Scheer was promoted to Lieutenant Commander and given command of the first torpedo boat flotilla. After being appointed to the rank of Commander in 1904, he assumed command of the cruiser *Gazelle*. One year later Scheer was a Kapitän zur See (Captain) and later the commanding officer of the battleship *Elsass*. In 1910 he was promoted to Rear Admiral and Chief of Staff of the Hochseeflotte (High Seas Fleet). Three years later he became a Vice Admiral and when the war broke out in 1914 he was commanding the 2nd Battle Squadron, although he took over the 3rd Battle Squadron at the end of 1914. Scheer believed the German Navy was fully capable of facing the Royal Navy and consequently was an advocate of the active use of the Hochseeflotte. He also supported the concept of unrestricted torpedo warfare. On 24 January 1916 he was appointed commander of the battle fleet, and on 31 May 1916, flying his flag in the battleship *Friedrich der Grosse*, Sheer commanded the German forces in the largest naval battle of the First World War. Around 246 British and German ships took part in this engagement which became known as the Battle of Jutland (to the British) or the Battle of the

Skagerrak (to the Germans). Although the German fleet did not achieve its goal of destroying or eliminating enough of the Grand Fleet to compel Britain to make peace, the tactics employed by Scheer resulted in the sinking of three British battlecruisers, three armoured cruisers and eight destroyers, compared to his own losses of one pre-dreadnought battleship, one battlecruiser, four light cruisers and five torpedo boats. On 5 June 1916 Vice Admiral Scheer was promoted to full Admiral and awarded the Pour le Mérite Order – he was called the Victor of the Skagerrak, but he refused to accept the title of Baron from the emperor. In August 1918 he was appointed the Chief of Admiralty Staff and at the end of the war the Chief of Staff of the Naval Warfare Directorate. In December 1918 Scheer resigned and retired from active duty, settling in his house in Martredwitz in Weimar. Here in 1920 he suffered a personal tragedy, when his wife, daughter and maid were murdered in this house by a burglar. He died on 26 November 1928 at the age of 65.

Photograph CAW

following sea trials in the Baltic, the ship then became part of the Baltenflotte which, together with the battleship *Tirpitz* and other ships, was employed keeping the Russian fleet in check.

In 1942 the ship was sent to Norway, taking part in Operations Rösselsprung and Wunderland but, as with *Lützow*, engine trouble forced the *Admiral Scheer*'s return to the Marinewerft shipyard in Wilhelmshaven at the end of December 1942. During the repairs the ship was bombed by British aircraft on 26 February 1943, so for greater safety it was decided to relocate the ship further to the east, to Swinemünde (Świnoujście). This turned out to be a very poor move as that port had no dry dock and no facilities to conduct the level of work

The capsized hull of the ship, July 1945.
Photograph by Drüppel, from the collection of M Skwiot

required, so the refit lasted until mid-1944. When the refit was finally complete, the ship was assigned to the Baltic, based at Gotenhafen (Gdynia). In 1945 the ship employed its main armament against Russian positions in the Sworbe (Sõrve) peninsula, operating until mid-March 1945 in the Bay of Gdańsk near Pillau (Baltiysk) and in the western Baltic. The bombardments wore out the main gun linings and on 18 March the ship was docked in Deutsche Werke in Kiel to replace these. However, an air raid on the shipyard on 9 April 1945 badly damaged the ship, which took on a list to starboard of about 18 degrees. Being in dockyard hands, the ship had no power so it was impossible to counterflood and the list soon increased to 28 degrees. At that point the order was given to abandon ship, and *Admiral Scheer* soon capsized and sank in the shallow dock basin. During a 48-hour rescue operation several men escaped from inside the cruiser's hull. The ship's story came to an unusual conclusion as a post-war salvage operation raised part of the ship – but the rest of the hull was covered with earth and a car park built on top of the wreck, which still exists today.

damage was done to the ship. However, this was an opportune moment to send the ship for a refit, which lasted until the end of the year. The bridge tower was replaced with a cylindrical structure similar to that on the *Deutschland*, and the anti-aircraft weaponry and fire control systems were modernised. At the same time the ship was reclassified as a heavy cruiser, as with the *Deutschland*. When the refit was complete, the ship

began a period of intensive exercises and sea trials in the Baltic before being sent to Norway. In October 1940 the ship left port for its first sortie against enemy shipping – a highly successful raid across three oceans in which sixteen merchant ships and the armed merchant cruiser *Jervis Bay* were sunk – the ship returning in triumph to Kiel on 1 April 1941. There *Admiral Scheer* underwent maintenance and repairs until the end of July and,

Hull of Panzerschiff B on the Number 2 slipway of the Marinewerft in Wilhelmshaven, photographed near the end of 1932.
S Breyer collection

The launching ceremony attracted numerous inhabitants of Wilhelmshaven, but surviving crew members of the ships commanded by Admiral Reinhard Scheer also participated in the event.
CAW

The hull was launched on 1 April 1933 at the Marinewerft in Wilhelmshaven. The guard of honour is inspected by the Reich's defence minister Werner von Blomberg followed by the head of the Reichsmarine Admiral Erich Raeder.
CAW

Unlike that of the *Deutschland*, the launching ceremony went off without a hitch. This photograph catches the moment when the champagne bottle, sent on its way by Admiral Scheer's daughter, hit the ship's hull.
CAW

The hull gained a lot of momentum during the launch and was not easy to stop. The tugs used their bows as buffers, hitting the hull sides hard enough to cause potential damage. It is this moment that was captured by the German photographer in the above picture.
CAW

Admiral Scheer at Wilhelmshaven, towards the end of 1934. To the left, behind the floating crane, is the old battleship *Hessen*; the *Admiral Scheer*'s crew was largely drafted from this ship when it decommissioned. This picture was taken a few days before commissioning of the new panzerschiff on 12 December 1934.
M Skwiot collection

Admiral Scheer in dry dock during the later stages of fitting out.
S Breyer collection

Admiral Scheer seen from the stern still flying the Reichsmarine ensign, photographed in Heikendorf Bay off Kiel.
M Skwiot collection

Admiral Scheer in Wilhelmshaven, towards the end of 1934.
CMM

The forward deck and the bridge tower (Kommandoturm) of *Admiral Scheer*, photographed in the Wilhelmshaven roadstead after the ship's commissioning.
A Jarski collection

A close-up of *Admiral Scheer*'s midship area with a floatplane on the catapult. The picture was taken in the summer of 1935 during the first trials of the catapult, which employed a Heinkel He 60 aircraft with civilian registration markings.
Photograph by Drüppel, from the collection of M Skwiot

Admiral Scheer during sea trials in the summer of 1935. In the first half of the year the ship received a refit, which included the installation of a seaplane catapult on the aft superstructure.
Photograph by Urbahns, from the collection of M Skwiot

MAIN PICTURE: *Admiral Scheer* during sea trials.
CMM

Admiral Scheer at sea, summer 1935.
S Breyer collection

Amidship area with the bridge tower prominent in the foreground. The picture was taken in summer or autumn of 1937.
Photograph by Klein, from the collection of T Klimczyk

Battleship *Admiral Scheer* dressed overall during the Kiel Navy Week (Kieler Woche) at a mooring buoy in Laboe in June 1935.
S Breyer collection

Admiral Scheer assisted by tugs navigates the channels to Holm island in the centre of Danzig (Gdańsk). The picture was taken during the ship's official visit on 30 August 1935 at the invitation of the Senate of the Free City of Gdańsk.
Daguerreotype from the collection of Z Bogdanowicz

Another view of the *Admiral Scheer* during her visit to the Free City of Gdańsk. This and all previous photos (daguerreotypes) of the panzerschiff's visit were taken on 31 August 1935 by the same man, a professional photographer working in Gdańsk.
T Klimczyk collection

Another view of the *Admiral Scheer* entering the port of Gdańsk. This photograph was reproduced from a daguerreotype and therefore has no traces of retouching: for example the Reichsmarine ensign was not replaced by the new Nazi ensign.
Daguerreotype from the collection of Z Bogdanowicz

Because of her deep draught the *Admiral Scheer* could not sail right into the city centre; the only place deep enough was opposite Holm island. In this picture the *Admiral Scheer* is moored at the nearby dolphins.
Daguerreotype from the collection of Z Bogdanowicz

On 1 September 1935 the *Admiral Scheer* completes her visit to Gdańsk. After being turned around, possibly near the F Schichau shipyard, as suggested by the buildings in the background, the battleship leaves Gdańsk and sails for Kiel.
Daguerreotype from the collection of Z Bogdanowicz

Admiral Scheer photographed at sea during gunnery practice. The main gun turrets were given individual names and crests: A turret carried the same crest as the ship and was named *Skagerrak* in memory of the 1916 battle the British call Jutland; B turret was called *Friedrich der Große*.
Photograph by Urbahns, from the collection of M Skwiot

Admiral Scheer in the Bay of Kiel.
Photograph by Urbahns, from the collection of A Jarski

This photograph was taken shortly after the previous one, but the angle of the word *Skagerrak* in the ship's crest was altered on the photograph, possibly to suggest that the photograph was taken on a later day.
Photograph by Urbahns, from the collection of A Jarski

Admiral Scheer in a spectacular shot from the bow taken during Navy Week at Kiel in June 1935. The cruiser *Köln* was moored on the other side of the same pier but is not visible in this photograph.
W Danielewicz collection

Panzerschiff *Admiral Scheer* (on the left) together with the cruiser *Köln* during Navy Week at Kiel in summer of 1935.
MMW

The portside ship's crest as it appeared before 1937. It was then reoriented, with the word *Skagerrak* running across the crest from the bottom left to the top right (*ie* it was rotated by 90 degrees compared to this earlier version). The starboard side was identical and not mirror-imaged.
S Breyer collection

Admiral Scheer's bridge tower photographed during a refit of the ship in the Deutsche Werke at Kiel. The refit was carried out from December 1936 to the end of February 1937.
M Krzyżan collection

Admiral Scheer passing under the Levensau bridge in the Kiel Canal en route for Wilhelmshaven. The photograph was probably taken near the end of February or in early March 1937, after the refit. The refit included the installation of two rangefinder platforms on the bridge tower; additionally the orientation of the band in the ship's crest was altered.
IWM

Admiral Scheer in the dock of the Marinewerft in Wilhelmshaven, September 1939.
S Breyer collection

Admiral Scheer photographed in 1939 after another refit. The refit included the modernisation of the bridge tower equipment and adding more elaborate masts and aerials on the funnel.
Photograph by Drüppel, from the collection of S Breyer

Launching of the He 60 seaplane (registration number 60 + D 91).
MMW

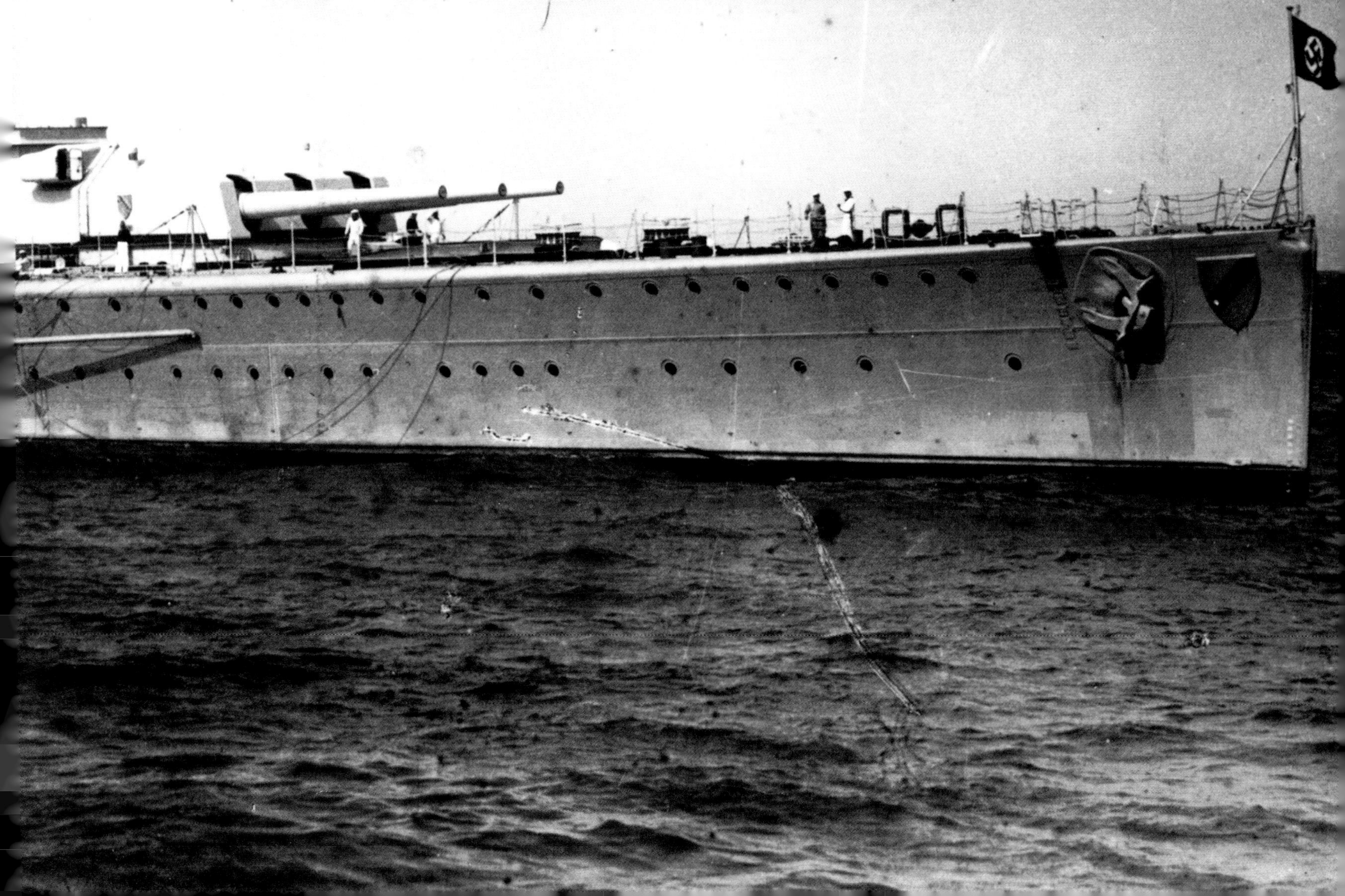

Admiral Scheer at Gibraltar photographed during one tour of duty in Spanish waters.
S Breyer collection

Admiral Scheer at the dolphins in the Kiel Canal photographed from *Admiral Graf Spee* en route to Hamburg. The flag of Vice Admiral Marschall, Commander of the Battleship Force, flies from the fore topmast.
MMW

Modernisation of the bridge tower being carried out in the Marinewerft in Wilhelmshaven in the winter of 1938/1939.
S Breyer collection

Admiral Scheer conducting exercises at sea.
CAW

Crew of *Admiral Scheer* manning the side during the launch of the battleship *Bismarck*, where the ship performed the function of flagship of the Commander of the Battleship Force, Vice Admiral Marschall.
CAW

Admiral Scheer visiting Hamburg, on 14 February 1939, for celebrations surrounding the launch of the battleship *Bismarck*. *Admiral Scheer* was the flagship of the Commander of Battleships, Vice Admiral Marschall. At this time the ship still carries a Heinkel He 60 floatplane (registration number 60 + D 91), but it was about to be replaced by a new type of aircraft, the Arado Ar 196.
S Breyer collection

Two views of the *Admiral Scheer* at Gotenhafen in the autumn of 1939.
A Jarski collection

Two views of *Admiral Scheer* moored at the French Pier in Gotenhafen Kriegsmarine base.
This was the Polish Gdynia occupied by the Germans. Note the 20mm anti-aircraft gun mounted on the forward main battery turret
A Jarski collection

A close-up of the breech ends of the starboard quadruple torpedo tube mounting. Note that the two outer tubes open to the left, and the two inner ones to the right.

After another major refit the *Admiral Scheer*, now classified as a heavy cruiser, sailed on 27 October 1940 for her first operation against enemy shipping. In this photograph the ship rolls in a North Atlantic swell.
ADM

Admiral Scheer photographed after the outbreak of war. In the upper picture the battleship meets a supply ship in the North Atlantic.
CAW

The meetings were usually very short but this was the moment to refuel, resupply, and transfer the letters from home, always eagerly awaited and highly valued by all seamen. Note the details of the 15cm mountings, the ship's secondary armament.
S Breyer collection

The monotonous search for enemy convoys was sometimes broken by a meeting with a supply ship or a submarine. In this picture the *Admiral Scheer* was photographed from the *U66*. Note the radical alteration to the ship's appearance as a result of the recent refit, the bridge being entirely rebuilt, the masts rearranged and a shallow cap fitted to the funnel.
S Breyer collection

One of many mid-ocean farewells, this time with *U66*.
ADM

Searching for convoys in the middle of the Atlantic was no easy task, and in most cases long weeks passed before any ships were found. However, the aircraft carried on board was very useful for finding lone ships sailing independently. This picture shows the retrieval of an Arado Ar 196 floatplane after one such reconnaissance.
ADM

The *Admiral Scheer* in new camouflage scheme, in which the ship was painted in May 1941.
IWM

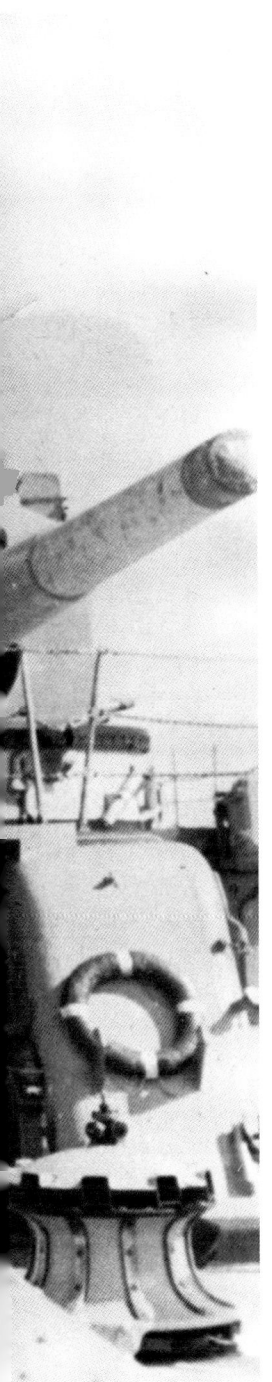

The photograph on the left shows Grossadmiral Erich M Raeder visiting the ship after the ship's successful commerce-raiding operation in the winter of 1940/41.
A Jarski collection

The heavy cruiser *Admiral Scheer* (in the background) during an operation by the Baltenflotte task force in September 1941 in the Baltic. In the foreground the roof and bevels of *Tirpitz*'s C turret are being repainted.
CAW

After a major reconstruction, the *Admiral Scheer* was redesignated a heavy cruiser, and began her first commerce-raiding sortie on 27 October 1940. This picture was taken in the North Atlantic, with the ship still painted light grey. Only the roofs of the gun turrets were painted in different colours.
A Jarski collection

The *Admiral Scheer* after the Atlantic commerce-raiding operation. The ship has a camouflage composed of dark grey lines on the superstructure. The roofs of the gun turrets are painted red, as a recognition mark for friendly aircraft.
M Skwiot collection

The heavy cruiser was successfully redeployed to Norwegian waters during Operation Sportpalast. *Admiral Scheer* moored to dolphins in Lofjord near Trondheim, March 1943.
S Breyer collection

The *Admiral Scheer* in Norwegian waters, wearing a new wedge-shaped camouflage, which was applied after the successful completion of Operation Sportpalast in May 1942.
Top: IWM; left and below: R Schmidt collection

This picture of *Admiral Scheer* was probably taken on 5 July 1942, probably from the *Admiral Hipper* during operations against the PQ17 convoy. She is wearing the new camouflage scheme designed for Norwegian conditions.
CAW

The *Admiral Scheer*, still in her 'wedge' camouflage, Norway 1942.
M Pocock collection

Before the next operation, codenamed Rosselsprüng, *Admiral Scheer* was painted in a camouflage scheme based on irregular wedge shapes intended to make it difficult to spot the ship against the background of the cliffs of the Norwegian fiords. The photograph shows the ship in Bogen Bay near Narvik in the summer of 1942.
S Breyer collection

A close-up of the *Admiral Scheer*'s superstructure as it appeared after the refit of December 1942 to March 1943. This photograph was taken in October 1943 as the ship left Swinemünde (Świnoujście) en route for the Gotenhafen (Gdynia) naval base.
S Breyer collection

Following the refit carried out at the Marinewerft in Wilhelmshaven between December 1942 and March 1943, the *Admiral Scheer* was painted dark grey overall.
S Breyer collection

While the *Admiral Scheer* was at the Deutsche Werke at Kiel to have the worn-out main gun barrel linings replaced, the ship was attacked by Allied bombers on 9 April 1945. Hit several times, the ship rapidly rolled over to starboard, but because the dock basin was not very deep the hull came to rest at about 120 degrees from the vertical. This aerial reconnaissance photograph shows the hull of the capsized *Admiral Scheer*.
Naval Museum, Kiel

A close-up of the capsized *Admiral Scheer* in the dock basin probably taken in early May 1945.
S Breyer collection

150

The dismantling of the heavy cruiser lasted until 1950, but the ship's history finally came to an end with the construction of a new naval base. The remaining sections of the ship were covered with gravel and a huge car park was built on top of it.
Photograph by Drüppel, from the collection of M Skwiot

The breaking up of the wreck began in July 1945.
Photograph by Drüppel, from the collection of M Skwiot

Admiral Graf Spee

A view of the ship during the celebrations of 29 May 1936.
A Jarski collection

The order for the third of the class, Panzerschiff C ('Ersatz *Braunschweig*') was placed on 23 August 1932 with the Marinewerft shipyard in Wilhelmshaven (hull number 124). The keel was laid on 1 October 1932 on the Number 2 slipway, as Panzerschiff B was under construction on the other slipway. The construction supervisor was once again director Lottman assisted by engineer Dykmann. The hull was launched on 30 June 1934, the name *Admiral Graf Spee* being given to the ship by Vice Admiral von Spee's daughter Huberta. The ceremony was held in the presence of the C-in-C of the Reichsmarine, Admiral Erich Raeder, and invitations went out to all surviving crew members from the armoured cruisers *Scharnhorst* and *Gneisenau* and the light cruisers *Leipzig* and *Nürnberg*, all sunk in 1914 under von Spee's command. After the ceremony the battleship's hull was towed to the B5 fitting-out berth.

Commissioned on 6 January 1936, *Admiral Graf Spee*'s first commander was Captain (Kpt z S) Conrad Patzig. The sea trials in January and February showed that the ship's seakeeping qualities were not as good as *Admiral Scheer*'s, but these trials were conducted without full water and fuel tanks, which affected the ship's stability. In February, on the Neukrug measured mile, the ship reached a speed of 28.5 knots at a displacement of 14,100 tons and a rated power of 53,650 HP. Compared to her sister the *Scheer*, the new ship did not handle as well, particularly in strong gusting winds. At deep draught the ship lost about 1 knot of speed and in shallow water the speed was further decreased by 2 or 3 knots. The different internal layout of the ship's engine rooms and equipment produced even greater vibration than that suffered by *Scheer*. And this was just the beginning of her problems: in heavy weather the captain's bridge was awash from waves breaking over the bow. As a consequence it was decided to modify the command tower on the *Admiral Scheer* and *Admiral Graf Spee* and to install additional wind deflectors on their bridges. It was also decided to remodel the superstructure to enlarge the chart room. All initial trials and crew training were declared complete on 9 May 1936, when the ship became the flagship of the Kriegsmarine.

Admiral Graf Spee completed several tours of duty in Spanish waters and was also present at King George VI's coronation review at Spithead in May 1937. After the ceremonies the ship returned to patrolling Spanish waters. During the two years prior to the outbreak of the Second World War *Admiral Graf Spee* made several international cruises, and in the second half of August 1939 the ship left Wilhelmshaven for the South Atlantic under the command of Captain (Kpt z S) H W Langsdorff. After hostilities commenced the ship was ordered to attack Allied merchant shipping, and its raider operations lasted from 30 September 1939 to 7 December 1939, sinking nine Allied merchantmen in the Atlantic and in the Indian Ocean. After returning to the Atlantic around the Cape of Good Hope, on 13 December 1939 the ship was intercepted off the estuary of the River Plate by a British cruiser squadron under the command of Commodore Henry Harwood. This consisted of the heavy cruiser *Exeter* and the light cruisers *Ajax* (flagship) and *Achilles* (New Zealand Division).

During the ensuing engagement – known to the British as the Battle of the River Plate – the tactics employed by the *Admiral Graf Spee*'s commander are open to criticism. By trying to close with the enemy he did not use the advantage of the battleship's heavier artillery, which could out-range the enemy cruisers. In addition, during the engagement he ordered the ship's fire to be split between two targets instead of first eliminating the strongest opponent and dealing with the weaker ships later. Nevertheless, the *Exeter* was heavily damaged and knocked out of the fight, but the ship was saved when the German commander ordered fire switched to the other two ships at the moment when it was becoming most effective against the heavy cruiser. The light cruisers remained in action and *Admiral Graf Spee* also sustained significant damage, which led Captain Langsdorff to break off the battle and enter the neutral port of Montevideo. Although the fighting was inconclusive, this is usually seen as a tactical victory to the British, who had forced the German ship to enter port and thus gained time to gather reinforcements. A diplomatic battle followed. The British ambassador in Montevideo tried to persuade the Uruguayan government that the German ship must

Maximillian Johannes Graf von Spee

Von Spee was born on 22 June 1861 in Copenhagen into a Rhineland family who could trace their ancestry back to the early twelfth century. At the age of 17, on 23 April 1878 he joined the Imperial Navy as a Cadet. One year later, after the probationary period he became a full Seekadett, learning his trade on the sail training ship *Niobe* and the gunnery training ship *Renown*. He received his first commission as a Sub Lieutenant in January 1882, together with his first posting to the armoured frigate *Friedrich Karl*. In the years 1884-1885 he took part in an expedition to West Africa on board the gunboat *Möwe*. In August 1885 he was promoted to Lieutenant Junior Grade, and served on the corvette *Vineta* and the armoured frigate *Deutschland*.

Two years later he was promoted to Lieutenant Senior Grade (Oberleutnant) and appointed to the post of port commander in Cameroon (a German West African colony); it was probably there that his hobby of collecting exotic fauna and flora was born. He then served on board the corvette *Moltke* as the deck training officer and later became a gunnery officer on the battleships *Baden* and *Bayern*. In November 1892 he was promoted to Lieutenant Commander and served as a staff officer in the Far East. At the end of May 1899 he was promoted to Commander and became the first officer of the battleship *Brandenburg*. From this ship he took part in the suppression of the Boxer Rebellion in China in 1900. After his return he assumed command of the light cruiser *Hela*. In the years 1901-1902 he commanded the minelayer *Pelikan* and then he worked for three years in the Coastal Defence Committee. In January 1905 he was promoted to Kapitän zur See and took command of the battleship *Wittelsbach* and in 1908 he was transferred to the post of the Chief of Staff of the North Sea Fleet Command. At the age of 49

he was promoted to Rear Admiral and three years later Vice Admiral. Following this promotion he became the commander of the East Asia Squadron stationed in Tsingtao (China). He defeated a British squadron off Coronel (Chile) in November 1914, but died on board his flagship, the armoured cruiser *Scharnhorst*, during the subsequent battle near the Falklands with the British squadron commanded by Vice Admiral Sturdee on 8 December 1914. Two of his sons served in the same squadron as Lieutenants – Heinrich (born 1893) on the armoured cruiser *Gneisenau* and Otto (born 1890) on the light cruiser *Nürnberg*: both died on the same day. Ironically, almost twenty-five years later, also in December and in the very same region, the battleship bearing his name was scuttled after a battle with British forces off the River Plate.

leave port within 72 hours so there would be no time to repair damages. In the meantime the *Ajax* and *Achilles*, together with the newly arrived heavy cruiser *Cumberland*, blockaded the estuary of the River Plate, with further reinforcements already on their way. While the British negotiated, the situation for the crew of the *Graf Spee* became ever bleaker. The ship was damaged and could not reckon on any outside help; exchanges with Berlin confirmed that. Having limited forces in the region, the British still considered the damaged *Graf Spee* a severe threat to shipping so would not give up their quarry easily. Needing more time, they switched tactics, invoking an international law that prevented a belligerent warship from sailing within 24 hours of an enemy merchant ship; to the annoyance of the Uruguayan authorities, the British were able to organise a stream of merchantmen to leave on a daily basis.

With some luck the panzerschiff might have slipped out of the trap, disappeared into the Atlantic and avoided pursuit. However, the British then allowed the Germans to intercept information which led them to believe that a strong force awaited the ship outside the harbour. Therefore, with no possibility of repairs and apparently facing overwhelming odds, Captain Langsdorff decided against trying to fight his way out into the Atlantic. On 17 December 1939 *Admiral Graf Spee* left Montevideo and anchored just outside territorial waters. Scuttling charges fitted in the ship were armed, the skeleton crew took to the boats and at 19.52 the charges were detonated. The whole operation was rather complicated by the fact that the ship did not carry enough explosives, so six of the torpedo warheads were used. The wreck of the battleship burned for another two days after settling on the bottom with the superstructure above water. This was not quite the end of the story as the British became interested in the wreck to investigate its construction and technology – especially the new radar – and organised the salvage of selected equipment.

As with previous warship launches, this one was well attended by the inhabitants of Wilhelmshaven. Here the ship has been christened and the nameplate revealed; the chocks have been released and the hull begins its first journey – down the Number 2 slipway.
CAW

The Reichsmarine C-in-C Admiral Erich Raeder receives a guard of honour before the launching ceremony of Panzerschiff C. The ceremony was held in the Marinewerft shipyard in Wilhelmshaven on 30 June 1934.
CAW

Battleship C ('Ersatz *Braunschweig*') was named *Admiral Graf Spee* by Huberta von Spee, the admiral's daughter, and surviving members of crews commanded by von Spee were present at the ceremony. After the formal christening the panzerschiff's name was unveiled.
CAW

Two stages in the fitting out of *Admiral Graf Spee* alongside in the Marinewerft in Wilhelmshaven: at the end of 1934 and in the middle of 1935.

S Breyer collection

Admiral Graf Spee leaving the shipyard for her first sea trials, at the end of 1935.
A Jarski collection

Admiral Graf Spee leaving the Wilhelmshaven naval base.
A Jarski collection

ABOVE AND BELOW: Two views of *Admiral Graf Spee* returning from sea trials conducted in November and December 1935. After these were complete the ship was formally accepted from the builders and commissioned.
S Breyer collection

The ensign was hoisted and the *Admiral Graf Spee* officially entered service on 6 January 1936. Captain (Kpt z S) Konrad Patzig gives a speech to the crew gathered on the quarterdeck.
CAW

Admiral Graf Spee photographed in early May 1936 at the A9 mooring buoy in Kiel. The crew is painting the ship before a fleet review planned for later that month.
Photograph by Klein, from the collection of T Klimczyk

The panzerschiff's crew manning the side on 29 May 1936 in the Bay of Kiel. The occasion was the dedication of a new monument commemorating German sailors who died in the Great War.
A Jarski collection

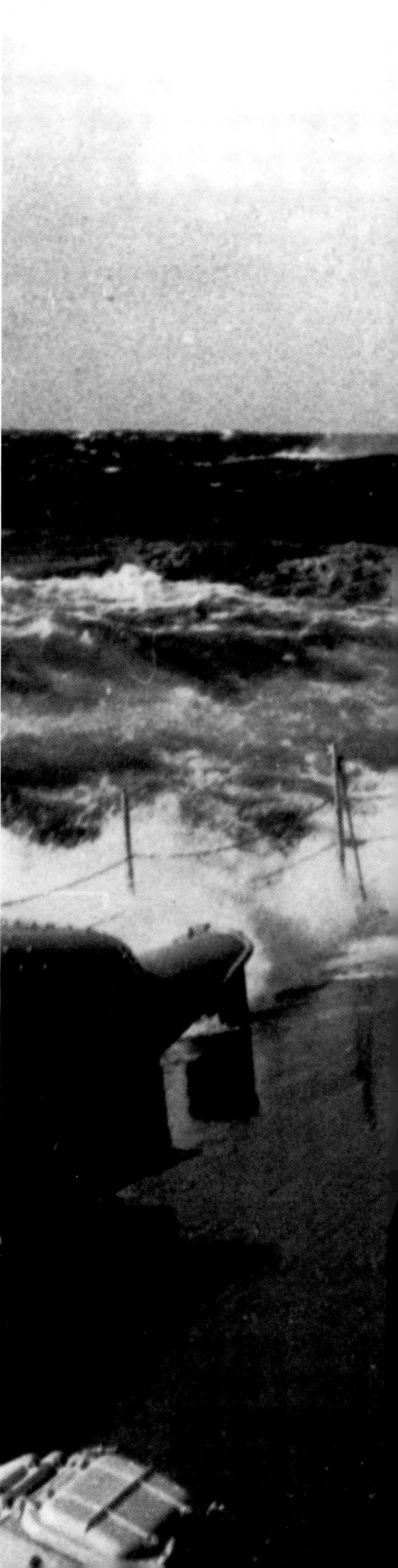

Conning tower of *Admiral Graf Spee*, flagship of the Kriegsmarine since 9 May 1936. On the bridge front is the battle-honour 'Coronel', celebrating von Spee's victory over a British squadron in 1914.
Photograph by Klein, from the collection of T Klimczyk

Admiral Graf Spee's quarterdeck photographed in rough weather. In such conditions the ship was very wet aft, and the operation of the torpedo tubes was very difficult.
S Breyer collection

Admiral Graf Spee alongside a quay in the naval arsenal at Kiel. This picture was probably taken in October 1936 when the ship returned from her first tour of duty off Spain. This is confirmed by the 'neutrality' stripes on A turret which were used to identify German warships in Spanish waters.
S Breyer collection

A close-up of the stem of *Admiral Graf Spee* at the A9 mooring buoy in Kiel Naval Arsenal during October 1936. The ship departed for another patrol off Spain on 14 December 1936. On board the ship was the new commander of German forces in Spain, Rear Admiral Hermann Boehem. The shield on either side of the stemhead carried the coat of arms of the von Spee family.
CAW

A gun salute from *Admiral Graf Spee* anchored in Kiel during the visit by American battleships in May 1937.
ADM

ABOVE: *Admiral Graf Spee* anchored in the roadstead of Kiel in May 1937. This photograph was taken from the Japanese heavy cruiser *Ashigara*, which also entered Kiel while on the way to Great Britain.
ADM

A visit to Kiel in May 1937 by three American battleships, *New York*, *Wyoming* and *Arkansas*. The American ships came to Europe for the Spithead naval review to celebrate the coronation of the British King George VI, but also called at Kiel. The *Admiral Graf Spee* can be seen behind the American battleships. The German panzerschiff also took part in these celebrations.
ADM

ABOVE: A quarter view of the *Admiral Graf Spee* at Spithead on 20 May 1937. Note the very large ensign the ship flew on this occasion.
M Skwiot collection

RIGHT: *Admiral Graf Spee* represented Germany at the Coronation Naval Review at Spithead between 15 and 22 May 1937.
CAW

TOP RIGHT: *Admiral Graf Spee* at sea. This picture was probably taken in mid-1937 after the ship had taken part in the naval review at Spithead.
T Klimczyk collection

CENTRE RIGHT: *Admiral Graf Spee* in the Bay of Kiel photographed at the turn of 1937/1938 before the reconstruction of the bridge tower.
A Jarski collection

LEFT: *Admiral Graf Spee* photographed from the deck of a German destroyer during her second deployment in Spanish waters. The ship now has the identification stripes painted on the front slopes of the main battery turrets, whereas previously they were towards the backs of the turrets.
A Jarski collection

The crew of *Admiral Graf Spee* lining the rails on 22 August 1938. The occasion was the launching of the new heavy cruiser *Prinz Eugen* and a visit by the Hungarian regent Admiral Horthy.
M Skwiot collection

RIGHT: Kriegsmarine ensign flown from the stump mast atop the after control position. The photograph shows the *Admiral Graf Spee* after her 1938 refit.
M Skwiot collection

A close-up of the panzerschiff after the reconstruction of the bridge tower in the Deutsche Werke at Kiel between March and May 1938. The changes included the replacement of two searchlight platforms on the sides of the tower with a new single searchlight platform on the front, as well as enclosing part of the captain's bridge.
Photograph by Klein, from the collection of T Klimczyk

Two views of *Admiral Graf Spee* in the roadstead of Kiel on 31 October 1938 during an inspection by the Fleet Commander Rear Admiral R Carls.
ABOVE: **CAW**; RIGHT: **S Breyer collection**

Admiral Graf Spee carries out a main battery practice shoot.
CAW

Admiral Graf Spee in the Bay of Kiel photographed in 1939.
CAW

The panzerschiffe *Admiral Graf Spee* (in the foreground) and *Deutschland* photographed on 1 April 1939 during the fleet review in the Wilhelmshaven roadstead.
CAW

LEFT: A closer view of the same event, 1 April 1939.
CAW

Admiral Graf Spee as fleet flagship towards the end of March 1939. The ship flies the flag of the fleet commander Admiral Herman Boehm at the foremast head.
Photograph by Urbahns, from the collection of A Jarski

Admiral Graf Spee in heavy weather in the middle of the Atlantic in May 1939. Together with the light cruisers *Köln*, *Leipzig* and *Nürnberg*, the panzerschiff sailed for major fleet manoeuvres in the central Atlantic on 17 April. When they were finished, the ships visited Spanish ports before returning to Wilhelmshaven.
A Jarski collection

Admiral Graf Spee at sea with the fleet commander Admiral Boehm on board.
Photograph by Urbahns, from the collection of A Jarski

Admiral Graf Spee in May 1939 after providing the guard of honour for the ship carrying the Condor Legion pilots returning from Spain. In the foreground is the *U14*, a Type IIB submarine.
M Krzy an collection

Admiral Graf Spee photographed in the Spanish port of Ceuta, which was visited between 27 April and 2 May 1939.
CAW

Another view of *Admiral Graf Spee* in the Spanish port of Ceuta (between 27 April and 2 May 1939).
S Breyer collection

Admiral Graf Spee photographed in the River Plate off Montevideo on 14 December 1939 after the battle with the British cruisers. Around the edges of this print are the autographs of the masters of British merchant ships captured by *Graf Spee*.
IWM

Capt. N. Edwards. m/v "Nueva"

Admiral Graf Spee after the Battle of the River Plate: top of the bridge tower and a close-up of damage to the hull amidships sustained during the uneven battle with the British ships.
National Archives

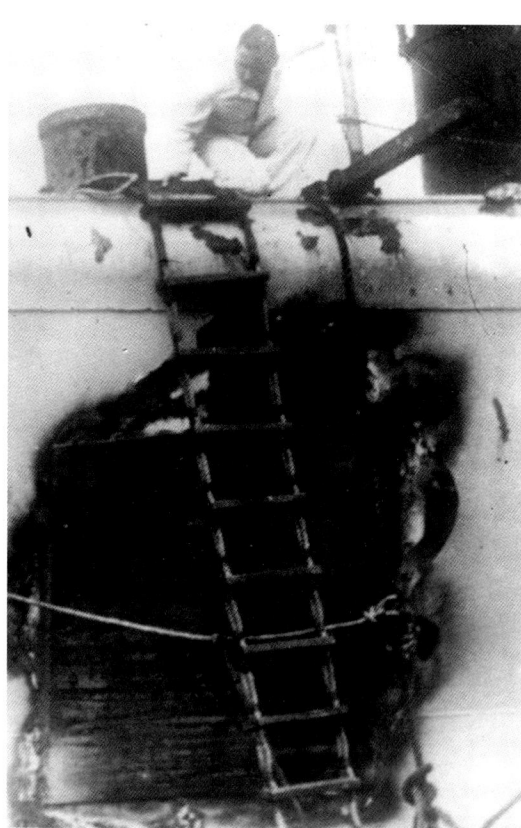

Another view of the *Admiral Graf Spee* in the roadstead of Montevideo, 14 December 1939.
A Jarski collection

Admiral Graf Spee after the River Plate engagement: close-ups of damage sustained during the battle.
A Jarski collection

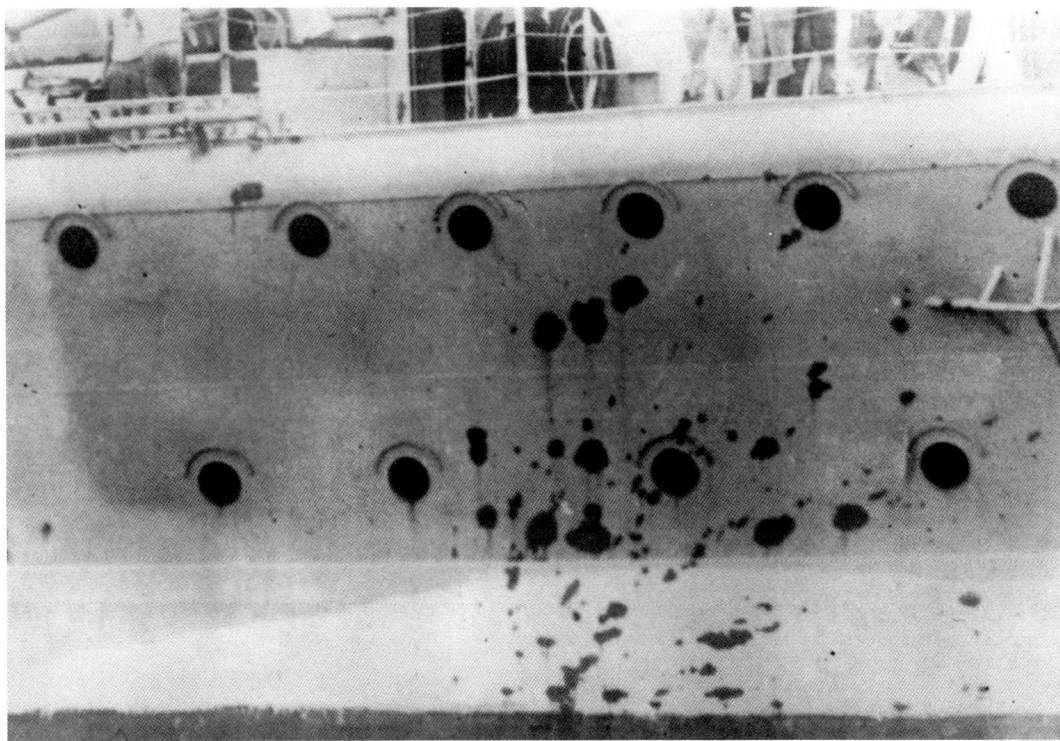

In the evening of 17 December 1939 the panzerschiff *Admiral Graf Spee* was scuttled just over a mile outside Uruguay territorial waters. The moment of the explosion of the scuttling charges was captured in the top right picture. The scuttling operation was more complicated than it looked because the ship did not carry enough explosives. It was decided to use torpedo warheads and six of them were detonated. As the other pictures show, the ship sank in shallow water, at a depth of 9 metres, and the wreck burned for another two days after settling on the bottom. This was not the end of the story as the British wanted to investigate the ship and its equipment – especially an early model radar the ship carried. A Uruguay businessman, Julio Vega Helguera, bought the wreck on behalf of the British shipbreaking company T W Ward and in March 1942 the Admiralty sent out two experts to supervise the removal of selected equipment. The salvaged material was loaded aboard ss *Princesa* and dispatched to Britain. U-boats attempted to sink this ship but were unsuccessful and the cargo arrived safely in Milford Haven on 15 June 1942.

Top: NARA; top right & bottom right: A Jarski collection; others: IWM

3 The Evolution of Battleships D and E
SCHARNHORST AND *GNEISENAU*

Gneisenau leaving for gunnery exercises in the North Atlantic, planned for the period 31 June to 8 July 1938. In the photograph the *Gneisenau* is depicted while leaving port, still in the waters of the Bay of Kiel.
Photograph by Klein, from the collection of M Skwiot

IN NOVEMBER 1932 a meeting between the C-in-C of the Reichsmarine, Admiral Raeder and the Reich's Minister of Defence, General Wilhelm Groener decided that the German fleet should be enlarged to six panzerschiffe, six cruisers, six destroyers, a flotilla of torpedo boats, three flotillas of patrol boats and, if the political situation permitted, sixteen submarines – all before the end of 1938. However, the plan to arm the Navy with *Deutschland* class ships ran into opposition. The construction of the third battleship (C) coincided with the laying down of the French battleship *Dunkerque*. Based on intelligence data, the displacement of the new French battleship was estimated at about 26,000 tons, but the biggest surprise was the ship's designed speed of 31 knots. If the ship was really armed with eight 33cm (13in) guns, it would be far more powerful than the *Deutschland* type panzerschiffe; therefore the German ship would be both slower and less heavily armed. This prompted the decision not to build any more ships of the *Deutschland* type, so Panzerschiff D ('Ersatz *Elsass*') that was part of the fleet development program for the years 1931–1934 had to be reconsidered.

The characteristics of Battleship D were the subject of intense discussions during 1933 where the final requirements were hammered out and three sketch designs proposed. The first variant had a displacement of 18,000 tons, the second carried 28cm guns and the third 33cm guns. Rear Admiral O Gross, director of the Marinekommandoamt, supported the construction of a battleship with a displacement of 26,000 tons armed with 33cm guns similar to the French battleship *Dunkerque*. The difficulty of determining the design was compounded by the estimated construction costs. The first variant (18,000-ton battleship) would cost about RM 120 million. Increasing the displacement to 22,000 tons would cost RM 150 million, and a battleship of 26,000 tons would cost RM 180 million. Considering the financial situation of the Reich and the disarmament treaties, the selection of the right variant was no easy task. An additional problem was the limitations of German shipyards: only slipway Number 2 in Wilhelmshaven was capable of building a 26,000-ton battleship. A related restriction was docking: only the Kaiserdock in Bremerhaven or the dock in Hamburg could handle ships of that size. Before Battleship D could be built, the shipyards and repair infrastructure in Germany needed attention, which also applied to the dredged channels, canals and anchorages in naval bases unequipped to handle such large ships. It may seem that these were only minor inconveniences, but they had a major influence on the characteristics of the future ship. An additional limitation was the height of the central span of the Levensau Bridge over the Kiel Canal, which restricted the 'air draught' of ships pass-

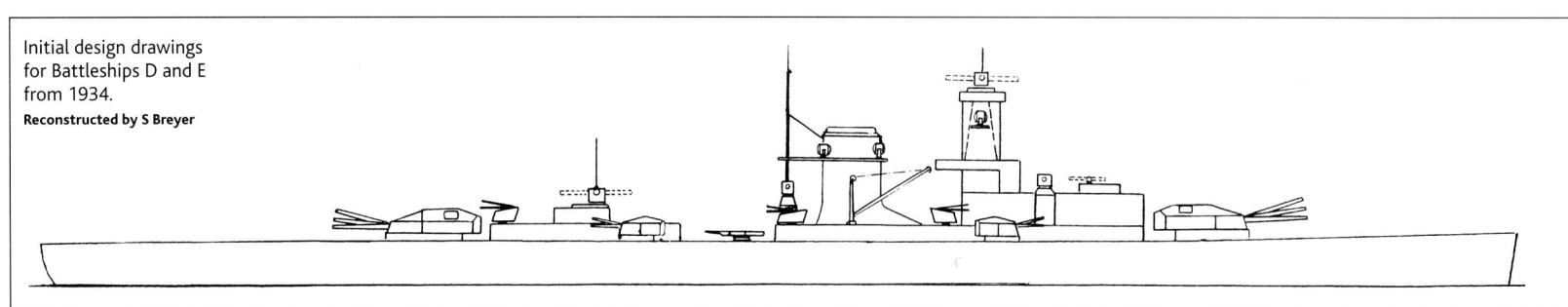

Initial design drawings for Battleships D and E from 1934.
Reconstructed by S Breyer

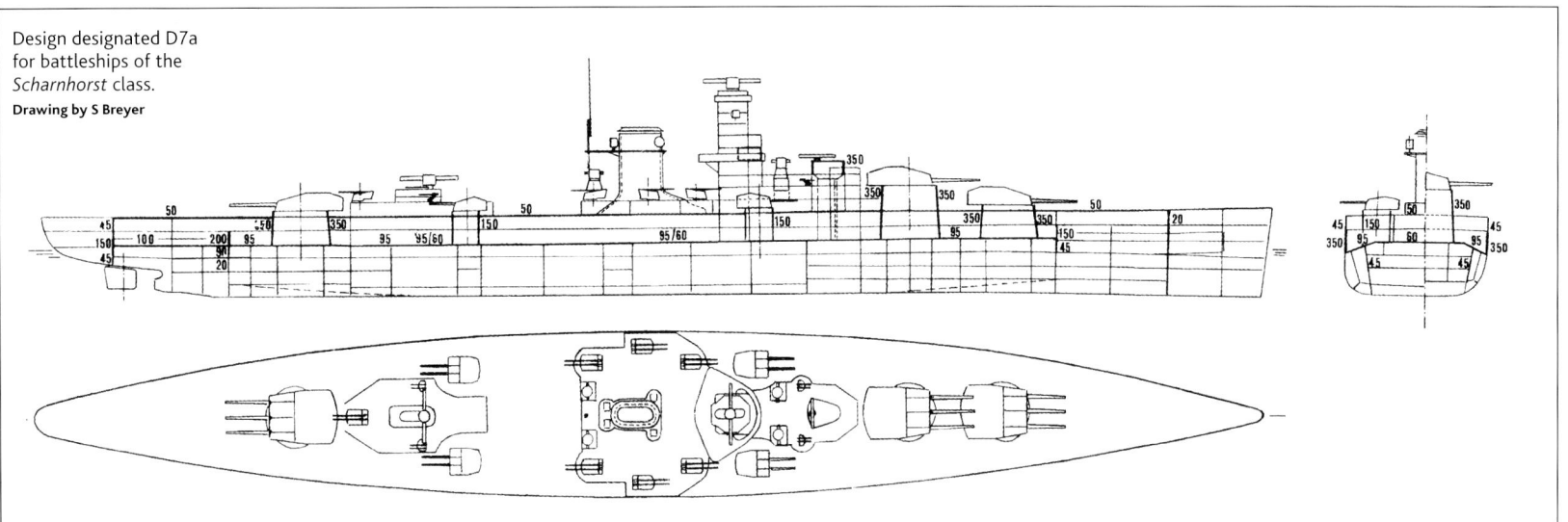

Design designated D7a for battleships of the *Scharnhorst* class.
Drawing by S Breyer

ing beneath it.

With these considerations in mind, Admiral Raeder, C-in-C of the Reichsmarine, ordered the preparation of several battleship designs. The basic requirement called for a ship of 26,500 tons armed with 33cm guns; the first variant had four twin turrets, the second mounted two quadruple turrets and the third three triple turrets. In deference to the delicate political situation of the German Reich, the Admiral also ordered a battleship design of 22,000 tons armed with 28cm guns. This design, designated 'Project XIII', was completed in 1934 so the keel could have been laid as early as that same year.

However, before this, on 23 June 1933 another conference devoted to Battleship D was held, in which the performance of the *Deutschland* was discussed. The initial sea trials had revealed both its strengths and, what is more important, its weaknesses. Each department of the construction office had suggestions for improvements that they wanted immediately introduced into the Battleship D design, which was largely based on the panzerschiffe. Everyone agreed that the ship's armour thickness had to be increased, but one matter of debate was the armament of the future ships. The armament office suggested altering the secondary battery from single open mounts to twin 15cm turrets: better from the point of view of crew protection and ease of operation. It was also planned to increase the number of heavy anti-aircraft guns. All these changes were supposed to be introduced while maintaining a displacement of 18,000 tons. The question of the machinery was left open – the decision to use diesel engines or replace them with another type of power plant would be made later.

Yet another conference about Battleship D took place on 11 October 1933. The armament office was critical of the twin 15cm turrets on the new battleship, the positions of the barbettes for the new turrets, as well as the weak anti-aircraft armament, which had been increased from three to four twin 8.8cm mountings. The question of torpedo armament was also raised, but at this stage of the design process it was considered an unimportant issue. The shape of the bridge tower (Kommandoturm) was a major point in the discussion. The design office opted for the cylindrical superstructure similar to that on the *Deutschland*, but it was not stable enough

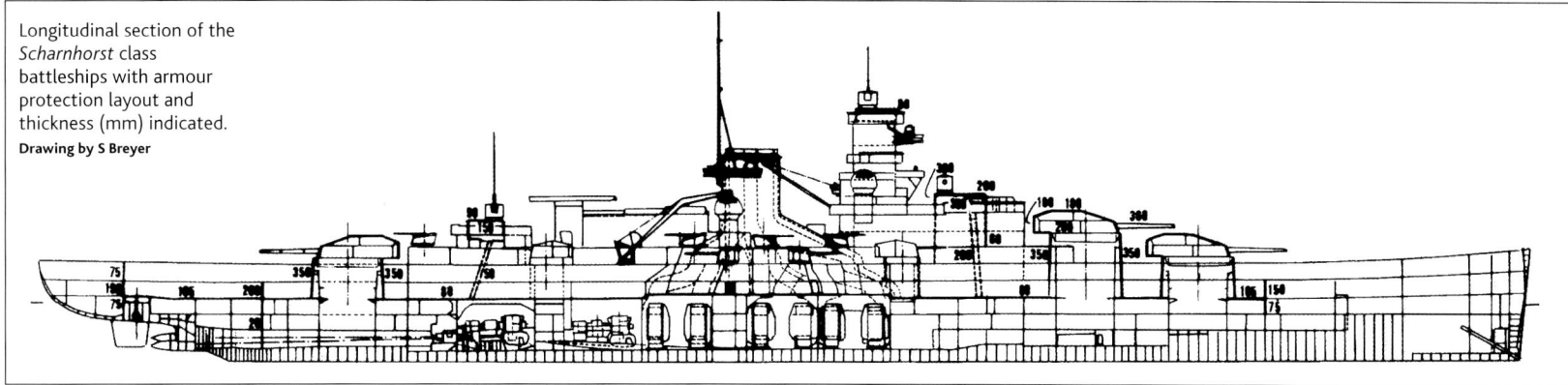

Longitudinal section of the *Scharnhorst* class battleships with armour protection layout and thickness (mm) indicated.
Drawing by S Breyer

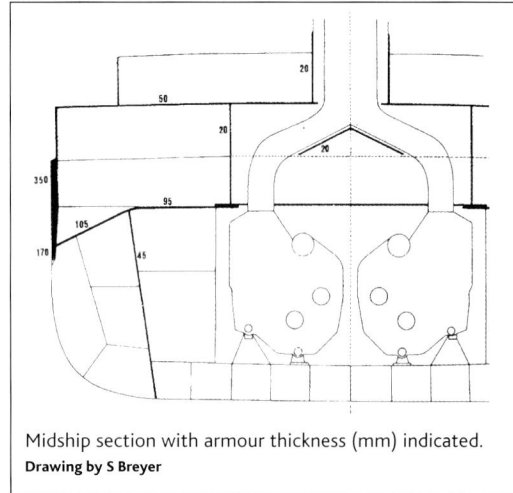

Midship section with armour thickness (mm) indicated.
Drawing by S Breyer

when fire control systems – the rangefinders and directors – were fitted on top of it. A solution was to move A turret closer to the bow, allowing the forward superstructure to be enlarged, and hence providing a more stable platform for the fire control systems, both optical as well as the future electronic systems. The final improvements included increasing the armour thickness on longitudinal bulkheads. If these changes to the design were approved immediately, it would be possible to order the 28cm turrets in November 1933 and the 15cm turrets in the beginning of January 1934. One week later, on 18 October 1933 the decision was made to order two ships with an official displacement of 17,000 tons – the original document actually gives it as 19,000 tons but it was crossed out and '17,000 tons' entered instead. As it transpired, this figure had no real significance as the machinery had yet to be decided and this would drastically affect the displacement of the new battleships.

In December 1933 the question of the battleship's main armament came up again. In the 1933 budget RM 1.4 million had been assigned for work on the 33cm guns. However, the Reich's political situation forced the reduction of the gun calibre to 30.5cm (12in). The armament office estimated that it would need about one year for the design work on the new gun turret and another three and a half years for their manufacture, so the construction of 25,000-ton battleships armed with six 30.5cm guns could not start until 1936/1935. The disarmament treaties were due to expire after 1936, so to begin the construction of the new ships a year earlier, in 1935, would allow the Germans to save a year on the ships' in-service date.

In December 1933 during a meeting with Adolf Hitler, the fleet commander Admiral Raeder was given permission to approve the construction of the fourth and fifth panzerschiffe, Battleships D and E (this latter, formally 'Ersatz *Hessen*') under the 1934 budget. During this meeting Admiral Raeder presented his proposals to improve the fighting characteristics of the future ships as compared to the *Deutschland* currently in service, but Hitler was not entirely convinced. Although the Chancellor approved the suggested increase in the ship's armour while at the same time enlarging the displacement to about 19,000 tons, he did not agree to the addition of a third 28cm turret. The order for both ships was placed on 25 January 1934, Battleship D to be built in the Navy's yard in Wilhelmshaven and Battleship E by the Deutsche Werke in Kiel. The shipyards were presented with a design for a ship of 18,000 tons displacement, and armament comprising two triple 28cm turrets, four twin 15cm turrets and four twin 8.8cm mountings. Keels for both ships were laid on the same day, 14 February 1934.

Admiral Raeder was not impressed with the design of the new battleships: the decision to build them was a result of political pressure and they were inferior to the *Dunkerque*, which was already considered their likely opponent. The view of the admiral, and most senior naval officers, was that the only way to make Battleships D and E satisfactory would be to give them an additional, third, 28cm gun turret. On this Raeder insisted, and the decision was finally made during a meeting with Hitler on 5 June 1934. Nevertheless, even though he agreed the third turret, Hitler was against increasing the gun calibre. Introducing the third turret meant ceasing all work on Battleships D and E, as it required radical changes throughout the design. The construction office estimated that the new battleship drawings would not be finished until October 1935 at best. The situation was worse for sub-contractors as their work was put on hold, and they faced cancelled and altered orders for parts and materials, all of which delays made the date of the ships' commissioning difficult to estimate.

On the next day, 6 June, a conference was held on the modification of the Battleship D design. The Marinekomandoamt opted to place one turret forward and two aft and to maintain a sustained speed of 28 knots and a maximum speed of 30 knots. The armour should protect the ship against a 33cm shell at a range of 15,000–20,000m; in addition 300–350mm side

TABLE : TECHNICAL DATA FOR BATTLESHIPS D AND E APPROVED IN THE 1932/34 DESIGNS.

Design displacement	about 23,000 tons
Standard displacement	about 19,700 tonnes (19,400 tons)
Length at waterline	207.00m (209.70m oa)
Beam at waterline	25.60m
Design draught	7.71m
Machinery	12-cylinder MAN diesel engines M 12 Z 42/58 rated 10,625 HP (total 85,000 HP)
Speed	26 knots
Armament	6 x 28cm (2 x III); 8 x 15cm (4 x II); 10 x 10.5cm (5 x II); 8 x 3.7cm (4 x II)
Torpedo tubes	8 (2 x IV)
ARMOUR	
Side armour	220mm
Armoured citadel	35mm side, 60mm bow, 80mm stern, 40mm inclined deck
Platform deck	45mm
Armoured deck	40mm
Armoured deck above engine rooms	80mm
Torpedo bulkheads	45mm
Main gun turret barbettes	220mm
Conning tower	300mm

armour, an armoured citadel and an armoured bow and stern were required. No aircraft equipment or torpedo armament were provided. The lack of reliable intelligence on the thickness of the *Dunkerque*'s side armour influenced the decision to postpone the selection of the main gun calibre, which was initially established at 28cm. The proposal to arm the battleship with twin 33cm turrets was rejected as the design, construction and installation of the new mounts would delay commissioning to at least mid-1939. The matter of main armament was not finally settled as it was assumed that it would be possible to re-arm the ship later with twin gun turrets and that the operation would not take longer than nine months to complete. However, the biggest problem was the main machinery, which still had not been decided. Two types of power plant were under consideration: geared steam turbines or turbo-electric drive. The use of diesel engines was rejected due to their excessive weight. The new battleship variants were designated Neuentwurft I and Neuentwurft II (New Design I and II).

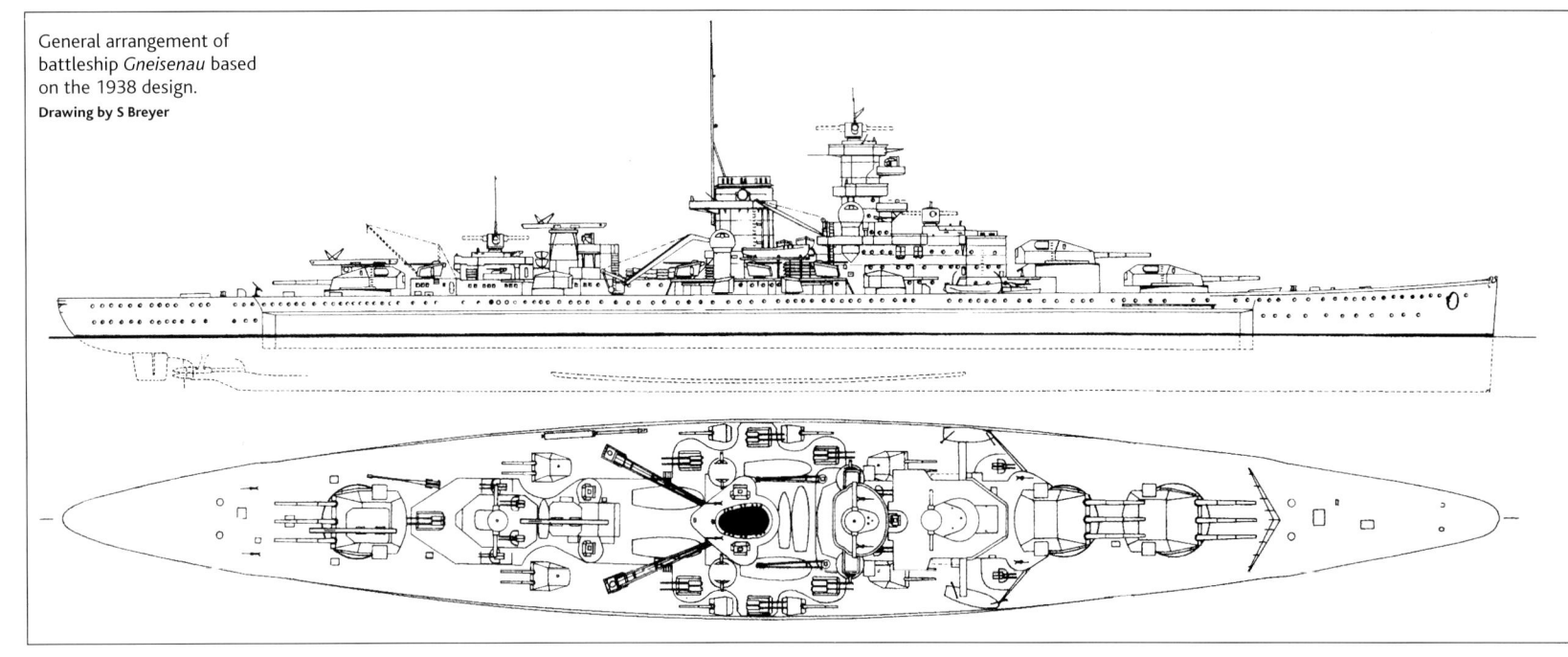

General arrangement of battleship *Gneisenau* based on the 1938 design.
Drawing by S Breyer

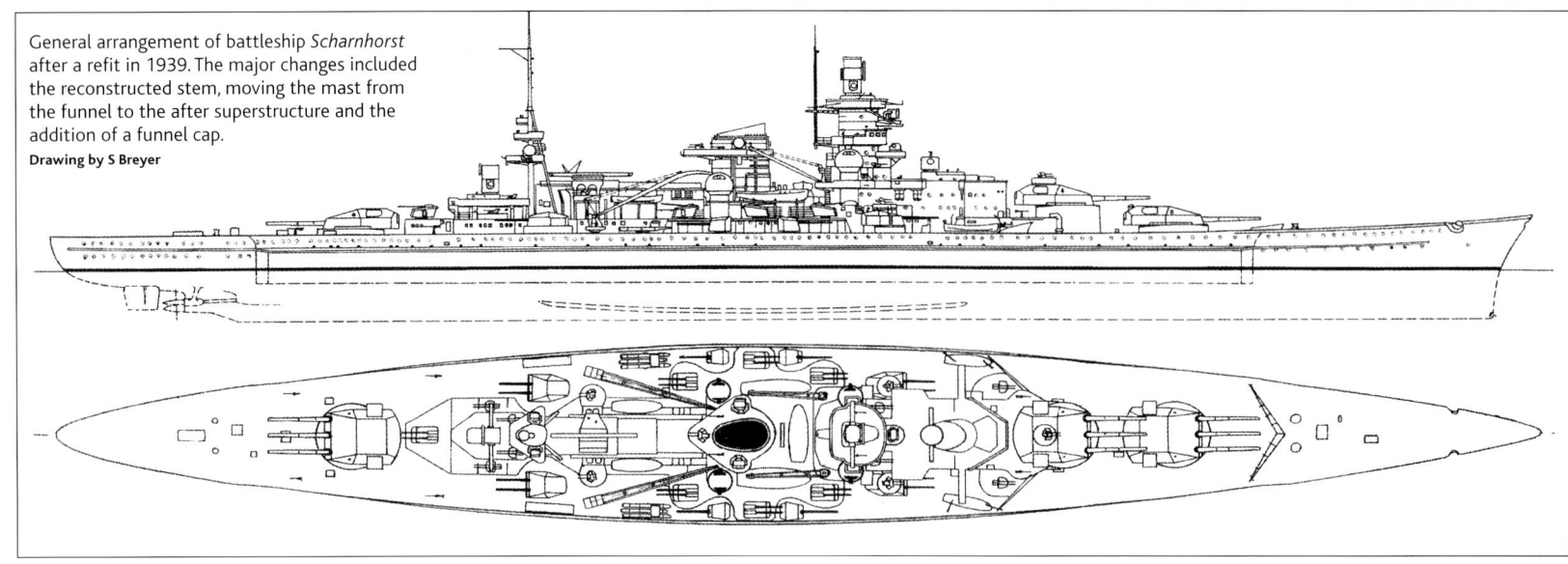

General arrangement of battleship *Scharnhorst* after a refit in 1939. The major changes included the reconstructed stem, moving the mast from the funnel to the after superstructure and the addition of a funnel cap.
Drawing by S Breyer

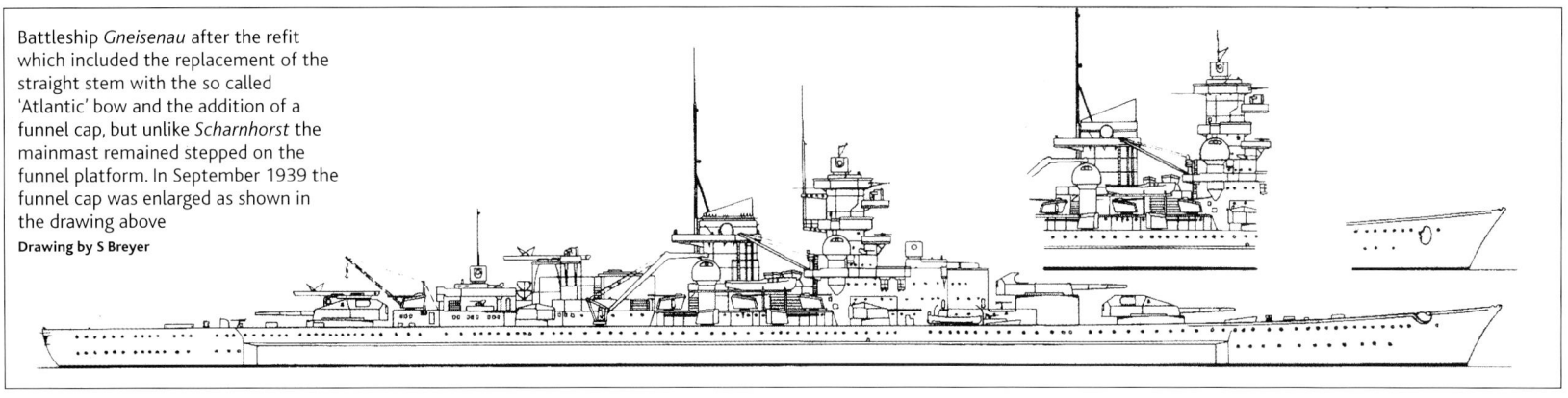

Battleship *Gneisenau* after the refit which included the replacement of the straight stem with the so called 'Atlantic' bow and the addition of a funnel cap, but unlike *Scharnhorst* the mainmast remained stepped on the funnel platform. In September 1939 the funnel cap was enlarged as shown in the drawing above
Drawing by S Breyer

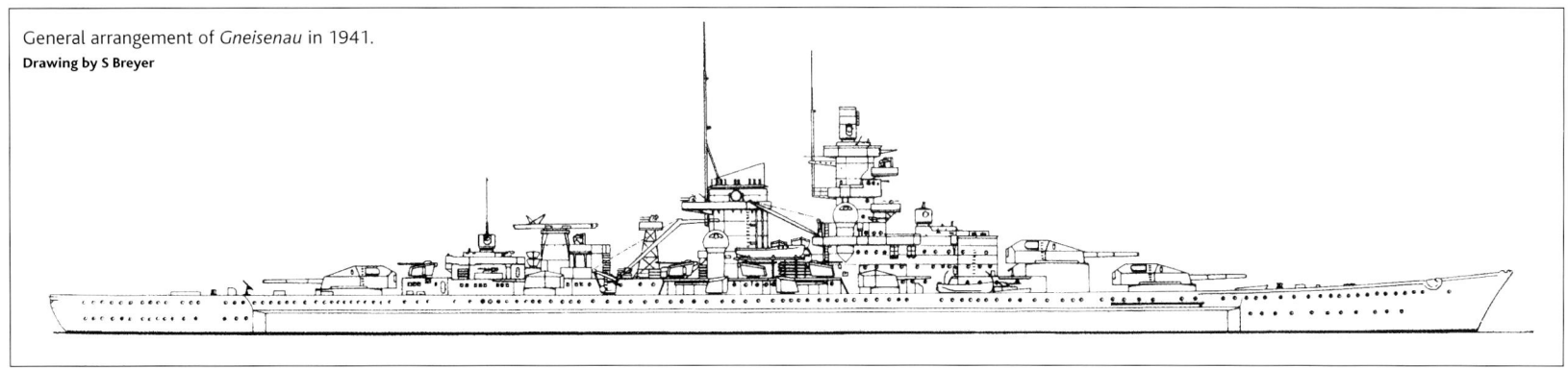

General arrangement of *Gneisenau* in 1941.
Drawing by S Breyer

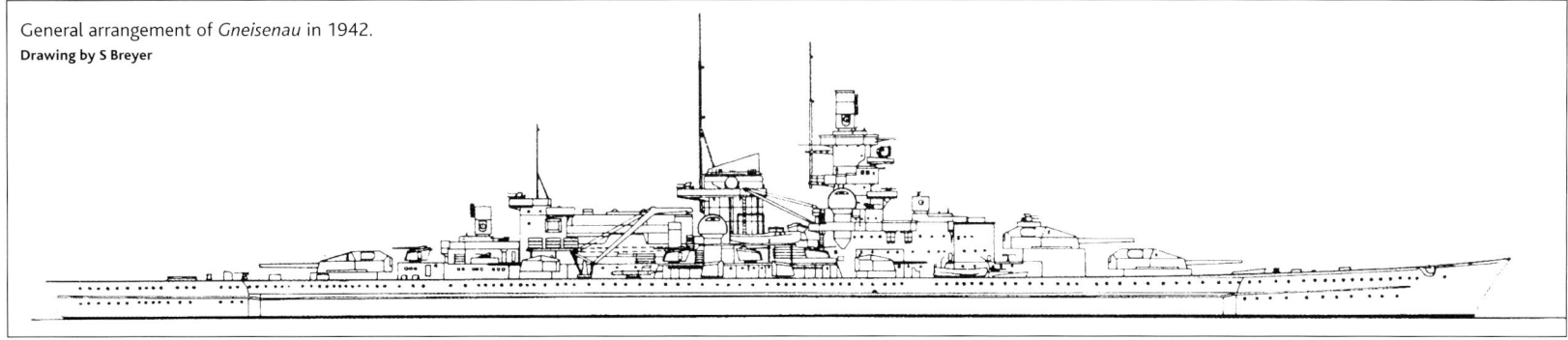

General arrangement of *Gneisenau* in 1942.
Drawing by S Breyer

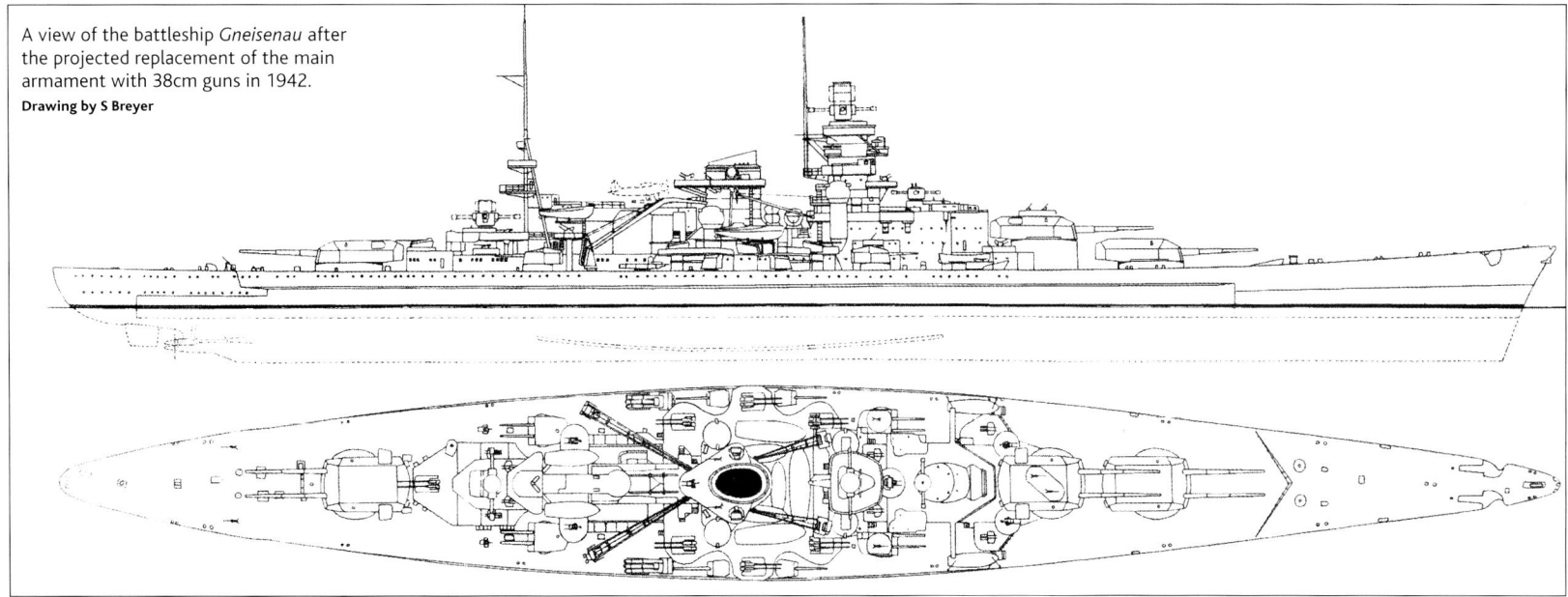

A view of the battleship *Gneisenau* after the projected replacement of the main armament with 38cm guns in 1942.
Drawing by S Breyer

TABLE: DESIGN TECHNICAL DATA APPROVED ON 19 JUNE 1934.

	New Design I (Neuentwurft I)	New Design II (Neuentwurft II)
Construction displacement	33,400 tons	30,950 tons
Standard displacement	30,400 tons	28,000 tons
Length at waterline	227.00m	223.00m
Beam at waterline	30.00m	29.30m
Design draught	8.70m	8.40m
Machinery	Steam turbines	Steam turbines
Rated power	125,000 HP	105,000 HP
Speed	30 knots	28 knots
Number of shafts	3	3
Armament	9 x 28cm (3 x III); 8 x 15cm (4 x II); 10 x 10.5cm (5 x II)	9 x 28cm (3 x III); 8 x 15cm (4 x II); 10 x 10.5cm (5 x II)
Torpedo tubes	none	none
ARMOUR		
Side armour	350mm	300mm
Armoured citadel	60mm bow, 90mm stern	60mm bow, 90mm stern
Platform deck	50mm	50mm
Armoured deck	60–100mm	60–100mm
Main gun turret barbettes	350mm	350mm
Conning tower	350mm	350mm

With all decisions now made and approved one might think that the construction of the battleships would begin quickly, but doubt about the main armament surfaced once again, which continued to hold up the resumption of work. In March 1935 five design variants with different main armament layouts were prepared:

a   nine 30.5cm (12in) guns in three triple turrets

b   nine 33cm (13in) guns in three triple turrets

c   six 38cm guns (15in) in three twin turrets

d   six 33cm (13in) guns in three twin turrets

e   six 35cm (14in) guns in three twin turrets

The first three designs assumed a displacement of 34,000–37,000 tons and the period required to design the turrets would be a year and a half, and adding the fitting-out period of three and a half years, the entire construction process would take five years. If work started in 1935 then the ship would enter service in 1940. The first armament variant was considered the best option as it assumed that Battleship D would complete in 16/17 months, and Battleship E would take a little longer, at 22/23 months. However, this would involve writing off RM 11 million already expended on the design and construction work on the 28cm gun turrets, which made this variant difficult to accept. An alternative would be to re-arm the battleships with 35cm guns at a later date, which would increase their displacement by 650 tons and increase the draught by 15cm. These figures were acceptable as they did not significantly affect the battleships' seagoing characteristics or their ability to use navigation channels, locks and canals. The only major consideration was a reduced ammunition capacity: for 28cm guns the ship would carry 150 shells per barrel but for the

35cm guns this number was only 130. However, raising the gun calibre automatically increased the distance at which it was possible to engage the enemy and, what was most important, allowed the guns to penetrate effectively the *Dunkerque*'s side armour. Balancing advantages and disadvantages in the choice of gun calibre was not as easy as hindsight might suggest, and in the end the armament of Battleships D and E was a compromise between the financial and political needs of the German Reich. The final decision was to arm the battleships with three triple 28cm turrets and in the near future replace them with 35cm guns. Later it turned out that the parameters of the 35cm guns were just slightly inferior to the more effective 33cm guns, and the question of re-arming the battleships was left open for further discussion.

At the beginning of 1935 German foreign policy shifted dramatically when on 16 March Hitler announced that Germany would no longer be bound by the terms of the Versailles Treaty. The quick diplomatic reaction by the British resulted in signing a bilateral naval agreement on 18 June 1935 that allowed Germany to build a fleet equal to 35 per cent of the size of the Royal Navy. When calculated, the limit for German battleships amounted to about 83,000 tons. In the case of Battleships D and E this agreement was irrelevant as these ships had already been laid down, respectively on 15 June 1935 in the Marinewerft at Wilhelmshaven and on 6 May 1935 in the Deutsche Werke at Kiel. After their complicated evolution, it is worth noting that the construction of the battleships took 42 months and cost RM 143.471 million for the *Scharnhorst* and 37 months and 146.174 million for the *Gneisenau*.

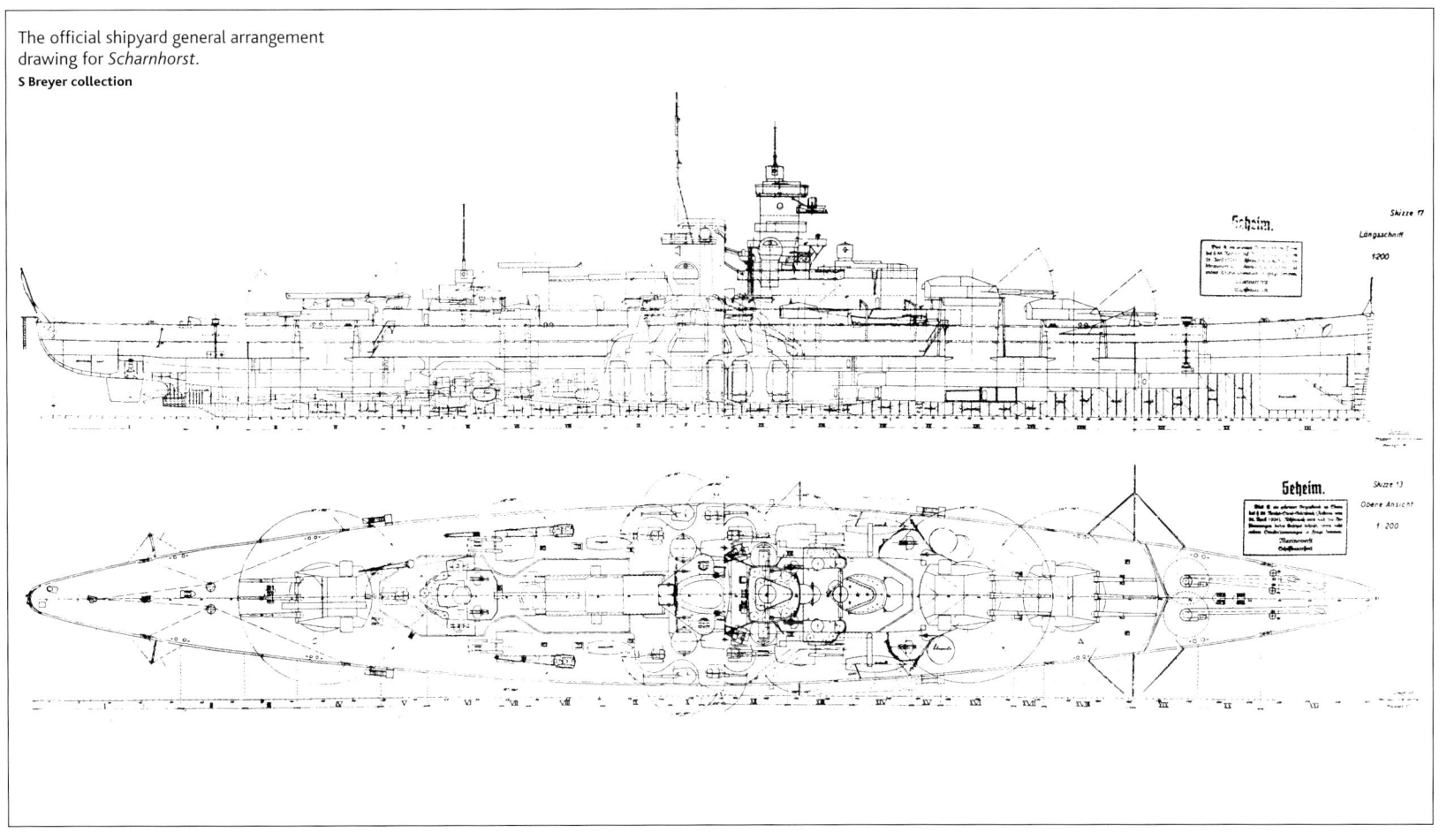

The official shipyard general arrangement drawing for *Scharnhorst*.
S Breyer collection

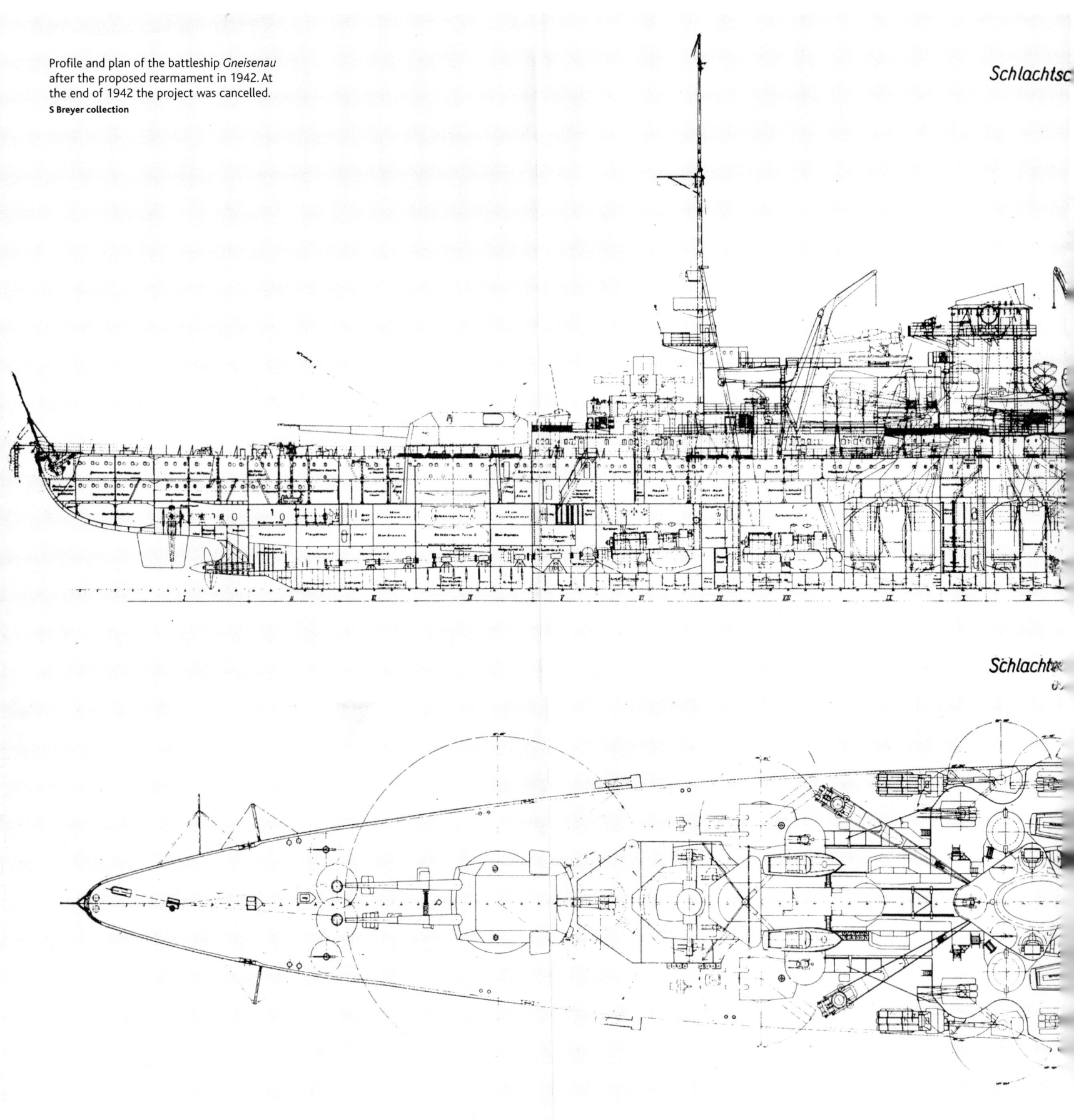

Profile and plan of the battleship *Gneisenau* after the proposed rearmament in 1942. At the end of 1942 the project was cancelled.
S Breyer collection

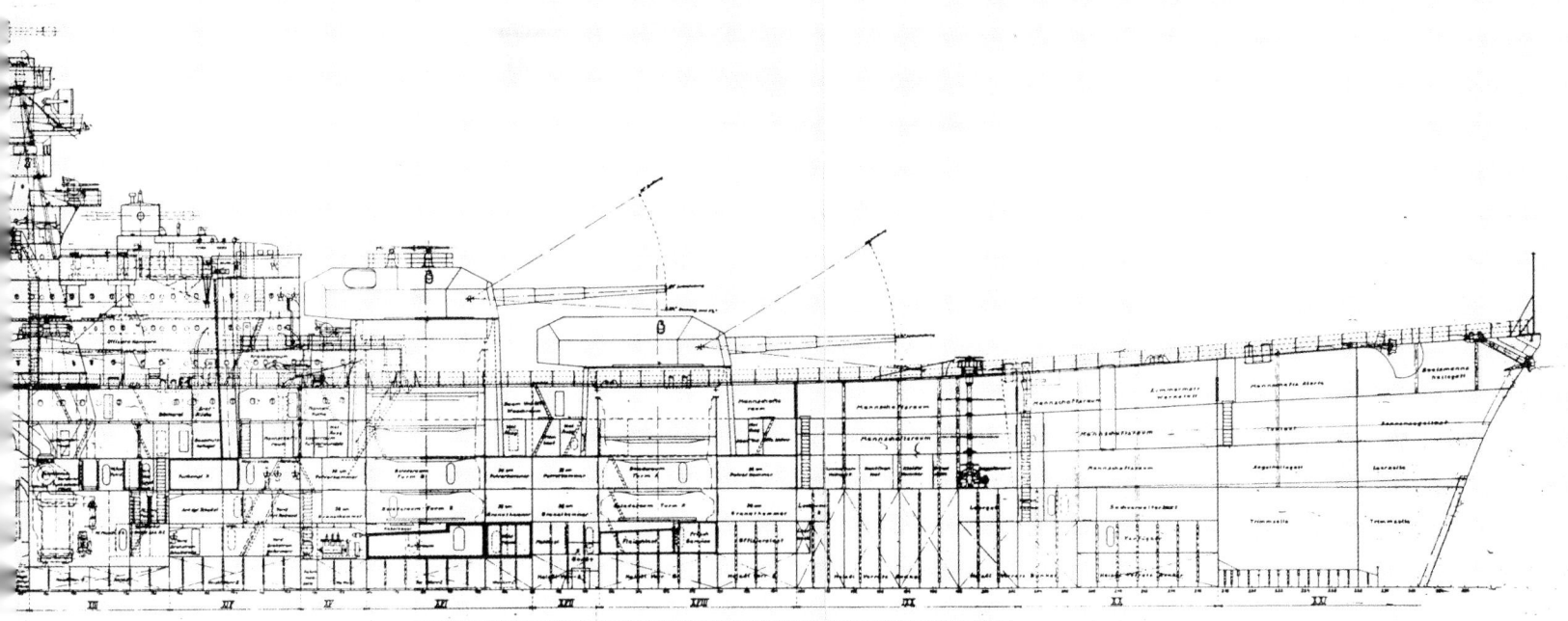

"nau" – K235/N4
Längsschnitt
1:100

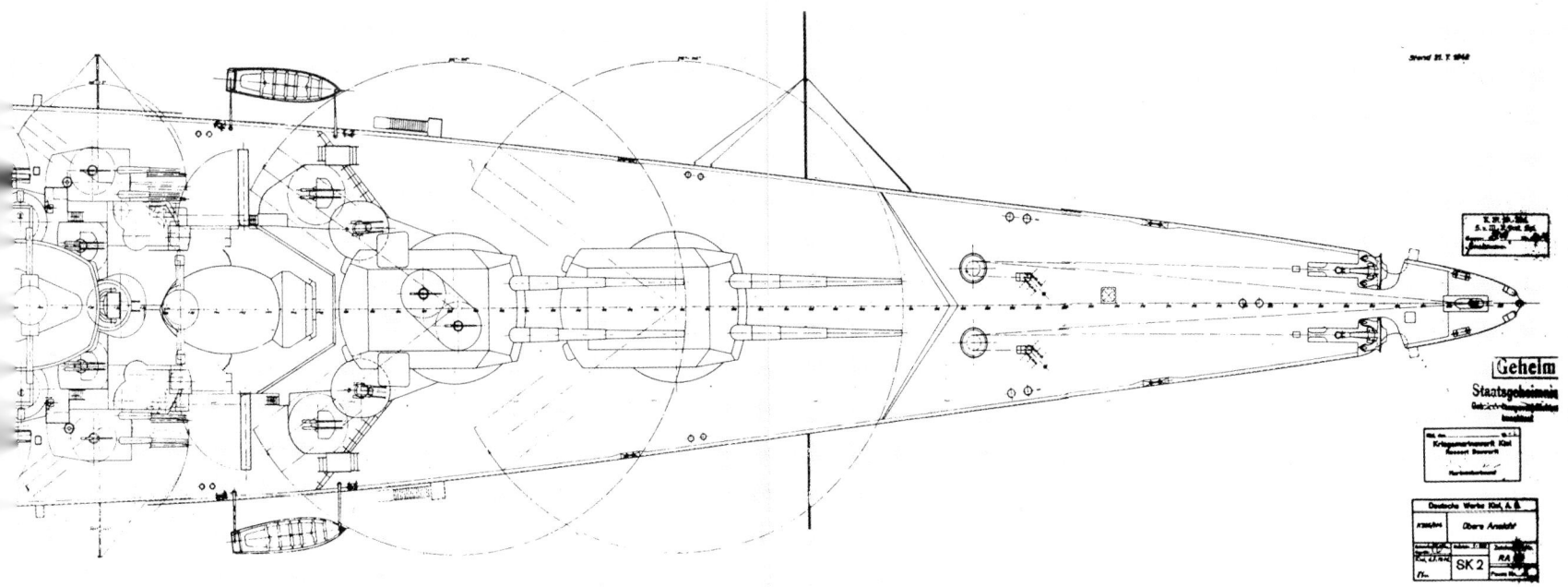

" K235/N4

SCHARNHORST

The hull of the new battleship was launched on 3 October 1936 in the Marinewerft in Wilhelmshaven, and named by the widow of Commander Felix Schultz who had commanded the armoured cruiser *Scharnhorst* sunk off the Falkland Islands during the Great War. The ensign was raised on 7 January 1939 and Otto Ciliax became the ship's first commander. The ship ran acceptance trials and work-up exercises in the Baltic until mid-1939, when she went back to the shipyard for modification of the bow. Between July and August 1939 the ship had a curved 'Atlantic stem' fitted, designed to keep excessive amounts of seawater from breaking over the forecastle. The replacement of a straight stem with an overhanging 'clipper' cutwater and the addition of a small bulbous forefoot solved this problem.

Scharnhorst's first operation was conducted with her sister *Gneisenau* against British convoys off Iceland, during which the German ships sank the British armed merchant cruiser HMS *Rawalpindi*. Another raid, codenamed Operation Nordmark, involved *Scharnhorst*, *Gneisenau*, the heavy cruiser *Admiral Hipper* and escorting destroyers, despatched to attack British

The roof of A turret is painted red, a colour that can be easily distinguished even in difficult weather conditions, and intended to identify a German ship to friendly forces without potential error.
Photograph by Dr Wehlau, from the collection of A Jarski

The ship spent her first months of service in the North Sea and the Baltic conducting sea trials. Here the *Scharnhorst* is seen in the estuary of the River Jade off Wilhelmshaven for another set of trials planned for 13 April 1939. Later the battleship sailed through the Kaiser Wilhelm Canal and anchored in the roadstead of Kiel for the celebrations of the Chancellor's birthday.
M Skwiot collection

convoys sailing between Bergen and British ports. This operation was less successful, as no British ship was sunk and the operation was cancelled after just two days. During Operation Weserübung, the invasion of Denmark and Norway, the *Scharnhorst* and *Gneisenau* belonged to the 1st Group, tasked with transporting German troops to Narvik. During this operation there was a brief inconclusive engagement with the British battlecruiser HMS *Renown* in heavy weather. When the operation was complete, the battleships were sent to Wilhelmshaven to prepare for another operation, codenamed Juno. The operation was a great success for the Germans as the battleships encountered the British aircraft carrier HMS *Glorious* sailing with only two

Gerhard Johann David von Scharnhorst

Gerhard Scharnhorst was born on 12 November 1755 in Bordenau on the River Leine near Hanover, where he spent his youth. At the age of 17 he entered the Count Wilhelm Schaumburg-Lippe's military school in Wilhelmstein Castle, where the future officers of the small Hanoverian army received very good education. After graduating in 1778 he served in the army of Hanover, transferring in 1783 to the artillery branch. He continued his military education and began to publish articles on military matters. His first experience of combat came during the Netherlands campaign in 1793, and a year later he took part in the defence of the city of Menin. Shortly after he was promoted to Major and, following the peace of Basel, he returned to Hanover In 1795. By now his military skills were highly regarded and he received offers to serve in several countries. In 1801 Scharnhorst entered the service of the Prussian king as a Lieutenant Colonel and was accepted as a lecturer in the Military Academy in Berlin, where he gained a reputation as a great teacher and military theorist. During the 1806 war with France he became the Chief of Staff for the Prince of Braunschweig. He was present at the battles of Jena and Auerstadt, where he was slightly wounded. Together with Blücher he was captured and became a prisoner of war during the capitulation of Ratkau but was later exchanged for some of Nepoleon's officers. He played a major role in the command of the Prussian L'Estocq corps serving with the Russians. For this campaign he was awarded the Pour le Mérite, Prussia's highest military Order (generally known as the Blue Max).

In 1806 Scharnhorst began a major program to modernise the Prussian army. After the Treaties of Tilsit he was promoted to Major

General and appointed to the post of Supervisor of the Army Reorganisation Committee, tasked with creating a modern national army. Diplomatic pressure from France after the lost war with Napoleon, however, limited the scope of the reforms. Two years later he was appointed the Minister of War and in 1810 he became the Chief of Staff. His further military career was determined by the current political situation – in 1811–12 Prussia was forced into an alliance with Napoleon against Russia, which Scharnhorst disapproved of, so he left Berlin and Prussian military service. This situation did not last long. During the French retreat from Moscow the Prussian king appointed him as Chief of Staff to replace Blücher. During the Battle of Lützen fought on 2 May 1813 he was wounded in the leg, and the subsequent lack of proper medical care brought about his death on 28 June 1813 in Prague.

destroyer escorts. During a short and uneven battle all three British ships were sunk. However, their loss came at the price of damage to the *Scharnhorst*, hit by a torpedo fired by HMS *Acasta*. The torpedo hit near C turret and 48 of the crew were killed and many more wounded. After some makeshift repairs in Trondheim the ship sailed to the Deutsche Werke at Kiel where she remained under repair until mid-December 1940. When these were complete the ship went for trials and exercises in the Baltic, followed by preparations for another sortie, codenamed Berlin. The first attempt was made on 28 December 1940, but *Gneisenau* was damaged in a storm and the German force withdrew. The second attempt was made on 22 January 1941 and this time the breakout succeeded. The German squadron passed the Denmark Strait and on 3 February reached southern Greenland. Their first target was convoy HX106, but it was left unmolested when the presence of the British battleship *Ramilles* was spotted. Between 7 and 9 March the German battleships stalked convoy SL67 but, as previously, when the battleship *Malaya* was sighted the attack was abandoned. Operation Berlin concluded with the ships entering Brest on 22 March 1941.

At Brest the *Scharnhorst* was bombed by the RAF, which was the reason that kept the ship in France until the end of the year. In July 1941 the heavy cruiser *Prinz Eugen* joined the two battleships in Brest. This assembly of ships made an attractive target within easy range of British bombers, so there was a high risk of severe damage or even loss. At the beginning of 1942, therefore, the decision was made to bring this force back to Germany and then the safety of the Baltic Sea. The shortest route was through the English Channel and between 11 and 13 February the *Scharnhorst*, *Gneisenau* and *Prinz Eugen* made their famous 'dash' up this narrow waterway to Germany in Operation Cerberus. During this passage the *Scharnhorst* twice hit a mine and was severely damaged, but she managed to reach Wilhelmshaven safely. The repairs lasted until the end of the year when the ship left the Deutsche Werke in Kiel and sailed to the Baltic for sea trials. At the beginning of January, Operation Fronttheater planned to relocate the ship from Gotenhafen (Gdynia) to Norway, but after receiving a warning of possible British attempts to intercept the battleship she returned to Gotenhafen. The second attempt was made towards the end of January during Operation Domino, but again the attempt was abandoned. The third operation, codenamed Paderborn, was successful and the battleship, together with the *Prinz Eugen*, entered a fjord near Bergen on 9 March 1943. Several days later the ship was moved to Altafjord where it remained, with the battleship *Tirpitz*, until the end of the year. In April several accidental explosions on board put the ship out of action for some time. In September 1943 the ship, together with the battleship *Tirpitz*, took part in Operation Sizilien (the attack on Spitsbergen).

When the *Tirpitz* was put out of action the *Scharnhorst* remained the strongest Kriegsmarine warship in the north. Immediately after the Russian-bound convoy JW55B was detected, the ship was despatched to intercept in a sortie codenamed Operation Ostfront. The German force consisting of *Scharnhorst* and escorting destroyers under the command of Admiral Erich Bey left the Kaafjord to attack the convoy. The vigilant British soon received intelligence from Ultra that the German ships were leaving harbour, so they were forewarned. In the initial phase of the operation the battleship engaged British cruisers, which knocked out the *Scharnhorst*'s radar, but they also sent information on her course and location to the battleship *Duke of York* coming up astern of the convoy. During the ensuing engagement with the British battleship and the cruisers on 26 December 1943, the *Scharnhorst* was hit by destroyer torpedoes and overwhelmed by gunfire, sinking with most of her crew after receiving the coup de grace delivered by torpedoes from the smaller craft. Only 36 men were rescued.

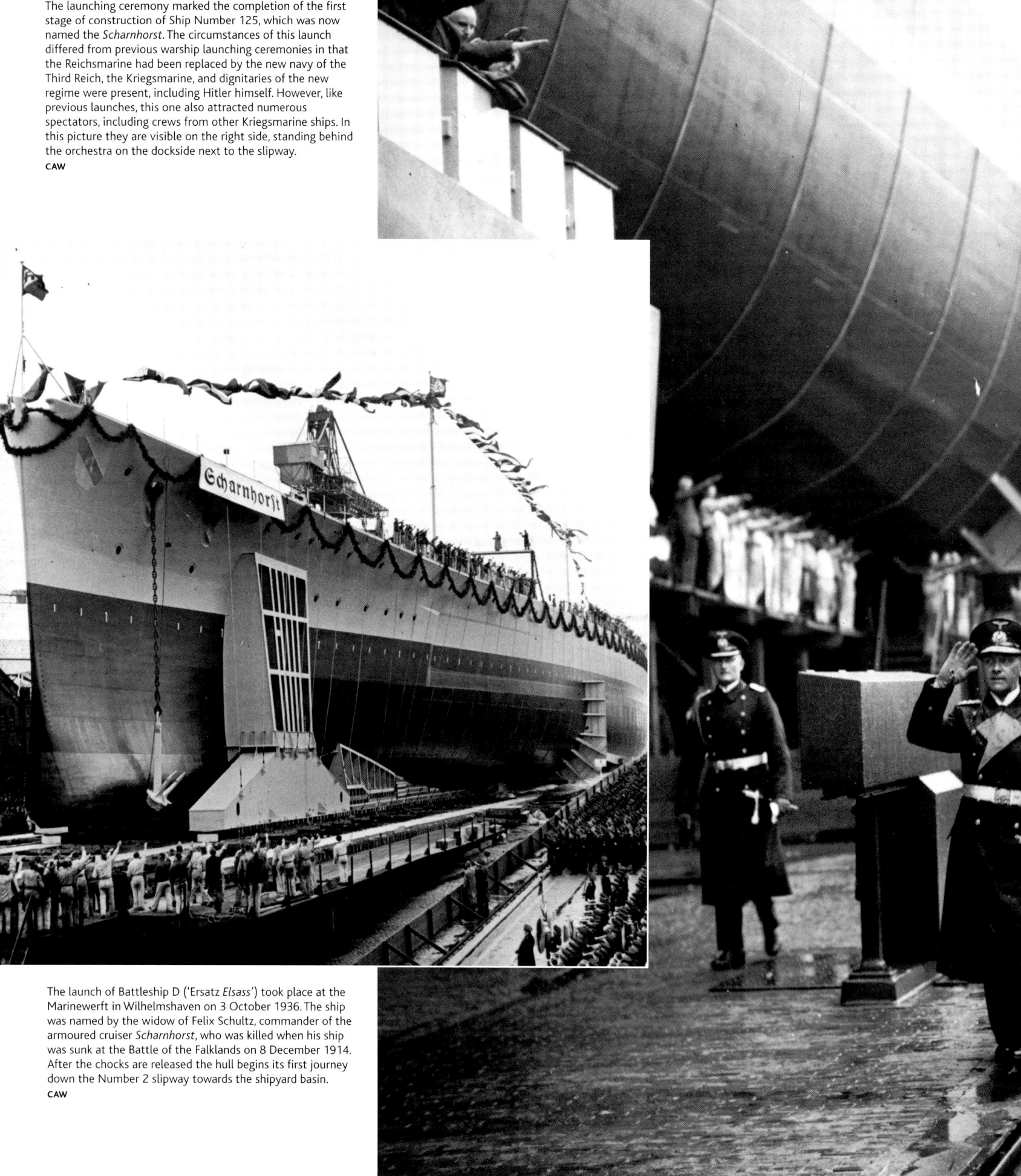

The launching ceremony marked the completion of the first stage of construction of Ship Number 125, which was now named the *Scharnhorst*. The circumstances of this launch differed from previous warship launching ceremonies in that the Reichsmarine had been replaced by the new navy of the Third Reich, the Kriegsmarine, and dignitaries of the new regime were present, including Hitler himself. However, like previous launches, this one also attracted numerous spectators, including crews from other Kriegsmarine ships. In this picture they are visible on the right side, standing behind the orchestra on the dockside next to the slipway.
CAW

The launch of Battleship D ('Ersatz *Elsass*') took place at the Marinewerft in Wilhelmshaven on 3 October 1936. The ship was named by the widow of Felix Schultz, commander of the armoured cruiser *Scharnhorst*, who was killed when his ship was sunk at the Battle of the Falklands on 8 December 1914. After the chocks are released the hull begins its first journey down the Number 2 slipway towards the shipyard basin.
CAW

The launching proceeds as planned and the *Scharnhorst* slides down towards the shipyard basin in Wilhelmshaven. Among the invited guests were also NSDAP (Nazi party) members who are gathered in a separate sector next to the slipway. In this picture they can be seen on the left of the Number 2 slipway.
CAW

Once afloat, the battleship hull is towed towards the fitting-out berth of the Marinewerft in Wilhelmshaven.
S Breyer collection

Fitting out the *Scharnhorst* in the summer of 1937. In the foreground is a complete-looking A turret covered with canvas. Work is proceeding on the first level of the forward superstructure and the conning tower is erected. Further aft is C turret, also apparently complete.
S Breyer collection

By the time this picture was taken at the end of 1937 the forward superstructure and the funnel were almost finished, but much remained to be done on the battleship's after superstructure.
S Breyer collection

The *Scharnhorst* was commissioned at a ceremony held on 7 January 1939 in the Wilhelmshaven naval base. The battleship's first commander was Otto Ciliax, seen here saluting on a specially built stand on top of the aircraft catapult installed on C turret. The photographer captured the moment when the Kriegsmarine ensign was hoisted for the first time on the ship.
CAW

Gunnery practice for the heavy anti-aircraft artillery on board the *Scharnhorst* conducted shortly after commissioning.
CAW

The *Scharnhorst*'s bow photographed in Wilhelmshaven during the commissioning ceremony on 7 January 1939. An interesting feature is the ship's crest newly installed either side of the stemhead – as can be seen in earlier photographs, between launching and fitting out the ship only carried a painted version of the shield, which eventually faded away with the paint. Just before the ship was commissioned a low-relief shield carrying the crest was installed, port and starboard.
WBB, from the collection of M Krzyżan

The ship spent her first months of service in the North Sea and the Baltic conducting sea trials. Here the *Scharnhorst* is seen in the estuary of the River Jade off Wilhelmshaven for another set of trials planned for 13 April 1939. Later the battleship sailed through the Kaiser Wilhelm Canal and anchored in the roadstead of Kiel for the celebrations of the Chancellor's birthday.
A Jarski collection

Dressed overall, *Scharnhorst* fires a gun salute in the roadstead of Kiel on 20 April 1939. The occasion for these celebrations was the birthday of the Chancellor Adolf Hitler. For propaganda reasons this photograph was heavily retouched.
Photograph by Urbahns, from the collection of M Skwiot

Scharnhorst's forward main gun turrets. As originally commissioned, the sisters could be differentiated by details of their A turrets – in the Scharnhorst there were lockers installed near the turret bases on both sides, but there were none in the Gneisenau. If visible, the crests on individual turrets could also distinguish the battleships.
Photograph by Urbahns, from the collection of T Klimczyk

A close-up of Scharnhorst's funnel and midships area, in a picture that was taken before the first refit.
S Breyer collection

Battleship *Scharnhorst* in the waters off Wilhelmshaven in the summer of 1939 shortly after the refit in the Marinewerft was completed. The most noticeable new features were the installation of the overhanging 'Atlantic' bow, addition of a funnel cap and replacement of the mast stepped on the funnel platform by a new tripod mast aft of the aircraft hangar. These modifications were carried out between June and August 1939 and significantly altered the appearance of the ship.
M Skwiot collection

The battleships *Scharnhorst* and *Gneisenau* photographed at Kiel in April or May 1939. In the foreground the *Scharnhorst* before the planned refit still sports the straight stem, and in the background the *Gneisenau*, with the new bow and the funnel cap already installed.
CAW

GERMAN CAPITAL SHIPS

In the foreground one of the many German submarines returning to base. Emerging out of the morning mist in the background is the battleship *Scharnhorst* anchored in Kiel.
S Breyer collection

LEFT: Another shot showing *Scharnhorst* setting out for sea trials. It was common practice by the censors to remove any military background from warship pictures – in this case the buildings of Wilhelmshaven were painted out. This was supposed to prevent the identification of the location and date of the picture.
M Skwiot collection

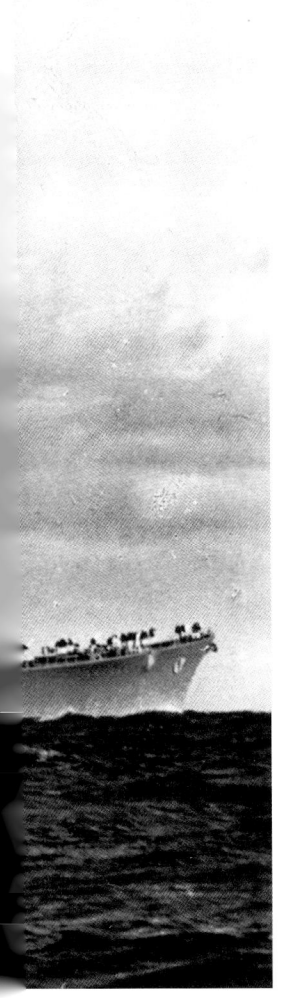

Scharnhorst in open water during September 1939 after embarking new floatplanes of the Ar 196 type. On 8 September 1939 the ship sailed out into the Baltic for gunnery practice against the target ship *Hessen*. The blast caused by firing the main guns damaged the midships hangar and the Arado aircraft stowed on top of it. This came as a surprise as it was usually the aircraft and catapult located on C turret that proved more vulnerable.
T Klimczyk collection

Scharnhorst during sea trials conducted in open water after the installation of the FuMO 22 radar at the Kiel shipyard. Over the hangar roof an Arado 196 A1 floatplane awaits launch from the catapult. Four of these aircraft were embarked on 8 November at Kiel.
S Breyer collection

View from the forecastle of the battleship anchored in Kiel prior to the installation of the radar. This photograph was taken near the end of November 1939 after the ship returned from a sortie against Allied shipping which resulted in the sinking of the armed merchant cruiser HMS *Rawalpindi* on 23 November 1939. The censor removed the naval base background (the inset shows the original photo) to create an impression that the battleship is at sea.
T Klimczyk collection

Drill on the forecastle deck, with B turret visible to the right.

Lowering one of the ship's boats by crane.

Off-duty men relaxing.

Work on one of the 10.5cm anti-aircraft gun mountings.

Signalmen in semaphore drills on the battleship's deck.

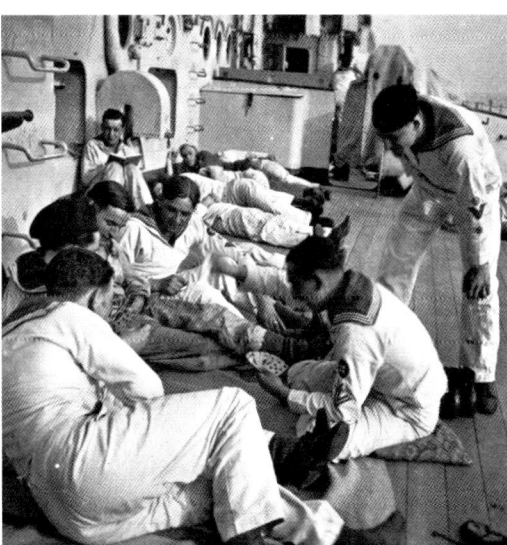
Playing cards, a popular off-duty pastime.

One of the many ship's offices on board.

Maintenance being carried out in the engine room.

Scrubbing the quarterdeck.
All photographs by Dr Wehlau, from the collection of A Jarski

Scharnhorst photographed in early December 1939 in the basin of the Marinewerft in Wilhelmshaven. Above the foretop and its 10.5m rangefinder is the FuMO 22 antenna. In the background the hull of the battleship *Tirpitz* is visible at the shipyard's fitting-out berth. When magnified, the photograph reveals that the superstructure of the *Tirpitz* is complete up to the level of the admiral's bridge.
Photograph by Drüppel, from the collection of S Breyer

Scharnhorst at sea in December 1939. This picture was taken during a test flight of an Arado Ar 196 A1 aircraft from a new catapult capable of launching heavier aircraft. One of the aircraft is being lifted from the water after the flight for repositioning on top of the battleship's hangar.
S Breyer collection

Scharnhorst photographed in Kiel in January 1940. The battleship spent the winter in Kiel together with her sister ship *Gneisenau* and only in late February did both ships sail for their first operation of the year, codenamed Nordmark.
S Breyer collection

LEFT: Releasing the crane hook after positioning the Ar 196 (T3+NH, as below) on the battleship's midships catapult. The replacement of older model floatplanes was not without difficulties – by the end of 1939 the Arado factory had only managed to complete 20 of these aircraft. The earliest version, A1, was used by the Kriegsmarine from June 1939.
S Breyer collection

Arado Ar 196 floatplane (registration number T3+NH) ready to be launched from the catapult. The aircraft does not carry the 1/196 Bordfliegerstaffel crest – a white seahorse on a silver background in black outline – so this aircraft was probably assigned to the *Scharnhorst* straight from the Arado factory.
S Breyer collection

The first of the *Scharnhorst*'s new Arado floatplanes is placed on the trolley and prepared for folding the wings before it is hauled into the aircraft hangar.
S Breyer collection

View of the battleship's aircraft hangar. In the foreground an Arado floatplane with its wings folded being pulled inside the hangar. The arrangement was awkward and the space very confined.
S Breyer collection

Scharnhorst alongside the H1 pier in the Hipper Basin in Wilhelmshaven. In this photograph, taken probably in early March 1940, new engine room staff are being instructed on the quayside. In the background the aircraft catapult is being removed from the battleship's C turret by the *Lange Heinrich* floating crane.
S Breyer collection

A view of engine room staff under instruction during the battleship's time in Wilhelmshaven in March 1940. In the background the catapult from C turret is being removed by the floating crane.
S Breyer collection

Another shot of the crew in training, this time against the backdrop of the ship's midship superstructure. The aircraft hangar is visible in the background, with an Arado Ar 196 floatplane, registration number T3+NH is being pulled into the hangar.
S Breyer collection

The searchlight and the anti-aircraft gun crews man their stations on the funnel platform during a simulated alarm. In the background the *Scharnhorst*'s mast and seaplane hangar roof are visible. The picture was taken in March 1940.
S Breyer collection

Forward superstructure of the *Scharnhorst*, April 1940, Wilhelmshaven. The ship now carries the instant recognition markings designed to make clear the ship's nationality to friendly aircraft. The markings included the national flag painted on the weather deck forward and aft, and the roofs and angles of the turret tops painted in a contrasting colour from the rest of the ship (usually red or yellow).
Photograph by Dr Wehlau, from the collection of A Jarski

Scharnhorst in the Wilhelmshaven roadstead, April 1940. Based on the camouflage pattern it is a reasonable assumption that the picture was taken prior to Operation Weserübung (the invasion of Norway, 7-12 April 1940).
Photograph by Dr Wehlau, from the collection of A Jarski

Scharnhorst at the H1 berth in Wilhelmshaven's Hipper Basin, photographed in March 1940 from *U50* as the submarine enters the dock. Although the weather is foggy, it is clear that the aircraft catapult has been removed from the battleship's C turret.
S Breyer collection

ABOVE: The crew drawn up on the battleship's quarterdeck. Note the large national flag towards the stern.
All photographs on this spread by Dr Wehlau, from the collection of A Jarski

LEFT: Scrubbing the deck was one of the many duties performed by the men while the ship was in port. This is one of the few unretouched photos which show a stripe painted on the battleship's forward superstructure. No previous publication has mentioned this stripe and even its colour remains unknown. The picture was taken during the ship's time in Wilhelmshaven roadstead during May 1940, prior to Operation Juno. This was an attempt to intercept troopships evacuating allied forces from Norway which ended in the sinking of the British carrier *Glorious* and her two escorting destroyers.

Removal of grease from a 10.5cm anti-aircraft shell. In the background is the 15cm training gun which was used by the gun crews for practice without wearing out or damaging a real gun.

ABOVE: A view of the *Scharnhorst*'s forward turrets during preparations for Operation Weserübung – maintenance of one of the capstans.

Scharnhorst's forward main gun turrets seen from the forward deck. Roofs and inclined parts of the turrets are painted red. This picture was taken near Wilhelmshaven in April 1940 before Operation Weserübung.

RIGHT: The aft side of *Scharnhorst*'s bridge structure with various platforms seen from the starboard boat deck.

Scharnhorst's boat deck between the bridge and the funnel. In the foreground is one of the motor boats on its chocks with the crane visible above. This picture, like the previous ones, was taken during preparations for Operation Weserübung.
All photographs on this spread by Dr Wehlau, from the collection of A Jarski

Repairs and painting of the funnel in April 1940.

Cleaning and washing of the forward turrets and main guns. For this task the A turret gun barrels are fully depressed to facilitate maintenance. This picture was taken during the ship's time in port, which is signified by the black ball hoisted under the foretop.

All photographs on this spread by Dr Wehlau, from the collection of A Jarski

Routine work on board – washing and scrubbing the deck. The photographer also took this picture during the ship's time in Wilhelmshaven.

LEFT: Signalmen participating in semaphore drills on the *Scharnhorst*'s weather deck aft. In the background note the vents and one of the mainmast tripod legs.

Drills by divisions on board the battleship: in this case the signal division practices Morse code signalling using semaphore. In the background is a 10.5cm SK C/33 gun on a twin LC/31 8.8cm mount.

Crew of an after 3.7cm anti-aircraft gun at their battle stations. One of the men is wearing sunglasses which allows for better observation of the horizon. This is another picture taken during the preparations for Operation Juno.

Another routine activity for the sailors were physical exercises on deck. Abreast A and B turrets special stays for gymnastic bars could be set up.

Painting the port aircraft and boat crane on board the *Scharnhorst*. In the *Scharnhorst* and *Gneisenau* the crane jibs were of different design, which allows for easy identification of each ship.

A salvo fired from the forward turrets at the British aircraft carrier HMS *Glorious* during the engagement of 8 June 1940. Note the markings used for identification by friendly aircraft applied on A and B turrets – the turret roofs are painted a dark colour (probably grey) and the 10m rangefinder covers are painted in a lighter colour, probably the light grey of the rest of the turret.
CAW

Another shot taken a few seconds after the previous one.
CAW

A salvo fired at the enemy during the engagement with HMS *Glorious* observed from the battleship's bridge.
S Breyer collection

In the background is the battleship *Gneisenau*, seen from the *Scharnhorst* during Operation Juno, but before the engagement with the aircraft carrier HMS *Glorious* and her two destroyer escorts.
S Breyer collection

Although the battle ended with German victory and the sinking of all three British ships, the *Scharnhorst* was hit by a torpedo fired by HMS *Acasta*. Almost 2500 tons of water entered the ship's hull, which forced the ship to return to Trondheim on 9 June 1940. In this picture, taken probably on the 10th or 11th, the *Scharnhorst* shows a slight trim by the stern.
S Breyer collection

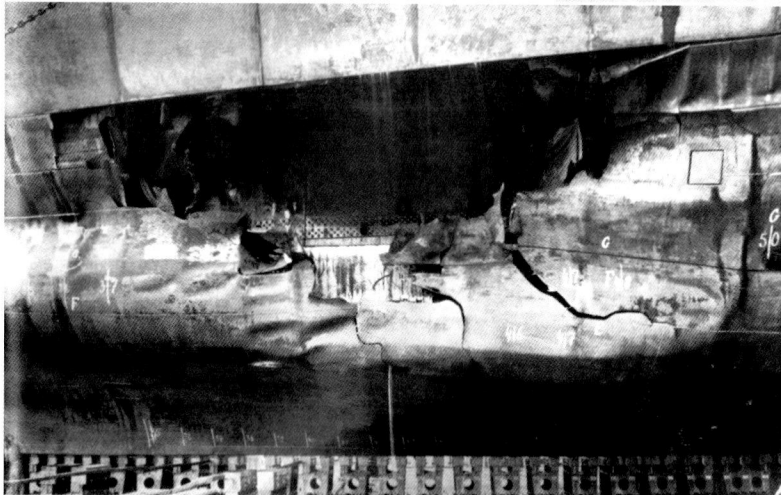

The torpedo damage was temporarily repaired and on 18 June 1940 the ship successfully conducted engine trials. On the 20th the ship left Trondheim for Kiel, arriving there on 23 June, and on the following day entered Dry Dock C in the Deutsche Werke shipyard. This close-up shows the damage to the ship's stern (frames 35–52).
S Breyer collection

Prisoners of war from sunken British merchant ships leaving the *Scharnhorst* when the ship docked in the occupied French naval base of Brest in March 1941 after Operation Berlin.
CAW

Scharnhorst alongside at Brest. This picture was taken after the ship returned from Operation Berlin towards the end of March 1941. British intelligence soon discovered the location of the *Scharnhorst* and *Gneisenau* and planned to remove the threat the ships posed at all cost; the only viable method was air attack with bombs or torpedoes.
S Breyer collection

The camouflaged *Scharnhorst* and the quay to which the battleship was moored seen from the forecastle. The picture was taken in April 1941 in Brest.
S Breyer collection

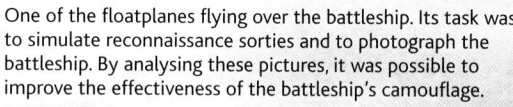

One of the floatplanes flying over the battleship. Its task was to simulate reconnaissance sorties and to photograph the battleship. By analysing these pictures, it was possible to improve the effectiveness of the battleship's camouflage.
S Breyer collection

Fearing that French agents might provide the British with useful information, all identification markings were removed from the ships during their time in Brest. In the foreground is one of the ship's aircraft with identification markings and crest painted over. Replacement Arado floatplanes were flown from Wilhelmshaven to Brest on 12 June 1941. As it turned out the protection offered by camouflage netting alone was insufficient, so the upper parts of the superstructures were painted in a camouflage pattern.
S Breyer collection

The first air strikes against the battleships at Brest were conducted during the last night of March 1941. To prevent the identification of the *Scharnhorst*, the ship was covered with camouflage netting. The anti-aircraft artillery was also reinforced by additional guns located on the quay. The picture shows the camouflaged *Scharnhorst* alongside a quay in Brest in mid-April 1941.
S Breyer collection

Aerial reconnaissance photograph of Brest taken in December 1941 shows both battleships in dry docks covered with camouflage netting. On the left, marked with '1' is the *Scharnhorst* and number '2', on the right, is the *Gneisenau*.
IWM

ABOVE: Operation Cerberus, the 'Channel Dash'. This picture was taken on 12 February 1942 from the heavy cruiser *Prinz Eugen* after the *Scharnhorst* hit a mine for the first time. The mines were dropped from British Hampden aircraft between 6 and 11 February during a mining operation codenamed Nectarine. The force commander, Vice Admiral Ciliax moved his flag to the destroyer Z29, assigning the 3rd Torpedo Boat Flotilla to protect the battleship.
S Breyer collection

Another view of the damaged *Scharnhorst* taken on 12 February 1942 from the heavy cruiser *Prinz Eugen*.
S Breyer collection

After makeshift repairs the battleship rejoined the force, but the damage continued to affect the ship and she soon began to fall behind; in the evening the distance was almost 30 miles. In this photograph taken from the destroyer *Z29*, the *Scharnhorst* is still making good speed but with a slight trim by the bow.
CAW

The passage of the three heavy German ships, *Scharnhorst*, *Gneisenau* and *Prinz Eugen*, through the English Channel in February 1942 was codenamed Operation Cerberus. This picture taken from the *Gneisenau* shows the *Scharnhorst*, flagship of the force commander Vice Admiral Otto Ciliax.
S Breyer collection

This was not the end of the *Scharnhorst*'s misfortunes during Operation Cerberus – at about 22.34 the ship hit another mine north of Terschelling. Almost 1000 tons of water entered the hull and the turbines and generators were damaged. The battleship was only good for 15 knots, but luck did not entirely desert the ship and on the next day at about 12.30 she entered the Wilhelmshaven naval base.
CAW

Aerial photograph of the Deutsche Werke shipyard in Kiel taken in March 1942 by British reconnaissance aircraft. At the left of the picture surrounded by ice is the battleship *Scharnhorst*, while at the bottom moored to a jetty is the cruiser *Nürnberg*.
S Breyer collection

As it soon transpired, the safest place to carry out a thorough repair was the Gotenhafen naval base. In this picture taken in autumn of 1942 the *Scharnhorst* is moored alongside the Passenger Terminal in Gotenhafen (Gdynia).
S Breyer collection

ABOVE: *Scharnhorst* in Bogen Bay near Narvik on 9 or 10 March 1943. The operation to transfer the battleship to Norwegian waters was codenamed Paderborn and was carried out successfully. The destroyer in the right background is the *Erich Steinbrink*.
S Breyer collection

LEFT: The *Scharnhorst* in winter paint scheme in 1943. The ship's outline is confused by the camouflaged destroyer *Z33* lying alongside.
M Skwiot collection

Battleships *Scharnhorst* (on the left) and *Tirpitz* photographed in September 1943 at the time of the attack on Spitsbergen. This operation, codenamed Sizilien, was conducted under the command of Vice Admiral Kummetz. The ships destroyed the coaling facilities, port amenities and cargo-handling equipment located on the island.
M Skwiot collection

Gneisenau

The hull of the battleship *Gneisenau* was launched on 8 December 1936, christened by the widow of Julius Marker, commander of the armoured cruiser *Gneisenau* sunk at the Falkland Islands in 1914. During the launching there was a minor accident when shipyard workers failed to stop the ship after the launch and the hull hit the quay on the opposite side of the basin; luckily, only the wall was damaged and the ship was unscathed. The fitting-out ran to schedule and on 21 May 1938 the ship was commissioned in the usual the ensign-raising ceremony, the commander of the new ship being Captain (Kpt z S) F Förste. Just one month later the *Gneisenau* sailed for the North Atlantic. It was during this cruise that the disadvantages of the straight stem became apparent: at high speed in rough seas the rangefinders in A and B turrets as well as the bridge were washed out, a situation that made main gunfire control a difficult task and in very heavy seas completely impossible. In October 1938 the *Gneisenau* was sent to the Deutsche Werke at Kiel to have her bow reconstructed in work that continued until the end of January 1939.

When war broke out the battleship's first mission was a raid against the shipping lanes between Great Britain and Norway that she conducted with the cruiser *Köln* and escorting destroyers. The plan was to lure the British into a trap set by the U-boats and the Luftwaffe, but the effort was futile, as the British, despite detecting the enemy force, did not attempt to intercept them. The German force returned to base. The *Gneisenau* left Wilhelmshaven for another operation with her sister *Scharnhorst* and the cruisers *Köln* and *Leipzig*. During this raid the force under the command of Vice Admiral Marschall sank the British armed merchant cruiser *Rawalpindi*. After the engagement the raid was cancelled due to structural damage inflicted on *Gneisenau* by a storm – a lot of water entered the ship through leaks in the hull, which was deemed dangerous enough to force the ships to return to base. Repairs were carried out in Wilhelmshaven and the ship was relocated to the Baltic for sea trials. In mid-January 1940 the *Gneisenau* returned to Kiel and was preparing for another raid in the Atlantic when this operation had to be postponed because one of the ship's propellers was damaged by ice. On 18 February the *Gneisenau* left for another sortie, codenamed Nordmark, but as with its predecessor, this operation was unsuccessful and after two days the ships returned to Wilhelmshaven. When back in port, *Gneisenau*, like other Kriegsmarine units, prepared for Operation Weserübung, the attack on Denmark and Norway. Vice Admiral Günter Lütjens assumed command of the German naval force. During this operation there was a brief engagement with the

Gneisenau at the fleet review, 22 August 1938. As the newest capital ship in the fleet, *Gneisenau* led the parade ahead of the three panzerschiffe.
CAW

British battlecruiser HMS *Renown* near the Lofoten Islands. This first gunnery duel with the enemy did not go well for the German ship: the *Gneisenau* was hit three times and had to withdraw. Furthermore, because of the damage sustained, the force commander decided to abandon the mission and ordered all ships to return to Germany. It seems that bad luck never left the ship. On 5 May during a routine transit to the Baltic, the *Gneisenau* set off a magnetic mine and had to be docked once again. The period of sea trials and exercises that followed was interrupted in June when the *Gneisenau*, together with the *Scharnhorst*, left Kiel on 4 June 1940 for Operation Juno. Against the run of bad luck, at the very beginning of the operation (on 8 June) the battleships sank the British aircraft carrier HMS *Glorious* and her two destroyer escorts. Although *Scharnhorst* was damaged, *Gneisenau* emerged unscathed – but not for long. The British had stationed a line of submarines across the assumed return course the battleships would have to take, and on 20 June the *Gneisenau* was torpedoed by HMS/M *Clyde* (Lieutenant Commander Ingram) about 40 miles north of Hapten Island. On the following day the damaged *Gneisenau*, with large amounts of water in the hull, reached Trondheim, where repairs began immediately. They continued until 21 July 1940, when sea trials were conducted in a fjord near Trondheim. The temporary repairs allowed the *Gneisenau* to sail safely to Germany for full repairs. Escorted by the light cruiser *Nürnberg*, the ship set out on 25 July for Kiel, which was reached safely on the 28th. The ship was put straight into B dock in the Howaldtswerke shipyard, where the repairs started immediately. The work continued into the second half of October and on 14 November the *Gneisenau* sailed for the Baltic and a regime of exercises and sea trials. After these were complete the ship returned to Kiel where she once again entered the dock and began preparations for another sortie – Operation Berlin.

The first attempt to sail was made on 28 December, but after two days it was abandoned because of the extreme cold and a forecast of heavy storms in the North Atlantic which would make the passage of the Iceland Gap impossible. Having no other option, the German force waited until the end of January for weather conditions to improve. The second attempt to begin the operation was made on 28 January 1941 and this time the breakout succeeded. The German attack on Allied merchant shipping in this operation lasted until the second half of March and was claimed by German propaganda to be a 'great success', with 22 enemy ships sunk or captured. However, when both ships arrived in Brest, the information about their whereabouts rapidly reached London. This was a great, and possibly one-off, opportunity to dispose of both ships, as they were well within range of RAF bombers. The most important information obtained by the British was that the ships would remain in Brest for at least three months, but the battleships were monitored closely by aerial reconnaissance and based on these regular reports air strike plans were adapted. At one point the ships left their docks and were moored alongside a jetty, whereupon the British took immediate advantage of the situation to carry out a torpedo attack on the *Gneisenau* by Beauforts of 22 Sqd. This was a true 'master plan', as the Germans never expected a torpedo attack on a ship moored in a harbour basin. No doubt there was too little time to deploy torpedo nets, while there must have been confidence that the Luftwaffe and the anti-aircraft defences would protect the ships. The heroic attack led by Flying Officer Kenneth Campbell on the *Gneisenau* resulted in his torpedo hitting the battleship, although his aircraft was shot down and he was killed (he was awarded the Victoria Cross posthumously). Four days later the British conducted another bombing raid on Brest and the *Gneisenau* was hit several more times, eliminating the ship from operations for several

August Wilhelm Anton Neidhardt von Gneisenau

Von Gneisenau was born on 27 October 1760 in Schildau near Torgau in Saxony. He came from a family with long military traditions so it was not surprising that the young August embarked on an army career with the help of his father, who was an artillery officer. In his youth von Gneisenau was educated by the Jesuit order and studied philosophy at Erfurt University from 1777. One year later he left the university and entered military service, joining an Austrian hussar regiment. The first real step in his military career came in 1780 when he was promoted to 2nd Lieutenant and became an officer in Markgraf Bayreuth-Anspach's army. Later he served in the British army in North America, and after his return in 1786 he entered the service of the Prussian king. One year later he was promoted to Lieutenant and assigned to staff duty. A breakthrough in his career came in 1796 when he was promoted to Captain and received a post in command of a fusilier company. During the Napoleonic Wars he was promoted to Major, and saw action at the battles of Saalfeld (1806) and Jena (1806). Soon after, he became the commander of a brigade in the Anthony Wilhelm L'Eestocq corps. In April 1807 he assumed command of the garrison in Kolberg (present-day Kołobrzeg). The defence of the Kolberg fortress was the most important event of his life and established von Gneisenau's reputation as an excellent commander. This opened the way to a brilliant career and the highest military ranks. On 25 July 1807 he became a member of the Modernisation Committee presided over by Gerhard von Scharnhorst. Only a month later, on 17 August 1807, he was awarded the Pour le Mérite Order for the defence of Kolberg (Kołobrzeg). His career advancement accelerated: on 26 August 1807 he was promoted to Lieutenant Colonel; in 1808 he was assigned the post of fortress inspector and the chief of the engineer corps; one year later he was assigned to the artillery and engineering department and was promoted to Colonel. After 1809 he left military service and travelled widely in Europe.

He returned to the colours during Napoleon's advance on Moscow: re-entering Prussian service, Gneisenau played his part in restoring the country's independence. In 1813 he was promoted to Major General and assigned the post of quartermaster-general of the Silesian Army under the command of Field Marshall

Gebhard von Blücher, seeing action at the Battle of Lützen. Shortly afterwards he became the Governor of Silesia and quartermaster-general of the army. In 1813 Gneisenau was promoted to chief of staff for Field Marshall Blücher. For his behaviour at the Battle of Leipzig he was promoted to Lieutenant General and received the Iron Cross 1st class. In 1814 he participated in the advance on Paris and after the fall of the First French Empire he received the title of Count. During Napoleon's Hundred Days, it was he who convinced Field Marshall Blücher to advance on Waterloo. For his actions in this battle he received the Order of the Black Eagle. Later, in 1815 as a General of Infantry he commanded the 8th Corps in Koblenz. This was to be his last active military appointment, and for a short period he retreated from public life. He returned to public service in 1817 when he became a member of the State Council, and a year later the governor of Berlin. For his services to the country he was promoted to Field Marshall in 1825. His last military action was as part of Prussia's response to the November Uprising in partitioned Poland. He was sent with his army to the Duchy of Poznań to await the further developments in the Kingdom of Poland (commonly known as Congress Poland). He died suddenly on 23 August 1831 in Poznań during a cholera epidemic that swept in the city. He was buried in the Sommerschenburg mausoleum.

months. This situation forced the Maritime Warfare Command (Seekriegsleitung, SKL) to change its plans. The inspection conducted on 14 April 1941 by Admiral Günther Lütjens confirmed that both ships needed repairs that would probably continue at least until the autumn of 1941. This forced Lütjens to alter the plans for Operation Rheinübung, the *Bismarck* sortie. The Admiral had to leave *Scharnhorst* and *Gneisenau* behind and instead sail with only the heavy cruiser *Prinz Eugen*, which was then completing her gunnery exercises and sea trials in the Baltic Sea.

The *Gneisenau* remained in Brest until the end of the year, before full operational capability was restored (officially declared on 5 November 1941). In February 1942 the ship took part in Operation Cerberus, the famous 'Channel Dash' with *Scharnhorst* and the heavy cruiser *Prinz Eugen*. During the transit, on the 12th, *Gneisenau* hit a mine but the damage was not very serious and on the next day the ship anchored at Brunsbüttel. During the next few days the ship passed through the Kiel Canal and on 15 February was docked in the Deutsche Werke shipyard in Kiel. Restoring the ship to full operational capability was a priority and the repair procedure was supposed to be completed by 6 March 1942, so permission was granted to leave all the ammunition on board. The one safety condition required was removing the fuses from the shells but, as was soon demonstrated, this did not protect the ship. The British did not wait long and on the night of 26/27 February 1942 carried out an air attack on the battleship, in the course of which the *Gneisenau* was hit by a bomb that exploded near the bow of the ship. The hot gas and shrapnel caused a fire and then an explosion of the propellant charges in A turret, which destroyed the entire bow of the ship. The damage was severe enough that the ship was unserviceable for several months.

When *Gneisenau* was moved to Gotenhafen (Gdynia) she was formally stricken from the fleet list on 1 July 1942, as the ship was intended to undergo a major refit, including the change of main armament that had been so much discussed during the design phase. However, in January 1943 Hitler ordered the withdrawal of all heavy Kriegsmarine ships from active duty. All work on the ship stopped. The two undamaged turrets were removed from the ship and installed as coastal artillery in Norway. During that period the *Gneisenau* was used as a storage hulk, being moved around the harbour basin in Gotenhafen (Gdynia) several times. When the Russian troops were liberating Pomerania (Pomorze Gdańskie), the ship was towed to the entry of the Gotenhafen port and scuttled on 27 March 1945. The post-war history of the ship is a series of attempts to remove the wreck and clear the port entry as soon as possible. First the superstructure was cut away and on 15 July 1949 the breaking up of the hull began. Taking the ship to pieces lasted until September 1951.

The launching ceremony of the battleship *Gneisenau* on 8 December 1936 in the Deutsche Werke in Kiel did not go well. The shipyard workers failed to stop the hull after it left the slipway and the stern rammed the opposite pier, although damage to the ship was negligible.
M Skwiot collection

Gneisenau leaving Kiel for her first sea trials photographed in early April 1938.
S Breyer collection

Gneisenau's forward superstructure with the main gun turrets photographed in summer 1938, before the ship entered service. The 6.5m rangefinder is already installed.
Photograph by Urbahns, from the collection of T Klimczyk

After leaving the Heikendorf roadstead *Gneisenau* sails past Möltenort en route to the Bay of Kiel for initial sea trials. The program included test running of the main engines and boiler room equipment. This picture was taken in late April or early May 1938 before the ship was commissioned.
CAW

Further speed trials were conducted after the ship formally entered service. The commissioning ceremony took place on 21 May 1938 and the battleship's first commander was Captain (Kpt z S) Erich Förster. A spectacular photograph of the *Gneisenau* working up to full speed.
IWM

Gneisenau during the major fleet review in the Bay of Kiel, photographed on 22 August 1938. The review was occasioned by the launch of the heavy cruiser *Prinz Eugen* and the visit of the Hungarian regent Admiral N Horthy von Nagybánya. The battleship flies the regent's flag on her mainmast which was later 'replaced' on the photograph with the flag of Adolf Hitler. This was to indicate his short stay on board the ship.
Photograph by Urbahns, from the collection of M Skwiot

Another picture taken just a few minutes later than the one opposite during the same review. The *Gneisenau*'s crew is manning the side.
CAW

Fleet review, 22 August 1938. This picture was taken from a civilian vessel present at the event. On the left is the aviso *Grille* – the Kriegsmarine's official yacht – with the invited guests and the Reich Chancellor Adolf Hitler. On the right the review is opened by the battleship *Gneisenau* followed by the *Admiral Graf Spee*, *Admiral Scheer* and *Deutschland*.
CAW

RIGHT: The battleship *Gneisenau* after the parade photographed en route to Kiel. In this picture the flag of the Regent of Hungary Admiral N Horthy von Nagybánya was 'touched out' from the head of the mainmast. It can be seen in the other photos.
Photograph by Urbahns, from the collection of T Klimczyk

BELOW RIGHT: A gun salute from the *Gneisenau* for the Hungarian guest of honour, Admiral Horthy von Nagybánya. The battleship is at a mooring buoy in Heikendorf roadstead off Kiel during the launching ceremonies for the heavy cruiser *Prinz Eugen*. On the battleship's catapult is a Heinkel He 60 floatplane with the civilian markings C-10GD??.
S Breyer collection

BELOW: After passing the aviso *Grille* carrying Adolf Hitler, *Gneisenau* heads towards Kiel.
CAW

Battleship *Gneisenau* at the A8 mooring buoy in the Heikendorf roadstead at Kiel. This picture was taken towards the end of August 1938, shortly after the launch of the heavy cruiser *Prinz Eugen*.
Photograph by Urbahns, from the collection of S Breyer

Two views of the *Gneisenau* at the A11 mooring buoy in Kiel. The picture showing the new 'Atlantic' bow and funnel cap was probably taken in spring 1939 during the ship's time at Heikendorf after the refit in the Deutsche Werke shipyard. Unfortunately the new bow proved less effective than was hoped and the ship had to be given another modification; this third version had even more overhang and flare.
MMW

This photograph was modified for propaganda purposes to show the *Gneisenau* at sea with the new bow. The B turret, which was rotated to port, was removed from the photograph and replaced by a new image of the turret trained fore and aft, transferred from the *Gneisenau* picture taken during the fleet review on 22 August 1938. Inset is the original photograph of the *Gneisenau* without the retouching.

Photograph by Urbahns, from the collection of T Klimczyk; inset: A Jarski collection

ABOVE: Battleship *Gneisenau* in the Bay of Kiel in May 1939 shortly after the completion of the refit in the Deutsche Werke shipyard. This shows the new anchor arrangements and the replacement of the foremast previously located on top of the rangefinder.
Photograph by Urbahns, from the collection of M Skwiot

LEFT: *Gneisenau* in the Bay of Kiel photographed shortly after the first modification of the bow. The anchors are still in hawse pipes, one on the starboard side and two on the port side. After the second modification of the stem the hawse pipes were welded up and the anchors moved to housings on the forecastle deck-edge, one on each side, reducing the number of anchors to two.
M Skwiot collection

Gneisenau in the Heikendorf roadstead at Kiel in summer 1939. The battleship has the new bow with the anchors placed on the deck-edge. The new foremast abaft the bridge can be seen clearly from this angle.
Photograph by Klein, from the collection of T Klimczyk

RIGHT Sea-level bow view of *Gneisenau* at the A10 mooring buoy in the Heikendorf roadstead at Kiel in summer 1939. The ship has the final variant of the Atlantic bow. As built, when the ship steamed into rough seas the 10m rangefinders in A and B turrets were smothered in spray on many occasions. The solution was to install this new stem and a small bulbous forefoot.
Photograph by Klein, from the collection of T Klimczyk

Gneisenau seen during a cruise in the Atlantic in July 1939. During this deployment the battleship entered Las Palmas in the Canary Islands on 1 July.
ADM

ABOVE *Gneisenau* entered the Deutsche Werke shipyard in Kiel on 10 October 1939 for the installation of FuMO 22 radar – despite the funnel smoke, it is just visible on top of the bridge tower. This photograph was probably taken in the Kiel roadstead in October 1939 during sea trials. Later the ship was relocated to the Baltic Sea together with her sister ship the *Scharnhorst*.
S Breyer collection

Gneisenau photographed from the quarterdeck during the ship's first combat operation in early October 1939. Together with the light cruiser *Köln* and destroyer escorts the ship sailed towards southern Norway. The operation was soon cancelled and the battleship returned to Kiel on 10 October. In the foreground C turret still carries the seaplane catapult, which was removed during a refit at the Deutsche Werke in February 1940.
S Breyer collection

Battleship *Gneisenau* photographed on 21 November 1939 from one of the destroyer escorts during the raid on allied convoys with the *Scharnhorst*, the light cruisers *Leipzig* and *Köln* and other destroyer escorts. During this operation the armed merchant cruiser HMS *Rawalpindi* was sunk.
CAW

ABOVE *Gneisenau* creating a smokescreen during exercises in the Bay of Kiel. The ship already has the covered admiral's bridge and the FuMO 22 radar installed on top of the superstructure. Based on the camouflage pattern it can be deduced that the ship is still based in Kiel – after relocating to Gotenhafen the ship received a new striped pattern.
CAW

RIGHT The after side of *Gneisenau*'s bridge photographed in spring 1940 while the ship was at Wilhelmshaven.
S Breyer collection

Detail of the battleship's funnel and mast seen from the midships hangar deck. This picture was taken shortly after the installation of the radar, barely visible here behind the cover of black funnel smoke. This photograph was probably taken in November 1939 during the sortie with the *Scharnhorst* under the command of Admiral Marschall, who replaced Admiral Boehm as the fleet commander.
S Breyer collection

The periods between operational sorties were used for intensive training to hone the crew's performance. One regularly practiced procedure was the launch and retrieval of the floatplanes. This required perfect synchronisation between by the battleship's crew, the pilots and the aviation mechanics, who were seconded to the ship from the Luftwaffe. In this photograph an Ar 196 (T3+A?) is hoisted on board the ship.
Photograph by Dr Wehlau, from the collection of A Jarski

Positioning the aircraft on the battleship's catapult.
Photograph by Dr Wehlau, from the collection of A Jarski

With the Arado floatplane successfully secured on the catapult, it is now ready for take off at short notice.
S Breyer collection

The battleship's forecastle deck photographed during the *Gneisenau*'s time at Wilhelmshaven.
Photograph by Dr Wehlau, from the collection of A Jarski

After Operation Nordmark (17-20 February 1940) the *Gneisenau* was sent to the Marinewerft in Wilhelmshaven for the removal of the seaplane catapult from C turret. As indicated by the absence of the catapult, this photograph was taken in spring 1940 during preparations for Operation Weserübung – the assault on Denmark and Norway.
Photograph by Dr Wehlau, from the collection of A Jarski

A view aft from the bridge. *Gneisenau* is leaving port for Operation Weserübung.
Photograph by Dr Wehlau, from the collection of A Jarski

The main artillery fires a salvo during the ship's encounter with the battlecruiser HMS *Renown*. Although both ships were hit, the battle ended indecisively.
CAW

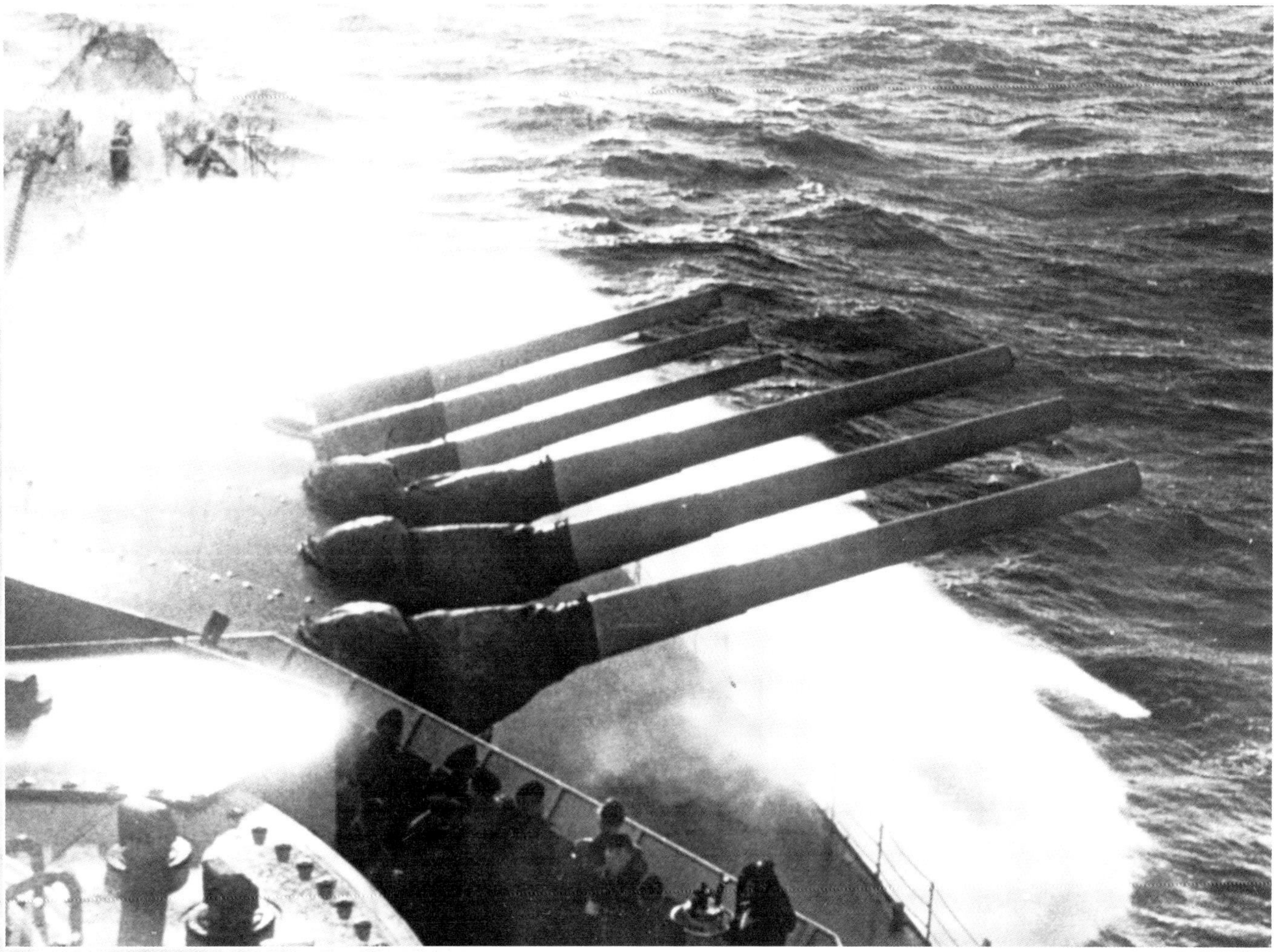

The battleship's forward main gun turrets are directed at her opponent, which will soon be identified as the battlecruiser HMS *Renown* and her escorting destroyers. The photograph was taken moments before the engagement with the British ship began.
Photograph by Dr Wehlau, from the collection of A Jarski

Decoration of gun crews with medals awarded on the recommendation of the battleship's commanding officer Harald Netzbandt (seen in the foreground with his back to the photographer). The ceremony was conducted on the battleship's quarterdeck after the ship returned from Operation Weserübung.
Photograph by Dr Wehlau, from the collection of A Jarski

Gneisenau's crew at battle stations during Operation Juno. The operation involved Luftwaffe units, so the main and secondary gun turret tops were painted red for easy identification by friendly aircraft. In the foreground of this view the roof of one of *Gneisenau*'s 15cm turrets is painted in this colour. This picture was probably taken on 8 June 1940.
CAW

Kiel roadstead in May 1940. On the left is *Gneisenau*, with the heavy cruiser *Admiral Hipper* ahead and between the two, in the background, the battleship *Scharnhorst*. The combat training and exercise program conducted by *Gneisenau* and *Scharnhorst* was to be completed by 2 June 1940.
S Breyer collection

The crew at battle stations. In the top view the funnel platform bulwarks still bear the remains of the striped camouflage pattern used by the ship for a short period when stationed in the Baltic.
Photographs by Krassman-Scherl, from the collection of CAW

Trondheim roadstead after the German invasion of Norway photographed on 11 June 1940. To the left is the anchored battleship *Gneisenau* and on the right the heavy cruiser *Admiral Hipper*.

LEFT: *Gneisenau* in dry dock in the Deutsche Werke shipyard in Kiel. After a successful torpedo attack by HMS/M *Clyde* on 20 June 1940, the *Gneisenau* retired to Trondheim roads. There the ship was patched up and prepared for the voyage home. On 28 June the ship reached Kiel and was docked in Dry Dock B of the Deutsche Werke where she remained until 21 October 1940. In this picture the extent of the damage sustained from the British torpedoes is clearly visible.
S Breyer collection

TOP: *Gneisenau* in Dry Dock B of the Deutsche Werke shipyard in Kiel: a close-up of the damage.
S Breyer collection

LEFT: The winter of 1940/1941 was very harsh throughout Europe, with very low temperatures prevalent everywhere. Consequently service on board ship was even more difficult as everything was covered in ice. This picture was taken during sea trials in the Baltic. On the top of A turret the crew of a 2cm Flak 38 anti-aircraft gun is busy removing the canvas cover.
S Breyer collection

RIGHT: After the cover was removed the seamen began the arduous task of cleaning the gun barrel. Normally, in warmer conditions this was not a very tricky thing to do, but working on an ice-covered turret roof made the task both difficult and unpleasant.
S Breyer collection

BELOW: Placing canvas covers on the muzzles of A turret's guns. They prevented seawater from entering the gun barrels while at sea.
Photograph by Krassman-Scherl, from the collection of CAW

Gneisenau's forward main armament fires at a target during gunnery practice in the Baltic during the winter of 1940/1941.
CAW

Gneisenau's A turret turns towards an 'enemy' during gunnery practice in the Baltic conducted in the winter of 1940/1941.
S Breyer collection

The ship on winter exercises in the Baltic, 1940/1941.
S Breyer collection

Gneisenau photographed in Hjeltefjord near Bergen at the beginning of Operation Berlin. On 30 December 1940 the operation was postponed because of storm damage sustained by *Gneisenau* and the ship, together with her sister, the *Scharnhorst*, returned to the Baltic.
CAW

Gneisenau seen from her sister ship *Scharnhorst* during their longest sortie, Operation Berlin, which finally began on 28 January 1941.
M Skwiot collection

The battleship searching for British convoys during Operation Berlin.
CAW

During Operation Berlin several submarines were transferred to the operational control of Admiral Lütjens commanding the battleships, to support and cooperate with the surface vessels. In this picture the *Gneisenau* is seen from *U124* in the central Atlantic on 6 March 1941.
M Skwiot collection

GERMAN CAPITAL SHIPS

BREAKS IN ROUTINE.
LEFT: Scenes of keep-fit and relaxation.
BELOW: A rendezvous with a friendly submarines was always welcomed by the crews of both ships. Each of them offered some respite in the monotonous search for enemy ships. The U-boot crew could refuel and receive supplies and the off-duty crews had their chance to chat with other seamen. However these meetings did not happen very often and were rather short. This meeting was no different – after exchanging information the submarine dives and goes its own way. In this photograph the crew bids farewell to *U124*.
S Breyer collection

ABOVE: *Gneisenau* photographed from her sister ship *Scharnhorst* in heavy weather in the Atlantic during Operation Berlin.
M Skwiot collection

FAR RIGHT: Another view of the *Gneisenau* during a storm. Before Operation Berlin the ship spent some time in the Deutsche Werke Shipyard in Kiel where she received additional quadruple anti-aircraft guns and a new radar. The radar was removed from this picture as well as from all other pictures taken during 'Berlin'.
CAW

MAIN PICTURE: *Gneisenau* partly hidden by a wave. Taken during Operation Berlin, this is one of the few photographs of the battleship showing her stern in a colour different from the rest of the hull; the other side of the ship was probably painted in a similar manner. The main and secondary gun turrets had their tops painted yellow to serve as recognition markings for their own aircraft.
CAW

LEFT: *Gneisenau* at Brest, having arrived on 22 March 1941. Operation Berlin lasted for 59 days and between them the two battleships sank or captured 22 ships of over 115,662 tonnes. After the ship entered port preparations began immediately to carry out the necessary repairs and modernisation, work which was to last for about three months. For the British this was a great opportunity to try and eliminate the threat posed by this ship.
S Breyer collection

Soon after the ship entered dock it was visited by a Japanese delegation.
S Breyer collection

LEFT: In this picture taken in March or April 1941 the *Gneisenau* is in a dry dock in Brest. Using intelligence and aerial reconnaissance data, the British soon located the *Gneisenau*'s dry dock. During the first air raid on the ship conducted during the night of 30/31 March no direct hits were scored. Some bombs exploded near the dock and some fell into the dock but did not explode. This potential threat forced the Germans to move the ship out of the dock to the Abri roadstead.
S Breyer collection

RIGHT: With the battleship again afloat came the idea of attacking *Gneisenau* with torpedoes. On 6 April 1941 No 22 Squadron flying Beaufort bombers took off from St Eval airfield in Cornwall and launched an attack on the *Gneisenau*. The aircraft piloted by F/O Campbell managed to fly through intense anti-aircraft fire and successfully torpedoed the battleship between frames 51 and 62. The damage was so severe that the battleship had to be returned to dry dock. This photograph was taken later in April 1941 when the battleship was painted in a camouflage pattern and covered with camouflage netting.
S Breyer collection

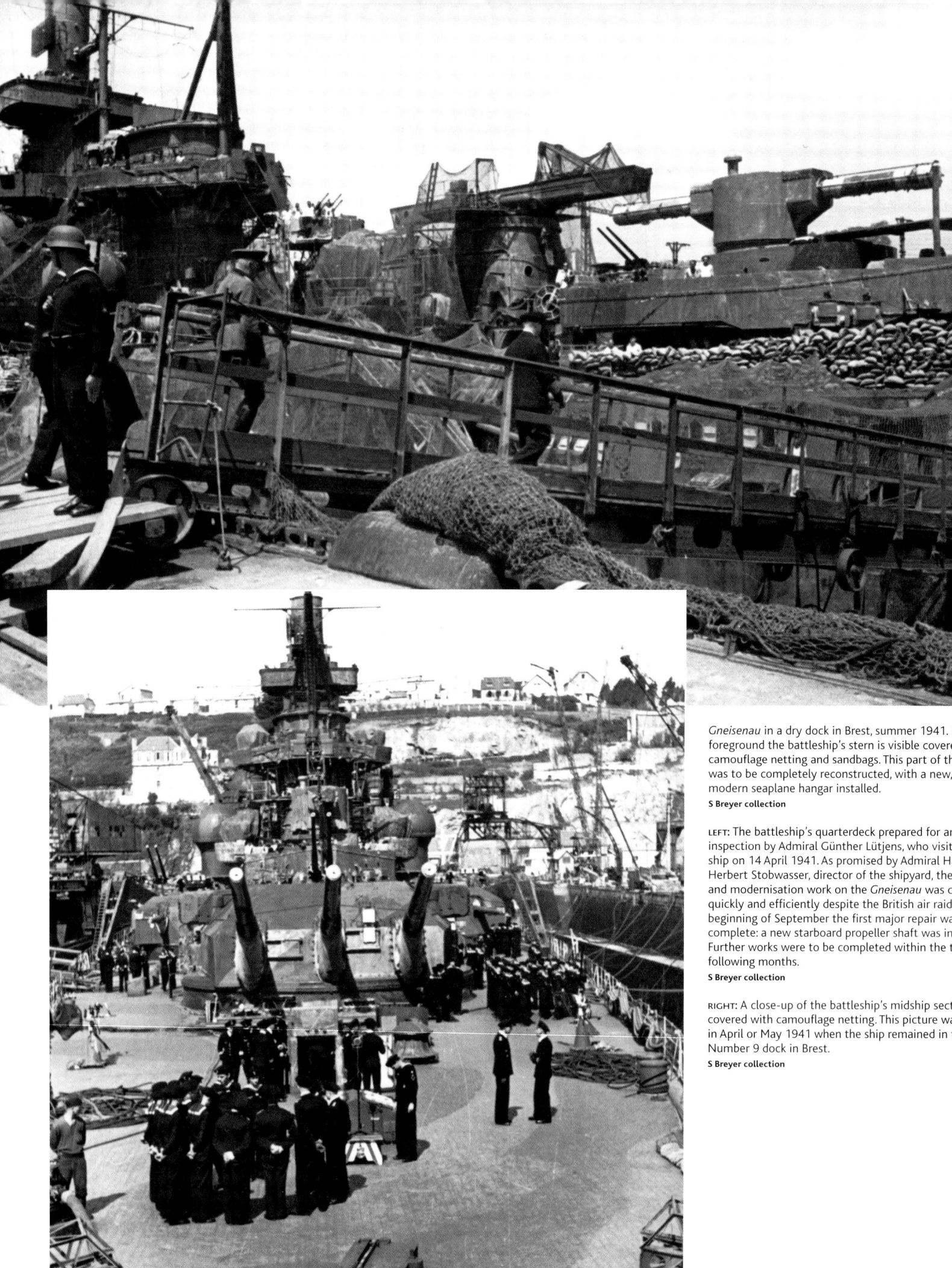

Gneisenau in a dry dock in Brest, summer 1941. In the foreground the battleship's stern is visible covered with camouflage netting and sandbags. This part of the ship was to be completely reconstructed, with a new, modern seaplane hangar installed.
S Breyer collection

LEFT: The battleship's quarterdeck prepared for an inspection by Admiral Günther Lütjens, who visited the ship on 14 April 1941. As promised by Admiral Hans-Herbert Stobwasser, director of the shipyard, the repair and modernisation work on the *Gneisenau* was conducted quickly and efficiently despite the British air raids. In the beginning of September the first major repair was complete: a new starboard propeller shaft was installed. Further works were to be completed within the two following months.
S Breyer collection

RIGHT: A close-up of the battleship's midship section covered with camouflage netting. This picture was taken in April or May 1941 when the ship remained in the Number 9 dock in Brest.
S Breyer collection

RIGHT: After Japan joined the war by attacking the American naval base in Pearl Harbor, the British stepped up the air raids, trying even harder to eliminate the three heavy German ships (from June, the heavy cruiser *Prinz Eugen* was also in Brest). At the end of the year the British decided to try air raids in daylight. Stirling and Halifax bombers were assigned to those missions as they were able to carry more bombs. The daylight air raids on Brest were codenamed Veracity I. Apart from one bomb which exploded near the *Gneisenau* on 17/18 December, the British did not manage to cause any serious damage to the German ships. This photograph taken from a British aircraft shows the moment of that bomb hitting the battleship.
IWM

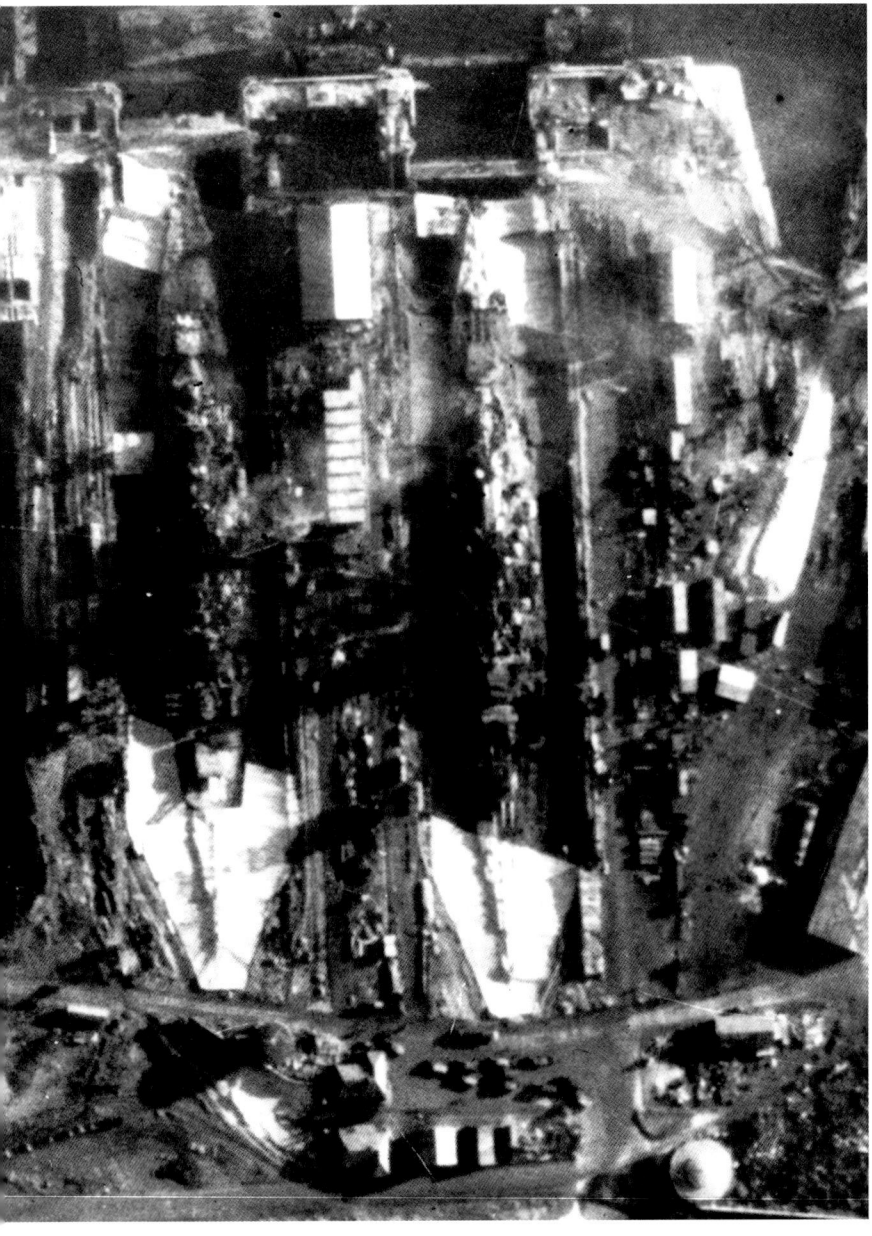

Battleships *Gneisenau* (on the left) and *Scharnhorst* in dry docks in Brest photographed by British aerial reconnaissance in December 1941. Both ships are covered with camouflage netting and sheets of canvas.
IWM

Operation Cerberus was the codename assigned to the passage of the three heavy German ships *Scharnhorst*, *Gneisenau* and *Prinz Eugen* through the English Channel in February 1942. In these photographs the battleship *Gneisenau* is seen from the heavy cruiser *Prinz Eugen*.
S Breyer collection

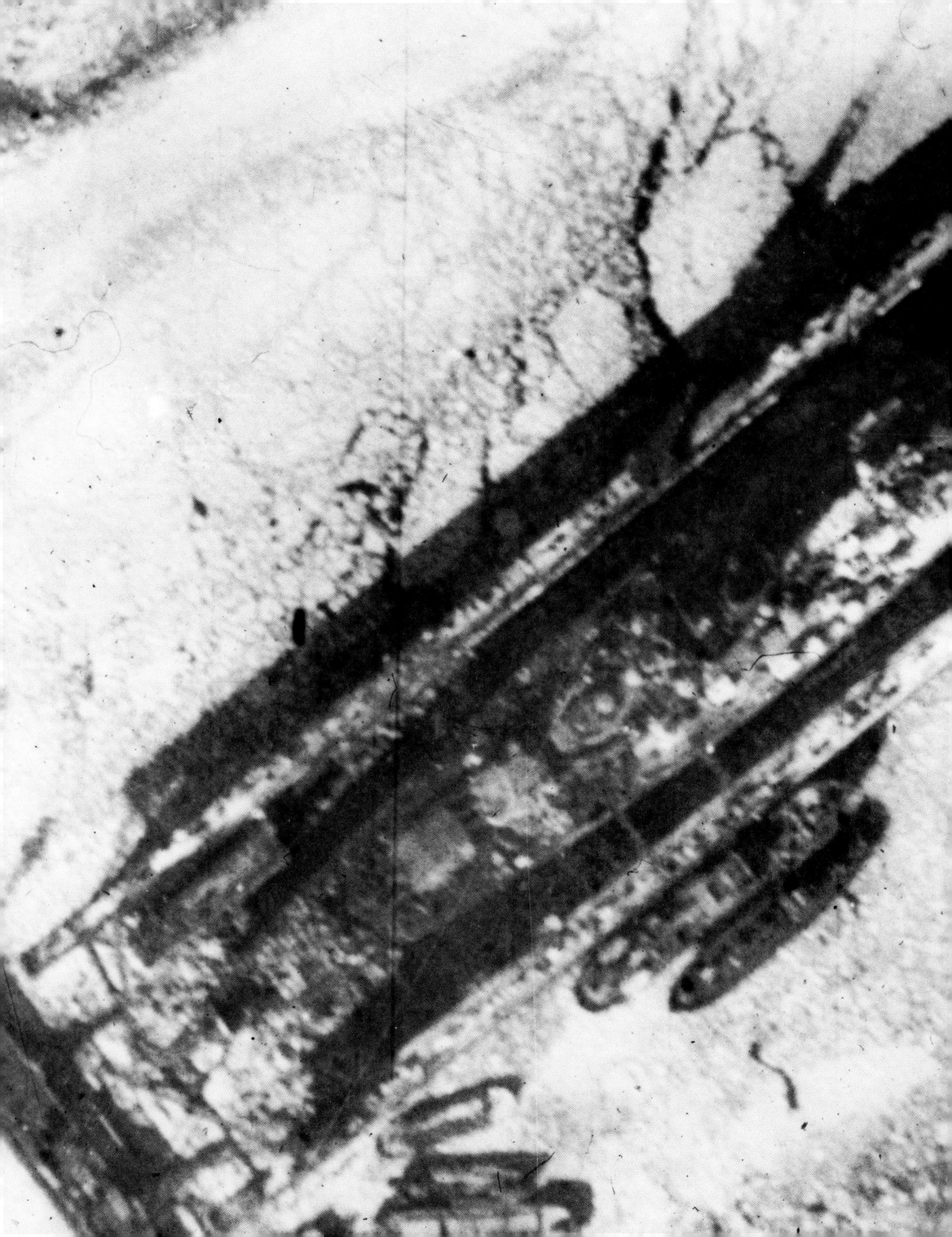

LEFT: After 'Cerberus' the ship needed a refit, but during an air raid on 25/26 February the ship was hit with a single bomb which caused an explosion of the propellant charges magazines and the destruction of the battleship's bow. This photograph shows *Gneisenau* inside the dock with part of the bow plating already removed. The systematic aerial bombardment of Kiel prevented proper repairs and the battleship had to be relocated to Gotenhafen. On 9 March 1942 the ship was floated out of the dock and prepared for the transfer voyage.
IWM

Gneisenau photographed at a pier in Gotenhafen by British aerial reconnaissance in August 1942. All main turrets have been removed as on 18 March 1942 the decision was made to rearm the battleship with new 38cm twin mounts. On 1 July 1942 the *Gneisenau* was formally decommissioned.
IWM

Another shot taken by British aerial reconnaissance in Gotenhafen, November 1942.
IWM

Gneisenau moored at a jetty in Gotenhafen, photographed in October 1943. All work on the ship has stopped and the vessel is masked with camouflage netting and wooden frameworks.
IWM

Two views of the wreck of the *Gneisenau* in the summer of 1946. Some of the equipment and material recovered from the wreck was used in rebuilding the city of Gdynia. Other parts of the ship became exhibits in the Navy Museum where they are kept to this day.
MMG

Salvage work continuing on the *Gneisenau* wreck.
Photograph by Uklejewski, from the collection of MMG

The *Gneisenau* was scuttled in the Gotenhafen port basin on 27 March 1945. The wreck completely blocked the southern access to the port, so after the war work started to remove the wreck, which lasted for several years. This picture shows the remains of *Gneisenau* as on 3 February 1946.
MMG

4 The Evolution of Battleships F and G
BISMARCK AND TIRPITZ

Bismarck at the end of 1940. Since commissioning in August the ship has had her fore and aft main directors fitted, but the third director (forward of the bridge) is still missing.
Photograph by Schäfer, from the collection of M Skwiot

ESIGN WORK ON NEW BATTLE-SHIPS of 35,000 tons displacement began in 1932, but these activities were kept secret until early 1934, because the Versailles Treaty prohibited the construction of such large ships in Germany. The Kriegsmarine Construction Office was instructed to prepare a preliminary design for Battleship F, planned to replace the obsolete pre-dreadnought *Hannover* of the *Deutschland* class. The new ship was to be armed with eight 33cm (13in) main guns and, more importantly, would be able to reach a speed of 30 knots; 'adequate' vertical and horizontal armour was stipulated for the new battleship class. At the same time even bigger 38cm and 40.6cm (15in and 16in) guns were being designed, to be mounted on future ships.

On 16 March 1935 the acting Reich Chancellor Adolf Hitler re-introduced compulsory military service in Germany. This, in effect, meant the unilateral abrogation of the Versailles Treaty. Germany's move triggered much diplomatic activity on the part of the United Kingdom, culminating in signing a bilateral British-German naval armaments agreement. Signed on 13 June 1935, this allowed German fleet tonnage to be increased to as much as 35 per cent of the Royal Navy's tonnage – totalling 184,000 tons of displacement for battleships. The ships laid down earlier, the three panzerschiffe (*Deutschland*, *Admiral Scheer* and *Admiral Graf Spee*) and the two *Scharnhorst* class battleships under construction, added up to 83,000 tons of declared displacement, leaving 101,000 tons for new ships. Two new battleships, Battleship F ('Ersatz *Hannover*') and Battleship G ('Ersatz *Schleswig-Holstein*'), took the majority of the nominal remaining tonnage. The Washington Treaty of 1922 and the First Naval Conference in London had set the maximum displacement for this type of ship at 35,000 tons, and Germany decided to comply with the existing international treaties for the two new battleships.

The Naval Staff initially insisted that the new

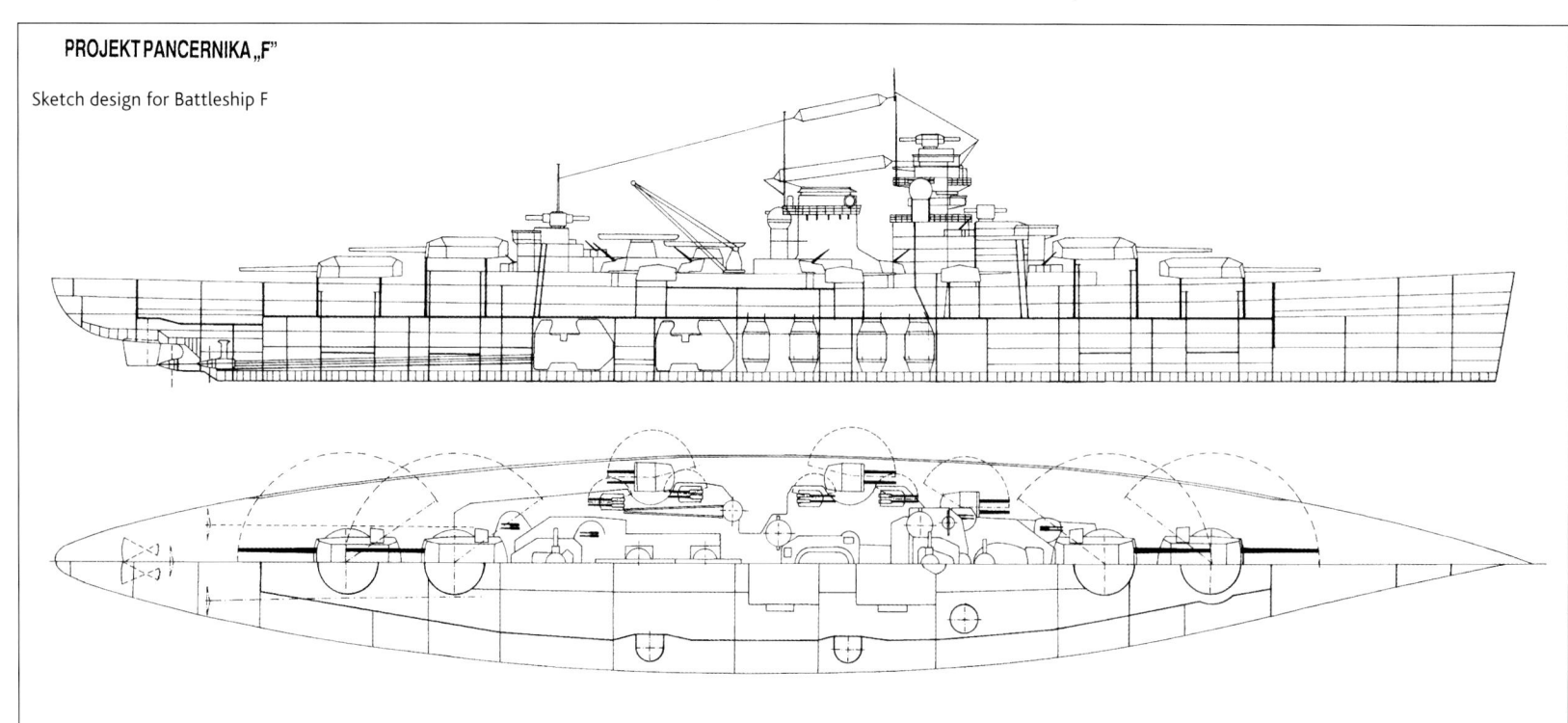

PROJEKT PANCERNIKA „F"
Sketch design for Battleship F

ships must not exceed the 35,000-ton limit. The planned armament comprised a main battery of eight 33cm guns and a secondary battery of twelve 15cm in twin turrets, as well as sixteen 10.5cm dual-purpose guns.

The Naval Staff specified the armour protection as in Table I below:

TABLE 1

Main armour belt (central citadel) (same as Battleships D and E)	350mm
Side armour at bow and stern	150mm
Main deck	50mm
Armoured (fourth) deck	100mm
Inclined sections of the armoured deck (also above magazines and steering room)	120mm
Main gun barbettes	330mm / 350mm
Secondary 15cm gun turrets	150mm / 150mm
Conning tower	400mm
Torpedo bulkhead	60mm
Splinter deck	60mm

The first calculations showed that it was impossible to give the ship the required armour protection within the displacement limit of 35,000 tons. The main armoured belt was accordingly thinned down from 350mm to 320mm, the bow side armour from 150mm to a mere 70mm, and the stern side armour from 150mm to 90mm. The improved preliminary design did not specify the type of machinery, which would also have a bearing on the final displacement figure. In autumn 1934 the Kriegsmarine Construction Office was busy working on a 35,000-ton battleship with eight 33cm main guns and with secondary and anti-aircraft artillery arrangements taken directly from the earlier D and E battleship design, but faster – capable of a sustained speed of 30 knots.

During a conference on the battleship design, held on 2 November 1934, it was laid down that the new ship must be faster and better armed than the newly commissioned French battleship *Dunkerque*, which was capable of touching 31 knots. Therefore, the speed requirements for the new battleship were even more demanding: a maximum speed of 33 knots, sustained speed of 30 knots and a cruising speed of 21 knots. Vice Admiral Guse, director of the Construction Office, protested

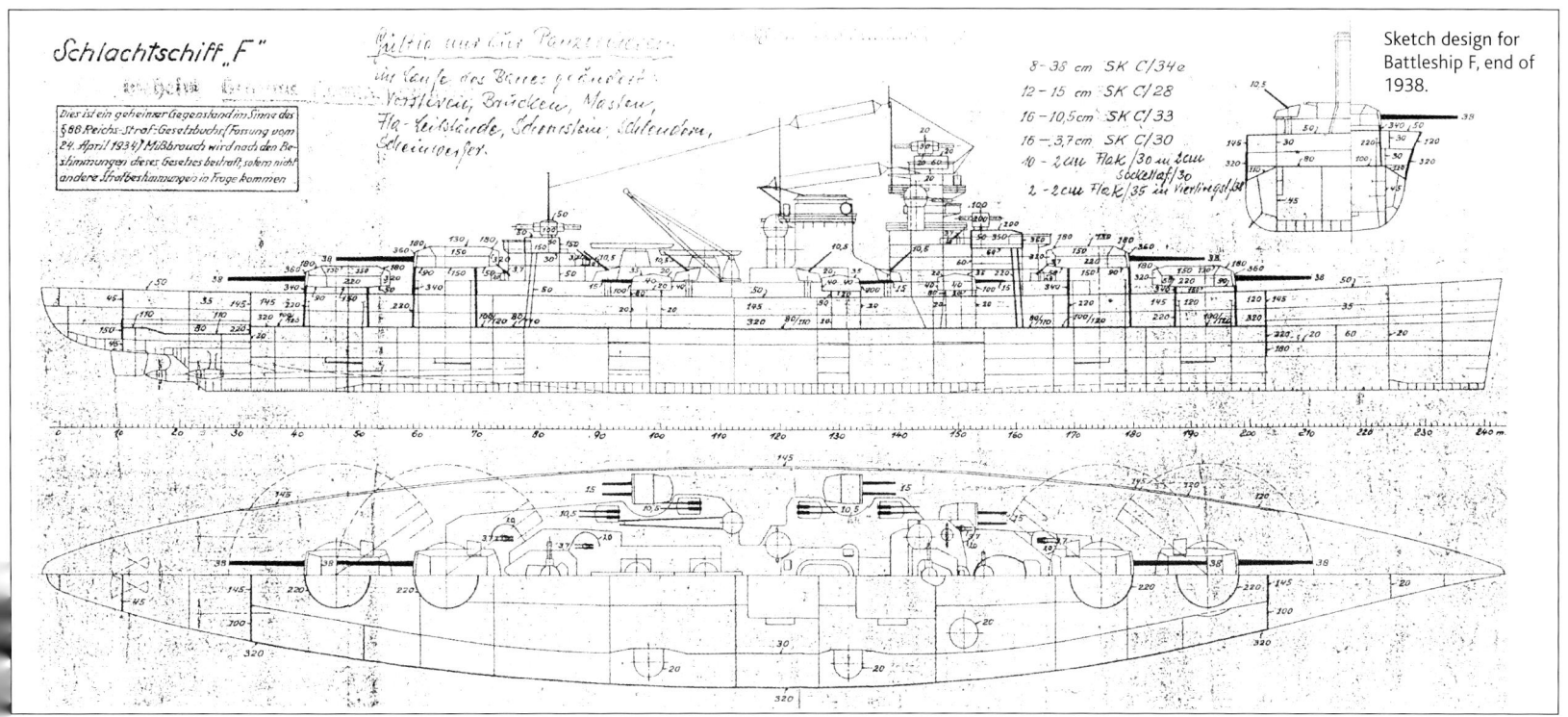

Sketch design for Battleship F, end of 1938.

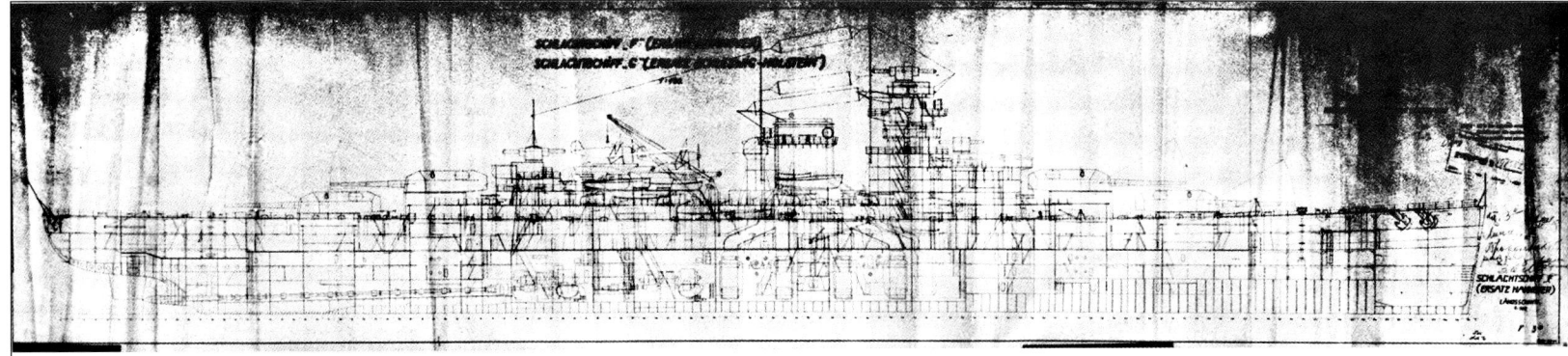

General arrangement of Battleship F design ('Ersatz *Hannover*'), dated 16 May 1936.
Bundesarchiv RM 25-6588

at such 'exorbitant' requirements, and because of his objections, the required speed values were reduced to 29/27/21 knots, respectively.

During another conference, held on 10 November 1934, the head of the German Navy, Admiral Raeder reiterated that in the current situation the projected displacement must not exceed the 35,000-ton figure. This limit was determined by both the external political factors and the physical capacity of the German naval infrastructure – canals and locks, existing dry dock facilities and the depth of the harbours and anchorages of the German coast. With these limitations in mind, all previous designs were again revised, while attempting to minimise the reductions in capabilities. Very little of the technical requirements could be safely sacrificed, so a partial solution would have been to allow money for the deepening and widening of the canals, locks, and roadsteads, as well building new facilities. This was only a partial solution because, whatever else was achieved, the Kiel Canal locks could not have been enlarged because of both technical and financial constraints.

On 21 December 1934, during another Battleship F design conference, Admiral Raeder summed up the project's latest requirements, of which the most important were:

A. The displacement figure for Battleship F could be exceeded
B. Turbo-electric propulsion for the Battleship F would be studied
C. Two parallel designs would be prepared:
   - with eight 33cm guns in four twin turrets and a turbo-electric power plant;
   - with eight 35cm guns in four twin turrets and a steam turbine power plant

At that time a discussion was still raging over the proposed main gun calibre: whether Battleship F should be armed with 33cm or 35cm (13in or 14in) guns; the bigger the guns, the higher the displacement figure. Studies conducted on the 35cm calibre indicated that the bigger guns would have better performance, but even the 33cm had enough power to defeat the main armour of any battleship then commissioned in any of the world's navies. Other figures such as the range, estimated time of flight, trajectory and barrel elevation values were also satisfactory. Fields of fire for both gun calibres were also comparable, but the barrel life of only 180 rounds was a great disadvantage of the 35cm gun.

The displacement limit was eventually lifted,

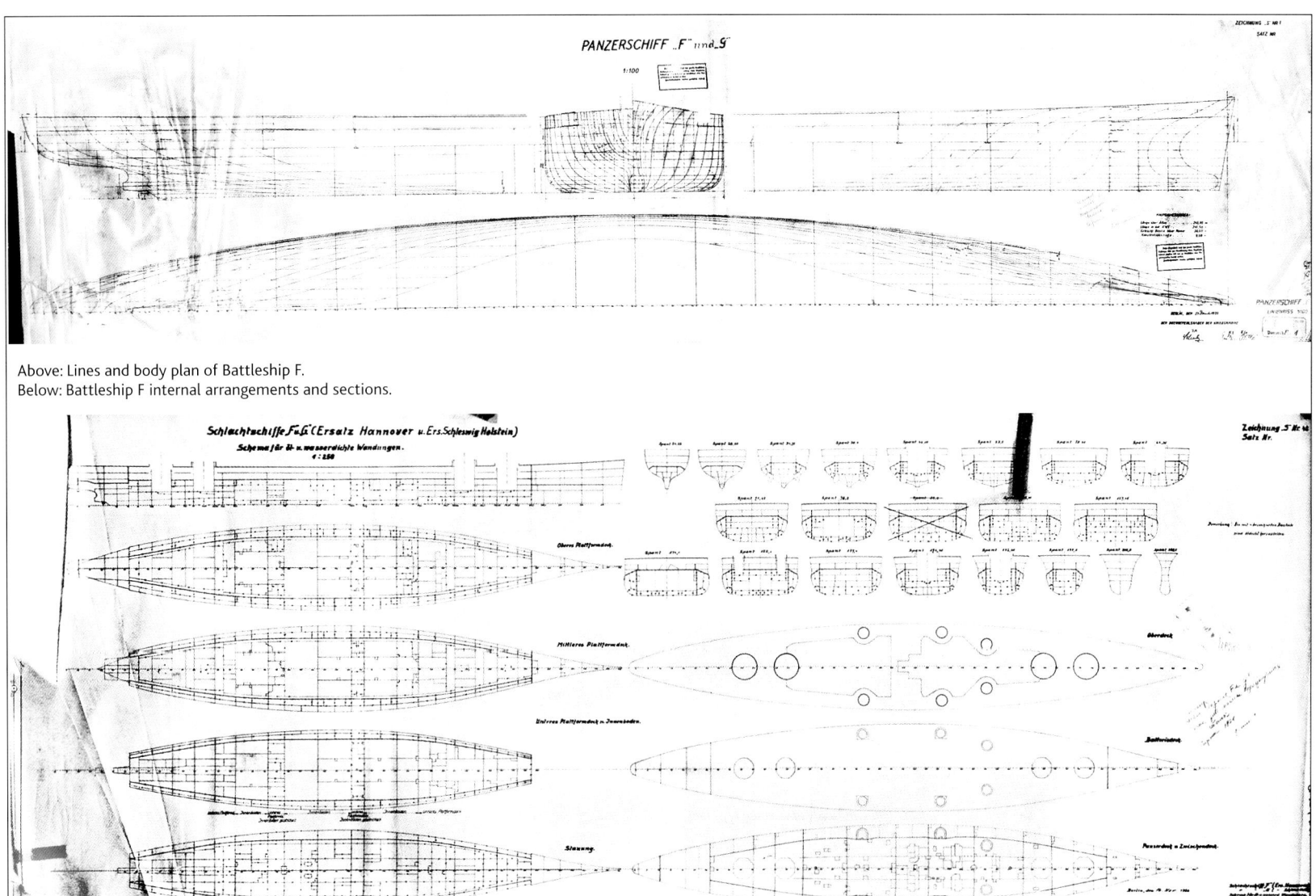

Above: Lines and body plan of Battleship F.
Below: Battleship F internal arrangements and sections.

so further studies on the main gun calibre, as well as new power plants, were soon initiated. A turbo-electrical drive capable of a combined 100,000 metric HP was planned and the design called for the use of three shafts. Two boilers and a turbo-generator were to drive each shaft and propeller. Such an arrangement had the advantage of allowing the use of relatively simple propulsion units capable of rapid speed and direction changes (ahead/astern), allowing greater agility in manoeuvring. This design also limited the shaft length in the future battleships.

Admiral Raeder closely supervised the battleship design process, constantly requiring improved characteristics. On 19 January 1935 he decided that Battleship F would be armed with 35cm guns (provided they met the estimated performance parameters listed in Table II) and agreed that the ship would be powered by three-shaft turbines. As for the armour protection, the main battery barbettes were to be 350mm thick above the main deck and 320mm below deck.

Table II 35cm Gun characteristics

Muzzle velocity	875m/s
Shell weight	625kg
Rate of fire	2.3 rounds/min
Gun weight	11,490 kg
Battery rate of fire	18.4 rounds/min
Explosive charge:	
armour piercing shell	232kg
high-explosive shell, nose fuse	804kg
high-explosive shell, base fuse	804kg

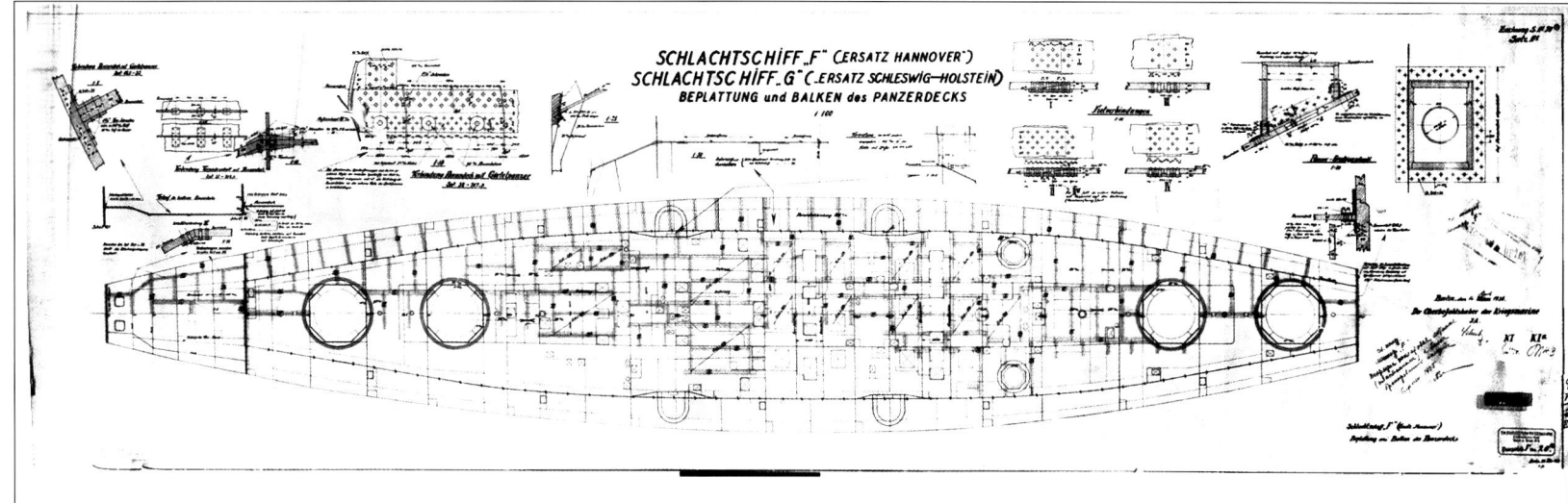

Above: Drawing S Nr 20, third copy, dated 16 April 1936 for Battleships F and G — armoured deck details.
Below: Torpedo bulkhead drawing. Drawing Nr 19, copy 14, dated 14 July 1936.

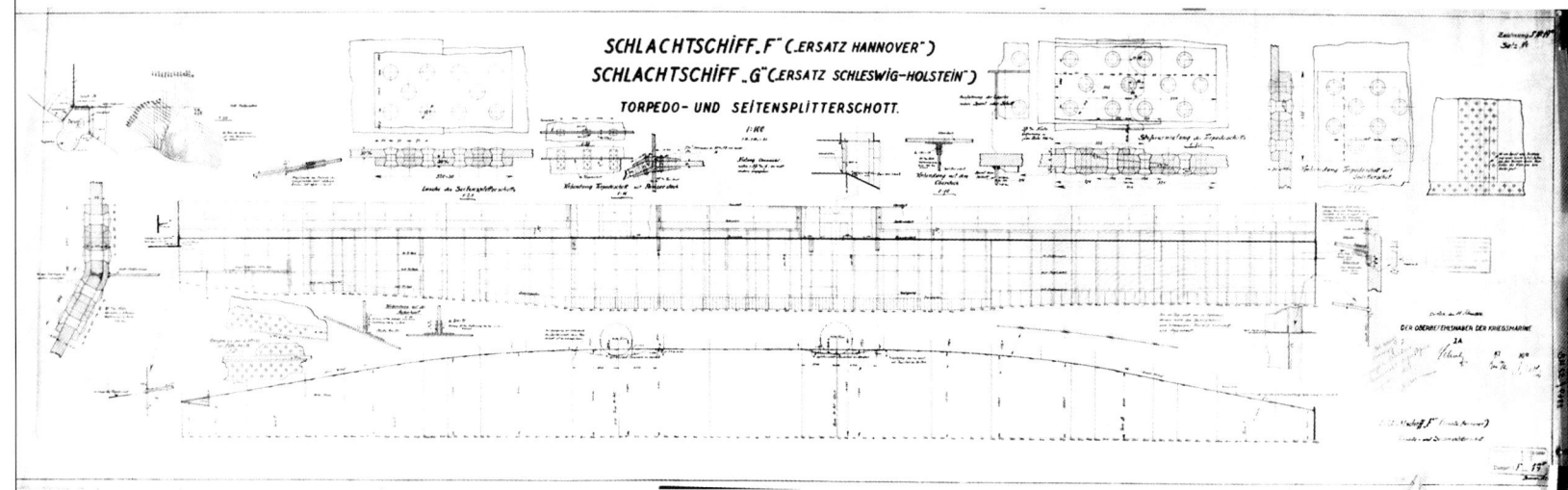

Admiral Raeder also insisted that the displacement figure in all documents be given as an 'unbreachable value of 35,000 tons'. The real value was higher and all planned displacement figures for the future Battleship F were eventually exceeded, reaching as high as 39,000 tons. The final calculations showed that the hull weight for Battleship F was same as that of the *Scharnhorst* and *Gneisenau*, making the displacement figure much higher than initially estimated. More reductions in armour protection were therefore ordered, but the problems with the Battleship F design were still far from over. Later on, the displacement figure had to be revised and increased once more, which resulted in the draught reaching 10 metres – the absolute maximum allowable. The Construction Office intended that the battleship would be based at Wilhelmshaven, which meant that the hull dimensions were limited to 242m in length, 36m in width and 10m draught, dimensions set by the Kiel Canal, which the ship needed to transit to reach its base.

In March 1935 the question of main gun calibre was broached once again. This time it was the possible mounting of 38cm guns, anticipating the abrogation of the Versailles Treaty, which soon came to pass. If the battleship was armed with such powerful guns, the final displacement figure was bound to rise again, by

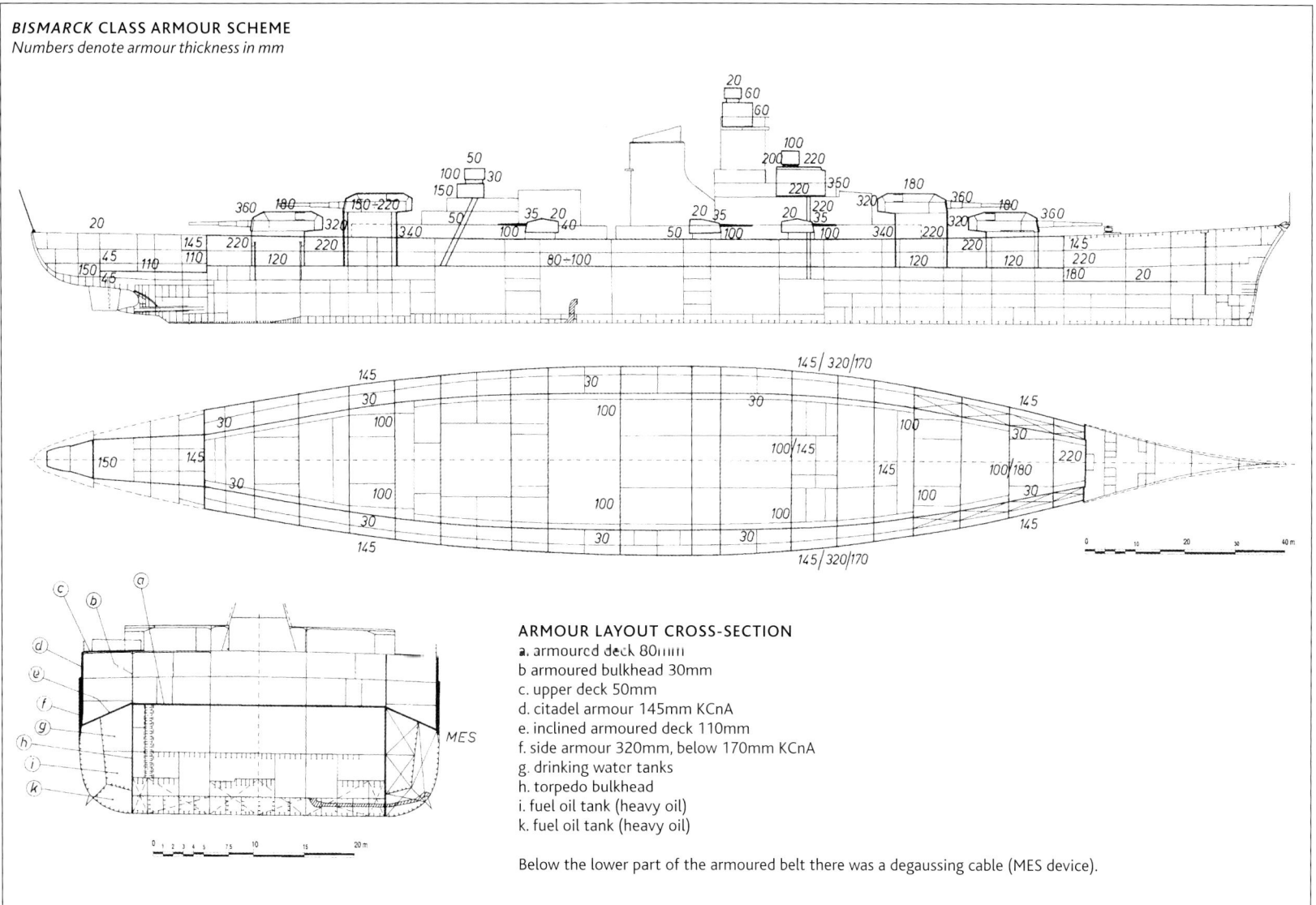

BISMARCK CLASS ARMOUR SCHEME
Numbers denote armour thickness in mm

ARMOUR LAYOUT CROSS-SECTION
a. armoured deck 80mm
b armoured bulkhead 30mm
c. upper deck 50mm
d. citadel armour 145mm KCnA
e. inclined armoured deck 110mm
f. side armour 320mm, below 170mm KCnA
g. drinking water tanks
h. torpedo bulkhead
i. fuel oil tank (heavy oil)
k. fuel oil tank (heavy oil)

Below the lower part of the armoured belt there was a degaussing cable (MES device).

1500 tons, to an astonishing 42,000–42,500 tons. A ship of that size would be even more difficult to handle in the shallow German ports, which was why the Construction Office insisted on returning to the 35cm calibre for the main guns. A battleship displacing 41,000 tons, armed with eight 35cm guns, would have a maximum draught of 9.25m, which would allow it to navigate the Kiel Canal and pass through its locks. The 38cm guns would set the hull deeper, at 9.4m, precluding the use of locks. On the other hand, arming the ship with guns of a lesser calibre would put it at a disadvantage when faced with French *Dunkerque* class battleships. Another suggestion was to mount the 38cm guns in triple turrets but this was no more realistic within the set displacement limit.

All variants of the battleship armament taken into consideration are listed in Table III.

TABLE III: COMPARISON OF VARIOUS BATTLESHIP F DESIGNS WITH ALTERNATIVE ARMAMENT ARRANGEMENTS

A. With 8 × 35cm guns	Original design	Reduced	B. With 8 × 38cm guns	Original design	Reduced
Side armour (citadel)	320mm	290mm	Side armour (citadel)	320mm	260mm
Bow armour	70mm	70mm	Bow armour	70mm	70mm
Stern armour	90mm	80mm	Stern armour	90mm	80mm
Main gun barbettes	320mm	290mm	Main gun barbettes	320mm	255mm
Secondary gun barbettes	150mm	125mm	Secondary gun barbettes	150mm	125mm
Conning tower	350mm	350mm	Conning tower	350mm	350mm
Torpedo bulkheads	45mm	45mm	Torpedo bulkheads	45mm	45mm
Armour over magazines	100mm	90mm	Armour above magazines	100mm	90mm
Armour over engine room and control room	100mm	85mm	Armour above engine room and control room	100mm	85mm
Upper deck	50mm	45mm	Upper deck	50mm	45mm
Displacement	41,000 tons	39,000 tons	Displacement	43,000 tons	39,800 tons
Design draught	9.25m	8.80m	Design draught	9.40m	8.80m
Length at waterline	243m	243m	Length at waterline	250m	250m
Beam	36m	36m	Beam	36m	36m
Designed speed	27kts/28kts	28kts	Designed speed	27kts/28kts	28kts

On 1 April 1935 Admiral Raeder consulted the heads of department and decided that the existing displacement limit could be exceeded and authorised the increase to 41,000 tons and the installation of eight 38cm guns in four twin turrets. The first ship, Battleship F, was ordered from the Blohm & Voss shipyard in Hamburg on 1 April 1936. This decision was based on the assumption that the current limits on gun calibre imposed by international agreements would soon be abandoned, allowing the 38cm guns to be installed in future battleships. The Armament Office was ordered to re-design the barbettes and turrets to accommodate the 38cm guns within six months, and on 9 May 1935 Admiral Raeder finally authorised this calibre for the new battleships.

The Construction Office prepared as many as four propulsion layouts with detailed plans for the following machinery configurations:

Project 1: high-pressure steam turbines with twelve boilers in six boiler rooms placed forward of the turbine rooms;

Project 2: high-pressure steam turbines with twelve boilers in three boiler rooms forward of the turbine rooms;

Project 3: high-pressure steam turbines with twelve boilers in one boiler room in between the turbine rooms;

Project 4: a turbo-electric power plant.

The Construction Office thought the best solution would be Project 2, while Project 4 was considered undesirable due to the weight of such machinery. The Construction Office's alternatives were detailed in designs A-3 to A-6, with different power plant arrangements and several variants of secondary battery positions, including locating this in broadside casemates. Further variants, A-7 to A-9, dealt mostly with generator location and employed a casemate-mounted secondary battery of 15cm guns. The latter idea was discussed and rejected.

Further design conferences led to the improvement of the armour protection and expansion of the armoured citadel to protect the secondary battery gun barbettes. The height of

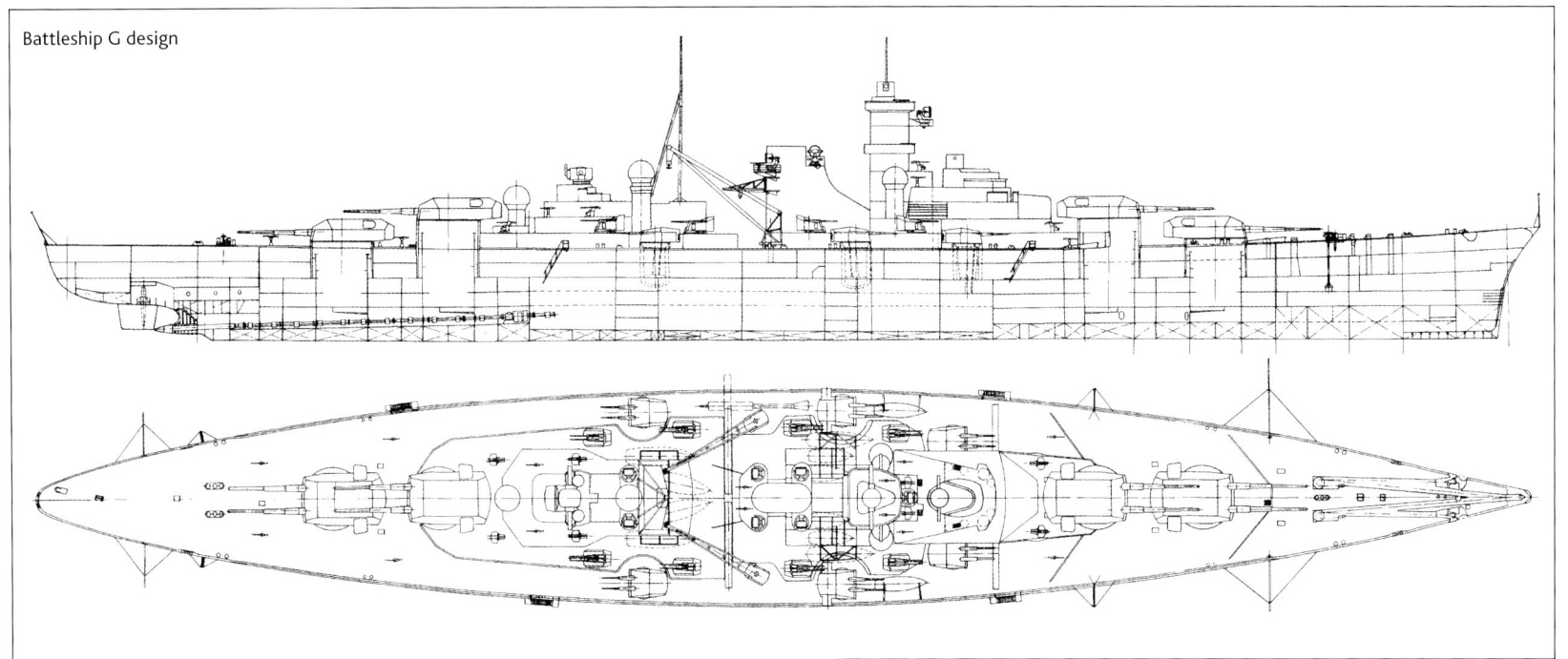

Battleship G design

the citadel was to be discussed later, with several design variants prepared showing the citadel covering varying lengths of the battleship. Under discussion were: a citadel extending beyond the main battery barbettes, protecting the ammunition magazines; shorter citadel designs protecting only the area between A and D main gun turrets; an even shorter citadel stretching between B and C turrets.

On 7 June 1935 another conference was held, this time to discuss the secondary battery arrangements and the battleship's machinery. At the same time an experimental turbo-electric power plant installed in the passenger liner *Scharnhorst* was being tested and the results were quite satisfactory. The turbo-electric power plant was once again discussed for both new battleships, even though it made them 600 tons heavier than the steam turbine variant. The Construction Office had serious doubts about the system and prepared a detailed analysis of this design. Admiral Raeder wanted his new ships to be as fast as possible – to match, or if possible exceed, the fastest battleships of their possible enemies. Several power plant variants were studied, even though it was plain for all to see that only the steam turbine machinery was capable of supplying the required power. The German designers, as well as Admiral Raeder himself, were impressed by the American turbo-electrical propulsion used in the aircraft carriers *Lexington* and *Saratoga*. Such power plants were easier to manage, more flexible in output, capable of going into reverse without changing the direction of the turbine shaft revolutions, and made more effective use of the power provided by the steam turbines.

On 23 August 1935 the Construction Office presented Admiral Raeder with the A-13 design using three turbo-electric units to propel the battleship. Raeder finally sanctioned this version, and pronounced it the definitive design, although some details were left to be specified during the later stages of the design and construction process, such as the anti-aircraft armament, the architecture of the bridge superstructure, placement of control positions, and aviation equipment. The Allgemeines Marineamt (General

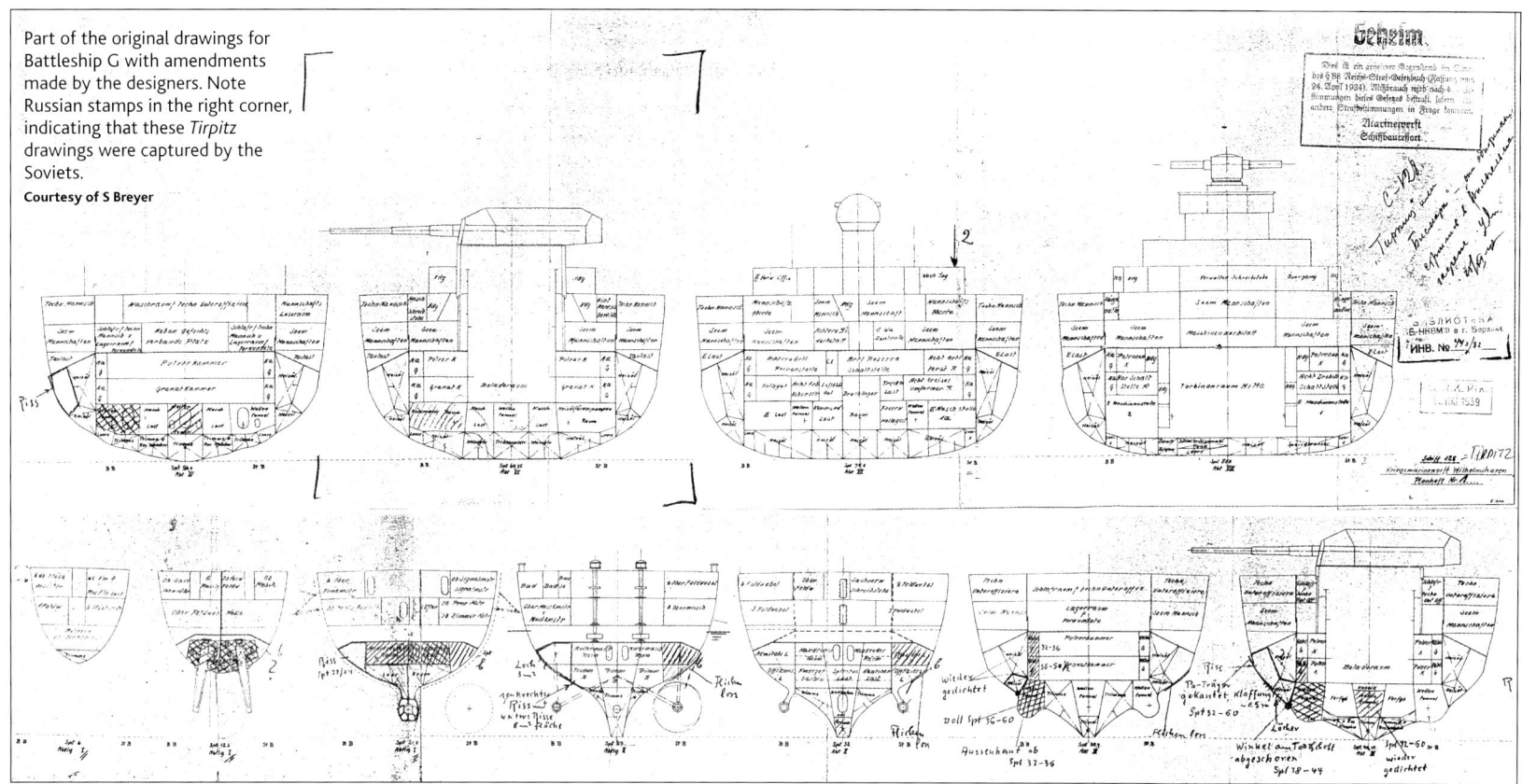

Part of the original drawings for Battleship G with amendments made by the designers. Note Russian stamps in the right corner, indicating that these *Tirpitz* drawings were captured by the Soviets.
Courtesy of S Breyer

Naval Office) wanted sixteen 3.7cm anti-aircraft guns in eight twin mountings instead of the eight single guns as designed. More space for the crew messes was required, and these were created by reducing the length of the armoured citadel. The final version of the armoured citadel extended from turret B to turret C, leaving the A and D turret barbettes outside. After another session of detailed analyses it was decided to move the crew berthing spaces outside the citadel as well. The length and shape of the citadel was finally approved on 23 January 1936.

However, drawbacks to the planned turbo-electric propulsion system began to emerge at this stage: such a system consists of numerous units – boilers, turbines, generators and electric motors – and although it may be a good solution for a commercial liner that has no armoured bulkheads, on a battleship the various elements had to be placed in separate compartments. Altering the power plant would require changing the entire internal layout of the ship and making the bulkhead design more complicated. After more in-depth analyses by the Berlin experts that weighed against turbo-electrical propulsion on a battleship, this design was rejected on the grounds of unnecessary complication and added weight. Thus it was back to the classic steam turbines again. The only problem was that no one in Germany had ever installed a power plant of such colossal output in a ship. The design was based on the turbine machinery of the earlier Battleships D and E but enlarged to provide the power required by the new ships. The turbine casings for what became *Bismarck* and *Tirpitz* were mostly welded, which made them lighter than traditional cast ones. The huge turbines for the *Tirpitz* were ordered from a Swiss firm, Brown-Boveri, while the *Bismarck*'s units were to be built at the Blohm & Voss shipyard in Hamburg.

The design phase for Battleship F (*Bismarck*)

was completed on 15 November 1935 and 14 June 1936 for Battleship G (*Tirpitz*). Admiral Raeder hoped that the first of the new class would be laid down before 1 June 1936. The increasingly aggressive foreign policy of the Third Reich led to the scheduled commissioning of the first battleship being brought forward to 1 October 1939 instead of 1 December as initially planned. In June 1936, after another reversed decision, the Construction Office sanctioned the installation of a modified turbo-electric power plant, but to avoid repeating the delays that occurred during the construction of Battleships D and E, Raeder suggested adapting the existing pure turbine designs to the new layout of the machinery rooms. This was approved on 6 June when Admiral Raeder ordered the drawings altered accordingly.

Choosing a lighter power plant did not reduce overall displacement, as the armour protection was increased at the same time – the main armour belt was reinforced from 300mm to 320mm. Some weight-savings were made possible by using welding instead of riveting the armour, which allowed the thickening of the armoured deck above the main magazines from 95mm to 100mm, with inclined sections reinforced from 110mm to 120mm. Rolling, a new technology of armour plate manufacture introduced in December 1936, made the plates lighter and helped keep the displacement down to the intended tonnage.

On 16 November 1935 the Blohm & Voss shipyard in Hamburg was selected to build Battleship F and the formal order was placed on 1 April 1936. The actual construction work commenced on 1 July 1936, when the first keel segments for the *Bismarck* were laid down on the Number 9 slipway. Two weeks earlier, on 14 June 1936, Battleship G had been ordered from the Marinewerft in Wilhelmshaven. Only the Number 2 slipway was large enough to accommodate the new battleship and this was still occupied by the hull that was to become *Scharnhorst* (although a bigger ship, the keel for Battleship G was to be of the same length as that of Battleship D). Battleship G was significantly larger and displaced more water than any ship built at the Marinewerft, and many yard engineers feared the problems that might occur during the launching of such a large ship into a confined dock basin. Numerous experiments were conducted with models to find the right angle between the slipway and the basin before a safe combination was found. Then it was necessary to reconstruct the slipways at that safe angle – but before that could be done the *Scharnhorst* had to be launched. This took place on 3 October 1936 and within hours of the launching ceremony ending, slipway Number 2 became a hive of activity when the construction workers set about reinforcing the foundation of the slipway, changing the angle to enable the safe launch of the giant 41,000-ton battleship that was to be the next ship built on it. As the delayed construction of the *Scharnhorst* held up work on the slipway, only part of the keel could be laid immediately. This took place on 2 November 1936 (though some sources give the earlier date of 24 October 1936), with an estimated completion date of 1 February 1940.

During Admiral Raeder's visit to the Naval Staff on 25 May 1938, a battleship construction conference was held involving representatives from all departments concerned. The goal of the meeting was to agree the contents of a report which Raeder was to prepare for Adolf Hitler. In the preliminary schedule the launch of both ships was planned for mid-March 1939,

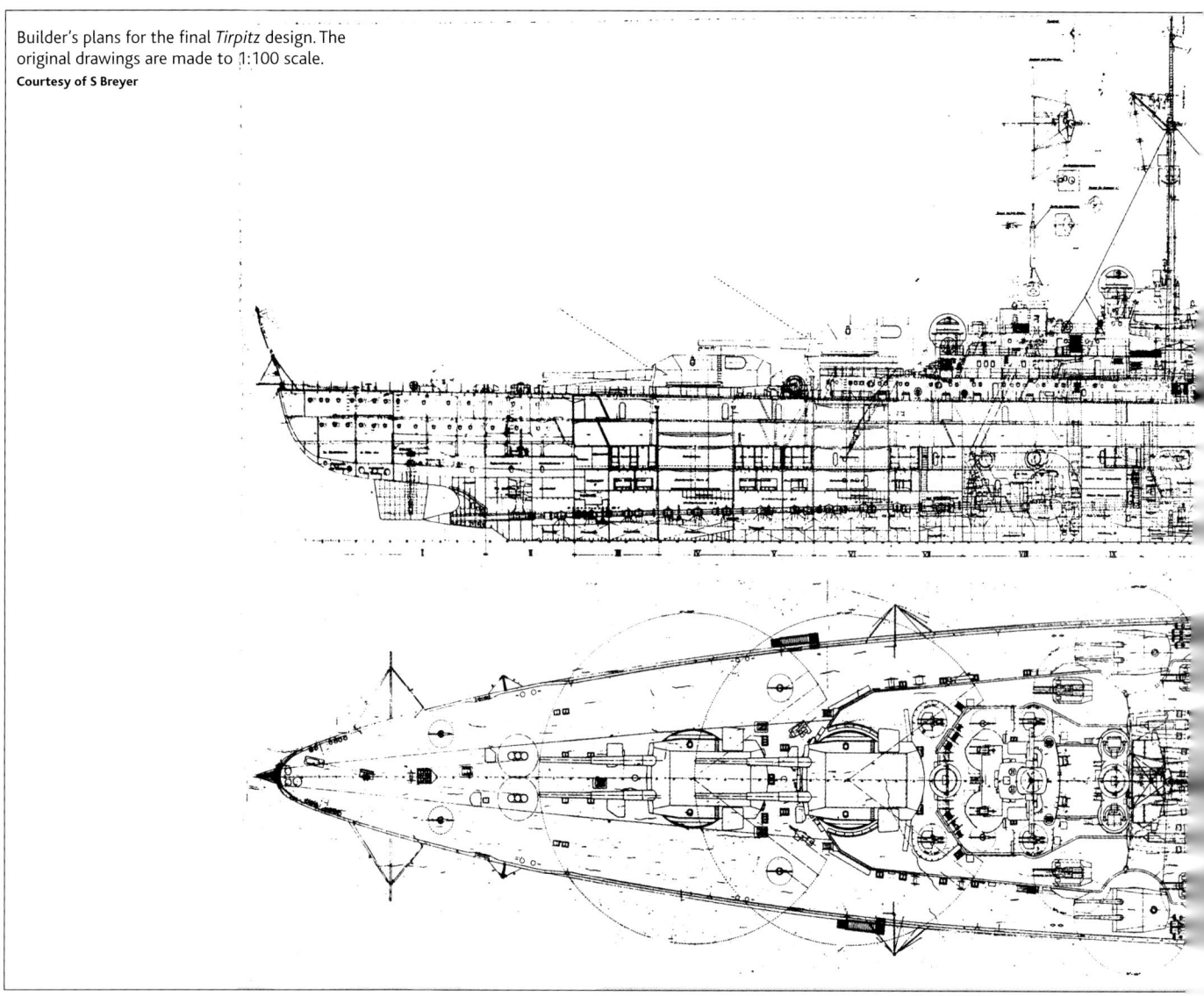

Builder's plans for the final *Tirpitz* design. The original drawings are made to 1:100 scale.
Courtesy of S Breyer

with initial fitting-out to last until the spring of 1940 and then the final fitting-out phase was to commence, lasting for another year and a half. The critical point in all timetables was the date of the machinery delivery and installation; all previous agreements had stipulated December 1939 as this deadline. On the existing schedule all construction works were to be completed within a year after the last boiler and the last piece of engine room equipment had been fitted on board the ships.

However, in the spring of 1939, Hitler suddenly ordered that Battleship F be ready and commissioned by 1 December 1940. This order, verbatim, simply read: 'The Naval High Command orders that the contract with the Blohm & Voss shipyard for the construction of Battleship F be amended so as to accelerate the construction closing date and commission the said battleship not later than 1 December 1940.' A similar order was issued to the Marinewerft in Wilhelmshaven concerning Battleship G. Here the initial date of 1 January 1941 had already been postponed to 1 April 1941; now this date too was brought forward. After numerous conferences the head of the Construction Office stated that, as the ships were almost identical design, the shortened deadline could be met, providing the engines were delivered on time.

However, the main battery turrets suddenly

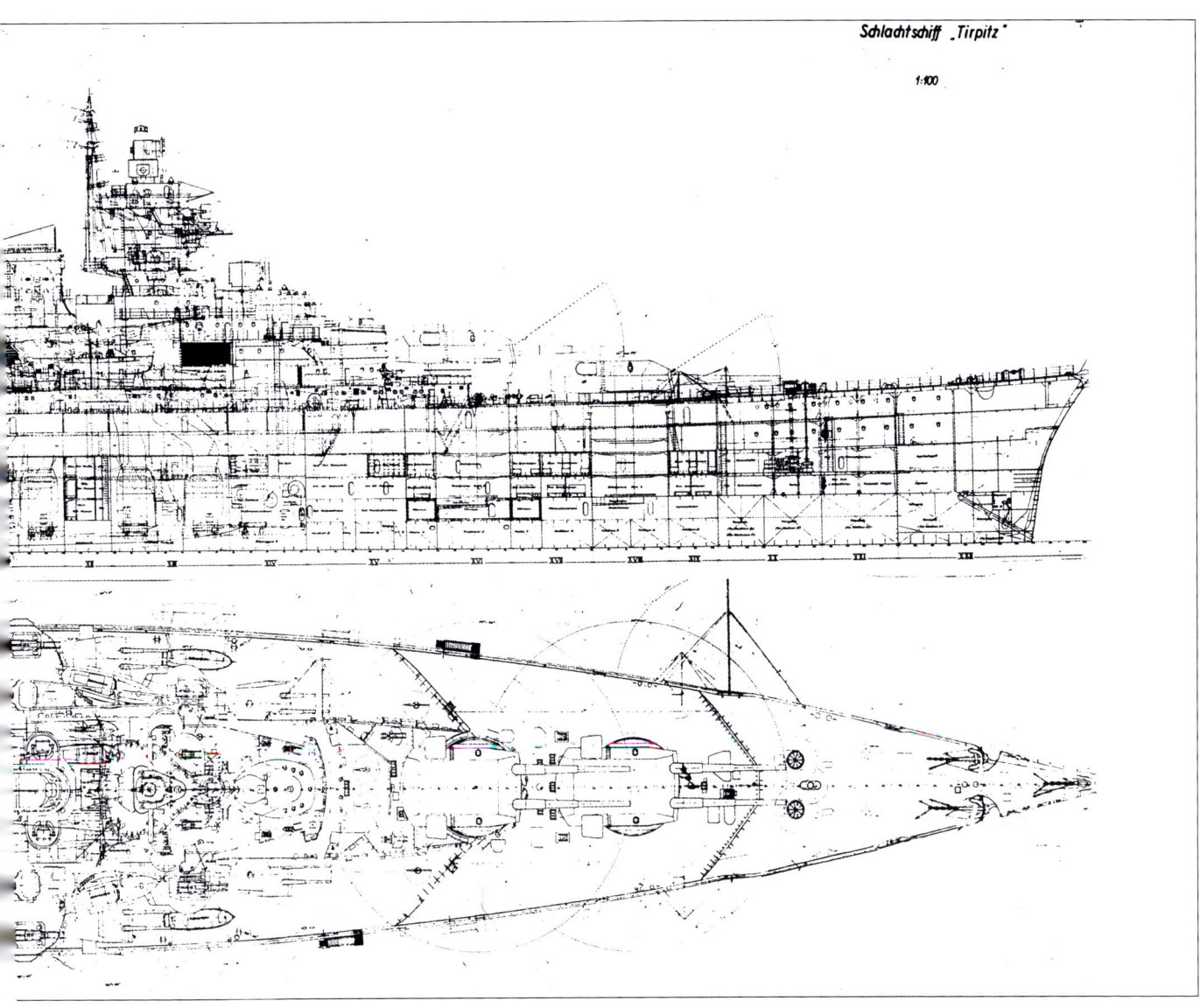

Schlachtschiff „Tirpitz"
1:100

became a new concern. The head of the Armament Office brought the bad news: his contractors were overloaded with other armament programs and had warned that the delivery of the main gun turrets would be delayed by four to five months. This in turn meant delays in hull construction work, as certain phases could not be finalised without the turrets being installed first. In December 1938 only the first of the eight turrets was ready for fitting. The head of the Armament Office suggested that increasing the contracted price could solve the problem, as it would enable Krupp to hire more workers and convert to a three-shift working day. This would overcome many of the difficulties and perhaps even allow some recovery from earlier delays and restore the original construction schedules for Battleships F and G. After Hitler's order to accelerate the construction of the battleships, both yards were ordered to strain their resources and work a three-shift pattern, but without any additional payment. Hitler's order, believed by many to be completely unrealistic, was not only carried out, but even exceeded. Both ships were ready before the scheduled dates. The first of them to be commissioned was the *Bismarck*, which hoisted the Kriegsmarine ensign on 24 August 1940, more than three months ahead of the Hitler's 'unrealistic' deadline of 1 December.

Bismarck

Bismarck photographed in the Bay of Kiel between 18 and 23 September 1940, awaiting the arrival of two Arado floatplanes assigned to the battleship.
Photograph by Schäfer, from the collection of M Skwiot

The construction of the battleship designated 'Ersatz Hannover' began on 1 July 1936 with the keel-laying at the Blohm & Voss shipyard in Hamburg. The ship was launched on 14 February 1939 and named by Dorothea von Loewenfeld, granddaughter of Otto von Bismarck. The *Bismarck* was commissioned on 24 August 1940 and Ernst Lindemann became her first and only commander. After the fitting-out was complete, the *Bismarck* made her first voyage to Gotenhafen (Gdynia) on 28 September 1940 to run sea trials on the sheltered waters of the Baltic. These trials lasted until the end of March 1941 with interruptions for the installation of the remaining optical and fire control equipment. The ship's first mission began on 22 April 1941 with the order to commence Operation Rheinübung, a breakout into the North Atlantic to attack Allied shipping. *Bismarck* was to be the flagship of the force commanded by Admiral Günther Lütjens that also included the heavy cruiser *Prinz Eugen*. Towards the end of April *Prinz Eugen* suffered an accident and the operation had to postponed to a later date. Hitler, disturbed by this turn of events, went to see for himself, inspecting the *Bismarck* and her sister ship *Tirpitz* at Gotenhafen (Gdynia) on 5 May 1941. There Lütjens convinced him that the future operation would be successful and Hitler returned to Berlin. Operation Rheinübung finally got underway on 19 May, when *Bismarck* set out for the Kattegat, being joined en route by the heavy cruiser *Prinz Eugen* and the escorting destroyers. The German force arrived in the Bergen fjord on the 21st, and in the afternoon of the same day they were detected by British aerial reconnaissance. Lütjens now knew that it was only a matter of time before British forces were sent against him, so without waiting for further intelligence he sailed as soon as refuelling was completed. In the meantime Admiral Sir John Tovey assigned the battleships *Prince of Wales* and *King George V*, the battlecruisers *Hood* and *Repulse* and the aircraft carrier *Victorious*, together with smaller craft, to the task of finding and destroying the German ships.

After leaving Norwegian waters the German force sailed north towards the entrance to the Denmark Strait, reached the edge of the pack ice, passed Iceland and sailed south. In the strait the *Bismarck* was spotted by the British heavy cruiser *Suffolk*, which notified the accompanying *Norfolk*. *Norfolk* in turn almost sailed into range of the *Bismarck*'s guns while searching for the battleship and avoided damage only by a quick escape into the fog. Both British cruisers followed the German force and sent its current course, speed and position to the Admiralty. In the meantime a British squadron of *Hood* and *Prince of Wales* commanded by Admiral Holland set course to intercept the Germans. On the morning of 24 May 1941 the German force engaged and during the short artillery duel the *Hood* was sunk and the *Prince of Wales* was damaged. The *Prince of Wales* also managed to hit the *Bismarck* with three 14in (356mm) shells, but this seemingly minor damage sustained by the *Bismarck* had a decisive influence on the outcome of Operation Rheinübung. The most important result was the limiting of the *Bismarck*'s maximum speed to 21 knots. In these circumstances Admiral Lütjens decided to make for St Nazaire to repair the damage. In the meantime the *Prinz Eugen* was detached to continue the operation.

The *Bismarck*, followed by the British ships, tried to shake off the pursuit, but thanks to their radar equipment the British stayed on the trail despite numerous evasive manoeuvres. It is important to note that after the sinking of the *Hood*, the Admiralty deployed all ships available in the Atlantic to take part in the hunt for the *Bismarck*.

On 25 May *Bismarck* finally managed to shake off her pursuers and break contact. For 31 hours she steamed undetected towards the French coast, but at 10.30 on the 26th the *Bismarck* was spotted by an RAF Catalina flying boat, which transmitted the ship's position. By the evening of the same day the cruiser *Sheffield* was close to the battleship and remained in contact until the end of the battle. Admiral Tovey had to slow down the *Bismarck* somehow so that she would not be able to reach port before the British ships caught up. Most of the British ships were low on oil and would have to refuel shortly, and at that time no tankers were at sea; furthermore, U-boats had been sent to help the *Bismarck*. An earlier torpedo bomber attack from the newly commissioned carrier *Victorious* had failed to do significant damage, so the admiral ordered another air strike from the more experienced aircrew of the carrier *Ark Royal*. During the briefing it was suggested that the pilots should target the battleship's rudder to destroy her manoeuvrability. Despite unfavourable weather conditions and heavy German anti-aircraft fire, a formation of Swordfish torpedo planes carried out a successful attack, one of their torpedoes hitting the *Bismarck*'s rudder. Soon the turbines lost power, the ship's speed slowly falling off, while the jammed rudder made steering nearly impossible. Even though the U-boats sent to help arrived in the vicinity, because of the stormy weather

Otto von Bismarck

Otto Eduard Leopold, Prince of Bismarck, Duke of Lauenburg is widely regarded as the architect of German unification and the creator of a Prussian-dominated German empire. Born on 1 April 1815 into a Junker family (the traditional landowning class of Prussia), his early career showed little promise of the greatness was to come. He followed a rather dissolute and ill-directed path through the legal profession, punctuated with much foreign travel, before turning to politics in 1847. In that same year he married Johanna von Puttkamer, who is credited with calming the rather wild young Bismarck and focusing his ambition.

In 1847 'Germany' was a geographical term only, covering a loose confederation of independent states, a relic of the medieval Holy Roman Empire, under the conflicting influence of Prussia and Austria. During the next decade Bismarck made a name for himself in the federal assembly at Frankfurt as a combative and ruthless Prussian representative of conservative, royalist views, fiercely opposed to Austrian dominance. Eventually he fell foul of Austrian pressure, and was transferred to the diplomatic service, becoming successively Prussian ambassador to St Petersburg and Paris, giving him deep insight into the foreign policy of both Russia and France. However, in 1862 he was appointed Minister-President of Prussia by the new king Wilhelm I, and became the champion of royal supremacy in the ensuing disputes with the increasingly liberal members of the elected Diet or parliament.

In the years following, Bismarck succeeded in keeping the calls for greater democracy at bay, while using diplomatic and military means to forward his policy of German unification. Following a dispute over the German-speaking duchies of Schleswig and Holstein, Denmark was invaded and rapidly defeated by the armies of Prussia and Austria in 1864. This in turn became the basis of an argument, and war, with Austria in 1866 that ended in a similarly quick and decisive victory by the newly reorganised Prussian army at Königgrätz (Sadowa). Thereafter Austrian influence in German affairs was severely curtailed, while Prussia annexed several small states and set up a new North German Confederation in 1867, with King Wilhelm as its president and Bismarck as chancellor.

The final barrier to German unification was likely to be the attitude of France, which needed to be isolated diplomatically before being beaten on the field of battle. This Bismarck adroitly achieved, manoeuvring the French emperor Napoleon III into declaring war in July 1870 over a dispute nominally about succession to the Spanish throne. The Franco-Prussian War was a disaster for France, which lost two whole armies at Sedan and Metz (including the capture of the emperor himself), saw Paris besieged, and eventually led to the loss of Alsace and Lorraine in the peace treaty. Most of the north German states had flocked to Prussia's side during the war, and this enabled Bismarck to cajole the southern German states into joining a unified German empire, declared in January 1871 in the famous Hall of Mirrors in Versailles when Wilhelm I assumed the title Kaiser (from Caesar, the German equivalent of Emperor).

The new German Empire was actually a federation, with many of its once-independent states retaining a degree of autonomy. Bismarck became its Chancellor while retaining his Prussian offices, so in a state now completely dominated by Prussia, Bismarck's personal hegemony influenced every aspect of German policy. For nearly twenty years the 'Iron Chancellor' dealt with domestic struggles over economic and welfare issues, while resolutely pursuing a foreign policy aimed at keeping the peace in Europe now that Germany had achieved its primary goal. Considering that Germany's most famous battleship was named after him, it is ironic that he was not a great supporter of naval expansion – which he knew would lead to conflict with Great Britain – and he was only a late convert to colonialism.

His downfall came in 1890 following a clash of wills with the new emperor Wilhelm II, who was determined to impose his own ideas on both domestic and foreign policy. The man who had steered Germany for three decades was forced into resigning, a situation *Punch* magazine appropriately, and famously, caricatured as 'Dropping the Pilot'. In retirement he devoted himself to writing his memoirs and was nominally reconciled to Wilhelm II, but after he died in October 1898 Bismarck's true opinion was revealed on his tombstone epitaph: 'Here lies a true servant of the Emperor Wilhelm I.'

they could not do much to help *Bismarck*.

By this time Lütjens knew that he had very little chance of saving the ship, so he decided to fly the ship's documents to safety using one of the floatplanes. However, an attempt to launch an Arado failed and the ship's war diary and film footage from the operation had to be picked up by a U-boat. In the meantime the British prepared for the final battle against the *Bismarck*. The destroyers had attacked during the night, firing flares so that the battleship would not be lost in the darkness, but good German defensive fire kept them at bay. On the morning of 27 May 1941 the Royal Navy battleships *King George V* and *Rodney* closed in on the slow moving, almost unmanoeuvrable *Bismarck*; they were soon joined by the heavy cruisers *Norfolk* and *Dorsetshire*. At 08.47 *Rodney* opened fire, to which *Bismarck* responded a couple of minutes later and a general battle ensued. The German ship was first hit shortly after 09.00 and within a quarter of an hour all her fire control equipment was knocked out and the ship became an easy target for all enemy ships, which closed to point-blank range. On board the *Bismarck* an order was given to set explosive charges in the engine room and open the kingston valves. *Bismarck*'s guns fell silent at 09.31. The British ceased fire at 10.16 and the heavy cruiser *Dorsetshire* was ordered to use torpedoes to finish off the *Bismarck*, whose blazing hulk still remained afloat. Finally the *Bismarck* rolled over and sank at 10.39, with the loss of 2106 men; only 115 survived.

1 Number 9 slipway in the Blohm & Voss shipyard photographed in autumn 1937. In the foreground the installation of the torpedo bulkheads continues amidships in the hull of Battleship F, which was to become *Bismarck*. The inclined armour is riveted to those bulkheads and stretches to the ship's side.

2 A very similar view of the slipway and building work on the hull taken a little later. Construction is picking up pace and part of the midships area already has the armoured deck in place.

3 This photograph was taken in the same period as the previous one but from a different position on the gantry crane. It shows more closely the work on the bow section and the armoured citadel. Further aft, progress is made on the armouring.

4 An overall view of Number 9 slipway in the Blohm & Voss shipyard, 26 January 1938. Work on the battleship's hull continues: the torpedo bulkhead and the bow section of the ship are under construction. Soon the first armoured bulkhead will be installed – this bulkhead was also the forward wall of the armoured citadel. Inside the hull the first two secondary armament barbettes are installed.

5 Dated 1 April 1938, this photograph documents progress on the armoured deck. Aft the main battery barbettes for C and D (Caesar and Dora) turrets have been completed.

6 A view from the after end of the hull in 1938. In the foreground the third armoured bulkhead is in position.

7 Construction work has moved up to the main deck level towards the end of 1938. This deck is almost complete.

8 In this picture taken on 10 September 1938 the battleship's hull is nearing completion. Almost all of the main deck is in place, with only a small amount of work to be done near A barbette. All main and secondary barbettes are complete.

Blohm & Voss, via Jörg Schmiedeskamp

The launching ceremony took place on 14 February 1939 at the Blohm & Voss shipyard in Hamburg. As was the case with previous battleship launching ceremonies, this one was attended by numerous guests, including high ranking officers, politicians, shipyard workers and inhabitants of Hamburg. In the foreground is the launching platform from which the ceremony will be conducted.
Blohm & Voss, via Jörg Schmiedeskamp

BELOW: The final moments before the battleship's launch. The hull (known in the shipyard as Number 509) will be named *Bismarck* and launched by Dorothea von Loewenfeld, granddaughter of Otto von Bismarck.
CAW

INSET: Adolf Hitler, Chancellor of the Third Reich, makes a speech before the ship received its name and the hull was launched.
CAW

Bismarck shortly after the naming ceremony and the release of chocks. The hull slides down the Number 9 slipway into the shipyard basin.
CAW

As the ship left the ways many must have thought the ship's name highly appropriate, but none of the guests could have known how the ship would so literally fulfil its patron's motto *Patriae inserviendo consumer*.
Blohm & Voss, via Jörg Schmiedeskamp

Immediately after the launch the *Bismarck*'s hull was towed to the fitting-out berth by the shipyard tugs visible in the foreground.
CAW

Following the experience of the earlier battleships *Scharnhorst* and *Gneisenau*, the stem was similarly altered to the so-called Atlantic bow, whose increased overhang and flare was intended to reduce the drenching of the forward rangefinders in A and B turrets by waves breaking over the bow. The reconstruction was performed in the Blohm & Voss shipyard and was completed in September 1939. In this photograph work on the forward superstructure has already started.
Blohm & Voss, via Jörg Schmiedeskamp

Bows of the *Bismarck* after the modification, indicated by the lighter coloured steel. The new Atlantic stem required altering the ship's anchor-handling arrangements, the conventional hawse pipes through the hull sides being replaced by deck-edge beds for the anchors, again as in *Scharnhorst* and *Gneisenau*.
S Breyer collection

The official photographer recording the progress of fitting-out.
S Breyer collection

The Atlantic bow as modified in the *Bismarck* resulted in an elegant clipper cutwater. The anchors were relocated to the deck-edge – in the conventional position they contributed to the spray thrown up at speed – and a third anchor was carried at the stemhead.
S Breyer collection

Details of the anchor-handling arrangements, for the stem anchor (bottom) and starboard bower anchor.

LEFT: Details of *Bismarck*'s stem after modification. The design improved the working condition for the turret rangefinder crews.
S Breyer collection

ABOVE: Stern of the *Bismarck*. Note the anchor on the port side only.
S Breyer collection

The battleship's forward superstructure in spring 1940. In the foreground A and B turrets look structurally complete.
Blohm & Voss, via Jörg Schmiedeskamp

RIGHT: Another view of the forward main gun turrets taken at the same period but from a different perspective, with the barbettes of A and B (Anton and Bruno) turrets in the foreground. Later the 10m rangefinder was removed from A turret and the openings were covered with armour plates.
Blohm & Voss, via Jörg Schmiedeskamp

An early 1940 view of a snow-covered ship during later stages of fitting out. Canvas covers protect some of the work from the conditions.
Blohm & Voss, via Jörg Schmiedeskamp

The fitting out of *Bismarck* continued in all weathers – the snow-covered view was taken in winter 1939/1940, although work at the time was largely confined to the ship's interior. The close-ups opposite show many details of the fittings, especially around the funnel cap.
S Breyer collection

Funnel cap and searchlight position.
S Breyer collection

Steering position during fitting out - not all equipment has been installed.
S Breyer collection

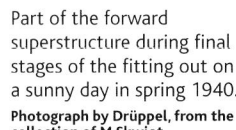

Part of the forward superstructure during final stages of the fitting out on a sunny day in spring 1940.
Photograph by Drüppel, from the collection of M Skwiot

ABOVE: View from the starboard side of *Bismarck*'s forecastle photographed in the summer of 1940 during the last phase of fitting out in the Blohm & Voss shipyard. In this photograph the ventilation ducts can be seen on the side of B turret barbette. Experience was to show that in rough seas these were often flooded with seawater from waves breaking over the bow, so the ducts were later reconstructed with the intakes facing aft and slightly raised.
Bundesarchiv, courtesy S Breyer

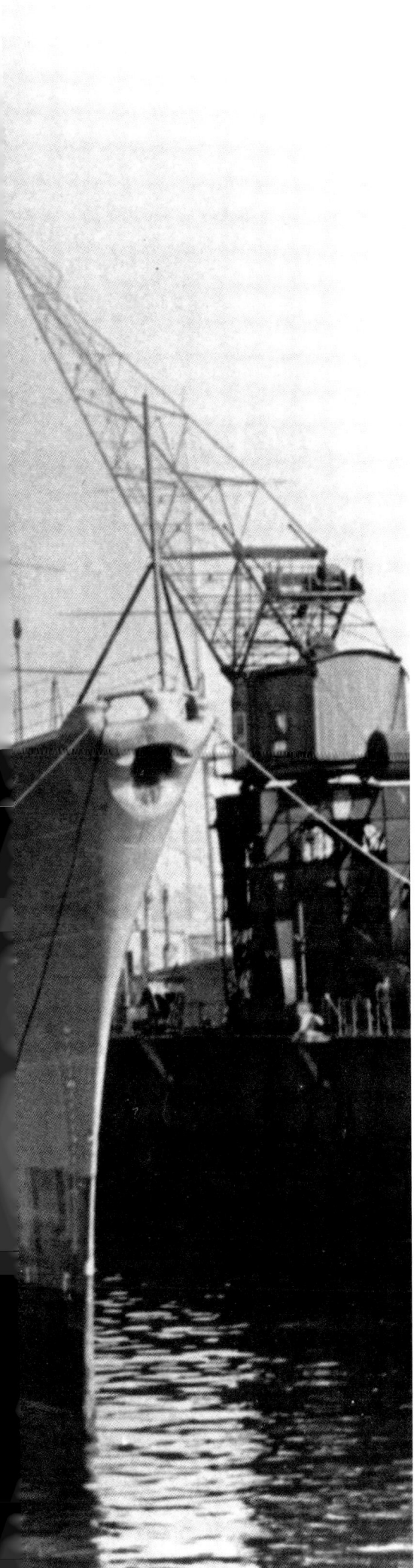

LEFT: *Bismarck* entering Dry Dock C in the Blohm & Voss shipyard on 23 June 1940. While in the dock the degaussing cable (or MES) was installed on the battleship's hull.
Blohm & Voss, via Jörg Schmiedeskamp

Port side of B turret barbette, also in the summer of 1940. As with the ducts on the starboard side, these were similarly heightened and reoriented to face aft.
Bundesarchiv, courtesy S Breyer

Looking forward at the back of the starboard fore 15cm gun turret. On the platform above, canvas covers a 10.5cmm anti-aircraft gun mount, 'Stb 2' according to the designation painted on its side.
S Breyer collection

A view from port of *Bismarck*'s forward superstructure in the later stages of fitting out in summer 1940. In the foreground is a Type SL-8 high-angle director on top of a tubular tower abreast the bridge; other fire-control directors and radar antennas have yet to be fitted.
S Breyer collection

Details of the funnel platform and port (No 2) aircraft hangar with boats nested on top, seen during fitting out. In the foreground is the top of a 15cm gun turret with storage bins on the roof.
S Breyer collection

Starboard No 2 15cm gun seen from the front. In the foreground is a 10.5cm anti-aircraft gun on a stabilised twin mount, formally designated 10.5cm SK C/33 on a 8.8cm Dopp. LC/31 mount. *Bismarck*'s heavy anti-aircraft battery was installed in two phases – the first four forward twin 10.5cm guns before the ship commissioned and the four after guns in November 1940.
S Breyer collection

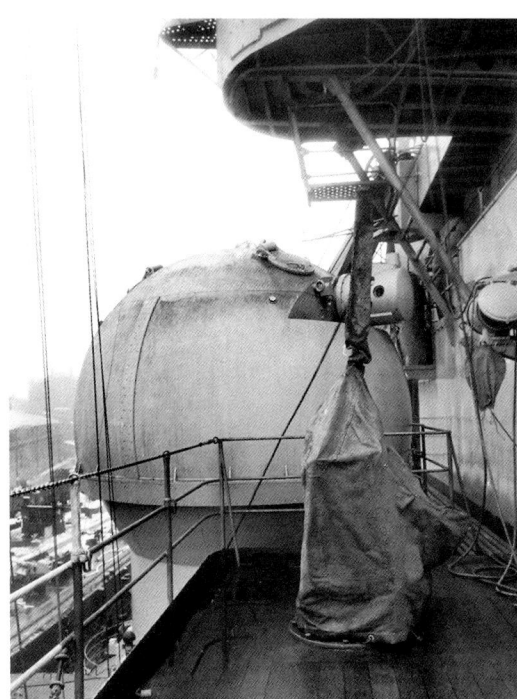

Details of the stabilised searchlight mountings and the high-angle directors.
S Breyer collection

RIGHT: Details of the ventilation shafts on C turret barbette. On the far right is part of the 10.5cm training gun; a 15cmm training gun was installed next to it.
S Breyer collection

LEFT: The catapult deck amidships, showing details of the cranes and the end of the catapult track. The main hangar is to the right with the doors partly open, but there were also narrow hangars further forward, abreast the funnel trunking. On the weather deck the seamen are standing at the end of a narrow athwartship passage under the aviation deck; *Bismarck* had this feature but not *Tirpitz*.
S Breyer collection

RIGHT AND BELOW: Details of the boat- and aircraft-handling crane.
S Breyer collection

BOTTOM RIGHT: Scuttle and vent details on a curved bulkhead behind one of the 15cm mountings.
S Breyer collection

RIGHT: Main aircraft hangar seen from the port side; the larger ship's boats are stowed on top of it. The absence of the after 10.5cm guns and the 10.5m rangefinder indicates that the photograph was taken in August 1940 when the *Bismarck* was still fitting out in the Blohm & Voss shipyard.
S Breyer collection

LEFT: Starboard shelter deck bulkhead just below B turret. The canvas cover shrouds a single 2cm gun.
S Breyer collection

BELOW: The after 38cm turrets.
S Breyer collection

The battleship's first commander, Kapitan zur See Ernst Lindemann, coming aboard. On taking command, Lindemann delivered a short speech urging the crew to make the *Bismarck* a battle-ready unit as soon as possible, and thanking the shipyard workers for their hard work during the ship's construction and fitting out. After his address the ensign was hoisted aft and the commander's flag broke out at the masthead.
S Breyer collection

During the first days of September the ship was made ready to leave the Blohm & Voss shipyard, and on 15 September the *Bismarck* finally cast off and sailed down the Elbe river observed by numerous inhabitants of Hamburg. This photograph was taken at approximately 14.20 as the battleship was manoeuvred out of the shipyard.
M Skwiot collection

ABOVE: The fitting out of the *Bismarck* was filmed for propaganda purposes from time to time. Here the film crew has just finished their assignment and is leaving the ship.
S Breyer collection

Bismarck during the final stages of fitting out in the Blohm & Voss shipyard, August 1940. Part of the crew had been assigned to the ship since mid-April. These were mainly technical branch officers, non-commissioned officers and 65 other ranks. Two months later the gunnery personnel, about 60 men, joined them, becoming the first to familiarise themselves with the equipment installed on board the ship. Because of the ongoing work on board the *Bismarck*, this skeleton crew was accommodated on two hulks, *Oceana* and *General Artigas*.
Blohm & Voss, via Jörg Schmiedeskamp

Close-up of the battleship's funnel. Beneath the rear platform is the gantry crane used to position the floatplanes on the catapult. Note forward searchlights with their 'Kalotten' ('skull-cap') covers abreast the front of the funnel. On the *Bismarck* these platforms were installed about 1.5 metres higher than on her sister ship *Tirpitz*, which had a flush platform for all searchlights, a useful identification feature.
S Breyer collection

Bismarck in the Elbe assisted by tugs, 15 September 1940. Unfortunately for the battleship the voyage was marred by a collision with the tug *Atlantik*, which occurred at about 16.58.
Photograph by Urbahns, from the collection of M Skwiot

Bismarck on passage to the Kiel Canal, photographed in the afternoon of 15 September 1940.
Photograph by Urbahns, from the collection of S Breyer

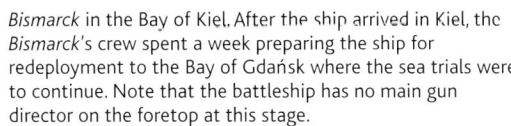

Bismarck in the Bay of Kiel. After the ship arrived in Kiel, the *Bismarck*'s crew spent a week preparing the ship for redeployment to the Bay of Gdańsk where the sea trials were to continue. Note that the battleship has no main gun director on the foretop at this stage.
Photograph by Urbahns, from the collection of M Skwiot

In the evening the battleship reached Brunsbüttel roadstead, where she anchored at 19.20. However, the night was not very peaceful as shortly after an air raid alarm was sounded in the city and on board the ship. Only on the next day did the *Bismarck* enter the Kiel Canal. After two days transiting the canal, on 17 September the *Bismarck* moored at the Scheerahafen pier in Kiel.
S Breyer collection

Bismarck at the A12 mooring buoy in the Heikendorf roadstead off Kiel between 25 and 27 September 1940. The two floatplanes have now been embarked and one of them is visible on the catapult. The aircraft carried the designations T3+IH (serial No 0052) and T3+AK (0110).
Photograph by Schäfer, from the collection of M Skwiot

Bismarck at the end of 1940. By this stage the ship has the after main director fitted and the full complement of 10.5cm anti-aircraft guns.
Photograph by Schäfer from the collection of Blohm & Voss via Jörg Schmiedeskamp

Bismarck in the Bay of Kiel en route to Gotenhafen. Near Cape Arkona the ship was joined by *Sperrbrecher 13*.
Photograph by Urbahns, from the collection of M Skwiot

LEFT: From the beginning of October the *Bismarck* conducted an intensive program of sea trials and combat training off Gotenhafen – full speed runs, fuel consumption measurements, manoeuvring trials and steering under emergency control. In this photograph taken in the second half of November 1940 the ship has the after 10.5cm guns installed. These four twin mounts were of a more modern model (1933) than the forward guns. They were designated 10.5cm SK C/33 on 10.5cm Dopp LC/37 mount. The guns had different barrels and gun hoods.
CAW

Close-up of the underside of the funnel platform, showing the port gantry crane used to lift the floatplanes from the transport trolley to the launching catapult. The gantry cranes were installed on special brackets that could support the weight of a loaded Arado Ar 196 floatplane. The striped camouflage (the white part is visible) on the funnel indicates that the picture was taken in February or March 1941 in Hamburg.
S Breyer collection

RIGHT: *Bismarck*'s searchlight platform seen from the aviation deck, February-March 1941. In the foreground the bracket system supporting the searchlight platform and the gantry crane are visible.
S Breyer collection

LEFT: During the main armament and anti-aircraft gunnery trials the superstructure, air conditioning system and the hangar door were damaged so severely that it could not be made good in Gotenhafen. In addition, the fitting out, still incomplete, had to finished. All this prompted the decision to return the ship to the Blohm & Voss shipyard in Hamburg, and on 5 December the ship left Gotenhafen for Kiel.
Photograph by Schäfer from the collection of Blohm & Voss, via Jörg Schmiedeskamp

ABOVE: The ship carried a varied outfit of boats, the majority stowed on top of the aircraft hangars forward of the funnel and aft of the catapult deck.
S Breyer collection

RIGHT: The aircraft hangars on either side of the *Bismarck*'s funnel were very small, each housing one Ar 196, but only with its wings fully folded. This is the after side of Number 2 Hangar, located on the battleship's port side.
S Breyer collection

TOP RIGHT: Two views of the after main fire control director with its 10.5m rangefinder and FuMO 23 radar aerial.
S Breyer collection

RIGHT: Abaft the catapults, the main aviation hangar (Grosse Flugzeughalle) was an irregular trapezoid when seen in plan view, divided in two by the mainmast. The area of the hangar was 120m^2, which provided just enough space for two Arado floatplanes with wings folded. The hangar was closed by two overlapping doors, the left one sliding outside the right.
S Breyer collection

FAR RIGHT: Trunking detail at the back of the bridge, beneath the platform on which the foremast was stepped.
S Breyer collection

BISMARCK

Bismarck seen from the heavy cruiser *Prinz Eugen*. This photograph was taken in May 1941 during tactical exercises in the Baltic designed to test the command structure of both ships and Admiral Lütjens' staff.
Photograph by Lagemann, from the collection of M Skwiot

Prinz Eugen towing the *Bismarck* during exercises before Operation Rheinübung on 13 May 1941. On the very same afternoon the *Bismarck* practised refuelling from the *Prinz Eugen*, transferring a fuel line from the *Bismarck*'s bow to the cruiser and taking fuel from its tanks. The exercise was specifically ordered by the force commander, Admiral Günther Lütjens, who anticipated that it might be necessary at some point during the long cruise that the ships were about to undertake.
IWM

RIGHT: Admiral Lütjens, the new force commander, inspects the crew.

BELOW: Accompanied by an entourage of officials, Hitler visited the ship on 5 May 1940. He was given an extensive tour of the ship and discussed the forthcoming Operation Rheinübung with the senior officers.
Both S Breyer collection

Another photograph of the *Bismarck* during exercises in the Baltic. This is one of the few shots where A turret's roof is clearly painted in a different colour from the other turrets. The colour was probably crimson, but it is impossible to be 100 per cent certain without consulting surviving crew members.
M Skwiot collection

Bismarck seen from the heavy cruiser *Prinz Eugen*. This picture was taken during exercises in the Baltic in May 1941.
Bibliothek für Zeitgeschichte

One of the best-known photographs of *Bismarck*, taken from the *Prinz Eugen*. It is usually captioned as depicting the ships setting out on Operation Rheinübung, but this cannot be the case. When leaving Rügen the two ships took up a line ahead formation at a distance of about a mile from one other, whereas in this photograph they are just a few cables apart.
M Skwiot collection

RIGHT: Hitlers' visit to the ship, 5 May 1940. Note the film cameraman recording the event.
S Breyer collection

BELOW: *Bismarck* sailing into Grimstadfiord on 21 May 1941 photographed from the heavy cruiser *Prinz Eugen*. The battleship still carries the Baltic striped camouflage, but the crew began to repaint the ship as soon as an order from the Fleet Command to change the colour scheme pattern to an overall grey was received. The uniform grey was better suited to the conditions in the Denmark Strait.
M Skwiot collection

Bismarck and the accompanying tankers photographed on 21 May 1941 in Korsofjord by a Spitfire reconnaissance aircraft piloted by Michael Suckling.
IWM

ABOVE AND RIGHT: Three views of *Bismarck* (seen from astern) in the early hours of 21 May 1941 leaving Korsofjord. Shortly afterwards the ship passed the southern fjord entry and turned for Bergen, finally dropping anchor in Fjörangerfjord.
Prinz Eugen archive

Bismarck photographed from the *Prinz Eugen* while firing at the *Hood*.
Blohm & Voss, via Jörg Schmiedeskamp

The battlecruiser HMS *Hood*, pride of the Royal Navy, sunk in the Denmark Strait.
IWM

This photograph taken shortly after the *Hood* blew up shows the burning remains of the battlecruiser (to the right) and the battleship *Prince of Wales* making a smokescreen.
IWM

Bismarck photographed on 24 May 1941 after the battle in the Denmark Strait. During this engagement the *Bismarck* was hit three times by heavy calibre shells from the *Prince of Wales*, and one of those hits was to have a major impact on subsequent events. This shell hit the fuel tanks in the forward compartments on the battleship's starboard side and continued through the ship, creating a 2-metre hole in the ship's bottom. Almost 2000 tons of seawater entered the forward hull compartments. This photograph taken from the *Prinz Eugen* shows the *Bismarck* with the resulting trim by the head.
IWM

RIGHT: A sequence of photos taken during the final battle. The top view shows *Bismarck*'s erratic course after the torpedo hit on the rudder by one of *Ark Royal*'s Swordfish. The second shows the immense columns of water thrown up astern of *Bismarck* by 16in shells from *Rodney* (seen in the third view), while the bottom picture records *Bismarck*'s final moments.
All IWM

Tirpitz

The construction of the battleship *Tirpitz* commenced in October 1936 in the Marinewerft in Wilhelmshaven. It was intended to build the ship on the same slipway from which the *Scharnhorst* had just been launched, and the first section of keel was laid on 24 October 1936. However, the angle of the slipway had to be altered for the larger ship, so it was only on 2 November, after the reconstruction of the slipway, that the rest of the keel was laid down. This explains why two different laying-down dates occur in the literature – and both are correct. The name of the new battleship was that of Grand Admiral Alfred von Tirpitz, the creator of German naval power. Enjoying peacetime conditions, the initial building stages went smoothly, but the impending launch was a source of concern, as there was very little space in the Wilhelmshaven basin to bring the hull to a stop after it left the ways. A series of tests was performed on models of both shipyard basin and the battleship, to avoid the embarrassment of hitting the pier opposite, as *Gneisenau* had. The official launching ceremony was performed on 1 April 1939, in the presence of Hitler and many high-ranking commanders of the Kriegsmarine and Wehrmacht. The ship was named by Mrs von Hassel, daughter of Admiral Tirpitz, and to the yard management's relief, the hull slid into the water without a hitch. On this occasion Admiral Raeder was promoted to Grand Admiral.

Tirpitz in the roadstead in the Bay of Kiel, photographed in May 1941 with the main director installed on the foretop (it incorporated a 10.5m rangefinder and a FuMo 23 radar aerial). A second FuMO 23 antenna is visible on the 7m rangefinder forward of the bridge.
Bundesarchiv

The beginning of the war in September 1939 did not immediately affect the building schedule, but when the RAF began intensive night raids on the Wilhelmshaven naval base, the ship's construction was speeded up. The ensign was formally hoisted on 25 February 1941 and Captain (Kpt z S) Karl Topp assumed command of the new battleship. For the following months the *Tirpitz* conducted sea trials in the Baltic and reached full combat readiness in September 1941. The ship remained in the Baltic until the end of the year, participating in the naval blockade of the Russian fleet in Leningrad. Since the sinking of the *Bismarck*, the idea of raids against merchant shipping by major surface units was considered too risky and the Kriegsmarine high command feared further losses. However, the intensified Lend-Lease support supplied to the Soviet Union via the 'northern route' to Murmansk influenced the decision to relocate the *Tirpitz* to Norway, where its new mission would be to attack the arctic convoys. From the safe base of a Norwegian fjord the ship could quickly sortie to intercept the convoy escorts while its supporting units, together with the U-boats, would sink the merchant ships.

The *Tirpitz* arrived in Trondheim on 16 January 1942 and other heavy German ships soon followed. Stationed in Norway for over three years, the battleship was a constant threat to convoys sailing the arctic route. The very fact of the ship's presence in Norway forced the Allies to employ numerous British and American heavy ships to protect the convoys. Each of the convoys sailing to or returning from the Soviet Union had to be accompanied by forces strong enough at least to deter the *Tirpitz* or, the British hoped, sink the ship. Deploying British capital ships in this region came at the expense of other theatres of operation, so even as a passive threat the *Tirpitz* had a significant impact on the war at sea. However, during her service in arctic waters, *Tirpitz* also took part in three major operations. The first of them, Operation Sportpalast in March 1942, was an attempt to intercept the convoys PQ12 and QP8. On this occasion, the battleship and her escorting destroyers did not manage to find the convoys, although they got very close. In July 1942 the battleship participated in Operation Rösselsprung, the attack on convoy PQ17. On the day before the *Tirpitz* sailed the British Admiralty received information from decrypted radio transmissions that German forces, including the *Tirpitz*, were putting to sea and based on this information made the disastrous decision to scatter the convoy, which was then decimated by the Luftwaffe and U-boats. When this information was intercepted on board the *Tirpitz*, it was deemed pointless to continue the operation and the battleship with its escorts returned to the fjords. In September 1943 the ship took part in Operation Zitronella (Sizilien), an attack on Spitsbergen, in company with *Scharnhorst* and escorting destroyers. After this operation the ship was attacked by six British X-Craft midget submarines while anchored in Altafjord. The operation was partially successful as the charges managed to damage the *Tirpitz* and put it out of action for several months. However, the ship was considered so valuable that it was gradually restored to combat readiness, without being docked, during a lengthy operation in Altafjord, codenamed Paul, which was completed by the end of March 1944. But the ship's

Alfred von Tirpitz

Battleship G was named after Grossadmiral Alfred von Tirpitz, the founder of German naval power. Born on 19 March 1849 in Küstrin (now Kostrzyn in Poland), Tirpitz passed the entrance exams in Berlin and became a Naval Cadet in April 1865. After four years of education, he graduated on 24 June 1869, entered the Prussian Navy and in September he was commissioned as a Sub Lieutenant. Improving the automobile torpedo became his professional obsession, and his work on torpedoes won him professional accolades from the German Admiralty. Later he served on numerous boards and committees dealing with underwater weapons (mines and torpedoes).

His first command was the *Ziethen*, a sloop that he commanded as a Lieutenant Junior Grade. Promoted to Lieutenant Senior Grade (Oberleutnant), he became the executive officer, and then the CO of the corvette *Blücher*. In September 1881 he was promoted Lieutenant Commander and given the post of Torpedo Weapon Development Supervisor. In 1885, as Commander, he took command of the Torpedo Boat Squadron. Excellent results, professional competence and organisational talents were awarded that same year with a promotion to Captain. In early April of 1889 he was appointed the CO of the battleship *Preussen* and soon after, in May 1890, he became captain of the brand-new battleship *Württemberg*.

In September of 1890 he began a period of staff appointments. First he served as a chief of staff, Baltic Regional Command (January 1891 to January 1892), then he became the Chief of the Naval Staff (January 1892 to September 1895), being promoted to Rear Admiral in May 1895. By now he had the ear of the Kaiser, who was impressed by his vision of Germany as a serious naval power, but his views were often at odds with the Navy's high command. As a temporary solution to one such political disagreement, Tirpitz was sent to command the Far Eastern

Cruiser Squadron (June 1896 to April 1897) pending his June 1897 appointment as a State Secretary in the Department of the Navy in Berlin. In March of the following year he became the Secretary of the Navy and was promoted Vice Admiral in December a year later. As a Secretary of the Navy Tirpitz was largely responsible for turning Germany into a naval power with a proper battle fleet, adumbrating his famous Risk theory – the Kaiser's navy did not have to equal the largest fleet but should be big enough that combat with it would bring an unacceptable risk to any country dependent on naval power. In June of 1903 he was promoted Admiral, and in 1911 he became a Grand Admiral (Grossadmiral), a grade invented especially for him by the grateful Kaiser.

In 1916 he fell from favour with the Kaiser for advocating unlimited submarine warfare and a pre-emptive strike against the United States. He was dismissed and retired. He died on 6 March 1930 in Ebenhausen.

serviceability did not last long as the vigilant British followed the repair works closely and as soon as the ship completed its machinery trials they launched another attack. In April Royal Navy carrier-based aircraft attacked the *Tirpitz* as part of Operation Tungsten and managed to damage the ship again. Further air strikes followed, but complete success came on 12 November 1944, when RAF Lancaster heavy bombers attacked the ship with specially designed 'Tallboy' bombs, each weighing 5 tons. *Tirpitz* was hit twice on the port side, once near the seaplane catapult and once near B turret; other bombs that did not hit the ship directly caused a shockwave that was stronger than usual as it rebounded off the shallow bottom of the fjord. At 09.45 the *Tirpitz* had an 11-degree list to port; tidal waves of water caused by the explosions flooded the ship and the list further increased. Counter-flooding did not help the battleship much and twenty minutes later the ship suffered an internal explosion in the magazines beneath C turret, tearing a huge hole in the *Tirpitz*'s port side and increasing the list to 30–40 degrees. The captain gave the order to abandon ship. Two minutes later the list reached 60–70 degrees and the ship rolled over and settled on the bottom with its superstructure at an angle of 135 degrees. Part of the battleship's hull remained above the water.

Hull construction works in the battleship's midships area. In the foreground the secondary armament barbettes are complete to the main deck level. In the background, behind the crane, is the old battleship *Hannover*.
Photograph by Schäfer, from the collection of S Breyer

The dignitaries gathered on the launching platform, with the Chancellor of the Third Reich, Adolf Hitler prominent.
CAW

The complete hull of the battleship *Tirpitz* ready for launching on 1 April 1939. The naming ceremony is about to begin on the Number 2 slipway of the Marinewerft in Wilhelmshaven
Photograph by Schäfer, from the collection of S Breyer

RIGHT: Because of the relative narrowness of the basin the Wilhelmshaven shipyard had to prepare very carefully for this launch. While the battleship was building, numerous tests were carried out with a shipyard model simulating the launch of the ship. On the day it went off perfectly – here the moment the hull left the ways.
Photograph by Drüppel, from the collection of CAW

The launch of the *Tirpitz* posed a considerable challenge, as the distance to the pier on the other side of the basin was really close. To avoid the hull hitting the pier it was necessary to reduce its speed promptly, and this photograph shows several of the tugs that were employed for this purpose.
Photograph by Drüppel, from the collection of S Breyer

The hull being towed to the shipyard's fitting-out berth. The picture was taken from the battleship *Scharnhorst*.
Photograph by Drüppel, from the collection of M Skwiot

The *Tirpitz*'s hull being turned in the narrow basin of the Marinewerft in Wilhelmshaven.
CAW

Tirpitz photographed on 2 February 1940 during fitting out in the Wilhelmshaven shipyard.
NHC

Fitting-out work proceeding on the *Tirpitz* in the Marinewerft in Wilhelmshaven. In the foreground is the cylindrical mast for the heavy cruiser *Admiral Scheer* undergoing a refit in the years 1939/1940.
S Breyer collection

The fitting out of the *Tirpitz* was closely monitored by the British, who wanted to prevent, or at least delay, the ship entering service, and to this end they conducted systematic air raids on Wilhelmshaven and the battleship moored in the shipyard. To render the assessment of the state of works more difficult for British aerial reconnaissance, the battleship was covered in the unusual camouflage shown here in which features of the surrounding buildings were painted on to the seaward side of the hull.
S Breyer collection

The incomplete *Tirpitz* being manoeuvred in the fitting-out basin at Wilhelmshaven. The 38cm guns have not yet been mounted in B turret.
S Breyer collection

One of the best shots of the camouflaged port side of the ship taken by Schäfer at the end of 1940. The quayside buildings are still painted on but repainting the ship into standard colours is just beginning.
Photograph by Schäfer, from the collection of S Breyer

Tirpitz during the fitting out of the forward superstructure in winter 1940/1941. In this photograph the camouflage pattern painted on A and B main gun turrets, funnel and upper parts of the superstructure is very clearly visible.
S Breyer collection

LEFT: Before commissioning the *Tirpitz* had to go into dry dock to have the underwater hull cleaned and repainted. Here the battleship is leaving the fitting-out berth assisted by tugs and heading towards the dry dock.
S Breyer collection

Entering the Scheer Basin en route to the 40,000-ton floating dry dock. Behind the ship is the Kaiser Wilhelm bridge.
S Breyer collection

Tirpitz during machinery trials in the Baltic, March 1941. The forward main director with its 10.5m rangefinder has not yet been installed on the foretop – this will be done in May.
S Breyer collection

The installation of the forward main director with its 10.5m rangefinder allowed some gunnery practice for A and B turrets main and the secondary armament, but the complete fire control system could not be tested as yet because the ship did not have the after directors for the main and anti-aircraft guns.
NHC collection

Photographed in May 1941 in the Baltic during sea trials. From this month until the end of the year the *Tirpitz*'s turret tops were painted dark grey.
S Breyer collection

Tirpitz during the second series of gunnery practice conducted in May 1941 in the Baltic Sea.
Photograph by Drüppel, from the collection of A Jarski

Adolf Hitler visiting *Tirpitz* at Gotenhafen on 5 May 1941.
S Breyer collection

Tirpitz in the Bay of Kiel, photographed in May 1941 during a brief respite in sea trials. The battleship does not yet have the after SL-8 HA directors nor the after main director with its 10.5m rangefinder.
S Breyer collection

Battleship *Tirpitz* seen from the port quarter during the first series of gunnery trials in May 1941. During a period in the Deutsche Werke shipyard in Kiel in April the ship received the two forward main directors; both carried FuMO 23 radar antennas, but the foretop director housed a 10.5m rangefinder, with a 7m rangefinder in the one ahead of the bridge. The installation of some fire control equipment allowed the battleship to conduct limited gunnery practice and calibrate the A and B turret mechanisms.

Photograph by Drüppel, from the collection of S Breyer

Tirpitz's stern photographed from the mainmast platform. In the foreground the EM II rangefinder installed on the after director platform is visible and in the background the C and D main gun turrets can be seen. This photograph was taken in June 1941 during a pause in the sea trials conducted in the Baltic Sea.
M Skwiot collection

Two further views of *Tirpitz* from the summer of 1941 during trials in the Baltic. The ship still does not have her after main director mounted.
S Breyer collection

RIGHT: *Tirpitz* photographed on 13 July 1941 in the Bay of Kiel between sea trials and exercises. The battleship's visits to Kiel were usually associated with the installation of new equipment, and on this occasion it was to receive the after SL-8 anti-aircraft directors
Bibliothek für Zeitgeschichte

BOTTOM: Another photograph taken on 13 July 1941 shows *Tirpitz* with the characteristically domed covers of the two newly installed SL-8 anti-aircraft directors aft.
Bibliothek für Zeitgeschichte

A fine portrait of *Tirpitz* between series of sea trials returning at slow speed to the Bay of Kiel, photographed in July 1941.
M Skwiot collection

Part of *Tirpitz*'s bridge and forward turrets photographed in the Baltic in September 1941. Note the navigating bridge-wings folded back against the main superstructure block.
M Skwiot collection

During the sea trials a film crew from the propaganda division visited the *Tirpitz* from time to time. Here the film crew records the floatplane launching practice.
S Breyer collection

The Ar 196 floatplane lands near the battleship during exercises conducted in September 1941.
S Breyer collection

The first trial aircraft launches were conducted on the battleship in September 1941 in the Bay of Kiel.
S Breyer collection

The first gunnery trials employing the entire main battery was only possible after all fire control equipment had been installed. At the end of September 1941 the *Tirpitz* began the first series of full gunnery exercises in the Baltic.
S Breyer collection

The after main director with its 10.5m rangefinder and FuMO 23 radar antenna was finally fitted in September 1941 at the Deutsche Werke shipyard in Kiel. Only then could the *Tirpitz* complete the second series of gunnery exercises and calibrate C and D gun turrets, integrating them into the fire control system.
S Breyer collection

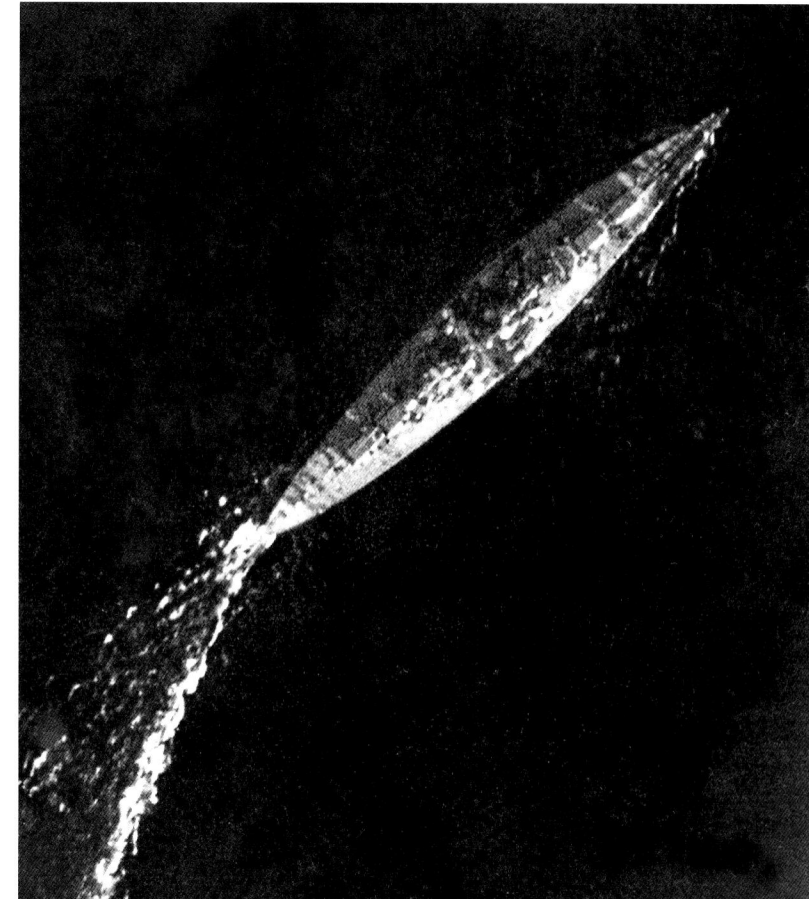

The sea trials and exercises were interrupted from time to time by bad weather. In this photograph the *Tirpitz* sails through a storm in the Baltic in September 1941.
Bundesarchiv

RIGHT: *Tirpitz*'s work-up was observed closely by the British. This picture shows the *Tirpitz* in September 1941 during exercises in Strander Bay before joining the Baltenflotte.
IWM

Tirpitz in September 1941 in the Baltic. Three *M35* class minesweepers are moored alongside the battleship.
S Breyer collection

FAR RIGHT: *Tirpitz* alongside at Kiel between series of gunnery practices, perfectly photographed by British aerial reconnaissance in September 1941.
IWM

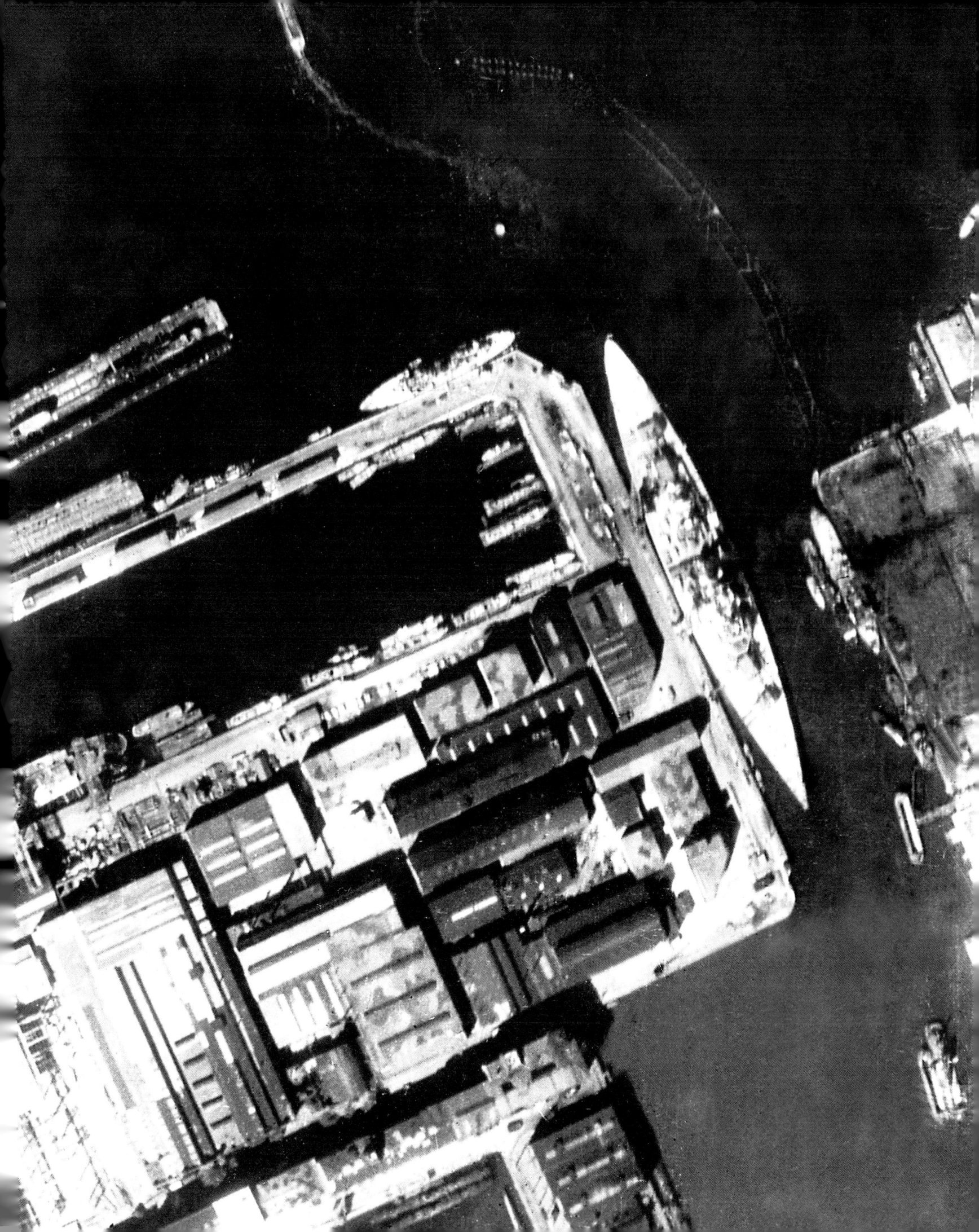

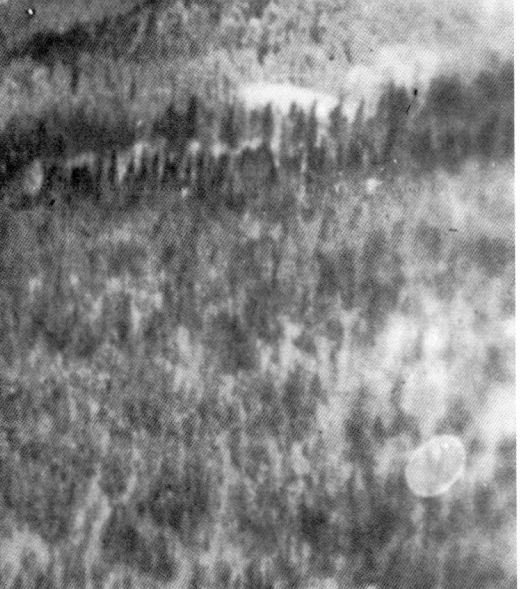

At the beginning of 1942 a decision was made to send *Tirpitz* to Norway. The operation, called Polarnacht, was completed without any interruptions. The British, vigilant as ever, searched for the battleship, but it took a week to locate the ship – she was finally spotted in Faettenfjord near Trondheim on 25 January 1942.
IWM

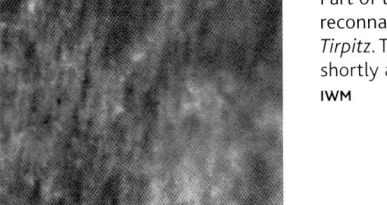

Part of the battleship's centre section photographed by a reconnaissance Spitfire that flew low over the unsuspecting *Tirpitz*. This photograph was taken near the end of January, shortly after the *Tirpitz* was relocated to Norway.
IWM

Tirpitz spent most of the initial period after the relocation to Norway moored to a jetty in Faettenfjord. The ship left the fjord for its first operation, codenamed Sportpalast, to attack convoy PQ12. The battleship sailed from Trondheim with Vice Admiral Ciliax as the task force commander. This photograph was taken a few days after the ship's return from this operation.
S Breyer collection

Tirpitz photographed by British reconnaissance aircraft moored in Faettenfjord. Judging by the camouflage scheme this photograph may have been taken shortly before Operation Sportpalast or, more probably, immediately afterwards.
S Breyer collection

Because of the increasing frequency of British air raids, the number of anti-aircraft guns on the ship was increased. The major changes in the battleship's AA armament occurred between March and June 1942. The *Tirpitz* was armed with the new quadruple Flak 35 guns (Vierling L38). The *Tirpitz* was equipped with eight of these mountings, which gave it 48 additional 20mm barrels. In this photograph the *Tirpitz* is anchored in Faettenfjord in the beginning of June 1942, with the new anti-aircraft guns installed on B turret and on the forward superstructure.
S Breyer collection

The battleship spent the majority of its time in Faettenfjord waiting for Allied convoys. The monotonous routine was sometimes interrupted by exercises with other ships that happened to be in the region, but fuel shortages suffered by the German navy in Norway caused the battleship to spend most of its time stationary in the fjord.
S Breyer collection

LEFT: A view from the captain's bridge of some of the *Tirpitz*'s crew going about their domestic duties – in the background the men are folding blankets after cleaning them.
NHC

RIGHT: The men were given various tasks to break the routine. One of the most regular was repainting the ship in a new camouflage pattern – here in Faettenfjord *Tirpitz*'s summer scheme is being changed because of the planned relocation of the battleship further north to Bogen Bay near Narvik.
S Breyer collection

The men could not go ashore for entertainment, so entertainment came to them – here a full house on the quarterdeck of the *Tirpitz* watches a dance routine.
NHC

RIGHT: Service on board the *Tirpitz* was not easy. The ship spent most of its time away from ports and bigger cities so the men were not allowed much leave. Work on the ship's camouflage helped deflect the monotony and discomfort suffered by men waiting for action.
NHC

Tirpitz needed tugs to navigate the narrow fjords. In this photograph one of the tugs, probably *Arngast*, is manoeuvring the *Tirpitz* with a stern line.
NHC

ABOVE: This photograph taken by Schäfer in Faettenfjord in July 1942 shows the modified superstructure after the ship was repainted in striped camouflage in preparation for Operation Rosselsprüng in early 1942.
Photograph by Schäfer, from the collection of S Breyer

Photograph of the remodelled superstructure made for the OKM (*Tirpitz* G.Kdos No 29). show the new superstructure. During the refit the side and the rear parts of the bridge superstructure were enclosed to protect against the weather.
Photograph by Schäfer, from the collection of S Breyer

ABOVE: Battleship *Tirpitz* in Bogen Bay near Narvik. The ship already has the new 'striped' camouflage with light grey C and D main gun turrets. They were repainted from time to time, covered with canvas or otherwise camouflaged depending on the battleship's area of operations. Based on these changes it can be quite accurately established where the ship operated in a given period.
S Breyer collection

LEFT: Another photograph taken during the ship's stay in Bogen Bay in July. This striped camouflage pattern is usually said to consist of four colours, but as suggested by this picture, there was also a fifth colour on the front part of B turret (a lighter shade of green). This colour can also be found in other parts of the ship seen on photographs and in films made in that period.
Photograph by Drüppel, from the collection of S Breyer

Battleship *Tirpitz* in Bogen Bay, before or after Operation Rösselsprung. In the background is the heavy cruiser *Admiral Hipper*.
M Skwiot collection

Tirpitz with destroyer escorts photographed in the second half of July 1942.
M Skwiot collection

Battleship *Tirpitz* surrounded by torpedo nets in Bogen Bay, photographed in the first half of July 1942 by British aerial reconnaissance. A small oil tanker is moored on the battleship's port quarter.
IWM

Tirpitz in Bogen Bay surrounded by torpedo nets. The light grey C and presumably D main gun turrets indicate that the picture was taken in the first half of July 1942.
IWM

LEFT: The *Tirpitz*, photographed from the heavy cruiser *Admiral Hipper*, returning from exercises conducted between 20 and 29 August 1942. The light cruiser *Köln* astern of the battleship also took part in those exercises.
CAW

Aft superstructure of the heavy cruiser *Admiral Hipper* photographed while returning from exercises in August 1942. In the background is the *Tirpitz*.
CAW

Two stern views of the battleship *Tirpitz* returning from exercises in August 1942 seen from one of the escorting destroyers.
M Skwiot collection; CAW collection

The battleship *Tirpitz* anchored in Kaafiord, winter 1942. Note the offset swastika painted on the starboard side of the quarterdeck.
O Dyvbig collection

A view from the forecastle of the *Tirpitz* anchored in Kaafjord in winter 1942.
S Breyer collection

The battleship *Tirpitz* anchored in Kaafiord, winter 1942. The summer camouflage is now clearly inappropriate.
O Dyvbig collection

September 1943, the *Tirpitz* is entering Altafjord after returning from Operation Sizilien/Zitronella, the attack on Spitsbergen.
M Skwiot collection

BELOW: The battleship photographed inside Kaafjord heading for the anchorage. The roofs and inclined parts of A and C turrets are painted dark grey.
S Breyer collection

The *Tirpitz* on her way back from an exercise, winter 1943. The ship is in new, winter camouflage.
CAW

Tirpitz anchored in Kaafjord, photographed by British aerial reconnaissance in the second half of September 1943 shortly before an attack by X-Craft midget submarines.
IWM

Tirpitz in Kaafjord, in September 1943, shortly before an attack by British midget submarines.
S Breyer collection

Tirpitz undergoing repairs after an attack by midget submarines in Kaafjord, photographed by British aerial reconnaissance. The operation to return the battleship to combat readiness was codenamed Paul.
IWM

Tirpitz in the summer of 1944, as repaired after the X-Craft attack.
S Breyer collection

As a result of Operation Paul, *Tirpitz* was successfully returned to combat readiness. In this photograph the ship is anchored in Kaafjord on 30 March 1944.
Bundesarchiv

Tirpitz during machinery trials on 16 March 1944 in Altafjord. The photograph was taken from the destroyer *Z30*.
S Breyer collection

The entire operation to return *Tirpitz* to combat readiness was closely observed by the British. Based on aerial reconnaissance photos and information sent by agents in Norway, they knew the pace of works and were aware that the ship would be quickly back in service. They decided to attack the battleship immediately, and the resulting carrier air strike on *Tirpitz* was called Operation Tungsten. In these photographs bombs can be seen exploding on the battleship during that raid on 3 April 1944. The photo below demonstrates how ineffective the smoke-making apparatus proved.
All IWM

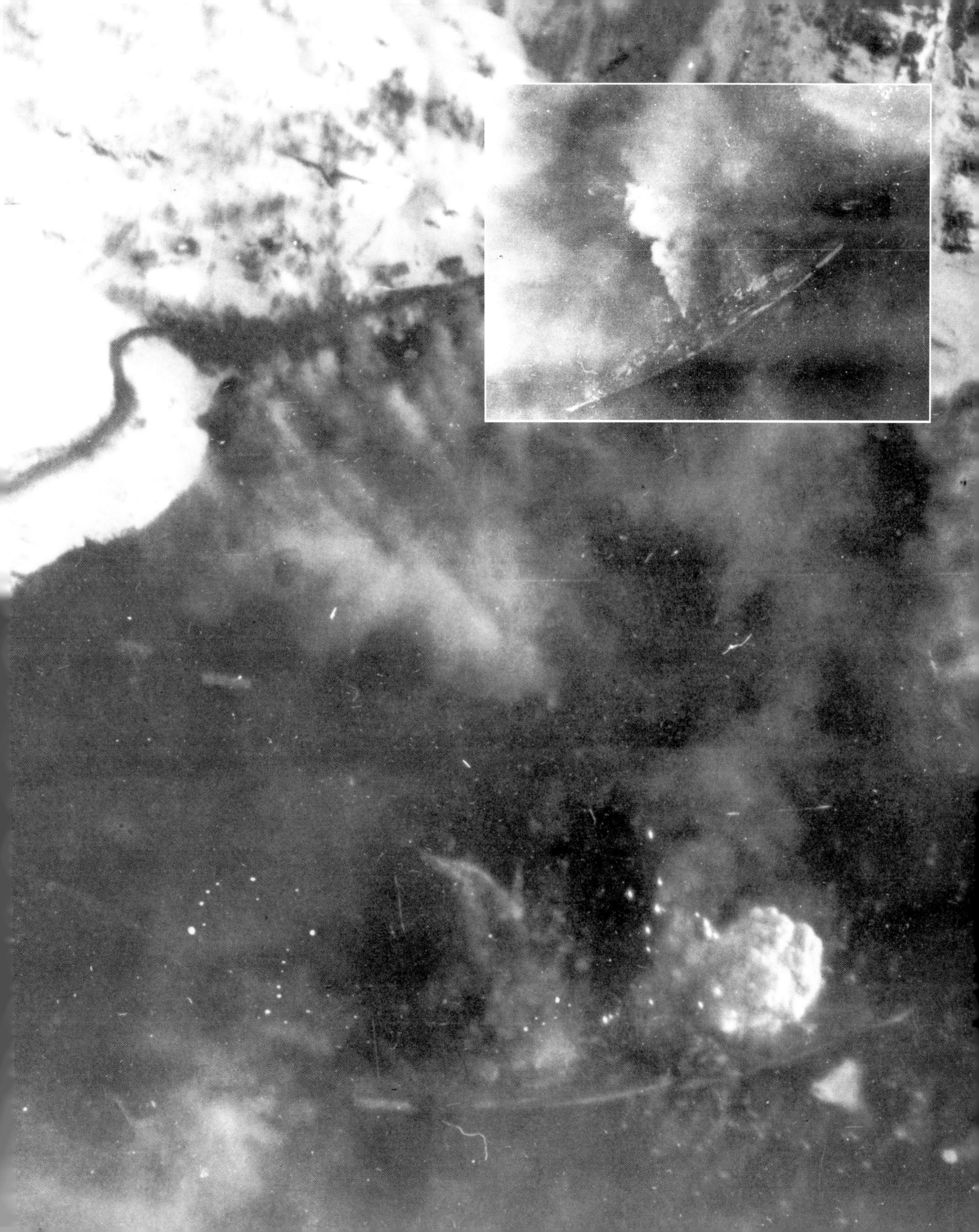

RIGHT: Two views of damage to the ship from the Tungsten raid.
S Breyer collection

BELOW: Further attacks on the battleship by both carrier aircraft and land-based bombers were so effective that from time to time the battleship was unserviceable. In this photograph taken in June 1944 the heavily damaged battleship is anchored in Kaafjord.
S Breyer collection

RIGHT: This picture, taken by British aerial reconnaissance on 12 July 1944, shows the ship in a new dappled camouflage designed to look like a peninsula of land. The ship had been damaged by carrier aircraft, but it was only with the introduction of a special heavier bomb, the Tallboy, that there was a strong possibility of actually sinking the *Tirpitz*. Bomber Command Lancasters carried out raids in September and October 1944, but despite hits by Tallboys, the ship remained afloat. However, the raids persuaded the Germans to relocate the ship further north.
IWM

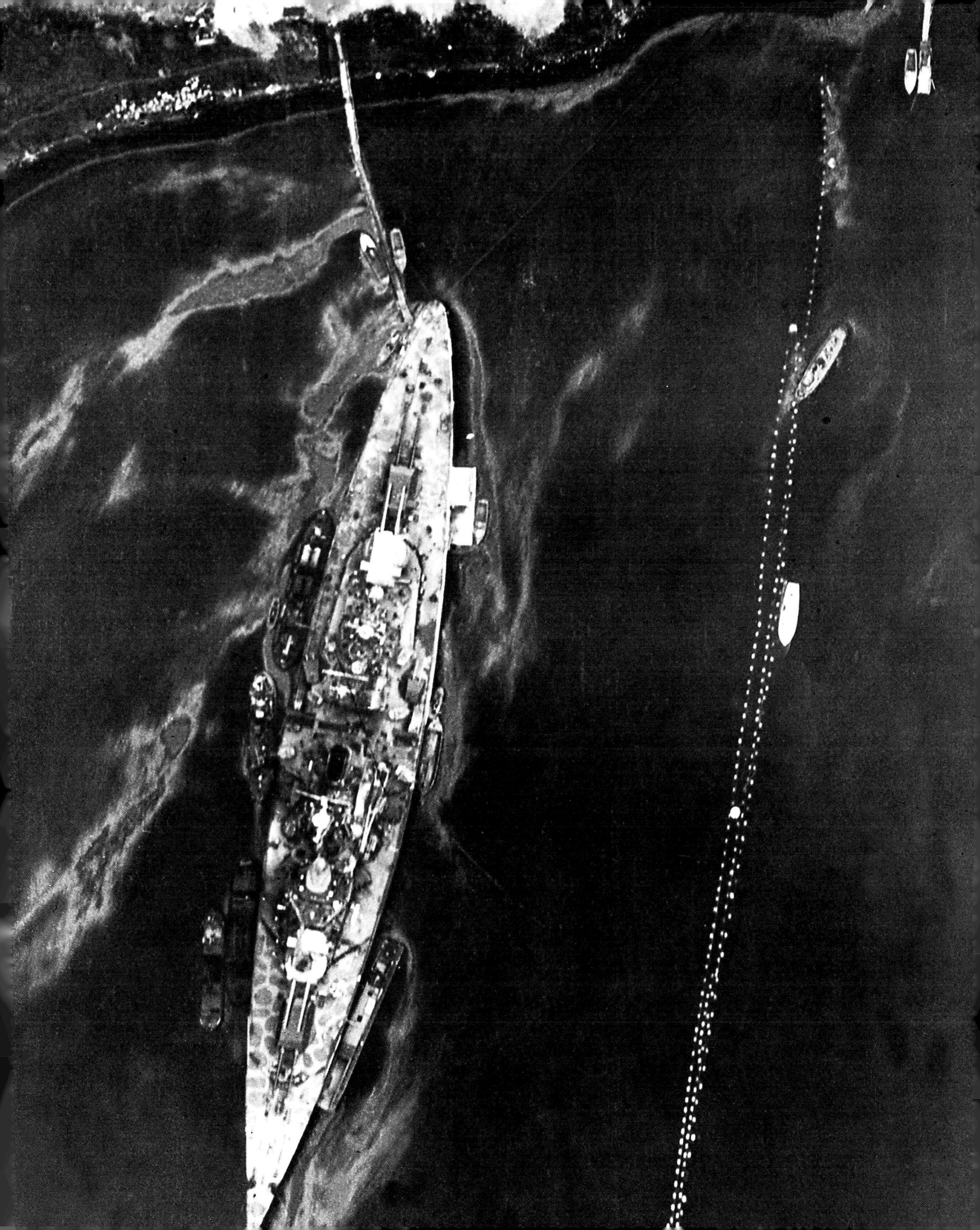

Tirpitz anchored on the landward side of Haakøy island photographed on 18 October 1944 shortly before Operation Catechism, which definitely ended the ship's operational career.
IWM

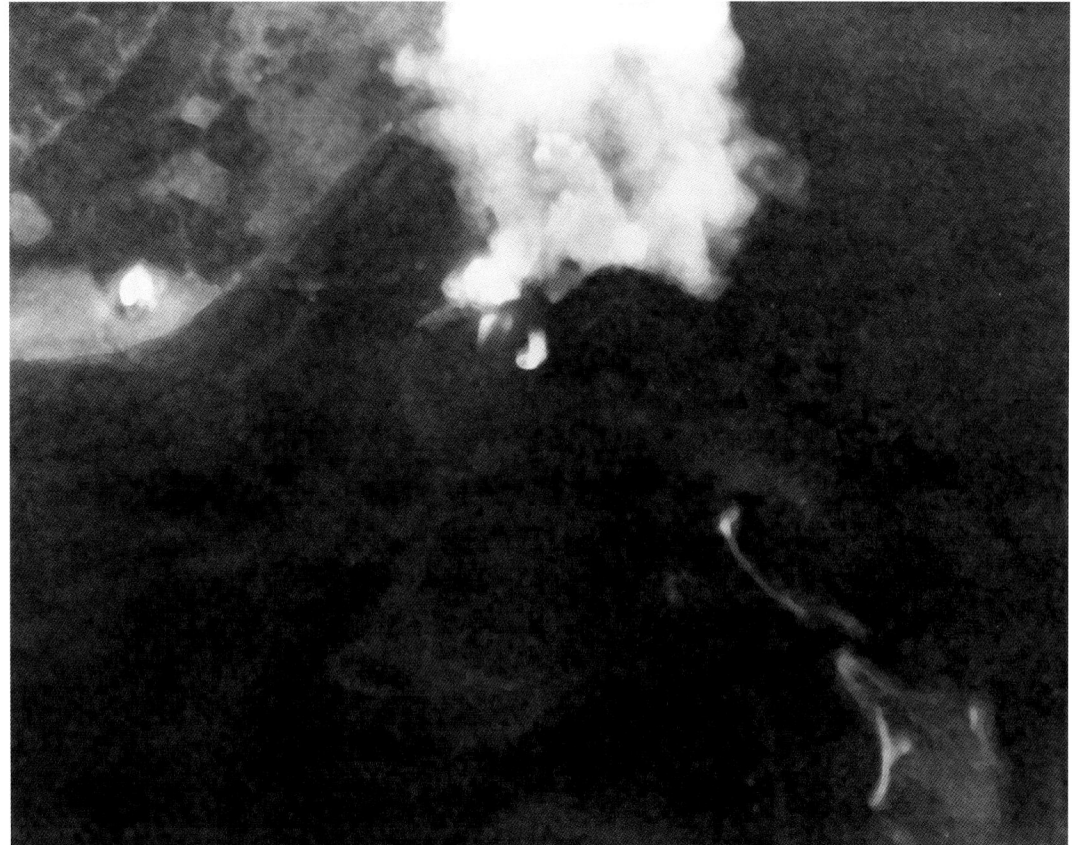

Explosion of two Tallboy bombs on the battleship during the final attack on 12 November 1944.
IWM

The capsized wreck of the battleship after two direct hits and several more near-misses by Tallboy bombs caused one of the ship's magazines to explode. The detail view shows one of the propeller shafts and its supports on the upturned hull.
IWM

APPENDIX: The Aircraft Carrier *Graf Zeppelin*

GERMAN INTEREST in the aircraft carrier can be traced to a First World War project to convert the incomplete liner *Ausonia* into a ship that could handle both seaplanes and wheeled aircraft. For the latter it featured a flying-off platform forward, with a larger landing deck above and abaft it, taking up most of the length of the ship. There were two hangar decks, and a small island to starboard built around the funnel uptakes.

The project was the work of an engineer called Jürgen Reimpell, who published a book titled *Die Unterbringen der Flugzeugen an Bord* (The Landing of Aircraft on Deck) that was promptly banned by the authorities in 1919 as a breach of security. Ever since, the project has been shrouded in mystery. It is not known if it was officially sponsored or whether the concept was Reimpell's own, but it is certain that no work was ever ordered on the 11,300grt liner. It is only

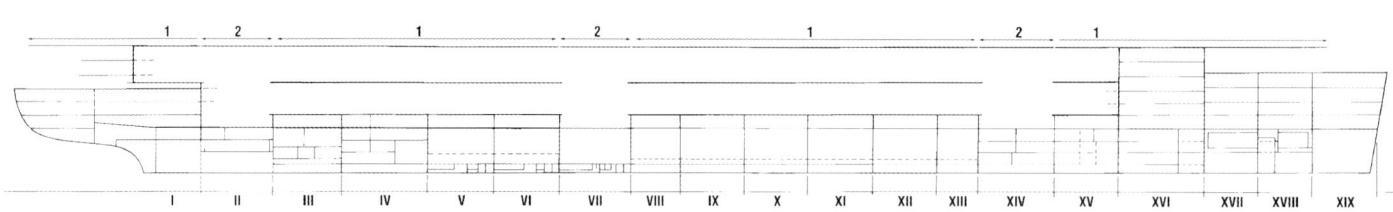

General arrangement of the carrier as first designed, with a straight stem. Later modifications included an additional, sixth, 10.5cm twin mounting forward (shown in dotted line), increasing AA firepower with quad Flakvierling 2cm mounts, strengthening the masts to carry radar and additional electronics and, most noticeably, a large funnel cap.
Drawing by S Breyer

Longitudinal section showing watertight compartments in roman numerals.
1 = flight deck.
2 = aircraft lifts.
Drawing by S Breyer

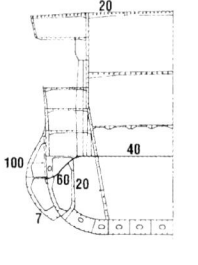

Armour thicknesses (in mm) shown at frame 137. The 100m main belt extended from frame 57 to frame 177 (covering 48 percent of waterline length), thinning to 60mm at the 15cm magazine forward and to 30mm at the bow; aft it was 80mm. A strake of 20mm horizontal armour backed the torpedo bulkhead, and the horizontal armour was thickest at the slope (and over the rudder compartment). The flight deck was armoured, but there was no protection to the hangar sides.
Drawing by S Breyer

The stern of the ship just prior to launching, taken from one of the assisting tugs. The propellers are not fitted, but note the twin rudders, angled outward as in the *Bismarck* design.
S Breyer collection

of interest in the *Graf Zeppelin* story because in 1934 the young engineer put in charge of preliminary design on the new carrier turned to Reimpell's work as a starting point – that, at least, was his intention, but when he searched, no copy of Reimpell's publication could be found in any official archive. The Naval Library's copy had been confiscated on the orders of Hermann Göring, who was not only the head of the Luftwaffe but also the Reich's Minister of Aviation; his famous dictum 'Everything that flies belongs to me' would reverberate through the history of the *Graf Zeppelin*.

The new carrier was one of a number of projects initiated shortly after Hitler came to power in 1933 and set Germany on the road to military expansion. The first requirements were defined in March 1934 and envisaged a ship of about 15,000 tons, a top speed of 33 knots and a range of 12,000 nautical miles designed to operate in the North Sea and the Atlantic. The ship would carry nine 15cm or six 20.3cm guns, plus a strong AA battery, and would be protected on a light cruiser scale; aircraft would number 60, one-third of which should have folding wings, and a flight deck of 180 metres minimum length would

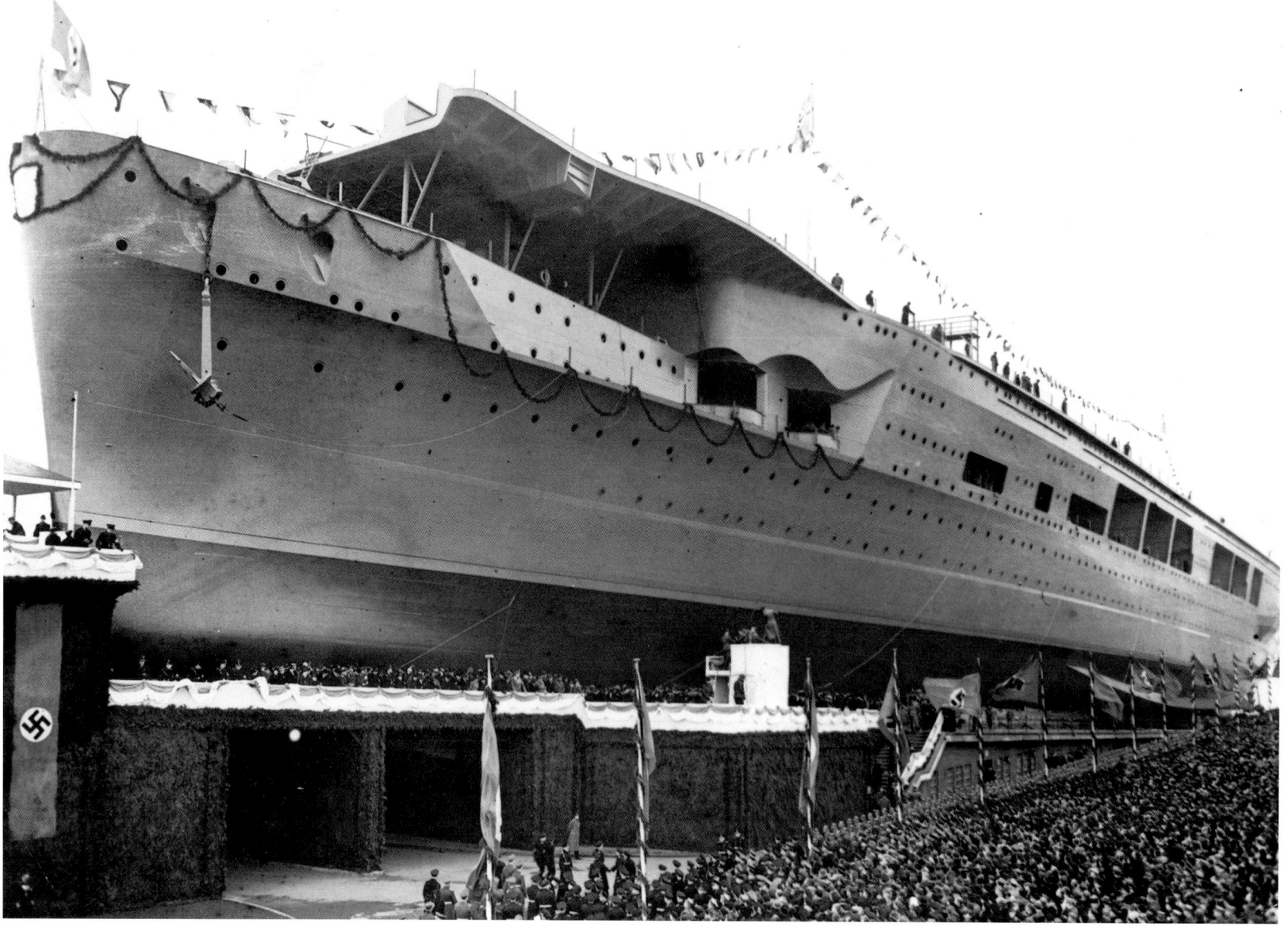

The launching ceremony, 8 December 1938. The ship was named by Countess Hella von Brandenstein-Zeppelin, the daughter of the famous airship pioneer. The principal guests were Hitler, Admiral Raeder and – demonstrating his control of everything to do with aviation – Field Marshall Hermann Göring, the C-in-C of the Luftwaffe.
S Breyer collection

Successfully launched, the hull of *Graf Zeppelin* is towed to the fitting-out berth.
CAW

The partially complete carrier moored at Stettin (Szczecin) during her temporary residence there in the summer of 1941. She had been moved west from Gotenhafen (Gdynia) when Germany invaded the Soviet Union, but returned once the German advance freed the area from the threat of Russian air attacks.
S Breyer collection

A view of the incomplete superstructure at Stettin in 1941.
S Breyer collection

BOTTOM: *Graf Zeppelin* being prepared for the return voyage to Gotenhafen in November 1941.
S Breyer collection

The carrier after her return to Gotenhafen.
M Twardowski collection

have two catapults. Preliminary design was placed in the relatively inexperienced hands of a junior constructor called Wilhelm Hadeler, and he was allowed just a year to complete the design study. This was a tough assignment given the Navy's total lack of a precedent, and inevitably a foreign ship became the model – the Royal Navy's *Courageous* class inspired the general layout, including a separate flying-off deck extending over the forecastle from the upper hangar.

At this stage there was still no clear idea how the carrier would be employed, nor could the aviation aspects be settled, since the Luftwaffe gave such a low priority to responding to the Kriegsmarine's requests for information. In an attempt to acquire some insight into technical details, one official paid a clandestine visit to HMS *Furious* during Navy Week in 1935 but gleaned little. More useful was the visit by a German commission to the Japanese carrier *Akagi* later that autumn. The Japanese Navy was apparently very open with their new Axis partners, giving them copies of plans for all the aviation deck fittings – but omitting to mention that the ship was about to be rebuilt and that all these details were already outmoded. However, as a result of this mission some modifications were made to the German design, including extending the flight deck and adding a third centreline aircraft lift.

The design was almost finalised by the end of 1935 and the first ship was ordered from Deutsche Werke, Kiel on 16 November, given the yard number 252. A second ship, known only as 'B', was planned for 1938, while the later Z Plan envisaged two more, 'C' and 'D', as well. Because Deutsche Werke was fully occupied, the keel could not be laid until 28 December the following year, after *Gneisenau* had been

Graf Zeppelin Specification

Design	1938/39	1942
Displacement (tons)	23,140	
Official standard	19,250	
Actual	23,200	c24,500
Construction	27,030	28,090
Full load	29,720	33,550
Length waterline/overall (metres)		
1938	250.00/257.30	
1939	250.00/262.50	
Breadth at waterline (metres)	27.00	31.50
Draught (metres)		
At construction displacement	7.35	
At full load displacement	7.60	8.50
Height of side (metres)	22.50	
Flight deck length (metres)	244.00	
Flight deck maximum width (metres)	30.00	
Flight deck height above waterline (metres)	15.60	
Total machinery output (shp)	200,000	
Shafts	4	
Boilers	16	
Speed (knots)		
Design maximum	35.0	
Design sustained	34.5	
Cruising (economical)	15.0	
Fuel oil capacity (tons)	5187	6740
Diesel oil capacity (m^3)	119	
Lubricating oil capacity (m^3)	222	
Fuel consumption (kg per hour)		
At cruising speed	7,800	
At 19 knots	15,200	
At sustained maximum	56,400	
Range (nm @ knots)	8,000 @ 19	
Endurance (stores and water)	7-8 weeks	
Complement (officers + men)	306 + 1720	

Armament and Equipment (1942 Design)

Main battery	16 – 15cm SK C/28 in eight MPL C/36 twin mounts
Heavy AA	12 – 10.5cm SK C/33 in six C/37 twin mounts
Light AA	22 – 3.7cm SK C/30 in eleven C/30 twin mounts
	28 – 2cm SK C/38 in seven C/38 quad mounts
Aircraft	30 Ju 87C + 12 Bf 109T
Sensors	3 radars

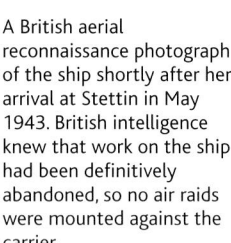

A British aerial reconnaissance photograph of the ship shortly after her arrival at Stettin in May 1943. British intelligence knew that work on the ship had been definitively abandoned, so no air raids were mounted against the carrier.
S Breyer collection

launched. The carrier was then two years on the stocks, being launched on 8 December 1938, the twenty-fourth anniversary of the 1914 Battle of the Falklands.

The design followed standard international practice in having an island superstructure on the starboard side, although this was longer and lower than those on most foreign carriers. There were two superimposed hangar decks which made the ship high-sided – indeed, the windage was calculated to equal the sail area of the huge five-masted windjammer *Preussen* – so handling the ship at slow speeds was a potential problem; this was ingeniously countered by fitting a Voith-Schneider bow thruster in a compartment right forward. Other features were less advanced, most notably the emphasis on surface gunfire: at one point in the process, in order to save space, the designer proposed placing the requested eight 15cm guns in twin mounts, which the gunnery-minded senior administrators turned into eight twin mounts, doubling the number of 15cm guns.

However, the most significant weakness of the design was the aircraft arrangements. There were two compressed-air catapults forward, but in order to use them, aircraft had to be secured to a fixed cradle in the upper hangar, moved to the flight deck and transported to the catapults on a system of rails; after launch the cradle was returned to the hangar via the rails and a special ramp. An optimistic interpretation of the launching cycle suggested one aircraft per minute could be flown off, but the compressed-air reservoirs of each catapult were exhausted after nine launches and it then took 50 minutes to recharge them. Nor were the intended aircraft ideal: the Luftwaffe was reluctant to devote much effort to the requirement for such a

A brief attempt was made to complete the ship at Kiel in late 1942, during which the bulges were added, but then Hitler decided to suspend building work on all major warships. *Graf Zeppelin* was ordered back to Gotenhaven and finally Stettin in an operation appropriately named Zugvogel (Wandering Bird). Seen here on 21 April 1943, the carrier is setting out, under tow, on her final relocation. The masts have been removed, but the new bulges can be seen.
S Breyer collection

small number of naval aircraft, so the main types were to be minimally modified versions of the Bf 109 fighter and the Ju 87 dive-bomber, although a multi-purpose bomber design (with a particular emphasis on the torpedo role) was put out to tender. The winner was the Fiesler 167, a biplane that enjoyed the short take-off characteristics its manufacturer was known for, but by the time the carrier was likely to enter service, the type would have been obsolescent. The maximum capacity of the hangars was 18 Fi 167s, 13 Ju 87s and 8 to 10 Bf 109s.

It was originally scheduled to complete *Graf Zeppelin* for sea trials in June 1940, with the ship ready for service by the end of that year, but the outbreak of war inevitably meant delays, mainly as a knock-on from the expanded U-boat building program. In September 1939 the ship was between 85 and 90 per cent complete, with main engines and boilers installed, and auxiliary machinery ready. At this point, work on the second carrier – fabricated up to the armoured deck – was stopped, to be finally abandoned in February 1940 when the steel was allocated to other uses.

After the German invasion of Norway, naval priorities changed, with greater emphasis on small craft, so in April 1940 work on the *Graf Zeppelin* was suspended and her 15cm and AA guns were removed to be employed in Norwegian coastal defences. The incomplete ship was towed to Gotenhafen (modern Gdynia) in July 1940 and laid up until just prior to the German invasion of the Soviet Union in June 1941, when the ship was moved west again (to Stettin) in case she became the target for Russian air attacks. Once the German army had penetrated deep into the USSR, the threat was deemed over and the ship was once again towed to Gotenhafen in November, where she served as a floating timber store.

By the end of 1941 the value of aircraft carriers in the naval war had been amply demonstrated at Taranto, Pearl Harbor and, most painfully for the Germans, during the pursuit of the *Bismarck*. Therefore the German naval command pressed for the completion of the *Graf Zeppelin* and at a meeting on 16 April 1942 Hitler agreed to an outline scheme for completion, as follows:

Hull and machinery (half to be operational) to be completed by summer 1943

Upgrading of aviation facilities to accommodate the only readily available aircraft types (Bf 109 and Ju 87). The Luftwaffe claimed no purpose-designed aircraft could be ready before 1946 and the ship was planned to be in service by the winter of 1943/44.

The Luftwaffe agreed to turn over 10 fighters and 22 bombers to the Kriegsmarine, but Hitler vetoed the development of a new torpedo aircraft, which he thought was of no value.

The go-ahead was given on 13 May, but it was also necessary to revamp the design, especially of the superstructure, which needed splinter-protection to the bridge and fire control centre, as well as more substantial masts to carry a fighter control station and the recently developed radar and other electronics. This in turn required a larger funnel cap to keep hot gases from the control positions. The additional weight of the island was offset by fitting asymmetrical bulges (of heavier construction on the port side), which also improved the ship's anti-torpedo protection. The AA firepower was also enhanced by adding quadruple Flakvierling 2cm mounts. At this time the plan was for the ship to carry 40 aircraft (12 Bf 109s and 28 Ju 87s) and

MAIN PICTURE: The hull was raised by the Russians and is seen here in 1947 at anchor in the Oder river. The framework forward supported camouflage netting.

RIGHT: The Russians carried out some limited repairs, as seen in this 1947 view of the flight deck aft from the searchlight platform on the funnel. The crane was a temporary addition to facilitate the work.

CENTRE: A stern view of the ship in 1947 anchored in the Oder. The port bulge is visible at the waterline, as is the framework for the camouflage netting.

FAR RIGHT: Probably taken in the middle of 1946, this view of the flight deck shows the damage caused when the Germans retreated from Stettin. On deck are the ship's four propellers, removed to prevent electrochemical corrosion to the hull. Although not obvious, the ship is lying on the bottom in shallow water.

All S Breyer collection

THE AIRCRAFT CARRIER GRAF ZEPPELIN

completion was now anticipated to be April 1943 for sea trials in August.

The ship left Gotenhafen under tow on 30 November 1942 and was docked at Deutsche Werke in Kiel for work to fit the bulges and make the two inboard shafts and their machinery operational; the ship would then be good for 25-26 knots. However, on 30 January 1943, following the humiliating Battle of the Barents Sea, Hitler issued his infamous order to decommission all the Kriegsmarine's capital ships and cancel further work on any under construction: it was, as the disgraced Admiral Raeder put it, 'the cheapest naval victory England ever won'. Work on the carrier stopped in February and in April the ship was towed to Gotenhafen in an operation appropriately codenamed Zugvogel (Wandering Bird), although she was eventually anchored off Stettin, camouflaged as a small island in a fork of the Oder river.

British aerial reconnaissance identified the carrier but it was known that the ship was neither operational nor ever likely to be, so no air attacks were thought necessary. The carrier was undisturbed until April 1945, when on the approach of Soviet forces the ship was scuttled in shallow water. On the 25th, shortly before the Red Army entered Stettin, a German demolition party set off a series of controlled explosions using depth charges that did significant local damage to parts of the ship. In the post-war Allied agreement on the disposal of German naval assets, the ship was ceded to the Soviets, who had little trouble refloating the hulk. Some in the Russian naval command wanted the ship refurbished to give them some experience of carrier operations, but this would have been a breach of the agreement, which stipulated that all damaged and incomplete ships should be scuttled in deep water.

The Soviets finally opted to use the hulk for a series of secret weapons trials, to test the resistance of the ship and the efficacy of their shells, aircraft bombs and torpedoes. Carried out in August 1947, the tests showed the ship – static, inert and unmanned as she was – to be quite tough. The bombing was neither very accurate nor, using practice bombs, very damaging, but twenty-four explosive devices of varying types and sizes up to 1000kg were set off on board; yet it still took two 53.3cm (21in) torpedoes to finish off the wreck. The battered remains of the *Graf Zeppelin* finally sank on 18 August 1947.

This section is an edited summary of Siegfried Breyers monograph Graf Zeppelin, *published by AJ Press, Gdansk in 2004. Readers are referred to that publication for further detail and more illustrations.*

TREKKING & RANDONNÉES
AUTOUR DU MONDE

directeur éditorial – STEVE RAZZETTI

TREKKING & RANDONNÉES AUTOUR DU MONDE

Directrices de la publication : Claudia dos Santos,
Mari Roberts
Directeur artistique : Peter Bosman
Directeur éditorial : Simon Pooley
Rédacteur : Ingrid Schneider
Cartographie : John Loubser, John Hall
Recherche iconographique : Sonya Meyer, Zuné Roberts
Illustrateur : Steven Felmore
Production : Myrna Collins
Indexation et correction : Sean Fraser

Reproduction par
Hirt & Carter (pty) ltd, Le Cap

Édition originale en langue anglaise
Top Treks of the World
© 2001 New Holland Publishers (UK) Ltd

Texte © 2001 : Steve Razzetti
et les autres, cités page 167
Illustrations © 2001 : New Holland Publishers
Photographies © 2001 : photographes individuels
et/ou leurs agents, cités page 167

Traduction : 5/5

© Édilarge S.A. – Éditions Ouest-France, Rennes 2001

Tous droits réservés.
Aucun extrait de cet ouvrage ne peut être reproduit, stocké dans une base
de données ou retransmis sous quelque forme ni par quelque moyen que ce soit,
électronique, mécanique, reprographique, magnétique ou autre, sans l'accord
préalable écrit des éditeurs et des détenteurs des copyrights.

N° d'éditeur : 4281.02.4,5.09.02
ISBN 2-7373-2917-5
Dépôt légal : octobre 2001

Imprimé et relié à Singapour par :
Tien Wah Press (pte) ltd
2 4 6 8 10 9 7 5 3

FAUX-TITRE *Le parc national du Tongariro, dominant le lac d'Emeraude. La forte teneur en minéraux de l'eau dans ces cratères volcaniques leur donne cette coloration unique.*

TITRE *Vus depuis une prairie parsemée de fleurs dominant le glacier de Biafo, dans le Karakoram central au Pakistan, l'Ogre et le Latok se détachent d'une manière extraordinaire.*

CI-DESSUS *Un guanaco solitaire pose devant les flèches de granit du massif de Paine, dans le parc national de Torres del Paine. Sur la droite, le curieusement nommé Nido Negro de Condores (le Nid Noir des Condors).*

PAGES SUIVANTES *Le Tongariro Crossing, l'une des randonnées d'une journée les plus appréciées en Nouvelle-Zélande, fait partie de l'itinéraire Autour de la montagne, dans le parc national de Tongariro.*

TABLE DES MATIÈRES

AVANT-PROPOS	11
INTRODUCTION	14

EUROPE 18

LA HAUTE ROUTE PYRÉNÉENNE
Pyrénées, France/Espagne — 22

LA HAUTE ROUTE CHAMONIX-ZERMATT
Alpes Pennines, France/Italie/Suisse — 26

ALTA VIA 2
Dolomites, Tyrol du Sud, Italie — 30

GRANDE RANDONNÉE 20 (GR 20)
Parc naturel régional de Corse — 34

AFRIQUE 38

DE TICHKA AU TOUBKAL
Mont Atlas, Maroc — 42

CHOGORIA ET LES ITINÉRAIRES DES SOMMETS
Parc national du mont Kenya, Kenya — 46

CANYON DE FISH RIVER
Namibie — 50

PISTES DES LOUTRES ET DU TSITSIKAMMA
Cap Sud, Afrique du Sud — 54

ASIE 58

LA ROUTE DE LYCIE
Lycie, Turquie — 62

GONDOKORO LA - DE HUSHE À CONCORDIA
Karakoram, Pakistan — 66

LA TRAVERSÉE BIAFO-HISPAR
Karakoram, Pakistan — 70

LADAKH & ZANSKAR
Himalaya, Inde — 74

DE SINGALILA À KANGCHENDZONGA
Himalaya Sikkim, Inde — 78

KANGCHENDZONGA
Kangchendzonga Himal, Népal — 82

DE JUMLA AU MONT KAILAS	
Himalaya, Népal/Tibet	86

CIRCUIT DU DHAULAGIRI	
Himalaya, Népal	90

CIRCUIT DE MANASLU ET DE L'ANNAPURNA	
Larkya Himal, Népal	94

LA RANDONNÉE DU « BONHOMME DE NEIGE »	
Himalaya, Bhoutan	98

AUSTRALASIE 102

LA PISTE DE LARAPINTA	
Chaine MacDonnell occidentale, Australie	106

DE EDEN À MALLACOOTA	
Côte Sauvage, Australie	110

LA PISTE TERRESTRE	
Tasmanie, Australie	114

TOUR DES MONTAGNES	
Tongariro, Ile du Nord, Nouvelle-Zélande	118

LA PISTE DE ROUTEBURN,	
South Westland, Ile du Sud, Nouvelle-Zélande	122

AMÉRIQUE DU NORD 126

LE GRAND CANYON	
Arizona, USA	130

LA PISTE DES APPALACHES	
De la Georgie au Maine, USA	134

AMÉRIQUE DU SUD 140

CIRCUIT DE HUAYHUASH	
Cordillère de Huayhuash, Pérou	144

CIRCUIT D'ALPAMAYO	
Cordillère Blanche, Pérou	148

CIRCUIT D'ILLAMPU	
Cordillère Royale, Bolivie	152

TORRES DEL PAINE	
Patagonie, Chili	156

BIOGRAPHIES DES AUTEURS	160
BIBLIOGRAPHIE	164
REMERCIEMENTS	165
INDEX	166

AVANT-PROPOS

« Le corps parcourt la montagne et l'esprit se libère... »

Ainsi s'exprimait Hsu Hsia-K'o, poète chinois du XVIIᵉ siècle. Il y a longtemps que j'ai fait mienne cette pensée mais je serais tenté de remplacer la montagne par le terme plus général de « grands espaces »...

J'ai passé le plus clair de ma vie à parcourir la montagne, mais j'ai aussi trouvé dans les grands espaces, dans la savane déserte ou sur l'océan un vrai ressourcement spirituel, même s'il manquait peut-être l'occasionnelle poussée d'adrénaline.

Nous passons tant de temps à nous efforcer de survivre, à supporter les contraintes de l'existence, qu'il serait trop facile de se prendre pour une fourmi insignifiante au sein de la fourmilière universelle. Perdant de vue la signification même d'Être, les grandes étendues sauvages nous permettent de retrouver nos repères.

Je connais en Angleterre une colline qui s'élève, telle la proue d'un grand navire, au-dessus d'une immense vallée verdoyante. Son sommet, entouré des remparts crénelés d'un fort préhistorique, se dresse à 190 m au-dessus du niveau de la mer, mais quand le vent couche l'herbe jaune et que les nuages bas défilent dans le ciel, l'endroit est tout aussi stimulant que n'importe quel sommet alpin. Je m'y rends souvent pour me rappeler qu'il y a autre chose dans la vie que des appareils photo, des ordinateurs, des e-mails et des factures.

Mais comment définir les « grands espaces » ? La beauté est dans l'œil de celui qui regarde. Tout est relatif. Nous n'avons pas souvent l'occasion de profiter de vraies grandes étendues sauvages – elles se font rares et distantes. Les nécessités fondamentales sont peut-être ce qui les définit le mieux : trouver à manger, à boire, par exemple, la quête d'un lieu pour se reposer ou dormir, trouver le bon itinéraire. Parfois même la simple survie. S'éloigner de la civilisation n'est pas fuir la réalité mais aller vers elle.

Cet ouvrage vous emmènera vers de tels endroits. Ces parcours de randonnées ont été soigneusement choisis par des voyageurs expérimentés. Ils constituent des objectifs concrets pour le marcheur enthousiaste, tout en présentant des difficultés suffisantes pour en faire des aventures mémorables. Mais avant tout, pour vous reposer l'esprit.

Le grand explorateur montagnard écossais Norman Collie a écrit :

« ... Il y a encore assez de mystère dans les forêts, les grands lacs, les montagnes et les torrents pour satisfaire tous ceux qui ont des yeux pour voir et qui veulent comprendre. »

Alors, en route, et profitez-en.

JOHN CLEARE, WILTSHIRE, ANGLETERRE

PAGES PRÉCÉDENTES, DE GAUCHE À DROITE *Un randonneur s'imprègne des merveilles du printemps sur les rives de l'Ordesa dans les Pyrénées ; l'arrivée est en vue ! Des randonneurs sur la piste des Loutres approchent de Nature's Valley.*
À GAUCHE *La piste de Manang à Thorung Phedi, Népal. Les premières neiges hivernales transforment la vallée de Marsyangdi, au-dessus de Manang, en un étincelant pays des merveilles.*
VERSO *Campement dans la vallée d'ablation du côté nord du glacier de Hispar, à Haghura Shanga Lichang, Pakistan. Une oasis de verdure bienvenue dans un paysage aussi désolé et sans vie apparente.*

INTRODUCTION
par Steve Razzetti

L'espèce humaine a toujours montré une nette tendance au nomadisme. La chasse entraîna l'homme préhistorique hors d'Afrique, à travers l'Europe et l'Asie, jusqu'en Australie où il arriva il y a 50 000 ans. De la même manière, il fit la traversée de Sibérie en Alaska, vers les Amériques il y a près de 14 000 ans. Les premiers récits d'explorations humaines sont relatés dans des hiéroglyphes égyptiens datant de 4 000 ans av. J.-C., et jusqu'à l'an 1500 de notre ère, les explorateurs et les cartographes les plus accomplis venaient des mondes chinois et arabe.

Au XIVe siècle, relativement tard dans la course à l'exploration de la planète, plusieurs personnages hauts en couleur appareillèrent des ports d'Europe avec comme motivations premières les sempiternelles justifications de tout effort humain : le développement commercial et le prosélytisme religieux. Avec le XVe siècle arriva la Renaissance, l'émergence d'États souverains puissants – Angleterre, Espagne, Portugal et France – et le début de l'ère coloniale. Au même moment, le développement d'une classe aisée de marchands dans toute l'Europe conduisit à l'épanouissement d'une activité artistique et stimula l'effort scientifique. Vers le XVIIe siècle, les idéaux de la Renaissance commencèrent à trouver leur expression dans les motivations des voyageurs, et depuis cette époque jusqu'à nos jours, une riche tradition littéraire rassemble les récits et les illustrations de ceux qui ont voyagé pour le simple plaisir, comme de ceux qui étaient en quête de connaissance géographique, anthropologique ou scientifique.

Les lieux les plus reculés et les plus exotiques deviennent de plus en plus accessibles, mais la facilité avec laquelle on se procure un billet d'avion ou une réservation de vacances ne signifie pas que le voyage à pied soit devenu plus facile que par le passé. Une part considérable de préparation et d'anticipation est nécessaire pour accomplir un voyage sans désagrément et en toute sécurité.

La plupart des destinations décrites dans cet ouvrage sont extrêmement lointaines, situées dans des régions inaccessibles du monde, dans des pays où il n'y a aucun moyen de transports intérieurs vraiment fiables et où l'eau potable et la nourriture sont presque un luxe. La planification et la réussite d'un tel voyage en de tels endroits demandent une bonne dose de patience et une grande faculté d'adaptation. Les appareils tombent en panne, la météo est capricieuse. Les moyens de communication sont peu fiables. Attendez-vous à devoir réfléchir en marchant, rester optimiste et adapter vos plans aux conditions trouvées sur place. La réussite de votre voyage ne se mesurera pas au nombre d'objectifs atteints, mais à la part de bonheur que vous en aurez retirée !

Tout d'abord, il faut choisir le mode ou le style de randonnée le plus approprié, et un choix éclairé et précoce optimisera singulièrement vos chances de faire un voyage qui vous satisfaira pleinement. Quatre options fondamentales s'offrent à vous : le « sac à dos » (vous emportez tout avec vous), les possibilités d'hébergement et de restauration locales (ce que l'on appelle les « tea-house » pour randonnées au Népal), le mode « expédition » (avec porteurs locaux ou bêtes de somme engagés par vous-même) ou enfin passer par un tour operateur (qui organisera tout pour vous). Il se peut que votre choix soit limité par le lieu où vous voulez voyager et le temps dont vous disposez, mais vous trouverez dans les pages suivantes un résumé des avantages concernant chaque solution.

CI-DESSUS *On goûte la cuisine locale dans une halte/salon de thé au Népal. Nourriture et hébergement requièrent peu d'effort ou de préparation avec ce mode de randonnée.*

CI-DESSUS *Des bêtes de somme sont mises à contribution pour transporter les bagages des randonneurs dans les espaces sauvages. Un conditionnement soigneux et des sacs solides sont essentiels.*

INTRODUCTION

LE SAC À DOS : c'est la souplesse et l'absolue liberté d'un côté, mais aussi l'obligation de vous « coltiner » des charges lourdes, et de vous nourrir presque essentiellement d'aliments lyophilisés. Vous ferez moins de kilomètres dans la journée, mais il vous faudra néanmoins encore assez d'énergie en arrivant pour établir votre campement, ramasser du bois, aller chercher de l'eau, cuisiner et tout remettre en ordre. Le temps que vous passerez dans la nature sera limité par la quantité de vivres et de combustible que vous pourrez transporter.

TEA-HOUSE : suivant le lieu où vous voulez voyager, cette méthode peut varier du plus grand luxe à la plus pénible des épreuves. Sur les parcours favoris du Népal, les auberges locales se sont transformées en hôtels sophistiqués, offrant des chambres individuelles, des chauffe-pieds, des douches chaudes, des solariums et une gamme de mets et de bières qui n'a rien à envier à n'importe quelle station des Alpes. Là, vous pouvez raisonnablement envisager une sortie de trois semaines avec pour seul bagage vos vêtements et votre sac de

couchage. Alors que dans le Karakoram, ce mode de déplacement vous imposera de connaître plusieurs langues locales, de dormir dans des taudis, et de faire d'un peu de pain et de lait de chèvre votre ration quotidienne. Votre rayon d'action dépendra de la disponibilité en vivres et en abris.

EXPÉDITION : pour un groupe d'amis partageant le même objectif, c'est certainement la meilleure manière et la plus économique de partir. En engageant des porteurs locaux et des bêtes de somme, vous serez effectivement autonome pendant un bon mois et adapterez vos plans aux conditions rencontrées au fil des jours. Ce mode de déplacement est particulièrement adapté dans l'Himalaya et dans les Andes, et une équipe d'autochtones

CI-DESSUS *Randonneurs près du camp de Mackinder, mont Kenya. Porter votre propre barda peut restreindre le temps passé en plein air, mais vous serez certain d'en profiter en solitaire.*

CI-DESSUS *Camp de base pour K2, sur le glacier Godwin-Austen. Des tentes pour le mode expédition dans de telles régions doivent pouvoir supporter de fortes chutes de neige et des vents très forts.*

vous apportera sa connaissance du terrain et vous familiarisera avec ses langues et coutumes.

TOUR OPÉRATEUR : « Le voyage aventure », organisé par l'une des multiples agences spécialisées dans la découverte des grands espaces, peut paraître paradoxal ; néanmoins, ce mode de déplacement est de plus en plus apprécié. En vous inscrivant pour un parcours préétabli à dates fixes, vous vous épargnerez la peine et le temps d'organiser la logistique du voyage, mais vous vous engagerez aussi à suivre un itinéraire préétabli en compagnie d'un groupe d'inconnus. C'est souvent la seule solution pour nombre de gens qui mènent une vie professionnelle très active, mais cela implique de bien choisir le tour opérateur et de posséder des qualités indéniables de sociabilité.

Dans la mesure où nous vivons presque tous des vies sédentaires, il conviendra de prêter une attention toute particulière à la forme physique, pour affronter une longue marche

dans la nature. Votre forme elle-même bénéficiera de la marche, mais meilleure sera votre condition physique au départ, meilleures seront vos chances de surmonter les rigueurs d'un exercice dur et prolongé. De même, rester en bonne santé dans un environnement sauvage demande quelques précautions et compétences. Le bon sens recommande de faire un bilan médical et dentaire complet avant le départ, et dans certains pays, un programme de vaccinations serait prudent, voire obligatoire. Il est essentiel d'emporter une trousse médicale complète de premiers secours.

La plupart des parcours décrits dans cet ouvrage atteignent des altitudes qui, sans une acclimatation correcte, feront sans doute apparaître le « mal des montagnes » dans tout ou partie du

CI-DESSUS *Alors que le côté festif de la randonnée « salon de thé » peut plaire à certains, ceux qui préfèrent la tranquillité choisiront de voyager dans un groupe autonome.*

CI-DESSUS *L'ascension d'un sommet qui ne pose pas de problèmes techniques particuliers, comme le Gondokoro au Pakistan, est une excellente acclimatation pour la traversée, plus difficile, du Gondokoro La.*

groupe. Prenez soin de bien comprendre la physiologie de base de cet état potentiellement grave. Le mal des montagnes peut être mortel. Soyez conscient qu'il n'a absolument rien à voir avec l'âge, le sexe, la forme physique ou l'expérience, et soyez prêt à revoir votre itinéraire pour prendre en compte les différences de temps d'acclimatation à l'intérieur de votre groupe. La règle est de ne jamais poursuivre une ascension en présence de symptômes du mal des montagnes, et de redescendre si ces symptômes s'aggravent alors que vous êtes resté à la même altitude.

De même, la plupart des parcours de cet ouvrage se situent dans des régions où soleil et sécheresse de l'air se conjuguent pour faire de la déshydratation un risque très réel. Les signes de déshydratation sont souvent les mêmes – et le mal tout aussi grave – que ceux du mal des montagnes. Il est primordial de boire beaucoup d'eau potable. Il est maintenant admis que porter de l'eau à ébullition suffit à la rendre stérile, mais cela n'est pas toujours possible en situation de campagne. La teinture d'iode est également fiable et la taille et la qualité des bou-

reurs si une évacuation d'urgence est nécessaire. Pensez aussi à la manière dont vous emporterez votre argent, et changez-le en monnaie locale. Il est en effet peu probable que les Indiens Quechua du Pérou acceptent les chèques de voyage ou les cartes bancaires…

Par souci de courtoisie et de conscience écologiste, prêtez l'attention qu'il convient à l'impact culturel et environnemental d'un voyage dans ces contrées lointaines. Par définition, beaucoup de ces lieux abritent des écosystèmes fragiles et des populations aux traditions et coutumes très éloignées des nôtres. Faites que votre voyage soit aussi écologique que possible en adoptant une stratégie appropriée d'élimination des déchets, des combustibles, etc., et en vous y tenant. N'ignorez pas les codes d'habillement locaux, l'étiquette du pays et les comportements qui conviennent, et si vous êtes photographe, préparez-vous à faire le sacrifice d'une excellente photo si le sujet indigène ne déborde pas de joie à l'idée d'être photographié. Demandez lui toujours la permission avant.

teilles d'eau feront l'objet d'un soin attentif. Les autres points à prendre en considération, avant de s'élancer vers les cimes, sont l'assurance et la manière d'organiser une opération de sauvetage en cas d'accident. Les assurances classiques ne suffiront sans doute pas, et vous devrez soigneusement choisir la police d'assurance approprié auprès des courtiers spécialisés en couverture d'expéditions. Lisez bien tout et prévoyez comment entrer en communication avec vos assu-

Enfin, partez et explorez. Découvrez de nouveaux sommets, embrassez du regard votre environnement, appréciez les cultures locales et prenez le temps de méditer sur les expériences exaltantes qui vous attendent.

Mais surtout, prenez du plaisir.

CI-DESSUS *Les indigènes, comme ces Indiens Aymara en Bolivie, mènent une vie simple et heureuse, et répondent avec enthousiasme à tous ceux qui manifestent un intérêt pour leur langue et leur culture.*

CI-DESSUS *Le besoin des Occidentaux de distribuer des bonbons a transformé les enfants, le long des pistes les plus fréquentées du Népal, en quémandeurs insistants, et devrait être fermement refréné. L'amitié suffit.*

EUROPE

LA HAUTE ROUTE DES PYRÉNÉES | LA HAUTE ROUTE DE CHAMONIX À ZERMATT | ALTA VIA 2 | SENTIER DE GRANDE RANDONNÉE 20

EUROPE

*Bouger est notre nature ;
le calme absolu, c'est la mort*

PASCAL

CI-DESSUS *La forme imposante et reconnaissable du Matterhorn est si saisissante qu'elle hypnotise, pour ainsi dire, pendant des heures les marcheurs à chaque passage.*
CI-CONTRE *Un marcheur se fraye un chemin le long des pistes herbues des Dolomites, avec les Stella Towers en classique toile de fond.*
PAGES PRÉCÉDENTES *Les vie ferrate (voies en fer), en Italie, ne sont pas faites pour les cœurs sensibles ! Souvent entièrement exposées aux éléments, elles offrent des passages mémorables le long des murailles surplombant le vide.*

Bien qu'il soit indéniable que la plupart des continents aient donné naissance à des civilisations sophistiquées, variées et magnifiques bien avant l'avènement de l'ère chrétienne et la montée en puissance de l'Europe, il est tout aussi indéniable que le monde dans lequel nous vivons, dans ce qu'il a de meilleur ou de pire, est principalement le produit des efforts européens.

Les valeurs économiques et culturelles de l'Europe furent exportées énergiquement et quelquefois violemment vers les contrées les plus reculées du globe pendant l'époque coloniale, et leur influence a été primordiale dans tous les domaines, de la démographie à l'architecture. La langue est peut-être le baromètre le plus simple et le plus éloquent pour refléter ce foisonnement d'idées. Pour voyager en Amérique du Sud, il faut parler espagnol ; en Amérique du Nord, dans tout le sous-continent indien, en Australie et en Nouvelle-Zélande, l'anglais suffira ; quant au vaste continent africain, le français, l'allemand, le portugais, l'anglais et le hollandais ont chacun leur place.

Avec en arrière-plan la reconstruction d'après-guerre, la dépression économique et la découverte soudaine que la domination du monde est une chose du passé, beaucoup d'Européens ont recherché dans leur propre pays des moyens d'évasion et d'aventures, et ils ont réalisé qu'ils étaient assis sur une mine d'or. L'alpinisme a peut-être commencé à l'époque victorienne, réservé d'abord aux classes moyenne et supérieure, mais après la Seconde Guerre mondiale les choses ont vite changé. Guides et magazines se sont mis à proliférer, des clubs d'escalade, de marche et de cyclisme ont surgi dans chaque ville, des sentiers de randonnée ont été imaginés, tracés et balisés, les journaux ont relaté abondamment les exploits téméraires de toutes sortes d'aventuriers, et ainsi a débuté l'engouement pour les grands espaces.

Cet ouvrage compte l'essentiel des randonnées au long cours dans les zones montagneuses sauvages les plus célèbres et les plus spectaculaires d'Europe. Toutes représentent des défis, physiques et logistiques, toutes ont beaucoup de succès et vous feront vous interroger sur les raisons qui ont pu donner envie aux Européens d'aller chercher l'aventure à l'étranger alors que de telles merveilles étaient à leurs portes.

Dans les Alpes, la traditionnelle Haute Route entre Chamonix et Zermatt – du mont Blanc au Mont cervin – représente 65 km, englobant onze cols parmi les plus hauts des Alpes. La « Alta Via 2 », traversant les Dolomites de Bressanone à Feltre, dans le Tyrol italien du Sud, est une féerie de tours perpendiculaires de calcaire rose, de *vias ferratas* et d'idylliques plaines boisées.

Arrivant juste après les Alpes en termes d'altitude et de majesté grandiose, les Pyrénées comprennent plus de 120 sommets dépassant les 3 000 m. Elles constituent une frontière naturelle superbe entre la France et l'Espagne. Ignorées par les amateurs de montagnes et les randonneurs pendant des décennies, alors que les Alpes occupaient la vedette, les vallées perdues et les vastes étendues désertiques et immaculées d'alpages qui constituent la plus grande partie de la chaîne pyrénéenne ne furent découvertes par les amateurs de plein air que relativement récemment. Dans les pages qui suivent, vous trouverez une description très stimulante d'une partie de la Haute Route des Pyrénées (HRP), une odyssée de 45 jours le long de la ligne de crêtes, de l'Atlantique à la Méditerranée.

La Corse est représentée comme une île dans votre atlas, mais en réalité c'est une chaîne de montagnes au milieu de la mer Méditerranée. Bien que sous administration française depuis 200 ans, la Corse appartient géographiquement, historiquement et linguistiquement à l'Italie et son histoire, toujours haute en couleur, fut souvent violente. L'intérieur se compose d'un inextricable labyrinthe de vallées, de pics arides et dénudés de granit rose et gris, dont beaucoup culminent à plus de 2 000 m. Tout le long des crêtes, de Calenzana à Conca, le sentier de Grande Randonnée n° 20 (GR 20) constitue une expédition sérieuse mais très appréciée de 180 km.

LA HAUTE ROUTE DES PYRÉNÉES

par Hilary Sharp

La Haute Route des Pyrénées s'étend de l'océan Atlantique à la Méditerranée, matérialisant la frontière entre la France et l'Espagne. D'après la légende, Hercule, en des temps anciens, ne put s'empêcher de séduire Pyrène, la ravissante fille du roi de Cerdagne, avant de partir pour une mission. Désespérée par le départ de son amant, la princesse partit sur ses traces et fut dévorée par des animaux sauvages. À son retour, ravagé par le chagrin, Hercule érigea une tombe pour sa bien-aimée en empilant d'énormes rochers qui formèrent les Pyrénées.

Les pics d'ici sont plus petits que ceux des Alpes, mais non moins impressionnants et le contraste est frappant entre les chaînes escarpées du versant espagnol et les vallées boisées et pentues du versant français du massif. Les Pyrénées comptent trois parcs nationaux, dont deux sont sur le parcours de la Haute Route Pyrénéenne : en France, le parc national des Pyrénées et en Espagne, le Parque Nacional de Ordesa y Monte Perdido.

Le premier véritable explorateur de ces contrées fut le géologue et botaniste français Louis-François Ramond de Carbonnières, qui, à partir de 1787, gravit de nombreux pics et cols. En 1802, il fut l'instigateur de la première ascension (par deux guides français, Laurens et Rondeau, et un berger espagnol) du mont Perdido, à 3 355 m, le troisième pic de la chaîne. L'une des fleurs indigènes des Pyrénées fut baptisée Ramondie des Pyrénées en son honneur.

La Haute Route Pyrénéenne commence au lac de Bious d'Artigues, un lac bleu profond dominé par le pic du Midi d'Ossau (2 884 m), imposant et facilement reconnaissable par son double sommet. La piste passe en bas de la face sud de la montagne et la contourne par l'est, traversant des prairies que les iris sauvages transforment, en été, en un superbe tapis bleu. Plus haut, les gentianes tachetées de jaune remplacent les iris, jusqu'au grand champ de bloc rocheux qui surplombe le lac de Peygeret. La difficulté de la montée est compensée par les magnifiques points de vue, et en arrivant au col de Peygeret (2 300 m) vous serez récompensés par le spectacle impressionnant qu'offre la face sud du pic du Midi d'Ossau, juste au-dessus. Plus loin, le Palas (2 974 m) et le Balaitous (3 144 m), vous indiquent la direction que vous suivrez le lendemain, et juste en dessous, près d'un lac scintillant, se trouve le refuge de Pombie.

Aux premières heures de la matinée, le soleil accroche le sommet du pic du Midi d'Ossau, faisant rougir son flanc à mesure que vous descendez les prairies parsemées de digitales et de chardons bleus des Pyrénées. Avec un peu de chance, vous verrez des troupeaux d'isards, le chamois des Pyrénées, galopant en haut des versants. Plus bas, des chevaux et des ânes broutent paisiblement pendant que des bergers gardent leurs moutons. La vallée de l'Arious sera la principale ascension de cette journée, une grimpette agréable et régulière débouchant de la forêt vers un paysage grand ouvert parsemé de grosses pierres rondes, vers le col d'Arrious (2 259 m).

EN HAUT *Les dernières pentes sous le col de la Fache (2 664 m) peuvent rester étonnamment enneigées. Glisser ici signifierait un bain forcé et glacial dans le lac de la Fache.*

ENCART *Un départ de bonne heure depuis le refuge de Pombie vous permettra d'admirer le lever du soleil au pic du Midi d'Ossau (2 884 m).*

À DROITE *Le Petit Vignemale est un bon détour, avec d'excellentes vues à 360 degrés. Ici, regardant en direction du nord par-dessus le parc national et le lac de Gaube.*

PYRÉNÉES, FRANCE/ESPAGNE

CI-DESSUS *Le passage d'Orteig termine la journée de façon spectaculaire, traversant bien au-dessus du lac d'Artouste pour atteindre le refuge d'Arremoulit.*

Deux itinéraires différents permettent d'accéder au refuge d'Arremoulit. Par temps humide ou orageux, vous devez prendre le sentier qui descend vers le lac d'Artouste, puis suivre un chemin dégagé et facile qui remonte vers le refuge. Mais par temps sec, il est beaucoup plus intéressant et moins pénible de prendre le passage d'Orteig, qui contourne le flanc de la montagne bien au-dessus du lac, avec une courte section assez scabreuse le long d'une main-courante en câble. Mais l'émotion est de courte durée et vous retrouverez très vite la sécurité d'un terrain relativement plat jusqu'au chalet, entouré de plusieurs lacs bleu azur.

Le col d'Arremoulit (2 448 m), que l'on atteint en suivant un sentier balisé de cairns, à travers de gros blocs de rochers, vous conduit à la frontière espagnole et vous découvrirez un panorama splendide – le sommet de Lurien (2 753 m) au loin derrière vous, et devant, le haut pic de Balaitous qui se reflète dans le lac en contrebas. Le chemin contourne les lacs Arriel puis bifurque vers l'est, contournant le flanc de la montagne, bien au-dessus du rio Aguas Limpias, vers le lac artificiel de Respumoso. Abondance de fleurs – barbajoue, gentiane, coquelicots, herbe aux panthères, arméria, ciboulette sauvage, et bien sûr les iris – et panorama sans fin de montagnes lointaines. Le nouveau refuge, au-dessus du lac, propose des boissons fraîches, qui sont les bienvenues en été, avant la remontée ardue vers la France. Le chemin passe à proximité d'un lac magnifique.

Le retour en France, au col de la Fache (2 664 m), offre une vue impressionnante sur le pic de Vignemale (3 298 m), le plus haut pic des Pyrénées françaises. La longue descente assez abrupte mettra les jambes, déjà fatiguées, à rude épreuve. Vous verrez le refuge Wallon bien avant de l'atteindre, mais alors que vous serez proches du découragement, les roches tout à coup laisseront la place aux verts pâturages et au chalet, dans un décor délicieux.

Au départ de Wallon, l'itinéraire traverse le torrent et se fraye un chemin vers la vallée du Gave d'Arratille. Un agréable sentier surplombe le torrent en longeant des pins chétifs jusqu'au lac d'Arramatille, colonisé par d'abondantes fleurs blanches. L'ascension vers le col d'Arratille (2 528 m) est assez difficile et vous fait repasser une fois de plus en Espagne, ne

LIEU La chaîne des Pyrénées qui sépare l'Espagne de la France.
QUAND PARTIR Juillet, août et la première quinzaine de septembre.
DÉPART Le Lac de Bious d'Artigues, on y accède en bus et taxi depuis les villes voisines, y compris Lourdes.
ARRIVÉE Gavarnie. Deux fois par jour, un bus fait la navette jusqu'à Lourdes.
DURÉE 10 jours. Ceci est seulement un tronçon de la longue Haute Route Pyrénéenne, qui représente environ 45 jours de marche.
POINT CULMINANT Monte Perdido (3 355 m).
ASPECTS TECHNIQUES Ce n'est pas une randonnée dans les glaciers, mais certains tronçons sont très impressionnants et dangereux. Il faut prévoir le mauvais temps. Le Monte Perdido peut être gravi sans crampons ni piolet plus tard dans la saison, lorsqu'il n'y a plus de neige. Le Taillon est une ascension relativement facile mais assez longue, elle requiert beaucoup d'attention. L'itinéraire du Petit Vignemale est indiqué jusqu'en haut, mais dans des endroits difficiles, une chute aura de graves conséquences. En cas de doute, adressez-vous à l'office de tourisme local.
MATÉRIEL Matériel de randonnée habituel. Les refuges fournissent des couvertures et de la nourriture.
MODE DE RANDONNÉE Sac à dos et camping, mais il est possible de passer la nuit dans des refuges. Prévoir toute la nourriture avant le départ. Le seul endroit de la randonnée où l'on peut s'approvisionner est Gavarnie.
AUTORISATIONS/RESTRICTIONS Aucune.

CI-DESSUS *Les iris bleus forment un premier plan coloré pour cette vue éloignée de la Brèche de Roland, prise ici depuis les pentes sous le refuge des Espuguettes.*

serait-ce que pendant une heure cette fois, avant de revenir vers le col des Mulets (2 591 m) et découvrir l'impressionnante façade nord du Vignemale et de son glacier. La première ascension de cette montagne a été réalisée par Henri Cazaux et Bernard Guillembet en 1837. Mais c'est le Franco-néerlandais Henri Russell qui, envoûté par ce sommet, rendit le Vignemale célèbre lorsqu'en 1899 il se porta acquéreur d'un bail de 99 ans pour ce pic, moyennant un loyer annuel de UN franc. Il creusa un certain nombre de petites cavernes dans la roche, tout autour du sommet, pour y séjourner et y accueillir des amis.

Le refuge des Ourlettes de Gaube est rudimentaire, racheté par sa position au pied du Vignemale et par l'accueil souriant des gardiens. Un sentier aménagé zigzague aisément depuis le chalet jusqu'à la Hourquette d'Ossoue (2 734 m) mais on progresse lentement car le regard est constamment attiré par la lueur orangée du soleil levant embrassant le sommet du Vignemale. À partir du col de la Hourquette, le refuge de Baysellance n'est qu'à une courte marche, mais le sommet du petit Vignemale (3 032 m), au sud, vous attend d'abord, vous offrant une brève montée et des vues bien dégagées sur le glacier d'Ossoue.

À partir du refuge, le chemin descend inexorablement et en haute saison on croise une multitude de marcheurs montant avec peine. Après une ou deux sections délicates, vous atteindrez une zone parsemée de pierres plates précédant le barrage d'Ossoue, un lieu de pique-nique idéal et l'occasion de décongestionner ses pieds endoloris dans les eaux glacées de la rivière. Le barrage est au détour de la route, mais Gavarnie est encore à plusieurs kilomètres. Sauf si vous aimez marcher sur route, il vaut mieux prendre le chemin qui serpente plus haut, à travers les prairies d'iris, de gentianes, de chardons bleus et d'orchidées. Cette route est longue, mais les points de vue sont très agréables. Derrière vous, le Vignemale et le Petit Vignemale dominent l'horizon, tandis que devant vos yeux s'offre la pyramide du sommet du Pimené, situé juste au-dessus de Gavarnie. Une dernière étape de 20 minutes sur le goudron vous conduit en ville, vers un retour un peu brutal à la civilisation – ici les rues grouillent de monde, et sont couvertes de crottin de cheval, puisque c'est le moyen de transport préféré pour se rendre au célèbre et impressionnant cirque de Gavarnie.

La randonnée pourrait s'achever ici, mais ce serait dommage de ne pas continuer pour découvrir la région espagnole d'Ordesa, juste de l'autre côté de la frontière franco-espagnole.

Comptant parmi les paysages les plus spectaculaires des Pyrénées, l'un des hauts lieux en est le canyon d'Ordesa, une profonde et impressionnante gorge sculptée.

On arrive en Espagne par le refuge des Espuguettes, le cirque d'Estaubé et la brèche de Tuqueroye (2 669 m) et on découvre le mont Perdido dans toute sa glorieuse splendeur. La « montagne perdue », ainsi nommée parce que, depuis la France, elle est cachée par les sommets frontaliers, offre une ascension très appréciée, que ce soit par son glacier ou par un autre itinéraire sans glaces, plus tard en saison. Mettez le cap vers le sud en dépassant le lac de Marboré jusqu'au cirque de Puneta et le refuge de Ronatiza Pineta, vous pourrez guetter une éventuelle apparition du célèbre lammergeier (vautour) au-dessus de vous.

La piste de Faja de Pelay emprunte la face sud du canyon d'Ordesa, son immense muraille rouge dominant tout alentour, tandis qu'en bas le rapide Rio Arazas creuse les gorges. Au bas de la gorge, deux itinéraires permettent d'atteindre le plus proche hébergement, dans la pittoresque Torla : une longue marche routière ou bien le GR 11 à travers bois. Ce tronçon sera à parcourir en sens inverse le lendemain, grimpant franchement sur les pentes du canyon, le long d'une via ferrata, pour rejoindre la piste Faja de las Flores, qui franchit la face nord du canyon et occupe une situation privilégiée. Ce tronçon est inoubliable, en raison à la fois de son exposition et des parois incroyablement sculptées du canyon en contrebas. Remontez par la grotte du Casteret, un réseau important de grottes où de la glace subsiste toute l'année, jusqu'à l'étonnante Brèche de Roland (2 807 m), avant d'atteindre de nouveau la France. Faites une pause pour savourer ce dernier point fort du parcours, et laissez votre regard se perdre vers les lointaines montagnes et les plaines embrumées d'Espagne.

CI-DESSUS *Les pentes nord en bas de l'impressionnante Brèche de Roland restent souvent enneigées tout l'été. La piste est ici elle-même bien enneigée.*

CI-DESSUS *Les impressionnantes falaises à pic du ravin d'Ordesa, vues depuis le sentier de Faja de Pelay, qui coupe juste au-dessus du ravin.*

LA HAUTE ROUTE DE CHAMONIX À ZERMATT

par Hilary Sharp

La Haute Route des glaciers Chamonix-Zermatt, qui passe par un grand nombre de pics de la chaîne Pennine, est l'une des plus belles randonnées des Alpes. Tracée en 1861 par des membres du Club alpin britannique, aidés par des guides locaux, cette route fut d'abord connue sous le nom de « Route de Haut Niveau ». Aujourd'hui, on la parcourt souvent à ski au printemps, mais elle reste une marche très appréciée en été.

En 1741, deux aventuriers britanniques, William Windham et Richard Pococke, débarquent à Chamonix dans le but d'explorer les glaciers qu'ils voyaient scintiller au loin depuis Genève. Leur expédition fut considérée comme imprudente et déraisonnable, car non seulement l'accès à la vallée de Chamonix est long et difficile, mais on croyait en plus que les glaciers étaient habités par de mauvais esprits, et s'y aventurer était aller au-devant de malheurs.

Cependant, les hommes et leurs escortes ne se découragèrent pas, et les brillantes descriptions qu'ils firent ensuite des glaciers amenèrent, au cours des décennies suivantes, un très grand nombre de visiteurs vers les Alpes. En 1786, Jacques Balmat et Gabriel Paccard, tous deux natifs de Chamonix, accomplirent la première ascension du mont Blanc, marquant ainsi le début de l'alpinisme moderne. Très rapidement, de nombreux sommets furent atteints, sauf le mont Cervin, dont les flancs abrupts restèrent invaincus jusqu'au XIXᵉ siècle. L'Anglais Edward Whymper, l'un des alpinistes les plus prolifiques de tous les temps, s'était promis de réaliser cette ascension. En 1865, en concurrence avec l'Italien Jean Antoine Carrel, Whymper et son équipe atteignirent le sommet du mont Cervin, mais furent victimes, pendant la descente, d'un terrible accident ou quatre membres de l'expédition trouvèrent la mort.

Il existe aujourd'hui plusieurs variations de la Haute Route, mais l'option de Chamonix à Zermatt semble bien la plus appréciée, pour son itinéraire et sa direction. Chamonix est une grande station française située à l'ombre du mont Blanc, le plus haut sommet d'Europe occidentale avec ses 4 807 m. Zermatt est la version suisse, avec à l'arrière-plan l'inoubliable mont Cervin, unique par sa forme pyramidale qui surgit brutalement. Rien ne s'oppose vraiment à ce que vous alliez de Zermatt à Chamonix, exceptée la tradition et la force de l'habitude.

L'itinéraire part effectivement du haut de la vallée de Chamonix, du village de Le Tour. Jusqu'au refuge Albert-Iᵉʳ, le sentier s'élève à flanc de montagne vers les moraines qui conduisent au chalet. Perché juste au-dessus du glacier du Tour, ce chalet jouit d'un point de vue

EN HAUT *La charmante station de Champex jouit de points de vue fabuleux sur le Grand Combin, dominant son lac parfaitement entretenu. Un endroit où il fait bon s'attarder un peu.*
ENCART *Les fleurs sauvages font partie des joies de la randonnée d'été. Ici, une ancolie alpestre poussant près de Zermatt, avec le mont Cervin en toile de fond.*
CI-DESSUS *Le mont Blanc domine Chamonix, ses immenses glaciers descendant en un désordre chaotique vers l'étroite vallée en contrebas.*
CI-CONTRE *Ici, sur le plateau de Trient avec le Chardonnet en arrière-plan, les randonneurs font une pause en milieu de matinée.*

LIEU Les Alpes Pennines, situées à l'ouest des Alpes françaises à la frontière triangulaire France-Suisse-Italie.

QUAND PARTIR Juillet, août ou début septembre. Au début de l'année, il est fréquent qu'il y ait de la neige fraîche, ce qui rend difficile la marche et peut être dangereux. Après le mois de septembre, le temps est moins stable et les refuges sont fermés.

DÉPART Le Tour dans le haut de la vallée de Chamonix. On y accède en bus au départ de Chamonix.

ARRIVÉE Zermatt. Il y a des trains au départ de Zermatt qui vont jusqu'à la vallée du Rhône.

DURÉE 8 jours. Comptez plus en cas de mauvais temps.

POINT CULMINANT La Pigne d'Arolla (3 796 m).

ASPECTS TECHNIQUES La randonnée se déroule principalement dans les glaciers, une connaissance des conditions météorologiques est donc nécessaire. Il faut aussi avoir une expérience des glaciers. Il est impératif de consulter un guide précis pour cette randonnée ainsi que la carte.

MATÉRIEL Équipement de base pour randonnée dans les glaciers : crampons, piolet (55-60 cm pour une personne de taille moyenne), harnais, équipement de secours pour les crevasses (minimum nécessaire : sels [acide prussique], une longue cordée, 5 mousquetons et une fiche à glace), et une corde (30 m de long et 8 mm de diamètre minimum).

MODE DE RANDONNÉE Sac à dos ou refuge. Les refuges que l'on trouve au cours de la randonnée fournissent de la nourriture et des couchages. Il est conseillé de réserver pendant les périodes de vacances.

AUTORISATIONS/RESTRICTIONS Aucune.

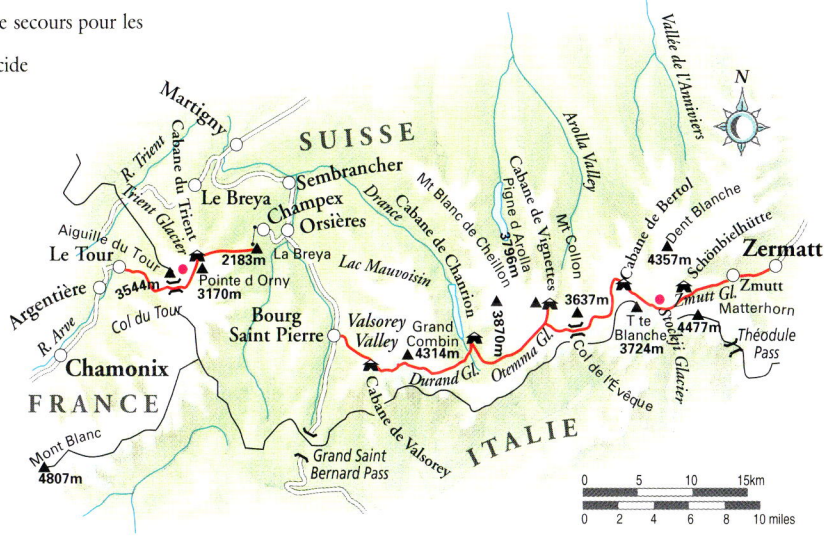

CI-DESSUS *Ces solides chaînes de la via ferrata permettent au randonneur de profiter pleinement du spectacle de la Dent Blanche depuis les environs du refuge de Bertol.*

spectaculaire sur le glacier et sur la chaîne de sommets. Mais c'est l'un des plus fréquentés des Alpes et il y a toujours beaucoup de monde. Si vous envisagez d'escalader l'aiguille du Tour (3 544 m), un bon sommet pour les débutants, nous vous conseillons de passer la nuit au chalet.

À peine parti du chalet, vous poserez le pied sur le premier glacier. Votre objectif, le col du Tour (3 280 m), se trouve à la tête du glacier, et permet d'accéder au glacier Trient, qui forme un immense plateau sur lequel il est assez facile de se perdre par mauvais temps. On trouvera le chalet du Trient sous la pointe d'Orny à 3 170 m, avec des vues incomparables sur la face nord de l'aiguille du Tour et les aiguilles Dorées – si c'est votre première nuit en montagne, vous ne serez pas déçu.

Le lendemain, pendant la descente le long de la rive gauche du glacier Orny, vous pourrez admirer le profil impressionnant de la flèche rocheuse des clochers du Portalet, avant de poursuivre par un sentier agréable et fréquemment emprunté qui vous conduira au télésiège de La Breya, lequel vous emmène à proximité de Champex. Champex est un endroit très agréable pour faire une petite pause avant de prendre le car ou le taxi vers Bourg-Saint-Pierre.

Un sentier très praticable part de Bourg-Saint-Pierre, montant doucement au début vers la vallée de Valsorey, pour devenir plus raide ensuite, avec un tronçon comportant une main courante. Le refuge de Valsorey est perché à 3 030 m, sous le versant sud-ouest de l'énorme masse du Grand Combin (4 314 m). L'étape suivante est plus délicate et ne doit pas être tentée par mauvais temps. Grimper vers le nord-est derrière le refuge et prendre à l'est vers le plateau du Couloir (3 664 m). Les conditions peuvent varier de façon spectaculaire : de la neige facile en saison à la glace et aux éboulis plus tard. Partant du plateau, qui se situe immédiatement sous le Grand Combin, vous descendez vers le glacier du Sonadon, qui est assez plat à cet endroit. Le col du Sonadon (3 504 m) se trouve juste devant vous, vers l'est, et on le traverse facilement, en route vers le glacier Durand.

Descendant le glacier vers la vallée au-dessus du lac Mauvoisin, vous en sortez au pont, à 2 182 m. Votre journée au cœur des glaciers étant maintenant terminée, vous pouvez vous détendre et profiter de la vue magnifique sur le Grand Combin, La Ruinette et, plus bas dans la vallée, le lac Mauvoisin lui-même, formé par le plus grand barrage de ce type au monde. Le chalet de Chanrion n'est que 280 m plus haut.

CI-DESSUS *Les marcheurs coupent à travers le Glacier du Tour. Un départ au petit matin vous garantira une neige dure et vous évitera la chaleur de la journée.*

ALPES PENNINES, FRANCE/ITALIE/SUISSE

CI-DESSUS *Le profil particulier du Cervin domine la dernière partie de la randonnée Chamonix-Zermatt, qui contraste avec les versants glacés du mont Blanc.*

Deux possibilités s'offrent à vous le lendemain, et le choix de l'itinéraire dépend surtout du temps. Le premier itinéraire, par le glacier Otemma, ne comporte pas de difficultés techniques et l'altitude reste relativement basse, ce qui en fait un bon choix si le temps n'est pas parfait ; le second, remontant le glacier Brenay, comprend un tronçon de terrain plus abrupt, traverse une barrière de séracs et permet l'ascension de la Pigne d'Arolla (3 796 m). Ce sommet mérite d'être inclus au programme, et ne présente aucune difficulté technique. Les splendides points de vue sont sans nul doute les points forts de ce parcours, avec le mont Blanc de Cheillon (3 870 m) à l'ouest et le mont Collon (3 637 m) à l'est.

Quel que soit l'itinéraire choisi, vous arrivez à la cabane des Vignettes, située sur un promontoire rocheux. Perchée bien au-dessus de la vallée d'Arolla, avec les sommets rocailleux de l'aiguille de la Tsa, les dents de Bertol et les Bouquetins, juste en face ; une nuit passée là vous laissera un souvenir inoubliable.

Repartant du refuge, il faut reprendre en sens inverse l'itinéraire Otemma jusqu'au col de la Chermotane (3 053 m), puis continuer sur le glacier sous le flanc occidental du mont Collon, jusqu'au col de l'Évêque (3 392 m), puis descendre le haut glacier d'Arolla jusqu'à ce qu'il rejoigne le sentier qui va vers les dents de Bertol. Prenez un repos bien mérité avant de vous attaquer à la piste rude mais bien balisée, puis à la neige du glacier Bertol jusqu'au col de Bertol à 3 279 m. Le chalet est situé juste au-dessus, au nord du col, perché sur la roche et accessible par des chaînes et des échelles et entouré d'une mer de glaciers.

Tandis que vous passerez de la Suisse francophone à la Suisse allemande, vous vous rapprocherez de Zermatt et vous vous assurerez que votre appareil photo est prêt à saisir et fixer votre premier aperçu du mont Cervin dans toute sa splendeur. Par beau temps, la traversée de la section supérieure plate du glacier du mont Miné ne posera aucun problème, empruntant généralement une orientation vers le sud-est pour découvrir le fantastique point de vue de la Tête Blanche (3 724 m). Et voilà enfin le point de vue dont vous rêviez : le mont Cervin et la dent Blanche, tout près, et les hauteurs de Zermatt dans le lointain.

Vous aurez du mal à vous arracher à cette contemplation pour continuer sur le glacier Stockji, très crevassé, et à détacher votre regard de ces superbes sommets pour consacrer votre attention aux crevasses. Depuis la masse rocheuse du Stockji, le sentier zigzagant et à pic descend vers les moraines qui conduisent au glacier Schonbiel. Traversez le glacier et reprenez le sentier qui serpente en remontant un terrain pentu jusqu'à la cabane.

Une étape à la Schonbielhutte est une expérience à ne pas manquer. Une équipe en bonne condition physique à la recherche de night-clubs et de boutiques pourrait certainement poursuivre jusqu'à Zermatt. Mais ce chalet occupe une position tellement merveilleuse, avec la face nord du mont Cervin juste en face de la porte d'entrée, qu'on n'imagine pas que quiconque puisse passer outre. Le mont Cervin (le Matterhorn en allemand, Monte Cervinon en italien [le mont aux Cerfs]) est un sommet tellement unique que l'on est totalement absorbé par l'étude de ses différentes faces et arêtes. Son voisin, la dent d'Herens (4 171 m), est aussi spectaculaire et ce bonheur visuel est tout simplement inoubliable.

Vous aurez tout loisir, le lendemain, de redescendre vers le « monde réel ». Une bonne piste coupe à travers la rive gauche du glacier Zmutt, traversant le charmant hameau du même nom, l'un des plus anciens de la région. Son importance remonte à l'époque romaine, quand il constituait le dernier camp de base avant la longue escalade vers le passage Théodule, itinéraire emprunté pour passer en Italie. Des rafraîchissements et la visite des maisons traditionnelles méritent une halte.

Déambulez tranquillement vers Zermatt, parmi les nombreux chalets anciens et les prairies éclatantes des couleurs de gentianes, d'orchidées, épervières et raiponces – un contraste bienvenu avec les journées passées au cœur de la neige et de la glace – et fêtez ça !

CI-DESSUS *Un repos bien mérité dans la montée du glacier du mont Miné. Marcher sur les glaciers, en plein soleil, est une épreuve très fatigante, mais les points de vue récompensent très largement des efforts fournis.*

ALTA VIA 2

par Hilary Sharp

Situés à l'extrémité orientale de la chaîne des Alpes, les Dolomites forment une partie de la région du Sud-Tyrol. Le Tyrol chevauche l'Autriche et l'Italie, et le Tyrol du Sud faisait partie de l'empire austro-hongrois jusqu'à la Première Guerre mondiale. En 1918, le traité de Versailles donna le Tyrol du Sud à l'Italie, mais sa population est restée germanophone. Dans cette région d'Italie, les habitants se sentent paraît-il plus Autrichiens qu'Italiens, et il faut savoir, avant de se rendre dans les Dolomites, que chaque lieu porte deux dénominations – une italienne et une autrichienne – et en règle générale, ces deux mots ne se ressemblent pas du tout. Par exemple, la ville de Bressanone s'appelle aussi Brixen, le Rifugio Genova est le Schluterhutte. Habituez-vous à ces particularités et vous serez sur la bonne voie pour comprendre les Dolomites.

Le nom de Dolomites viendrait de celui du marquis de Dolomieu, un géologue français qui, au XVIIIe siècle, entreprit d'analyser les roches particulières à cette région. Mais l'appellation originelle de la région, Monti Pallidi (les Montagnes Pâles), fait référence aux clochers de roche calcaire qui font la célébrité de cette région. La présence de magnésium dans la roche lui donne une tonalité rose et les levers et couchers de soleil spectaculaires sont à eux seuls une bonne raison de venir jusqu'ici. La Première Guerre mondiale fut l'occasion de batailles acharnées et interminables entre l'Autriche et l'Italie dans cette chaîne de montagne, et les troupes durent souvent surmonter les obstacles rocheux au moyen de câbles, d'échelles métalliques et autre « quincaillerie » fichée dans la roche. Ces *via ferrata* sont devenues une tradition dans les Dolomites, où bon nombre de parcours a été équipé de la sorte pour encourager la varappe de plaisance. Néanmoins, malgré un paysage aride et nu, le marcheur des Dolomites pourra aussi traverser des prairies parsemées de fleurs et de verdoyantes vallées pastorales. La région est très propice à la promenade, avec un réseau très étendu de sentiers magnifiquement entretenus et très bien signalés, dont plusieurs *Alta via* (route d'altitude) qui traversent la région. L'une des meilleures est la *Alta via 2*, dont une partie est décrite ici.

La *Alta via 2* commence dans la partie nord-ouest des Dolomites, descendant à travers la région pour s'achever à son extrémité sud. Elle traverse un certain nombre de massifs en chemin. Une randonnée d'une semaine sur une partie de la *Alta via 2* pourra englober les massifs Odle, Puez, Sella et Marmolada (dans les Dolomites, on les appelle aussi des « groupes »).

EN HAUT *Ascension d'une via ferrata. Bien qu'extrêmement impressionnants, ces parcours ferrés s'escaladent facilement et offrent de fabuleuses marches très exposées.*
ENCART *L'édelweiss – étoile blanche – d'aspect relativement banal à première vue, révèle, après un examen plus approfondi, de minuscules fleurs jaunes dissimulées dans les grandes bractées velues et argentées.*
À DROITE *De la neige fraîche recouvre le Marmolada, le point culminant des Dolomites. On peut l'admirer depuis un certain nombre de points de vue, le plus apprécié étant celui de Vial del Pan.*

La randonnée commence à Bressanone (Brixen), une charmante et élégante ville dont l'histoire remonte à plus de 1 000 ans. Bressanone possède d'intéressantes rues pavées, d'étroites allées et des porches qui expriment, avec les culottes de cuir et l'abondance des gâteaux aux pommes (Apfelstrudel), la forte empreinte du Tyrol autrichien. La première journée, hors de la ville, implique une marche relativement longue vers le Rifugio Plose. Accessible par remonte-pente ainsi que par la route, le sentier est bon, mais la plupart des randonneurs choisit de ne pas l'emprunter la nuit, préférant prendre le remonte-pente et se diriger vers le Rifugio Genova (Schluterhutte).

Tout de suite, les vues sur le massif Odle sont spectaculaires, avec le sommet du Sass de Putia apparaissant parmi les autres pics aux formes acérées. Une agréable promenade le long d'un chemin bordé de genièvres et de myrtilles constitue une bonne mise en forme jusqu'au Passo Rodella, au-delà duquel une montée plus raide vous donnera l'avant-goût d'une vraie randonnée dans les Dolomites. Ce sentier, bien tracé, serpente au départ à travers des forêts de pins pour déboucher sur des rochers et des éboulis. Bien que parfaitement entretenu, le chemin est très fatigant par sa déclivité. Les marcheurs sont généralement ravis d'atteindre la Forcella della Putia à 2 361 m, pour y prendre un repos bien mérité.

Si vous avez le temps et l'énergie nécessaires, il est fortement recommandé de continuer sur cet excellent chemin vers le Sass de Putia. À 2 875 m d'altitude vous attend un très beau pic, avec une courte via ferrata pour atteindre le dernier sommet. Toutes les *via ferrata* mentionnées ici peuvent être empruntées sans équipement spécial, mais peuvent comporter du danger. La prudence doit être de tous les instants. Par mauvais temps, la roche devient très rapidement glissante, et une chute pourrait vous entraîner vers la façade abrupte côté ouest.

La seconde journée débute tranquillement, avec des panoramas superbes, vers le Piz Duleda (2 909 m) devant vous et le Sass Putia derrière. L'objectif suivant, la Forcella della Roa (2 616 m) est presque trop évident – une grande saignée droit devant – mais pour l'instant, profitez du paysage pastoral en guettant le chamois matinal ! On atteint la Forcella par un raidillon d'éboulis abrupt mais court. Les points de vue sur la vallée lointaine et le Piz Duleda sont fabuleux. À partir d'ici, il y a au moins deux itinéraires pour traverser la chaîne et atteindre les Alpes de Puez ; le plus direct comprend quelques mains courantes dans les parties abruptes et arrive à la crête sous le Piz Duleda, qui peut faire l'objet d'un détour agréable. Une promenade au travers des pentes parsemées de minuscules fleurs alpestres (comme le muflier, la renoncule, le jasmin), surplombant un à-pic impressionnant vers le Vallunga, offrant des points de vue sur le massif Sella et sur le sommet du Sassolungo (3 181 m), vous amènera rapidement jusqu'au Rifugio Puez. Ce chalet facilement accessible attire une clientèle impressionnante pour le déjeuner, mais la plupart de ces marcheurs redescendront avant la fin de la journée.

À partir de Puez, la piste vers le sud, au petit matin, est un vrai délice avec les premiers rayons du soleil et des vues sur les sommets enneigés des Alpes Otztal scintillant dans le lointain. Devant, le massif Sella que l'on atteint en descendant depuis le Passo del Cir (2 466 m) en traversant une forêt de colonnes calcaires d'un rouge orange inhabituel. Le Passo Gardena offre une forme de civilisation – assez chaotique en été – et l'on peut s'y procurer les provisions de base.

Un sentier bien balisé encourage de nombreux marcheurs à faire l'ascension du val Setus. Assez curieusement numéroté 666, le chemin zigzague inexorablement à travers une zone d'éboulis, vers une *via ferrata* existante sur un plateau rocheux à côté du Rifugio Pisciadu

CI-DESSUS *La randonnée dans les Dolomites n'est pas que rocaille et désolation. La piste, jusqu'au refuge Falier, vous emmène à travers de magnifiques forêts et prairies.*

À DROITE *Composées d'éléments métalliques allant du câble aux échelles de fer, les via ferrata permettent d'emprunter des itinéraires qui, autrement, ne seraient pas accessibles aux randonneurs.*

et son lac. Une étape à cet endroit vous donne le temps de faire l'ascension de la Cima Pisciadu (2 985 m), juste au-dessus. Poursuivant la grimpette d'une zone d'éboulis, vous accédez à un plateau dénudé et à un paysage lunaire. De là, l'ascension rapide du Piz Boe (3 152 m), qui comprend un court tronçon de *via ferrata*, est un « must ». Ce sommet ne ressemble à aucun autre, avec son chalet et cette étrange antenne métallique rectangulaire, évocatrice d'un écran de cinéma en plein air – on ne s'y attardera pas.

Soit en revenant du chalet ou en faisant la traversée du pic, le prochain objectif sera la sombre Forcella Pordoi (2 829 m). De là, la descente emprunte des couloirs étroits d'éboulis, très raides et assez impressionnants – la sensation est la même que lorsque l'on contemple une piste de ski avant de s'élancer dans sa descente. Au début des années quatre-vingt, un original entreprit de descendre les pentes d'éboulis des Dolomites à skis, et il est presque aisé de comprendre ses raisons.

Le célèbre sentier, le Vial del Pan, continue à partir du Passo Pordoi ; c'était au XVIIe siècle la route du grain, empruntée par les contrebandiers. Ce sentier peut être très encombré – d'une part en raison des points de vue qu'il offre sur le Marmolada, à 3 343 m, le plus haut sommet des Dolomites, et d'autre part parce qu'il est plat. La vue sur le glacier de Marmolata et sur l'imposant sommet rocheux du Gran Vernal voisin, s'allie avec les nombreuses fleurs de montagne que l'on trouve ici (gentianes, anémones, edelweiss et orchidées) pour en faire une marche mémorable. Passez la nuit dans un des hôtels, sur les bords du Lago di Fedaia, sur les pentes couvertes de glace de la face nord du Marmolada. Avant 1919, ce sommet constituait la frontière entre l'Autriche et l'Italie, et de ce fait fut le témoin de nombreuses batailles. À mesure que le glacier Marmolada s'amenuise, les galeries taillées dans la roche et des vestiges d'abris en bois refont surface, à partir de 3 000 m et au-dessus, témoignant de l'immense effort fourni par les troupes qui se sont battues ici.

Il existe deux options pour traverser le Marmolada. On peut faire la traversée du glacier lui-même via la Forcella della Marmolada (2 910 m), après quoi une descente à pic et une *via ferrata* conduisent au Rifugio Contrin. L'autre possibilité est une route longue mais incroyablement spectaculaire qui fait le tour de la montagne par Malga Ciapela puis remonte par le Rifugio Falier, sous les murailles orange et grises de la face sud du Marmolada, un lieu d'escalade réputé. Le Passo di Ombretta (2 702 m), avec son chalet rose vif, se trouve au bout d'une longue montée, et des prairies couvertes d'edelweiss, gentianes et barbajoues descendent vers le Rifugio Contrin, grand bâtiment appartenant à l'armée italienne, planté dans un cadre superbe sous la Cima Ombretta (2 931 m).

À partir du Rifugio Contrin, un sentier agréable remonte vers un terrain plus rocailleux, passant à côté de vestiges de fils barbelés et de boîtes de conserve, reliefs poignants de la guerre, vers le Passo Cirelle (2 683 m) et un panorama sans fin de montagnes embrumées. La descente vers le Rifugio Fochiade sera l'occasion d'une dernière descente assez raide avant de déjeuner à Fochiade, après quoi la fin de votre randonnée au Passo di San Pellegrino (1 919 m) n'est plus qu'une flânerie.

À GAUCHE *Après avoir atteint le Passo di Ombretta et admiré de près le Marmolada, la piste vers le Rifugio Contrin laisse en arrière le profil rocailleux de la Cima Ombretta.*
CI-CONTRE *L'exaltante vue depuis le Passo Cirelle est en poignant contraste avec les tristes souvenirs des atrocités commises pendant la Première Guerre mondiale sur ce champ de bataille majestueux.*

DOLOMITES, TYROL DU SUD, ITALIE

LIEU Extrémité est des Alpes, au sud de la frontière austro-italienne.

QUAND PARTIR De juillet à début septembre. Avant, les cols les plus hauts peuvent être trop enneigés. Plus tard, les refuges risquent d'être fermés et la nouvelle neige peut tomber d'un moment à l'autre à basse altitude.

DÉPART Bressanone (Brixen). Accessible par la route au départ de l'Italie ou de l'Autriche. Chemin de fer au départ d'Innsbruck.

ARRIVÉE Passo di San Pellegrino. Services de cars directs vers Bolzano et vers Bressanone en juillet et en août seulement. Hors saison, il est recommandé de prévoir un taxi avant de partir.

DURÉE 6 à 8 jours, environ 75 km.

POINT CULMINANT Forcella della Marmolada, 2 910 m.

ASPECTS TECHNIQUES La plus grande prudence est recommandée au passage des *via ferrata* – ces itinéraires sont déconseillés aux marcheurs timorés. La traversée du Marmolada (facultative) nécessite en général un piolet à glace, des crampons et une corde, ainsi que des connaissances concernant la randonnée sur glacier. L'escalade est de difficulté moyenne. Plusieurs descentes et montées longues et à pic nécessiteront des bâtons de marche.

MATÉRIEL Les chalets offrent lits, couvertures et oreillers. Les « sacs à viande » sont indispensables. La nourriture est excellente et cuisiner soi-même n'est en général pas une option retenue sur ce parcours.

MODE DE RANDONNÉE Sac à dos, ou de chalet en chalet. Fournitures élémentaires pour pique-nique disponibles dans les chalets et aux cols desservis par des routes.

AUTORISATIONS/RESTRICTIONS Aucune.

SENTIER DE GRANDE RANDONNÉE 20 (GR 20)

par Hilary Sharp

La Corse, que les Français appellent l'île de Beauté, et connue des anciens Grecs sous le nom de *Kalliste* – la plus belle –, est située à 160 km au sud de la côte française méditerranéenne et à 80 km à l'ouest de la côte italienne. Département français, la Corse est un massif rocheux en plein milieu de la mer. Bien que ses plus hauts sommets culminent à 2 700 m, ils restent enneigés pendant une grande partie de l'année. Malgré cette situation méditerranéenne et ses magnifiques plages de sable, les montagnes corses sont réputées pour la soudaineté des changements de temps.

En les parcourant, vous aurez l'impression d'avoir remonté le temps. La plus grande partie de la population vit sur la côte, et il y a moins de dix personnes au kilomètre carré en montagne, où la vie est rude, les modestes revenus des agriculteurs provenant de l'élevage de moutons, chèvres ou bovins. Les bandits corses et leurs *vendettas* font maintenant partie de l'histoire, même si elle n'est pas très ancienne, et les villages dans les collines sont désertés au profit des grandes villes côtières, voir du continent.

Avec une distance d'environ 180 km et un dénivelé total de 9 700 m, la randonnée en Corse est considérée comme l'un des itinéraires les plus difficiles d'Europe. Mais également comme l'un des plus beaux. Officiellement appelé Sentier de Grande Randonnée 20 (GR 20), cet itinéraire commence dans le Nord-Ouest et se fraye un passage le long de l'épine dorsale la plus montagneuse de l'île, presque toujours en altitude, pour émerger finalement près de ces jolies plages de la côte sud-est. Le Parc Naturel régional de Corse (PNC) fut créé en 1972 pour protéger toute la chaîne de montagnes, et tous les refuges sur ce parcours en font partie.

EN HAUT *Le lac de Capitello, dominant la vallée de Restonica, paraît tentant vu d'en haut, mais un examen plus rapproché révélera la vraie température de ces eaux glacées !*

ENCART *Les aiguilles de granit et les pins corses de Bavella forment l'une des attractions les plus classiques de l'île.*

EN HAUT À DROITE *On quitte le refuge de Carozzu par un nouveau pont suspendu splendide, ce qui provoque une certaine excitation matinale.*

La randonnée commence dans le petit village de Calenzana, au nord de Calvi. Partant de l'altitude modeste de 275 m, la première journée de marche vous conduit à une altitude déjà importante de 1 570 m. Vous échapperez rapidement à la chaleur oppressante de l'été à mesure que vous monterez vers les collines, et les points de vue magnifiques vers le nord seront d'excellentes excuses pour souffler un peu. Après avoir laborieusement passé deux cols, vous arriverez à la crête de Fuca, où le terrain devient plus praticable, et une promenade agréable vous conduira jusqu'au refuge de Ortu di u Piobbu.

Bien que les chalets gardés soient fréquents sur cet itinéraire, il n'existe pas de source fiable d'approvisionnement alimentaire. On fournira des réchauds et des gamelles, mais au plus fort de la saison il faut parfois faire la queue pour s'en servir. Les places dans les chalets sont accordées selon le principe du « premier arrivé, premier servi », et il est toujours envisageable qu'il n'y ait plus de place. Il est essentiel d'emporter un minimum de matériel de camping. Des sacs de couchage sont nécessaires même dans les chalets, de même que des tapis de sol, même si les bas flancs des chalets comportent des matelas.

La marche du lendemain est plus douce, bien que tout aussi spectaculaire et variée ; rocailleuse par moments, entourée de genièvre et de buissons parfumés à d'autres, et avec des points de vue dominés par les sommets du Monte Cintu à 2 706 m, le plus haut de Corse. Le refuge de Carrozzu (connu aussi comme le refuge de Spasimatu) est entouré de falaises,

À partir du chalet de Pietra Piana, il y a deux options possibles : soit par la vallée en passant par la bergerie de Tolla, ou bien une version plus courte le long de la ligne de crête, vers le sud. Le refuge de l'Onda marque le dernier arrêt avant la plaine, où vous retrouverez la civilisation. Vizzavona, à un peu plus de la moitié du parcours, marque le point de séparation entre les tronçons nord et sud. Le paysage de la partie sud du GR 20 est très différent, avec des collines herbues et des vues magnifiques sur la côte.

Une forêt pentue conduit hors de Vizzavona, passe le Bocca Palmente et le refuge assez ancien de Capanelle. La traversée continue entre les hêtres et vous amène au col de Verde, où il y a encore un refuge. La montée suivante est particulièrement gratifiante. Après un long et pénible effort, on atteint le col de Prati à 1 840 m et la vue est à couper le souffle – vous apercevez la côte sud-est pour la première fois – et c'est alors que vous commencez à réaliser tout le chemin parcouru. Une ligne de crête extraordinaire vous offre un parcours touristique jusqu'à la Bocca Usciolu, et des points de vue panoramiques sur la côte. De nouveau entourée d'une forêt de hêtres, la piste débouche sur un plateau où des ruisseaux se frayent un chemin au travers d'une herbe verdoyante et grasse, parsemée d'aconit bleu. À partir du col de Luana, l'itinéraire s'impose de lui-même, et monte vers le seul vrai sommet du GR 20, le Monte Incudine (2 134 m).

Une descente rapide conduit au refuge Asinao, lui-même à une très courte distance de l'un des endroits les plus célèbres de l'île, le cirque de Bavella. Le sentier se fraye un chemin entre des formations rocheuses à la fois étranges et splendidement sculptées, les aiguilles de granit parfois couronnées de lambeaux de brume matinale qui montent de la vallée. Bavella offre hébergement et service d'autocars, mais le prochain chalet, le refuge de Paliri, mérite une halte, ne serait-ce que pour le point de vue sur la côte italienne, Monte Christo et la Sardaigne voisine. Le dernier jour n'a rien à envier aux autres, avec de nombreuses et impressionnantes flèches de granit, orangées dans le soleil matinal. Une fois atteint l'étroit passage de la Bocca Usciolu, il suffit de descendre, la côte sud-est vous faisant signe, jusqu'à ce que soudain, vous débouchiez du sentier sur la route, tout près de la fontaine de Conca, appréciée de tous.

CI-CONTRE *Petit matin au cirque de Bavella. Un randonneur savoure quelques minutes de solitude avant de redescendre vers la réalité au col de Bavella.*

CI-DESSUS *L'impressionnant trou érodé dans le Capu Tafanatu, vu depuis le Paglia Orba voisin, constitue un bon objectif pour une marche d'une journée.*

AFRIQUE

E TICHKA AU TOUBKAL | CHOGORIA ET LES ITINÉRAIRES DES SOMMETS | LE CANYON DE FISH RIVER | LES PISTES DES LOUTRES ET DU TSITSIKAMMA |

AFRIQUE

*Celui qui ne voyage pas ne connaît pas
la valeur de l'homme.*

PROVERBE MOORISH

CI-DESSUS *Le lac Mickaelson, la perle de la vallée des Gorges, est un endroit bienvenu pour faire une halte d'une nuit sur la route de Chogoria au mont Kenya.*
CI-CONTRE *Les traversées d'estuaires constituent l'une des caractéristiques de la fameuse piste des Loutres d'Afrique du Sud – ici à Elandsbos.*
PAGES PRÉCÉDENTES *Un reflet de l'aube des temps. Le plus ancien canyon du monde fut creusé par la Fish River en Namibie.*

Peu d'endroits au monde suscitent des émotions aussi intenses et variées que l'Afrique. Il est maintenant reconnu que l'histoire de l'humanité a commencé ici, où les travaux archéologiques et anthropologiques de Leakeys au Kenya et en Tanzanie ont confirmé que la vallée du Rift (ou fossé tectonique) était effectivement le berceau de l'humanité.

Les voyageurs d'aujourd'hui peuvent contempler avec admiration l'incroyable diversité et l'immensité du paysage, s'émerveiller de la faune sauvage et envier l'exubérance du peuple africain, mais en réalité, ces pays figurent parmi les plus pauvres du monde. La détresse et les privations quotidiennes sont presque inconcevables, et pourtant, confronté à tant d'adversité, l'esprit humain trouve le moyen de s'épanouir, et la vie est riche, colorée et joyeuse.

Dans les remous des siècles de colonisation et d'exploitation, il n'est pas surprenant que la libération de l'Afrique ait laissé une bonne partie du continent dans un état de misère. Les communications, l'électricité, l'eau potable, les transports, autant de services considérés comme acquis en Occident, se font encore attendre sur les immenses territoires africains.

Le tourisme bien géré constitue l'un des meilleurs espoirs de l'Afrique de sortir du chaos post-colonial et les gouvernements les plus éclairés du continent en ont pris conscience et ont officialisé la création de parcs et de réserves pour préserver leur patrimoine naturel. Le « voyage aventure », loin des lieux de villégiature et des hôtels de luxe, contribue à l'abolissement des barrières culturelles et au recul de l'ignorance qui alimente les préjugés. Il n'est pas de meilleure façon pour découvrir une Afrique authentique, que de faire l'expérience physique du paysage et de ressentir les textures et couleurs uniques de la brousse africaine, ces randonnées révèlent la glorieuse splendeur des paysages de ce continent.

La côte méditerranéenne du Maroc n'est peut-être qu'à une heure de l'Espagne en bateau, mais la vie dans le Haut Atlas aride et sans voies de communication, se poursuit à un rythme inchangé depuis des siècles. Au milieu de ces sommets inaccessibles, sur la frange nord du Sahara, dans des villages pittoresques de glaise et de pierres,

vivent les Berbères, les occupants originels du Maroc. L'Atlas est la plus haute chaîne de montagne d'Afrique du Nord, et bien que la plupart des marcheurs se focalisent sur le massif du Toubkal, la traversée de toute la chaîne fera découvrir un tableau beaucoup plus vaste et stimulant.

A environ 6 400 km au sud de l'Atlas, en Namibie, entre les déserts de Namib et du Kalahari, le canyon de la Fish River s'étend sur une bande de terre peut-être encore plus inhospitalière que le Sahara. La route en direction du canyon à partir de la ville de Keetmanshoop a souvent été décrite comme la plus désolée mais la plus magnifique de Namibie, et bien que la piste de randonnées pédestres de 86 km qui traverse le canyon lui-même ne soit certainement pas faite pour les timorés, c'est sans aucun doute l'une des randonnées les plus extraordinairement belles du sud de l'Afrique.

Contrastant complètement avec le dénuement provocateur de Namibie, la côte de l'océan Indien de la région du Cap, en Afrique du Sud, est un véritable jardin d'Eden, avec de fraîches et verdoyantes clairières et des plages abritées, derrière lesquelles se dressent les montagnes idylliques de la chaîne du Tsitsikamma. En associant deux des pistes bien établies de cette région, un circuit qui comprend tous les hauts lieux de cette enclave immaculée peut s'accomplir en dix jours.

Aucun choix d'itinéraire en Afrique, quelle que soit sa longueur, ne peut omettre les fantastiques collines de la vallée du Rift (fossé tectonique), au Kenya, et même si le Kilimandjaro, en Tanzanie voisine, se glorifie d'être le plus haut sommet du continent, les chemins de randonnée autour du mont Kenya lui sont indubitablement supérieurs. S'élevant au-dessus d'une étendue de forêts presque impénétrables, la montagne elle-même est entourée de chaparal et de magnifiques bruyères d'altitude, et offre des points de vue splendides, accompagnés d'une impression d'espace et de perspective jamais atteinte sur le « Kili ». En combinant les deux approches les plus spectaculaires de la montagne avec un circuit englobant les trois principaux sommets, vous tirerez un maximum de plaisir de cette perle d'Afrique orientale.

DE TICHKA AU TOUBKAL

par Hamish Brown

Le pôle Sud fut vaincu douze ans avant que des alpinistes européens n'atteignent le point culminant du Maroc, le Djebel Toubkal (4 167 m). L'hostilité des tribus berbères avait conservé à l'Atlas son statut de terres inconnues jusqu'à ce que la France envahisse le pays en 1912, faisant du Maroc l'une des dernières colonies d'Afrique. La première ascension du Toubkal fut effectuée en 1923 par une expédition française. Dix ans plus tard, une mission polonaise explora l'Atlas occidental et on pourrait compter sur les doigts d'une main ceux qui avaient vu le plateau de la Tichka avant la Seconde Guerre mondiale, qui mit un frein à l'exploration des montagnes. Après-guerre, le combat pour l'indépendance maintint les Européens à distance jusqu'en 1956, et c'est pour cette raison que cet univers montagneux, pratiquement inchangé depuis des siècles, n'est mieux connu que depuis quarante ans. Le premier parcours complet de Tichka au Toubkal, surnommé « la marche merveilleuse » fut entrepris par moi-même en 1992. Les montagnes de l'Atlas s'étendent en travers du sud marocain, séparant les plaines et les villes des déserts qui bordent le Sahara. Marrakech est la porte d'accès vers l'Atlas, et de ses terrasses, on aperçoit l'horizon bordé de sommets enneigés, selon la saison. Des tribus berbères occupent l'Atlas depuis des millénaires, et forment une société agricole rude, amicale et hospitalière. Sur les parcours, leurs mules garantissent une liberté de mouvement sans fardeau, avec des installations de camping et de cuisson renforcées.

Les randonneurs apprécieront, sur ce parcours, les paysages variés et spectaculaires qui, jour après jour, les conduiront, du lointain plateau de la Tichka, par les forêts, les gorges et les villages sur l'Oued Nfis, par des cols et des lacets jusqu'à Imlil, au Toubkal, le point culminant d'Afrique du Nord. Ce parcours demande en général deux semaines, plus deux jours de voyage aller-retour.

EN HAUT *Il fut un temps où chaque vallée, clan ou tribu avait sa propre casbah, un poste fortifié pour stocker le grain et les biens de valeur. Cette ruine au-dessus d'Imlil est maintenant restaurée.*

ENCART *Les chameaux sont omniprésents au Maroc ; ils sont encore largement utilisés pour le transport tout-terrain et pour tirer les charrues dans de minuscules champs en terrasse.*

À DROITE *L'un des attraits de la randonnée dans l'Atlas est la fiabilité de la météo. Les couchers de soleil sont souvent très colorés, comme le montre cette vue de la chaîne de l'Aksoual et du Toubkal.*

MONT ATLAS, MAROC

Les randonneurs prennent l'avion jusqu'à Marrakech, en changeant à Casablanca. Plusieurs hôtels offrent un service de minibus et emmèneront les randonneurs de l'autre côté de l'Atlas par la spectaculaire route de Tizi n'Test jusqu'à Taroudant, empruntant un court moment l'itinéraire de randonnée qui passe par l'oued Nfis. Après Taroudant, une camionnette emmènera l'équipe à travers l'unique forêt d'argan, de palmiers dattiers, d'orangeraies et de noyers, jusqu'aux hauts pâturages irrigués de la vallée de la Medlawa, enchâssée au cœur des montagnes. On passe la nuit dans le village le plus élevé, Awsaghmelt, dans une amicale maison berbère, avec cuisine traditionnelle et thé à la menthe.

Tôt le lendemain matin, les randonneurs repartent. Les muletiers s'occupent des tentes, chargent les mules et plus tard rejoindront et dépasseront les randonneurs jusqu'au site suivant, où ils leur prépareront un thé de bienvenue. Une fois les tentes installées, il reste généralement un peu de temps pour explorer la flore et la faune locales, et rencontrer les gens du coin.

Au départ d'Awsaghmelt, le sentier de Medlawa grimpe et serpente pendant des heures, pour atteindre le Tizi n'Targa, une encoche dans le bord du plateau de la Tichka. À 3 000 m, il est possible que certains se sentent essoufflés. Le plateau de la Tichka à la forme d'une cuvette rectangulaire ; la source de l'Oued Nfis est bordée de sommets dont les faces extérieures forment des précipices de centaines de mètres de profondeur. Le campement occupe une bande herbue le long du torrent, parsemée de petites jonquilles en début de saison.

Le plateau dégage un réel sentiment de monde perdu, qui s'intensifie encore le lendemain lors de l'ascension du plus haut sommet, l'Imadarene (3 351 m). La crête, quelque peu scabreuse, implique un peu d'escalade Pendant la traversée du sommet, les muletiers transfèrent le campement vers l'extrémité inférieure du plateau. L'oued Nfis apporte une heureuse succession de forêts de chênes, de villages et de forêts de sapins avant de se retrouver parallèle à la longue et sinueuse route de Tizi n'Test, passant les sites historiques de Tinmal et la kasbah Goundafi, pour

enfin arriver à Ijoukak, où l'itinéraire quitte le Nfis. En quittant le plateau, la forêt de Tiziatin (chênes verts) est surplombée par des sommets rocailleux et la rivière entaille profondément une gorge granitique sur une portion du parcours. Les sommets deviennent de plus en plus sauvages ; les trois sommets d'Oumzra, au nord, se laissent apercevoir en haut d'une vallée latérale à l'approche du premier village, Agadir. Les villages, reliés par des chemins muletiers, sont perchés et espacés de quelques kilomètres du côté nord, l'hébergement chez l'habitant reste une possibilité. L'architecture locale est entièrement fondée sur la pierre et le bois du pays, avec des rigoles d'eau, des champs en terrasse.

Quelques villages après Souk Sebt, le sentier pénètre dans des forêts de pins. Dormir à la belle étoile, se baigner dans les cuvettes des torrents, autant de moments privilégiés qui font que chaque campement semble plus agréable que le précédent. Les terres rouges d'Afrique remplacent les abords escarpés de la vallée et on suit la rivière sur sa rive nord, alors que la route goudronnée, au sud, se remarque à peine. Tinmal, avec sa mosquée fortifiée et restaurée dans les années quatre-vingt-dix, est un lieu d'une beauté étonnante. C'est à partir de là qu'au XIIe siècle, les Almohades envahirent la région pour conquérir Marrakech et créer un empire tout le long de l'Afrique du Nord et jusqu'à la moitié de l'Espagne.

Au bord de la rivière, la kasbah Goundafi est en fait le palais en ruine de l'un des chefs de tribus, appelés aussi « seigneurs de l'Atlas », qui contrôlaient le Nfis et le Tizi n'Test, au grand dam des explorateurs britanniques Cunninghame Graham et Joseph Thomson. C'est la construction de routes goudronnées dans l'Atlas qui a vraiment mis un terme aux puissances tribales.

L'essentiel du trafic routier fait halte à Tjoubak, qui, plein d'étals alimentaires et de cafés, vous offre une nouvelle fois la tentation d'un toit pour la nuit et d'un tagine épicé. Une longue montée vous attend, avec deux options possibles. L'une, praticable lorsqu'il n'y a pas de neige, remonte la vallée du côté d'Agoundis et enjambe le Tizi n'Ouagane (3 750 m) jusqu'au chalet du Toubkal. L'autre itinéraire, plus classique, monte plus haut au travers des pentes nord du Tazharhat (3 980 m), la montagne qui se trouve entre les vallées du Nfis et d'Agoundis, avec quelques beaux passages entre les éperons nord. La montée est éprouvante pour gagner de l'altitude par la piste en lacets qui ensuite traverse le Tizi n'Iguidi et le Tizi n'Ouarhou avant de redescendre vers le village de Tizi Oussem. De là, une dernière grimpette jusqu'aux 2 489 m du Tizi Mzic surmonte et redescend vers le bassin Imlil (1 750 m) et le monde animé de la piste du Toubkal. Imlil est appelé le Chamonix du Maroc.

À une heure d'Imlil, se trouve Around, le dernier village en direction du Toubkal. Les montagnes se resserrent et le sentier zigzague jusqu'au temple sacré de Sidi Chamharouch. Le passage vers l'est, le Tizi n'Tagharat (3 442 m), fut le point le plus éloigné et le plus haut que Hooker et Ball atteignirent lors de la première vraie expédition dans l'Atlas, en 1871. La piste du Toubkal monte en s'enroulant comme une corde, avant une transversale jusqu'au refuge du Club Alpin Français, à 3 207 m.

À partir de ce chalet, le sommet du Toubkal (4 167 m) est encore à trois ou quatre heures de marche. La piste coupe à travers une pente abrupte jusqu'à la vallée suspendue d'Ikhibi Sud, puis suit une crête jusqu'au sommet de la montagne. Peu de randonnées se terminent de manière aussi grandiose – tous les sommets du pays atteignant 4 000 m, sauf un – sont rassemblés là.

Le Toubkal ne marque pas la fin de la randonnée, bien entendu. Il faut encore descendre parmi les monotones blocs rocheux, mais comme ce sentier semble facile vers la verdoyante Imlil ! Même le retour en voiture vers Marrakech est fascinant et une nuit ou deux dans cette cité magique complétera l'impression de « grand tableau final ».

EN HAUT *Le chalet du Toubkal fut construit pour faciliter l'ascension du Djebel Toubkal, le plus haut sommet d'Afrique du Nord (6 167 m), très fréquenté toute l'année.*
AU CENTRE *Les bergers berbères sont souvent semi-nomades, conduisant les troupeaux dans les alpages en été, et séjournant dans des abris de pierres rudimentaires ou sous les tentes noires des nomades.*
CI-CONTRE *Les maisons des villages berbères sont toujours groupées ; jadis pour se défendre, aujourd'hui pour économiser la précieuse terre agricole.*

LIEU Les montagnes du Haut-Atlas au Maroc, Afrique du Nord.

QUAND PARTIR De mai à octobre.

DÉPART/ARRIVÉE Plateau de la Tichka, au nord de Taroudant ; redescendre vers Marrakech depuis le Djebel Toubkal. Liaisons aériennes avec Marrakech et minibus de l'hôtel vers départ/arrivée.

DURÉE 14 à 18 jours, 140 km ; ajouter les jours d'approche au départ et à l'arrivée. On peut au besoin faire l'impasse sur les sommets principaux de l'Imaradene (départ) et du Toubkal (arrivée), mais leur ascension n'est pas très technique.

POINT CULMINANT Djebel Toubkal (4 167 m).

ASPECTS TECHNIQUES Une randonnée essentiellement estivale, toutes les dates antérieures étant conditionnées par l'accès muletier au plateau de la Tichka, et le sommet du Djebel Toubkal peut être enneigé en juin. Suivre les conseils locaux. Les sentiers sont généralement en bon état et conviennent à toute personne en forme, mais quelques montées vers les tizis sont particulièrement longues. Les nuits peuvent être fraîches, les journées chaudes, et bien que le temps soit généralement clément et ensoleillé, des orages peuvent se produire en toutes saisons.

MATÉRIEL Des vêtements pour toutes saisons, tente, sac de couchage et tapis de sol. Pas de shorts. Une grande bouteille d'eau, un écran solaire et des lunettes de soleil sont indispensables.

MODE DE RANDONNÉE Sac à dos ou expédition.

AUTORISATIONS/RESTRICTIONS Aucune restriction ni droits à payer, frais de randonnée très modestes.

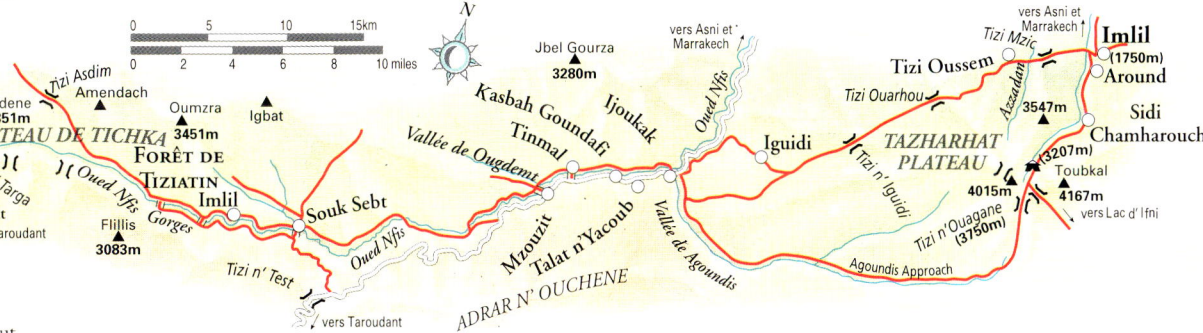

CHOGORIA ET LES ITINÉRAIRES DES SOMMETS

par Steve Razzetti

S'étendant en un énorme arc de cercle de la Syrie au Mozambique, le Grand Fossé est l'une des manifestations les plus spectaculaires des mouvements tectoniques de la planète. Formé par la cassure et l'enfoncement de la croûte terrestre le long d'une ancienne faille tectonique, le Grand Fossé s'étend sur plus de 4 800 km et son fond varie en altitude de 400 m en dessous du niveau de la mer Morte jusqu'à 1 800 m d'altitude au Kenya. La grande majorité de l'activité volcanique et sismique du globe se produit à proximité de telles failles, et bien qu'aucune éruption volcanique ou tremblement de terre important ne se soit produit au Kenya depuis des siècles, de petites secousses peuvent encore être ressenties dans les hauteurs du pays.

En Afrique orientale, le Grand Fossé se divise en un fossé occidental et un fossé oriental, le second séparant les montagnes du Kenya entre la chaîne Aberdare et l'escarpement Mau. De nombreux volcans éteints jalonnent la grande fosse, les plus hauts étant le mont Kenya (5 199 m) et le mont Elgon (4 321 m). Le mont Kenya, deuxième sommet du continent africain, se situe derrière le Kilimandjaro (5 895 m), en Tanzanie, le pays voisin ; il est aujourd'hui constitué du noyau de magma érodé d'un volcan qui jadis dépassait les 6 500 m d'altitude.

Le Kenya a pris le nom de cette montagne, et le mot est une déformation du terme Kikuyu Kere Nyaga, (la montagne de la lumière). Les Kikuyus croient que la montagne est la demeure de leur dieu Ngai, qu'ils appellent aussi Mwene Nyaga (le professeur de lumière). Situé à quelque 150 km au nord de Nairobi et offrant un spectacle inoubliable, le mont Kenya a donné à l'Afrique beaucoup plus que sa seule luminescence. De nombreuses rivières naissent dans son voisinage immédiat, alimentées par la fonte de ses neiges. Parmi celles-ci, la plus longue du pays, la Tanna, qui produit une bonne part de l'énergie électrique du Kenya.

De la neige à l'équateur ? Ludwig Krapf, voyageant vers l'intérieur des terres depuis Mombassa, en 1849, n'en crut pas ses yeux quand le Kenya lui apparut plus distinctement, avec ses deux grandes cornes ou piliers s'élevant au-dessus d'une montagne énorme « recouverte d'une substance blanche » dans le nord-ouest du Kilimandjaro. L'idée selon laquelle il

EN HAUT *Les marcheurs fêtent l'apogée de leur randonnée au mont Kenya au lever du soleil, sur le sommet rocheux de Point Lenana.*

ENCART *Lobella keniensis, l'un des trois types de roses géantes que l'on trouve en Afrique de l'Est. Les autres s'appellent Carduus et Senecio.*

CI-DESSUS À GAUCHE *Une grotte glaciaire sous le glacier Lewis, près de Curling Pond, à une courte distance du refuge des Autrichiens (Austrian Hut).*

CI-DESSUS À DROITE *A l'assaut des pentes rocheuses et sans piste, au-dessus du lac Mickaelson, la journée la plus dure à l'approche du refuge des Autrichiens.*

CI-DESSUS *Le soleil du matin ravive les couleurs des roches escarpées et abruptes du Nelion, vues ici depuis la plus haute crête de Point Lenana.*

existait des sommets enneigés en Afrique équatoriale fut longtemps tournée en ridicule par les institutions géographiques européennes, jusqu'à ce que, 33 ans plus tard, l'affable Écossais Joseph Thomson s'en approcha encore plus, et confirme la ressemblance avec de la neige !

Le premier Européen qui parvint à traverser la jungle alentour jusqu'à la montagne elle-même fut un Autrichien, le comte Samuel Teleki. Vint ensuite le géologue britannique J. W. Gregory qui, en 1893, étudia la structure physique de la montagne et attribua des noms européens à un certain nombre de sites importants, comprenant la vallée Teleki du côté du Naro Moru.

Sir Halford Mackinder fit la première ascension du plus haut pic du mont Kenya en 1899, accompagné par les guides de montagne Ollier et Brocherel. À cette époque, le chemin de fer arrivait à Nairobi, mais il n'y avait aucune route. Éléphants, lions, buffles et rhinocéros parcouraient alors la brousse, ainsi que les tribus Kikuyus qui n'appréciaient guère que les Européens viennent piétiner leurs terres sacrées. Pour apaiser les indigènes, Mackinder donna au plus haut sommet (5 199 m) le nom d'un sorcier massaï appelé Mbatiang. Il donna au deuxième sommet (5 598 m) le nom du frère de Mbatiang, Neilieng, puis aux troisième (4 985 m) et quatrième (4 704 m) ceux de ses fils, Olonana et Sendeyo. Les trois premiers ont été anglicisés pour devenir Batian, Nelion et Lenana.

Trente ans plus tard, le 6 janvier 1929, les Anglais Éric Shipton et Percy Wyn Harris ouvrirent ce qu'il est maintenant convenu d'appeler la Route Normale vers le Nelion. Shipton y retourna en compagnie de Bill Tillman en août 1930, et accomplit à la fois la première traversée de la montagne et le premier circuit des sommets. Après la Deuxième Guerre mondiale, l'intérêt pour ces montagnes fut de plus en plus vif. En 1949, le territoire situé au-dessus de 3 400 m fut officiellement

CI-DESSUS *La récession glaciaire apparaît clairement depuis cet endroit isolé et venteux sur une crête juste au-dessus du refuge des Autrichiens.*

déclaré Parc national et la zone fut cartographiée par les services coloniaux. Cette même année, le club alpin du Kenya fut constitué et très vite des chalets furent bâtis en différents points stratégiques.

Planté seul au-dessus des plaines du Grand Fossé (Rift Valley), le mont Kenya ne permet pas de s'acclimater à l'altitude lors des marches d'approche, comme c'est le cas pour les autres sommets de même stature dans les grandes chaînes de l'Himalaya ou des Andes. De nombreux randonneurs sous-estiment à la fois cet état de fait et la nature du terrain, qui se souviendront peut-être davantage de leurs membres endoloris et d'épouvantables maux de tête, que des points de vue splendides qu'ils auront rencontrés. La route de Chogoria, ouverte dans les années vingt par Earnest Carr, constitue en trois jours la plus belle approche, et de loin la plus aisée. Tenez-en compte, surtout en l'absence d'acclimatation préalable.

Ainsi que pour tous les voyages au sein de montagnes fréquentés, on ne peut que recommander d'éviter les voies principales. Au lieu de vous diriger directement vers le chalet de Minto (4 300 m) en empruntant le sentier bien signalisé depuis la Chogoria Park Gate et la Mount Kenya Lodge, prenez donc votre temps et empruntez la piste plus petite, traversant la lande jusqu'au lac Ellis pour votre premier campement de nuit. Passez la deuxième nuit sur le rivage idyllique du lac Michaelson et prenez la direction de la Top Hut (4 790 m) en passant par Square Tarn et Tooth Col à partir de là. La splendeur immaculée de ces lacs et du pays qui les entoure est bien éloignée de la malpropreté et de l'entassement qui caractérise une nuit chez Minto.

Point Lenana vous offre des vues sur les sommets voisins, qui vous couperont le souffle, après seulement 45 minutes de montée facile depuis la Top Hut. La plupart des gens gravissent cela à la lumière de leur torche frontale, avant l'aube, et s'arrêtent au sommet, dans le froid pinçant du matin, pour admirer le spectacle glorieux du soleil d'Afrique s'élevant dans le ciel. Il s'ensuit une folle ruée vers le chalet, l'on peut dévorer un copieux petit déjeuner, avant de descendre tout droit vers la vallée Teleki et la station météorologique sur la route du Naro Moru, bien plus bas. C'est bien dommage, car un ou deux jours de plus pour terminer le circuit des sommets couronnent vraiment ce qui est sans aucun doute la plus belle randonnée en haute montagne de toute l'Afrique de l'Est.

Quelle que soit la direction, le circuit des sommets peut être parcouru en moins de huit jours par des marcheurs acclimatés et en bonne condition. Toutefois, pour bien profiter de tout, une nuit supplémentaire au chalet de Two Tarn Hut (4 990 m) ou celui de Kami Huts (4 425 m) est chaudement recommandée. Le premier offre des vues époustouflantes sur le glacier Tyndall et la face ouest du Batian, tandis que le second est tourné vers les sommets de Sendeyo et Terere. Les sentiers sont étroits et traversent un sol instable. L'orientation peut poser quelques problèmes lorsque la brume enveloppe quotidiennement les pics, cachant les marques de parcours ; le circuit des sommets constitue certainement l'apogée spectaculaire et stimulant d'une traversée du mont Kenya. Quelle que soit l'option que vous prendrez, ne vous précipitez pas pour descendre vers le Naro Moru – un dernier regard en arrière sur les principaux sommets, depuis le camp Mackinder, vous vaudra les plus belles vues du parcours, et la végétation sur la dernière descente abrupte vers la station météo par le Vertical Bog est absolument fantastique. Ceux qui, après tous ces efforts, seraient en manque d'un peu de luxe débridé, ne seront pas déçus par le Naro Moru River Lodge.

CI-DESSUS *Batian et Nelion, séparés par la Porte des Brumes, offrent une vue magnifique sur le Hut Tarn depuis la Two Tarn Hut (4 990 m).*

LIEU Est du Grand Fossé, Kenyan Highlands.

QUAND PARTIR Janvier à février, août à septembre.

DÉPART Mount Kenya Lodge (3 000 m). Vols internationaux sur Nairobi, puis trajet routier (3 h) jusqu'à l'ancienne mission écossaise de Chogoria. Il y a là un hôtel de transit et on peut y recruter des porteurs. Les cases du Mount Kenya Lodge se trouvent 3 h 30 plus loin par 4 x 4 si la route est sèche.

FIN Station météo de Naro Moru. L'hôtel Naro Moru River Lodge exploite un terrain de camping sommaire à cet endroit. L'hôtel River Lodge est à 1 h de jeep, et le trajet de Naro Moru à Nairobi prend 3 h.

DURÉE 6 jours minimum.

ALTITUDE MAXIMUM Point Lenana (4 985 m).

ASPECTS TECHNIQUES Acclimatation indispensable.

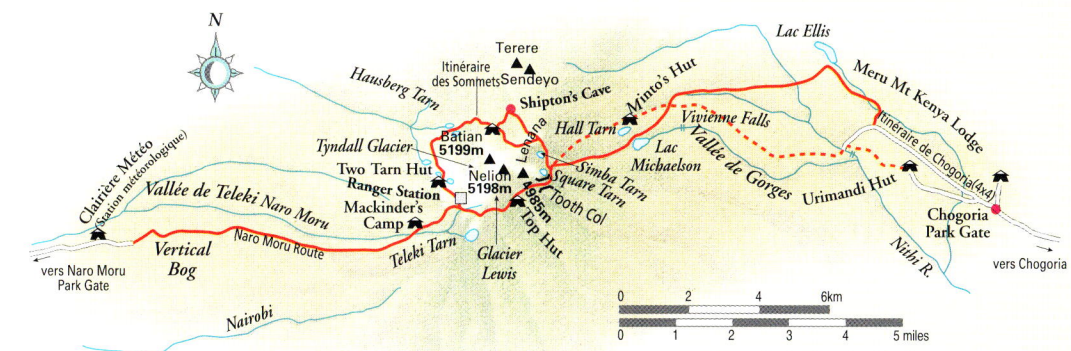

ÉQUIPEMENT Matériel de camping autonome recommandé, surtout si le détour par les lacs Ellis/Michaelson est envisagé, soit par l'intermédiaire d'une agence à Nairobi, ou organisé sur place à Chogoria.

MODE DE RANDONNÉE Sac à dos ou expédition.

AUTORISATIONS/RESTRICTIONS Aucune, mais les droits d'accès aux parcs, camps/chalets sont payables d'avance.

LE CANYON DE FISH RIVER

par Mike Lundy

Le canyon de Fish River est l'un des plus grands du monde, devancé seulement par le Grand Canyon d'Arizona, USA. Comme les Victoria Falls et le Kilimandjaro, il fait partie des grandes merveilles naturelles de l'Afrique. Le silence total, la solitude inviolée et les milliards d'étoiles se conjuguent chaque soir pour créer une expérience profondément inspiratrice, et purifier l'âme.

Les anciens sédiments de lave qui forment le fond du canyon furent déposés initialement entre 1 800 et 1 000 millions d'années avant notre ère. Il y a environ 300 à 500 millions d'années, pendant la période glaciaire du Gondwana, de nombreuses failles orientées nord-sud furent creusées plus profondément encore par des glaciers en mouvement vers le sud. L'entaille effectuée par la rivière Fish en des temps plus chauds, depuis près de 50 millions d'années, a donné au canyon sa forme actuelle.

Proclamé monument naturel en 1962, le Fish River Canyon fut, six ans plus tard, déclaré réserve animalière par le gouvernement sud-africain qui, à l'époque, administrait le territoire sous mandat de l'Afrique du Sud-Ouest. Le canyon se situe dans la partie sud-ouest de ce qui, en mars 1990, devint la Namibie, un pays plus grand que le Royaume-Uni et la France réunis, mais avec une population n'atteignant qu'un million et demi d'habitants. La profondeur du canyon excède 600 m par endroits et il s'étend sur plus de 160 km. Le parcours lui-même couvre plus de la moitié de cette distance, et il faut cinq jours pour l'accomplir. Certains tronçons sont si étroits que l'on a parfois l'impression de pouvoir presque toucher les deux falaises en tendant les bras. A mesure que l'on descend le torrent, le canyon s'élargit jusqu'à atteindre 27 km dans sa plus grande largeur.

Avant de commencer votre descente, arrêtez-vous pour regarder cet impressionnant spectacle depuis le belvédère le plus au nord. Le Coin du Diable vous renvoie son regard noir, mais un peu plus loin en aval la vue vous coupe le souffle, surtout au petit matin, quand les falaises abruptes

EN HAUT *A l'approche de la moitié du parcours, les parois du canyon dominent toujours les marcheurs partagés entre un sentiment de respect et de total désintérêt.*
ENCART *Descente dans les profondeurs du Fish River Canyon, avec l'aide de chaînes. Les bâtons de marche sont une aide précieuse pour enjamber les blocs rocheux et pour les passages à gué.*

sont inondées de couleur. L'abrupte descente jusqu'au fond du canyon vous entraîne dans un voyage dans le temps, à travers des centaines de millions d'années d'histoire géologique de la terre. Le ruban argenté de la rivière se rapproche de plus en plus, pour qu'enfin, une heure environ après le début de votre descente à l'aide de mains courantes, vous puissiez piquer une tête dans l'énorme cuvette naturelle qui vous attend en bas, dans les entrailles du plus vieux canyon du monde.

Les premiers 16 km, jusqu'à Palm Springs, sont notoirement escarpés et lents, le terrain étant principalement composé de gros blocs rocheux en alternance avec du sable mou – sans parler de l'occasionnel passage à gué. Bien qu'elle demande de nombreux efforts, il s'agit là de la partie la plus intéressante et la plus belle du canyon. Le balisage n'est pas nécessaire, puique la piste chemine entre les deux énormes murailles qui canalisent l'itinéraire. Il n'y a pas de point d'arrêt nocturne établi, aussi, arrêtez-vous pour la nuit à n'importe quel endroit convenable, au moins une heure avant le coucher de soleil (après quoi il fait vite très sombre et la température tombe).

Peu de temps après avoir entamé votre descente du canyon, vous serez surpris de rencontrer les vestiges de deux scooters. Ils sont le résultat d'une expédition insensée, organisée en 1968 contre l'avis de toutes les autorités, par le Vespa Club du Cap.

Quelque temps avant d'apercevoir les palmiers de Palm Springs, votre odorat vous en annoncera la proximité. L'eau des sources à 57 °C est riche en fluorure, chlorure et sulfure, ce dernier étant responsable de cette odeur d'œuf pourri. Malgré cela, cet endroit est parfait pour une pause ou même pour y passer la nuit, et les membres fatigués peuvent se délasser dans les eaux bien chaudes. Les palmiers, bien qu'étant de magnifiques spécimens, paraissent un peu incongrus à cet endroit. Ils ne sont pas originaires d'Afrique du Sud et

CI-DESSOUS *Le Fish River Canyon, ne donnant qu'un aperçu de sa pleine majesté. Une randonnée en montagnes russes pour descendre dans le plus ancien canyon du monde, le deuxième par la taille.*

CI-DESSUS *Reflets dans le temps et dans l'espace. Juin et juillet sont les mois idéaux pour éviter l'excès ou le manque d'eau.*

leur origine a suscité diverses hypothèses. La plus populaire et la plus vraisemblable veut qu'ils aient poussé à partir de noyaux de dattes jetés par des prisonniers allemands évadés d'un camp durant la Première Guerre mondiale, situé non loin, au lieu-dit « Aus ».

Après Palm Springs, la progression devient plus facile, et la montagne de la Table, une grande montagne au sommet aplati (à ne pas confondre avec la bien plus grande « Table Mountain » reconnue comme le symbole international de la ville du Cap, quelque 900 km au sud) apparaît, aidera à se diriger le temps de parcourir les quelques méandres de la rivière.

Le troisième jour, vous rencontrerez une série de formations rocheuses et de cimes intéressantes, prenant la forme de curieuses créations comme « Les trois sœurs » et le « Rocher à quatre doigts ». Une fois ce dernier dépassé, le canyon commence à s'élargir, les falaises s'éloignant progressivement. C'est là, dans cette région de formations rocheuses, que vous pourrez apprécier à quel point les relations tendues entre les léopards et les babouins peuvent parfois devenir dangereuses. Il n'est pas rare que le silence du soir soit rompu par les hurlements à vous glacer le sang des babouins attaqués, tandis que la nature s'exprime dans une promiscuité peu rassurante !

Après un ou deux raccourcis coupant au travers des épingles à cheveu, par-dessus les crêtes, le canyon commence à s'élargir et il se peut que vous tombiez sur quelque chose qui ressemble à du crottin de cheval. Malheureusement, c'est probablement tout ce que vous verrez du timide zèbre de la montagne de Hartmann, dans la mesure où il ne se désaltère que sous couvert de l'obscurité. Il existe deux autres espèces de zèbre en Afrique du Sud, mais celle-ci ne vit que dans les zones montagneuses isolées de Namibie et d'Angola du Sud. Vous avez plus de chance de voir le majestueux kudu, une grande antilope aux cordes torsadées.

Le quatrième jour, vos pas vous mèneront peut-être vers une tombe allemande, son occupant profitant pour l'éternité de la solitude que lui offre cette étendue déserte. L'Allemagne a occupé la Namibie comme puissance coloniale pendant environ trente ans, avant la Première Guerre mondiale, et des combats acharnés avec les tribus Nama se déroulèrent dans cette région. Le lieutenant von Trotha fut abattu d'une balle dans le dos en 1905, pendant une échauffourée, et fut enterré sur le lieu de sa mort.

Le dernier jour, le canyon se transforme en un grand espace ouvert et la piste continue principalement sur du sable mou. A ce stade, vous aurez certainement entendu l'appel de l'Afrique – le son plaintif et obsédant du pyrargue vocifère, sans doute l'oiseau de proie le plus majestueux et le plus impressionnant – et aperçu quelques-unes de ses vedettes : l'oréotrague (ou

NAMIBIE

saute-rochers) se dressant gracieusement sur la pointe de ses sabots, tel un danseur de ballet. Vous aurez sans doute reconnu, parmi la rare végétation, l'arbre qui symbolise le mieux la Namibie, l'arbre carquois, ainsi nommé parce que les peuplades indigènes Khoi utilisaient le tronc creux de cette euphorbe en forme d'aloès comme carquois pour transporter leurs flèches. Principalement concentrée sur les berges, l'alhagi ou épine de chameau apporte une ombre bienvenue ainsi que l'ébène qui, avec ses branches pendantes, donne l'impression de dépérir sous la chaleur. Il n'en est rien. Il faut être immortel dans cette nature hostile.

La randonnée du canyon de Fish River se termine à Ai-Ais, qui paradoxalement signifie « eaux brûlantes » en langage nama, et les sources chaudes cicatrisantes de cet oasis luxuriant soulageront vos articulations endolories. Cette station, établie en 1971, fut presque entièrement emportée par la rivière un an plus tard, lors de la plus forte crue jamais enregistrée.

La Namibie est un pays qui voit toujours revenir ses visiteurs. Difficile de savoir pourquoi. Il y a des kilomètres et des kilomètres de « rien », mais ce désert a une allure, un mystère. Les verdoyantes collines boisées du nord, les plaines désertes et arides du sud et la « Skeleton Coast » si bien nommée, en constante opposition avec l'Atlantique sud si froid, nous dévoilent quelques-unes de ses facettes. Pourtant, le titre d'un ouvrage récent sur la Namibie veut tout dire : « Namibie – la terre que Dieu créa dans sa colère ». Faites la randonnée du canyon de la Fish River, et vous verrez ce dont Dieu en colère est réellement capable...

CI-DESSUS, DE GAUCHE À DROITE *Après une journée étouffante avec une température de 40 °C, un feu de camp maintient les randonneurs au chaud dans la nuit glaciale du désert – les extrêmes sont monnaie courante dans le Fish River Canyon ; une météo fiable dispense les marcheurs d'emporter des tentes et leur permet d'apprécier la magnificence du ciel nocturne en dormant à la belle étoile ; le but est en vue – Ai-Ais attend les marcheurs avec ses sources chaudes, de la bière fraîche et des lits confortables. Et cette oasis n'est pas un mirage !*

LIEU Namibie, près de la frontière sud-africaine.
QUAND PARTIR De mi-avril à mi-septembre. Juin et juillet sont les meilleurs mois. En raison de conditions météorologiques extrêmes, le canyon est fermé pendant le reste de l'année.
DÉPART Hobas, à 10 km du canyon, 650 km de Windhoeck, 900 km du Cap ou 1 200 km de Johannesburg.
ARRIVÉE Ai-Ais, oasis de sources chaudes dans un semi-désert. Moyens d'hébergement allant d'appartements luxueux aux cases primitives, et tentes permanentes avec lits de camp. La station thermale compte un restaurant, une station-service et une piscine.
DURÉE 5 jours, 100 km tout au long du cours de la rivière, ou environ 86 km par les raccourcis.
POINT CULMINANT 820 m.
ASPECTS TECHNIQUES Néant.
ÉQUIPEMENT Bottes légères, vêtements toutes saisons, lotion solaire, lunettes de soleil et chapeau absolument indispensables. La tente n'est pas nécessaire, car on peut dormir à la belle étoile, mais un kit de survie est recommandé. Le bois est rare, donc prévoyez un réchaud. Grande bouteille d'eau recommandée.
MODE DE RANDONNÉE Sac à dos.
AUTORISATIONS/RESTRICTIONS Les groupes peuvent compter 3 (minimum) à 40 personnes (maximum). Certificat médical de bonne forme physique datant de moins de 40 jours, à fournir au ranger à Hobas avant le départ. Demandes d'autorisations auprès du bureau central de réservations de la Namibia Wildlife Resorts Ltd, à Windhoek.

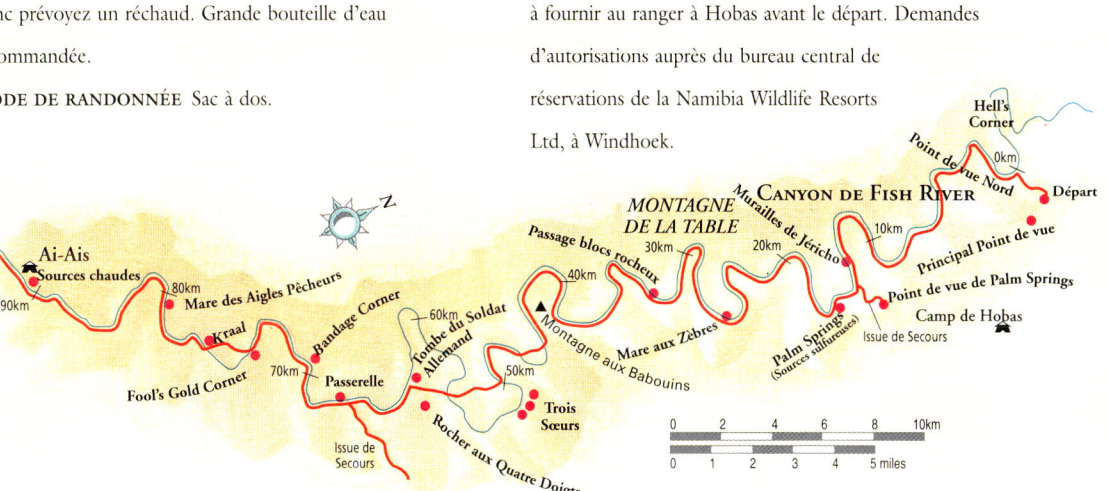

LES PISTES DES LOUTRES ET DU TSITSIKAMMA

par Mike Lundy

Les premiers habitants de cette extrémité sud-est de l'Afrique étaient les Khoisans ou Bushmen (Hommes de la Brousse). La peau claire et de petite taille, ils compensaient ce dernier handicap par leurs talents de chasseurs et leur instinct de conservation. Ils appelaient cet endroit Tsitsikamma – *là où commencent les eaux claires* – parce qu'un grand nombre de rivières prennent leur source dans ces montagnes verdoyantes.

Situé aux deux tiers environ de la distance entre les villes côtières du Cap et Port Élisabeth, le circuit des pistes des Loutres et du Tsitsikamma est la conjugaison de deux parcours sud-africains très appréciés – la piste montagneuse du Tsitsikamma, à l'intérieur du pays, et la spectaculaire piste côtière des Loutres. Cette aventure de dix jours nous conduit de la beauté sauvage de la côte déchiquetée jusqu'aux hautes montagnes du Tsitsikamma, avec ses sombres forêts primitives de fougères arborescentes et de *fynbus*.

Le *fynbus*, que l'on trouve exclusivement dans ce petit coin d'Afrique, est un groupe de fleurs arborescentes qui constituent un véritable trésor botanique, sans égal sur la planète. Le monde végétal est divisé en six régions distinctes et séparées, appelées royaumes floraux. Le royaume floral du Cap est la plus petite de ces six régions – mais c'est aussi la plus riche, avec près de neuf mille espèces différentes de plantes à fleurs concentrées. La richesse et l'abondance de la flore sont très bien illustrées par les bruyères, du genre Erica. La bruyère européenne bien connue comprend vingt et une espèces d'Erica. Ici on n'en compte pas moins de six cent cinquante-sept.

Le parc national du Tsitsikamma fut créé en 1964, suivi peu de temps après, en 1968, par le réseau de pistes. Le parc est adossé à la montagne et comprend 80 km de côte immaculée ; il s'étend même sur trois milles nautiques en mer, avec l'unique piste sous-marine d'Afrique.

Les pistes du Tsitsikamma et des Loutres furent les premières composantes d'un véritable réseau de pistes de randonnée dans toute l'Afrique du Sud. Le réseau national de voies pédestres, comme il devait s'appeler, n'a en fait jamais été raccordé mais a donné naissance à un grand nombre de parcours à travers le pays. Au dernier recensement, on comptait trois cent soixante-quinze pistes dans la seule Afrique du Sud, et soixante-dix-huit autres dans les pays avoisinants.

La randonnée de dix jours part du spectaculaire camp de repos situé à l'embouchure de la rivière Storm. De là, les randonneurs partent vers l'ouest le long de la côte sauvage, se déplaçant à travers une forêt dense d'où ils débouchent, de temps à autre, sur une plage isolée avec un point de vue à vous couper le souffle. D'énormes rochers aux formes acérées surgissent de la mer, telles des sentinelles gardant la côte. Ce n'est pas l'endroit que vous choisiriez pour faire naufrage ! Le sentier tourne, monte et redescend des collines boisées, occasionnellement coupé par une rivière. Les 43 km du tronçon côtier pourraient laisser penser à une simple promenade de cinq jours, eh bien, non ! En fait, la deuxième partie du parcours, la piste du Tsitsikamma, est beaucoup plus longue avec ses 72 km, mais plus facile. Prenez votre temps sur la section côtière.

La première partie du parcours comprend une bonne part de varappe et de sauts de bloc en bloc, sur et juste au-dessus de la marque des pleines marées. Ce court tronçon jusqu'à la

EN HAUT *La deuxième journée apporte la paisible harmonie des cascades argentées et de la verdure. L'une des nombreuses chutes – celle-ci entre Ngubu Huts et Kleinbos.*
ENCART *À cause de son odorat très développé et de son ouïe très fine, la loutre du cap se montre très rarement. Malgré cela, cet animal insaisissable a donné son nom à cette piste.*
CI-CONTRE *Le deuxième jour, à Kleinbos, un marcheur fait une pause pour admirer le paysage – un véritable jardin d'Éden avec piscine.*

CI-DESSUS *La piste des Loutres serpente le long de la côte, débouchant souvent de la brousse sur des falaises qui offrent le spectacle grandiose de l'océan Indien s'y brisant.*

première case étape pour la nuit (4,8 km) est un peu un baptême du feu. En tout cas pour les randonneurs inexpérimentés, qui semblent incapables de sauter sur le prochain rocher sans descendre et remonter laborieusement à l'assaut du suivant. Mais toutes les difficultés seront vite oubliées, « lavées » par une cascade magnifique.

A peine trois heures après le départ, vous atteindrez les premières cases où passer la nuit – Ngubu Huts – du nom du garde forestier qui participa à la création de la piste et périt dans un incendie. Chaque bivouac côtier comprend deux cabanes en bois au confort spartiate. Chacune peut accueillir six personnes. Eau et bois de chauffage sont théoriquement fournis, mais sans garantie.

Le deuxième jour du parcours est une alternance spectaculaire de montée et descente à pic, avec comme point fort les falaises peintes de Skilderkrans. De là, vous pouvez voir la quasi-totalité de la piste des Loutres dans les deux directions. Écartez-vous un instant de la piste pour gagner la Baie Bleue, un « must ». Ce n'est qu'à dix minutes, en direction d'une superbe plage de sable – l'une des rares existantes sur cette côte déchiquetée. Profitez-en au maximum avant d'affronter la laborieuse remontée vers la piste principale.

Le jour suivant, vous aurez peut-être l'impression d'être observé. Et ce sera vrai, par un espiègle petit singe vervet ou par les *Knysna loeries* au plumage chatoyant. Cette journée s'achève par la traversée de l'embouchure de la rivière Lottering pour atteindre les cases Oakhurst sur la rive opposée. On ne peut pas être plus près des vagues fracassantes où les dauphins batifolent dans les brisants translucides.

Le quatrième jour vous rencontrerez l'obstacle le plus redouté du parcours : la traversée de la Bloukrans River (rivière des Falaises bleues). Les risques en sont presque déraisonnablement amplifiés, et les randonneurs, la nuit précédente, dorment souvent d'un sommeil agité par l'appréhension. Le fort courant et l'important dénivelé à marée haute sont des facteurs à prendre en considération, mais si l'on traverse à marée basse, il n'y a pas beaucoup de soucis à se faire.

Le dernier jour sur la côte commence par l'ascension d'un haut plateau, avant de redescendre très vite vers la plage sans fin de la Nature Valley au point intermédiaire de la randonnée. Les mouettes chamailleuses, les rares huitriers noirs d'Afrique qui tentent de vous éloigner de leurs poussins sans défense, le cormoran solitaire qui, tel

QUAND PARTIR Bien que cette région soit soumise à des précipitations toute l'année, évitez la période d'août à novembre. Les mois les plus chauds sont ceux de décembre à mars, avec une température moyenne autour de 20 °C.

DÉPART/ARRIVÉE Embouchure de la Storm River ; 500 km à l'est du Cap ; 250 km à l'ouest de Port Élisabeth.

DURÉE 10 jours. La piste des Loutres fait 43 km de long, la piste du Tsitsikamma en compte 72.

POINT CULMINANT 740 m.

ASPECTS TECHNIQUES Néant.

MATÉRIEL Équipement de randonnée standard, plus sac de couchage. Il faut être autonome sur le plan alimentaire.

MODE DE RANDONNÉE Sac à dos, bien que les deux pistes offrent des cases pour passer la nuit. Les cases de la piste des Loutres comptent chacune six bat-flanc (deux cases à chaque bivouac) ; les cases de la piste du Tsitsikamma comptent trente lits chacune.

AUTORISATIONS/RESTRICTIONS Des permis sont nécessaires pour chacune des pistes et on peut les obtenir auprès de SA National Parks pour la piste des Loutres et auprès de SA Forestry Co, Ltd (SAFCOL) pour la piste du Tsitsikamma. En raison de son succès, il n'est pas facile d'obtenir un permis pour la piste les Loutres.

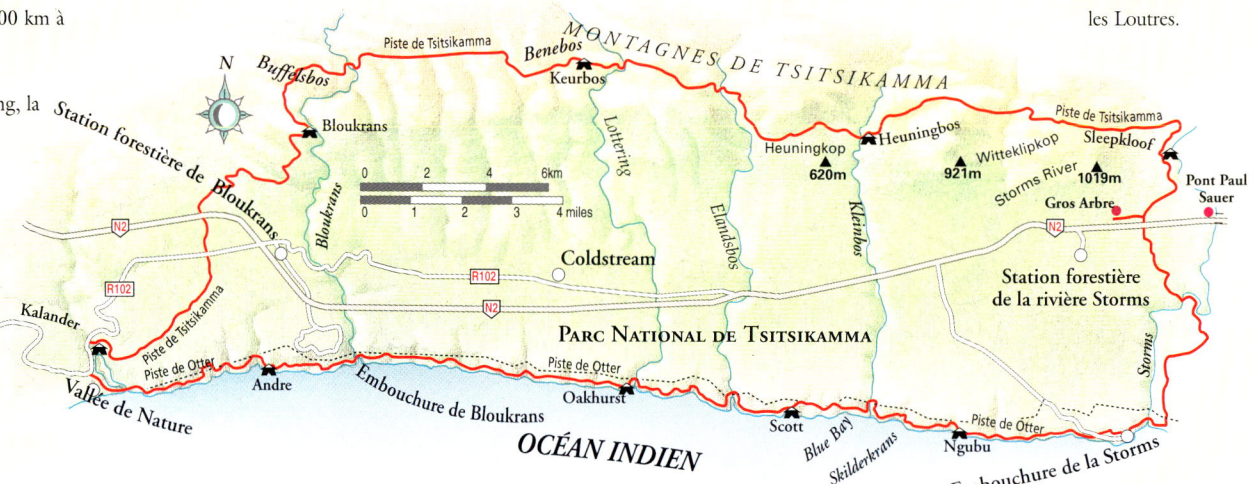

CI-CONTRE *La marée montante n'est pas le meilleur moment pour traverser l'embouchure de la Bloukrans; mais ces marcheurs savent que c'est bien moins dangereux qu'à marée descendante!*

CI-DESSUS *Les rayons du soleil filtrés par la canopée ajoutent une note de paix et de tranquillité au parcours intérieur de la piste Tsitsikamma, en vif contraste avec la côte très bruyante de la piste des Loutres.*

un crucifix, fait sécher ses ailes – tous ces oiseaux côtiers ne vous suivront pas dans la montagne.

Refaites vos provisions à la boutique locale, et poursuivez jusqu'aux montagnes du Tsitsikamma, qui cachent jalousement leur forêt vierge, leurs *fynbus* et leurs pétillantes baignoires naturelles. Les chalets de montagne peuvent accueillir trente personnes ; attendez-vous par conséquent à cohabiter avec d'intéressants inconnus. Votre première nuit dans la montagne au chalet de Bloukrans, précairement accroché au bord d'une falaise, conclura en beauté votre journée, et la vue vous laissera des souvenirs inoubliables.

A l'instar de la piste côtière, la seconde journée alterne montées et descentes, vous traverserez les forêts de Buffelbos (forêt des Buffles) et de Benebos (forêt des Os). Éléphants et buffles les parcouraient jadis en très grand nombre ; hélas ! en moins de cent ans, les colons européens les ont anéantis. Un grand nombre de fougères arborescentes ont subsisté, qui donnent aux clairières l'aspect d'un décor vieux de trois millions d'années. Les rochers sont décorés par la nature – les lichens de tous les tons de jaune, rouge, orange, noir, blanc et gris.

Le jour suivant vous conduira au-delà du pic Formosa, le point culminant de la chaîne du Tsitsikamma, avec ses 1 675 m. Trois traversées de rivière et une marche le long d'une ancienne voie de wagonnets vous amènera jusqu'au bivouac ultime, dans la forêt de Heuningbos (forêt du Miel). La voie fut construite en 1834 dans le but d'exploiter la forêt locale.

Le neuvième jour du parcours atteint le point culminant de la piste (740 m), faisant probablement de cette journée la plus fatigante du trajet. Le point de vue sur la forêt qui s'étend jusqu'à la Storm River Gorge est superbe, avec votre dernier bivouac dans la case perchée sur le rebord d'un promontoire, à Sleepkloof, dans le lointain contrebas. Là, vous dormirez sans doute, mais le nom en fait signifie « ravin attirant » et évoque les rondins qui s'en sont détachés.

Le « sprint final », une descente qui traverse assez tristement une route nationale, vous ramènera à la réalité du monde. Le franchissement de l'embouchure de la Storm River sur un pont de lianes dont on se demande s'il est vraiment solide, constitue le clou du périple. Vous venez de savourer dix jours de ce que l'Afrique compte de meilleur.

ASIE

LA ROUTE DE LUCIE | GONDOKORO LA – DE HUSHE À CONCORDIA | LA TRAVERSÉE BIAFO–HISPAR | LADAKH ET ZANSKAR | DE SINGALILA À KANGCHENDZONGA
GCHENDZONGA | DE JUMLA AU MONT KAILAS | LE CIRCUIT DE DHAULAGIRI | CIRCUIT DU MANASLU ET DE L'ANNAPURNA | LA RANDONNÉE DU « BONHOMME DE NEIGE »

ASIE

*Je suis un voyageur, et toujours je parcourrai
le monde pour en voir les merveilles*

SHIHABUDDIN SUHRAWARDI, 1153-1191

CI-DESSUS *Les conditions de randonnée dans les déserts montagneux du Pakistan diffèrent totalement de celles du Népal – moins de montées et de descentes importantes, mais un terrain beaucoup plus dur sous le pied.*
CI-CONTRE *Marcheurs franchissant un pont sur la Dudh Khola supérieure, juste au-dessous de Bimthang, au Népal. Au-delà, l'imposant Himlung Himal offre l'un des plus vastes panoramas sur les stupéfiants sommets révélés pendant le passage du Larkya La.*
PAGES PRÉCÉDENTES *À Dzong Ri, les drapeaux colorés du bouddhisme tantrique flottent au vent, envoyant des prières aux dieux.*

Avec des côtes sur les océans Arctique, Pacifique et Indien et sur les mers Rouge et Méditerranée, l'Asie est le plus grand des continents. Ses limites englobent les immenses péninsules d'Arabie, de l'Inde et d'Indochine, et son sol fut le berceau des civilisations anciennes de Mésopotamie (Irak) et de la vallée de l'Indus, plus de 4 000 ans av. J.-C.

Les empires et les invasions, tels les mouvements des marées, ont déposé et laissé dans les divers pays du continent une fantastique diversité culturelle, et la nature y a apporté une main complice pour enrichir plus encore le monde en créant la plus haute et la plus formidable frontière naturelle de la planète – l'Himalaya – à l'assaut de laquelle montent depuis des siècles les vagues du commerce, de l'islam, de l'hindouisme et du bouddhisme. Nulle part ailleurs, sur terre, alpinistes et randonneurs ne pourront conjuguer les joies que leur procurent l'exercice de leur passion et l'exaltation de voyager au milieu de montagnes et de vallées si imprégnées de spiritualité.

Une simple évocation du Pakistan ou du Karakoram devant ceux qui y ont déjà voyagé leur rappellera l'hospitalité des musulmans rustiques des régions du nord. L'infrastructure touristique est peut-être primitive, mais ceux qui s'aventurent en ces lieux de soleil intense, de chaleur torride et de montagnes incroyablement escarpées à l'infini, éprouvent un profond bonheur. Les parcours décrits ici – vers K2 par le Gondokoro La et la traversée du Biafo-Hispar –, sont les plus difficiles de cet ouvrage, mais également les plus spectaculaires.

Le Cachemire, le paradis himalayen pour lequel le Pakistan et l'Inde se querellent depuis si longtemps, est malheureusement hors limites pour les randonneurs aujourd'hui, mais au-delà s'étend l'aride contrée des montagnes de l'Inde, tout aussi attirantes.

Le Ladakh et le Zanskar n'ont peut-être pas de sommets de 8 000 m ou les immenses glaciers du Karakoram, mais ils sont habités par un peuple noble, d'obédience bouddhiste tibétaine, qui a su garder vivaces toutes ses traditions. De tous les itinéraires de randonnée possibles dans la région, aucun n'est plus étincelant ni plus stimulant que le long passage sud de Lamayuru au Ladakh jusqu'à Manali, en traversant le cœur du Zhankar.

Il est inutile de présenter le Népal aux randonneurs. C'est ici, dans les années soixante, que les premières sociétés commerciales d'organisation de randonnées ont vu le jour, et le Népal est toujours «la Mecque» des amoureux de la montagne du monde entier. À Katmandou, la capitale bouillonnante de ce petit royaume de montagne, des temples médiévaux côtoient des cybercafés et les randonneurs découvriront que les Népalais ont appris à satisfaire leurs moindres besoins. Bien qu'un grand nombre de pistes renommées soit maintenant très encombré, il est encore possible de fuir la foule.

À l'est du Népal, plus près du courant de mousson porteur de vie qui souffle depuis le golfe du Bengale, la chaîne de l'Himalaya offre ici son aspect le plus verdoyant et le plus secret. À Sikkim, on a pu récemment approcher l'énorme Kangchendzonga le long de la chaîne Singalila, tandis que dans le Bhoutan, le Snowman Trek (la randonnée du Bonhomme de neige) est sans doute la piste la plus spectaculaire et la moins connue de tout le massif himalayen.

Enfin, un pied en Europe et l'autre en Asie, la Turquie est depuis longtemps le point de rencontre de l'histoire des deux continents. Sur la côte méditerranéenne de l'Asie Mineure – aujourd'hui la péninsule d'Anatolie – la province antique de Lycie fut successivement convoitée par les Perses, les Rhodiens et les Romains. La piste récemment ouverte le long de la côte déchiquetée deviendra certainement un classique du genre.

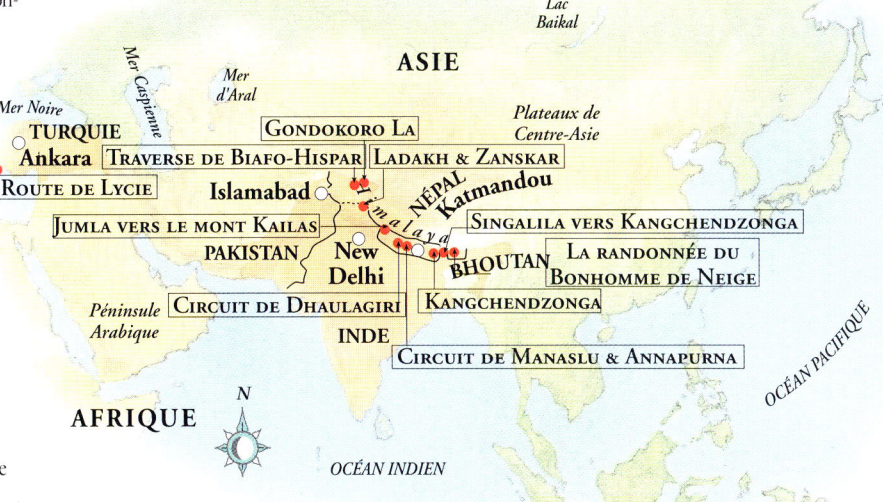

LA ROUTE DE LYCIE

par Kate Clow

La Lycie est un chaos montagneux sur la côte sud de la Turquie, où la chaîne du Taurus plonge dans la scintillante Méditerranée. La route de Lycie suit les anciennes routes et aqueducs grecs et romains, les pistes traditionnelles des nomades et les chemins forestiers qui contournent la côte, surmontant des chaînes et évitant le delta. Des pistes existantes ont été reliées pour former un itinéraire continu de marches couvrant plus de 530 km, surgissant des falaises, serpentant à travers bois, où s'arrêtant sur des plages désertes en faisant plusieurs détours à l'intérieur du pays. D'anciens villages de pêcheurs, maintenant « pièges à touristes », comme Kemer, Kas et Kalban, proposent provisions, hébergement et une pause dans la solitude de la piste. La plupart des Turcs travaillent encore la terre, certains comme bergers. Plus récemment, néanmoins, les citadins de deuxième génération ont redécouvert leurs territoires ancestraux ; la route de Lycie constitue une nouvelle mode récréative. Elle est sponsorisée (et signalisée) par une grande banque et jalonnée de marques rouges et blanches, semblables à celles des sentiers de grande randonnée français. Les randonneurs sont encore rares sur cette nouvelle route ; on peut y marcher toute une semaine sans rencontrer âme qui vive. La partie la plus appréciée est la déviation vers le mont Olympos – le haut lieu spirituel et matériel du parcours.

La Lycie fut tout d'abord un État dépendant de l'Empire hittite, établi en Anatolie centrale aux alentours de 1800 av. J.-C. Repoussés vers le sud par de nouveaux envahisseurs, les Lyciens

EN HAUT *Bas-relief (IV ou V siècle) sur la tombe de la dynastie royale à Xanthos, représentant des lions attaquant un daim.*

CI-DESSUS *Un groupe de marcheurs se repose sur un yayla (alpage d'été) après la rude montée des pentes du Musa Dagi.*

se mélangèrent avec les colons grecs et établirent une culture riche, artistique, complétant l'agriculture et la pêche par la guerre mercenaire. Les troupes lyciennes combattirent à Troie et à Salamis. Après la mort d'Alexandre (323 av. J.-C.), les Séleucides, puis les Romains gouvernèrent l'Anatolie, mais laissèrent aux Lyciens, qui maintenant parlent grec, la liberté de constituer une ligue démocratique unique. Après des siècles de prospérité, la population, aux environs du XVe siècle, avait presque entièrement succombé à la peste et aux pirates arabes. La péninsule de Lycie resta presque totalement déserte jusqu'à l'arrivée des Turcs, au XVe siècle.

Le premier véritable héros à emprunter la route de Lycie fut le roi de Macédoine, Alexandre le Grand. Ayant pour mission la libération des Grecs d'Asie Mineure du joug perse, il entra en Lycie à l'endroit appelé aujourd'hui Fethiye avec son armée de dix mille fantassins. Il traversa la montagne de Baba Dagi, en route pour la superbe place forte de Xanthos, où il accepta la reddition de la capitale lycienne. L'une après l'autre, les villes se soumirent et les représentants de Phaselis lui offrirent une couronne d'or. Alexandre passa l'hiver à Phasalis et, assis dans l'arène en plein air, put contempler le mont Olympos et les gorges qui lui barraient la route, au nord. Après être sorti vainqueur de quelques accrochages locaux, il envoya des ingénieurs tailler des marches dans la montagne pour le passage de son armée.

Alexandre lui-même, accompagné de ses plus proches compagnons, passa par les plages pour rejoindre son armée dans la plaine d'Antalya.

L'itinéraire de la Route de Lycie part du croissant de sable doré appelé Olu Deniz, où la prolifération récente d'hôtels et de pensions aurait permis de loger toute l'armée d'Alexandre !

L'itinéraire emprunte d'abrupts chemins muletiers sur les pentes du Baba Dagi, où les parapentistes profitent des brises d'ouest tandis qu'en dessous, les vagues martèlent les rochers. La descente du premier jour passe devant un moulin restauré et conduit jusqu'à Faralya, où une sympathique pension de village proposant une cuisine locale excellente est perchée sur la falaise qui domine Butterfly Valley – la vallée des papillons. Après une nuit confortable, vous serez pratiquement seuls sur les sentiers serpentant à travers champs et bois, apercevant par moment la mer immense et les quelques bateaux de passage. La montée en lacets, qui grimpe entre les fusains et les pins depuis la vallée de Kabak, est sans doute la plus belle piste de Turquie.

La première ville de Lycie est Sidyma, où les vieilles pierres ont été adaptées aux besoins quotidiens de cette communauté agricole et apicole ; l'arche d'un temple supporte des chaumières branlantes ; quelques inscriptions sont incluses dans les murs de la mosquée et un sarcophage de pierre sert de cabane à outils.

EN HAUT *Une vue au-dessus Yedi Burun (les sept caps), une série de pointes spectaculaires faisant face au vent d'ouest dominant pour abriter des plages désertes.*

CI-DESSUS, AU CENTRE *La route de Lycie s'embrase de fleurs sauvages au printemps – entre janvier et mai, selon l'altitude.*

CI-DESSUS *L'explorateur Charles Fellows rapporta que ces tombes lyciennes taillées dans la roche au-dessus du théâtre romain de Myra étaient jadis peintes aux couleurs de l'arc-en-ciel.*

Une piste côtière descend de Sidyma vers le fort antique de Pydnai et représente un bon test pour un randonneur muni de son équipement complet – la piste est glissante, les rochers instables et les anciennes pierres de chaussée se sont effondrées depuis longtemps. L'itinéraire plonge vers une forêt d'orchidées et traverse des champs de blé jusqu'au village de Gavuragili (ce qui signifie « l'Enclos des Chrétiens »), où les descendants des anciens Grecs avaient coutume d'abriter leurs troupeaux, jusqu'à ce qu'ils retournent en Grèce dans le chaos qui suivit la Première Guerre mondiale.

De l'autre côté de la pointe, au-delà du fort de Pydnai, s'étend une plage de 12 km de long qui mène à Patara, jadis le principal port du pays de Lycie. Le sable, poussé par le vent, ainsi que la vase, ont étendu le delta du fleuve Xanthos jusqu'à la mer, ensablant le site de Patara et créant un sol fertile pour la culture des tomates. La route lycienne fait le tour du delta, tout d'abord au travers d'une plantation de mimosas, puis en suivant le parcours des aqueducs qui alimentaient Xanthos et Patara depuis les collines avoisinantes. L'aqueduc de Patara enjambe des vallées asséchées, soutenu par un système de siphon constitué de mille blocs de pierre, chacun pesant six cents kilos et vieux de 2 000 ans.

En suivant les pistes nomades vers les alpages de Bezirgan, la piste pénètre dans un monde désertique. Des formations rocheuses sculptées par le vent dominent des sources jaillissantes et des anémones, d'un pourpre vif, parsèment les sentiers retirés. Le sommet de la colline de Phellos, où un énorme bas-relief représentant un taureau témoigne du talent des artistes de l'Antiquité, offre des points de vue sur les îles grecques et constitue le point de départ d'une descente à pic vers la station de Kas.

À partir de là, l'itinéraire longe la côte, serpentant à travers un maquis parfumé de thym, jusqu'aux ruines d'Aperlac où d'antiques pierres tombales montent la garde devant une baie peu profonde. Juste après, on trouve le village de pêcheurs abondamment fleuri d'Uçagiz, puis Myra, demeure légendaire de saint Nicolas. Au-dessus de Myra, au mois de mai, les randonneurs sont les premiers témoins des migrations. L'itinéraire remonte et dépasse les ruines d'une église byzantine et d'une cellule d'ermite jusqu'à la colline d'Insegeris à 1 811 m. La côte, des îles d'Uçagiz jusqu'à la chaîne calcaire du cap Gelidonia, s'étend en contrebas. Une descente régulière par la voie romaine conduit à Finike, une ville d'orangeraies, et à travers le delta vers le point le plus au sud de Lycie. Le cap est signalé par un phare isolé où l'on peut passer la nuit. Montez au sommet de la tour pour regarder le soleil levant peindre le monde de rose et d'or.

Au nord, les choses se compliquent. Après quelques jours passés à monter et descendre énergiquement par-delà les crêtes boisées, l'itinéraire atteint les contreforts du mont Olympos, où d'immenses cèdres gardent le col à environ 1 800 m d'altitude. Les plus courageux et les plus chevronnés auront une chance d'atteindre le sommet à 2 366 m, pour être récompensés par des points de vue sur les crêtes sans fin d'un bleu indigo profond se découpant sur la mer d'argent. Les moins aventureux peuvent contourner le pic, visiter le théâtre de Phaselis et se détendre à l'endroit même où Alexandre s'assit un jour. Au-delà du mont Olympos, une succession de petits villages vous offre la possibilité de côtoyer les habitants. L'itinéraire s'achève par la descente d'une vallée profonde et silencieuse jusqu'à la mer, puis une dernière montée de deux jours jusqu'à 1 500 m. On arrive alors sur une étroite crête avec un à-pic à vous couper le souffle qui surplombe le ravin, des points de vue sur la baie et sur votre prochaine destination, la ville d'Antalya. À deux heures de marche se trouve le plus proche village de Hisarçandir, où vous retrouverez la civilisation.

CI-DESSUS *Suleyman, l'un des quatre habitants restés à Gavuragili, parcourt chaque vendredi un tronçon de la route de Lycie pour se rendre à la mosquée.*
CI-CONTRE *Le phare du cap Gelidonia. Jadis, le cap et les cinq îles qui l'entourent constituaient un danger pour la navigation entre l'Égypte ou la Syrie et la Grèce ou Rome.*

LYCIE, TURQUIE

LIEU Côte méditerranéenne de Turquie ; la piste passe entre le Fethiye et Antalya.

QUAND PARTIR Soleil et couleurs sont au rendez-vous de mi-septembre à novembre. De février à mai, les fleurs printanières sont magnifiques.

DÉPART Olu Deniz, 20 min de Fethiye par minibus public. L'aéroport le plus proche est Dalaman, à 2 h de voiture de Olu Deniz.

ARRIVÉE Hisarçandir, 30 min en taxi ou minibus depuis Antalya. L'aéroport le plus proche est à Antalya.

DURÉE 30 jours, 530 km.

POINT CULMINANT Mont Olympos (2 366 m).

ASPECTS TECHNIQUES Le parcours, de difficulté moyenne au départ, devient plus difficile ensuite ; les parties les plus reculées ne seront pas tentées en solitaire. Prenez le temps de vous acclimater et emportez beaucoup d'eau. Aucune carte locale à grande échelle n'est disponible. Pour tous renseignements récents concernant la piste, consultez www.lycianway.com.

MATÉRIEL Tente légère, sac de couchage, matériel de cuisson, chaussures à semelles épaisses, vêtements légers en fonction de la saison, lunettes de soleil, écran solaire, maillots de bain. Fournitures disponibles dans les villages du parcours.

MODE DE RANDONNÉE Sac à dos.

AUTORISATIONS/RESTRICTIONS Camping interdit sur les sites historiques du ministère de la Culture, mais possible en de nombreux endroits le long du parcours. Les énormes chiens de berger d'Anatolie peuvent être menaçants ; un sifflet dissuasif est recommandé.

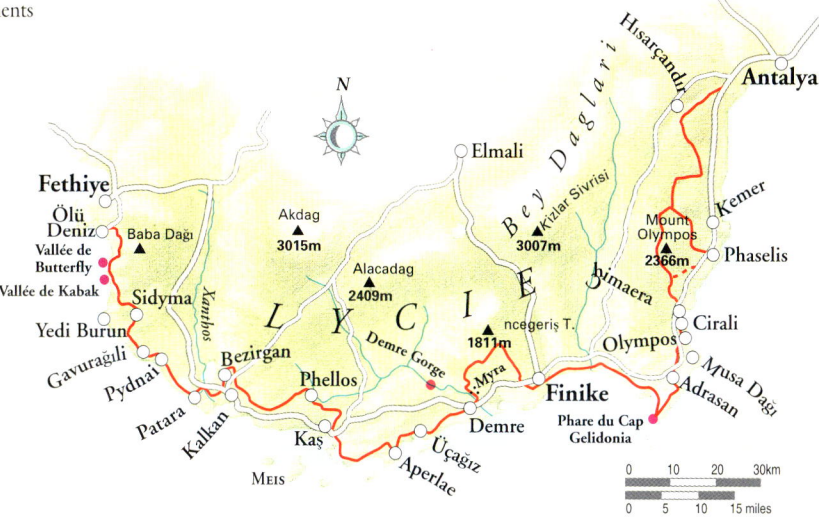

GONDOROKO LA – DE HUSHE À CONCORDIA

par Steve Razzetti

Nom de l'ancien col qui franchit la ligne de partage des eaux entre l'océan Indien et l'Asie centrale, le Karakoram est, sans nul doute, la chaîne de montagne de la beauté la plus sauvage au monde. S'étendant sur quelque 320 km de l'Hindu Kush à l'ouest vers la chaîne du Ladakh et le Grand Himalaya à l'est, des sommets du Karakoram sont situés sur l'une des failles les plus actives du globe, et tandis que les forces tectoniques poussent les sommets vers le ciel, de gigantesques glaciers et des torrents tumultueux les rabaissent inlassablement. Voyager dans le Karakoram, est sans doute assister à la plus grande démonstration de géologie active que le monde puisse nous offrir.

Tout ce qui touche le Karakoram est extrême. Quatre des quatorze sommets de 8 000 m du monde – K2, Broad Peak, Gasherbrum I et Gasherbrum II – dominent un seul réseau de glaciers, le Baltoro. Pas moins de trente-six sommets dépassent 7 300 m d'altitude, et on compte par centaines ceux de plus de 6 000 m. Il y a là quelques-unes des plus hautes montagnes glaciaires hors des régions polaires, et les sept plus grands glaciers (Biafo, Hispar, Baltoro, Gasherbrum, Chogo Lungma, Siachen et Batura) dépassent tous 350 km^2 de superficie. En été, les températures dans les vallées dépassent fréquemment 40 °C, la chaleur incroyablement forte du soleil fait fondre les hauts glaciers et les champs de neige à une vitesse incroyable, transformant les rivières d'aval en torrents rugissants qui transportent le plus fort volume de sédiments de toutes les rivières du monde. La puissance de ces impressionnants cours d'eau est telle, que des blocs de rochers de la taille d'un immeuble se retournent et roulent dans leurs lits comme des feuilles mortes emportées par un courant d'air.

Bien que l'Anglais Godfrey Thomas Vigne fût le premier Européen à pénétrer réellement dans le Karakoram, ce fut Thomas Montgomerie, dans le cadre de son étude topographique de l'Inde, qui le premier prit conscience de sa vraie dimension. En 1856, depuis une station géographique au sommet du pic Haramukh au Cachemire, il positionne par triangulation une série de trente-deux sommets auxquels il attribue le préfixe « K » pour Karakoram. Une fois ses observations recalculées en 1858, K2 se révéla être la deuxième plus haute montagne au monde, et on lui attribue aujourd'hui l'altitude de 8 611 m.

Henry Haversham Godwin-Austen fut le premier à voir de près le K2 en 1861. Au terme d'une expédition épique, au cours de laquelle il découvrit le glacier de Hispar et franchit le col du même nom (*voir page 70*) avant de redescendre le glacier Biafo jusqu'au village d'Askole, il fit une petite incursion sur le glacier Baltoro. Vraiment décidé à voir vérita-

EN HAUT *La redoutable face nord du Masherbrum (7 821 m) et les sommets alignés au sud du glacier Baltoro après les neiges de printemps.*

ENCART *Les aiguilles de granit des Trango Towers constituent indubitablement le chef-d'œuvre de l'architecture montagneuse de la face nord du Baltoro.*

CI-DESSUS *De retour du camp de base de K2 vers Concordia, par une section très crevassée du Baltoro, avec l'imposant pic de la Mitre au-dessus.*

blement le K2, il renonça au Baltoro et escalada un éperon au-dessus du camp, connu aujourd'hui sous le nom d'Urdokas, jusqu'à l'endroit d'où il put dessiner un croquis du sommet de l'énorme pyramide qui surplombe les crêtes afférentes.

Les premiers documents photographiques de ces sommets, pris par le célèbre photographe italien, Vittorio Sella, au cours de l'expédition du duc des Abruzzes en 1909, portèrent les alpinistes du monde entier à s'intéresser réellement à cette région. Utilisant un appareil photo capable d'exposer des plaques de verre de 30 x 40 cm, Sella prit près de huit cents clichés exceptionnels pendant l'expédition, et des tirages furent ensuite achetés par des institutions aussi respectées que la Royal Geographic Society et le Club Alpin à Londres et la National Geographic Society à Washington. L'intérêt des Italiens pour le K2 n'a jamais faibli, et en 1954 Ardito Desio conduisit l'expédition qui réussit la première ascension.

La randonnée pédestre jusqu'à Concordia, au confluent des glaciers de Baltoro et de Goldwin-Austen, au cœur même du Karakoram, est une entreprise difficile. Bien que Skardu, la capitale endormie de la province pakistanaise du Baltistan, où se trouvent les plus hauts pics du Karakoram, soit desservie par des vols quotidiens au départ d'Islamabad, la météo de montagne est notoirement capricieuse et des vols sont souvent annulés. Jusqu'en 1986, ceux qui cherchaient à approcher le K2 et ses puissants voisins se trouvaient confrontés à

CI-DESSUS *La traversée par jhola des eaux tumultueuses de la rivière Braldu à Chongo. Une nécessité qui dépend de l'état de la route.*

CI-DESSOUS *Une ascension en terrain rocailleux au-dessus du glacier de Gondokoro, avec le Layla Peak au loin. Le port de casque est recommandé sur ce tronçon, car les chutes de pierres sont fréquentes.*

GONDOKORO LA – DE HUSHE À CONCORDIA

LIEU Domaine de Karakoram, province de Balistan, zone nord, Pakistan.

QUAND PARTIR De début juin à début septembre.

DÉPART Hushe village ; vols internationaux vers Karachi ou Islamabad (conseillé), puis par avion (1 h) ou par la route (autoroute Karakoram, 18-30 h) jusqu'à Skardu. Nuit étape à Skardu, puis transport en jeep jusqu'à Hushe (10 h).

ARRIVÉE Askole village ; transport en jeep jusqu'à Skardu (6 à 10 h selon l'état de la route), puis par avion ou par la route jusqu'à Islamabad-Rawalpindi.

DURÉE 22 jours ; 130 km.

POINT CULMINANT Gondokoro La (5 585 m).

ASPECTS TECHNIQUES Les randonneurs doivent être expérimentés et équipés pour la traversée de glaciers en cordée et le sauvetage dans les crevasses. Quelques cordes fixes peuvent être nécessaires dans les parties plus hautes du Gondokoro La. Il peut aussi y avoir quelques chutes de pierres – les casques sont recommandés.

MATÉRIEL Bottes en caoutchouc, crampons, harnais et équipement de sauvetage pour randonnée dans les glaciers.

MODE DE RANDONNÉE Expédition. Doit être totalement autonome.

AUTORISATIONS/RESTRICTIONS Un permis de randonnée et un officier de liaison sont désormais exigés pour cette excursion (elle se déroule près de la frontière indienne, zone de conflit). Au Pakistan, les permis peuvent être obtenus seulement auprès d'un agent de randonnée. *Note* Les guides de montagne pakistanais ayant un permis peuvent aussi faire fonction d'officiers de liaison.

---

une expédition exténuante, considérée à juste titre comme la plus difficile du monde. Au départ de Skardu, que l'on atteignait, comme maintenant, par avion ou au terme de deux jours épiques de voiture par une branche de l'autoroute – fréquemment coupée – de Karakoram, des jeeps faisaient la navette dans l'aride vallée du Shigar jusqu'à Dassu, la porte d'accès aux gorges du Braldu. En trois jours, la piste précaire, parfois emportée par le fleuve tumultueux, ou quelquefois par de dangereuses chutes de pierres, conduisait à l'oasis d'Askole. La route continuait sous la chaleur étouffante le jour, les nuits glaciales, les effrayants passages de rivières et les moraines tortueuses de Baltoro jusqu'à Concordia, les Gasherbrum, Broad Peak et K2. Les expéditions empruntaient la même route pour le retour. C'est alors qu'arriva, du village de Hushe, un homme appelé Ali Mohammed.

Son pays s'étend en haut d'une vallée, jadis inconnue, au sud du Masherbrum, qui, jusqu'aux années 1980, ne reçut qu'une brève visite du tristement célèbre couple d'Américains Fanny Bullock Workman et son époux William Hunter Workman en 1911, et de quelques expéditions sporadiques vers la face sud du Masherbrum. Les robustes hommes de Hushe travaillaient régulièrement comme porteurs en altitude sur le Baltoro et, en 1985, Ali Mohammed fut engagé par une expédition vers le Chogolisa, un pic de 7 654 m du Haut Baltoro. Regardant vers le sud au-delà d'un col voisin, depuis un camp avancé assez haut sur le pic, il fut sidéré de découvrir la forme caractéristique du pic Layla, une élégante flèche sur le glacier de Gandokoro, juste au-dessus de son village. Il décida de tenter de rentrer chez lui par ce raccourci très tentant, réussit et découvrit ainsi le Gandokoro La (5 585 m).

La réputation de Hushe s'amplifia auprès des randonneurs et des alpinistes vers le milieu des années quatre-vingt, et la découverte d'Ali Mohammed ouvrit du même coup la possibilité de créer un circuit pédestre englobant les plus pittoresques des quatre glaciers au-dessus du village de Hushe, un col d'altitude offrant des panoramas à vous couper le souffle sur le K2, Broad Peak et tout le groupe des Gasherbrums, ainsi qu'une visite à Concordia se terminant par une marche descendant de Baltoro vers Askole. Cet itinéraire est devenu un « must » pour les fervents de grands espaces et les aventuriers.

Le village de Hushe peut être atteint en jeep en dix heures environ au départ de Skardu, et les locaux se sont organisés pour apporter aux randonneurs et alpinistes qui souhaiteraient emprunter cet itinéraire tous les services dont ils auraient besoin. Se faisant appeler

CI-CONTRE *Le Baltoro Kangri (7 312 m), souvent surnommé le « Trône doré », au-dessus de Concordia appelée à son tour « la Salle du trône du dieu des montagnes ».*

Hushe Mountain Rescue Team, au début de chaque saison (fin mai), ils fixent des cordes sur les sections difficiles, construisent des ponts de bambou à travers les crevasses et établissent des camps permanents de part et d'autre du col. Moyennant rétribution, ils pourront même vous guider de l'autre côté.

Cet itinéraire est déconseillé à ceux qui ont le vertige, et il est essentiel de posséder un minimum de compétences en matière de navigation et traversée de glaciers. Il s'agit d'une expédition sérieuse, et pour ceux qui souhaitent faire l'expérience de la montagne sans pour autant s'aventurer vers un grand sommet, ce circuit représente la meilleure opportunité. Beaucoup débutent la traversée en faisant l'ascension, sans difficulté particulière, du pic du Gandokoro (5 656 m), au-dessus du glacier du Gandokoro et, après avoir traversé vers Concordia, passent quelques jours là pour visiter les camps de base des Gasherbrums, Broad Peak et K2, avant de redescendre vers le Baltoro. Vous bénéficiez ainsi, jusqu'au bout, d'un incroyable défilé de montagnes, avec les Mustagh Towers, la face nord du Masherbrum, les Trango Towers, Uli Biaho, les Cathedral Spires (Flèches de cathédrale) et le pic Piaju, autant de moments de bonheur que vous aurez gardés pour les quelques derniers jours.

EN HAUT *Campement sur le Baltoro à Concordia, avec Crystal Peak et Marble Peak sur la gauche, et l'imposante pyramide du K2 dans le lointain, à distance du glacier Godwin-Austen.*
CI-CONTRE *Une jeep se fraye un chemin par la route nouvellement dynamitée, mais souvent impraticable, de la gorge du Braldu, entre Dassu et Chongo.*

LA TRAVERSÉE BIAFO-HISPAR

par Steve Razzetti

K2 et la multitude d'autres pics impressionnants qui entourent le glacier de Baltoro attirent depuis longtemps l'attention des grands explorateurs et alpinistes du monde entier, mais une énigme de plus sur le Karakoram central a laissé les géographes dans le doute quant à son identité jusqu'au XXᵉ siècle.

Lupke Lawo, ou « Lac des Neiges », le vaste névé à partir duquel rayonnent les glaciers de Biafo et Hispar, personnifie, peut-être plus qu'aucune autre des magnifiques montagnes de la région, tout ce qu'il y a d'unique dans le Karakoram.

Taillant un énorme chemin au cœur du Karakoram central, la traversée Biafo-Hispar constitue l'une des plus longues étendues de glace hors des régions polaires – environ 130 km au total. Pendant des années, on a cru que le Lac des Neiges était une véritable calotte glaciaire, et bien des légendes fantastiques y sont nées et s'y sont nourries avant que sa véritable nature soit établie. Le premier explorateur qui posa les yeux sur le glacier Biafo fut un sportif britannique du nom de H. Falconer, en 1838, pendant que Henry Haversham Godwin-Austen découvrait l'Hispar en atteignant la crête du Nushik La par le sud, en 1861. Pourtant, la vraie dimension de cette « superautoroute » glaciaire resta méconnue en attendant une expédition de l'Anglais sir Martin Conway, trente et un ans plus tard.

Conway fut le premier à franchir le col d'Hispar (5 151 m), le 18 juillet 1892. Bien qu'il traversât aussi le glacier Biafo vers Askole, il ne tenta pas d'étudier le Lac des Neiges. Cette mission, et les descriptions alléchantes qu'il fit de l'endroit, attira un couple d'Américains, Fanny Bullock et son mari William Hunter Workman, dont les noms resteront à jamais associés aux premières explorations de la région. Ils consacrèrent leur vie au Karakoram. Entre 1898 et 1908, ils n'effectuèrent pas moins de sept grandes expéditions vers cette région, et publièrent un grand nombre d'ouvrages richement illustrés, et d'articles sur leurs voyages. En 1908, ils suivirent Conway par le col d'Hispar, à partir duquel Fanny réalisa sa fameuse ascension du pic Woodman et évalua la surface du Lac des Neiges à plus de 700 km².

Ce n'est qu'en 1939, la veille de la déclaration de la Seconde Guerre mondiale, que cette énorme étendue glaciaire fut cartographiée avec précision, au cours d'une expédition phénoménale qui représenta l'apogée de la carrière du plus célèbre et plus accompli des explorateurs alpinistes de Grande-Bretagne. Au cours du second de leurs voyages épiques vers le Karakoram, Éric Shipton et ses collègues entreprirent une étude géographique qui devait donner naissance à une carte d'une extraordinaire précision. Ce travail allait être la phase initiale d'une odyssée montagnarde de seize mois, mais même aux confins du Karakoram, les événements graves ne pouvaient rester ignorés des hommes. Le groupe s'était partagé en plusieurs unités pour les besoins de ses travaux, et, à l'approche du point de ralliement prédéfini sur le Lac des Neiges, Shipton fit le point : « Lorsque enfin nous fûmes à portée de voix, Russell nous hurla l'accablante nouvelle : l'Angleterre était en guerre avec

EN HAUT *Une vue panoramique de Namla, le premier campement dans la montée du Biafo depuis Askole. Au fur et à mesure que l'on avance dans l'été, les crevasses s'élargissent pour se transformer en gouffres béants.*
ENCART *Un groupe de marcheurs encordé sur le glacier Biafo, où l'échelle du paysage est presque étourdissante.*
À DROITE *Les champs irrigués du village d'Askole se détachent, en un contraste verdoyant, des splendeurs dénudées de la vallée du Braldu, avec l'entrée de la gorge du Braldu au loin.*
CI-CONTRE *Voyager sans s'encorder au-dessus de la ligne de neige devrait être exclu. Toutefois, si vous ne voyagez qu'avec un seul compagnon, c'est peut-être l'option la plus sûre.*

LIEU Central Karakoram, Pakistan.

QUAND PARTIR De juin à septembre.

DÉPART Askole village. Vols internationaux vers Karachi ou Islamabad, puis par avion (1 h) ou par la route (KKH, 18-30 h) jusqu'à Skardu. Nuit étape à Skardu, puis transport en jeep jusqu'à Askole (6-10 h).

ARRIVÉE Nagar village. Transport en Jeep jusqu'à Karimabad (sur la route KKH dans la Vallée Hunza), puis en bus ou en jeep jusqu'à Gilgit (3-4 h). Gilgit-Islamabad en bus (14-18 h) ou par avion (45 minutes).

DURÉE 14-20 jours, selon les équipes d'excursion, le rythme et la météo.

POINT CULMINANT Col d'Hispar (5 151 m).

ASPECTS TECHNIQUES Les randonneurs doivent être expérimentés et équipés pour la traversée de glaciers en cordée et le sauvetage dans les crevasses.

MATÉRIEL Harnais et matériel de secours et de traversée des glaciers.

MODE DE RANDONNÉE Expédition. Doit être autonome tout au long du parcours.

AUTORISATIONS/RESTRICTIONS Zone ouverte, aucune autorisation nécessaire.

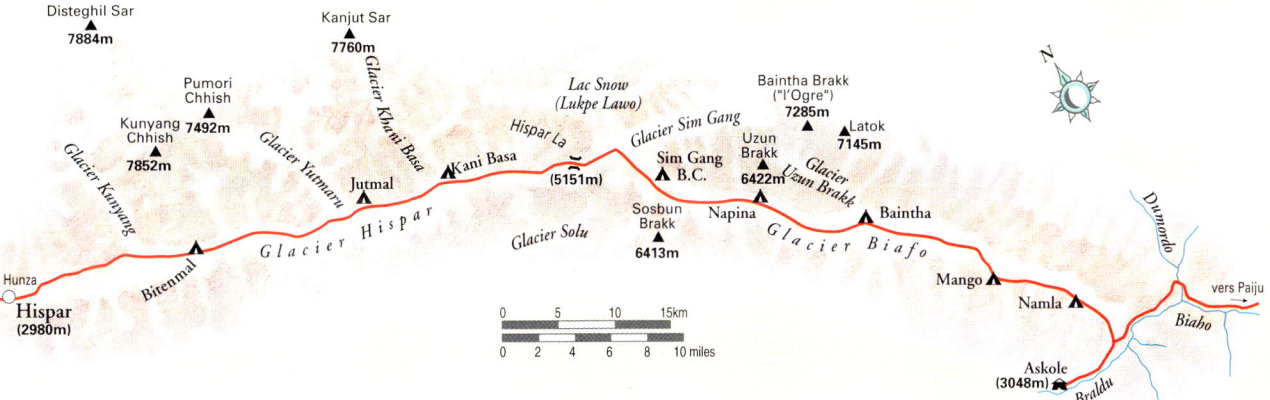

CI-DESSUS *La pleine lune se dressant derrière la terrible face nord de l'Ogre, vue d'un camp sur la crête du col de l'Hispar. Sur la droite, Uzun Brakk (« l'Ogre de Conway »).*
CI-DESSOUS *Une vue sur la vallée vers Braldu, Mango et Namla de l'autre côté de la zone d'ablation, à Baintha, sur le glacier Biafo.*

l'Allemagne. Il venait de l'entendre sur le petit récepteur TSF que nous avions emporté pour pouvoir recevoir des signaux horaires nécessaires à nos travaux astronomiques. Nous eûmes du mal à réaliser la portée du désastre. Peut-être que Londres, la ville où nous avions préparé cette entreprise, n'était plus que chaos, ruines et terreur. Comme cela paraissait irréel et suprêmement ridicule, dans notre univers merveilleux et lointain de glace et de neige ! Comme pour appuyer ce contraste, les brumes se levèrent et pour un moment le glacier fut inondé d'un coucher de soleil dont la lueur était renvoyée par les grands sommets. Les grandes flèches de granit du Biafo se détachaient du ciel bleu foncé. Au moins, cet univers de montagnes, auquel je devais tant de vie et de bonheur, survivra-t-il au-dessus des espoirs ruinés des hommes, en héritage aux générations plus sages. »

Alors, pendant un demi-siècle, les ours solitaires et les panthères des neiges du Biafo-Hispar furent pratiquement les seuls occupants de l'endroit, observant depuis leurs promontoires solitaires, au milieu d'un paysage montagneux immense, les occasionnelles expéditions alpines venues prendre la mesure des cimes et des aiguilles qui entourent ces glaciers. Les statistiques sont la preuve de la grandeur glaciaire mais ne peuvent traduire l'impact des lieux en termes de sensations vécues. L'étude Shipton montra que la superficie du Lac des Neiges n'était que le dixième de celle avancée par les Workman, mais néanmoins, là où le Biafo s'écoule du Lac des Neiges au sud, il fait près de 5 km de large, 1 000 m de profondeur et il se déplace de 200 m par an. Ses immenses crevasses pourraient engloutir des immeubles entiers.

Aujourd'hui encore, avec des vols vers Gilgit et Skardu et de rudes pistes tout-terrain serpentant vers les vallées désolées et sauvages de la chaîne, le Karakoram reste une entreprise difficile pour ceux qui envisagent de venir l'escalader. Pourtant, la route d'Askole à Nagar est reconnue par beaucoup comme la quintessence de la traversée du Karakoram.

Partant des contreforts de K2 jusqu'au-delà d'Askole, cette stimulante randonnée ne rencontre aucune installation humaine jusqu'au tout dernier jour, en arrivant au village d'Hispar. Quittant la piste relativement encombrée des alpinistes, qui remonte la vallée de Braldu, elle tourne vers le nord-ouest et les premiers contreforts empierrés du Biafo, puis pénètre d'un seul coup dans un autre monde. Le sommet de ce glacier, comme la plupart des flots de glace du Karakoram, est caché derrière une énorme masse de débris charriés des hauteurs, et dépasse dans la vallée de Braldu, presque au point de la barrer entièrement. Ce n'est qu'en de très rares endroits que la glace, noircie et fondue par endroits, peut être aperçue sous les graviers et les rochers ; la marche s'y révèle épuisante au début. Ce n'est que le troisième jour, lorsque l'itinéraire traverse le flanc nord, qu'une bande de glace propre et blanche apparaît au centre, rendant l'avancée plus facile.

Dès le début de la montée vers le Biafo, apparaît à l'horizon un éventail spectaculaire de sommets enneigés. Ce sont les Latoks et le Baintha Brakk, surnommés « l'Ogre » par sir Martin Conway. À partir du camp n°3, à Baintha, une ascension relativement facile vers le sommet de Baintha Peak (5 100 m) est possible offrant des vues panoramiques sur la splendide architecture montagneuse qui décore le haut Biafo et son affluent, le Uzun Brakk. À partir des pentes douces qui dominent ce camp, où une journée de repos est presque obligatoire afin de permettre aux porteurs de faire du pain et de se nourrir, en prévision des rigueurs qui les attendent, la pleine dimension des défenses formidables de l'Ogre se révèle. La première ascension épique de cette montagne résolument hostile fut réalisée en 1977 par les alpinistes britanniques Doug Scott, Chris Bonnington et Mo Antoine, et n'a jamais été réitérée.

Aussi impressionnante que puisse paraître la face sud de l'Ogre vue d'au-dessus de Baintha, elle est battue par la perspective de la face nord vue depuis le col de Hispar même, où on ne manquera pas de dresser un camp si le temps le permet. On ne peut imaginer un lieu plus sensationnel, où les pentes enneigées et apparemment interminables qui conduisent au col s'adoucissent progressivement, et le terrain, imperceptiblement, recommence à descendre vers l'ouest. À l'est, les blanches étendues du bassin Sim Gang et du Lac des Neiges sont entourées par une multitude de pics perpendiculaires, sur lesquels la face nord de l'Ogre, dans l'ombre, veille comme un spectre menaçant.

Cette vue d'ensemble, au lever et au coucher du soleil, est époustouflante. Pourtant, aussi incroyable que cela puisse paraître, les plus hautes montagnes restent encore à découvrir. Le glacier de Hispar est plus difficile que celui de Biafo, et ses gigantesques affluents du nord descendent d'une chaîne de montagne ininterrompue qui comprend les sommets de Kanjur Sar, Disteghil Sar, Pumori Chhish et Kunyang Chhish, tous dépassant largement 7 000 m d'altitude. Quand vous aurez rejoint les touristes qui se détendent dans les confortables hôtels de Karimabad à Hunza, vous aurez certainement mérité vos galons de Karakoram.

CI-DESSOUS *Traversée du glacier de Kani Basa, le premier des quatre principaux affluents de l'Hispar, qui devront être négociés sur cet itinéraire.*

LADAKH ET ZANSKAR

par Steve Razzetti

Zanskar et Ladakh sont les deux régions les plus reculées de toute la chaîne himalayenne de l'Inde. Dissimulé au milieu de défilés déchiquetés, domaine de nombreux torrents et de montagnes arides et désolées, le précieux patchwork de champs irrigués qui entoure les villages disséminés dans toute la région ressemble à d'éclatantes émeraudes serties dans une couronne d'épines. Perchés au sommet d'éperons et de falaises invraisemblables, bénéficiant souvent de points de vue à vous couper le souffle sur la campagne alentour, de nombreux monastères bouddhistes ou *gompahs* ponctuent d'un blanc brillant le fond brun ou gris du tableau. Dans un paysage qui appelle souvent des comparaisons avec la lune, les hauts déserts montagneux du Ladakh ne correspondent peut-être pas à l'idée qu'on se fait de la béatitude, mais la région dégage certainement une puissante et indéniable magie.

Limitées au nord et à l'est par les chaînes du Karakoram et du Kailas, et au sud par la grande chaîne de l'Himalaya, les chaînes du Ladakh et du Zanskar ne sont pas aussi élevées que leurs voisines. Mais elles sont tout aussi découpées et comptent assez de sommets de plus de 6 000 m pour recueillir de très fortes chutes de neige en hiver. Étant situées au nord, abrités des pluies par l'Himalaya, le Ladakh et le Zanskar ne sont pas affectés par la mousson, mais l'ardent soleil d'été fait rapidement fondre les champs de neige et les glaciers, changeant les ruisseaux en torrents tumultueux.

Beaucoup de ses vallées deviennent pour cette raison impraticables, et les principales pistes traversent souvent d'immenses crêtes pour éviter des gorges dangereuses. Le nom de Ladakh signifie le « pays des cols », et la randonnée d'été implique souvent des traversées de rivières à vous faire dresser les cheveux sur la tête, en particulier sur les itinéraires les moins fréquentés.

L'histoire du Ladakh n'est que conquêtes et acquisitions, les maîtres des lieux devant constamment repousser les prétentions tibétaines et cachemiri sur leur territoire. En raison de son riche et vigoureux passé culturel bouddhiste, le Ladakh est souvent surnommé le « Petit Tibet », alors qu'en fait il n'a jamais été sous l'autorité du dalaï-lama de Lhassa. La conversion forcée du Cachemire voisin à l'islam au XIIIe siècle rapprocha effectivement les royaumes séparés du Ladakh et de Zanskar, et la puissance du Ladakh fut à son zénith au XVIIe siècle, au début duquel le roi, Senge Namgyal, édifia à Leh une imitation du palais de Potala. Le Zanskar est effectivement un territoire dépendant depuis cette époque.

Le premier Européen à avoir atteint le Ladakh était un laïc portugais du nom de Diogo d'Almeria, qui passa deux ans dans la région aux alentours de l'an 1600. Il fut suivi brièvement par les prêtres jésuites Francesco de Azavedo et Giovanni de Oliviero en 1631, puis par Ipolito Desideri en 1715, pendant son interminable voyage de Srinagar à Lhasa. Un autre siècle s'écoula avant que l'influence de la Compagnie britannique des Indes orientales ne parvint jusqu'à Leh, par le truchement de William Moorcroft et George Trebeck. Ils trouvèrent les autorités du Ladakh très soupçonneuses face à leurs motivations, et dans sa relation des événements, Moorcroft raconte comment le Khalun (le roi) de Ladakh s'était laissé dire « qu'il est pratique courante chez les Anglais de se faire passer pour des marchands, simplement pour mettre un

EN HAUT *Le labyrinthe de monastères et de temples qui composent Phuktal Gompah, accroché à la falaise au-dessus de Biri Chhu.*
ENCART *Le drapeau de prières flotte sur un sanctuaire de la vallée de l'Indus, près de Leh.*
EN BAS, À GAUCHE *Il y a un monastère à Lamayuru depuis le Xe siècle. Jadis important relais de poste sur la route caravanière de Srinagar à Leh, il abritait autrefois plus de deux cents moines, réduits maintenant au nombre de trente. C'est le point de départ de la randonnée sud à travers le Zanskar.*

HIMALAYA, INDE

pied dans le pays, pour ensuite exercer leur autorité ». Il fallut à peine deux décennies pour que les appréhensions du Khalun se vérifient.

L'intérêt de l'Occident pour l'histoire des Zanskar débuta par la rencontre inopinée d'un Anglais et d'un Hongrois sur l'itinéraire des caravanes, entre Srinagar et Leh, en 1822. William Moorcroft voyageait pour le compte de la Compagnie des Indes orientales, tandis que Alexander De Koros revenait de Leh après avoir échoué dans sa tentative de gagner le Yarkand pour y retrouver les origines du peuple hongrois. Moorcroft éveilla l'intérêt de De Koros pour les choses tibétaines, et en juin 1823 ce dernier arriva à Zanskar, où il passa seize mois à compiler une grammaire tibétaine pour le compte du gouvernement britannique.

Le Ladakh est peut-être lointain, mais le Zanskar est non seulement lointain, mais presque inaccessible. Traduit du tibétain « Zang-dkar » (cuivre blanc), en raison du précieux minerai que l'on trouve dans cette région, le territoire se compose essentiellement de terres drainées par les deux affluents principaux du fleuve Zanskar, et recouvre 4 800 km² de terrain extrêmement montagneux à une altitude moyenne de 4 000 m.

Avant l'arrivée de la route sommaire de Kargil vers Zanskar, sur « l'Autoroute des Balises » (Beacon Highway) de Srinagar à Leh, la minuscule capitale Padum était effectivement coupée du monde extérieur la plus grande partie de l'année. L'isolement et l'ignorance entourant le Zanskar ont contribué à le préserver comme une enclave de culture tibétaine sans

CI-DESSUS *Les murs blancs de Karsha Gompah accroché à la roche au-dessus du fleuve Zanskar, en face de Padum. Le plus grand monastère du Zanskar, demeure de cent cinquante moines gelup-pa (à chapeau jaune) sous l'autorité du frère cadet du dalaï-lama.*

CI-DESSOUS, DE GAUCHE À DROITE *Un groupe de femmes ladakki au festival de Hemis, au Ladakh ; la superbe statue du nouveau Maitreya, ou futur bouddha, au Thikse Gompah ; un homme masqué participe aux danses rituelles du festival de Hemis.*

CI-DESSUS *Ces ruines dans la vallée du Spantang, sur l'itinéraire de Hanupatta au Sirsir La, témoignent du passé plus prospère de la région.*

aucune entrave, apportant son patrimoine de bouddhisme tantrique à peu près intact dans le XXI⁰ siècle. Les monastères cachés dans les replis des montagnes arides sont des exemples vivants d'une tradition ancienne qui s'est trouvée violemment coupée de son Tibet d'origine.

Les montagnes et les vallées du Ladakh et de Zanskar sont découpées par un réseau complexe de pistes et de cols, faisant de cette région un paradis pour les randonneurs prêts à improviser leurs itinéraires. Les touristes peuvent parcourir les régions découvertes sans aucun permis ou autres tracasseries administratives, mais la faible population et le dénuement du sol rendent essentielle l'autonomie du voyageur. Un grand nombre d'itinéraires agréables est possible, adaptables à la condition physique de l'équipe et à son intérêt pour la culture bouddhiste, mais rien ne vaut la traversée du Zanskar entre Lamayuru et Darcha, qui combine la beauté de la montagne et les splendeurs monastiques. Très peu de parcours offrent les attraits combinés d'un intérêt culturel certain et d'une diversité de paysages tout au long d'une marche aussi longue et stimulante.

La marche commence sous le spectacle extraordinaire de Lamayuru, où les constructions médiévales superbement conservées du monastère sont perchées sur un éperon, au milieu d'un paysage étrange de falaises sculptées et de collines érodés par le vent. De nos jours, la piste contourne à la fois le village et le monastère, mais il est toujours possible de suivre l'ancienne route des caravanes, à pied, un peu plus haut, en passant devant les ruines des remparts de *mane* vers le Fatu La depuis le monastère. La piste vers Zanskar quitte la basse vallée de Lamayuru, avant de se faufiler vers le sud, remontant un défilé pierreux et sec vers le Prinkiti La, le premier de huit cols entre Lamayuru et Padum. Comptez au moins dix jours pour terminer ce tronçon et préparez-vous à de nombreuses montées ardues et autant de descentes brise-genoux. Les guides locaux sont fortement recommandés car les pistes et les ponts sont souvent emportés par les eaux. La cartographie disponible est très imprécise et il est essentiel de se procurer les derniers renseignements mis à jour sur le parcours. Les points forts de cette marche vers Zanskar sont sans nul doute le fabuleux monastère de Lingshot et le point de vue depuis le Sini La à 5 060 m d'altitude. Immédiatement à l'est du col, se trouve un spectaculaire pic rocheux, mais ce sont les vues vers le nord, sur le col précédent, le Sirsir La, puis devant vers Lingshot, qui vous éblouiront vraiment.

Enfin, à partir du Purfi La, la vallée de Zanskar apparaît, et à partir d'un point juste sous la crête, lors de la descente, on découvre une impressionnante vue plongeante dans les formidables gorges par lesquelles la rivière Zanskar s'échappe au nord vers l'Indus et le Ladakh. Pendant les longs mois d'hiver, quand les cols sont fermés, c'est sur la surface gelée de cet immense fleuve que des Zanskaris mènent leurs yaks vers les marchés de Leh.

HIMALAYA, INDE

LIEU Himalaya du Ladakh, Jammu et Cachemire et Himachal Pradesh, Inde.

QUAND PARTIR Juin à novembre. Comme le Karakoram pakistanais, les chaînes du Ladakh et du Zanskar sont des déserts montagneux abrités des pluies par la chaîne principale de l'Himalaya, et sont à peine touchées par la mousson.

DÉPART Gompah de Lamayuru, vols internationaux vers New Delhi, puis par avion (1 h) ou par la route (3 jours) jusqu'à Leh. Les moyens de transport locaux (jeep ou bus) jusqu'à Lamayuru prennent une demi-journée.

ARRIVÉ Darcha ; bus local vers Manali (10 h). Puis par la route jusqu'à Delhi (18 h) ou Kulu (3 h de route) puis avion (1 h) jusqu'à Delhi. Alternative : par la route jusqu'à Chandigar (8 h) puis par avion jusqu'à Delhi (35 min).

REMARQUE La route entre Chandigar et Delhi est extrêmement dangereuse.

DURÉE 23 jours au minimum.

POINT CULMINANT Shin-Kun (5 096 m) ou Phirtse La (5 250 m).

ASPECTS TECHNIQUES Néant.

MATÉRIEL Autonomie recommandée pour l'hébergement, la nourriture et le combustible. Emportez de solides paquetages. Des poneys de somme sont utilisés sur cet itinéraire.

MODE DE RANDONNÉE Sac à dos ou expédition. Un hébergement local est possible, mais rudimentaire et insalubre.

AUTORISATIONS/RESTRICTIONS Aucune autorisation nécessaire.

Le rythme de la vie à Padum s'est trouvé quelque peu accéléré avec l'arrivée de la route, mais c'est encore un coin perdu et poussiéreux. Il y a toutefois dans le voisinage plusieurs monastères importants, qui justifient largement d'y passer deux jours supplémentaires. En face de la ville, sur un flanc de collines incroyablement abrupt, siège Karsha, le plus grand monastère de Zanskar, où vivent cent cinquante moines. La salle basse (*labrang*) est sombre et inutilisée aujourd'hui, mais une torche révèle des murs croulants, recouverts d'adorables fresques et peintures murales, datant de près d'un millénaire.

Padum est situé au confluent des deux principaux affluents de la rivière Zanskar, la Doda et la Tsarap Chhu, et la piste sud vers Darcha et Lahaul via le Shingo La commence par suivre le dernier. Prévoyez un minimum de sept jours pour atteindre Darcha. Comparée aux crêtes dentelées et aux gorges profondes traversées sur la première partie du parcours, ce tronçon traverse d'immenses paysages de plaines ventées ponctuées de fermes isolées. Malgré le court détour vers la vallée du Biri Chhu, on ne manquera pas de visiter le *Gompah* de Phuktal. On ne peut imaginer décor plus spectaculaire pour un monastère. Les constructions badigeonnées de blanc semblent sortir en cascade d'une énorme caverne au-dessus des eaux rugissantes du torrent.

Le dernier village du Zanskar est Kargyak, et au sud de ce hameau d'une vingtaine de maisons, la piste passe sous le Gumbarajon, un splendide monolithe de plus de 1 000 m de haut qui ne déparerait pas le parc du Yosemite. Plus loin, le Shingo La (5 096 m), le seul col à traverser entre Padum et Darcha. Il peut être enneigé à tout moment de l'année, et après cinq heures de descente vers le minuscule terrain de camping de Ramjak, vous ne regretterez pas d'avoir choisi de terminer votre itinéraire dans cette direction.

EN HAUT À GAUCHE *L'éclairage de fin d'après-midi met en relief les collines avoisinantes, vues depuis la crête du Sirsir La.*

À GAUCHE *Plusieurs espèces du pavot bleu de l'Himalaya poussent au Ladakh et au Zanskar, apportant une touche de couleur vive dans le désert montagneux à la fin de l'été.*

DE SINGALILA À KANGCHENDZONGA

par Steve Razzetti

Alors que l'Himalaya du Népal et le Tibet étaient hors d'atteinte pour les explorateurs européens pendant tout le XIXe siècle et une bonne partie du XXe, ce n'était pas le cas de l'Himalaya du Sikkim. Le tracé des frontières actuelles de cette minuscule principauté fut défini par un traité avec les Britanniques en 1861, mettant fin à près de 200 ans d'invasions et d'incertitudes pendant lesquelles le pays fut envahi à la fois par les Bhoutanais et les Népalais.

En 1888, une tentative d'invasion par les Tibétains fut repoussée avec l'aide d'une force expéditionnaire indienne, précipitant enfin l'instauration du Sikkim en état protectorat protégé. Il fait depuis partie de l'Inde. En termes géographiques, le pays correspond très précisément au bassin hydrographique du fleuve Teesta, bordé à l'ouest par le Kangchendzonga et la chaîne du Singalila, et à l'est par le Pauhunri et la chaîne de Donkya.

Le premier Européen qui explora réellement les montagnes du Sikkim fut le major L.A. Waddell. Entre 1888 et 1896, il effectua divers voyages et franchit la chaîne du Singalila via le Kang La To pour explorer le glacier de Yalung. Toutefois, le développement du Sikkim comme terrain de jeux pour les sportifs du Raj victorien fut principalement le fait d'un seul homme : Claude White. Celui-ci fut nommé premier « officier politique » du Sikkim après qu'il eut accompagné la force expéditionnaire envoyée pour repousser les Tibétains en 1888. Ce fut lui qui le premier traversa le Goecha La de Dzong Ri au glacier de Talung en 1890, explora les gorges entre Pandim et Simvu et acheva son voyage par la descente du fleuve Talung.

Vers 1930, Sikkim était devenu la destination favorite des alpinistes et des naturalistes britanniques. Les fonctionnaires de Calcutta affluaient dans les stations de montagne de Darjeeling et de Kalimpong, fuyant la moiteur et la chaleur oppressantes de la mousson indienne, et le tourisme dans les districts montagneux du Sikkim était en pleine vogue. Les

EN HAUT *Les sommets de la haute crête du Singalila – Kokthang, Rathong et Kabru – vus depuis le campement de Dzong Ri dans le Sikkim.*
AU MILIEU *L'apogée de ce trek – un groupe de marcheurs sur le Goecha La, en bas de la face est du Kangchendzonga.*
À DROITE *Regardant vers le Kangchendzonga et le Jannu au petit matin, depuis le Phalut, sur la crête de Singalila.*

bulletins des clubs alpins himalayens regorgeaient de récits d'exploits, tandis que Sikkim devenait l'une des régions himalayennes les mieux connues.

Aujourd'hui, le gouvernement indien n'accorde pas aux étrangers autant de liberté pour parcourir ces montagnes. Il y a peu de régions de l'Himalaya qui nécessitent autant de procédures administratives pour la délivrance des autorisations nécessaires, mais les randonneurs ne doivent pas se décourager pour autant. L'itinéraire offre des points de vue sur les pics de la chaîne Singalila, Pandim et la face est du Kangchendzonga, avant d'atteindre le cœur de l'Himalaya Sikkim.

Jusqu'en 1999, la marche de cinq jours jusqu'au Goecha La (4 800 m), à partir du village de Yoksum, était habituellement précédée d'une agréable promenade de trois ou quatre jours le long de la partie Sandakphu de la chaîne Singalila, entre Mani Banjang et Phalut, avec une étape de nuit dans la ville de Pemayangtse. De courtes mais très plaisantes randonnées étaient ainsi entrecoupées d'un jour ou deux de route et d'une nuit d'hôtel. La deuxième moitié de la randonnée commençait par un parcours le long de pistes forestières infestées de sangsues dans les profondes gorges du Rathong Chhu, suivie par l'ascension d'une crête abrupte apparemment interminable, qui sépare les vallées du Churong Chhu et du Prek Chhu. Sortant des bois à Dzong Ri, les randonneurs se trouvaient face à un panorama montagneux aussi impressionnant que dans tout le reste de l'Himalaya. Devant, la forme pyramidale du Kangchendzonga surmonte une crête intermédiaire. Vers l'ouest, Kothang, Rathong et Kabru, ces pics magnifiques qui forment la partie nord de la chaîne du Singalila, s'élevant en une série d'impressionnantes marches enneigées.

Comme par miracle, au cours du printemps 2000, les autorités indiennes ont annoncé l'ouverture de la zone antérieurement interdite de la chaîne du Singalila, entre Phalut et Dzong Ri. S'en était fini de la frustrante obligation de quitter le magnifique parcours des

DE SINGALILA À KANGCHENDZONGA

CI-DESSUS *Sous un manteau de neige, les redoutables pyramides de la face est du Kangchendzonga vues de Thanshing, Sikkim.*

crêtes à Phalut. On peut maintenant accomplir l'intégralité du parcours de Mani Banjang au Goecha La via Dzong Ri, en une randonnée sensationnelle de quinze jours, avant de revenir sur ses pas pendant une journée ou deux pour terminer par la descente vers Yuksom.

Au printemps, la chaîne du Singalila n'offre que quelques échappées sur les sommets enneigés étincelants, alors que la piste suit la crête vers le nord, dans les brumes tourbillonnantes et les nuages épais, puis traverse des flancs entiers de montagne parsemés d'énormes azalées et de rhododendrons en fleurs. Des orchidées exotiques fleurissent dans des grottes humides tandis que, sous les arbres, des fougères luxuriantes recouvrent le sol d'un épais tapis vert. Mais il faut cependant abandonner la crête, car la piste de Dzong Ri et de Kangchendzonga plonge vers le Churong Chhu pour le traverser.

À partir du camp de Dzong Ri, au pied de la sombre face est du Kangchendzonga, on peut jeter un coup d'œil vers la vallée interdite et attirante qui conduit, tout de suite à l'ouest, vers le Kang La et le Népal. Au nord, le Prek Chhu se présente sous la forme d'une spectaculaire crevasse sous les murailles acérées de Pandim (6 691 m) puis vers le Goecha La. Trois jours plus tard, se tenant sur ce col enneigé, la plupart des randonneurs déploreront les contraintes imposées par la politique moderne, qui interdit de parcourir plus complètement le sensationnel Himalaya Sikkim.

CI-DESSUS *Depuis Dzong Ri, l'approche du Kangchendzonga descend dans la vallée du Prek Chhu et passe au-dessous de la face ouest du Pandim.*

LIEU Himalaya Sikkim, Inde.

QUAND PARTIR De mars à mai ou de septembre à décembre.

DÉPART Mani Banjang ; vols internationaux vers Delhi, Bombay ou Calcutta, puis par le train, car ou avion jusqu'à Bagdogra (Bengale occidental) et jusqu'à Darjeeling par train miniature, bus ou jeep. Nuit étape à Darjeeling, puis par la route (4 h) jusqu'à Mani Banjang.

ARRIVÉE Yuksom ; jeep ou bus jusqu'à Kalimpong ou Darjeeling, puis jusqu'à Bagdogra pour correspondances par rail, route ou avion sur Delhi, Bombay ou Calcutta.

REMARQUE La traversée par l'intérieur vers le Népal occidental est aussi possible depuis Darjeeling.

DURÉE 18 jours.

POINT CULMINANT Goecha La (4 800 m).

ASPECTS TECHNIQUES Après les chutes de neige, le Goecha La peut ne pas être accessible sans un piolet à glace au minimum.

MATÉRIEL Il est indispensable d'être autonome tout au long du parcours.

MODE DE RANDONNÉE Sac à dos ou expédition. Quelques auberges sur la chaîne de Singalila entre Mani Banjang et Phalut, mais sans restauration.

AUTORISATIONS/RESTRICTIONS On ne peut pas faire ce voyage sans guide ou représentant local. Les permis pour la section Phalut-Dzong Ri ne sont disponibles qu'auprès de l'Office de Tourisme de Gangtok. Les permis sont gratuits, mais des taxes journalières sont perçues pour les yaks, porteurs, appareils photo et tentes.

KANGCHENDZONGA

par Steve Razzetti

Hope Leezum Namgyal, la princesse héritière du Sikkim, était catégorique. Voyant mes notes de voyages au Kangchendzonga, elle s'exclama : « vous ne pouvez pas écrire ce nom comme cela ! Ça ne veut rien dire ! Le vrai nom de la montagne en tibétain "Kang-Chen-Dzong-Nga" se traduit par "le Pic aux Cinq Grands Trésors des Neiges". Par correction, on n'anglicise pas les noms des montagnes au pays de Galles et en Écosse, alors pourquoi le faire avec ceux du Sikkim et du Tibet ? » Ce sera donc Kangchendzonga !

Séparé des grands sommets du tronçon Khosi de l'Himalaya népalais par l'Arun, le plus puissant des fleuves transhimalayens du pays, le Kangchendzonga est souvent considéré comme faisant partie de l'Himalaya Sikkim. Contrairement aux autres grands sommets du Grand Himalaya, le Kangchendzonga représente non seulement une chaîne de crêtes est-ouest, mais forme également le centre d'une croix géante dont les bras gigantesques s'étendent à l'est, à l'ouest, au nord et au sud depuis son sommet de 8 598 m. Avec seulement 13 m de moins que le K2, c'est la troisième plus haute montagne du monde.

Le bras occidental de cette intersection monumentale se termine par le sommet du Jannu, lui-même l'un des pics les plus spectaculaires de tout l'Himalaya, tandis que le bras oriental descend vers la trouée de Zemu Gap au Sikkim. Vers le sud, la chaîne de Singalila s'étend sur 80 km, formant la frontière entre le Népal et le Sikkim. Au nord, une chaîne complexe et inaccessible de sommets se termine par le pic Jongsang et la frontière avec le Tibet. Émergeant directement des plaines de l'Inde, le massif du Kangchendzonga se situe à l'est de la barrière protectrice des collines de Siwalik, qui arrêtent les nuages apportant la mousson avant qu'ils ne puissent déverser leur déluge sur le reste de l'Himalaya népalais. Ces montagnes reçoivent donc les plus fortes précipitations du Népal, leur sommet étant coiffé de

EN HAUT *Coucher de soleil sur la face sud du Kangchendzonga vu depuis le sanctuaire isolé d'Oktang, sur le glacier de Yalung.*
ENCART *Jeunes filles bhotia au village de Phole, dans la vallée de la Ghunsa Khola. La partie supérieure de cette vallée faisait jadis partie du Sikkim voisin.*
À DROITE *Traversée d'un ruisseau dans la vallée d'ablation du flanc nord du glacier Kangchendzonga à Ramtang. Les pierres sont entièrement serties dans la glace.*

phénoménales formations neigeuses, tandis que les vallées, en bas, sont couvertes d'une jungle luxuriante et incroyablement dense.

Bien visible depuis la station de Darjeeling, au Bengale occidental, le Kangchendzonga attira l'attention des explorateurs bien avant les autres régions du Népal. C'est vers cette ville que les sportifs, les oisifs et les dames de la colonie fuyaient la chaleur et l'humidité oppressantes de Calcutta. Le Népal et le Tibet étaient tous deux interdits aux étrangers pendant le XIXᵉ siècle, et les premiers voyageurs qui pénétrèrent à l'intérieur de leurs frontières le firent clandestinement, prenant de grands risques, pour eux-mêmes et pour leurs porteurs locaux.

Le premier explorateur à visiter le versant népalais du Kangchendzonga fut le botaniste britannique sir Joseph Hooker. Ses récits, publiés sous le titre « Himalayan Journals », attirèrent l'attention de la Royal Geographic Society et du Survey of India, et ce dernier envoya les experts Sarat Chandra Das et Rinzin Namgyal pour en savoir plus. Chandra Da se rendit deux fois au Népal, en 1879 et en 1881, y pénétrant à chaque fois par la chaîne du Singalila via le Kang La, mais en traversant le Tibet par le Jongsang La en 1879 et par le Nago La en 1881. En 1833, Rinzin Namgyal entra aussi au Népal en traversant le Kang La depuis Sikkim, puis explora la partie inférieure du glacier de Yalung par le Jongsang La, dans les pas de son prédécesseur.

En 1899, ce fut Rinzin Namgyal que l'Anglais Douglas Freshfield choisit pour accompagner son groupe international dans une expédition qui fut sans nul doute la plus importante de l'histoire du Kangchendzonga. Partant de Darjeeling, leur objectif était de faire le tour complet du massif. Flanqué du célèbre photographe de montagne Vittoria Sella et de son frère Erminio, du guide de montagne Angelo Maquignaz, du professeur Edmund Garwood et M. Dover, l'inspecteur des Routes du Sikkim indépendant, le groupe emprunta finalement l'itinéraire suivi par Rinzin en 1883, en sens inverse, entrant au Népal par le Jongsang La. De là, il descendit vers le village isolé de Ghunsa, dont les habitants, à sa grande surprise, ne furent en rien déconcertés de compter parmi eux toute une bande de « visages pâles ».

Poursuivant vers l'est en direction de la vallée du Yamatari Chhu, Freshfield et son groupe traversèrent vers le glacier Yalung et la face sud du Kangchendzonga, empruntant le plus bas des deux itinéraires, celui du Chunjerma La. Leurs provisions s'amenuisant et Rinzin craignant de plus en plus de se faire arrêter par les gardes frontaliers népalais, ils ne s'attardèrent point sur le versant Yalung du col. Ne s'octroyant que quelques regards furtifs vers le glacier Yalung et les pics alentour, à travers la brume de plus en plus épaisse, ils descendirent jusqu'à Tseram, franchirent la Simbua Khola et campèrent dans la vallée, au pied du Kang La. Deux jours plus tard, ils sirotaient leur café en lisant le courrier d'Angleterre à Dzong Ri, au Sikkim.

Les randonneurs qui, aujourd'hui, souhaiteraient explorer le côté népalais du Kangchendzonga, trouveraient les autorités de Katmandou bien plus obligeantes, à condition que toutes les autorisations nécessaires aient été demandées et que les conditions d'autonomie en nourriture, combustible et hébergement soient remplies. Du fait de l'extrême éloignement de cette région, une visite complète occupera cinq bonnes semaines (trente jours de marche). Ceux qui ne disposeraient pas de tout ce temps peuvent envisager d'utiliser la liaison aérienne quotidienne vers la minuscule piste d'atterrissage de Suketar, au-dessus de Taplejung, le centre administratif du district. En utilisant les liaisons aérienne, il est tout à fait possible de visiter le glacier Yalung et la face sud du Kangchendzonga, de traverser l'une ou l'autre des routes vers Ghunsa et de remonter vers Pang Pema, au pied de l'impressionnante face nord, avant de rentrer sur Taplejung en un peu plus de trois semaines (vingt-trois jours de marche).

Le meilleur point de départ est Tumlingtar, dans la vallée de l'Arun. De là, la piste mène à Taplejung par la crête de Milke Danda, d'où le massif du Kangchendzonga se révèle dans toute sa splendeur quelque 64 km plus loin. Ramze, le camp de base du glacier Yalung pour la face sud du Kangchendzonga, est à huit jours de marche de Taplejung. N'offrant aucun salon de thé ou auberge, cet itinéraire constitue une alternative rafraîchissante au mercantilisme des régions plus touristiques du pays. Toutefois, cette traversée du pays à contre-courant n'est pas une entreprise facile. La première moitié de la piste serpente à travers une région de culture intensive, avec de curieuses fermes au toit de chaume entourées de jardins soignés, à l'ombre des plus grands arbres que vous ne verrez jamais. Témoignant du travail acharné des populations montagnardes du Népal, les immenses étendues de rizières en terrasses restent uniques. Au-delà de Yamphudin, le hameau le plus isolé de cet itinéraire, la piste pénètre dans une région montagneuse sauvage et désolée, grimpant parmi les forêts de

KANGCHENDZONGA

CI-DESSUS *Bien que le Lapsang La soit plus élevé, le spectacle saisissant du Jannu vu du Mirgin La fait de cet itinéraire plus bas une attrayante alternative.*

bouleaux, de conifères et de rhododendrons, puis traversant à nouveau d'autres crêtes avant de se rapprocher enfin du versant sud du Kangchendzonga, en haut de la pittoresque vallée du Simbua Khola. L'étonnant éventail de sommets qui domine le glacier Yalung à Ramze n'est qu'un avant-goût des splendeurs à venir.

Deux itinéraires sont possibles pour passer la ligne de séparation des eaux entre le glacier Yalung et la vallée de Ghunsa Khola au nord. Le Lapsang La (5 100 m) est plus haut et implique de traverser d'abrupts champs d'éboulis et de blocs rocheux des deux côtés, mais ses paysages sont indubitablement moins beaux. L'itinéraire de Chunjerma, appelé localement la route du Selele (du nom des alpages d'été sur le versant de Ghunsa), n'atteint que 4 500 m d'altitude, mais la piste est bien meilleure et garde une bonne altitude beaucoup plus longtemps. Cet itinéraire emprunte en fait deux cols, le Sinion La (4 440 m) et le Mirgin La, plus élevé (4 570 m). La montée raide au-dessus de Tseram, du côté de Yalung, offre d'extraordinaires panoramas sur tout le côté sud du Kangchendzonga, tandis que des crêtes du Mirgin La, les points de vue vers l'ouest sur l'Arun et au nord sur les murailles impressionnantes de Jannu sont tout simplement magnifiques.

Après avoir marché jusqu'à Ramze, et avoir passé là un ou deux jours avant de traverser vers le nord jusqu'à Ghunsa, vous serez suffisamment acclimatés pour profiter au maximum de ce qui constitue le « bouquet final » de de cette randonnée : la remontée de trois jours du glacier de Kangchendzonga depuis Ghunsa. Sur cette partie du parcours, chaque tournant dévoile une vue nouvelle toujours plus étonnante jusqu'à ce qu'enfin, lorsque la minuscule piste surmontant le glacier du Kangchendzonga atteint le camp de base de Pang Pema, apparaisse l'impressionnante face nord du Kangchendzonga. Aucune perspective montagneuse au monde n'est aussi écrasante, s'élançant vers les cieux dans une ombre perpétuelle, menaçante, et très impressionnante. Pour avoir une vue d'ensemble, faites l'ascension du Drohmo Ri, la « colline » de 6 200 m située juste au-dessus du camp. Le retour à Taplejung prendra encore sept jours.

LIEU Kangchendzonga Himal, Népal oriental.

QUAND PARTIR Avril à juin ou octobre à décembre.

DÉPART/ARRIVÉE Deux vols internationaux sur Katmandou, puis par avion (45 min) ou par la route (car de nuit, 14 h) jusqu'à Biratnagar pour la nuit. Avion STOL au petit matin vers Taplejung (30 min). Retour idem.

DURÉE 23 jours minimum.

POINT CULMINANT Pang Pema (5 100 m).

ASPECTS TECHNIQUES En cas de neige, les groupes optant pour la traversée du Lapsang La (la route haute de Tseram à Ghunsa) devront s'équiper de piolets à glace pour tailler des marches, en particulier pour les porteurs.

MATÉRIEL Autonomie nécessaire en hébergement, nourriture et combustible sur tout le parcours. Les personnes organisant leur propre randonnée devront s'assurer que leurs porteurs disposent des vêtements d'altitude et des chaussures appropriés. Si vous les fournissez vous-même, remettez-les aux intéressés le jour où ils en ont besoin.

MODE DE RANDONNÉE Sac à dos ou expédition.

AUTORISATIONS/RESTRICTIONS Permis de randonnée nécessaire. Doit être obtenu auprès d'une agence accréditée.

KANGCHENDZONGA HIMAL, NÉPAL

CI-DESSUS *Approchant Pang Pema par la minuscule piste au-dessus du glacier Kangchendzonga, avec à l'arrière-plan le pic du Népal et les Jumelles (The Twins).*

85

DE JUMLA AU MONT KAILAS

par Steve Razzetti

L'Himalaya entretenait déjà des mythes et légendes lorsque la première vague d'Indo-Aryens traversa le Pendjab 2 000 ans av. J.-C. Découvrant l'Himalaya, ils mirent au point une cosmographie qui reconnaissait à ces montagnes enneigées un caractère divin, et aux rivières qui en étaient issues, le don de vie.

Les religions hindoue, bon, bouddhiste et jaïn développèrent ces notions en une mythologie fondée sur l'idée qu'une montagne particulière de l'Himalaya était le pilier du Monde, autour duquel s'établissait toute existence. Les jaïns vénèrent la montagne comme une *Astapada*, où ils croient que Rishaba, le fondateur de leur foi, a trouvé la lumière. Les hindous, pour leur part, appellent ce pic mythique le *Meru*, et croient que le dieu Shivah est assis sur son sommet, méditant, s'ébattant avec la déesse Parvati et fumant la *ganja* (marijuana). Leur fleuve sacré – le Gange – coulerait directement sur son sommet depuis le paradis, où il se divise en quatre cours d'eau qui vont purifier les quatre coins de la Terre.

Le temps a prouvé que ces légendes fantastiques reposaient sur de surprenantes bases géographiques. Au nord de la chaîne principale de l'Himalaya, dans la province éloignée du Tibet oriental de Ngari, se dresse effectivement une montagne unique, le Kailas, au pied de laquelle naissent quatre des fleuves les plus importants du sous-continent indien – l'Indus, le Sutlej, le Karnali et le Trangpo-Bramaputra. Les plaines entourant le Kailas forment le point culminant du haut plateau tibétain, et les rivières qui naissent ici rejoignent les océans en des points aussi éloignés que le golfe Arabique et le golfe du Bengale.

L'ancienne religion pré-bouddhiste bon considérait les montagnes comme des points forts reliant le Ciel et la Terre, et le mont Kailas comme la montagne-esprit du royaume de Zhang Zhung. La guerre spirituelle entre les traditionalistes tibétains bon et le bouddhisme moderne était centrée sur le Kailas, et on raconte encore aujourd'hui l'histoire du combat pour le pouvoir magique entre la divinité bon Naro Bon Chung et le saint bouddhiste Milarepa, qui devait décider laquelle des deux cultures pourrait prétendre à la montagne sacrée. La légende veut que Milarepa l'emportât, mais qu'il fut assez magnanime dans sa victoire pour léguer un sommet voisin au Bon-po et leur permettre de continuer à marcher autour du Kailas.

L'occupation du Tibet par la Chine en 1951, les troubles internes qui en découlèrent et la destruction systématique de la culture monastique tibétaine pendant la Révolution cultu-

EN HAUT *Point de vue sur les montagnes de la région de Mugu depuis la berge nord du lac Rara, bordée de roseaux.*

ENCART *Une enfant tibétaine sur le Kailas kora. L'énergie et le moral des pèlerins qui se rendent au Kailas depuis tout le sous-continent indien sont étonnants.*

À DROITE *Un paysage idyllique et des pistes peu pratiquées font de la montée du Humla Karnali vers Simikos une expérience inoubliable.*

relle entraînèrent la fermeture hermétique des frontières avec l'Inde et le Népal. Les anciennes relations commerciales et les pèlerinages furent instantanément abolis et un grand nombre de communautés frontalières, isolées, tombèrent dans l'oubli économique.

En un remarquable geste de conciliation, les Chinois acceptèrent, en 1993, d'ouvrir la frontière du Humla Karnali, au nord-ouest du Népal, permettant aux étrangers, pour la première fois de l'histoire, d'accéder légalement au mont Kailas à pied. Vous pouvez aujourd'hui faire votre propre pèlerinage jusqu'au Kailas en passant par l'un des lieux les plus enchanteurs et les plus authentiques du Népal, au lieu d'endurer la corvée d'une semaine de voyage depuis Lhassa. Il y a là une opportunité unique pour les voyageurs passionnés par l'histoire ancienne et la culture himalayenne.

La plupart des gens qui, aujourd'hui, se rendent à Kailas, arrivent par avion à l'aérodrome de Simikot, la capitale du Humla. Pourtant, en partant de Jumla plus au sud et en suivant les anciens itinéraires commerciaux vers Humla au nord, par le lac Rara, on transformera une visite rapide du Tibet et du Népal en une approche plus adaptée pour des montagnes aussi vénérées que le Kailas.

Le lac de Rara se trouve au cœur du parc national le moins visité du Népal – ces eaux scintillantes apparaissant comme un havre de paix au milieu de forêts primitives et de colline à perte de vue – et à trois jours bien pleins de Jumla. La piste est parfois à peine visible, toujours fatigante, et la campagne traversée est très peu peuplée, mais Rara est un merveilleux trésor. Quittant le Parc national de Rara vers le nord, la route vers Humla plonge pour traverser le Humla Karnali avant la longue remontée vers le Chankel Lekh (3 640 m), pour se rapprocher de Simikot en longeant la vallée du Humla Karnali. À l'approche de la crête du Chankel Lekh, le paysage se transforme instantanément, la ligne bleue des crêtes de l'Humla s'estompant au loin sous une barrière de sommets enneigés qui marque la frontière du Tibet.

CI-DESSUS *À une altitude de 4 150 m, le lac Manasarovar est particulièrement vénéré par les Hindous. Beaucoup d'entre eux effectuent la difficile kora de 85 km autour du lac.*

La vie à Humla s'écoule hors du temps et échappe aux pressions du monde extérieur. Ici, les villages sont médiévaux et la vie de leurs habitants est étroitement liée au rythme de la nature. Avant de grimper laborieusement les derniers 1 000 m jusqu'à Simikot et de poursuivre par les villages montagneux bothia (peuple originaire du Tibet) jusqu'au col de Nara Lagna et au Tibet, le charme subtil de Hulma vous aura envoûté.

LIEU Province de Ngari, au sud-ouest du Tibet. Approche par Humla, au nord-ouest du Népal.

QUAND PARTIR Mai à juin ; fin septembre à décembre.

DÉPART Vols internationaux vers Katmandou puis avion jusqu'à Nepalganj (50 min) ou par la route (car, 14 h) pour la nuit. Vol matinal jusqu'à Jumla (25 min).

ARRIVÉE Simikot, avion jusqu'à Nepalganj (50 min) puis Katmandou par avion ou par la route (car de nuit 12-14 h).

DURÉE 28-30 jours.

POINT CULMINANT Dolma La (5 600 m).

ASPECTS TECHNIQUES Compte tenu de l'éloignement du Kailas et des altitudes extrêmes atteintes sur ce parcours, on sera très attentif à l'apparition de signes du mal des montagnes. Redescendre à moins de 4 000 m dans cette partie du Tibet ne sera pas facile et une évacuation par hélicoptère est impossible.

MATÉRIEL Totale autonomie indispensable sur tout le parcours

MODE DE RANDONNÉE Sac à dos ou expédition.

AUTORISATIONS/RESTRICTIONS Permis de randonnée népalais ordinaire nécessaire pour le tronçon Jumla-Simikot. Doit être obtenu auprès d'une agence accréditée. Le tronçon de Simikot à la frontière nécessite un permis spécial. Les formalités des visas pour le secteur de Kailas doivent être accomplies à l'avance par l'intermédiaire d'une agence accréditée au Népal ou au Tibet. Onéreux.

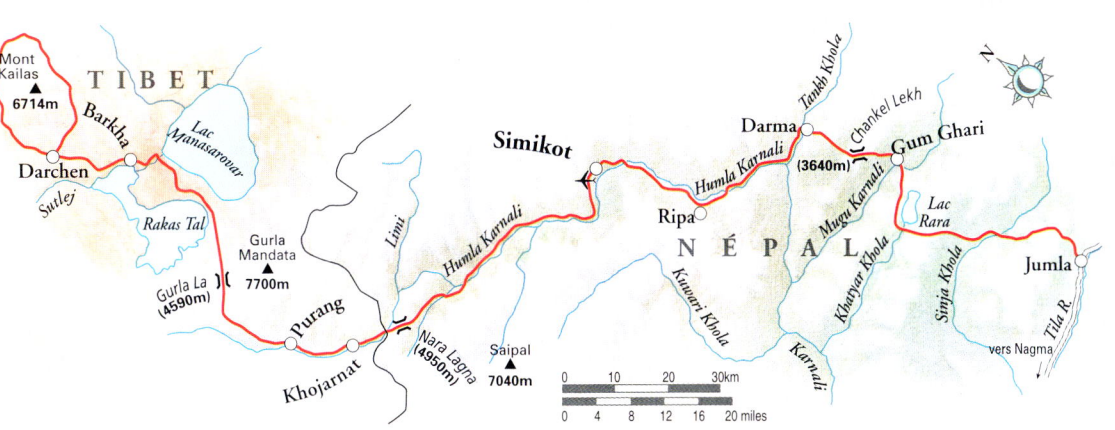

CI-DESSUS *L'étrange symétrie du mont Kailas (6 714 m), vu ici se dressant au-dessus des plaines de Barkha depuis le Chiu Gompah, sur les rives du lac Manasarovar, a inspiré l'architecture de temples aussi lointains qu'Angkor Vat au Cambodge et Borobudur en Indonésie.*

HIMALAYA, NÉPAL/TIBET

Formé du plus haut dépôt au monde de conglomérats de l'époque tertiaire, le mont Kailas offre un spectacle impressionnant en s'élevant de façon spectaculaire au-dessus des plaines désolées de Barkha. Les voyageurs approchant la montagne sacrée par le sud en auront la première vision en atteignant la crête de Gurla La (4 950 m), d'où il semble flotter sur l'horizon, au-dessus des lacs irisés de turquoise de Manasarovar et Rakas. Partant du poussiéreux poste avancé de Darchen, les Tibétains parcourent les 56 km autour de Kailas en une seule journée. La plupart des étrangers s'accordent quatre jours, en tenant compte de l'altitude extrême, des visites de monastères et du temps nécessaire pour apprécier pleinement ce paysage étourdissant.

Le vent cinglant mugit alors que le soleil brûlant frappe à travers l'air raréfié. Des chapelles surgissent à chaque tournant du sentier et des drapeaux de prière flottent et se détachent du ciel d'azur. Dans un paysage aussi austère, et après des décennies de répression, l'expression joyeuse des Tibétains qui, par centaines, parcourent chaque jour ces 56 km, est extrêmement émouvante et témoigne de la détermination de l'esprit humain.

CI-DESSOUS *Cornes de yaks et pierres taillées sur lesquelles est gravé le proverbe universel tibétain Om Mane Padme Hum (Vive le joyau dans le Lotus) au Chiu Gompah.*

CI-DESSUS *Vers le sud et Purang, avec le lointain Garwal Himalaya en Inde, depuis la route poussiéreuse du Gurla La (4 590 m).*

CIRCUIT DE DHAULAGIRI

par Steve Razzetti

D'une manière générale, des habitants du haut Himalaya ne partagent pas le goût de la classification qu'éprouvent les Occidentaux, et bien souvent, quand on s'enquiert du nom d'un des sommets enneigés, les Sherpas répondent innocemment « Dhaulagiri, Monsieur » (Montagne blanche). Dans le cas du massif que nous connaissons aujourd'hui sous le nom de Dhaulagiri, cette anecdote entraîna une confusion quant à la topographie du Népal, résultant d'une cartographie particulièrement imaginative.

Le Dhaulagiri I (8 167 m) est le point culminant d'un massif complexe qui s'étend sur plus de 55 km en largeur et comprend les six sommets Dhaulagiri et leurs voisins de l'ouest, Churen Himal et Putha Hiunchuli, qui tous dépassent 7 200 m. Le pic de Tukuche est l'un des plus spectaculaires de cet ensemble, manquant de 80 m seulement l'altitude des 7 000 m.

Le géologue suisse Arnold Heim fut le premier Européen à s'approcher des sommets du Népal central, alors qu'il effectuait une reconnaissance aérienne de la région en 1949. Un an plus tard, l'expédition de Bill Tilman aperçut le Dhaulagiri depuis Muktinath, après avoir passé le Thorung La au départ de Manang, mais c'est l'expédition du Français Maurice Herzog, cette même année, qui approcha réellement le plus intimidant et le plus splendide des mastodontes himalayens.

Herzog conduisait une équipe brillante, organisée sous les auspices du Club Alpin Français, et qui comprenait des alpinistes aussi célèbres que Gaston Rebuffat, Lionel Terray et Jacques Oudot. Leurs efforts n'étaient qu'une affaire d'escalade, entreprise dans l'intention d'atteindre le premier sommet de 8 000 m « pour l'honneur de la France ». Ils s'étaient fixé le Dhaulagiri et l'Annapurna comme objectifs, et ils choisirent le village de Tukuche, dans la vallée du Kali

EN HAUT *Une marche dans les nuages à l'approche de la crête acérée du col de Budzunge Bara, en route pour le Kaphe Khola et le camp de base de Putha Hiunchuli.*
AU MILIEU *Un solide déjeuner sur la piste de Gurja Gaon. Une nourriture copieuse et de bonne qualité est l'une des raisons pour organiser votre voyage par l'intermédiaire d'un tour-opérateur connu.*
À DROITE *Un repos bien mérité hors de la neige lors de la descente du col de Damphus vers le Kali Gandaki au-dessus de Marpha. On peut voir le Thorung La de l'autre côté de la vallée.*
CI-CONTRE *Coucher de soleil sur la muraille Puchhar du Dhaulagiri I depuis le camp de base italien – le dernier endroit avec encore quelque végétation jusqu'à Marpha, à quatre bons jours de marche.*

Gandaki, pour y établir leur camp de base. Les approches vers les deux pics étaient inconnues, et l'équipe se trouva confrontée à un colossal travail de reconnaissance. Choisissant de se concentrer d'abord sur le Dhaulagiri, ils se divisèrent en petits groupes et se mirent en quête d'un chemin vers la montagne. Ayant basé leur stratégie sur une carte indienne erronée, ils effectuèrent plusieurs percées infructueuses vers la vallée du Damphus Khola et remontèrent le terrible glacier du Dhaulagiri oriental avant d'atteindre la ligne de partage des eaux à l'ouest du Kali Gandaki, au point que nous connaissons maintenant sous le nom de Damphus ou col de Thapa.

Néanmoins, les glaciers au nord du Dhaulagiri gardèrent leur secret. Ce n'est que lorsque Lionel Terray et Jacques Oudot réussirent enfin à traverser la vallée Secrète (Hidden Valley), et parvinrent au col surmontant le glacier de Chhonbardan et la face nord du Dhaulagiri, que le problème fut résolu : le glacier s'écoulait dans les redoutables ravins du Myagdi Khola. Bien que le col français fût baptisé après cette héroïque exploration, Herzog et son équipe finirent par battre en retraite,

CIRCUIT DE DHAULAGIRI

LIEU Dhaulagiri Himal, Népal.

QUAND PARTIR Avril à mai et septembre à décembre.

DÉPART Beni, vols internationaux vers Katmandou puis avion ; ou par la route jusqu'à Pokara, puis car ou jeep jusqu'à Beni (mauvaise route).

ARRIVÉE Jomsom ; avion jusqu'à Pokara (20 min) puis Katmandou par avion (25 min) ou par la route (8 h).

DURÉE 21-23 jours au minimum.

POINT CULMINANT French Pass (col des Français, 5 300 m).

ASPECTS TECHNIQUES Le col des Français par mauvais temps demande une « navigation » adroite. Bien qu'ostensiblement proche de quelques-unes des pistes les plus fréquentées et des aérodromes du Népal, une bonne partie de cet itinéraire est extrêmement isolée et l'organisation d'un repli ou d'une évacuation en cas d'urgence serait très longue. Les groupes voyageant ici devront se préparer, s'équiper et se diriger en gardant cela présent à l'esprit.

MATÉRIEL Autonomie d'hébergement, de nourriture et de combustible indispensable sur tout le parcours. Il peut y avoir un problème de sécurité dans la région de Pokhara, où sévissent des voleurs ; gardez un œil sur vos biens à tout moment.

MODE DE RANDONNÉE Sac à dos ou expédition.

AUTORISATIONS/RESTRICTIONS Permis de randonnée nécessaire. Doit être obtenu auprès d'une agence accréditée.

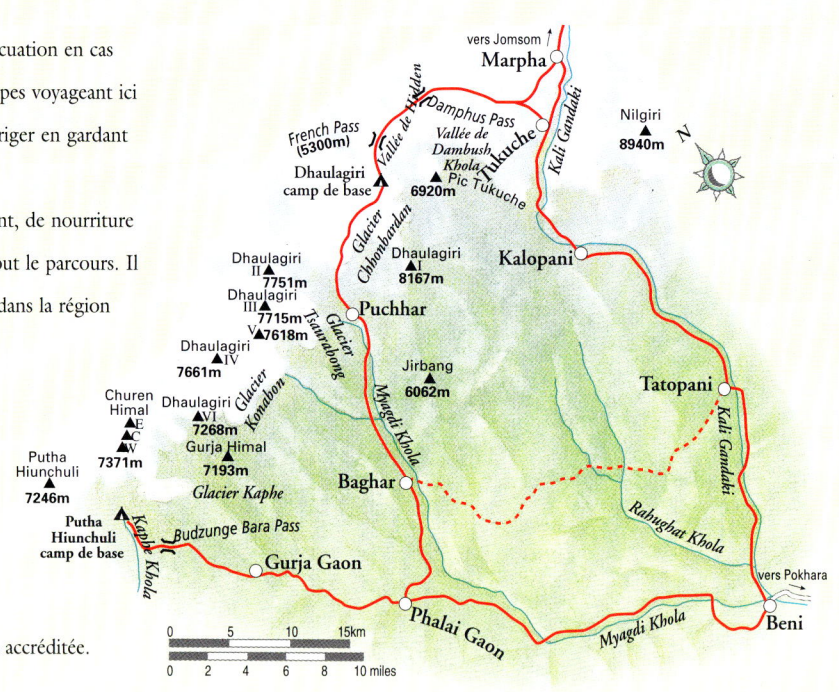

CI-DESSUS *Une pause pour admirer le paysage de la vallée Dara Khola, en direction du Gurja Himal et du col du Budzunge Bara, non loin du village de Lurang.*

proclamant ce pic « inescaladable ». La première expédition qui approcha le Dhaulagiri par le Myagdi Khola fut conduite par l'alpiniste suisse, Bernhard Lauterburg, en 1953. Ne disposant pour toute indication que d'une photographie (prise par Terray depuis le French Pass en 1950), le Suisse entreprit d'explorer le glacier de Chhonbardan en essayant de trouver une voie d'accès vers le Dhaulagiri lui-même. Une reconnaissance minutieuse fut effectuée jusqu'à l'altitude de 7 200 m au sommet, mais tandis que plusieurs membres de l'équipe repartaient par le French Pass (col des Français) et le col du Damphus, la difficulté à escalader la face nord restait évidente.

En 1960, une deuxième expédition suisse finit par vaincre la montagne. Ses membres avaient apporté avec eux un avion monomoteur équipé pour atterrir sur les glaciers, avec un pilote chevronné et un mécanicien. Après avoir établi un système de navette et aéroporté l'équipe entière jusqu'au col de Damphus, le pilote Ernst Saxer établit un nouveau record d'altitude d'atterrissage sur glacier, en déposant Kurt Diembeurger et Ernst Forrer sur le col du nord-est, d'où ils entreprirent leur ascension.

Le circuit de base du Dhaulagiri I reste l'un des itinéraires les plus gratifiants du Népal et un véritable défi. La piste la plus connue part de Beni et se termine par le franchissement du col du Damphus pour retrouver le Kali Gandaki à Tukuche ou à Marpha, vous obligeant à une marche longue et difficile, comprenant deux cols éloignés et le plus haut des camps de base, celui du Dhaulagiri, tout au bout de la piste. Les voies de dégagement sur cet itinéraire devront être soigneusement pesées..

Par beau temps et dans de bonnes conditions d'enneigement, le passage des cols des Français et de Damphus restera inoubliable, avec d'impressionnantes perspectives sur la face nord du Dhaulagiri, alors que la navigation peut s'avérer extrêmement difficile dans le blizzard. De même, il est absolument impératif de choisir le bon col pour passer de la vallée Secrète vers le Kali Gandaki, car une erreur pourrait mener vers des à pic dangereux.

Pour un groupe voyageant en mode expédition, la meilleure option est peut-être celle du circuit de base, en commençant par une variante vers la vallée du Khafe Khola et le camp de base de Putha Hiunchuli. La première ascension par le nord de ce sommet fut effectuée en 1954 par une

expédition britannique conduite par Jimmy Roberts, mais ce furent les seconde et troisième ascensions, réalisées toutes deux par des équipes japonaises en 1972, qui ouvrirent la route du village de Phalai Gaon, dans la vallée du Myagdi Khola, par Gurja Gaon et le col de Budzunge Bara.

La piste en montagnes russes qui constitue cette marche spectaculaire sur les crêtes, s'élève vers le ciel depuis Gurja Gaon puis vers le Budzunge Bara. Sous la neige, cela constituerait une aventure périlleuse, mais par beau temps, un camp d'altitude juste à l'est du col reste possible. Blottie immédiatement sous la face sud du Gurja Himal, cette position offre des couchers de soleil spectaculaires sur le Dhaulagiri et le Nilgiri ; et sans aucun autre point élevé sur des kilomètres vers l'est ou vers l'ouest, on a vraiment l'impression de marcher sur les nuages.

L'étroite piste qui monte vers le Myagdi Khola, au-dessus du village de Baghar, traverse une épaisse forêt vierge. La piste monte et descend en zigzaguant, traverse le torrent tumultueux au moyen de frêles ponts de bambou, franchit des parois verticales de roche au moyen d'échelles de bambou amarrées par des lianes, puis disparaît sous d'énormes blocs rocheux en équilibre précaire pour réapparaître au-dessus des troncs pourrissants de gigantesques arbres morts.

Ce n'est que le quatrième jour que les arbres aux feuillages caducs feront place aux conifères et que les murailles rocheuses de chaque côté de la vallée s'écarteront à une distance plus respectable. Soudain, la piste débouche sur une clairière, avec Pucchar droit devant. Ce camp minuscule, connu comme le camp de base italien, est situé sur une petite prairie située immédiatement sous la face ouest – ou la paroi Pucchar – du Dhaulagiri I. Il est difficile d'imaginer un endroit plus impressionnant : avec la face Rupal du Nanga Parbat au Pakistan, cette muraille compte parmi les plus hautes du monde, s'élevant vers les cieux jusqu'à plus de 4 600 m. Les eaux du Myagdi Khola, maintenant réduites à un filet, s'échappent entre les parois glacées d'une gorge sombre et inhospitalière vers le nord, et la beauté sauvage du décor s'intensifie chaque soir lorsque le soleil couchant projette son spectacle de lumières sur toute la face de la montagne.

CI-DESSUS *L'ascension des dernières pentes neigeuses, au-dessus du glacier Chhonbardan et du camp de base du Dhaulagiri avec, au loin, la face nord du Dhaulagiri I.*

CIRCUIT DE MANASLU ET DE L'ANNAPURNA

par Steve Razzetti

Le royaume du Népal englobe 800 km des plus hauts sommets de la chaîne himalayenne d'est en ouest, et sur 220 km du nord au sud dans sa plus grande largeur. D'après les dernières statistiques, près de 400 000 touristes visitent ce royaume montagneux chaque année. Parmi eux, environ 80 000 parcourent les collines à pied, profitant du splendide paysage montagnard qui fait la renommée de ce pays dans le monde. Le Népal s'ouvrit aux étrangers en 1949, et la randonnée telle que nous la connaissons aujourd'hui vit le jour dans les années soixante. Les quarante années qui ont suivi ont vu d'étonnants changements affecter le Népal. Le tourisme est une manne à double tranchant. Des visiteurs indélicats ont concouru à l'érosion écologique de plusieurs des régions très fréquentées et brisé le charme naturel de leurs habitants. Heureusement, les Népalais ont assez de caractère pour faire face à ces agressions culturelles, et d'innombrables mystères captivent encore les explorateurs avisés.

La partie centrale de l'Himalaya népalais est connue sous le nom de Section Gandaki, car elle englobe les chaînes de montagnes d'où coulent les affluents du fleuve Gandaki – les Kali Gandaki, Seti Gandaki, Marsyangdi, Buri Gandaki et Trisuli Gandaki. La chaîne de sommets la plus haute, s'étendant d'est en ouest d'une extrémité à l'autre du Népal, est connue comme le Grand Himalaya, et au nord s'étend une chaîne secondaire quelquefois appelée la chaîne du Ladakh ou la Chaîne Marginale Tibétaine. La plupart des fleuves importants prennent leur source en amont de la chaîne du Grand Himalaya et, actuellement, la coupent littéralement, tandis que quelques-uns drainent des régions du Tibet au nord des deux chaînes. Le résultat concret de cette géographie physique est que la frontière népalo-tibétaine longe les crêtes du nord par endroits, et le Grand Himalaya à d'autres. Dans le premier cas, il est souvent possible de parcourir les circuits des pics les plus élevés du Grand Himalaya tout en restant à l'intérieur du Népal. Partons donc pour le Manaslu et l'Annapurna.

EN HAUT *Citrouilles séchant au soleil d'automne sous les avant-toits d'une maison de Gurung. Avec le riz, les fruits et légumes secs, elles forment la base de l'alimentation des montagnards.*
AU MILIEU *Dans toutes les régions d'altitude inhabitées du Népal, les poinsettias apportent une touche colorée bienvenue dans les vallées automnales.*
À DROITE *Premier aperçu de la face est du Manaslu, dominant le village de Lo, dans le haut Buri Gandaki.*

L'exploration de la région par les Européens commença modestement en 1864, quand Nain Singh Rawat, « l'administrateur en chef » de la Grande Étude Géographique (GET) et trigonométrique de Montgomerie, se rendit au Buri Gandaki supérieur, en route pour le Tibet. « Numéro 1 », comme on le surnomma bientôt, et son cousin Mani avaient été détachés au quartier général de la GET à Dehra Dun, pour être formés comme géomètres clandestins. Après deux ans de formation à l'utilisation du sextant et du compas, ils n'essayèrent pas de s'infiltrer au Tibet depuis leur territoire natal, en raison de leur renommée dans la région. Ce n'est qu'après plusieurs tentatives que Nain Singh parvint, du Népal, en remontant la vallée du Trisuli Gandaki, à pénétrer au Tibet par Rasua Garhi.

Il fallut près d'un siècle pour que débute la seconde phase de l'exploration de la région. En 1950, au départ de leur deuxième expédition vers le Népal, les alpinistes britanniques Bill Tilman, Jimmy Roberts et leur équipe passèrent plusieurs semaines aux alentours de Bimtakhoti, les prairies en contrebas des flancs ouest du Larkya La. Signalé sur les cartes modernes comme le Bimthang, c'était encore à l'époque un centre d'affaires important. Le

véritable objectif de Tilman, pendant cette expédition épique était de trouver des approches possibles vers l'Annapurna et le Manaslu en prévision de futures expéditions, mais l'équipe parvint également à cartographier dans le détail ce qui est maintenant l'un des parcours de montagne les plus appréciés au monde. Une fois à Manang, l'équipe se sépara par groupes de deux qui, à eux tous, découvrirent la haute vallée du Marsyangdi, franchirent le Thorung La jusqu'à Multinah, parvinrent à l'altitude de 7 200 m lors d'une tentative d'ascension de l'Annapurna IV, franchirent le col du Larkya La jusqu'à Nupri pour enfin quitter la région en redescendant par l'impressionnant défilé de la vallée du Buri Gandaki.

De nos jours, pour vivre la stupéfiante révélation qui accompagnait le franchissement des cols isolés au cœur de l'Himalaya népalais, et apprécier le contraste entre la randonnée réellement sauvage et les pistes touristiques, la conjugaison des circuits du Manaslu et de l'Annapurna est sans égal.

Trois des principaux affluents du Gandaki sont au programme de cet itinéraire. Dans l'est, le Buri Gandaki sépare les sommets du Gurkha Himal (Manaslu, Himalchuli et leurs satellites) du Ganesh Himal. Ensuite, le Marsyangdi sépare le Gurkha Himal des Annapurnas, et enfin la grande gorge du Buri Gandaki coupe les Annapurnas du Dhaulagiri. Au nord de Manaslu s'étend Nupri, et Manang et Mustang – des étendues d'alpages dénudées sous contrôle népalais, encore peuplées aujourd'hui par les Bhotias (peuple d'origine tibétaine) Ceux qui entreprennent ce périple partent généralement de Gorkha, accessible depuis Katmandou en 6 h par une route goudronnée. Partant de la poussiéreuse et chaotique place principale de Gorkha, également gare routière, la piste remonte une chaîne basse vers l'est avant de replonger dans la chaleur étouffante du Buti Gandaki, accédant à la vallée par la ville-marché d'Arughat Bazaar. Le périple vers le nord, longeant la rivière jusqu'à Nupri, est un véritable défi de huit jours à travers l'une des plus longues et des plus spectaculaires vallées transhimalayennes du Népal.

Bien que la piste empruntant les gorges ait été utilisée pendant des siècles comme route de commerce, elle est régulièrement dévastée par les pluies de mousson et certaines sections sont toujours délicates. Attendez-vous à perdre beaucoup de temps et d'énergie en détours

et à escalader à quatre pattes les débris de la jungle décimée par les avalanches, avant d'atteindre le délicieux air frais des régions plus élevées. Ceux qui se risqueront sur cet itinéraire vers Nupri seront largement récompensés de leurs efforts : ils découvriront une multitude de sommets extraordinaires, des villages non dénaturés et fragilement blottis entre forêt vierge et terres agricoles, de minuscules gompahs (monastères) isolés où ils pourront s'asseoir et siroter une chang (bière) en compagnie de lamas venus d'aussi loin que Lhassa ou Sikkim.

Pour ceux qui ont le temps, le plus grand village du Nupri, Sama Gaon, et ses environs ne manquent pas d'intérêt. Niché dans la partie supérieure et aride du Buri Gandaki, ce lieu tout à fait bizarre se compose d'un agglomérat serré de maisons tibétaines en bois et s'enorgueillit de son pittoresque gompah et de ces impressionnantes perspectives vers le nord et l'est du Manaslu. Les ruines de Larkya Bazaar, ville jadis prospère, ne sont pas très loin vers le nord.

CI-DESSUS *Les murailles du Buri Gandaki sont incroyablement abruptes. En l'absence presque totale de terrain plat dans la vallée, les campements sont rares et les terres cultivables presque inexistantes.*
CI-CONTRE *Des porteurs franchissent le Larkya La. Moins célèbre que le Thorung La au nord de l'Annapurna, ce col est plus agréable grâce à la solitude qui règne au sommet.*

LIEU Larkya Himal, Népal.

QUAND PARTIR Mars à mai ou septembre à décembre.

DÉPART Vols internationaux vers Katmandou puis par la route jusqu'à Gorkha par l'autoroute de Prithvi (7 h).

ARRIVÉE Jomsom, avion jusqu'à Pokhara (20 min) puis Katmandou par avion (25 min) ou par la route (8 h).

DURÉE 22 jours.

POINT CULMINANT Thorung La (5 400 m).

ASPECTS TECHNIQUES Néant.

MATÉRIEL Autonomie d'hébergement (tentes), de nourriture et de combustible.

MODE DE RANDONNÉE Gorkha-Thonje : sac à dos. Thonje-Jomsom : auberges ou salons de thé sur tout le parcours. La plupart des randonneurs qui font le circuit du Manaslu et de l'Annapurna campe sur tout le parcours.

AUTORISATIONS/RESTRICTIONS L'étape Gorkha-Thonje est une zone soumise à déclaration, et permis et agent de liaison sont nécessaires. Thonje-Jomsom est libre et aucun permis n'est exigé.

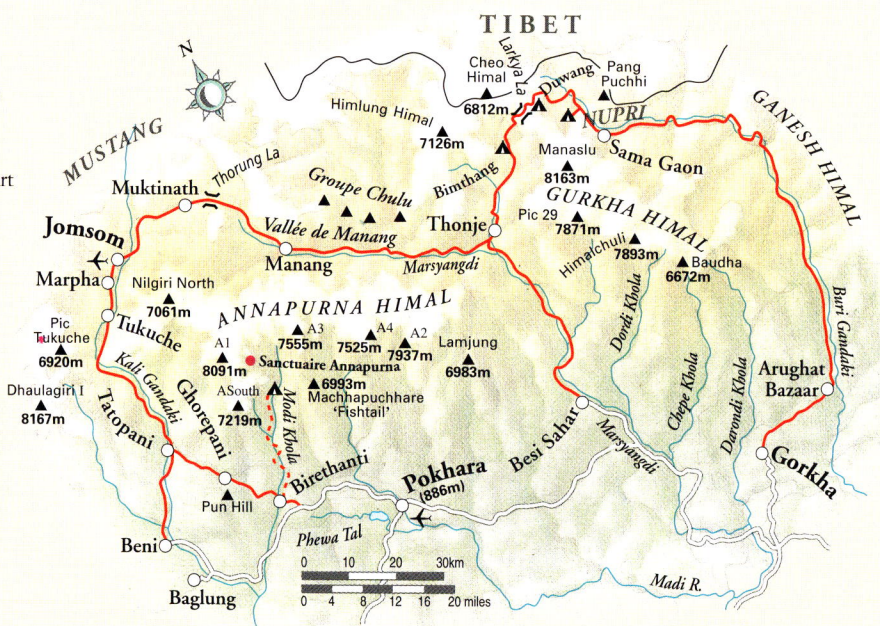

PAGE DE GAUCHE *L'Annapurna III et le Gangapurna dominent le paysage de carte de Noël de la vallée du Marsyangdi et de Manang après une première chute de neige.*

CI-DESSUS *Randonneurs cheminant à travers les champs de neige, dans la montée vers le Thorung La depuis Phedi. Cet itinéraire peut être barré à tout moment par des chutes de neige hors saison.*

Le Larkya La (5 100 m) entre Nupri et Manang ne pose pas de sérieux problème par beau temps mais comme tous les cols de cette altitude dans l'Himalaya, une randonnée court le risque de se transformer en une épopée héroïque dans le blizzard. La piste serpente entre le Cheo et le Manaslu Himalaya, offrant des points de vue étonnants sur les Annapurnas et le Himlung Himal devant vous, et sur le Pang Puchhi et le Ganesh Himal derrière. À Duwang (4 480 m) on trouve un petit abri de pierre du côté est, puis une longue et rude descente au travers de blocs rocheux instables, en venant de l'ouest, jusqu'aux prairies verdoyantes et idylliques de Bimthang. Un endroit spectaculaire pour camper – une surface parfaitement plate abritée derrière d'anciennes moraines glaciaires, et littéralement écrasée par le cirque des géants himalayens.

Dans de nombreux endroits décrits dans cet ouvrage, il y a beaucoup à gagner en s'attardant ici pour y conduire sa propre « exploration ». Ceux qui pourront s'accorder un peu plus de temps pour flâner trouveront suffisamment de matière à aventure autour du Larkya La. Le village de Thonje, la rivière de Marsyangdi et le circuit principal de l'Annapurna sont à deux bons jours de Bimthang, en descendant la vallée du Dudh Khola.

On pourrait terminer ce parcours en deux jours à partir de Thonje, en bifurquant au sud vers la ville de Besi Sahar, d'où part la route, mais ce serait vraiment dommage de ne pas profiter des splendeurs de la haute vallée. La vallée du Marsyangdi est beaucoup moins difficile que celle du Buri Gandaki, et bien que les villages le long de la piste se consacrent de plus en plus à satisfaire les caprices des touristes, offrant le spectacle clinquant de terrasses-solariums bardées de réclames de bières, de paraboles satellites, de bazars et de boutiques, le paysage des montagnes alentour est toujours magnifique.

Le passage du Thorung La (5 400 m) depuis l'auberge surpeuplée de Thorung Phedi n'aura rien d'une aventure paisible et solitaire (cinq cents randonneurs y passent en haute saison, et il y a maintenant un salon de thé au sommet), mais c'est le haut lieu et l'apogée de cet itinéraire. Le Larkya La est sans doute plus isolé et plus spectaculaire, mais le contraste, que vous découvrez au Thorung, entre les profonds défilés de Manang et les grandes étendues désertiques du Kali Gandaki et du Mustang La justifie pleinement sa renommée. D'un point de vue purement esthétique, la vue sur le Dhaulagiri et le pic de Tukuche depuis la descente est unique.

Ne manquez pas de visiter le beau complexe religieux du temple de Muktinah en redescendant du col. C'est un des lieux les plus sacrés du Népal. On peut maintenant prendre l'avion à Jomsom, à un jour de marche de Muktinah, mais ce serait vous priver du bonheur que procure la descente du Kali Gandaki à pied et de la célèbre hospitalité des auberges Thalaki, dans des villages comme Marpha et Tukuche. Pour terminer en beauté et garder de cette région un souvenir inoubliable, prenez à l'est depuis Tatopani, en direction de la route à Birethanti, par Ghorepani et Pun Hill. Levez-vous tôt pour être au sommet avant l'aube. On ne peut trouver plus beau lever de soleil, même si on doit le partager avec quelques centaines d'autres personnes.

À DROITE *Regard vers le nord dans le kaléidoscope de sable et d'éboulis de Mustang depuis la piste au-dessus de Kagbeni, qui contourne la colline vers le Kali Gandaki.*

LA RANDONNÉE DU « BONHOMME DE NEIGE »

par Steve Razzetti

Shangri La est peut-être devenu un cliché facile, mais s'il est un endroit sur terre qui mérite cette épithète, c'est bien le Bhoutan. Comme bon nombre de principautés satellites du Tibet, le Bhoutan dut souvent se battre pour préserver son indépendance économique et spirituelle contre ses puissants voisins. Cela a inculqué au peuple de ce pays un très fort sentiment de fierté et d'identité culturelle, et c'est maintenant le seul pays au monde qui ait fait du bouddhisme tantrique sa religion d'État.

Peu de pays peuvent s'enorgueillir d'un tel patrimoine traditionnel, et le Bhoutan est certainement le seul pays où coutumes et valeurs anciennes guident toujours la vie quotidienne du gouvernement comme celle du peuple, à presque tous les niveaux. Cela est dû en grande partie aux efforts éclairés du roi, Jigme Singye Wangchuk, et de quelques personnages-clés.

Fuyant la persécution au Tibet, Ngawang Namgyal, honoré du titre de Shabdrung (« celui aux pieds duquel on se prosterne »), arriva au Bhoutan au XVIIe siècle. Il réussit à unifier le pays du Dragon en trente jours, en créant un État politique et religieux qui durera jusqu'au XXe siècle. Les plus célèbres témoignages du legs de Shabdrung sont les élégants *dzongs* aux allures de forteresses, qui servent aujourd'hui de centres administratifs et de monastères.

Le père du Bhoutan moderne serait Jigme Dorje Wangchuk, qui régna de 1952 à 1972. Sous sa direction, la longue et totale isolation du pays prit fin et le gouvernement aborda le tourisme avec prudence. Les voyages individuels n'étaient pas autorisés mais un nombre limité d'étrangers était admis dans la mesure où ces derniers participaient à des voyages organisés payés d'avance. Cette situation est encore en vigueur, et près de 5 400 touristes ont visité le pays en 1999.

La randonnée au Bhoutan est soumise aux mêmes réglementations que le tourisme en général, rendant les randonnées exploratoires presque impossibles. Ceux qui souhaiteraient voyager à pied à travers la région montagneuse préservée du Bhoutan devront prendre toutes dispositions par l'intermédiaire d'une agence accréditée, et emprunteront l'un des itinéraires fixes approuvés par l'Office touristique du Bhoutan. L'organisation de toute activité touristique au Bhoutan, randonnée ou autre, coûte 200 dollars américains par jour, rendant les longs parcours en montagne très onéreux. Quoi qu'on puisse en penser, on ne peut nier l'attrait qu'il y a à parcourir ces montagnes vierges. De même que de tous les itinéraires actuellement autorisés au Bhoutan, les 400 km de la randonnée du Bonhomme de Neige sont les plus rudes, les plus difficiles, les plus longs, mais aussi les plus gratifiants.

À partir des ruines de Drukyel Dzong, dans la vallée du Paro, vers Bumthang dans le Bhoutan central, cet itinéraire ne franchit pas moins de onze cols, dont trois au-dessus de 5 000 m. Il comprend également le plus spectaculaire paysage de montagne du pays, avec le Chomolhari (7 315 m) et le Ganker Punzum ou le Rinchita (7 541 m), probablement le plus haut sommet invaincu au monde.

Drukyel Dzong, construite pour commémorer la victoire de Shabdrung sur les maraudeurs tibétains en 1644, est située au sommet d'un éperon rocheux qui occupe une position stratégique, quelque 20 km au nord de l'aéroport de Paro. Une route goudronnée

EN HAUT *Lingshi Dzong sur le chemin de Chomolhari à Laya. Ces imposantes forteresses sont les symboles de la puissance Drukpa au* XVIIe *siècle.*

AU MILIEU *Bharals (moutons bleus) tibétains à flanc de collines au-dessus du Gombu Le gouvernement bhoutanais a contribué à préserver la flore et la faune locales.*

À GAUCHE *Battage de l'orge dans le village de Woche au Lunana. L'agriculture de subsistance est essentielle dans ces régions éloignées, et les villageois peuvent rechigner à se joindre aux marcheurs pendant la période des moissons.*

conduit même jusqu'à cette ancienne forteresse, jadis puissante, et par beau temps, l'imposant sommet du Chomolhari domine les crêtes avoisinantes, point d'orgue aux paysages de pure magie du Bhoutan. Escaladé pour la première fois en 1937 par l'Anglais Freddy Spencer-Chapman et le Népalais Pasang Dawa Lama, le Chomolhari est un pic sacré dont le sommet est encore vierge.

Au Bhoutan, les bagages et le matériel des randonneurs sont traditionnellement portés par des yaks. Après avoir harnaché ces impressionnants animaux au pied des remparts croulants de Drukyel Dzong, et attaqué la remontée de la vallée du Paro Chhu, une marche idyllique de trois jours vous conduira au camp de base du Chomolhari à Jangothang (3 960 m). Les pistes, tout le long de cet itinéraire, ne sont pas vraiment difficiles, les yaks et leurs fardeaux nécessitant une grande largeur de passage, mais les flancs de la vallée sont à pic, les forêts impénétrables, les habitants rares et les camps peu nombreux et éloignés. On marche plus longtemps en une journée au Bhoutan qu'au Népal, et les installations ainsi que la communication en montagne sont beaucoup plus primitives. Les autorités bhoutanaises ont construit des chalets sur les principaux sites de campement, dans la partie Chomolhari du parcours, mais en fait, ils sont maintenant utilisés par les personnels de randonnée, insalubres, ils ne constituent qu'une alternative peu séduisante.

La remontée de la vallée du Paro Chhu est un vrai délice. Les eaux turquoise du fleuve s'écoulent paisiblement dans une vallée boisée de bouleaux et de mélèzes qui, fin octobre, offre

CI-DESSUS *Une caravane de yaks transportant du matériel progresse vers le col de Jazela (5 050 m) dans la partie Lunana de la randonnée du Bonhomme de Neige.*

CI-DESSOUS *Un groupe de randonneurs savourant le petit déjeuner au pied de l'imposante face est du Chomolhari*

une splendide palette de couleurs automnales. Approchant de Jangothang, les forêts s'éclaircissent, et les branches de bambou, de genièvre et de rhododendrons se détachent de la toile de fond que forment les impressionnantes pentes enneigées du Jitchu Drake (6 790 m), devant vous. Le Chomolhari demeure caché jusqu'aux approches du camp, quand soudain l'énorme face apparaît, en haut de la vallée glaciaire dont l'entrée est sous la garde d'un antique dzong en ruines. En une journée de marche sur les pentes herbeuses, immédiatement au nord de Jangothang, on atteint facilement des altitudes dépassant 5 000 m, permettant une excellente acclimatation, et on se délecte du formidable panorama à 360° sur les sommets alentour.

Poursuivant vers le nord-ouest et parallèlement à la frontière tibétaine, l'itinéraire vers Laya et Lunana franchit une série de hauts cols, offrant de superbes points de vue sur le Chomolhari, le Jitchu Drake, le Kang Bum (environ 6 500 m), le Gang Chhen Ta (6 794 m) et le Masa Gang (7 194 m). Le seul village important rencontré sur ce trajet de six jours entre Jangothang et Laya, est Lingshi, où un magnifique dzong badigeonné de blanc, perché sur le bord d'une corniche abrupte, offre un spectacle inoubliable.

Laya (à environ 3 800 m) est un gros village prospère, situé immédiatement au sud du Masa Gang, dont les habitants font commerce depuis longtemps avec leurs cousins du nord, au-delà des cols, au Tibet. L'agriculture et l'élevage des yaks constituent le pilier de l'économie locale, mais la contrebande fait partie des mœurs. De nombreuses maisons dans le village arborent des panneaux solaires, et en cherchant un peu vous trouverez une variété surprenante de marchandises chinoises ou tibétaines à vendre. Les femmes sont vêtues de longues robes noires en poil de yak et portent des chapeaux coniques en bambou très typiques ; elles fabriquent la chang (bière) qui amadouera les visiteurs.

Au-delà de Laya, la randonnée du Bonhomme de Neige continue vers l'est en franchissant le col du Kanglakachu La (5 105 m) vers la fabuleuse région de Lunana. D'aucuns traversent cette importante ligne de partage des eaux en une seule journée, depuis le camp d'altitude de Rodophu (4 350 m) jusqu'à Tarina, mais un groupe bien acclimaté et disposant du temps nécessaire envisagera de faire une pause à Narithang (environ 4 800 m). Cheminant entre des lacs irisés et l'ancien lit du glacier encombré de blocs rocheux, sous les hauts sommets enneigés, la piste est quelquefois étroite, mais c'est toujours un vrai bonheur de la parcourir.

Narithang est perché sur une moraine juste en face des contreforts nord enneigés du Gangla Karshung (6 395 m). En passant la nuit à cet endroit, un marathon de 13 h peut se transformer en une randonnée de deux jours tout à fait agréables. Au nord de l'itiné-

CI-DESSUS *Pendant la descente du Kanglakachu La vers la vallée de la Tarina, les sommets du Lunana se découvrent dans toute leur splendeur. Au centre, le Jejekangphu Gang.*

LIEU Bhoutan, Himalaya oriental.

QUAND PARTIR Mai à juin, ou octobre. La mousson est beaucoup plus sensible au Bhoutan qu'au Népal. Le temps est en général moins stable, plus venteux et plus froid.

DÉPART/ARRIVÉE La seule compagnie aérienne desservant Bhoutan est Druk Air. Flotte de deux BAe 146, assurant des liaisons avec Bombay, Delhi, Bangkok et Katmandou. La plupart des gens parcourent Paro-Bumthang à pied et tous les transports sont organisés par leurs hôtes bhoutanais.

DURÉE 25 jours minimum, de Drukyel à Dzong-Dhur. Ajouter 5 jours pour repos/imprévus/excursions latérales.

POINT CULMINANT Gophu La (5 230 m).

ASPECTS TECHNIQUES Néant.

MATÉRIEL Le matériel doit être soigneusement emballé dans des sacs solides qui seront transportés par les yacks. Tout le matériel de cuisine et de camping sera fourni par les hôtes bhoutanais.

MODE DE RANDONNÉE Sac à dos ou expédition.

AUTORISATIONS/RESTRICTIONS Aucun permis n'est délivré pour les voyages individuels dans tout le pays. Toutes les randonnées doivent faire l'objet de réservations auprès d'une agence accréditée. Obligation de respecter les itinéraires fixes approuvés par l'Office du Tourisme du Bhoutan.

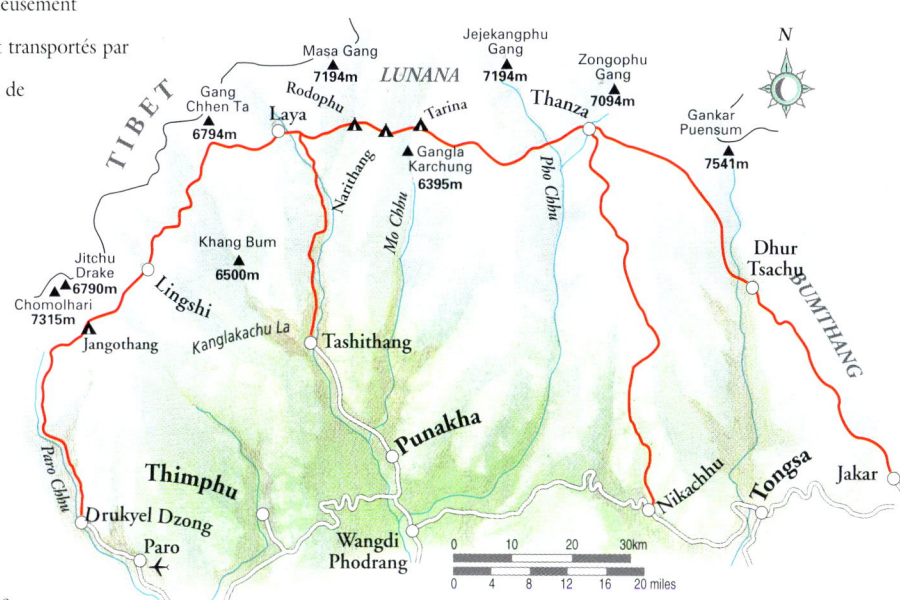

EN HAUT *Le Gangkar Puensum ou Rinchita, et les sources du Mangdi Chhu, vus depuis un éperon rocheux au-dessus du Wartang La, lors de la randonnée de Thanza à Bumthang.*

CI-DESSUS *Mauvaise surprise ! On aperçoit au sud la longue montée vers le col enneigé de Djule La, le dernier sur la route quittant Lunana pour Bumthang.*

raire de descente, un éperon rocheux proéminent peut s'escalader facilement, offrant un panorama impressionnant sur les montagnes entre Lunana et le Tibet.

Depuis la splendide vallée de la Tarina et à travers une série de falaises abruptes qui descendent de Jejekangphu Gang (7 194 m) vers les sources de Pho Chhu et Thanza, on découvre Lunana, une terre arcadienne à la lumière intense, ponctuée de hameaux médiévaux et habitée par une population rustique et pastorale. Approchant de Thanza, le long de la vallée encombrée de débris, la colossale face sud du Zongophu Gang (7 094 m) se cabre au-dessus des moraines abandonnées par d'invisibles glaciers. Plusieurs immenses lacs d'eau glacée sont retenus par ces amas instables de gravats, qui périodiquement provoquent des inondations cataclysmiques semant la destruction aussi loin que Punakha Dzong.

Coupés du reste du monde par l'épaisse neige qui recouvre les cols entre novembre et avril, les habitants de Thanza (environ 4 100 m) vivent dans l'un des lieux les plus hostiles, mais néanmoins magiques, de la planète, en une collectivité unique et intéressante sur le plan génétique. Grands et forts, ils sont indemnes de la maladie de Mong et des malformations cardiaques généralement observées chez les peuples qui passent toute leur vie en altitude. Bien sûr, ils rechignent à conduire leurs précieux yaks hors de Lunana à l'approche des neiges hivernales, et une préparation logistique soignée sera nécessaire pour éviter tout retard en fin de saison.

Il existe deux possibilités pour effectuer la dernière partie de la randonnée du Bonhomme de Neige. L'itinéraire ouest, de Thanza vers Nikachhu, est assez élevé et sauvage, et passe par un chapelet de lacs, brillants comme des bijoux, mais ceux qui tiennent à voir le Gankar Puensum de plus près choisiront l'itinéraire est, plus escarpé, jusqu'à Bumthang. Les deux itinéraires représentent chacun la partie la plus éprouvante du trajet, et comprennent un campement à plus de 5 000 m, mais nous offre au moins par trois fois sur ce parcours de sept jours jusqu'à Dhur en Bumthang, une vue absolument inouïe sur le Gankar Puensum. Les variantes sont multiples, et un bain chaud chez Guru Rinpoche à Dhur Tsachu parachèvera ce que beaucoup considèrent comme la randonnée la plus difficile et la plus belle du monde.

AUSTRALASIE

LA PISTE DE LARAPINTA | DE EDEN À MALLACOOTA | LA PISTE OVERLAND | AUTOUR DES MONTAGNES | LA PISTE ROUTEBURN |

AUSTRALASIE

Ces étendues sauvages nous sont nécessaires, car elles sont peut-être un moyen de nous rassurer sur notre équilibre, un élément géographique de l'espoir…

WALLACE STEGNER, 1909-1993

CI-DESSUS *La vallée des Cascades, la bien nommée (piste Overland, Tasmanie) est un pays enchanté avec ses jeux d'eau naturels et sa végétation luxuriante.*
CI-CONTRE *Le gouffre de Standley, point de départ de la piste du Larapinta, crée une oasis bienvenue au cœur aride de l'Australie.*
PAGES PRÉCÉDENTES *Les ponts et les passerelles du parc près du mont Ngauruhoe facilitent la marche et protègent les précaires rivières de montagne et les terres marécageuses.*

Entourés par les plus grands océans du monde, l'Australie et la Nouvelle-Zélande sont, malgré leur isolement géographique, des destinations touristiques très populaires, offrant aux amateurs de plein air un puissant cocktail de nature, de grands espaces et installations modernes.

L'Australie est le sixième plus grand pays du monde, et l'intérieur de cette île-continent est constitué en grande partie d'un désert inhospitalier que très peu de gens s'aventurent à traverser pendant les mois d'été torrides. Pourtant, il s'agit de l'une des terres les plus anciennes de la planète, sur laquelle une faune et une flore extrêmement variées ont su évoluer et survivre dans les conditions les plus difficiles. Ici, les montagnes furent formées il y a plus de 300 millions d'années, et celles qui subsistent aujourd'hui ne sont que les squelettes érodés des grandes chaînes d'alors. Presque exactement au centre de l'Australie se trouve la ville d'Alice Springs, et les montagnes de la MacDonnell Range voisine comprennent les plus hauts sommets à l'ouest de la Great Dividing Range (la Grande Séparation). Bien que la reconnaissance du caractère sacré de ces terres aborigènes ait empêché la construction de pistes centrales, celle de Larapinta passe par plusieurs points dignes d'intérêt, parmi les plus appréciés du Territoire du Nord, et a déjà été reconnue comme l'une des plus belles randonnées du monde dans un désert. Sans doute, l'étendue sauvage côtière la plus précieuse d'Australie s'étale-t-elle sur la Côte de Saphir, en Nouvelle-Galles du Sud, ainsi qu'en atteste la création de deux extraordinaires parcs nationaux – Ben Boyd et Nadgee. Les marcheurs allant d'Eden à Mallacoota apprécieront les plages de sable immaculé, les pointes rocheuses et les landes de ce littoral.

La Terre de Van Diemen, appelée aujourd'hui Tasmanie, fut au XIXe siècle une colonie pénitentiaire britannique de triste notoriété. C'est aujourd'hui le plus petit État d'Australie, mais le fait que 20 % de son étendue sauvage soient inscrits au patrimoine mondial par l'Unesco témoigne de son importance écologique.

Plages désertes, falaises imposantes, forêt tropicale dense, montagnes découpées et landes à perte de vue, tout contribue à faire de la Tasmanie un paradis pour les randonneurs. Dans l'ouest de l'île, le parc national de Cradle Mountain et du lac Saint-Clair comprend la plus spectaculaire de toutes les pistes de la région, la piste Overland, connue dans le monde entier.

Les Néo-Zélandais sont particulièrement fiers du patrimoine naturel de leur pays et sont depuis longtemps d'ardents protecteurs de la nature. Plus d'un tiers de toute la surface de la Nouvelle-Zélande est également classé réserve naturelle. Le département gouvernemental de protection de la nature administre le réseau très étendu de pistes et de cases du pays, et l'accès aux parcs nationaux est gratuit, sauf pour l'utilisation des différentes installations.

En 1887, le parc national de Tongariro, au centre de l'Ile du Nord, devint le premier parc national de Nouvelle-Zélande et le quatrième du monde. L'Unesco a fait de ce parc le tout premier patrimoine mondial naturel et culturel, en raison à la fois de la splendeur naturelle et unique de ce paysage volcanique, et de la présence du peuple maori. La randonnée qui fait le tour des montagnes explore les forêts et les steppes, les cours d'eau, les lacs et les cascades des trois montagnes volcaniques qui constituent le noyau de parc.

L'Ile du Sud de la Nouvelle-Zélande est dominée par la grande barrière montagneuse appelée Alpes du Sud/Ka Tiritiri o te Moana. Une série de parcs nationaux protège les glaciers, les champs de neige, les rivières, les lacs, les forêts et la faune sauvage de ces montagnes, tandis que les cols et les vallées sont devenus des itinéraires de randonnées populaires et stimulantes. La piste de Routeburn, qui traverse les étendues sauvages de deux des plus grands parcs nationaux du pays, Mount Aspiring et Fiordland, est l'un des parcours de Nouvelle-Zélande les plus spectaculaires et les plus appréciés.

LA PISTE DE LARAPINTA

par John Chapman

La piste de Larapinta suit l'épine dorsale de la chaîne occidentale MacDonnell, une série de crêtes parallèles qui s'élèvent au-dessus des déserts intérieurs rouges de l'Australie centrale. Ce continent est le plus sec du monde et la piste offre une opportunité unique de traverser une région désertique à pied. Bien que la piste soit encore en construction, elle est déjà bien connue des marcheurs et des voyageurs.

En 1989, le gouvernement décida de raccorder des réserves existantes (manquent ici le nom des réserves mal lisibles sur les photocopies du texte anglais en ma possession ! et plusieurs parcs plus petits) en un seul grand parc national unifié. Cet ambitieux projet comprenait, entre autres, la création d'un chemin pédestre de 220 km sur toute la longueur de la chaîne. Partant de la station télégraphique proche de Alice Springs, la piste du Larapinta devrait se prolonger à l'ouest jusqu'au mont Razorback à l'autre extrémité de la chaîne. Le premier tronçon fut ouvert en 1990, et dix ans après, huit des treize tronçons sont ouverts aux marcheurs. Le nom Larapinta est le nom aborigène de la rivière Finke, qui réunit la plupart des cours d'eau de la chaîne. Un grand nombre d'Aborigènes vivent encore dans la région et les derniers tronçons ne peuvent être achevés sans leur accord ; cela demandera peut-être trois ans.

La piste de Larapinta a été conçue pour attirer les randonneurs et les marcheurs désireux de faire l'expérience du désert sans avoir à se livrer à des préparatifs et à une planification complexes. L'une des particularités de la région est une série de failles profondes creusées par les cours d'eau à travers la chaîne. Lorsque celle-ci se souleva, les torrents continuèrent à éroder la roche et, au lieu d'être détournés, ils conservèrent leurs tracés. Il en résulte une série de gorges où la nappe phréatique est visible par des trous d'eau permanents. Ces points d'eau sont de la plus grande importance pour la population aborigène locale, pour les animaux sauvages de la région ainsi que, maintenant, pour les marcheurs. L'eau est aussi fournie par des réservoirs à chaque campement. La piste elle-même est en général bien balisée, et bornée tous les kilomètres.

En attendant que les quatre tronçons centraux de la piste du Larapinta soient terminés, la plus belle randonnée est celle qui va de Standley Chasm à Alice Springs, soit 60 km. Pour faciliter les problèmes de transport, prenez un car d'excursion jusqu'à Standley Chasm de bonne heure, puis revenez à pied vers Alice Springs. Le trajet en car vous offrira d'excellentes vues sur la chaîne de montagnes au nord.

La marche commence par un détour vers Standley Chasm elle-même. Cette gorge étroite aux parois parallèles attire beaucoup de visiteurs et il vaut mieux l'éviter vers la mi-journée,

EN HAUT *FishHole, une cuvette permanente sur la rivière Jay est sacrée pour les Aborigènes et marque la fin du deuxième tronçon de la piste de Larapinta.*

ENCART *Un jeune aborigène piste un « bush tucker », en suivant la trace laissée par le lézard.*

CI-DESSUS *Les parois du gouffre de Standley font plus de 150 m de haut, et le gouffre lui-même moins de 10 m de large.*

CI-CONTRE *La piste du Larapinta suit une crête élevée de la Chewings Range, à l'ouest de Fish Holem, entre Tangentyere Junction et Millers Flat.*

CHAÎNE MACDONNELL OCCIDENTALE, AUSTRALIE

LIEU Australie centrale.

QUAND PARTIR Mai à septembre. Éviter les mois d'été, quand la température peut dépasser 40°C.

DÉPART Standley Chasm. Des excursions en car partent d'Alice Springs plusieurs fois par jour ; réservations à l'Office du Tourisme.

ARRIVÉE Alice Springs.

DURÉE 4-6 jours ; 60 km.

POINT CULMINANT Lorettas Lookout (1 150 m).

ASPECTS TECHNIQUES Niveau moyen. La Commission de Protection de l'Environnement publie un ensemble de cartes de la piste. Les cartes n° 1 à 3 sont nécessaires pour cette randonnée.

MATÉRIEL Tente, matériel de camping léger. C'est une marche dans le désert – prévoir suffisamment d'eau pour chaque jour.

MODE DE RANDONNÉE Sac à dos. Camping sauvage interdit.

AUTORISATIONS/RESTRICTIONS Aucune autorisation nécessaire ; camping interdit près des points d'eau ; utiliser un réchaud à pétrole pour la cuisine.

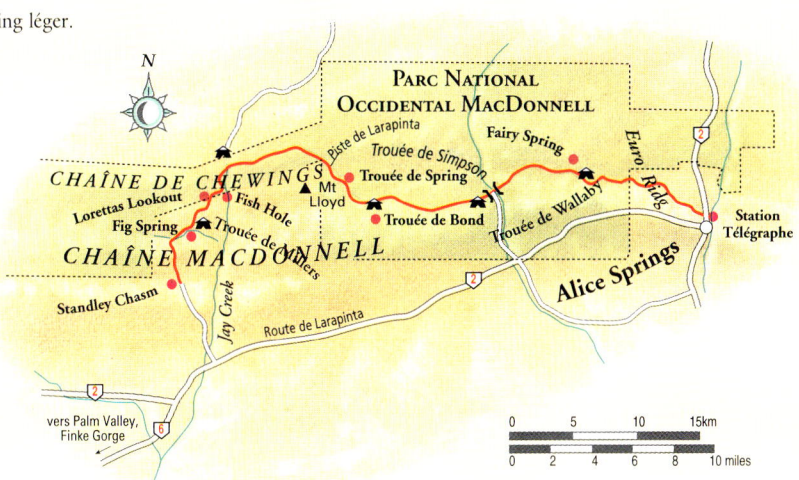

quand les touristes affluent. Aux autres heures de la journée il y a moins de monde et vous aurez tout loisir de patauger dans la piscine naturelle et de profiter des deux côtés de la gorge.

Après avoir quitté le gouffre, la piste principale grimpe régulièrement, offrant des points de vue intéressants sur le paysage alentour. Seuls quelques buissons et une herbe rare poussent ici, les pentes arides constituées de roches rouges dominent l'endroit. Prenez garde de ne pas vous asseoir sur l'herbe spinifex, dont les feuilles sont aussi pointues que des aiguilles ! En pénétrant au cœur de la chaîne, la piste mène à un col, avant de s'orienter au nord-est, en descendant le lit asséché d'un ancien ruisseau. Tout aux alentours montre des signes d'inondations, mais pas d'eau ! Les pluies, par ici, sont rares, et quand elles se produisent, c'est souvent sous forme d'orages violents, pouvant entraîner des crues soudaines – c'est pourquoi il vaut mieux éviter de planter sa tente pour la nuit dans le lit d'une rivière. Sur le parcours, il faut descendre le lit d'anciennes cascades asséchées, offrant chacune un aspect différent – la première est une falaise toute droite, puis une série de dalles inclinées et enfin un ensemble de cuvettes profondes séparées par des marches verticales. La piste, habituellement bien balisée, se détériore légèrement à mesure que l'on descend le lit du ruisseau, quelques pancartes ayant été emportées par les pluies torrentielles, mais elles ne sont pas vraiment indispensables. Il suffit de marcher vers l'aval.

Les seuls points d'eau sont à Refuge et à Fig Springs ; n'oubliez pas de vous approvisionner en eau car il n'y en aura pas d'autres avant Fish Hole. Non loin de Fig Springs, traversez le camping ouvert de Millers Flat. Les campements eux-mêmes n'apportent rien de particulier mais le panorama alentour sur les pentes et les falaises de roche rouge forment un décor agréable pour un bivouac de nuit. Avec la proximité des sources, la vallée abrite également une grande variété de plantes, y compris le cycas de la chaîne MacDonnell, le buisson vénéneux aux feuilles de pêcher, le plectranthus d'Australie centrale, et la fougère tendre. Beaucoup de ces plantes, typiques des climats humides, ne se trouvent que dans ces gorges étroites. Leur extrême diversité et le paysage découvert où elles poussent constituent l'une des particularités de la chaîne.

La piste se divise en deux itinéraires, l'un en haut et l'autre en bas. L'itinéraire bas a été prévu pour ceux qui ont horreur de gravir des collines, et il n'est pas spectaculaire. Prenez plutôt la route haute vers le nord. Elle passe par une petite gorge où poussent des palmiers, spectacle inattendu dans ce paysage aride. Une montée délicate passant par une grande cascade asséchée conduit à un col. La piste vire vers le nord-est et grimpe jusqu'à Loretta's Lookout (1 150 m), au sommet de la chaîne Chewings. C'est la plus belle vue du parcours. En se retournant pour regarder la crête de la MacDonnell, on découvre à quel point la chaîne est formée d'une série de crêtes et de sommets non reliés entre eux. Des panoramas sur les déserts sans fin se prolongent au nord comme au sud.

Une descente régulière rejoint la piste basse et conduit au fameux et spectaculaire Fish Hole, un profond trou d'eau entouré de falaises. Ce site est sacré pour les Aborigènes, qui permettent aux randonneurs de le visiter à condition qu'ils respectent quelques règles simples : pas de camping, et en repartant vers l'amont, ils doivent rester dans le lit du ruisseau. Suivre ce lit en amont jusqu'à Jay Creek par une gorge pittoresque sur 2 km. La piste contourne alors le côté nord du

CI-DESSUS *Le paysage aride de la trouée de Simpson, la plus importante trouée de la chaîne MacDonnell occidentale, ne comporte que quelques trous d'eau pour abreuver la faune et la flore.*

mont Lloyd (1 045 m), le sol devenant trop rocailleux et abrupt pour en faire une piste. Plusieurs crêtes de granit offrent de beaux points de vue sur ce sommet déchiqueté. La piste passe du nord au sud de la chaîne, par le Spring Gap, une autre source permanente. Quelques kilomètres plus loin, se trouve Mulga Camp. Le château d'eau et quelques arbres inhabituels en ce lieu abritent un peu du soleil brûlant du désert, et c'est un bon endroit pour faire une pause. Prenez de l'eau et marchez encore une heure pour camper au pied de l'Arenge Bluff. C'est là, sans nul doute, le meilleur endroit de la chaîne pour admirer le soleil couchant et les roches découpées virant à l'orange, puis au rouge.

Le jour suivant, on accède au Bond Gap par une piste secondaire signalisée. Ce point d'eau extrêmement étroit et profond est idéal pour s'asseoir et observer les oiseaux. La piste continue vers l'est, serpentant à travers une plaine désertique qui offre de très belles vues sur les montagnes alentour. Au Simpson's Gap, un campement pour les randonneurs a été installé, avec un abri ombragé et un sol ferme pour camper.

Simpson's Gap est le trou d'eau le plus important de la chaîne, ainsi qu'un lieu touristique fréquenté, avec une route d'accès contrôlée. L'altitude offre d'excellents points de vue jusqu'au-delà des plaines, et, à la fin de la chaîne, la piste redescend et continue au pied des montagnes. Quelques petites sources donnent parfois de l'eau, et une piste secondaire, à suivre vers le nord pendant une dizaine de minutes jusqu'à Fairy Spring, vaut réellement le détour.

Le camping à Wallaby Gap dispose d'un abri ombragé, d'un château d'eau et de toilettes. Le lendemain matin, la piste grimpe sur la Euro Ridge (790 m). Malgré sa faible altitude, cette crête et ses falaises offrent de beaux points de vue sur Alice Springs et les alentours. Passé Euro Ridge, la chaîne West MacDonnell se transforme en une série de collines basses. La piste serpente parmi ces collines jusqu'à la Telegraph Station.

La Telegraph Station fut la première implantation européenne permanente au centre de l'Australie. Installée en 1872, elle servit de réémetteur télégraphique pour la transmission des messages entre Adélaïde et Darwin. Alice Springs n'est qu'à 3 km, et une promenade facile par de bons sentiers le long de la rivière conduit au centre-ville. Des douches gratuites sont disponibles aux toilettes publiques qui jouxtent les bureaux de l'administration locale. Débarrassez-vous de la poussière rouge, mais n'oubliez pas les collines rougeoyantes, le piquant spinifex et les gorges colorées de la piste de Larapinta.

CI-DESSUS *La station télégraphique d'Alice Springs, érigée en l'honneur des premiers colons européens, est un spectacle pour les randonneurs qui terminent la piste du Larapinta.*

AU MILIEU *La crête des Euros (790 m) doit son nom au kangourou de taille moyenne appelé « Jurus » par les Aborigènes, souvent vu ici parmi les spinifex (herbe hérisson).*

DE EDEN À MALLACOOTA

par Peter Cook

La randonnée de huit jours entre les villes de Eden et Mallacoota, qui vivent de la pêche et du tourisme, vous fera traverser les plus belles étendues sauvages côtières de la côte est de l'Australie. Un des principaux attraits de cette randonnée réside dans le sentiment particulier qu'elle procure, de parcourir un environnement non dénaturé et non pollué, vierge de toute civilisation et progrès.

L'histoire de la région est fascinante, principalement en rapport avec des naufrages dont le plus célèbre fut celui du *Sydney Cape*, qui s'échoua sur une petite île entre Victoria et la Tasmanie en 1796, à l'époque où Sydney était la seule implantation coloniale d'Australie. Le capitaine envoya dix-sept hommes sur la chaloupe de sauvetage ; ils devaient ramer jusqu'à Sydney et prévenir les secours, mais l'embarcation fit naufrage sur la côte victorienne. Ayant tous survécu, les dix-sept hommes entamèrent une marche forcée le long de la côte victorienne et de celle des Nouvelles-Galles du Sud. Trois seulement survécurent et parvinrent à Sydney. Ces hommes furent donc les premiers Européens à parcourir la côte sauvage à pied. Il n'est pas difficile, en marchant aujourd'hui dans leur pas, de se rendre compte de leur exploit.

Le meilleur endroit pour entreprendre cette randonnée est le quai des pêcheurs à Eden, où vous pouvez louer un bateau qui vous emmènera, à travers la baie de Twofold, jusqu'à Fisheries Beach (Plage des Pêcheries), point de départ de la marche. Les trois premiers jours vous feront traverser le parc national de Ben Boyd, du nom de l'entrepreneur écossais haut en couleurs, Benjamin Boyd, arrivé en Australie en 1842. Boyd établit deux implantations sur la baie de Twofold, qu'il appela Boydtown et East Boyd. Elles étaient les pièces maîtresses de l'empire commercial qu'il comptait développer à partir de ses participations croissantes dans l'agriculture, la chasse à la baleine et le transport maritime. En 1849, l'empire commercial de Boyd s'écroula et il appareilla pour la dernière fois de Twofold Bay, à des-

tination des champs aurifères de Californie. Il disparut en 1851 sur une île du Pacifique, où il aurait été assassiné par des indigènes.

Peu après le début de la randonnée, vous passez devant la tour de Boyd (Boyd's Tower) à Red Point, l'une des imposantes structures érigée par Boyd en un lieu alors très isolé. Cette tour était sensée signaler, avant tout le monde, aux équipages des baleiniers de Boyd, la présence de baleines dans les parages, leur donnant un avantage sur leurs concurrents. Évoquant la pierre rose vif qui caractérise cette pointe, Red Point donne un aperçu intéressant du passé géologique de cette région. La pierre, provenant de fines cendres volcaniques, avait été répandue, au dévonien, en couches horizontales qui furent ensuite compressées par de puissants mouvements géologiques.

Un peu plus loin sur la piste, à Bittangabee Bay, se trouvent les ruines d'une station baleinière construite par les frères Imlay, principaux concurrents de Boyd. Ces bâtiments ne furent jamais achevés car, comme Boyd, ils essuyèrent une crise financière qui les obligea à réduire leurs activités.

Le parc national Ben Boyd comprend d'impressionnantes falaises maritimes que la piste longe souvent, offrant de très belles vues de la côte dans les deux sens. Le point le plus

EN HAUT *Brumes matinales sur le quai des pêcheurs de Snug Cove, Eden. Ici, des bateaux peuvent être affrétés pour emmener les marcheurs au départ de la piste à Fisheries Beach.*

AU MILIEU *Un autre jour tranquille s'achève sur les rives du lac Nadgee. L'abondance de la faune aviaire en fait un campement favori des randonneurs.*

CI-DESSUS, À DROITE *Seulement entachées par des traces de pas sur le sable, et rien d'autre, les plages du parc national Boyd forment une étendue sauvage vierge.*

CÔTE SAUVAGE, AUSTRALIE

connu de ce tronçon du parcours est Greencape et son phare. Ce dernier fut érigé en 1886, juste avant le naufrage du *Ly-ee-moon*, où soixante et onze personnes périrent. Plusieurs tombes sont encore visibles près du phare.

En allant du parc national Ben Boyd jusqu'à la réserve naturelle de Nadgee, vous pénétrez dans une nature sauvage. Nadgee n'a jamais été colonisée ou aménagée, et jusqu'aux années quatre-vingt, seuls les chercheurs en histoire naturelle y avaient accès. Tous ces facteurs ont préservé le caractère relativement vierge de cette réserve.

Nadgee comprend beaucoup de sites particuliers, comme l'embouchure de la Merrica, une magnifique anse dissimulée dans une côte rocheuse, fabuleux endroit pour pique-niquer, et la plage de Newton, avec ses grottes que l'on explore à marée basse et un chœur d'oiseaux-lyres tous les matins. Les oiseaux-lyres imitent à merveille le chant d'une multitude d'autres oiseaux et leur répertoire mélodieux fera de votre réveil à Newton un souvenir inoubliable.

Osprey Lookout est un autre point fort, et les vues qu'il offre sur la mer et les falaises alentour ainsi que sur les cuvettes de rochers en contrebas sont splendides. Non loin de Osprey Lookout, on trouve Nadgee Beach, où la rivière Nadgee traverse la plage jusqu'à la mer. Le lac Nadgee, résidence d'un grand nombre de cygnes noirs et de pélicans, est l'un des campements favoris des randonneurs. Ici, on appréciera les couchers de soleil magiques au-dessus du lac, avec la silhouette de Howe Hill se détachant de la ligne d'horizon. Les oiseaux prennent une part importante dans la randonnée à Nadgee. Traversant les champs de bruyère de Nadgee Moor et Endeavour Moor, il n'est pas rare d'apercevoir très furtivement le perroquet terrestre, en voie de disparition. Pendant la nuit que vous passerez au lac de Nadgee, vous pourrez entendre le hurlement des dingos. Les dingos se font rares en Australie du Sud-Est, et les spécialistes d'histoire naturelle étudient cette espèce à Nadgee depuis vingt ans.

Après trois jours de marche d'une extrémité à l'autre de Nadgee, on pénètre dans le parc national de Croajingolong, et le paysage se transforme entièrement, la nature sauvage prenant une forme nouvelle – les estuaires, falaises et landes cédant la place aux dunes et aux plages interminables. Le nom de Croajingolong est dérivé du nom d'une tribu aborigène appelée Krowathunkoolung, ce qui signifie « pays appartenant aux hommes de l'Est ».

Les dunes de sable que vous traverserez le septième jour, entre Cape Howe et le lac Wau Wauka sont les plus grandes dunes côtières d'Australie et créent un paysage absolument renversant. Le meilleur moment pour traverser les dunes est le matin très tôt ou tard en fin de jour-

CI-DESSOUS *Des dingos ont pris en chasse un lace monitor dans les eaux peu profondes du lac Nadgee. La population des dingos étant en diminution, ils font l'objet d'une surveillance particulière.*

111

Les fougères arborescentes (Cyatheaceae), comme ces spécimens dans la forêt tempérée près d'Eden, ont des tiges aussi grosses que des troncs, avec au sommet le feuillage.

née, quand le soleil est bas et que l'absence de réverbération facilite la découverte des dessins laissés par le vent sur le sable blanc. Le sable provient de l'île de Gabo, les vents dominants de sud-ouest renvoyant ce même sable à la mer à l'extrémité nord-est des dunes, non loin de Bunyip Hole. La progression à travers les dunes ne pose pas de problème, l'itinéraire choisi cheminant parallèlement à la plage, laquelle est visible sur la plus grande partie du parcours. La marche est aisée, en dépit de quelques montagnes russes, et l'on remarque d'intéressants paysages. Se laisser rouler en bas de la dune devient le passe-temps favori à chaque pause.

Au-delà du lac Wau Wauka, il y a Gabo Island, Tullaberga Island, le lac Barracoota et la Grande Plage. Le lac Barracoota est un endroit magnifique pour camper la dernière nuit, avec des points de vue et des perspectives différents jusqu'à Howe Hill. Cette région compte aussi son contingent de récits de naufrages, comme celui du *Monumental City*, qui s'échoua sur l'île de Tullaberga en 1853, faisant trente-sept victimes. Suite à cette catastrophe, on édifia le phare de Gabo Island neuf ans plus tard.

La randonnée s'achève sur la Grande Plage à l'est du Mallacoota Inlet. À Mallacoota, les randonneurs pourront fêter leur arrivée par un somptueux repas de fruits de mer, dans un restaurant avec vue sur les espaces sauvages que l'on vient d'explorer.

La marche d'Eden à Mallacoota ne représente qu'un tronçon d'une randonnée bien plus longue le long de la côte sauvage, entre les Lacs Entrance en Victoria et Pambula en Nouvelles-Galles du Sud. C'est certainement entre Eden et Mallacoota que la côte est la plus variée, mais une fois dans la région, vous trouverez de nombreux sites magnifiques dignes d'une visite. Le paysage non dénaturé, l'histoire et la géomorphologie intactes, l'abondance d'oiseaux, de la faune en général et de la flore, sont autant de raisons qui font que les randonneurs reviennent pour arpenter la côte sauvage.

Lorsque les marcheurs pénètrent dans le parc national de Croajingolong, la lande de bruyère et les falaises cèdent la place à de spectaculaires dunes et de très longues plages de sable blanc.

LIEU À peu près à mi-chemin entre Sydney et Melbourne, sur la côte.

QUAND PARTIR Mars à septembre.

DÉPART Quai des pêcheurs, Eden. Prendre un bateau de Twofold Bay jusqu'à Fisheries Beach, où commence la randonnée.

ARRIVÉE Big Beach, du côté est du Mallacoota Inlet. Des bateaux-taxis peuvent être réservés par l'intermédiaire du Centre de Renseignements Touristiques.

DURÉE 8 jours ; 95 km.

POINT CULMINANT 260 m.

ASPECTS TECHNIQUES Néant.

MATÉRIEL Équipement sac à dos standard. Autonomie alimentaire obligatoire. Vêtements imperméables et protection solaire. Les cartes nécessaires sont disponibles auprès des boutiques spécialisées de Melbourne, Sydney et Canberra.

MODE DE RANDONNÉE Sac à dos. Au début de la randonnée, la marche s'effectue sur des pistes de 4 x 4 ou sur des pistes étroites. Le sixième jour, après Bunyip Hole, la marche s'effectue principalement sur la plage.

AUTORISATIONS/RESTRICTIONS Le nombre de personnes autorisé à visiter Nadgee et Croajingolong est limité quelle que soit la période. Une autorisation est exigée et peut être obtenue auprès des Parcs nationaux de la Nouvelle-Galles du Sud et des Services de Protection de la nature ou des Parcs Victoria.

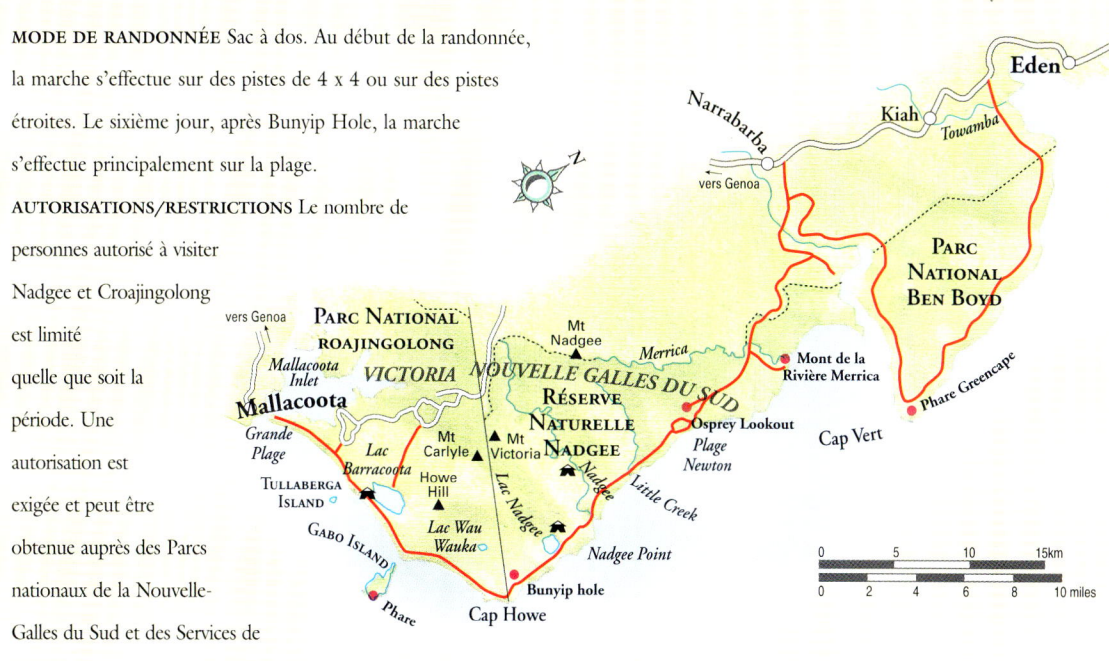

LA PISTE OVERLAND

par Shaun Barnett

La piste Overland de Tasmanie est devenue depuis quelques années la plus populaire d'Australie. Ses 73 km de randonnée en font un lieu idéal, avec la spectaculaire Cradle Mountain, de nombreux lacs de montagne, une faune et des forêts sauvages très spécifiques à ce continent, et une histoire européenne et aborigène intéressante. Ces montagnes sont parmi les plus escarpées d'Australie, et la piste passe non loin du point culminant de Tasmanie, le mont Ossa (1 617 m). Il n'y a plus aucun glacier aujourd'hui, mais le paysage porte encore les marques d'une glaciation intense, lors de la dernière période glaciaire qui se termina il y a environ 10 000 à 14 000 ans.

La piste traverse une partie importante de la Tasmanie, la plus vaste des régions sauvages qui subsiste en Australie. En 1982, en même temps que plusieurs régions du Sud-Ouest de la Tasmanie, la Cradle Mountain, dans le parc national du lac Saint-Clair, se vit attribuer le statut de patrimoine mondial, juste reconnaissance de son importance à l'échelle planétaire.

Les peuples aborigènes vivent en Tasmanie depuis plus de 30 000 ans, et survécurent à la dernière période glaciaire en s'abritant dans des refuges côtiers. On a l'impression de pénétrer pour la première fois dans un espace sauvage intact et originel, mais en fait la plupart des plaines herbues qui caractérisent la partie centrale du parcours sont le résultat d'incendies allumés jadis par les Aborigènes. En allumant ces feux, les chasseurs aborigènes provoquaient la pousse de ces herbes sur le sol humide et tourbeux, en déplaçant la forêt d'eucalyptus. Les espaces qui en résultaient faisaient d'excellents terrains où chasser le wombat, le wallaby et le kangourou.

Les Européens, arrivant entre la fin du xviiie et le début du XIXe siècle, ne tardèrent pas à découvrir eux-mêmes les possibilités de chasse qu'offrait le haut plateau, et des trappeurs y chassèrent – pour leur peau –, l'opossum, le wallaby, le wombat ou le loup de Tasmanie. C'est un Autrichien qui jouera un rôle déterminant pour obtenir la protection de la Cradle Mountain. Gustav Weindorfer émigra en Australie en 1900, et avec son épouse Kate, il se rendit sur la montagne à plusieurs reprises. Subjugué par la beauté du site, il nourrit la conviction que cette région méritait le statut de parc national. Pour encourager les visiteurs, Gustav construisit un chalet, qu'il appela Waldheim, non loin de la montagne. Il fut à la fois guide et hôte, tout en poursuivant sa campagne pour que la région soit déclarée zone protégée, jusqu'à sa mort en 1932.

La Cradle Mountain fut déclarée réserve touristique en 1922, mais n'acquit le statut de parc national qu'en 1971. Le trappeur Bert Nicholls ouvrit la piste Overland proprement dite en 1930 et la première randonnée du parcours entier fut achevée en janvier 1931.

Bien que l'on puisse la parcourir dans les deux sens, la plupart des gens s'attaquent à la piste Overland depuis Cradle Mountain, un impressionnant sommet crénelé qui porte les marques de la dernière période glaciaire. Officiellement, la piste Overland commence à Waldheim, mais on n'a pas, de cet endroit, de belles vues sur la montagne. Un panorama bien plus impressionnant se découvre depuis les berges du lac Dove voisin, et les randonneurs peuvent choisir d'y commencer leur parcours en suivant les sentiers qui relient la piste principale au Crater Lake (lac du Volcan).

Que l'on adopte l'un ou l'autre itinéraire, les pistes traversent des forêts associant hêtres et eucalyptus, enjambent des torrents bouillonnants, et montent régulièrement jusqu'à Marion's Lookout (1 200 m). Là, par beau temps, des vues panoramiques sans fin de la Cradle Mountain

EN HAUT *Au cours de la dernière période glaciaire, un épais glacier s'était formé sur les flancs de la Cradle Mountain et creusa le lit du Dove Lake, aujourd'hui l'un des meilleurs points de vue du parc.*
AU MILIEU *L'opossum est le moins craintif des marsupiaux de Tasmanie, et sa curiosité le conduit souvent à venir reconnaître cases ou tentes pendant la nuit.*
CI-DESSUS *Walheim, le chalet de Gustav Weindorfer, non loin du départ du parcours, ouvrit en 1912. Le chalet d'origine fut démoli en 1976 et remplacé par son exacte réplique.*

TASMANIE, AUSTRALIE

La Cradle Mountain, comme beaucoup d'autres sommets de Tasmanie, est composée de dolérite, une roche volcanique particulièrement résistante aux intempéries.

LA PISTE OVERLAND

CI-DESSUS *Alors que les myrtes poussent en un grand et bel arbuste persistant, d'autres espèces de hêtre Nothafagus prennent plus une forme de buissons et perdent leurs feuilles en automne.*

(1 545 m), maintenant beaucoup plus imposante, et du monolithe de Barn Bluff (1 559 m) dans le lointain s'offrent à vous. Pourtant, la visibilité est souvent mauvaise. Les vents d'ouest peuvent apporter neige, grêle et pluie à tout moment de l'année en Tasmanie, justifiant la réputation climatique de l'île. Un tel climat peut paraître froid et inhospitalier, mais les forêts tropicales si caractéristiques de Tasmanie ont nécessairement besoin de beaucoup d'eau.

Depuis Marion's Lookout, la piste se faufile tout le long du flanc ouest de la Cradle Mountain, en passant par l'abri rustique de Kitchen Hut avant de retrouver les arbustes subalpins endémiques appelés pandanni.

La flore de Tasmanie à la même origine que celles de Nouvelle-Zélande et d'Amérique du Sud. Depuis la séparation des continents, il y a 80 millions d'années, de nombreuses plantes du Gondwana ont survécu dans le climat relativement frais de Tasmanie, tandis que beaucoup ont cédé la place à des espèces plus récentes sur le continent australien ensoleillé.

Après une bretelle indiquant la direction de Barn Bluff, la piste Overland entame une descente vers les deux cases de Waterfall Valley (vallée des Cascades). Le jour suivant couvrira une distance considérable de plaines herbeuses, avec le mont Pelion (1 554 m), massif et visible pratiquement toute la journée. Presque toute la piste est maintenant constituée d'une passerelle en bois, rendue nécessaire par la présence notoire de tourbe. Les passages antérieurs ont transformé la piste en un bourbier, et les planches, bien que très dures à la marche, sont indispensables, pour protéger l'environnement et pour permettre aux randonneurs de maintenir leur moyenne.

La case du lac Windermere semble enchâssée dans une enclave accueillante et boisée, blottie non loin du lac Windermere si attrayant. Les randonneurs qui se sont fixé comme objectif d'accomplir le parcours en cinq jours devront poursuivre jusqu'à Pelion Hut, tandis que les moins pressés préféreront peut-être passer la nuit ici.

Traversant la Pine Forest Moor (la Lande des pins), la piste se rapproche des contreforts du mont Pelion, où elle arrive enfin aux marécageux Frog Flats (marécages aux Grenouilles). Depuis Pelion Plains, la piste grimpe au cœurs des plus hauts sommets de Tasmanie. Une mon-

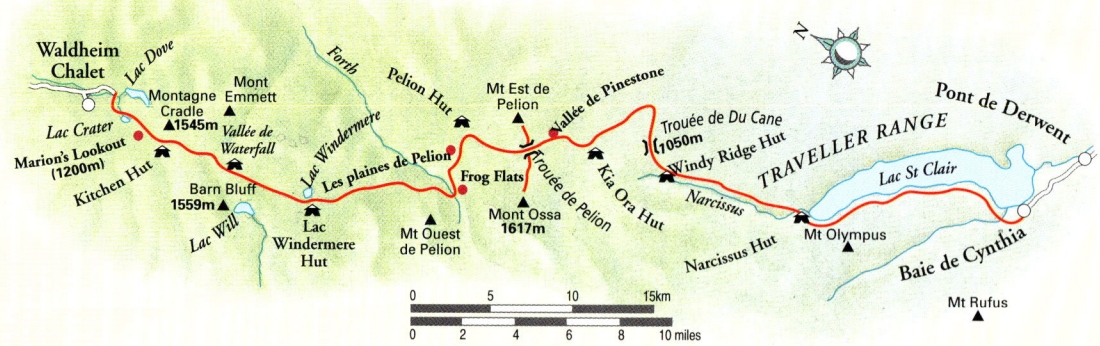

LIEU Cradle Mountain, parc national du lac Saint-Clair, Tasmanie centrale.

QUAND PARTIR Toute l'année. La haute saison se situe de décembre à mars, mais la piste peut être surchargée. En hiver, la neige peut recouvrir de longues sections du parcours.

DÉPART Cradle Mountain, près de Devonport, Tasmanie du Nord.

ARRIVÉE Lac Saint-Clair, à quelque 100 km de Hobart, capitale de l'État. Service quotidien de cars tout l'été au départ de chaque extrémité du parcours.

DURÉE 5-7 jours ; 73 km.

POINT CULMINANT Marion's Lookout (1 200 m).

ASPECTS TECHNIQUES Pente modérée, convenant aux personnes ayant une forme moyenne. Aucune escalade ou varappe n'est nécessaire. Tasmap publie une carte du parc à l'échelle 1 : 100 000.

MATÉRIEL Chaussures solides, sac de couchage et tapis de sol, nourriture, vêtements chauds et vêtements de pluie.

MODE DE RANDONNÉE Sac à dos. Piste bien tracée et signalisée, avec plusieurs cases sur le parcours. Camping possible à proximité de la plupart des cases, ainsi qu'en quelques autres emplacements. Des randonnées guidées, avec cases privatives et repas fournis sont également disponibles.

AUTORISATIONS/RESTRICTIONS Il n'existe pas pour l'instant de système de réservation pour les randonneurs individuels, mais cela peut changer dans un futur très proche. Des droits d'entrée modiques sont perçus pour tous les parcs nationaux de Tasmanie. Les randonneurs envisageant de visiter plusieurs parcs s'intéresseront au Backpacker Pass (Permis Sac à dos) valable deux mois, économique.

CI-DESSUS *Tout au long de l'année, le Pelion Gap est couvert de plantes-coussins, qui ont adopté une forme basse qui résiste mieux au vent et à la neige.*

tée régulière avec de nombreuses marches conduit à l'espace découvert de Pelion Gap (1 126 m), un col qui offre des panoramas à ne pas manquer. Portant des noms antiques empruntés à la mythologie grecque, les monts Thétis, Achille et Ossa remplissent l'horizon. On ne peut pas dire que le mont Ossa soit gigantesque avec ses 1 617 m, mais ses contreforts et ses accès abrupts appellent le respect des candidats à l'escalade. En été, le sommet est accessible par un passage depuis Pelion Gap, mais en hiver la neige peut décourager toute tentative.

Depuis Pelion Gap, le chemin redescend vers la vallée Pinestone pour arriver à la Kia Ora Hut. Voici une bonne occasion d'observer les wallabies de Bernett, l'une des trente et une espèces de marsupiaux de Tasmanie. Les wombats sont des créatures plus farouches, au corps court et trapu ; vous verrez surtout leurs crottes carrées très caractéristiques !

Traversant des forêts d'eucalyptus géants, la piste commence par franchir un col peu élevé appelé Du Cane Gap (1 050 m), puis redescend la Narcissus Valley (vallée des Narcisses), bordée par les escarpements abrupts de la Traveller Range. Les eucalyptus, qui sont les plus grandes plantes à fleurs du monde, peuvent atteindre 90 m de haut, leur tronc se débarrassant de son écorce en longs lambeaux pendant. Des oiseaux bruyants, comme le cacatoès à crête soufrée, sont susceptibles d'interrompre votre contemplation silencieuse dans ces bois. Les autres oiseaux susceptibles de se faire connaître sont les currawongs noirs – une sorte de corbeau aux yeux jaunes perçants et aux réflexes très rapides.

Au bout de la vallée, les eaux sombres de la rivière Narcisse se déversent dans la partie supérieure du lac Saint-Clair. De nombreux cours d'eau de Tasmanie traversant des plaines herbeuses sont colorés par les tanins concentrés et recueillis dans ces herbes, qui font ressembler l'eau à du thé bien fort. La Narcissus Hut est tout près.

Le bleu du lac Saint-Clair est plus classique, bien qu'il recueille plusieurs cours d'eau chargés de tanin. Après que la dernière période glaciaire ait creusé son lit entre le mont Olympus et la Traveller Rang, le lac Saint-Clair est devenu le plus profond d'Australie (167 m). Là, les platypus, mammifères ovipares primitifs, sont assez courants, et c'est au petit matin qu'on a le plus de chance de les voir se mouvoir tranquillement sur le lac.

Sur le bord du lac, Narcissus Hut est la dernière case sur le parcours de la piste Overland dans la direction nord-sud. Une piste contourne le lac Saint-Clair par Echo Point, jusqu'à la fin de la piste, à Cynthia Bay. Ou bien offrez-vous une tranquille croisière sur le lac sur la vedette qui appareille à la demande en été. C'est là une manière agréable de conclure l'une des plus belles expériences de plein air de Tasmanie.

AUTOUR DES MONTAGNES

par Kathy Ombler

Le paysage volcanique du parc national de Tongariro, en Nouvelle-Zélande, occupe une place particulière sur la scène mondiale de la protection de l'environnement. Le parc, dominé par trois magnifiques montagnes volcaniques, fut le premier parc national jamais créé et le premier site classé au patrimoine mondial pour ses exceptionnelles richesses naturelles et culturelles.

Ruapehu, Tongariro et Ngauruhoe se situent à l'extrémité septentrionale de la Ceinture de Feu du Pacifique, une immense zone d'activités volcanique et sismique. Le mont Ruapehu, le plus élevé des trois avec ses 2 797 m, domine la campagne alentour et c'est la seule montagne de l'Ile du Nord comptant de véritables glaciers. En effet, de la glace entoure complètement le lac volatil et fumant du Crater Lake, créant là un des très rares phénomènes du genre dans le monde. Le Ruapehu est un volcan extrêmement actif, qui entre en éruption tous les trois ou quatre ans. Pas plus tard qu'en 1996, une formidable pluie de cendres, de roches et de vapeur fut projetée à des centaines de mètres du Crater Lake et des fleuves de boue dévalèrent les flancs de la montagne.

Le mont Tongariro (1 968 m) est sans doute plus petit que le Ruapehu mais son massif immense s'étend sur plus de 18 km en longueur et englobe un grand nombre de cratères, de fumerolles bouillantes, de sources géothermiques et d'évents volcaniques, dont l'un n'est autre que le Ngauruhoe, plus haut mais de forme conique traditionnelle (2 291 m). La randonnée autour des montagnes passe par des paysages volcaniques variés, arides et désertiques, des hêtraies, des alpages, des lacs et des vallées creusées par d'anciens glaciers. La randonnée totale prend entre 7 et 9 jours, mais il existe plusieurs points d'accès offrant des options plus courtes.

Le circuit nord comprend la traversée du Tongariro, sans aucun doute la plus populaire et la plus spectaculaire marche d'une journée en Nouvelle-Zélande. Cette randonnée de 6 à 8 h grimpe entre les monts Ngauruhoe et Tongariro, passe par des accidents volcaniques tels que geysers de vapeur, anciennes coulées de lave et cratères inondés qui changent de couleur. La partie sud de cette randonnée traverse à mi-pente le mont Ruapehu, où le paysage volcanique s'adoucit quelque peu. Les pentes sont recouvertes d'une alternance de hêtraies, de champs de tussock et de plantes alpestres, ponctuées de torrents et de cascades.

Les volcans du Tongariro ont une grande signification spirituelle pour les Ngati Tuwharetoa, le peuple maori qui habite la région depuis près de mille ans. Les montagnes représentent la demeure de leurs ancêtres, des lieux sacrés à traiter avec respect. Des légendes traditionnelles donnent leur version des origines de l'activité volcanique dans le parc.

Quand les ancêtres de Ngati Tuwharetoa arrivèrent en Nouvelle-Zélande, le navigateur de leur canoë, Te Arawa, n'était autre que le grand prêtre Ngatoroirangi. Après avoir atteint le rivage, il conduisit son peuple à l'intérieur des terres, en quête de territoires. Ils s'établirent à côté du grand lac de Taupo, et Ngatoroirangi poursuivit sa route vers le sud pour prendre possession du sommet du Tongariro. Alors qu'il traversait le désert aride, il remar-

EN HAUT *Le mont Ruapehu est le plus haut et le plus récemment actif des trois volcans composant le noyau du parc national de Tongariro.*

AU MILIEU *Les ancêtres de Ngati Twharetoa, les Maoris locaux, sont immortalisés par des sculptures situées au centre d'informations du parc.*

CI-DESSUS, À DROITE *Les marcheurs font une pause bien méritée parmi les étendues de rochers et de tussock, entre le mont Ngauruhoe et le village de Whakapapa.*

qua un autre prêtre qui se dirigeait vers la montagne. Il appela les dieux à son secours, et ceux-ci déclenchèrent une violente tempête pour anéantir son rival. Plus tard, alors que Ngatoroirangi approchait du sommet couvert de glace, il fut frigorifié par une tempête de neige et invoqua ses sœurs prêtresses à Hawaiiki, sa patrie polynésienne, pour se réchauffer. Le nom de Tongariro, qui évoque le vent froid du sud, provient de ces incantations. Les sœurs prêtresses de Ngatoroirangi répondirent avec ferveur, envoyant du feu par un passage souterrain – connu aujourd'hui comme la Ceinture de Feu du Pacifique – qui fit éruption par un nouveau cratère appelé aujourd'hui le mont Ngauruhoe.

Ainsi furent allumés les feux d'occupation du peuple de Ngatoroirangi. Les années passant, le statut spirituel des volcans prit encore plus d'importance. Il était interdit de les escalader ; les voyageurs qui traversaient les déserts le long des pentes est du Tongariro utilisaient des feuilles en guise d'œillères pour ne pas même risquer un œil vers le sommet sacré. Les premières tentatives, entreprises par les explorateurs européens pour faire l'ascension des montagnes sacrées, furent contrecarrées par les Maoris, ou bien furent gardées secrètes. Vers 1800, l'immigration européenne s'accrut et les lois foncières européennes furent introduites dans toute la Nouvelle-Zélande, remettant en cause les bases mêmes de la propriété traditionnelle des tribus maories.

En 1887, pour empêcher la « vente » des sommets de la montagne sacrée, un descendant de Ngatoroirangi prit une décision héroïque en faisant don des trois sommets à la Couronne de sorte qu'ils demeurent à jamais des lieux sacrés. C'est ainsi qu'ils devinrent le noyau, l'essence même du parc national du Tongariro.

CI-DESSOUS *La randonnée « Autour de la montagne » explore le parc national de Tongariro, où cohabitent trois volcans : le Tongariro (premier plan), le Ngauruhoe (à mi-distance) et le Ruapehu (au loin).*

CI-DESSUS *Les lacs d'altitude du mont Tongariro, le lac Emeraude et le lac Bleu, d'anciens cratères remplis d'eau chargée en minéraux, apportent une note de couleur contrastée au paysage volcanique dénudé.*

À partir du village de Whakapapa, le circuit nord du Tongariro traverse une alternance de champs de tussock et de petites hêtraies, au pied des pentes du mont Ruapehu. Le classique cône géant du Ngauruhoe surgit devant vous, à côté de la masse moins élevée mais plus imposante du Tongariro. La piste contourne le Pukekaikiore, l'un des plus anciens évents du complexe volcanique du Tongariro, puis pénètre dans la vallée du Mangatepopo, non loin de la Mangatepopo Hut.

De là, la piste tourne en direction de la vallée, en suivant maintenant l'itinéraire d'une journée pour la traversée du Tongariro, escaladant une succession de coulées de lave déversées par le Ngauruhoe lors des éruptions de 1949 et 1954. Un détour de cinq minutes par le haut de la vallée conduit à Soda Springs, qui semble émerger de sous une ancienne coulée de lave, et qui forme, au milieu de ce paysage volcanique par ailleurs sinistre, une petite oasis fertile pleine de fleurs en été.

C'est ici que commence l'escalade la plus difficile du parcours, la piste rocailleuse se frayant un chemin vers un col élevé, entre les monts Tongariro et Ngauruhoe, puis traversant le cratère sud, plat, poussiéreux et à l'aspect lunaire, avant de monter à nouveau vers le point culminant de la randonnée, le Red Crater (cratère Rouge, 1 800 m). La pente est raide, mais la vue qui vous attend récompensera vos efforts. En effet, vous découvrirez ici un paysage volcanique dans sa plus grande beauté : les noirs, rouges et bruns crus de la roche volcanique contrastent fortement avec les eaux vertes et bleues des lacs Émeraude (Emerald Lake) et Bleu (Blue Lake), d'anciens cratères, à côté de ce massif comme arraché de l'écorce terrestre qu'est le cratère Rouge. Si le temps est clair – indispensable pour s'attaquer à ce tronçon exposé du parcours – la vue s'étend vers l'est, au-delà du paysage volcanique, vers les chaînes boisées de Kaimanawa, qui délimitent l'Ile du Nord.

Des excursions latérales au départ du cratère Rouge comprennent une marche jusqu'au sommet du Tongariro (environ 2 h aller-retour) ou une marche pour redescendre la face nord du Tongariro jusqu'à Ketetahi Hut (2 h dans chaque sens). On peut voir, depuis la case, la vapeur qui s'échappe des Ketetahi Springs, deux crêtes plus loin. Ces sources sont situées dans une enclave privée appartenant au peuple Ngati Tuwharetoa.

De retour sur la partie principale du parcours, la piste vers Oturere Hut s'oriente au sud-est, depuis les abords des Lacs Émeraudes, puis descend à travers des champs de lave déchiquetés, jusqu'à la vallée de l'Oturere. De nouveau, les hêtraies de la vallée de Waihohonu apportent un peu de répit, après l'itinéraire rocailleux et découvert. Il y a là une case historique, restaurée, d'où part une piste vers l'ouest, franchissant le col entre les monts Ngauruhoe et Ruapehu.

La randonnée autour des montagnes continue à travers le désert de Rangipo. C'est ici le seul vrai paysage désertique de Nouvelle-Zélande, l'altitude et le climat s'étant alliés pour

empêcher la repousse des forêts dévastées par les éruptions volcaniques. La case de Rangipo est située non loin de l'extrémité sud du désert, et de là, la piste continue, par les pentes du mont Ruapehu, ondulant à travers les hêtraies, touffes d'herbe et gorges abruptes vers la case de Mangaehuehu, à partir de laquelle on descend progressivement à travers de nouveaux champs d'herbes alpestres et de hêtraies. À environ 3 h de Mangaehuehu, la piste passe par les chutes les plus hautes du parc, les Waitonga Falls, qui bondissent par-dessus le rebord d'une coulée de lave, puis traversent une clairière tourbeuse où une passerelle protège les plantes aquatiques des chaussures des randonneurs. Par temps clair, on peut apprécier d'ici la vue sur les sommets enneigés du Ruapehu.

La piste rejoint un court moment la route contrôlée de Ohakune Mountain, qui donne accès à l'un des domaines skiables privés du Tongariro. Puis elle descend dans une vallée pentue, franchit une crête de lave recouverte d'herbes alpestres et plonge dans la vallée du Mangaturuturu, où est nichée, au bord de la brousse, la case du même nom.

Le dernier jour de marche vous fera passer par un délicieux mélange de lacs de montagne, de gorges abruptes d'où déferlent torrents et cascades, de hêtraies, d'herbes subalpestres, de buissons et de marécages, un tapis d'herbes aromatiques fleurissant en été. Par beau temps, les points de vue sont illimités : les sommets du Ruapehu dominent, et loin à l'ouest le cône volcanique du mont Egmont domine l'étendue sauvage boisée du parc national de Whanganui.

Vous avez le choix entre deux options pour terminer la randonnée depuis Whakapapaiti Hut : une piste haute qui grimpe au-dessus de la ligne de brousse pour atteindre la route Bruce (qui donne accès au domaine skiable du nord du parc), 4 km au-dessus du village de Whakapapa, ou bien la piste forestière en bas, qui mène directement au village. À Whakapapa Village, il existe un centre de visite du parc, un terrain de camping, un motel, des cafés et l'hôtel historique du Grand Château. On peut y effectuer plusieurs promenades, avec des panneaux d'informations sur les caractéristiques historiques et naturelles du parc.

LIEU Ile du Nord centrale.

QUAND PARTIR décembre à mars est la période la plus sûre, et la plus fréquentée. En hiver, risque de neige, de verglas et d'avalanches.

DÉPART/ARRIVÉE Whakapapa Village, à 40 min en voiture de Turangi. Transports publics réguliers et navettes.

DURÉE 7-9 jours ; 85 km.

POINT CULMINANT Red Crater (cratère Rouge), mont Tongariro (1 800 m).

ASPECTS TECHNIQUES L'itinéraire est balisé par des perches et par endroit il s'agit d'une passerelle ou d'un chemin aménagé. La plus grande partie du parcours est soumise toute l'année aux changements de temps intervenant en montagne. Neige et verglas peuvent recouvrir une grande partie du parcours en hiver, nécessitant du matériel d'escalade et... de l'expérience. Certains passages de rivières peuvent se révéler impossibles pendant ou après de fortes pluies.

MATÉRIEL Chaussures de marche solides, vêtements imperméables et chauds, ainsi que vêtements de marche ordinaires.

MODE DE RANDONNÉE Sac à dos. Neuf cases avec commodités comprenant toilettes, matelas, eau potable et appareils de cuisson. En été, les trois cases du mont Tongariro disposent également de gazinières et de radiateurs à gaz. Camping autorisé.

AUTORISATIONS/RESTRICTIONS Les cases sont attribuées selon le principe du premier arrivé ; séjour maximum de deux nuits. Tickets à acheter à l'avance. Pendant la saison estivale, des permis « Great Walks » (Grandes Randonnées) sont obligatoires pour utiliser les cases du circuit nord du Tongariro et le camping est interdit sur les 500 m de la piste, sur ce tronçon-là.

LA PISTE ROUTEBURN
par Kathy Ombler

La piste Routeburn est l'une des randonnées les plus spectaculaires et les plus fréquentées de Nouvelle-Zélande. Au cœur de la zone faisant partie du patrimoine mondial du South Westland/Te Wahipounamu, cette piste historique parcourt les montagnes du Sud-Ouest de la Nouvelle-Zélande, en passant par deux grands parcs nationaux du pays, Fjordland et Mount Aspiring.

Les randonneurs de Routeburn traversent un véritable kaléidoscope de paysages naturels. Chaque jour, voire chaque heure, passé sur la piste révèle un nouveau décor : forêts tropicales, prairies et champs de fleurs estivales alpines, torrents, cascades et lacs, marécages de plaines, cols de montagne, vestiges de glaciers et sommets vertigineux. La faune aviaire est aussi variée que le paysage, comptant plus de trente espèces d'oiseaux indigènes qui vivent dans la forêt, dans les marécages ou dans des enfractuosités de montagne tout au long du parcours.

Le climat montagnard imprévisible, lui aussi, compte pour beaucoup dans l'expérience Routeburn. Soleil brûlant, brume et crachin, pluie torrentielle, vent et neige ; il est fréquent de trouver tous ces éléments sur la durée du parcours Routeburn, même en été.

En raison de sa beauté et de son succès, la randonnée de Routeburn est bien desservie par la direction des parcs et les tour-opérateurs. La piste, les ponts, les cases et les camping sont en très bon état, conçus dans un souci de protection de l'environnement, et bien entretenus.

Aucune piste de première classe ni chaussures hi-tech ne faisaient honneur à la roche et aux touffes d'herbe des pentes lorsque les hommes franchirent ces montagnes pour la première fois. Les premiers colons de Nouvelle-Zélande, les Maoris, étaient des voyageurs acharnés et tenaces, en particulier quand ils recherchaient la pounamu – une pierre verte ou un jade de néphrite très recherché pour en faire des bijoux, des outils et des armes – que l'on trouvait dans les rivières de la côte ouest. Dans leur quête du précieux jade, ces peuples anciens modelèrent un certain nombre de « pistes pounamu » à travers la grande chaîne montagneuse de l'Ile du Sud.

On a trouvé des traces de la précieuse pounamu dans la rivière Routeburn aussi, ce qui explique comment la Routeburn devint l'une de ces pistes. Pendant des siècles, les voyageurs maoris chaussés de sandales de lin ont négocié les hêtraies de la vallée du Routeburn,

LIEU Sud-ouest de l'île du Sud.

QUAND PARTIR Novembre à avril. En hiver, la piste peut être barrée par la neige, et ne s'y attaqueront que ceux qui auront un minimum d'expérience en alpinisme.

DÉPART/ARRIVÉE On peut faire le parcours dans l'une ou l'autre direction, de Routeburn Shelter (72 km de Queenstown) ou depuis « The Divide » (85 km de Te Anau). Plusieurs entreprises de transports et/ou tour-opérateur assurent des liaisons au départ de Queenstown ou Te Anau, vers l'une ou l'autre des extrémités du parcours.

DURÉE 4 jours, 33 km. Le mauvais temps peut entraîner des retards sur les tronçons découverts et exposés.

POINT CULMINANT Harris Saddle (col Harris, 1 280 m).

ASPECTS TECHNIQUES Des orages peuvent se déclencher à tout moment de l'année sur cette piste de montagne. Les marcheurs seront prudents et emporteront des vêtements contre le froid, la pluie et le vent.

MATÉRIEL Paquetage, sac de couchage, chaussures de marche, vêtements imperméables, nourriture, vêtements chauds et séchant vite, insectifuge.

MODE DE RANDONNÉE Sac à dos. L'itinéraire compte quatre cases, chacune avec gazinière, eau courante froide, éclairage, chauffage, dortoirs et toilettes. Deux campings sur le parcours.

AUTORISATIONS/RESTRICTIONS Réservations indispensables. Les réservations de logement sont nécessaires entre octobre et avril. Camping interdit dans les 500 m de la piste, sauf dans les deux campings indiqués.

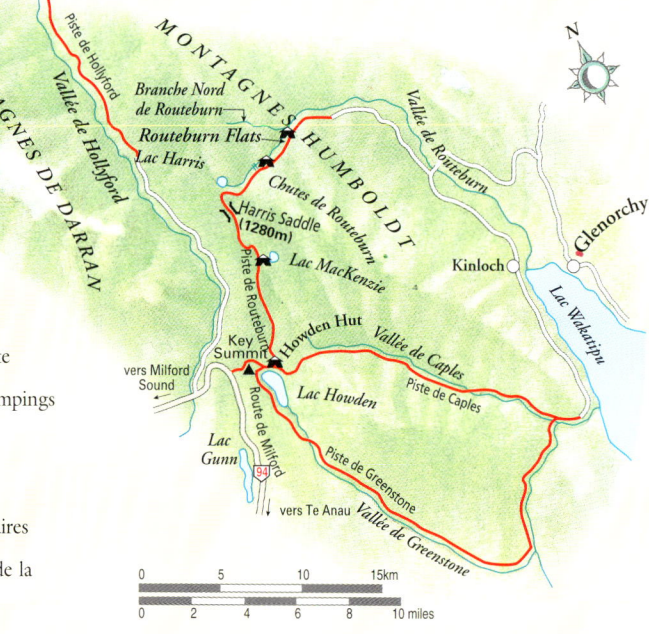

avant de gravir les montagnes abruptes par le col de Harris (1 280 m), appelé alors Tarahaka Whakatipu, aujourd'hui le point culminant de la piste de Routeburn.

Plus tard, les géomètres britanniques firent appel aux Maoris pour qu'ils les conseillent sur les itinéraires à prendre à travers la montagne. En 1870, dans le plus grand optimisme, une colonie fut établie à Martin's Bay, sur la lointaine côte du Sud-Ouest. Le projet du gouvernement provincial était de construire une route à travers la montagne, par la vallée de Routeburn et le col Harris, mais les travaux furent longs et difficiles.

Dans le même temps, les accès maritimes étant impossibles à cause des conditions climatiques épouvantables, la nouvelle colonie se trouva isolée. Un colon, William Homer, désigné comme celui connaissant le mieux la brousse, partit à travers le pays, en direction de Queenstown. C'était en septembre, quand la neige et les risques d'avalanches atteignent un point culminant ; Homer grimpa pendant deux jours pour atteindre le col Harris. Il progressa péniblement à travers de profondes congères, s'enfonçant souvent jusqu'à la taille, quand soudain le sol se déroba sous ses pieds et il tomba dans une crevasse profonde de 3 m. Il parvint à remonter à la surface, mais battit en retraite et redescendit, pour trouver enfin un chemin vers la vallée voisine de Greenstone, puis jusqu'à Queenstown, où il fut décrit comme « un paquet de guenilles, d'égratignures et d'ecchymoses qui bougeait ». Toute nouvelle tentative de construction de route et de colonies fut abandonnée, et c'est ainsi que la vieille piste au pounamu de Routeburn traverse encore des montagnes sauvages, appréciées aujourd'hui par des milliers de marcheurs. Les noms de sites reflètent les ententes qui eurent lieu par le passé avec les premiers voyageurs maoris, puis avec les explorateurs britanniques.

La piste du Routeburn commence doucement. Un chemin bien tracé, à la pente facile, suit le fond de la vallée de Routeburn à travers des hêtraies qui laissent passer la lumière pommelée du soleil - et des oiseaux indigènes peu farouches, pigeons – paons et merles, collent au pas des marcheurs, en quête du moindre insecte. Des passerelles enjambent les ruisseaux, et pendant un moment la piste s'aventure à suivre la gorge de Routeburn, un étonnant amalgame d'énormes blocs de pierre et de précipices profonds. Après environ 1 h 30 de marche, la piste quitte la brousse pour déboucher sur la vaste étendue marécageuse des Routeburn Flats. Les impressionnantes murailles montagneuses dominent les marécages herbus, et donnent un avant-goût de la splendeur alpestre qui vous attend plus loin.

CI-CONTRE *La piste Routeburn traverse deux des plus grands parcs nationaux de Nouvelle-Zélande. Depuis Conical Hill, au-dessus de Harris Saddle, le panorama embrasse les monts Darran du parc national de Fjordland.*

CI-DESSUS *Le lac Harris, niché entre les montagnes non loin du point culminant du parcours, commence à perdre sa couverture de neige. Même en été, il peut neiger sur la piste Routeburn, mais les chutes sont généralement de courte durée.*

CI-DESSUS *Earland Falls*, ces cascades dévalant une falaise à pic juste au-dessus de la piste sont particulièrement impressionnantes après de fortes chutes de pluie.

CI-DESSUS *Key Summit*, où les lacs alpestres sont entourés de fragiles tourbières couvertes de fleurs et d'où l'on découvre un superbe panorama, est un détour obligatoire.

La case et le camp de Routeburn sont nichés en lisière de la brousse, là où on peut entendre le cri particulier – qui évoque celui d'un klaxon – des tadornes, se propageant sur les marais. À partir des marais, la piste Routeburn s'attaque véritablement à la montagne. La première heure se passe à travers une hêtraie pentue, empruntant un tronçon de piste rénové à la suite d'un glissement de terrain en 1994. La partie supérieure de la piste est ici à portée d'avalanche, rappelant qu'il vaut mieux éviter cet itinéraire en hiver et au début du printemps.

La case de Routeburn Falls (1 000 m) est située au-dessus de la ligne de brousse, sur un site imposant qui domine les Routeburn Flats (500 m) en contrebas. Derrière la case, la rivière Routeburn dévale une série de seuils formés de roche avant de s'enfoncer plus profondément dans la vallée, plus bas. Au-dessus de la ligne des arbres, la piste franchit un terrain rocailleux, parmi de courtes plantes herbacées, des arbustes subalpestres, et du chiendent. Le chiendent, avec son étonnante fleur d'été, reste la hantise des marcheurs qui, par mégarde, touchent ses feuilles acérées. Au-dessus de la ligne de brousse prolifèrent de très nombreuses espèces différentes d'oiseaux : de minuscules fauvettes de roche se blottissent dans les pierres et les touffes d'herbe, le faucon de Nouvelle-Zélande plane dans les airs, et le kéa, le perroquet des montagnes de Nouvelle-Zélande, ne manquera pas de faire connaître insolemment sa présence.

Par temps clair, la montée vers le point culminant, le col Harris (1 280 m) peut s'effectuer sans le moindre problème, et offrir des panoramas spectaculaires, qui s'étendent de plus en plus loin à mesure que l'on gagne de l'altitude. Toutefois, pluie, nuages et vent peuvent très vite se conjuguer pour faire de cette partie exposée de la piste une expédition risquée, nécessitant des vêtements appropriés et une navigation attentive entre les marques de parcours.

Au col Harris, si le temps le permet, le décor magnifique offert par les flancs de diorite des montagnes de Darran, les plus hautes du parc national de Fjordland, se dévoile par-delà l'étendue boisée de la vallée de Hollyford. Le mont Tutoko (2 746 m) est le plus haut som-

À DROITE *L'un des quatre chalets sur la piste Routeburn, blotti contre les rives du lac MacKenzie, où se reflètent les montagnes.*

met des 1,2 millions d'hectares que compte le Fjordland, et la rivière Hollyford, dont le lit fut creusé par les glaces, est l'une des plus longues. Plus près, dans un bassin marécageux voisin du col, on trouve à profusion des plantes comme les roseras, les orchidées, les marguerites et les utriculaires, qui s'épanouissent dans ces espaces marécageux.

Après cette montée régulière jusqu'au sommet, un petit abri de jour offre un répit bienvenu aux marcheurs, surtout si le temps n'est pas clément. Par contre, par beau temps la montée de 250 m du col à la Conical Hill (montagne Conique) offrira une variante splendide à ceux qui possèdent une bonne condition physique. Les points de vue, encore plus vastes depuis ce lieu plus élevé, s'étendent jusqu'à la côte occidentale de l'Ile du Sud.

De là, la piste Routeburn ne fait que descendre. Depuis le col assez franchement, pour ensuite serpenter en pente plus douce, toujours au-dessus de la ligne de brousse, longeant la face exposée de Hollyford Face en haut de la vallée de Hollyford. Là encore, le beau temps est synonyme de vues splendides sur ce terrain subalpestre. Mais si la brume et les nuages décident de cacher les montagnes, vous pourrez tout de même admirer les ourisias, gentianes, marguerites d'été et l'éclatant Ranunculus lyalli, appelé vulgairement à tort le lys du mont Cook.

La piste fait une série de zigzags en descendant vers l'abri boisé du bassin MacKenzie, où, par temps calme, les sommets étincelants alentour se reflètent dans les eaux bleu foncé du lac MacKenzie. À 3 ou 4 h de marche du col Harris, se trouvent la case et le camping du lac MacKenzie, blottis à la lisière de la forêt, à côté du lac. La Lake MacKenzie Lodge, hôtel privé, se trouve juste derrière le lac, dans une clairière.

Depuis la beauté dénudée et sauvage des hauteurs exposées, la piste continue dans un espace plus abrité, flirtant avec la limite de la brousse à travers un mélange de hêtres de montagne et de touffes d'herbe enneigées, et côtoie de petits lacs de montagne. Après avoir passé une petite clairière parsemée d'arbustes indigènes très reconnaissables, la piste coupe carrément, s'accrochant à des falaises presque verticales, en aval des chutes de Earland Falls. Ces cascades de 80 m de haut constituent le point fort du parcours, surtout après de fortes précipitations.

Continuant à descendre, la piste pénètre dans une forêt plus dense, où les hêtres argentés dominent une multitude de petits arbres et d'arbustes, fougères, lichens et mousses fleurissant à leur pied. Les vues sur la montagne sont maintenant cachées, jusqu'à ce que la piste débouche sur une clairière proche de Howden Hut, blottie à proximité du lac du même nom.

Une variante à ne pas manquer, à un quart d'heure à peine de Howden Hut : l'ascension d'une demi-heure vers le sommet de la Clé (Key Summit). Une fois de plus, les montagnes alentour se révèlent dans toute leur splendeur, et en bas, des passerelles de bois conduisent les marcheurs autour de charmants petits lacs, au-dessus de zones marécageuses fragiles matelassées d'herbes aromatiques alpestres, de mousses et de plantes des marais.

La piste Routeburn s'achève à côté de la route de Te Anau à Milford, au lieu-dit The Divide, le passage est-ouest le plus bas des Alpes de l'Ile du Sud. De là, des correspondances sont possibles avec Te Anau, la vallée de Hollyford (un autre itinéraire majeur qui commence à quelques kilomètres de là), ou bien vers les pittoresques merveilles du Milford Sound, l'une des destinations néo-zélandaises les plus recherchées.

AMÉRIQUE DU NORD

| LE GRAND CANYON | LA PISTE DES APPALACHES |

AMÉRIQUE DU NORD

Que ferait l'homme, s'il était contraint à vivre dans la chaleur étouffante de la société, sans pouvoir jamais se rafraîchir dans un bain de solitude ?

NATHANIEL HAWTHORNE
AMERICAN NOTEBOOKS

EN HAUT *Un marcheur fait une pause à Gogswell's Butte (rive nord) pour contempler l'itinéraire qui plonge vers le vide.*
CI-CONTRE *Descendant de la Blood Mountain (1 360 m) en Georgie, un marcheur passe par le tunnel de verdure de la piste des Appalaches. On distingue les marques blanches signalant la piste sur les arbres et les rochers, dans onze États.*
PAGES PRÉCÉDENTES *Il est recommandé de partir à plusieurs pour parcourir la piste des Appalaches, en particulier dans les parties sauvages, comme ici dans les Great Smoky Mountains dans le Tennessee.*

En 1689, le philosophe britannique John Locke écrivait : « Au début, tout était Amérique, et bien plus que ça ne l'est maintenant. » Aujourd'hui, les États-Unis consomment plus de nourriture, d'électricité et de pétrole par tête que n'importe quelle autre nation sur terre. La technologie joue peut-être un plus grand rôle dans la vie des Américains, mais comme le disait l'historien américain Peter Caroll, l'identité de cette nation, la plus puissante du monde, s'articule autour du souhait que ses régions rurales restent dans un état mythique naturel, virtuellement incorrompues par la civilisation et pratiquement dénuées de lois et de gouvernement.

La notion de « frontière » en est sans doute le meilleur résumé ; il existe là, à la frontière de la civilisation, un endroit sauvage et naturel où les animaux vivent en liberté et où l'homme ne peut survivre que sur ses propres ressources. Cela obsède les producteurs de films hollywoodiens depuis des décennies, comme en témoigne le genre western et l'exprime l'introduction de chaque épisode de « Star Trek » : « L'espace - L'ultime frontière ». Afin de sauvegarder ce qui est indiscutablement un patrimoine naturel absolument extraordinaire, les USA ont protégé leurs sites sauvages et magnifiques en constituant le réseau de parcs nationaux le plus varié, le mieux géré et le plus visité du monde.

L'Amérique est grande. Tout, en Amérique, est grand. Les voitures, les steaks, les immeubles de bureaux et les panneaux publicitaires. L'exploration de cette vaste contrée par les pionniers du XIXe siècle a donné lieu à des épopées qui n'auraient rien eu à envier aux annales des expéditions d'Asie. Meriwether Lewis, William Clark et leur équipe de solides chasseurs triés sur le volet, costauds, en bonne santé, célibataires et habitués à la nature, entreprirent de remonter le Missouri au printemps de 1804, avec comme objectif de traverser les montagnes Rocheuses. En novembre 1805, ayant remonté le fleuve jusqu'à sa source, traversé la chaîne du Bitterroot puis suivi successivement les rivières de Clearwater, Snake et Columbia vers l'ouest, il atteignirent la côte pacifique et s'installèrent pour l'hiver. Lorsqu'ils furent enfin de retour à Saint Louis, en septembre 1806, cela faisait deux ans et demi qu'ils étaient partis, avaient parcouru 13 000 km et établi le contact avec plus de cinquante nations d'Indiens d'Amérique. Chaque enfant américain apprend l'histoire de l'expédition Lewis-Clark à l'école, et il ne fait pas de doute que cette histoire a semé la graine du voyage et conduit bon nombre de leurs héritiers à parcourir leur pays.

Aujourd'hui, les USA possèdent la plus grande longueur de pistes balisées au monde, et tous ceux qui les empruntent constituent une contre-culture unique et colorée, riche en littérature et en anecdotes. De tous ces itinéraires, la Piste des Appalaches de 3 460 km, de la Georgie au Maine, inspire à ses anciens baroudeurs le plus fort sentiment d'appartenance à la même confrérie. La plupart des librairies d'Amérique spécialisées en activités de plein air disposent de rayons entiers de guides, d'histoires, de souvenirs personnels, d'anthologies et d'illustrations. Chaque randonneur a son surnom de piste, et vous découvrirez comment « Départ au frein », « Le philosophe », « Lo-Tech », « Le cavalier chantant » et bien d'autres ont acquis leurs galons. Que vous entrepreniez une randonnée complète ou juste un tronçon de ce parcours marathon, dès l'instant où vous prenez la route, vous mettez le pied dans quelque chose de beaucoup plus vaste qu'un simple sentier.

Près de 3 200 km à l'ouest des Appalaches, le Colorado arrive en Arizona et presque immédiatement pénètre dans ce qui est sans aucun doute l'une des grandes merveilles naturelles de la planète. Sur une distance de 450 km, les eaux du puissant Colorado serpentent au fond du Grand Canyon, bordé de ses imposantes falaises multicolores en substrat rocheux fantastiquement érodé. Le Parc national du Grand Canyon est peut-être parmi les attractions les plus visitées d'Amérique, mais il suffit de descendre au fond, sur l'une des pistes escarpées jusqu'à la rivière, pour très vite oublier le monde des voitures et des badauds bruyants.

LE GRAND CANYON

par David Emblidge

Presque toutes les randonnées nous emmènent toujours plus haut. Paradoxalement, une marche dans le Grand Canyon nous fait redescendre vers de nouvelles découvertes, dans un monde si extraordinairement beau qu'aucun superlatif du langage quotidien ne suffit à le qualifier. En effet, « Grand » (n.d.t. : en anglais = grandiose) est un qualificatif modeste pour l'une des merveilles naturelles du monde inscrite au Patrimoine mondial en 1979.

Une randonnée par ici laisse une empreinte indélébile. Souvent aussi, elle vous laissera les pieds et les genoux endoloris, la gorge brûlante et la peau brûlée par le soleil. Le climat du Canyon est rude, avec une chaleur intense, un air sec, et des dénivelés incessants et abrupts. Mais la récompense est toujours à la mesure de l'effort, principalement pour ceux qui viennent ici, bien préparés à affronter les éléments, et qui savent apprécier la beauté silencieuse et envoûtante des roches antiques, sculptées par le vent et l'eau, l'acharnement vital des plantes dans cet environnement désertique, et le spectacle des lumières en perpétuel changement, quand le soleil estampille chaque pouce du Canyon. Bien que de courtes promenades dans les parties supérieures du Canyon, sur la rive sud, soient les plus fréquentées, le grand jeu consiste à traverser d'une rive à l'autre, en plusieurs jours, avec une escale au « Ranch du Fantôme », sur les berges du torrentueux Colorado qui se rue dans le fond lointain du canyon.

L'histoire géologique du Grand Canyon remonte à plus de deux milliards d'années. Des hommes vécurent ici bien avant l'arrivée des explorateurs européens. À première vue, le Canyon asséché peut paraître figé dans le temps, alors qu'il s'élargit et s'approfondit encore, imperceptiblement. Au début, des éruptions volcaniques soulevèrent les montagnes, qui s'érodèrent puis se reformèrent après de longues périodes. Les sédiments de l'érosion furent comprimés, puis, sous l'effet de la chaleur, se métamorphosèrent pour former les rochers de soubassement que nous voyons aujourd'hui, très bas dans le canyon.

EN HAUT *Les randonneurs font une pause à Ooh Aah Point sur la rive Sud dont la brousse contraste avec la forêt de la Rive Nord.*
ENCART *L'eau de pluie, précieuse et rare, ainsi que les eaux de fonte des glaces sont captées dans des cuvettes de grès sur les innombrables corniches du Grand Canyon.*
À DROITE *La plupart des pistes de randonnée du Grand Canyon sont assez larges pour que les bêtes de somme et les marcheurs puissent se croiser en toute sécurité.*

En tout juste six millions d'années, la rivière que nous appelons maintenant Colorado a creusé le Canyon et entaillé toute cette région. Au cours des millénaires, le vent et la pluie ont creusé, sculpté et remodelé les impressionnantes murailles du Canyon. Profond de 1500 m et large de 30 km par endroits, l'échelle des dimensions du Grand Canyon est difficile à appréhender, que ce soit visuellement ou intellectuellement.

Les Anasazis (Indiens d'Amérique) s'établirent ici il y a environ 11 000 ans. Jusqu'à la moitié du XIIIe siècle ils partagèrent le canyon avec les Indiens Coconino. Des villages, du commerce et un peu d'agriculture se développèrent. Une période de sécheresse au XIIIe siècle les força à quitter le canyon et d'autres Indiens d'Amérique, les Cerbats, remplacèrent les Anasazis.

L'explorateur espagnol Garcia Lopez de Cardenas fut le premier Européen à voir le Grand Canyon, en 1540, mais la plus ancienne exploration documentée nous vient de l'intrépide John Wesley Powell, ancien combattant manchot de la guerre de Sécession qui, en 1869, conduisit une expédition de bateaux sur le Colorado. Le récit coloré que Powell fit de ses deux périples dans le Canyon lança la machine du tourisme et de la prospection. Lorsque la compagnie de chemin de fer de Santa Fe posa les derniers rails de la voie ferrée, aux alentours de 1911, l'accès public du Canyon fut considérablement amélioré et le tourisme prit une grande impor-

LIEU USA, nord-ouest de l'Arizona, 126 km.

QUAND PARTIR Mai à juin, et octobre à novembre.

DÉPART/ARRIVÉE L'itinéraire peut être parcouru dans les deux sens. Partez de la rive sud, Grand Canyon Village, par navette bus jusqu'à l'entrée Sud de la de piste de Kaibab. Terminez à la sortie vers North Kaibab Trail, Rive Nord, puis navette jusqu'à Grand Canyon Lodge ou sortie par transports en commun.

DURÉE 5 jours (35 km).

POINT CULMINANT 2400 m.

ASPECTS TECHNIQUES Les randonnées dans le Grand Canyon peuvent être rendues impossibles en été comme en hiver. Neige et verglas sur les points culminants des rives sont courants jusqu'au printemps bien avancé. La chaleur écrasante dans le Canyon, à partir de la fin du printemps, augmente la probabilité de coups de soleil et de déshydratation. Boire beaucoup d'eau, même sans soif. Les sentiers sont en général larges et plats, mais comportent des étranglements particulièrement escarpés. Tous les déchets doivent être remportés.

MATÉRIEL Chaussures confortables, abri d'urgence (bâche légère), filtre à eau, lampe torche, écran solaire et chapeau.

MODE DE RANDONNÉE Sac à dos.

AUTORISATIONS/RESTRICTIONS L'administration du parc limite l'accès aux parties les plus profondes du Canyon pour empêcher l'encombrement, mais cela ne facilite pas les réservations. Permis (gratuits) nécessaires pour toute marche de plus d'une journée dans le Canyon.

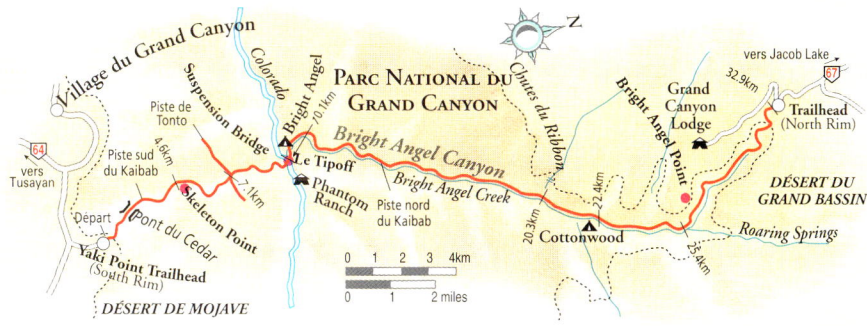

CI-DESSUS *Ribbon Falls, une source jaillissant de la rive nord du Grand Canyon sur la piste Kaybab, laisse des dépôts de travertin composé de carbonate de calcium.*

tance économique. Le village de Grand Canyon, sur la rive sud, prit forme après l'arrivée du chemin de fer, et constitue encore le point de départ de la plupart des randonnées.

Quels que soient l'heure où le moment auxquels vous arriverez au Grand Canyon, votre premier regard vers le vide vous coupera le souffle. L'aube et le crépuscule habillent le Canyon de son plus riche habit de lumière. La rive sud, au village de Grand Canyon, affiche une activité intense, encombrée de véhicules de toutes sortes et de cars de touristes pendant tout l'été. Ne désespérez pas. La rive nord n'en accueille que dix fois moins.

La traversée du Canyon peut s'effectuer du sud au nord ou du nord au sud. Dans un cas comme dans l'autre, les modalités de transport de ou vers la rive nord sont problématiques. L'accès par l'autoroute au Canyon lui-même est beaucoup plus facile en venant du sud ; l'accès nord est fermé en hiver, et en été, il implique un trajet assez long en territoire désert. Mais il vous faudra quand même une bonne journée, depuis le village de Grand Canyon, pour atteindre les entrées de pistes de la rive nord par les routes de services du parc national, soit avec votre propre voiture ou une voiture de location (350 km). Les randonneurs qui ont le temps et les moyens de positionner une voiture sur chaque rive avant de partir peuvent faire à leur guise, mais la plupart arrivent sur la rive sud, passent une nuit sur place, puis s'enfoncent avec la foule dans le Canyon par la piste de Bright Angel (la plus fréquentée) ou bien par celle de South Kaibab, un peu plus isolée. Après deux heures au fond du Canyon, quand la fatigue et la chaleur ont persuadé la plupart des marcheurs « journaliers » de remonter, les randonneurs auront les lieux presque entièrement pour eux, suivant la saison.

Partir du côté sud vous permet de vous éloigner de la civilisation plutôt que d'y revenir. La randonnée décrite ici emprunte la piste du Sud Kaibab, dont le point d'entrée, Yaki Point, est accessible par navette bus à partir du village de Grand Canyon. Le panorama, depuis Yaki, est superbe et la dénivellation pose un vrai défi. Priez pour que vos chaussures soient à votre pied – vous êtes sur le point de faire un « plongeon » de 1460 m vers la rivière du Colorado, sur les dix prochains kilomètres, presque toujours en forte pente. Il n'y a presque pas d'ombre et l'eau est, dans le meilleur des cas, très rare. Emportez une carte et utilisez-la. Bien que le sentier soit facile à suivre, il faut une grande concentration pour garder la notion du temps passé et de la distance parcourue, le soleil écrasant et la chaleur pouvant même étourdir les randonneurs les plus en forme. Il n'est pas recommandé de partir seul.

La Cedar Ridge (Crête des cèdres) apparaît après 2,4 km de sentier. Le Skeleton Point est à 4,6 km. La Vast Redwall Formation (immense muraille de grès rouge sculptée par le vent) accueille, dans ses immenses lacets, la piste du Sud Kaibab sur un grand nombre de kilomètres.

Malgré la délimitation nette de ses flancs abrupts, le Grand Canyon, est en fait un désert entre deux autres déserts, celui – chaud – du Mojave et celui – froid – du Grand Bassin. La caractéristique la plus frappante est la sécheresse. La flore du désert est une merveille d'adaptation. L'arbuste dominant, le blackbrush, projette de petites feuilles velues pour capter et retenir l'eau. En période de sécheresse, la plante devient caduque et interrompt son métabolisme. Environ tous les dix ans, il se produit une émergence de plantes désertiques, avec une abondance de phlox et de lupins.

La Toronto Trail Junction, à 7 km, est suivie de près par le Tip-off, le dernier plongeon vers la gorge du Colorado. À ce stade, vous entendrez la rivière, si vous ne la voyez pas encore. Quand vous serez arrivés au Colorado, vous aurez marché plus de 9 km et l'envie vous viendra peut-être de prendre un bain. Ne le faites pas. Le courant est traitre. Traversez le pont suspendu et continuez soit jusqu'au terrain de camping de Bright Angel, soit jusqu'au Phantom Ranch, où vous pourrez rafraîchir et soulager vos pieds fatigués dans un ruisseau tranquille en toute sécurité. On ne peut atteindre le ranch qu'à pied, à cheval ou par la rivière. Au milieu des peupliers, sur le bord du chantant ruisseau de Bright Angel Creek, cette « oasis dans un canyon » est bien loin du monde extérieur. Ici, on peut faire le plein d'eau mais on ne peut y acheter aucune nourriture. Le Ranch n'est pas une station thermale, les conditions sont spartiates, mais le privilège de séjourner ici vous laissera une collection d'excellents souvenirs.

La rivière Colorado fait l'objet d'un débat politique sans fin. Construit en 1963 quelque 140 km en amont, le barrage de Glen Canyon a modifié l'écologie du bassin versant du

Colorado d'une manière imprévisible. Le flux de sédiments qui auparavant creusait le Canyon a été stoppé. La flore et la faune ont été très durement affectées, et d'aucuns, maintenant, prétendent que le barrage devrait être détruit. Les amateurs de rafting se délectent de leurs chevauchées sauvages sur le Colorado, et nombre d'entre eux réclament qu'on laisse la nature reprendre ses droits. Plus loin en aval, les États d'Arizona, du Nevada et de Californie pompent, presque jusqu'à la dernière goutte, l'eau du Colorado, au point qu'il n'est plus qu'un filet d'eau quand il arrive à la mer.

La randonnée vers la rive nord, sur la piste du Nord Kaibab par le Canyon de Bright Angel, consiste en une longue ascension qu'il est préférable de partager en deux. À 10 km en amont depuis le Colorado, on trouvera répit à Ribbon Falls. Pour passer une nuit au camping de Cottonwood (12,2 km) il vous faut apporter tout votre équipement et votre nourriture, et remporter tous vos déchets. Mais l'effort en vaut la peine, d'une part parce que vous prolongerez d'autant votre séjour dans le Grand Canyon et d'autre part parce que l'escalade du côté nord du Canyon en une seule traite est généralement au-dessus des forces la plupart des randonneurs.

Le carrefour Roaring Springs/Bright Angel Creek Junction, à 15,3 km, sera la prochaine marque de parcours, mais 7,6 km restent encore à parcourir avant l'entrée de la piste. L'auberge Grand Canyon Lodge est à 3 km au-delà de l'entrée de la piste, après une telle distance, vous serez prêts pour une bonne nuit de repos dans un lit avant de reprendre votre voiture. Il y a de fortes chances pour que – nonobstant les ampoules, la gorge sèche et les courbatures – vous ayez du mal à vous arracher à ces images du Grand Canyon, vu depuis la rive nord. Mais vous serez conscient d'avoir traversé une véritable merveille naturelle.

CI-DESSUS *Des marcheurs pénètrent dans le Grand Canyon sur la piste du sud Kaibab, qui commence à Yaki Point sur la rive gauche et descend jusqu'au Colorado, à 10 km.*

CI-DESSUS *Le Grand Canyon intérieur, où lumière intense et zones d'ombre forment un contraste saisissant dans le labyrinthe de sentiers, ici au-dessus de Deer Creek.*

LA PISTE DES APPALACHES

par David Emblidge

L'ancêtre des grands sentiers d'Amérique du Nord, la piste des Appalaches, PA (The Appalachian Trail) est également la plus fréquentée. Avec ses 3460 km, traversant onze États et une variété de paysages et de climats non loin de la côte atlantique, la piste accueille chaque année quatre millions de marcheurs. Quelques-uns tentent un parcours intégral. Sur 2 500 marcheurs par an, à peine 10 % parviennent à l'autre bout, quatre à six mois plus tard.

La plupart des randonneurs sont les promeneurs de la journée, ou du week-end, et ceux en expédition pour une semaine ou deux. Un kilométrage important de la piste traverse des zones naturelles protégées, garantissant une solitude extrême et un certain nombre de défis à relever entre deux points de réapprovisionnement.

Boisée d'arbres caducs et de conifères, la région des Appalaches abrite des centaines d'espèces d'oiseaux et une multitude de mammifères, y compris des ours noirs et des originaux. Dans les États du Nord comme du Sud, les panoramas, la flore alpestre, la météo et la marche au-dessus de la ligne des arbres, sont au menu. L'hiver, la piste est fermée dans presque tous les États sauf les plus au sud, mais même dans ces derniers, des précipitations de neige de plusieurs pieds peuvent se produire en altitude.

La piste suit à peu près la ligne de crêtes des monts Appalaches, qui forment un arc depuis l'État de Georgie, au sud, vers les États de la façade atlantique, jusqu'en Nouvelle-Angleterre, culminant dans les régions sauvages et escarpées du New Hampshire et du Maine. Les parcs nationaux de Great Smoky Mountains et de Shenandoah, ainsi qu'un certain nombre de parcs d'États, ponctuent la piste sinueuse. Une prolongation vers le nord est en cours – la Piste nationale des Appalaches – jusqu'au Canada et la péninsule de Gaspésie.

EN HAUT *Un randonneur solitaire contemple les lumières de Waynesboro, Virginie, avant de bivouaquer pour la nuit.*

AU MILIEU *Quittant les étendues sauvages, les randonneurs de la piste des Appalaches rencontrent d'occasionnelles collectivités montagnardes comme celle-ci, dans la Laurel Valley, Virginie.*

À DROITE *Un randonneur trouve son chemin à travers la vieille forêt de spruce rouge dans le parc national des Great Smoky Mountains, Tennessee.*

CI-DESSUS *Un marcheur solitaire contemple la Blue Ridge Mountain depuis le Hanging Rock, un surplomb de 60 m en Caroline du Nord, d'où le nom de « Hanging Rock State Park ».*

Contrairement à ce que l'on croit souvent, la PA n'est pas un sentier d'Indiens d'Amérique. Cette réalisation moderne naquit de l'imagination de marcheurs enthousiastes à la fin du XIXe et du début du XXe siècle. Le très vénérable Appalachian Mountain Club de Boston et le Vermont's Green Mountain Club commencèrent à construire des pistes de randonnées pendant l'âge d'or (1880).

En 1921, un forestier sorti de Harvard, Benton McKaye, publia son « Appalachian Trail, A Project in Regional Planning » dans une revue scientifique, le « Journal of the American Institute of Architects ». Benton voyait un parc tout en longueur, de la Georgie ou Maine, comprenant le sentier de randonnée, des campings et des chalets de montagne avec activités récréatives pour les citadins fatigués. MacKaye, lecteur assidu de David Thoreau, Emerson et John Muir, célébra les vertus esthétiques et morales de la nature sauvage américaine.

Des milliers de bénévoles et de nombreux législateurs collaborèrent pendant vingt-cinq ans pour faire de la PA une réalité. Pendant la dépression, un programme de création d'emplois à l'intention des jeunes chômeurs – le Civilian Conservation Corps (CCC) – participa à la construction de nombreux tronçons, de camps et de chalets. Ce n'est qu'en 1948 que les premières tentatives sur l'intégralité du parcours furent mises à l'ordre du jour ; l'honneur en revient à Earl Shaffer, devenu héros légendaire de la PA.

La loi de 1968 sur le Réseau National de Chemins de Randonnées plaça la piste sous l'autorité du Service des Parcs nationaux, qui en 2000 avait pratiquement terminé son programme d'acquisitions foncières pour créer un couloir d'au moins 300 m de large, pouvant atteindre plusieurs kilomètres par endroits. Les écologistes et le législateur entamèrent des débats passionnés sur les problèmes d'impact sur l'environnement et ceux liés à la gestion des marcheurs.

Le randonneur appalachien « intégral » partira entre mars et avril de Springer Mountain, en Georgie, après une montée jusqu'au sommet, par le parc d'État d'Amicalola Falls. La piste est un étroit sentier, souvent escarpé et rocailleux, passant par les plus hauts sommets et les

CI-DESSUS *Parmi les fragiles fleurs alpestres, des randonneurs à sac à dos progressent le long de la piste venteuse des Appalaches du New Hampshire. La couverture nuageuse fait suite à l'ouragan Danny.*

plus belles vallées qu'il est donné de rencontrer sur l'itinéraire vers le nord. Les fleuves sont franchis par des ponts mais un grand nombre de ruisseaux nécessitent d'être traversés à gué.

Dans les États du Sud – Georgie, Caroline du Nord et Tennessee – la piste traverse plusieurs forêts nationales et parcourt 110 km dans le Parc national des Great Smoky Mountains, où elle franchit le Clingman's Dome (2024 m), le point culminant du parcours, décevant par la proximité de la route et son affluence. À l'exception de ce type de randonneurs, ce territoire, le plus au sud de la piste, est le plus souvent désert. Attendez-vous quand même à quelques paradoxes – le Parc National des GSM est le plus fréquenté du pays et la piste est particulièrement encombrée aux croisements des principales autoroutes. Mais à peine 1 ou 2 km plus loin, les foules auront disparu.

La chaleur, la moiteur et les pluies abondantes, s'ajoutant à la latitude, sont favorables au développement de forêts mélangées d'essences variées de bois, avec une profusion de fleurs sauvages, abondance de chants d'oiseaux et de fréquents passages d'ours noirs. Des preuves du malencontreux effet des pluies acides (provenant des cheminées des complexes industriels) sont apportées par les nombreux troncs d'arbres morts. Des parasites ont décimé l'orme et le châtaignier d'Amérique et s'en prennent aux baumiers. Rhododendrons, cornouillers et un nombre incalculable d'autres plantes à fleurs décorent le sentier, attirent des foules de marcheurs journaliers au moment de la pleine saison de floraison.

En plus d'un certain nombre de sommets du sud des États-Unis, dont la plupart sont « arrondis » (ce sont de très vieilles montagnes), il existe de vastes régions découvertes – les « chauves » – qui offrent des points de vue spectaculaires. On ne connaît pas l'origine de ces « chauves ». Malgré leurs 1500 m d'altitude, ils ne se situent pas au-dessus de la ligne des arbres en raison du climat chaud. Des légendes indiennes prétendent que les dieux embrasaient les sommets pour pouvoir garder l'œil sur les activités des hommes dans les vallées. Les botanistes savent que certains peuples indigènes faisaient paître leurs troupeaux sur les « chauves », sans que l'explication complète en soit connue.

Avec plus de 640 km, c'est en Virginie que la piste des Appalaches couvre la plus grande distance dans un même État. Damascus, Virginie, accueille les « Trail Days » (Journées Randonnée), saluant la marée de randonneurs, en mai de chaque année. Les collines du sud de la Virginie s'élèvent à plus de 1500 m. La proximité de Washington et de Baltimore,

DE LA GEORGIE AU MAINE, USA

s'ajoutant à l'attrait de cette piste facile et de faible dénivelé, fait que les tronçons situés en Virginie septentrionale sont très encombrés. L'été peut être terriblement chaud en Virginie, mais les randonnées d'automne sont longues et magnifiques. Le point le plus photogénique du parcours est indiscutablement le McAfee Knob (Bouton de McAfee), un promontoire de Virginie centrale, flanqué d'un gigantesque surplomb rocheux d'où l'on admire le panorama vers l'ouest.

Quelques kilomètres de piste sont situés dans l'ouest de la voisine Virginie, jusqu'au Parc historique national du Village de Harper's Ferry, où la Conférence de la PA a installé ses bureaux pour accueillir et renseigner tous les randonneurs par une documentation abondante sur la piste. De l'autre côté du fleuve Potomac, très large, la piste fait un bond de 60 km à travers le Maryland avant de passer la frontière de Pennsylvanie et la Mason Dixon Line chargée d'histoire qui sépare les États confédérés du Sud (esclavagistes) de ceux de l'Union, du Nord (abolitionnistes). La frontière politique est un vestige de la guerre de Sécession.

La mi-parcours de la PA se trouve juste au nord de la frontière sud de Pennsylvanie. Accent, cuisine, climat et architecture changent de façon remarquable dans les états de la façade atlantique. Les Appalaches de Pennsylvanie s'incurvent légèrement vers le nord-est, mais la marche est pénible en « Rocksylvanie ». De longues crêtes, souvent sans arbres, encombrées de rochers aux arêtes aiguës projetés vers le haut par la collision des plaques tectoniques, puis chamboulés par les glaciers. Les sites historiques de la guerre de Sécession et la beauté des paysages pastoraux rachètent cependant la difficulté du tronçon pennsylvanien. La limite nord de l'État est marquée par un puissant fleuve coulant dans une très belle gorge, dans la Zone nationale de Loisirs de la Delaware Water Gap.

Le New Jersey, un État à forte densité de population, offre quelques tronçons de la PA dans les montagnes de Pocono et le long de la chaîne de Kittatinny qui sont à la fois calmes et magnifiques. Les altitudes culminent à 520 m sans sommet particulier, mais certains bijoux comme la Sunfish Pond sont particulièrement intéressants. La piste contourne une

CI-DESSUS *Le village d'Harper's Ferry propose aux randonneurs isolés contacts et convivialité, et offre également de nombreux renseignements sur les sentiers de randonnée.*

partie de l'État de New York à environ 80 km au nord de la « Grosse Pomme », trouvant le moyen d'offrir des vues saisissantes sur les parcs d'État de Bear Mountain et de Harrison and Hudson Highlands, de part et d'autre du fleuve Hudson. Les moments d'isolement sont plus rares par ici, mais les randonneurs apprécient les paysages reproduits par les peintres célèbres de la Hudson River School au XIXe siècle, qui définirent la perception américaine romantique de la nature : sublime et effrayante.

Pénétrant dans le Connecticut, la piste parvient enfin en Nouvelle-Angleterre, sa dernière région typique, alors qu'il reste encore cinq États et des centaines de kilomètres à parcourir, et le plus gros de l'escalade. Les villages de Nouvelle-Angleterre constituent les plus charmantes

LIEU USA, onze États de la côte est (Georgie, Caroline du Nord, Tennessee, Virginie, Virginie-Occidentale, Maryland, Pennsylvanie, New Jersey, New York, Connecticut, Massachusetts, Vermont, New Hampshire, Maine).

QUAND PARTIR Printemps à automne : État du Sud de mars à novembre ; État du Nord d'avril à mi-octobre. Toute l'année dans les plaines du sud. La meilleure époque est de mi-août à l'automne pour les couleurs, en particulier dans les États de New York et de Nouvelle Angleterre.

DÉPART/ARRIVÉE Les grands randonneurs partent généralement de Georgie et marchent vers le nord jusqu'au Maine. Nombre de gens parcourent la totalité de la piste par tronçons sur plusieurs années.

DURÉE 4 à 6 mois pour un parcours continu et complet. Des tronçons isolés (par exemple, l'un des parcs nationaux) peuvent constituer d'excellentes randonnées de deux à trois semaines.

POINT CULMINANT Clingman's Dome, Caroline du Nord (2 024 m).

ASPECTS TECHNIQUES Les conditions hivernales peuvent entraîner la fermeture de la piste au début du printemps ou à la mi-automne. Toute la Piste des Appalaches est signalée par un trait vertical rouge sur fond blanc, peints sur les arbres et les rochers. Les pistes secondaires sont signalisées en bleu, orange et rouge, etc. Des appentis disposent souvent de toilettes extérieures et d'eau de source, mais les randonneurs « hors-piste » devront s'attendre à camper à bonne distance de la piste et sans commodités.

MATÉRIEL Sac à dos, sac de couchage, chaussures de marche, vêtements de pluie, nourriture (faible poids, énergétique) vêtements chauds et séchant vite, insectifuge.

MODE DE RANDONNÉE Sac à dos.

AUTORISATIONS/RESTRICTIONS Aucun permis n'est nécessaire pour la Piste des Appalaches. A l'intérieur du Parc national des Great Smoky Mountains, les appentis sont réservés aux grands randonneurs. Pour les parcours plus courts, emporter une tente.

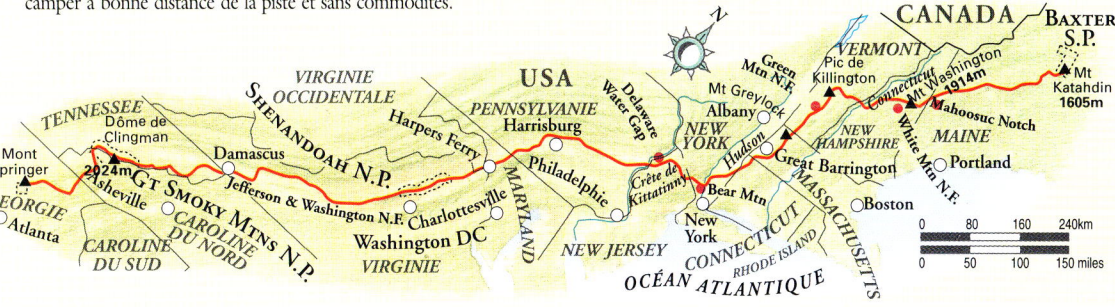

escales, puisque le sentier serpente à travers une campagne enchanteresse. Progressant vers le nord, la piste grimpe vers les toutes premières montagnes depuis la Virginie. Les hautes terres du nord-ouest du Connecticut sont les Litchfield Hills, où la piste fait des montagnes russes, de crête en vallée, tout en restant proche de la rivière Housatonic. Entre Salisbury l'embourgeoisée et le comté du sud Berkshire dans l'État du Massachusetts voisin, la piste parcourt une superbe forêt et un sentier de crête sur la Taconic Range, dans les parcs d'État, au travers le Sage's Ravine, un paradis de botaniste, avec cascades, et de brèves images du mont Everett (793 m).

De l'autre côté de la Housatonic, la piste passe non loin de Great Barrington, Massachusetts, puis s'élève vers le massif de Berkshire tout au long de ces 130 km de parcours. Les randonneurs attirés hors-piste par le patrimoine culturel adoreront les collines du Berkshire, où de nombreuses petites villes se vantent de tout avoir, depuis l'Orchestre symphonique de Boston, jusqu'au Festival de « Pillow dance », divers théâtres et plusieurs musées superbes. Le mont Greylock, dans le nord-ouest du Massachusetts, est le plus haut sommet de Nouvelle-Angleterre avec ses 1064 m, et le premier endroit où une météo incertaine peut poser des problèmes. Bascom Lodge, au sommet du Greylock, propose des couchettes, onéreuses mais appréciables.

La Forêt nationale de Green Mountain accueille la plus grande longueur de piste du Vermont, ici orientée presque plein nord. La Longue Piste du Vermont (Vermont's Long Trail) côtoie la PA depuis le Massachusetts jusqu'au Killington Peak, au centre de l'État. La Longue Piste est antérieure à la PA et possède ses propres héros légendaires, ceux qui vont à pied jusqu'à Québec, au Canada. Les étendues sauvages fédérales du Vermont, vierges de toute mécanisation, ne possèdent que très peu de routes, et proposent de s'échapper des terrains de camping. Une grande surprise attend les marcheurs sur les mon-

CI-DESSUS *En atteignant la zone alpine au-dessus de la limite des arbres sur le mont Madison dans les Montagnes Blanches, les randonneurs ont peu de place pour s'abriter du froid et des vents particulièrement violents.*

tagnes fréquentées du Vermont – Stratton (1200 m) et Killington (1293 m). L'étang de Stratton Pond, magiquement isolé, avec des abris et des tentes éparpillés autour d'un plan d'eau immaculé, est tout bonnement un petit coin de paradis.

Au nord de Killington, la PA vire à l'est, quitte la Longue Piste et s'enfonce vers la vallée du Connecticut. Il faut parcourir 80 km pour y parvenir, à travers une forêt sans fin, sur une piste peu utilisée et passant par une seule et unique ville intéressante, Woodstock, lieu saturé de boutiques à la mode et d'élégantes maisons de maîtres de l'époque fédéraliste. Dartmouth College, Hanover, New Hampshire, une université vénérable de la Ivy League, est située sur la PA. Réapprovisionnement et repos sont faciles à organiser ici pour les grands randonneurs. Après une promenade à basse altitude dans le nord-est de Hanover, la PA entame ses premières et plus difficiles ascensions et descentes, par la Forêt nationale de la Montagne Blanche (White Mountain National Forest). Le mont Moosilauke (1464 m) emmène la piste au-dessus de la ligne des arbres jusqu'à la zone alpine. Après une des-

cente éprouvante de Franconia Ridge jusqu'à Crawford Notch, la piste remonte encore plus haut, sur la Presidential Range, pour la randonnée la plus longue de toute l'Amérique de l'est, sans doute les plus belles vues et indubitablement la météo la plus risquée. Au mont Washington (1914 m), la piste atteint son deuxième point culminant, plus exposé aux éléments que le premier. Une construction bizarre gâche le paysage du sommet sans arbres (les aménageurs touristiques du XIXe siècle avaient taillé une route jusqu'au sommet). Un groupe de superbes chalets, gérés par le Appalachian Mountain Club (AMC) propose un peu de répit en s'abritant des vents forts. Le camping est interdit, dans cette zone extrêmement fragile où diapensia, rhododendrons de Laponie, azalées des montagnes et lichens s'agrippent aux rochers, survivant grâce à une étonnante chimie d'adaptation.

Les marcheurs qui n'utilisent pas les chalets AMC, onéreux et réservés des mois à l'avance, doivent en général descendre assez bas pour retrouver des sites où ils auront le droit de piquer leur tente. Une randonnée le long de la Presidential Range implique une préparation soignée de l'expédition, et une grande attention à la sécurité. Plusieurs victimes trouvent la mort chaque année, accidentellement ou par témérité dans ces montagnes, où la foudre, les vents très violents, les chutes de pierres, les avalanches et les chutes ont parfois des conséquences tragiques. Pourtant, un voyage sûr et bien planifié reste, le nec plus ultra de la PA.

La Mecque des randonneurs, c'est Pinkham Notch, sur la PA, dans la vallée en aval des Presidentials, où un chalet, restaurant, librairie, offre des programmes d'histoire naturelle et un service de navettes desservant des douzaines d'entrées de piste et attire ainsi des foules exubérantes et des passionnés d'alpinisme. La piste monte de nouveau rapidement, passe dans le Maine et se trouve confrontée au Mahoosuc Notch tristement célèbre, le mille le plus difficile de toute la PA, un fatras monstrueux de blocs de pierre colossaux, d'étroits et sombres passages tortueux. Quelques sommets encore dans le Maine occidental se dressent furtivement, mais bientôt les altitudes faiblissent et une randonnée d'une semaine à travers les étendues sauvages les plus lointaines de l'est américain commence. À quelques heures des principales villes des USA ou du Canada, les bois du Maine sont essentiellement le domaine d'entreprises d'abattage de bois, des chasseurs et des pêcheurs. Des lacs limpides et glacés parsèment le paysage de collines interminables, des élans paissent dans les régions marécageuses, et des ours noirs circulent en toute liberté. Le « 100-mile Wilderness » nécessite un approvisionnement complet. Le franchissement des fleuves et rivières du Maine peut être très dangereux. Sur la rivière Kennebec, où des randonneurs ont péri noyés en tentant de la traverser, le Maine Appalachian Trail Club assure un service de passeur gratuit par canoë.

Le parc d'État Baxter, vaste territoire occupant le centre nord du Maine, apportera l'épilogue qui convient, avec le Mouny Katahdin, ce qui veut dire en indien Abenaki « la plus haute montagne ». Avec ses 1605 m, le Katahdin est le sommet le plus isolé de tout le parcours, sans routes, sans abri ni refuge, et sans protection contre les éléments. Neige et glace s'attardent parfois jusqu'à mi-mai, puis reviennent au début ou à la mi-octobre. Les dernières heures de la PA se passent vers le nord, bien au-dessus de la ligne des arbres, pour culminer à Baxter Peak (1605 m), où bien des bouchons de champagne ont sauté pour fêter le succès des grands randonneurs, bien souvent dans un brouillard glacial et un vent à vous geler les os. Par temps clair, la descente par la face nord, après avoir franchi la crête « en lame de couteau » et ses précipices, offrira aux randonneurs une belle prime. Pourtant, une fois l'ascension du Katahdin bouclée, les randonneurs peuvent rentrer chez eux avec un sentiment de grande satisfaction. Si vous avez parcouru à pied toute la distance de Georgie au Maine, vous venez d'entrer dans la légende de la Piste des Appalaches.

AMÉRIQUE DU SUD

LE CIRCUIT HUAYHUASH | LE CIRCUIT ALPAMAYO | CIRCUIT D'ILLAMPU | TORRES DEL PAINE |

AMÉRIQUE DU SUD

Pour ma part, je voyage non pas pour aller quelque part, mais pour partir... Je voyage pour voyager. Ce qui compte, c'est bouger.

ROBERT LOUIS STEVENSON, 1850-1894

EN HAUT *Huascaran (6 768 m), le plus haut sommet du Pérou, ici vu depuis le col Alto de Pucaraju, cordillère Blanche.*

CI-CONTRE *Des ânes se désaltèrent dans la Guanacpatay. Bien que les ânes puissent porter des charges plus lourdes que les lamas, ces derniers restent les favoris en raison de leur résistance inégalée au froid et à l'altitude.*

PAGES PRÉCÉDENTES *Une enfant Aymara avec un jeune lama accorde un rare cliché sur les rives du lac Titicaca.*

Entre les douces plages bordées de cocotiers et les eaux languissantes des Caraïbes et les monstrueux piliers de granit de Patagonie, ravagés par les perpétuelles tempêtes des Quarantièmes Rugissants, l'Amérique du Sud est le quatrième continent du monde par sa taille. L'élément physique prédominant de cette vaste étendue de terre est sans contestation possible la cordillère des Andes, une chaîne de montagnes étonnamment belles qui longe tout le rebord occidental du continent. Bordées par les déserts de la bande littorale pacifique à l'ouest et par les forêts tropicales du bassin amazonien à l'est, les Andes comprennent de nombreux volcans et quelques-uns des plus célèbres paysages de montagne.

Bien que ne remontant pas aussi loin dans la nuit des temps que celles d'Asie, les civilisations anciennes qui naquirent en Amérique du Sud ont produit des quantités de merveilles architecturales et des trésors matériels qui n'ont rien à envier à ceux d'Asie. Les Incas symbolisent l'apogée d'une culture urbanistique qui se développa en plus de 3 000 ans, pour se trouver brutalement écrasée par l'arrivée des conquistadores espagnols au XVIe siècle. Les destructions provoquées par les conquistadores et la férocité avec laquelle ils traitèrent les Indiens d'Amérique du Sud sont sans équivalentes dans toute l'histoire de la colonisation européenne.

La randonnée en Amérique du Sud attire de plus en plus d'adeptes enthousiastes. Contrairement au sous-continent de l'Inde, la plupart des pays d'Amérique du Sud sont relativement développés et modernes. Les moyens de communication sont semblables à ceux que l'on trouve en Europe et en Amérique du Nord. Cela est vrai pour le Chili et l'Argentine, moins pour le Pérou et la Bolivie, où les Indiens des hautes contrées parlent leurs propres langues. Visualisez cela devant une toile de fond d'architecture coloniale espagnole, et vous commencerez à vous faire une idée de la scène sud-américaine.

Le Pérou, qui est fier de posséder les plus impressionnantes ruines incas, des réserves de forêt tropicale riches en faune sauvage et – dans la cordillère Blanche – la plus haute montagne de toute la ceinture tropicale (Huascaran,

6 768 m), offre des parcours de randonnée qui rivalisent avec les parcours himalayens. Alpamayo (5 947 m) ne figure peut-être pas parmi les géants de la cordillère Blanche, mais on le décrit souvent comme la plus belle montagne du monde, et le parcourir en randonnée permet de profiter de vues sans égales de la chaîne tout entière. Tout aussi impressionnant et superbe, le circuit de la cordillère Huaybuach est le prochain groupe de montagnes au sud de la cordillère Blanche. L'accès en est un peu plus difficile, et les itinéraires moins fréquentés, mais avec le Yerupaja (6 634 m) et une multitude d'autres sommets, cette chaîne serrée ressemble aux dents d'une scie géante retournée. Une vue inoubliable.

Au sud du Pérou, la chaîne des Andes entre en Bolivie, où la frontière sépare les eaux scintillantes du lac Titicaca entre deux nations. La Bolivie possède la plus forte proportion d'Indiens de tous les pays d'Amérique du Sud. Une démographie faible et un développement économique lent font de la Bolivie l'un des pays les plus pauvres du continent, mais en contrepartie, la beauté naturelle du pays n'a pas été dégradée par l'activité des hommes. La Cordillera Real est le bijou dans la couronne montagneuse de la Bolivie, et le circuit d'Illampu, au départ de Sorata, baignée de soleil et ombragée de palmiers, avec ses cours de style colonial espagnol, reste unique.

Il est peu d'endroits dans le monde avec lesquels la Patagonie n'offre pas un contraste total. Cinglée par les plus féroces intempéries imaginables, ce pays des merveilles de glaciers et de lacs, de forêts vierges atrophiées et de pampas infinies définit le mot « élémentaire ». Sous des cieux en perpétuel changement, avec des formations nuageuses surréalistes de cirrus et de nuages divers, on en parle souvent comme de la partie la plus lointaine du monde. Bien que marcher là-bas ne soit pas affaire de routine, ceux qui sont correctement préparés et équipés y vivront une expérience totalement captivante. Aucun itinéraire ne peut mieux afficher les multiples facettes de la Patagonie que celui du circuit de Torres del Paine.

LE CIRCUIT HUAYHUASH

par Chris Hooker

La cordillère Huayhuash se voit à peine sur la plupart des cartes du Pérou, avec ses 30 km en tout du nord au sud. Pourtant, cette chaîne compacte est l'une des plus magnifiques des Andes. L'une des vingt chaînes glaciaires du Pérou, le massif de Huayhuash surgit brutalement des prairies, 50 km au sud de la cordillère Blanche et, comme celle-ci, constitue la ligne de partage des eaux de l'Amazone. De loin, son profil ressemble à une scie géante – une douzaine de sommets acérés flanquent une chaîne unique et habillée de glace, avec le Yerupaja (6 634 m), le deuxième sommet du Pérou en altitude, dominant tout le reste.

Au cœur de la cordillère, on découvre une nature sauvage intacte. Sous les glaciers crevassés, des cirques et des vallées s'étendent, garnis de lacs éclatants et d'un faune aviaire abondante. Les alpages sauvages (puna) prédominent, ponctués par d'occasionnelles forêts de bois de rose (quenual). Le fugace *vicuna* sauvage (lama) est aperçu à l'occasion, bien que ce terrain pauvre accueille plus communément des troupeaux éparpillés de bovins conduits là par de petits éleveurs saisonniers. C'est là le décor d'une randonnée spectaculaire et extrêmement intéressante, le circuit de 170 km de Huayhuash, l'un des très rares parcours faisant le tour complet du massif montagneux. Bien que fatigant, et nécessitant 12 jours pour franchir plusieurs cols au-dessus de 4 500 m, il emmène les marcheurs vers un univers de beauté naturelle inégalée.

Les anciens peuples des Andes vénéraient certains des sommets enneigés, leur conférant d'importants pouvoirs. Si un *apu* (esprit des montagnes) devait apparaître, le prêtre pouvait escalader ses flancs pour y pratiquer un sacrifice. De nombreuses découvertes archéologiques d'altitude suggèrent même que ces prêtres furent peut-être les premiers humains à atteindre l'altitude de 6 000 m. Il n'existe cependant pas de preuve, aujourd'hui, d'exploits d'alpi-

EN HAUT *Une paysanne et sa fille gardent leurs chèvres sur un alpage estival à quelque 4 200 m d'altitude, non loin du col de Punta Llamac.*

AU MILIEU *Randonneur dans une forêt de quenual. Cette espèce rustique à l'écorce rouge est endémique dans les hautes Andes, où elle pousse au-dessus de 4 000 m.*

AU CENTRE *Des randonneurs au-dessus du lac Carhuacocha. À l'arrière-plan et au centre, la face est du Yerupaja Grande (6 634 m), le point culminant du bassin hydrographique de l'Amazone.*

nisme dans le Huayhuash ; et il n'y en aura sans doute jamais, considérant la verticalité absolue de ses sommets et les compétences techniques requises.

L'équipe géographique autrichienne de Erwin Schneider et A. Awerzger réalisa la première ascension dans le massif de Huayhuash, atteignant le sommet du Siula Grande (6 344 m) en 1936. Schneider poursuivit en solo avec le Rasac (6 017 m) et le Yerupaja fut escaladé pour la première fois par les Américains David Harrah et Jim Maxwell, mais une épopée associée à l'escalade dans le Huayhuash reste un récit particulièrement effrayant. En 1986, la face ouest du Siula Grande, inexplorée, fut la scène d'un exemple de survie exceptionnel, relaté dans le livre remarquable de Joe Simpson *Touching the Void*. Grièvement blessé après une chute près du sommet, Simpson était redescendu par son partenaire Simon Yates, dans le blizzard. Le jour baissant, Simpson suspendu au-dessus du vide, Yates commença à glisser. Il fut contraint de couper la corde. Simpson disparut dans une crevasse, laissé pour mort. Malgré plusieurs fractures, il parvint miraculeusement, pendant les deux jours suivants, à se traîner en rampant hors du glacier, et survécut. Une endurance si extraordinaire n'est sans doute pas nécessaire pour le circuit Huayhuash, mais une dose de persévérance peut être utile !

Chiquian, la porte vers le Huayhuash, est accessible par les transports publics. De la route, le massif s'aperçoit d'abord depuis un haut plateau, mais ce n'est que plus tard que la muraille et sa croûte de glace apparaissent. La ville est à deux bons jours de marche du flanc nord de la chaîne. Une piste bien rodée descend à pic du plateau de Chiquian (3 400 m) dans la vallée chaude et sèche du Pativilca, 500 m plus bas. Là, la piste vire à l'est et traverse un paysage poussiéreux de cactus et de broussailles. Au cours des deux semaines à venir, le randonneur va découvrir des exemples de la quintessence des écosystèmes des Andes, car la gamme des altitudes, combinée à la latitude, produit une variété fascinante d'environnements.

À deux heures de Chiquian, des campings abondent sur les rives du fleuve, mais avec très peu d'ombre car la piste suit le Pativilca dans la brousse aride vers l'aval pendant deux heures avant de s'orienter au nord. Ainsi commence les deux jours d'ascension, par les vallées du Pacllon et du Llamac, vers le cœur de la *cordillera*. Une fois dans la vallée du Llamac, le paysage change et la piste passe des bosquets d'eucalyptus, de bons vieux noyers et une grande variété d'arbustes à fleurs. Des colibris butinent des *cantuta*, splendides trompettes rouge vif considérées comme fleur sacrée des Incas, et devenue l'emblème du Pérou.

Llamac (3 200 m), l'un des trois villages rencontrés sur le circuit, est entouré de champs de maïs, à environ sept heures de Chiquian. Une heure en amont, la piste passe Popca – ses deux minuscules boutiques étant les dernières avant une semaine – et bientôt les randonneurs retrouvent une piste carrossable et la suivent pendant cinq heures. C'est sur ce tronçon que les premiers effets de l'altitude peuvent se faire sentir. Il importe de ne pas en faire trop. Il faut adapter son pas à la raréfaction de l'oxygène : à l'altitude des plus hauts cols du parcours, l'organisme n'absorbe plus que soixante pour cent de la quantité d'oxygène disponible au niveau de la mer.

À trois heures dans l'est de Pocpa, le terrain change de nouveau. Aux environs de 3 800 m, des punas d'herbe pâle et rêche (*ichu*) prédominent. Des taches de forêt sombre de *quenual* jalonnent également le paysage. Cette espèce à écorce rouge, propre aux Andes, prospère jusqu'à 4800 m d'altitude et prolifère ici. De nombreuses espèces de mammifères vivent ici, y compris le fugace puma et le lynx des Andes.

Les randonneurs quittent la route à Cuartel Huain (4 150 m), un petit rassemblement de granges au pied de la première ascension majeure du circuit, pour franchir la haute crête vers l'est. Cuartel Huain apporte aussi les tout premiers gros plans sur le massif. Au sud-est, Rondoy (5 870 m) et Ninashanka (5 607 m) dominent tout le champ de vision. L'endroit convient pour camper, bien qu'il soit un peu exposé. Par temps clair, la température peut descendre jusqu'a moins 4° au petit matin, donnant ainsi un avant-goût de ce qui vous attend, le parcours désormais ne devant redescendre qu'une seule fois au-dessous de 4 000 m.

On pourra repérer des condors géants tournoyant plus haut, pendant la montée vers le col de Cacanampunta (4 700 m). La flore est variée et inclut plusieurs plantes médicinales, la *wamanripa* (pour soigner la pneumonie) et la *anqush* (expectorant) notamment. Le col marque la ligne de partage des eaux de l'Amazone et la transition de la *puna* sèche à la *puna* humide. Une heure et demie plus loin, des panoramas époustouflants, par-dessus le lac Mitucocha, sur plusieurs pics enneigés dont se distinguent les sommets jumeaux de Jirishanka et Jirishanka Chico (6 094 m). La luminosité, ici, est intense et avive la netteté du paysage.

CORDILLÈRE HUAYHUASH

LIEU Les Andes du nord du Pérou. Les villes les plus proches sont Chiquian et Cajatambo.

QUAND PARTIR Mai à septembre, saison sèche.

DÉPART/ARRIVÉE Chiquian ; plusieurs cars quotidiens au départ de Lima (8 h) et Huaraz (3 h). Quand la route de Chiquian à Llamac sera terminée, Llamac deviendra le point de départ/arrivée idéal, réduisant la durée de toutes les randonnées de deux jours.

DURÉE 11-14 jours ; 160 km. Plus longue si on explore les vallées secondaires. Demi-circuit alternatif (7-9 jours) de Chiquian à Cajatambo ou inversement.

POINT CULMINANT Punta Cuyoc (4950 m). L'altitude moyenne est bien supérieure à 4000 m.

ASPECTS TECHNIQUES Acclimatation progressive essentielle avant d'entreprendre la randonnée. Pour des raisons sanitaires et de sécurité, la randonnée ne devrait être entreprise qu'en groupe.

MATÉRIEL Emportez toute votre nourriture. Sac à dos, tente, sac de couchage et tapis de sol, chaussures de marche, coupe-vent imperméable, vêtements thermiques, multicouches et blouson chaud, puissant écran solaire, insectifuge. Huaraz dispose de plusieurs agences qui louent du matériel de camping et de randonnée.

MODE DE RANDONNÉE Sac à dos ou expédition. Il est recommandé de louer des ânes pour transporter le matériel. Pas de terrains de camping signalés mais de nombreux sites de camping sauvage sont disponibles. Pas de chalets sur le parcours.

AUTORISATIONS Le Huayhuash ne fait l'objet d'aucune protection et aucun permis n'est requis.

Mitucocha offre d'excellentes possibilités de camping et une petite excursion de trois heures jusqu'à la moraine latérale au-dessus du lac Ninacocha est toujours possible. Pour reprendre le circuit, on contournera la limite sud de la plaine tourbeuse de Janca pendant 45 minutes, puis la piste coupe au nord, remontant une vallée étroite pour grimper tranquillement jusqu'à Punta Carhuac (4650 m). De là, l'imposante forme du Yerupaja se détache parmi une rangée de pics gigantesques. Redescendant vers l'étonnant Laguna Carhuacocha (4200 m), vous aurez un grand choix de campements avec Carnicero (5960 m), Siula Grande (6344 m) et Yerupaja en majestueuse toile de fond.

Reprenant la boucle, l'itinéraire le plus intéressant passe par Laguna Siula Grande, en montant rudement vers la crête de Carnicero (4850 m). Avec un peu de patience, on pourra apercevoir le vicuna dans le lointain. Dans l'ombre du Carnicero, du Jurao (5600 m) et du Trapecio (5644 m), de l'herbe en coussins tapisse le fond de la vallée inondée, et il est étonnamment facile de traverser la vallée en sautant de coussin en coussin ! Le hameau à deux maisons de Huayhuash (4350 m) offre un bon campement.

La montée de 400 m vers le col de Portachuelo est aisée. Depuis le col, la spectaculaire chaîne Raura est visible. De grands troupeaux d'alpaga (apparentés au lama) sont souvent visibles entre ici et Laguna Viconga (4450 m), au bout de la descente. Une trempette dans le bassin naturel proche apporte une détente musculaire bienvenue avant de s'attaquer à la Punta Cuyoc (4950 m). L'ascension de trois heures jusqu'au point culminant de la randonnée se dédouble à mi-chemin : prenez à gauche pour découvrir des vues extraordinaires

CI-DESSUS *Des ânes de somme franchissent le Cacanampunta, l'un des deux seuls cols qui enjambent la chaîne du Huayhuash. L'étroite crête de craie est la ligne de démarcation continentale.*

CI-DESSUS *Le lac Siula et le flanc est acéré de la cordillère Huayhuash. Les randonneurs progressent lentement vers la crête du Carnicero (4850 m).*

CORDILLÈRE DE HUAYHUASH, PÉROU

sur les *cordilleras*. La descente de retour vers le côté ouest de la chaîne conduit jusque dans la longue vallée de Huanacpatay, puis trois heures plus tard, une descente assez raide et poussiéreuse aboutit à la vallée de Huayllapa. L'air se réchauffe comme la piste, prenant à l'ouest sous une cascade impressionnante, vous vous rapprocherez du village de Huayllapa (3 550 m), le point le plus bas depuis Pocpa. Quelques provisions sont disponibles, et le camping est autorisé sur le terrain de football.

La montée de 1 250 m jusqu'au col de Tapush est longue et raide. Elle s'adoucit après Huatia (4 300 m), où le campement est bon, et se termine après cinq heures de marche. Il y a maintenant encore une heure pour descendre jusqu'au plateau de Cashpapampa, puis une autre demi-heure jusqu'au point de jonction avec la vallée de Yaucha. En marche vers l'est, une ascension de deux heures culmine par un passage d'éboulis jusqu'au col de Yaucha (4 800 m), où une rangée de pics enneigés splendides compose une toile de fond idéale pour un bivouac. Le dernier col, Pampa Llamac (4 300 m), est atteint par un sentier serpentant à travers une forêt de *quenual*. Puis c'est une descente de trois heures dans la poussière vers Llamac, suivie d'une heure en aval jusqu'au terrain de camping de Huarangallo. La dernière étape de cinq heures jusqu'à Chiquian culmine par une montée de 500 m qui vous fera transpirer.

CI-DESSUS *Le col de Punta Cuyoc (4 950 m), le point culminant de la randonnée avec à droite le versant est et à gauche le versant ouest des Andes.*

CI-DESSUS *Une* choza *(grange d'alpage) à Jahuacocha, et l'arrière-plan dominé par le double sommet des Jirishanka et le glacier qui alimente le lac Solterococha.*

LE CIRCUIT ALPAMAYO

par Kathy Jarvis

La randonnée de l'Alpamayo est l'un des itinéraires les plus spectaculaires des Andes, ce qui n'est pas peu dire, compte tenu du choix infini qu'offre cette extraordinaire chaîne de montagnes. Les Andes jaillissent de l'océan Pacifique, sur le rebord occidental du continent sud-américain. Elles s'étendent depuis le massif de Santa Marta en Colombie jusqu'au cap Horn au sud, pour une distance totale de plus de 7 000 km. La cordillère Blanche, juste une petite partie de l'ensemble, comprend 33 pics immenses qui s'élèvent à plus de 6 000 m. C'est là qu'est situé le Huascaran, le plus haut sommet du Pérou (6 768 m).

La région ne fut explorée qu'assez récemment – la première ascension de l'Alpamayo fut faite en 1957 par une expédition allemande – mais la *Cordillera Blanca* a, depuis, acquis une renommée comme lieu d'alpinisme et de randonnée d'altitude. Longtemps avant que d'aventureux étrangers ne débarquent pour se rendre compte de la beauté des Andes, des générations d'Indiens avaient vécu, combattu et travaillé au pied de ces pics impressionnants. Rendre visite à certaines des communautés indiennes encore en place est un des points forts de cet itinéraire.

On peut parcourir le circuit Alpamayo à pied dans les deux sens. Du point de vue paysage, il vaut mieux partir du nord et marcher vers le sud, mais les randonneurs doivent être parfaitement acclimatés en raison de l'ascension très rapide les deux premiers jours. Il n'y a aucune voie de dégagement entre les deux premiers cols, rendant impossible l'évacuation éventuelle d'une personne souffrant du mal des montagnes. On achètera toute la nourriture à Huaraz car aucun réapprovisionnement n'est possible sur le parcours. On trouve sur le marché local une grande variété de produits de bonne qualité.

EN HAUT *Les lambeaux d'écorce cuivrés du quennal (Polylepis sericea) encadrent les eaux de saphir du Laguna Chinacocha, au cœur de la cordillère Blanche.*
ENCADRÉ *Les viscacha, qui ressemblent à des lapins, sont souvent visibles, prenant le soleil entre eux parmi les blocs de roche, dans toutes les hautes Andes.*
CI-DESSUS, À DROITE *Les Indiens Quechua, qui habitent la fertile Callejon de Huaylas, vivent de l'élevage et de la culture d'une étonnante variété de plantes des Andes.*

Il est recommandé de partir tôt de Huaraz pour atteindre la piste. Un moyen de transport de location est nécessaire pour les 4 heures de route vers Hualcayan. Ce trajet le long de la vallée agricole de Callejon de Huaylas offre des vues très tentantes de certains des plus hauts sommets de la *Cordillera Blanca*. Copa (6 188 m), Hualcan (6 122 m), la forme impressionnante du Huascaran (6 768 m), les trois pics déchiquetés de Huandoy (6 359 m pour le plus haut) et le Santa Cruz élancé (6 259 m). À Hualcayan (3 000 m), on chargera le matériel et la nourriture pour les neuf jours à venir sur des ânes de location. Le sentier monte, en zigzags abrupts, et offre de magnifiques points de vue sur le Callejon et la vallée du Rio Santa. La gorge de Quebrada de los Cedros plonge vers l'ouest, en longeant les forêts de *quenual* à l'écorce rouge qui tapissent les pentes de la vallée, avec des lagons d'un bleu profond en contrebas. On aura un avant-goût de la beauté de cette randonnée en établissant le campement assez haut à flanc de montagne, à Huishca (4 000 m).

Le deuxième jour, après avoir traversé la Laguna Cullicocha (barrage hydroélectrique sur la rivière) la piste prend un raccourci très près des trois pics acérés et spectaculaires de Santa Cruz ressemblant à des lapins qui vont et viennent entre les blocs de pierre. Le premier col, Paso de los Cedros, nous défie de ses 4 850 m, le plus haut du parcours. Ensuite, on apprécie la descente vers le camp d'Osoruri (4 600 m).

Le lendemain, une courte ascension emmène les randonneurs de l'autre côté du col d'Osoruri (4 750 m) puis dans une longue descente vers la Quebracha de Los Cedros, en contrebas. Il y a là une collectivité agricole, avec des maisons en pisé nichées sur le fond de la vallée, des champs de pommes de terre en terrasse périlleusement perchés en haut des flancs de la vallée, et des chèvres sous la garde d'enfants remarquablement jeunes. La marche sérieuse étant terminée pour la journée, on prendra le temps d'apprécier les alentours au cours d'une promenade tranquille vers le haut de la vallée. La piste suit les rives de la rivière de Los Cedros, avec des cascades dévalant des glaciers de Milluacocha à l'ouest, et un superbe panorama de sommets enneigés apparaissant devant. Cette promenade culmine au camp de Jancarurish (4 200 m) juste sous le fameux pic d'Alpamayo (5 947 m), élu plus belle montagne du monde lors d'un concours organisé en Allemagne en 1966. L'Alpamayo se dresse de manière spectaculaire, telle une pyramide de glace aux formes parfaites, plus petit que ses voisins, mais unique et incomparable par ses formes : deux sommets aigus reliés par une crête-corniche en lame de rasoir.

Le quatrième jour débute par une sérieuse grimpette jusqu'au col de Jancarurish (4 830 m), offrant d'excellents points de vue en arrière, par-dessus les moraines rocailleuses et les lacs brillants comme des bijoux, sur les immenses glaciers et sommets de l'Alpamayo, Jancarurish (5 578 m) et Santa Cruz. Après le col, la piste oblique vers le nord-est et le Pucajirca (6 050 m) apparaît au loin. Une descente douce mène les randonneurs à travers des paysages vallonnés qui peuvent faire penser aux Highlands d'Écosse, avec des vues vers le Callejon de Conchucos, une zone d'agriculture productive s'étendant entre les hauts pics des Andes et les plaines du bassin amazonien. Une brève montée de 400 m conduit à Quebrada Tayapampa et au hameau de Huillca (4 000 m), où on campe pour la nuit.

À DROITE *La rude montée hors de la Quebrada de Los Cedros vers le col de Jankarurish procure aux marcheurs de très beaux points de vue sur la pyramide caractéristique de l'Alpamayo.*

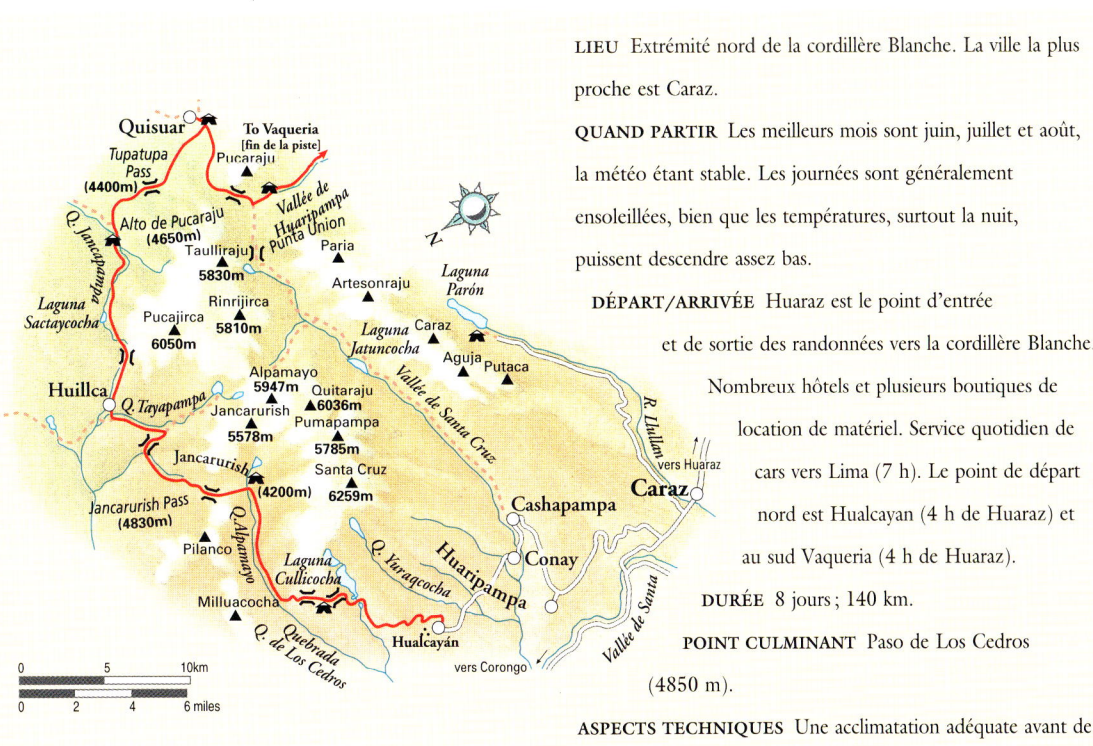

LIEU Extrémité nord de la cordillère Blanche. La ville la plus proche est Caraz.

QUAND PARTIR Les meilleurs mois sont juin, juillet et août, la météo étant stable. Les journées sont généralement ensoleillées, bien que les températures, surtout la nuit, puissent descendre assez bas.

DÉPART/ARRIVÉE Huaraz est le point d'entrée et de sortie des randonnées vers la cordillère Blanche. Nombreux hôtels et plusieurs boutiques de location de matériel. Service quotidien de cars vers Lima (7 h). Le point de départ nord est Hualcayan (4 h de Huaraz) et au sud Vaqueria (4 h de Huaraz).

DURÉE 8 jours ; 140 km.

POINT CULMINANT Paso de Los Cedros (4 850 m).

ASPECTS TECHNIQUES Une acclimatation adéquate avant de partir est indispensable. Les conditions météo en montagne peuvent changer très vite, donc emportez des vêtements pour faire face à toutes les éventualités. L'eau abonde dans les torrents, mais devra être purifiée avant d'être bue.

MATÉRIEL Sac à dos, tente imperméable légère, sac de couchage et tapis de sol, chaussures et vêtements imperméables, thermiques, chapeau, gants, aliments de faible poids et hautement énergétiques, protection solaire, carte, boussole, trousse de secours.

MODE DE RANDONNÉE Sac à dos ou expédition. Il n'y a ni refuge, ni terrains de camping matérialisé sur cet itinéraire ; camping sauvage dans des vallées isolées et magnifiques.

AUTORISATIONS/RESTRICTIONS Le parcours se trouve dans les limites du Parc National de Huascaran et un permis est nécessaire. Disponible auprès du bureau du Parc National à Huaraz, 25 dollars américains.

LE CIRCUIT ALPAMAYO

De Huillca, la piste grimpe régulièrement, traversant des herbages de puna d'altitude, jusqu'au col suivant à 4 600 m. Un panorama surprenant se dévoile sous le magique Laguna Sactaycocha, ses pentes boisées de *quenual* abritant le *oso de anteojos* (Ours des Andes) et le timide daim des montagnes. Le pucajirca se dresse au-dessus du col. La piste descend à travers ce pays des merveilles jusqu'à la vallée plate et large de Jancapampa (3 500 m) au pied du taulliraju (5 830 m) et du Rinrijirca (5 810 m). La cinquième nuit se passera en cet endroit spectaculaire, où on aura établi le campement.

La montée hors de la vallée conduit au travers d'un village d'altitude de chaumière de pisé. Par leurs méthodes de culture traditionnelles, les Indiens quechuas cultivent des espèces nutritives locales comme les haricots, les pommes de terre et les lupins, avec la seule aide de bœufs et de charrues en bois. L'un des points forts de la randonnée est le col de Tupatupa (4 400 m), d'où un panorama embrassant l'intégralité du massif nord de la *Cordillera Blanca* s'ouvre devant vous. Ce panorama sera la toile de fond spectaculaire de la descente vers le village de Quisuar (3 800 m). Le lendemain, le départ en douceur vers le col Alto de Pucaraju (4 650 m) prend plus de pente en zigzaguant. En haut, un autre panorama à vous couper le souffle se dévoile, sur les pics enneigés, récompensant amplement les efforts déployés dans la montée – le sommet déchiqueté du pic de Taulliraju au nord-ouest est impressionnant.

Une piste rocailleuse et raide descend en serpentant pour rejoindre la vallée de Huaripampa et le dernier jour consistera en une douce promenade jusqu'à la route, au bas de la vallée. Quittant la randonnée à Vaqueria, prenez un car au village pour effectuer un mémorable voyage de retour vers Huaraz. L'étroite route de montagne retraverse vers la vallée de la Santa en passant par le col de Portachuelo (4 767 m), avec des vues de cartes postales sur les lacs de Llanganuco au loin, et sur Huascaran en gros plan.

CI-DESSUS *Le majestueux condor des Andes, dont l'envergure excède souvent 1 m, plane au-dessus des pentes abruptes, en quête d'une charogne pour se nourrir.*

CI-DESSOUS *Les chevaux sont utilisés comme bêtes de somme par les communautés locales des Andes. De nombreuses familles complètent leurs revenus en travaillant comme arrieros (conducteurs d'ânes) pendant la saison des randonnées.*

CI-DESSUS *Les randonneurs admirent la profonde vallée du Llanganuco. Des promeneurs journaliers font souvent le déplacement depuis Huaraz jusqu'aux lacs pittoresques d'Orcancocha et de Chinacocha.*

LE CIRCUIT ILLAMPU

par Kathy Jarvis

La cordillère Royale émerge de la rive est du lac Titicaca, sur les hauts plateaux boliviens appelés altiplano. L'impressionnante chaîne de pics déchiquetés couverts de glace fait partie de l'immense chaîne des Andes, qui se prolonge sur 7 000 km, autrement dit toute la longueur du continent sud-américain. La cordillère Royale s'étend sur 150 km entre le sud-est de la plus grande ville de Bolivie, La Paz, et le massif d'Illampu (6 368 m) et Ancohuma (6 427 m) au nord-ouest. Plusieurs anciennes routes empierrées franchissent la chaîne, témoins de l'existence de civilisations précolombiennes. Ces routes laborieusement construites vont de l'altiplano aux plaines tropicales fertiles à l'est des Andes, et on les attribue habituellement aux Incas, qui aux XVe et XVIe siècles contrôlaient presque toute la Bolivie et le Pérou. On pense que la plupart de l'or inca de l'ancienne capitale Cusco provenait de la région de Tipuani, à l'est des Andes. Il y a toujours des mines d'or dans cette région. De solides routes empierrées étaient également utiles pour le déploiement des armées incas à mesure qu'ils étendaient leur empire. Depuis, tout un système de routes a été mis au point pour le commerce ainsi que pour transporter les minerais de valeur comme l'or et l'argent. Un tel labyrinthe de sentiers constitue la seule ligne de communication entre les villages indiens isolés et le monde extérieur.

Le circuit Illampu suit ces pistes bien rodées pendant sept jours, conduisant les randonneurs assez haut, autour des flancs du massif Illampu Ancohuma. Le parcours normal peut être rallongé si on s'accorde le temps de monter bien au-dessus de la Sorata de Laguna Chillata (4 204 m) et Laguna Glaciar. À l'altitude essoufflante de 5 038 m, le Laguna Glaciar est alimenté directement depuis celui d'Illampu. Pour les Indiens locaux Aymara, il est recommandé de s'attacher les services d'un guide local pour ce détour de trois jours. La piste principale

EN HAUT *Dans la cordillère Royale, les lamas servent encore de bêtes de somme, comme au temps des Incas. Il faut parfois plusieurs jours aux locaux pour transporter leurs produits depuis les plus lointains villages.*

CI-DESSUS *Les Indiens Aymara qui vivent sur le haut plateau sur les rives du lac Titicaca utilisent pour la pêche des embarcations de roseaux faites à la main.*

d'Illiampu traverse des fermes isolées, des zones de végétation variée allant des palmiers subtropicaux luxuriants, à des vallées semi-arides, cultivées en terrasses depuis des millénaires, jusqu'à la forêt féerique de polypepis noueux et rabougris. La piste finit par arriver dans une *puna* (haut plateau froid et sec) de type alpin, où seules quelques plantes bien acclimatées s'agrippent au sol gelé en permanence. Plus bas, sur la piste, où la flore est abondante, il y a aussi une faune très variée : les membres craintifs de la famille des camélidés, les *vicuna*, paissent avec méfiance, jadis chassés jusqu'à leur quasi-extinction pour leur belle fourrure ; les *viscachas* (rongeurs ressemblant à des lapins) vont et viennent parmi les blocs de pierre ; les oies des Andes et autres oiseaux aquatiques peuplent les nombreux lacs. Le plus majestueux de tous, le condor des Andes, plane au-dessus, en quête d'une charogne pour son repas.

Tournant le dos aux palmiers de la douce Sorata (2 678 m), la piste remonte assez rudement hors de la ville, serpentant au-dessus de la vallée de la Lakathia, vers le petit village de Quilambaya. À ce stade, trouver sa route peut encore être délicat, et il est fortement recommandé de s'attacher les services d'un guide local et d'ânes, au moins pour ce premier jour. À Quilambaya, prenez à gauche à l'embranchement, le long d'une avenue de grands cactus, et continuez à grimper. Le sentier retrouve l'horizontale, puis vire à gauche, puis à droite pour passer le pont qui enjambe la Lakathiya. Continuer la montée par la piste sinueuse jusqu'au village de Lakathiya. Traversant le village, gardez l'œil vers la gauche, guettant le confluent de deux bras de la rivière. Suivez la rive gauche du bras gauche, traversant la rivière par un petit pont de pierre, puis continuer sur la piste jusqu'à ce que la vallée s'élargisse et vous propose d'excellentes zones de camping tapissées d'herbe bien grasse (4 000 m).

CI-DESSUS *La face ouest de l'Ancohuma. Après avoir fait le tour de ses versants glacés, les randonneurs passent le dernier jour de piste dans les jardins subtropicaux et les verdoyantes terrasses un peu plus bas.*
CI-DESSOUS *Une montée à pic amène les randonneurs assez haut sur les pentes de l'Illampu, jusqu'au lac de Laguna Glaciar (5 038 m), souvent encombré d'icebergs provenant du glacier qui le surplombe.*

CI-DESSUS *Sur les versants est des Andes, l'ichu, l'herbe caractéristique des alpages andins, laisse la place aux pentes verdoyantes et boisées des Yungas, une région agricole fertile.*

Le lendemain, la montée vers le col se poursuit. Alors que la vallée s'élargit, l'itinéraire vire vers le nord, le long d'un ruisseau. La piste devient plus raide, zigzaguant presque verticalement jusqu'au premier col de la randonnée, Abra Illampu (4 741 m). Des troupeaux de lamas relèvent la tête, délaissant pour un temps leur pâture d'herbe dure *ichu*, semblant admirer le paysage splendide, indifférents à la présence des randonneurs fatigués. En avant, la vue du pic recouvert de glace d'Illampu est exaltante. De profondes vallées verdoyantes redescendent derrière, et la vaste mer intérieure que forme le lac Titicaca scintille dans le lointain.

À partir du col, la piste descend la vallée herbue de Quebrada Illampu jusqu'à la rivière Chuchu Jahuira et la piste de Sorata à Ancohuma et Cocoyo. Suivre la route qui descend doucement avant de prendre la direction du sud-est à partir du hameau d'Estancia Utana Pampa. Des maisons d'apparence antique, bâties de pierre et couvertes de chaume, flanquées d'enclos labourés et plantés d'espèces indigènes. *Quinoa*, une céréale riche en protéines aux feuilles rouges caractéristiques, est la principale culture. On en fait une soupe délicieuse. Prenez garde de ne pas marcher sur des pommes de terre éparpillées sur le sol, en train de se lyophiliser en *chuno*, qui sera stocké pour être reconstitué en ragoût plus tard. La vie dans les alpages n'a que peu changé dans ces vallées lointaines des Andes. Traversez la rivière Anco Huma Jahuira par un pont de pierre et continuez vers le haut de la vallée pour trouver de bons lieux de campement pour la nuit.

Le lendemain, continuez à marcher vers le sud-est, en une montée assez raide vers la vallée suspendue sous Abra Korahuasi (4 479 m), le deuxième col. Après le passage du col, suivez la piste qui redescend à travers une végétation luxuriante, une dénivellation de 1 000 m jusqu'à la vallée verdoyante et plate et le village de Cocoyo un peu plus loin. Il est parfois possible d'acheter des truites fraîches aux enfants qui gardent les troupeaux de lamas, et qui les pêchent dans le torrent qui serpente à travers la vallée. Cocoyo est un village d'éleveurs de lamas et de mineurs ; peu habitués à voir des randonneurs, des enfants ricanant et curieux tendent nerveusement le cou au coin des rues. Suivez les eaux tumultueuses du Sarani, en gardant la rivière sur votre gauche. De nombreux et excellents sites de camping sont à moins d'une heure du village. Quatre heures de montée douce depuis Cocoyo amènent les randonneurs au col Paso Sarani (4 600 m). En grimpant à pic hors de la vallée de la Sarani quelques heures plus tard, regardez au-dessus de vous : l'eau dévale d'une manière spectaculaire vers la pampa tourbeuse en tête de la vallée. Guettez les condors au-dessus de vous et les viscachas sur les blocs rocheux en montant au col.

De l'autre côté du col, la piste descend à pic vers le village isolé de Chajolpaya, qui comporte plusieurs maisons mais peu de signes de vie à part les lamas et les moutons. Aymara est la seule langue que l'on parle ici, et la plus proche boutique est à deux jours de marche, dans la ville d'Achacachi, bien au-delà d'Abra Calzada. Des panoramas spectaculaires sur les lacs de Carrizal et Khota, d'un bleu-vert profond, récompensent les randonneurs de leur longue et régulière ascension du village jusqu'au col le plus haut, et le dernier du parcours, Abra Calzada (5 045 m). Les lieux de camping abondent dans la montée, et il y en a même quelques-uns au sommet, tout contre les glaciers, les sommets glacés dominant le tout. Le col lui-même est large et presque dénudé, juste quelques plantes rustiques et l'omniprésent *ichu* s'accrochent à la terre, luttant pour survivre parmi les rochers érodés par les glaces et les lacs d'eaux de fonte.

La première partie de la descente depuis le col est à pic et délicate pour les ânes. La piste se rétablit bientôt et passe non loin des lacs Carrizal et Khota, traversant un pierrier d'un rouge profond. De Laguna Khota, dirigez-vous vers Laguna San Francisco, à travers la pampa herbue de la Quebrada de Kote, puis vers la crête herbue sur la droite. Du haut de la crête, un panorama impressionnant s'ouvre sur 360 degrés ; le vaste océan intérieur du lac Titicaca dans l'ouest, les hauts sommets de la Cordillera derrière vous. La couleur du paysage, accentuée par la luminosité unique qui baigne l'altiplano, est d'une inégalable beauté. Il y a plusieurs endroits où camper avant d'atteindre Laguna San Francisco, bien qu'il vaille mieux ne pas camper en vue des habitations, les paysans locaux n'étant pas toujours amènes.

En traversant Laguna San Francisco dans son extrémité nord, gardez un œil pour les grandes oies noires et blanches des Andes, qui souvent se nourrissent le long des berges du lac. La piste se porte vers le sommet de la crête, à distance, du côté où se dresse un cairn (4 867 m). À partir de là, l'itinéraire continue hors piste, sans aucune marque. Traversez la prochaine petite vallée avant de virer vers l'ouest, descendant à travers la pampa et dépassant la tête de la vallée de Quebrada Tiquitini. On finit par retrouver un sentier. Suivez le jusqu'a ce que vous rencontriez un chemin de terre, qui conduit au village de Alto Lojena. Vous pourrez peut-être y attraper un camion pour Sorata. Autrement, une autre journée de marche par la route vous amènera à Sorata, en passant par le petit village de Millipaya. Il existe de bons endroits pour camper sur le parcours ; essayez juste après la vieille mine, à une heure de Millipaya, avant le village de Cochipata.

Le paysage change radicalement à mesure que l'on descend des *puna* herbues des cols alpins vers les champs cultivés qui jouxtent de petits villages colorés. Il reste encore quelques points de vue fabuleux sur les imposants massifs glacés de Ancohuma et Illamp en haut, les eaux de fonte cascadant dans de profonds ravins vers le fond de la vallée. La végétation devient prolifique, la température monte et les chants d'oiseaux prolifèrent à mesure que l'on approche de Sorata et d'un repos bienvenue.

CI-DESSUS *Les fêtes folkloriques, souvent inspirées des traditions hispaniques, sont toujours gaies et hautes en couleurs. Les Indiens Aymara viennent de partout pour défiler dans les rues de Sorata.*

LIEU Cordillère Royale, Bolivie occidentale. Environ 150 km de La Paz.

QUAND PARTIR Mai à septembre (saison sèche) sont les meilleurs mois pour la randonnée. Journées ensoleillées et nuits froides.

DÉPART/ARRIVÉE La randonnée part et revient à Sorata (2 695 m, subtropical) au pied des montagnes Illampu et Ancohuma. Cars depuis La Paz (4 h).

DURÉE 6-7 jours ; 90 km.

POINT CULMINANT Abra Calzada (5 045 m).

ASPECTS TECHNIQUES La randonnée passe par des régions d'altitude isolées. Passez plusieurs jours en altitude avant de partir, pour vous assurer d'être bien acclimaté. Soleil puissant et altitude élevée se conjuguent pour augmenter le risque de déshydratation ; buvez beaucoup d'eau. L'eau de torrent est à portée de la main, mais devra être stérilisée avant d'être bue.

MATÉRIEL Emportez toute votre nourriture, sac à dos, tente imperméable légère, sac de couchage et tapis de sol, chaussures et vêtements imperméables, thermiques, chapeau, gants, aliments de faible poids et hautement énergétiques, protection solaire, carte, boussole, trousse de secours. On peut acheter des cartes et louer du matériel à La Paz, guides et ânes sont disponibles à Sorata.

MODE DE RANDONNÉE Sac à dos ou expédition. Camping sauvage, aucun endroit réservé. Ne campez pas près des villages.

AUTORISATIONS/RESTRICTIONS Aucune restriction n'affectant la randonnée ou l'escalade dans la région. Aucun permis n'est requis.

TORRES DEL PAINE

par Chris Hooker

Le Parc national de Torres del Paine s'étend dans les étendues sauvages au plus profond du Chili occidental, en sandwich entre la steppe ventée de Patagonie à l'est et l'énorme calotte glaciaire continentale au nord et à l'ouest. Au sud-ouest, il y a les fjords et les îles de l'archipel du Chili. Le Paine fait partie des Parcs nationaux d'Amérique les plus spectaculaires. Une merveille de sculpture naturelle, ses 2 422 km² présentent un grand nombre des paysages caractéristiques et spectaculaires de Patagonie : flèches de granit élancées, glaciers, lacs brillants comme des joyaux, de forêt Magellanique dense. Quant à la faune sauvage, les zones de végétation contrastées abritent de nombreuses espèces aviaires et mammifères, dont certaines sont endémiques. L'Unesco reconnaîtra cette particularité unique en 1978, en accordant au parc le statut de Patrimoine mondial.

Il y a quelque chose d'un autre monde dans le massif Paine aux contours invraisemblables (3 000 m). Il se dresse à pic depuis un plateau de faible altitude, et constitue la pièce centrale, le pivot du Parc. C'est également la plaque tournante du grand circuit de randonnée de Paine, une boucle exigeante de 10 jours qui emmène les randonneurs au cœur immaculé de l'une des étendues sauvages les plus époustouflantes du monde. Les vents d'ouest féroces font partie intégrante de l'expérience Paine. Ils sont principalement dus à la présence assez proche du grand glacier sud de Patagonie, une énorme anomalie considérant la latitude modeste – quelque 50 degrés sud. À une époque relativement récente (en termes de géologie), toute cette région était étranglée par les glaces ; les glaciers colossaux qui se frayent un chemin dans le parc aujourd'hui sont l'héritage de cette époque révolue.

L'époustouflant mur de granit de la chaîne de Paine est d'abord vu de loin, lorsqu'on approche de Puerto Natales, et ses traits particuliers se révèlent clairement lorsqu'on contourne les berges est du Lago Sarmiento. Le Cerro Paine Grande (3 000 m) domine son

EN HAUT *Le massif Paine vu du sud par-dessus les eaux de fonte des glaces du Lago Pehoe. En arrière-plan, les Cuernos (à droite) et le Cerro Paine Grande caché par les nuages.*

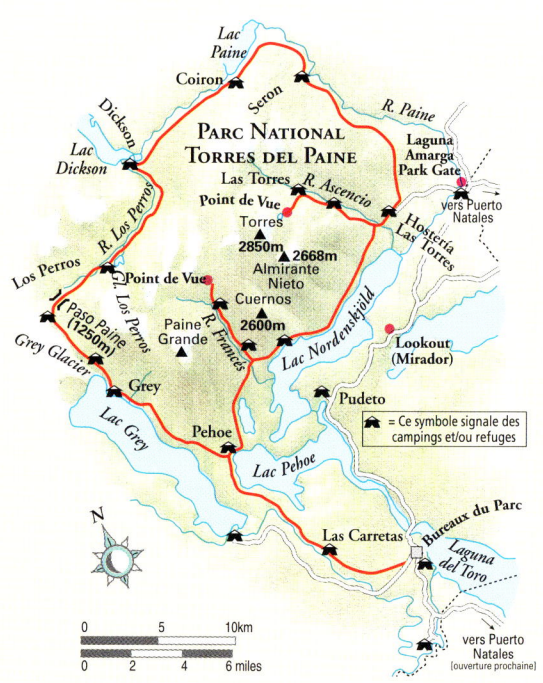

LIEU Sud Chili, 12ᵉ Région. 110 km au nord de Puerto Natales, 400 km au nord de Punta Arenas.

QUAND PARTIR Octobre à avril, jours très longs.

DÉPART/ARRIVÉE Plusieurs liaisons quotidiennes par car de Punta Arenas au Parc. Arrêts à Laguna Amarga, Pudeto (3 traversées de lac par jour) et au QG du Parc. Sortie par les mêmes.

DURÉE 10 jours ; 135 km, y compris excursions et jour(s) de repos. Option 5 jours, Randonnée « W » : Grey-Pehoe-Valle Francés-Torres, sortie par Laguna Amarga.

POINT CULMINANT John Gardiner Pass (1 250 m).

MODE DE RANDONNÉE Sac à dos.

ASPECTS TECHNIQUES Les pistes signalées par des marques de peinture orange sont encombrées. Il y a des tourbières à traverser, des rivières à franchir, et des ravins à négocier. Parcours à contre sens recommandé, évitant de commencer par les montées les plus dures.

Des vents de plus de 160 km/h peuvent retarder votre avance et nécessitent une grande prudence en terrain exposé. La neige peut être très profonde près des cols et peut masquer la piste, surtout en début de saison.

MATÉRIEL Emportez toute votre nourriture (énergétique et de faible poids), cartes d'état-major, sac à dos, tente, sac de couchage et tapis de sol, chaussures de marche, vêtements imperméables et coupe-vent, thermiques, vêtements à séchage rapide, protection solaire, insectifuge. On peut louer presque tout le matériel de camping à Puerto Natales.

AUTORISATIONS/RESTRICTIONS Droit d'entrée au parc national (16 USD) payable en pesos chiliens. S'inscrire avec son passeport à l'arrivée, émarger en partant. Le parc est bien géré par CONAF. Les gardes sont serviables.

flanc occidental tandis que sur sa droite, le Cuernos (Cornes) le bien nommé s'élance vers le ciel. Le Cerro Almirante Nicto forme l'épaule orientale du massif, masquant l'éponyme Torres. Ces trois colonnes polies par le gel de granit rose apparaissent au loin quand on approche de Laguna Amarga, point d'entrée dans le parc national, en venant de l'est. Dans le parc, l'herbe grise *cuiron* cède la place à la bruyère pré-andine à perte de vue, l'une des quatre communautés florales de Paine. Nous sommes au pays du *guanaco*, et les rencontres inopinées avec des groupes de ces camélidés (antérieurement en voie de disparition) ne sont pas rares.

Une fois à l'intérieur du parc national, et faisant route vers le nord, vers le refuge de Pudeto et le poste forestier, le chemin de terre serpente à travers une zone qui se caractérise au printemps par ses fleurs de *calafate* jaune vif et le *notro* (buisson ardent) rouge feu. L'itinéraire vire à l'ouest et passe bien au-dessus du Lago Nordenskjold bleu turquoise, qui brille aux éclats à la base du massif. Les spectateurs ébahis sont, pour la première fois ici, confrontés avec l'extraordinaire échelle du paysage : le lac n'est qu'à 60 m au-dessus du niveau de la mer tandis que les fantastiques sommets de granit au nord s'élancent jusqu'à 3 000 m plus haut. Pudeto n'est qu'à un peu plus de trois heures de Natales en car. De forts vents d'ouest peuvent changer Lago Pehoe en un chaudron bouillonnant de moutons, mais par beau temps clair, la traversée en catamaran de Pudeto à Refugio Pehoe est un vrai plaisir. Au nord, les Cuernos se projettent à 2 600 m vers le ciel. Leur stratification et conicité inhabituelles – couronnes en forme de tétine – résultent d'un schiste sombre et friable qui recouvre leur base de granit. Les Cuernos, en fait le massif tout entier, trouvèrent leurs origines géologiques il y a 12 millions d'années lors d'une convulsion tectonique qui projeta violemment vers le haut un vaste bloc de roche en fusion. (Cette chaîne compacte n'appartient pas strictement à la chaîne des Andes, bien plus ancienne, dont la médiane est plus à l'ouest.) Depuis, l'action de la glaciation et l'érosion par les glaces ont fendu et poli le batholite, lui donnant son merveilleux profil actuel. Cap à l'ouest, le bateau arrive bientôt dans l'ombre du Cerro Paine Grande, souvent pris dans les nuages.

La disposition du refuge de Pehoe est spectaculaire mais exposée. Le campement dispose de coupe-vent, mais les tempêtes peuvent arracher une tente mal plantée en quelques minutes. Le circuit commence par une

EN HAUT *Panorama sur la vallée Francés. Dans le lointain (à droite), les formes granitiques des Cerro Castillo, Cota, Catedral, Aguja de los Quirquinchos et Genelos.*

AU CENTRE *Un lenga (hêtre du sud) définitivement courbé par des décennies de vent à 160 km/h. Le lenga à feuilles caduques domine dans la dense forêt de Paine.*

157

marche ondulatoire vers les Cuernos, à travers une alternance de prairie mélangée et de forêt éparse, passant deux petits lacs investis par les canards, les foulques et d'occasionnels grèbes. Au bout de deux heures, la piste descend jusqu'au Rio Francés et emprunte un pont suspendu. À gauche, le Campamento Italiano consiste en plusieurs clairières entourées de forêt Magellanique d'arbres caducs. La première excursion, abrupte par endroits, va vers la spectaculaire Valle Francés.

Une bonne partie de la principale ascension traverse des forêts de *lenga* (hêtre du sud). La piste quitte bientôt la forêt pour tomber sur des blocs de moraines, nécessitant quelques courtes séances de varappe à pic. Des explosions périodiques et effrayantes annoncent la mise bas de glaces par les glaciers de la face est du Paine Grande, à gauche. Les glaciers en désintégration sont en principe libres de tout nuage car la vallée se trouve généralement sous le vent de la montagne. Par temps entièrement dégagé, des champignons de glace, une exclusivité des sommets patagoniens, perchent sur les sommets du Paine Grande, là-bas, très haut. La montée se poursuit en passant par une cascade, puis vers une crête de moraines fouettée par le vent. On doit vaincre une tourbière avant d'atteindre le Campamento Britanico, deux heures plus tard. Une cabane branlante se tient au milieu d'une clairière. Un point de vue, immédiatement après, offre des panoramas frappants sur les Cuernos, dans l'est. Au nord, une paroi de granit recouvert de schiste a été sculptée par la glace et le vent en d'étranges formes, parmi lesquelles l'Aleta de Tiburon (aileron de requin). Le trajet de retour au Campamento Italiano prendra une heure et demie.

L'étape suivante, une longue marche contournant la rive nord du Lago Nordenskjold, traverse un terrain varié avant d'atteindre le refuge et le camping de Los Cuernos. Deux heures encore vers le nord-est à travers un terrain ondoyant, avant que la piste ne débouche sur des pâturages de plaine, tout près de l'Hosteria Las Torres. Si vous avez encore assez d'énergie, l'itinéraire recommandé part sur la gauche et monte dans la vallée d'Ascencio, emprunte un sentier raide et zigzagant qui bifurque vers le ravin où bouillonne le torrent, beaucoup plus bas. La piste redescend et arrive au Refugio Chileno. Il faudra encore une heure et demie de montée et deux traversées de rivière avant d'arriver au camping de Las Torres. Avec un peu de patience, vous pourrez peut-être apercevoir (ou entendre) l'un des oiseaux extravertis qui peuplent la forêt patagonienne : le strident perroquet austral (l'espèce de perroquet vivant le plus au sud au monde), le pivert couronné ou le Pic Chilien marbré.

CI-DESSUS *La magnifique Torres del Paine. Ces parois sont soumises à des conditions climatiques extrêmes et offrent des escalades qui comptent parmi les plus difficiles au monde.*

CI-DESSUS *Franchissement précaire du Rio Los Perros non loin de Laguna Los Perros avant la longue ascension vers le col John Gardiner. De tels passages sont caractéristiques de l'arrière-pays de Paine.*

PATAGONIE, CHILI

Le sentier débouche sur une pente sablonneuse, au-dessus du camping dissimulé dans les bois. Les marques de la piste conduisent, à gauche, vers une large pente de blocs rocheux, puis remonte jusqu'à l'observatoire Laguna Torre. Fixez-vous comme objectif d'y être le matin, quand le soleil est sur les Tours. Une dernière escalade par-dessus les blocs de pierre s'achève au bord de la moraine (1 000 m), avec des vues spectaculaires des trois piliers surgissant au-dessus du cirque incrusté de glace. La descente sur l'hôtel Hostería Las Torres, refuge et terrain de camping privé prendra trois heures, puis la piste du Circuit continue à contre sens jusqu'à Campamento Seron. Des ibis hululants au cou chamois et des vanneaux plongeurs prolifèrent dans la partie est du parc. Il est également courant de voir des couples d'oies des montagnes. La piste suit le Rio Paine, traversant des prairies en fleurs. Des plantations de lenga squelettiques rappellent les traditions de culture sur brûlis des fermiers. Ce secteur ne fut déclaré site protégé qu'en 1975.

À une heure de Seron, la piste remonte sur la gauche jusqu'à un épaulement, puis descend vers l'ouest, dévoilant d'autres panoramas dans le nord. Deux heures plus loin, Campamento Coiron, puis une marche de trois heures sur plat, à travers des tourbières, s'achève au Refugio Dickson. Des icebergs gros comme des maisons traversent le Lago Dickson, la source du système hydrologique du parc national.

La montée de 1 000 m qui part du Refugio Dickson est la plus difficile du circuit. Le sentier suit le torrent de Los Perros à travers une forêt dense. Cinq heures plus tard, la piste arrive au Laguna Los Perros, plein d'icebergs, et au camping de Los Perros, à la situation spectaculaire. Au-dessus de la ligne des arbres, les quelques dernières centaines de mètres sont parcourues sur la roche nue. Une navigation attentive est nécessaire par temps bouché ou dans la neige profonde. Prenez garde aussi aux vents violents au Paso Paine (1 250 m). Par temps clair, la vue récompense amplement les efforts : le vaste glacier bleu-gris dégringolant 1 000 m plus bas.

La piste signalisée redescend, puis continue à travers une forêt. Humide, le sol y est très glissant. Le premier campement, Campamento Paso, est à deux heures du col, et Campamento Los Guardas encore trois heures plus loin. La piste s'améliore dans le dernier tronçon forestier, jusqu'au fameux Refugio Grey, situé non loin du « museum » du glacier en récession rapide.

Les dernières quatre heures jusqu'au Refugio Pehoe sont fabuleuses. Après une heure de montée, d'abord régulière, puis abrupte, les randonneurs ont une vue frappante sur le glacier Grey bordé de forêts. En automne, quand les feuilles de lenga tournent au rouge vif, le spectacle est étourdissant. Un peu plus loin, la partie sud, couverte d'icebergs, du Lago Grey apparaît. Un des signes alarmants de l'accélération de la fonte des glaces polaires. Enfin, le sentier franchit une crête basse, vire au sud-est et descend pendant une heure jusqu'au Refugio Pehoe. On sort soit par le QG du parc, soit en bateau en traversant le Lago Tahoe.

CI-DESSOUS *Des icebergs géants se détachent du Grey Glacier avant de dériver sur toute la longueur du lac Grey et de s'échouer sur la rive sud, quelque 7 km plus loin.*

159

BIOGRAPHIES DES AUTEURS

SHAUN BARNETT

La passion de **Shaun Barnett** pour les montagnes et la randonnée s'est développée à l'adolescence en Nouvelle-Zélande. Depuis, il a parcouru toute la Nouvelle-Zélande, l'Australie, l'Amérique du Sud, le Canada, le Népal et l'Alaska. Écologiste de formation, Shaun a travaillé pour le Département néo-zélandais pour la protection de la nature. Depuis 1996, il est écrivain et photographe à temps plein, et son premier ouvrage *Classic Tramping in New Zealand*, écrit en collaboration avec Rob Brown, s'est vu décerner le *2000 Montana Book Award* dans la catégorie Environnement. Il vit à Wellington avec sa femme Tania.

Hamish Brown est un écrivain, alpiniste, photographe, éducateur et conférencier professionnel, devenu l'autorité anglophone en ce qui concerne l'Atlas marocain. Né à Colombo, il découvrit très tôt la vie au grand air et, depuis, il n'a cessé de parcourir le monde. Ses ascensions et ses expéditions l'ont conduit de l'Arctique à la cordillère des Andes, des Alpes à l'Himalaya, mais ce sont les montagnes de l'Atlas marocain qui ont « volé son cœur ». Il conduit maintenant de petites randonnées exploratoires dans l'Atlas pendant cinq mois de l'année. Avec le guide local Ali, de Taroudant, il fut le premier à prendre conscience du potentiel de l'Atlas occidental et, toujours avec lui, Hamish a parcouru à pied l'intégralité de l'Anti-Atlas et du Haut Atlas, cette dernière expédition ayant duré quatre-vingt-seize jours, parcouru 900 km et franchi trente sommets. Il a tenu le rôle principal d'une émission de télévision sur l'Atlas occidental et en 2000 il fut consacré *Honorary Fellow of the Royal Geographic Society*. Il travaille actuellement à un ouvrage consacré aux premières explorations dans les montagnes de l'Atlas.

HAMISH BROWN

JOHN CHAPMAN

John Chapman est l'un des photographes et écrivains d'Australie les plus expérimentés en randonnée de brousse. En plus de mille six cents jours de marche, il a largement exploré tous les États d'Australie. Au cours des vingt-deux dernières années, il a écrit cinq livres, partagé pendant cinq ans une rubrique sur les randonnées en brousse dans un quotidien important, *The Age*, et il a écrit plus de cent articles pour des magazines spécialisés. Il a aussi guidé de nombreuses randonnées commerciales en Tasmanie, au Népal et en Inde. Ses photographies sont présentes dans nombre de publications. John a remporté de nombreux concours internationaux de photographie, et il est maintenant lui-même juge-arbitre de tels concours. Il s'est vu décerner diverses distinctions en tant que photographe, y compris celle de l'*Australian Photographic Society*.

KATE CLOW

Kate Clow naquit et grandit au Royaume-Uni, puis fit carrière dans l'informatique tout en s'adonnant à la moto « tout-terrain ». Au cours de voyages en moto à travers la France et l'Espagne, elle a parcouru le réseau des voies romaines et visité de nombreux sites historiques dans les montagnes. En poste à Istanbul, elle apprit le turc en vendant des ordinateurs au gouvernement et en poursuivant des études à l'université d'Istanbul. Il y a huit ans, elle déménagea pour Antalya, au pied de la fabuleuse chaîne du Taurus. Elle commença à collectionner les cartes et à rechercher le réseau routier antique, à pied ou à moto. La première randonnée au long cours de Turquie, la Route de Lycie, est le fruit de ses recherches. Aujourd'hui, elle vit de son écriture et de ses photographies, tout en conduisant des groupes de randonneurs sur les sentiers antiques.

Peter Cook développa son goût pour le plein air et son vif intérêt pour la faune et la flore d'Australie dès son plus jeune âge. Depuis plus de vingt-cinq ans, il parcourt toute l'Australie en sa qualité d'instructeur en formation de plein air, de dirigeant d'un club récréatif de plein air, ainsi que pour ses propres de loisirs. Il a mis au point des brevets de qualification pour l'encadrement et la sécurité en plein air. Il est membre actif et bénévole d'organisations de sauvetage. En 1993, il publia un ouvrage intitulé *Walking in the Wilderness Coast*, en collaboration avec son ami et collègue Chris Dowd.

PETER COOK

David Emblidge a passé le plus clair de sa vie d'adulte avec des chaussures de marche aux pieds. Né à Buffalo, New York, il grandit en faisant de la voile sur le lac Erié, à partir de la résidence d'été canadienne de sa famille. Il associe souvent son passé littéraire et journalistique à des aventures montagnardes ou maritimes. Sur la Piste des Appalaches, il a parcouru à pied sept des onze États, et le Connecticut, Massachusetts et le Vermont dans leur totalité, tout en écrivant *Hikes in the Southern New England* pour une collection appelée Exploring the Appalachian Trail (Stackpole). Emblidge a aussi créé The Appalachian Trail Reader (Oxford). Il effectua sa randonnée dans les profondeurs du Grand

Canyon et sa croisière des Bermudes au Connecticut à la voile parce que « l'occasion était trop belle pour la manquer ». La vie urbaine l'attire aussi. Il a travaillé à New York comme rédacteur pour Cambridge University Press. Emblidge vit maintenant à Seattle, Washington, où il est rédacteur en chef de *The Mountaineers Books*.

DAVID EMBLIDGE

L'amour de **Chris Hooker** pour les grands espaces et son métier de guide l'ont conduit vers de nombreuses régions perdues de par le monde. Mais son grand amour reste l'Amérique latine, où il est né, a grandi et passé le plus clair de sa vie d'adulte.

Des années à faire le guide, des randonnées, de l'escalade et du cyclisme, de l'Amazone aux Andes, du Pérou en Patagonie, lui ont permis d'acquérir une connaissance approfondie de ce continent. On le trouve généralement (ou on ne le trouve pas !) quelque part loin de tout, soit conduisant des randonnées ou préparant de nouveaux itinéraires.

Chris est copropriétaire de Andean Trails, une société de voyages basée au Royaume-Uni, spécialisée dans les expéditions vers les grands espaces d'Amérique du Sud.

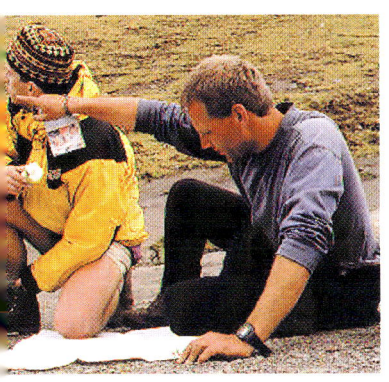

CHRIS HOOKER

Kathy Jarvis a grandi en Écosse, où elle fut initiée aux joies de la randonnée en montagne. Sa carrière en Amérique du Sud débuta quand elle partit travailler comme guide touristique au Chili et au Pérou dans les années 90. Pendant quelques années, tout son temps libre fut employé à explorer les Andes, mais elle passe maintenant de plus en plus de temps à son bureau en tant qu'associée de Andean Trails, une société spécialisée dans les randonnées à pied et à bicyclette qui organise des circuits au Pérou, en Bolivie et en Patagonie. Cela lui fournit d'excellentes occasions pour conduire des groupes sur ses parcours favoris, et passer quelques mois par an à explorer de nouveaux itinéraires à travers les Andes. Kathy n'a pas de préférence particulière parmi les pays des Andes, du moment qu'on y trouve des paysages spectaculaires, des espaces déserts, des populations locales, une faune sauvage et la liberté de marcher.

KATHY JARVIS

Mike Lundy a passé sa vie à parcourir de nombreuses régions d'Afrique du Sud. Il a écrit cinq livres et de nombreux articles de magazines sur le sujet. Il a été chroniqueur pour deux quotidiens sud-africains, produisant plus de deux cents articles sur la marche, ainsi que des émissions de radio hebdomadaires sur le sujet. En 1996, il reçut la médaille du mérite de la part de la fédération de randonnées d'Afrique du Sud, pour les services exceptionnels rendus à la communauté des marcheurs d'Afrique du Sud. Mike vit au Cap, qu'il décrit comme la capitale mondiale de la randonnée touristique. Ayant parcouru au moins cinquante pays dans le monde, il espère être assez qualifié et qu'on lui pardonne d'être si chauvin.

MIKE LUNDY

Kathy Ombler est un écrivain indépendant dont les intérêts englobent l'écotourisme, le voyage et la protection de la nature. Au cours des vingt dernières années, elle a séjourné ou visité tous les parcs nationaux de Nouvelle-Zélande. Elle a aussi profité de nombreuses années de randonnée et de camping avec des amis ou en famille dans les grands espaces sauvages magnifiques et variés de son pays. Elle a écrit plusieurs ouvrages et articles de magazine sur la protection de la nature et a participé à l'écriture et à la recherche sur la gestion des parcs nationaux et autres organisations de protection de la nature. Son ouvrage le plus récent s'intitule *National Parks and other Wild Places of New Zealand* (New Holland).

KATHY OMBLER

Hilary Sharp aime marcher dans la montagne depuis l'enfance. Professeur qualifié d'éducation de plein air, Hilary a passé plusieurs années dans des centres de plein air en Grande-Bretagne avant de s'installer dans les Alpes françaises, près de Chamonix. A partir de ce point de départ, elle conduit des randonnées dans toutes les Alpes européennes, les Pyrénées, en Corse et dans les autres îles méditerranéennes.

Également fervente adepte du ski et de la course à pied, elle passe beaucoup de son temps, hiver comme été, à explorer les montagnes autour de chez elle et plus loin. Elle a beaucoup marché et escaladé en Europe, Afrique, Amérique du Nord, Australie et Thaïlande, et elle s'intéresse particulièrement à la flore et la faune des régions montagneuses qu'elle visite.

HILARY SHARP

Hilary est l'auteur du *New Holland Globetrotter Adventure Guide – Trekking and Climbing in the Western Alps* et elle travaille actuellement à la préparation d'un guide de marche en raquettes dans les Alpes. Elle travaille régulièrement pour le magazine britannique *High*.

PAGES SUIVANTES *Les porteurs Balti sur le Snow Lake dans le Karakoram. Emmener des hommes de la région dans les hauts glaciers est une très lourde responsabilité – ils doivent être correctement équipés et encadrés à longueur de temps.*

BIBLIOGRAPHIE

AMERIQUE DU SUD

BRADT, HILARY. *Peru and Bolivia Backpacking and Trekking*, Bradt Publications, Bucks, RU (1999)

JARVIS, KATHY. *Ecuador, Peru and Bolivia The Backpacker's Manual*, Bradt Publications, Bucks, RU (2000)

AFRIQUE

ALLAN, IAIN. *Guide to Mount Kenya & Kilimanjaro*, Mountain Club of Kenya, Nairobi (1998)

BRISTOW, DAVID. *Best Hikes in South Africa*, Struik Publishers, Cape Town (1992)

BURMAN, JOSE. *Cape Trails and Wilderness Areas*, Human & Rousseau, Cape Town (1992)

ELSE, DAVID. *Walking in Africa 1 – Kenya*, Robertson McCarta, Londres (1991)

FINLAY, HUGH & CROWTHER, GEOFF. *Kenya – A Travel Survival Kit*, Lonely Planet, Australie (1997)

GRAHAM, ROBERT CUNNINGHAME. *Mogreb-el-Acksa*, Heinemann, Londres (1898)

MAXWELL, GAVIN. *Lord of the Atlas*, Cassel, Londres (2001)

OLIVIER, WILLIE & SANDRA. *The Guide to Backpacking & Wilderness Trails*, Southern Book Publishers, Johannesburg (1989)

OLIVIER, WILLIE & SANDRA. *The Guide to Hiking Trails*, Southern Book Publishers, Johannesburg (1988)

THOMSON, JOSEPH. *Travels in the Atlas & Southern Morocco*, George Philip & Son, Londres (1889)

The Rough Guide to Morocco. Rough Guides, Londres (2001)

WAGNER, PATRICK. *The Otter Trail*, Struik Publishers, Cape Town (1993)

EUROPE

CASTLE, ALAN. *The Corsica High Level Route*, Cicerone Press, Cumbria, RU (1992)

REYNOLDS, K. *Walks and Climbs in the Pyrenees*, Cicerone Press, Cumbria, RU (1993)

TOWNSEND, CHRIS. *Long Distance Walks in the Pyrenees*, The Crowood Press, Swindon, RU (1991)

Translated by PRETTY, HARRY & MCPHAIL, HELEN. *Walks in Corsica GR20*, Robertson McCarta, Londres (1990)

ASIE

ARMINGTON, STAN. *Trekking in the Nepal Himalaya*, Lonely Planet, Australie (1997)

ARMINGTON, STAN. *Trekking in Bhutan*, Lonely Planet, Australie (1999)

BEAN, GEORGE. *Lycian Turkey*, Ernest Benn, Londres (1971)

BEZRUCHKA, STEPHEN. *Trekking in Nepal*, Cordee, Leicester (1997)

BOOZ, ELIZABETH. *A Guide to Tibet*, Collins, Londres (1986)

CLOW, KATE. *The Lycian Way*, Upcountry (Turkey) Ltd, Buxton, RU (2000)

DUBUN, MARK & LUCAS, ENVER. *Trekking in Turkey*, Lonely Planet, Australie (1989)

JACCARD, PIERRE & FOLLMI, OLIVIER et al. *Ladakh-Zanskar*, Artou, Genève (1984)

KAPADIA, HARISH. *Across Peaks & Passes in Ladakh, Zanskar & East Karakoram*, Indus, New Delhi (1999)

MACDONALD, DAVID. *Touring in Sikkim and Tibet*, OBS, Siliguri (1943)

NAKANO, TORU. *Trekking in Nepal*, Yama Kei, Tokyo (1984)

POMMARET, FRANÇOISE. *An Illustrated Guide to Bhutan*, The Guidebook Company, Hong Kong (1990)

RAZZETTI, STEVE. *Trekking and Climbing in Nepal*, New Holland, London (2000)

SHAW, ISOBEL. *Pakistan Handbook*, John Murray, Londres (1989)

SHAW, ISOBEL & BEN. *Pakistan Trekking Guide*, Odyssey, Hong Kong (1993)

SNELLING, JOHN. *The Sacred Mountain*, East/West, Londres (1990)

STARK, FREYA. *Alexander's Path*, John Murray, Londres (1958)

SWIFT, HUGH. *Trekking in Nepal, West Tibet & Bhutan*, Hodder & Stoughton, Londres (1990)

SWIFT, HUGH. *Trekking in Pakistan and India*, Hodder & Stoughton, Londres (1990)

VERMA, RAJESH. *Sikkim, Darjeeling, Bhutan – A Guide and Handbook*, Verma, Gangtok (1996)

AUSTRALASIE

BELL, CHRIS. *Beyond the Reach, Cradle Mountain-Lake St Clair National Park*, Laurel Press, Tasmanie (1990)

CHAPMAN, JOHN & SISEMAN, JOHN. *Cradle Mountain-Lake St Clair and Walls of Jerusalem National Parks*, John Chapman, Melbourne (1998)

COOK, PETER & DOWD, CHRIS. *Walking the Wilderness Coast: Lakes Entrance to Pambula. A Bushwalking, Canoeing and Holiday Guide*, Wildcoast Publications, Victoria, Australie (1995)

GIORDANO, MARGARET. *A Man and a Mountain, The Story of Gustav Weindorfer*, Regal Publications, Launceston, Tasmanie (1987)

GREENAWAY, ROB. *The Restless Land – Stories of Tongariro National Park*, Department of Conservation/Tongariro National History Society, Turangi (1998)

OMBLER, KATHY. *National Parks and Other Wild Places of New Zealand*, New Holland, Cape Town (2001)

PEAT, NEVILLE. *Land Aspiring – The Story of Mount Aspiring National Park*, Craig Potton Publishing, Nelson (1994)

The Overland Track, A Walkers Notebook. Parks and Wildlife Service, Tasmanie (1996)

AMERIQUE DU NORD

BRUCE, DAN 'WINGFOOT'. *The Thru-Hiker's Handbook*, Center for Appalachian Trail Studies, Hot Springs, Caroline du Nord (annuel)

CHAZIN, DANIEL. *Appalachian Trail Data Book*, Appalachian Trail Conference, Harpers Ferry, Virginie Occidentale (annuel)

EMBLIDGE, DAVID (Series Editor). *Exploring the Appalachian Trail*, Stackpole Books, Mechanicsburg, Pennsylvanie (1998)

EMBLIDGE, DAVID (Editor). *The Appalachian Trail Reader*, Oxford University Press, New York (1996)

HOUK, ROSE. *Grand Canyon Trail Guide: South Kaibab*, Grand Canyon Natural History Association, Arizona (1981)

O'BRIEN, BILL (Editor). *Appalachian Trail Thru-Hiker's Companion*, Appalachian Trail Long Distance Hikers Association, Harpers Ferry, Virginie Occidentale (annuel)

WHITNEY, STEPHEN. *A Field Guide to the Grand Canyon*, The Mountaineers Books, Seattle, Washington (1996)

Grand Canyon Magazine, Pali Arts Communications, San Francisco, Californie (1989)

REMERCIEMENTS

Les éditeurs souhaiteraient remercier toutes les personnes qui ont participé à la création de cet ouvrage, tant pour leur enthousiasme que pour leurs efforts soutenus.

Steve Razzetti : j'aimerais remercier Jon Tinker, Val Pitkethly, Kate Harper, John Cleare et Pete Royall pour leur soutien moral et créatif, merci particulièrement à KE pour m'avoir guidé pendant ces années, merci aussi à New Holland pour m'avoir chargé de ce projet et à Natalie Hawkrigg pour m'avoir supporté pendant ces nuits interminables passées devant l'ordinateur. Merci aussi à tous mes amis et camarades en Asie ; merci à Shuckor Ali pour les six voyages fantastiques à travers l'Hispar, à Anwar Ali et Abdullah Javed de Hushe, à Bikrum Pandey et tout son personnel de Katmandou et merci à Dago Beda et tout son personnel de Thimpu. Je vous suis très reconnaissant.

IDENTIFICATION DES PHOTOGRAPHES

*Les droits d'auteur reviennent **aux photographes suivants et/ou leurs agents.***
Légende des emplacements : h = en haut ; hg = en haut à gauche ; hm = en haut au milieu ; hd = en haut à droite ; b = en bas ; bg = en bas à gauche ; bm = en bas au milieu ; bd = en bas à droite ; g = à gauche ; d = à droite ; m = au milieu ; e = encart.
(Il n'y a pas d'abréviation pour les pages avec une seule image, ou les pages sur lesquelles toutes les photographies sont du même photographe.)
Photographes : AB = Andy Belcher
ABQ = Anders Blomquist
AC = Auscape (JPF = Jean-Paul Ferrero)
AW = Art Wolfe
BB = Bill Bachman
BBC = British Broadcasting Corporation (JF = Jeff Foott; PO = Peter Oxford; JBR = Jose B Ruiz; SW = Staffan Widstrand)
BCC = Bruce Coleman Collection (JF = Jeff Foott; JC = Jules Cowan)
BO = Bill O'Connor
BP = Bigpie Pictures (NS = Nicholas Sumner)
CH = Chris Hooker
BR = Black Robin (SB = Shaun Barnett;
DP = Darryn Pegram)
COP = Christine Osborne Pictures
DR = David Rogers
DW = David Wall
ES = Edward AM Snijders
FF = ffotograff (MG = Mike Greenslade)
GG = Gary Gentile
HB = Hamish Brown
HG = Henry Gold
HH = Hedgehog House (BA = Bill Atkinson; SB = Shaun Barnett;
RB = Rob Brown; JM = Jim Harding;
LH = Lynda Harper; CM = Colin Monteath;
AR = Andy Reisinger)
HL = Holger Leue Photography
HS = Hilary Sharp
JDP = Jeff Drewitz Photography
KJ = Kathy Jarvis
LE = Leopard Enterprises (JK = Johann Kloppers)
LT = Lochman Transparencies (JL = Jiri Lochman; ML = Mari Lochman)
MB = Marco Borello
MC = Mountain Camera (CC = Chris Craggs; JC = John Cleare)
NG = National Geographic (SA = Sam Abell; SLA = Steven L Alvarez; RG = Raymond Gehman; LG = Lowell Georgia; DH = David Hiser; CJ = Chris Johns; TL = Timothy Laman; JR = Johan Reinhard)
NHIL = New Holland Image Library (SA = Shaen Adey; AJ = Anthony Johnson)
NV = Neil Vincent
PAPL/G = Photo Access Picture Library/Getaway (DB = David Bristow; DP = D Pinnock)
PM = Peter Mertz
RDH = Roger de le Harpe
RS = Robin Smith
SAP = South American Pictures (KJ = Kathy Jarvis; KM = Kimball Morrison; TM = Tony Morrison; KR = Kim Richardson)
SC = Sylvia Cordaiy Photo Library (AB = Anthony Bloomfield)
SR = Steve Razzetti
TI = Travel Ink (MD = Mark Dubin; AW = Andrew Watson)
TR = Terry Richardson
WK = W Koch

Pages de garde		NV	35–36		HS	89	hd	SR		bd	HH/SB	142–143		KJ
1		BR/SB	37		PM		b	HH/CM	115		HH/SB	144	h	MC/JC
2–3		SR	38–39		PAPL/G/DP	90–93		SR	116–117		BR/SB		e/d	KJ
4–5		BBC/JF	40		SR	94	h	FF/MG	118	h/g	AB	146	bg	MC/JC
6–7		DW	41		LE/JK		e	BR/SB		e	BR/SB		bd	KJ
8		BBC/JBR	42	h/e	HB		bd	SR	119		DW	147		KJ
9		LE/JK		d	BR/DP	95–97		SR	120–121		HL	148	h	SAP/KJ
10–13		SR	44–45		HB	98	h	SR	122		HH/AR		e	BBC/PO
14		ABQ	46	h/e/bd	SR		e	HH/CM	123		HH/CM		hd	SAP/TM
15	g	WK		bg	PAPL/G/DB		bg	SR	124	g	HH/CM	149		SAP/KJ
	d	SR	47–48		SR	99	hd	HH/JH		d	HH/LH	150	h	BBC/SW
16		SR	49		WK		b	HH/CM	125	bd	HH/CM		b	SAP/KR
17	g	SAP/TM	50–52		LE/JK	100–101		SR	126–127		GG	151		KJ
	d	SR	53	hg/hm	PAPL/G/DP	102–103		HH/RB	128		NG/JR	152	h	SAP/KM
18–21		BO		hd	LE/JK	104		LT/JL	129		NG/SA		b	SAP/TM
22–24		HS	54	h/bg	LE/JK	105		AC/JPF	130	h	NG/DH	153	h	KJ
25	hg	HS		e	RDH	106	h	BB		e	BCC/JF		b	BR/SB
	bd	TI/MD	55		LE/JK		e	COP		d	NG/TL	154–155		SAP/TM
26	h	MC/CC	56		DR		g	AC/JPF	131		BCC/JC	156		HH/CM
	e	BO	57		LE/JK	107		BB	132		NG/DH	157	h	HH/CM
	d	AW	58–61		SR	108		NHIL	133	bg	NG/DH		b	KJ
27–29		BO	62–63		KC	109	h	NHIL/AJ		hd	NG/JR	158	g	BR/SB
30	h	WK	64	hg	SC/AB		b	BB	134	h	NG/CJ		d	MC/JC
	e	HS		bd	KC	110	h	NHIL/SA		e	TI/AW	159		RS
	d	MB	65		KC		e	HG		d	NG/SA		b	HH/CM
31	hg	HS	66–74		SR		g	JDP	135		NG/RG	162–163		SR
	bd	BO	74	m	COP	111		AC/JPF	136		NG/SA	168		SR
32–33		HS	75	h	SR	112		LT/ML	137		GG			
34	h/e	PM		bg/m/bd	BP/NS	113		JDP	138–139		GG			
	d	HS	76–88		SR	114	h/e	HL	140–141		ES			

165

INDEX

Les chiffres en caractères gras se rapportent aux sujets des photographies

Abra Calzada 154, 155
Abra Illampu 154
Abra Korahuasi 154
Afrique 38-57
Afrique du Sud 54-57
Aguja de los Quirquinchos **157**
Ai-Ais **53**
Aiguille du Tour 28
Aksoual **42**
Alexandre le Grand 63, 64
Alpamayo **143**, 148-151
  Circuit 148-151
Alpes 15, 21, 26
Alpes du sud (Île du Sud, Nouvelle-Zélande) 125
Alpes Pennines 26-29
Alta Via 2 21
Alto de Pucaraju, col **142**, 150
Amazone 144, 145
  Bassin **142**, 149
Amérique du Nord 126-139
Amérique du Sud 140-159
Amicalola Falls, Parc d'État 136
Anasazi 130, *voir aussi* Indiens d'Amérique
Ancohuma 152, **153**, 154
  Montagnes 155
Andes 15, 48, 142-146, **147, 148, 149, 150**, 152-154, 157
Angel Point **131**
Annapurna 94-97
Antalya 63, 64, 65
Appalachian Mountain Club (AMC) 135, 139
Arizona 130-133
Arremoulit, Refuge d' **23**
Arughat Bazaar 95
Arun, Vallée d' 83
Arun, Rivière **82**
Asie 58-101
Askole 67, 68, **70**, 71, 73
Atlas, Monts de l' 40, 41, 42-45
Australasie 102-125
Australie 102-117
Australiens aborigènes 114
Austrian Hut **46**, 48, 49
Aymara, Indiens (Amérique du Sud) **17, 140-141,** 152, 154, **155**
Baba Dagi 63
Baintha **72**
  Brakk **73**
  Pic de **73**
Baltoro, glacier de **66, 69**, 70
Barkha **88**, 89
Barn Bluff 114, 116
Batian 47, **49**
Bavella **34**, 36
Baxter, Pic 139
Beacon Highway 75
Berbers 40, 42, 43, **45**
Bertol Hut **28**
Bhoitias 95
Bhutan 61, 78, 98-101
Biafo, Glacier **2-3,** 66, 67, **70-73**
Biafo-Hispar 60

Traversée 70-73
Bimthang 61, **94**
Blood Mountain **128**
Bloukrans Hut 57
Bloukrans River **55, 56**
Blue Lac **120**
Blue Ridge Mountains **135**
Bolivie **17,** 142, 143, 152-155
Bonhomme de Neige, Randonnée du 61, **98-101**
Braldu, Gorge du **68, 69,** 70
Braldu, Rivière **67**
Braldu, Vallée du **70, 72,** 73
Brèche de Capitello **35**, 36
Brèche de Roland **24, 25**
Brèche de Tuqueroye 25
Bressanone 21
Bright Angel, piste de 132
British Alpine Club 26, 67, 79
British East India Company 74, 75
Broad Peak 66, 68, 69
Budzunge Bara, col de **90**, 92, 93
Buri Gandaki **94, 95,** 97
  Vallée de 95
Butterfly, vallée de 63
Cacanampunta 145, **146**
Cajatambo 146
Calenzana 21 34, 36
Callejon de Huaylas 148
Camp de base italien (Dhaulagiri) **91,** 93
Cap Gelidonia 64, **65**
Capu Tafunatu 35, **37**
Carnicero 146
  chaîne 146
Caroline du Nord **135,** 136, 137
Caroline 146
Catedral **157**
Ceinture de Feu du Pacifique 118, 119
Cerbats 130, *voir aussi* Indiens d'Amérique
Cerro Almirante Nieto 157
Cerro Castillo **157**
Cerro Paine Grande **156,** 157, 158
Chamonix 21, **26-29**
  vallée de **26,** 27
Chamonix-Zermatt Haute Route 26-29
Champex, station de montagne **26,** 28
Chardonnet 27
Chhonbardan, glacier de **91,** 92, 93
Chili 142, 156-159
Chinacocha Lac 151
Chiquian 145, 146, **147**
Chiu Gompah **88**
Chogoria 46-49
  Circuit 46-49
  Entrée du parc de 48
  Itinéraire de **40**, 48
Chomolhari 98, **99,** 100
Chongo **67,** 69
Cirque de Bavella 36, **37**
Clingman's, dome de 136, 137
Club Alpin Français (CAF) 44, 90
Coconino, Indiens 130
Cogswell's Butte (North Rim) **128**
Col d'Arratille 23

Col d'Arremoulit 23
Col de Bavella **36**
Col de Bertol 29
Col de l'Eveque 29
Col de la Fache **22**, 23
Col de Luana 37
Col de Peygeret 22
Col de Verde 36, 37
Col du Sonadon 28
Col du Tour 28
Colorado River 129, 130, 132, 133
  Gorge 133
Concordia 66-69
Condor des Andes **150,** 153
Conical Hill **122,** 125
Connecticut 137
  River, vallée de 138
Continental Divide **146**
Conway, Sir Martin 70, 73
Cordillera Blanca **142, 143, 144,** 148-151
Cordillera Huayhuash 143, 144-147
Cordillera Real 143, 152-155
Corse 21, 34-37
Cradle Mountain **114, 115,** 116
Crater Lac 114, 118
Cuernos **156, 157,** 158
Curling Pond **46**
Dalai Lama 74, 75
Damphus 90-92
Dara Khola, vallée de **92**
Darjeeling 78, 81, 83
Darran Mountains **122,** 124
Delaware Water Gap 137
Delhi 77, 81, 101
Dent Blanche **28,** 29
Dhaulagiri 90-93, 95, 97
  Circuit 90-93
  Dhaulagiri I **91,** 92, **93**
Djebel Toubkal 41, 42, **44,** 45
Dolomites 21
Dove Lac **114**
Drukyel Dzong 98, 99, **101**
Du Cane Gap 117
Dudh Khola 61, 97
Dzong Ri **58-59,** 78, 79, **81,** 83
Earland Falls **124,** 125
Elandsbos 41
Emerald Lac 1, **120**
États Unis d'Amérique 126-139
Europe 18-37
Faja de las Flores **25**
Faja de Pelay 25
Fethiye 63, 65
Fiordland, Parc National **122,** 124-125
Fish River **38-39, 50-53**
  Canyon 41, **50-53**
Formosa Peak 57
Four Fingers Rock 52
French Pass 91, 92, **93**
Freshfield, Douglas 83
Gangapurna 97
Gange, Fleuve 86
Gangkar Puensum **101,** *voir aussi* Rinchita

Garwal Himalaya **89**
Gasherbrum 66, 68, 69
  Gasherbrum I 66
  Gasherbrum II 66
  Glacier 66
Gaspé, Presqu'île de 134
Gavarnie 23, 25
Gavuragili **64**
Georgie 128, 129, 134-139
Glacier du Mont Miné **29**
Glacier du Sonadon 28
Glacier du Tour 28
Godwin-Austen, Glacier **15,** 67, **69**
Godwin-Austen, Henry Haversham 66, 70
Goecha La **78,** 81
Gompah 74, 95
Gondokoro La 60, 66-69
Gondokoro, glacier de **67,** 69
Gondokoro, Pic de **16,** 69
Gorkha 95, 96
GR20 *voir* Grande Randonnée
Graham, Cunninghame 44
Grand Canyon 50, **128, 129, 130-133**
  Lodge 131, 133
  Parc National 129
  Village 130, 131, 132
Grand Combin 26, 28
Grande Randonnée (GR20) 21, 34-37
Grande Vallée du Rift 41, 46, 48, 49
Great Smoky Mountains **126-127,** 136
  Parc National **134,** 136, 137
Grey, glacier de **159**
Grotte de glace **46**
Guanaco **4-5**
Guanacpatay River **143**
Gurja Himal 92, 93
Gurja Gaon **90,** 93
Hanging Rock **135**
  Parc d'État **135**
Harpers Ferry 137
Harris Saddle **122,** 123, 124-125
Haut Asco 35, 36
Haut glacier d'Arolla 29
Haute Route Pyrénéenne (HRP) 21, 22, 23
Hemis, festival d' (Ladakh) **75**
Himalaya 15, 48, 60, 61, 66, 74-77, 78-81, 86-89, 90-93, 98-101
Himalayan Club 79
Himlung Himal 61, **97**
Hindu Kush 66
HÁsar-andÁr 64, 65
Hushe 66-69
Hispar 70-73
  Glacier **12-13,** 66
  Col de 66, 70, 71, **72,** 73
  Rivière **73**
Hollyford Face 125
Hollyford, vallée de 124-125
Hooker, Sir Joseph 83
Hosteria Las Torres 158, 159
Housatonic River 137
HRP *voir* Haute Route Pyrénéenne

Hualcayan 148, 149
Huaraz 146, 148, 149, 150, 151
Huascaran **142,** 148, 150
  Parc National 149
Huayhuash 144-147
  Circuit 144-147
Hudson, fleuve 137
Huillca 149-150
Humla Karnali **86,** 87
Hushe Mountain Rescue Team 69
Hut Tarn **49**
Île du Nord (Nouvelle Zélande) 118-121
Île du Sud (Nouvelle Zélande) 122-125
Illampu **143,** 152-155
  Circuit 152-155
Imaradene 43, 45
Imlil **42,** 44
Inde 60, 68, 74-77, 78-81, 82, **89**
Indiens d'Amérique 129, 130, 135, 136
Indus, fleuve 76, 86
  Vallée de 74
Islamabad 67, 68, 71
Italie **18-19,** 21
Itinéraire des Sommets 46-49
Jahuacocha **147**
Jancarurish 149
  Camp 149
  Col de 149
Jangothang **99,** 100
Jannu **78,** 82, **84**
Jazela, col de **99**
Jejekangphu Gang **100,** 101
Jirishanka 145, **147**
Jirishanka Chico 145, **147**
John Gardiner, col 156, **158**
Jomsom 92, 96, 97
Jumla 86-89
K2 **15,** 60, 66, 67, 68, 69, 70, 73, 82
Kabru 78, 79
Kagbeni 97
Kaibab, piste 131, **132**
Kaimanawa Ranges 120
Kali Gandaki **90,** 92, 94, **97**
  Vallée de 91
Kangchendzonga 61, 78-81, **82-85**
  Glacier **85**
  Himal 82-85
Kanglakachu La **100**
Kangri 97
Kani Basar, glacier de 73
Kaphe Khola **90**
  Vallée de 92
Karakoram **2-3,** 15, 60, 66-69, 70-73, 74, 77
  Highway 68
Kasbah Goundafi 43, 44
Kashmir 60, 66, 74, 77
Kas 62, 64
Kathmandu 61, 83, 84, 92, 95, 96, 101
Kenya 41, 46-49
Key Summit **124**
Khoisan 53, 54
Khota 154, 155
Kia Ora Hut 117
Kikuyu 46, 47

INDEX

Kilimanjaro 41, 46, 47, 50
Kittatinny Ridge 137
Kleinbos 54
klipspringer 52-53
Knysna loerie 55
Kokthang 78, 79
La Paz 152, 155
Lac Carhuacocha **144**
Lac d'Arratille 23
Lac d'Artouste 23
Lac de Capitello **34**, 35
Lac de Gaube 22
Lac Dickson 159
Lac Ellis 49
Lac Grey **159**
Lac Harris **123**
Lac Jahuacocha 147
Lac MacKenzie **125**
Lac Manasarovar **87**, 88
Lac Michaelson **40**, **46**, 49
Lac Ninacocha 146
Lac Nordenskj-ld **157**, 158
Lac Pehoe **156**, **157**, 159
Lac St Clair 116, **117**
   Parc National 114, 116
Lac Sarmiento 156
Lac Siula **146**
Lac Solterococha **147**
Lac Taupo 118
Lac Titicaca 140-141, 143, **152**, 154, 155
Lac Windermere 116
Ladakh 60, 61, 74-77
   Chaîne du 66
Laguna Amarga 156, 157
Laguna Carhuacocha 146
Laguna Chillata 152
Laguna Chinacocha **148**
Laguna Glaciar 152, **153**
Laguna Los Perros **158**, 159
Laguna Torre 159
Lamayuru 61, **74**, 76
   Gompah 77
Lapsang La **84**
Larkya Himal 94-97
Larkya La **61**, 94, **95**, 97
Latok **2-3**, 73
Laurel Valley **134**
Layla, Pic de **67**, 68
Le Tour **26**, 27
Leh **74**, 75, 76
Lewis, glacier de **46**, 48
Lhassa 74, 87, 95
Little Haystack Mountain **139**
Llanganuco Lacs 150
Llanganuco, vallée de **151**
Lobella keniensis **46**
Los Cedros River 149
Los Cuernos 158
Los Perros 159
Loutre du Cap **54**
Lunana **98**, **99**, **100**, 101
Lycie 61, 62-65
   Route de 62-65
MacKenzie, Bassin 125
Mackinder, Sir Halford 47
Mackinder's Camp **15**, Camp 49
Magellanic forest **157**
Maine 129, 134-139
   Appalachian Trail Club 139
Mal des montagnes 16-17
Manali 61, 77
Manang 90, 95, 97
Manang-Thorung Phedi trail **10-11**

Manaslu & Annapurna Circuit 94-97
Mangaehuehu Hut 121
Mangatepopo, vallée de 120
Mangdi Chhu **101**
Mango 72
Maori 118, 119, 122, 123
Marble Peak **69**
Marion's Lookout 114, 116
Maroc 40, 42-45
Marpha **90**, **91**, 92, 97
Marrakech 42, 43, 44, 45
Marsyangdi **94**, 95
Maryland 137
   River 97
   Vallée de **10-11**, 95, **97**
Masherbrum **66**, 68, 69
Massachusetts 137
Matterhorn **20**, 21, **26**, **29**
Mauvoisin, Lac 28-29
McAfee Knob 137
Milford Sound 125
Milke Dande 83
Minto's **48**, 49
Mirgin La **84**
Missouri 128
Mitre Peak **66**
Mohammed, Ali 68
Mont Aspiring 122
Mont Blanc 21, **26**, **29**
Mont Blanc de Cheillon 29
Mont Cervin 29
Mont Egmont 121
Mont Elgon 46
Mont Everett 137
Mont Garfield **139**
Mont Greylock 137
Mont Kailas **86-89**
Mont Katahdin 139
Mont Kenya **15**, **40**, 41, 46-49
   Lodge 48, 49
   Parc National 46-49
Mont Liberty **139**
Mont Lincoln **139**
Mont Ngauruhoe **118**, **119**, 120
Mont Olympos **62**, 63, 64, 65
Mont Pelion 116
Mont Ruapehu **118**, **119**, 120, 121
Mont Tongariro 118, **119**, **120**, 121
Mont Washington 138
Monte Christo 37
Monte Cintu **34**, 35
Monte Perdido 22, 23, 25
Montgomerie, Thomas 66, 94
Moorcroft, William 74, 75
Mugu Karnali, vallée de **86**, 87
Muktinath 90, 95, 97
Musa Dagi **62**
Mustagh Tower **69**
Mustang 95, **97**
Myagdi Khola 91, 92, 93
Myra **64**
Nairobi 46, 47, 49
Namgyal, Hope Leezum 82
Namgyal, Rinzin 83
Namibie **38-39**, 41, 50-53
   Désert de 41
   Wildlife Resorts 53
Namla **70**, **72**
   Vallée de 117
Naro Moru 47, 49
   Station Météorologique 49
   River Lodge 49
National Trails System Act (USA) 135
Nature, vallée de la **9**, 55

Nelion **47**, **49**
Nepal 14, 15, **17**, **60**, **61**, 78, 81, 82-85, 86-89, 90-93, 94-97
   Pic de 85
New Hampshire 134, 137, **138**, **139**
Ngati Tuwharetoa **118**, 119, 120
Ngubu Huts **54**, 55
Nido Negro de Condores **4-5**
Nouvelle Angleterre 134, 135, 136, 137
Nouvelle Zélande **1**, **6-7**, 118-125
North Kaibab Trail 131, 133
Oakhurst Huts 55
Ogre, L' **2-3**, **72**, 73
Oktang **82**
   Ölü Deniz 63, 65
Ooh Aah Point **130**
Ordesa, Canyon d' **25**
Ordesa, Rivière **8**
Orny, glacier de 28
Otemma, glacier de 29
Oturere, vallée de 120
Oued Nfis 42, **43**, 44
Padum **75**, **76**, 77
Paglia Orba 35, **37**
Paine, massif de **4-5**, **156-159**
Pakistan **2-3**, **12-13**, **16**, 60, 66-69, 70-73, 77, 93
Palm Springs (Namibie) 51, 52
Pandim 79, **81**
Pang Pema 83, 84, **85**
Parc National des Pyrénées 22
Parcs Nationaux d'Afrique du Sud 56
Parc Naturel Régional de la Corse (PNR) 34-37
Parque Nacional de Ordesa y Monte Perdido 22, 23
Parque Nacional Torres del Paine 156-159
Paso de Los Cedros 148, 149
Paso Paine 159
Paso Sarani 154
Passage d'Orteig **23**
Patagonie 143, 156-159
Pelion Gap **117**
Pelion Plains 116
Pennsylvanie 137
Pérou 142, 143, 144-147, 148-152
Petit Vignemale 22, 23, 25
Phalut **78**, 79, 81
Phantom Ranch 130, 133
Phedi **97**
Phole **82**
Phuktal Gompah **74**, 77
Pic du Midi d'Ossau **22**
Pigne d'Arolla 27, 29
Piste des Appalaches **126-127**, **128**, 129, **134-139**
Piste des Loutres **9**, **41**, 54-57
Piste Overland 114-117
Point Lenana **46**, **47**, 49
Pointe d'Orny 28
Pokhara 92, 96
Potomac, fleuve 137
Prek Chhu 79, **81**
Presidential Range 139
Puchhar 93
   Wall **91**, 93
Pudeto 157
Puerto Natales 156, 157
Punta Arenas 156
Punta Carhuac 146
Punta Cuyoc 146, **147**
   Col de 146, **147**

Punta Llamac **144**
Putha Hiunchuli **90**, 92
Pyrenees **8**, 21, 22, 23
   Parc National 22
Quebrada de Los Cedros 148, **149**
Quebrada Illampu 154
Quechua Indiens **148**, 150
Ramtang **82**
Randonnée Salons de Thé **14**, 15, **16**
Rara Lac **86**, 87
   Parc National 87
Rathong **78**
Red Crater 120, 121
Refuge de Carozzu **34**, 35
Refuge de Espuguettes **24**, 25
Refuge de Pombie **22**
Refugio Chileno **158**
Refugio Dickson 159
Refugio Grey **159**
Refugio Pehoe **157**, 159
Restonica, vallée de **34**, 35
Ribbon Falls **132**
Rinchita 98, **100**
Rio Franc-s 158
Rio Los Perros **158**
Rio Paine 159
Rive nord (Grand Canyon) 130, 131, **132**, 133
Rive sud (Grand Canyon) **130**, 131, 132, **133**
Rockies 128
Round the Mountains **6-7**, **118-121**
Route de Lycie, 62-65
Routeburn Falls 124
Routeburn Flats 123, 124
Routeburn Gorge 123
Routeburn River 124
Routeburn Shelter 122
Routeburn Track, The **122**-125
Routeburn, vallée de 122, 123
Sahara, désert 40, 41, 42
Schönbiel, glacier de 29
Schönbielhütte 29
Sella Towers **21**
Shenandoah, Parc National 134, 137
Shipton, Eric 47, 70-72
Sikkim 61, 78, 82, 83, 95
   Himalaya **78**, **79**, **81**
Singalila 61, 78-81
   Ridge **78**, **79**, 81, 82, 83
Sirsir La **76**, 77
Siula 145, 146
   Grande 145
Skardu 67, 68, 71, 73
Skilderkrans 55
Snow Lac **70**, 72, 73
Sorata 143, 152, 153, 154, **155**
South African Forestry Co Ltd (SAF COL) 56
South Kaibab Trail 132, **133**
South Westland (Nouvelle Zélande) 122-125
   World Heritage Area 122
Southern Cape (South Africa) 54-57
Spantang, vallée de **76**
Srinagar **74**, 75
Stockji, glacier de 29
Storms River 54, 56, 57
   Gorge 57
   Embouchure 54, 56, 57
Talung, glacier de **78**
Taplejung 83, 84
Tarina, vallée de **100**, 101

Taroudant 43, 45
Tasmanie 114-117
Te Anau 122, 125
Te Wahipounamu 122
Teleki, vallée de 47, 49
Tennessee **126-127**, **134**, 136, 137
Thikse Gompah **75**
Thonje 96, 97
Thorung La **90**, 95, 96, **97**
Three Sisters 52
Tibet 61, 74, 75, 76, 78, 82, 83, 86-89, 94, 98, 100
Tichka 42-45
   Plateau de 42, 43, 45
Tilman, Bill 48, 90, 94
Tizi n' Tagharat 44
Tizi n' Test 43, 44
Tongariro 118-121
   Crossing **6-7**, **118**, 120
   Parc National **1**, **6-7**, **118**, **119**
   Northern Circuit 119, 121
Torres 156-159
   Del Paine 143, **156-159**
   Del Paine Parc National **4-5**
Toubkal 42-45
   (Neltner) Hut **44**
Trango Towers **66**, **69**
Traveller Range 117
Trient, glacier de 28, **28**
Trient Plateau **27**
Tsitsikamma 41, 57
   Montagnes 57
   Parc National 54
   Circuit de la Piste des Loutres 54-57
   Piste 54-57
Tukuche 91, 92, 97
   Pic de 90
Twins, The **85**
Two Tarn Hut **49**
Uzun Brakk **72**, 73
Valle Frances 156, **157**, 158
Vermont 135, 137, 138
Victoria Falls 50
Vigne, Godfrey Thomas 66
Virginie **134**, 136, 137
Waldheim **114**
Wartang La **101**
Washington National Forest 137
Waterfall Valley 116
Waynesboro **134**
Weindorfer, Gustav 114
Whakapapa, village de **118**, 119, 121
Whakapapaiti Hut 121
Whanganui, Parc National 121
White Mountain National Forest 138
Whymper, Edward 26
Woche **98**
Workman, Fanny Bullock 68, 70, 72
Workman, William Hunter 68, 70, 72
Xanthos **62**, 63
   River 64
Yaki Point Trailhead 132, **133**
Yalung, glacier de 78, **82**, 83
Yedi Burun **63**
Yerupaja Grande **144**
Yerupaja 143, **144**, 145, 146
Yungas **154**
Zanskar 60, 61, 74-77
   River **75**, 76, 77
   Vallée de 76
Zermatt 21, **26-29**
Zmutt 29
   Glacier 29

*Ils disent que les voyages
élargissent l'esprit ;
mais pour cela vous devez d'abord
avoir l'esprit du voyage.*

GK CHESTERTON